SBS

STORIES OF MARINES

SHAUN CLARKE
IAN BLAKE
DAVID MONNERY

BLITZ EDITIONS

This edition published in 1996

Published by Blitz Editions
an imprint of Bookmart Limited
Registered Number 2372865
Trading at Bookmart Limited
Desford Road, Enderby
Leicester, LE9 5AD

ISBN 1 85605353 9

Typeset by Hewer Text Composition Services, Edinburgh
Printed in Great Britain by Cox and Wyman Limited, Reading

MARINE A: SBS

TERRORISM ON THE NORTH SEA

Shaun Clarke

1

'Is it true the Prime Minister's in the VIP lounge?' McGee asked, wiping his lips with his hand and glancing idly around the crowded heliport lounge.

'That's right,' Tony Masters replied, studying the bottles along the bar. 'Why do you ask? Want to shake the great man's hand?'

McGee laughed sardonically and turned his head to grin at Masters. The Englishman was leaning against the counter, sipping his whisky.

'Ackaye,' McGee said. 'I'd like to shake his hand all right. Then I'd push him off the edge of the drilling floor. For that I'd give my right arm.'

'You're a republican,' Masters said.

'Sure I am,' McGee replied. 'Me and a lot of other right-minded Paddies. Our day will come.'

Masters glanced at the other waiting men with an air of impatience. The heliport lounge was packed and the men on the chairs were surrounded by luggage. Mostly under thirty, they were wearing jeans and anoraks, and were all now hazed in a fog of cigarette smoke. Outside, the weather was filthy, with the airstrip covered in a silvery, wind-blown drizzle. Grounded, the Wessex Mk 3 transport helicopters were parked in well-spaced rows and the drifting clouds cast shadows on their Perspex windows. Masters was annoyed: he wanted to get moving. All the men in the lounge had been there for hours and were no less impatient.

'Look at them,' McGee said softly. 'The scum of the land.'

'Being one of them, you should know,' Masters replied.

The Irishman smiled tightly. His eyes were dark and intense. He had a rough, wind-whipped face, a short, wiry body, and the sort of restless energy that betrays unreleased inner tension.

'I come from them, all right. Sure, I haven't forgotten that. I'm a working-class Paddy and proud of it. But that doesn't mean I'm one of this rubbish.'

'Rubbish?' Glancing around the crowded lounge, Masters saw the unshaven faces of the other men through a veil of cigarette smoke, framed by the windows that looked out on the windy, cloud-darkened heliport. There was a storm over the North Sea, raging around the oil rigs, and the men in the lounge were waiting to board the grounded helicopters. They had been here, in the Bristow Heliport in Aberdeen, for almost five hours.

'Sure they're rubbish,' McGee insisted. 'The dregs

of the working classes. They only work on the rigs because they can't find employment elsewhere.'

'*You* work on the rigs,' Masters said. 'And *I* work on the rigs.'

'Right, Tone. But not because it's the only work we can find. The rigs attract the worthless, the North Sea attracts the debris. Sure, it's a job where you're not asked for your past record or credentials, which is why it appeals to this scum.'

'This is 1982,' Masters said. 'There are approximately *three million* unemployed. The first time since the 1930s. That makes it very easy to be scum.'

After sipping some more beer McGee put his glass down and lit a cigarette with abrupt, nervous movements. Knowing that Masters didn't smoke, he didn't offer him one.

Tony Masters was a bit of a mystery, being a wizard on the oil rigs, seemingly obsessed with work, and rarely discussing his onshore life. McGee was wary of Masters because most of the rig-workers revered him. The Englishman was a tool-pusher, one of the élite of the North Sea: in charge of the drilling, he was tough, efficient and ruthless when it came to hiring and firing. He demanded hard work and obedience from the roughnecks and roustabouts, but he had an almost puritanical sense of justice, which had gained him respect. Too much respect, McGee thought, for a man who had only been on the Frigg Field for six months, reportedly having spent the previous couple of years on the Beryl Field.

'Just think of it,' McGee said. 'Three million unemployed. And that bastard, the Prime Minister, is in the VIP lounge right now, filling his belly.'

'You're not unemployed,' Masters reminded him.

'I'm just a roughneck, Tone. I'm not unemployed, but I could be any day now, just like the others.'

'It's not that bad,' Masters insisted.

'It's that bad and you know it. Sure, with all that unemployment a man can't risk losing his job and the oil companies exploit it to the hilt. We used to have strong unions on the rigs. We still have unions, but they're no longer strong. With unemployment going up by forty thousand a month, the bosses have the whip hand and the unions can't afford to take chances. You're an English tool-pusher. That's a double advantage. You'll have a job as long as there's drilling, but we're not all so lucky.'

If only you knew, Masters thought, resisting the urge to smile.

'As for the oil,' McGee continued, 'it's really in Scottish waters, but the Scots don't get a penny out of it. They're being bled by the fucking Brits, just like the Irish.'

'So what's that got to do with your precious job?' Masters growled. 'You're in charge of every roustabout on your rig. You should be laughing, my friend.'

'Tell us another,' McGee retorted. He took a swig of beer, inhaled on his cigarette and nervously drummed his fingers on the bar. 'The oil beneath the North Sea is estimated at about £2000 million a year. If that revenue went to Scotland, it could meet their national budget *and* give them a healthy balance of payments surplus. I'm amazed the Scottish National Party, who're getting close to a majority, haven't formed their own band of paramilitaries to get that money back from the thieving Brits by taking over the oil rigs. That's what we would do.'

'You back the IRA, then?' Masters asked distractedly, as if making idle conversation.

'No,' McGee said promptly. 'Sure, I'm sympathetic to the cause, but I don't hold with the way they go about it. I'm not into violence.'

'It's comforting to know that,' Masters said sardonically.

'Ackaye, sure it is. They don't trust Irishmen on these rigs. They think all of us back the terrorists, murdering Englishmen in their sleep, so if they need to get rid of the odd worker they always drop the Irish or Scottish first.'

'I don't think that's true,' Masters replied.

'It's true enough,' McGee said.

Masters knew what McGee meant. The oil boom

of the late 1970s had given a lot of men employment, but not all that many had been Scots, let alone Irish. Although the oil was in Scottish waters, ironically the Scots had been forced to take second place to an enormous influx of American, French, Spanish, Norwegian and English workers, with the odd Scot and Irishman thrown in for the sake of appearances. Recently, however, after the Scottish National Party had created a political scandal out of the issue, the oil companies had been bending over backwards to take on more Scottish and Irish workers. In that sense, then, McGee was wrong – or at least out of date.

'Maybe things will change,' Masters said. 'Rumour has it that the real reason the Prime Minister is visiting Bravo 1, in the Forties Field, is for a discussion on the possibility of reducing taxes to encourage the big oil companies to do more drilling. Everyone knows they're deliberately building up huge tax losses in the Middle East and setting the revenue against liability for tax in the UK. They'll carry on like that until the British government reduces tax, and the Prime Minister is obviously aware of the fact.'

'Fuck dealing with them,' McGee retorted. 'The government should nationalize the oilfields and *force* the bastards to drill.'

'They can't do that, McGee. It was the British government that originally granted exploration licences to the oil companies, selling them off by means of an auction with sealed bids. The British sector of the North Sea now belongs legally to them, so if the government stepped in and nationalized, it would lead to an international scandal.'

'Ackaye,' McGee said, glancing around the smoky lounge. 'They're desperate for money, so they sell off the North Sea. Now they're even more desperate and they can't get their hands on the oil. There'll be no sense in this country until Parliament's dismantled and a whole new system introduced. British governments, be they Labour or Conservative, are just capitalist lackeys.'

'You keep talking like that,' Masters said, 'and you *will* lose your job.'

McGee finished his beer. 'Sure, you're not wrong there. A man on the rigs should be tight-lipped. He'll last longer that way.'

Glancing about him, Masters saw the tables piled high with beer cans and crumpled newspapers, the ashtrays overflowing, the cigarette smoke drifting above the heads of the men, whose conversation was a constant, edgy murmuring. Those men worked a fortnight on and a fortnight off. Once on the rigs they would work twelve hours a day, seven days a week, in wet, freezing weather and filth. Since smoking was allowed only when they were off duty, and since the only permissible alcohol was their allowance of two cans of beer a day, they were now doing as much smoking and drinking as possible before going back.

Gazing beyond their heads, out through the plate-glass windows of the lounge, Masters saw the Wessex helicopters parked on the landing pads along the runway, which was also used for light aircraft. Black clouds hung low above them, the rain continued to pour down, and a fierce wind was howling across the airstrip. Out in the North Sea there were Force Nine winds – fifty miles an hour – hurling huge waves against the rigs. The weather ruled the North Sea. It made work costly and dangerous. The men were used to long delays, but that didn't prevent annoyance; and Masters, like the rest of them, was growing edgy.

'I'm going for a piss,' McGee said. 'That should help pass a minute or two. Christ, this business is desperate!'

He slung his rucksack over his shoulder and lumbered off through the milling men, towards the toilet. Masters watched him go, a small smile on his lips, then he surveyed the noisy lounge once more.

Most of the men were quite young. They were a rough-looking bunch. They had come from building sites, from the armed forces or merchant navy, and they were generally the kind of men who, even if married, spent too much time away from home. Work on the rigs, though tough and dangerous, wasn't too highly paid; it appealed to men who could not get work elsewhere or who simply disliked the routine of onshore life. It wasn't a nine-to-five job, you had to serve no apprenticeship, there was no attention paid to previous history or qualifications, and a man with something to hide had to answer few questions.

In a sense they were the last of the brigands. They weren't colourful, but they were distinctive. They were returning, now, after two weeks on shore, where they would have visited families and girlfriends, bought sex in sleazy bedsits, or got drunk in the pubs of Peterhead or Aberdeen. An insular breed, they lived in a small world, working like navvies on the rigs, seldom seeing their relatives, and developing an underplayed camaraderie that gave them moral support.

This mutual support was something that Masters understood, given what he really was and where he came from. He was, in fact, a sergeant with the Royal Marines Special Boat Squadron (SBS), working for the intelligence branch and assigned secretly to the rigs to check out the very real threat of terrorist infiltration, either by Scottish nationalists or by the IRA.

However, his skill as an oil worker was genuine enough. Masters had been a tool-pusher for the oil companies until 1975, when a bad marriage and acrimonious separation had driven him to making his escape by enlisting in the Army, after which he eventually ended up in the Royal Marine Commandos. Soon bored even with that, and wanting to use the knowledge he had picked up on the North Sea rigs, he had applied for the notoriously difficult SBS Potential Recruits' Course (PRC).

After the usual physical and psychological tortures at the Commando Training Centre, Royal Marines, at Lympstone in Devon, he had passed the even more demanding three-week selection test, then undergone a fifteen-week training course in seamanship, navigation, demolition, diving and advanced weapons handling. Among the craft he trained in were paddle-boards, specially-made Klepper Mark 13 collapsibles, Geminis powered by 40bhp outboard motors, and glass-fibre Rigid Raiders powered by 140bhp outboard motors, as used by the specialists of the Royal Marines Rigid Raider Squadron. The main weapons employed by the SBS, he had learned during training, were the US 5.56mm M16 Armalite rifle with M203 grenade-launchers, the 9mm L34A1 Sterling submachine-gun, the standard-issue 9mm Browning High Power handgun, and a variety of plastic explosives. He had also learned to use laser designators, burst-transmission radios, and his extensive survival kit, similar to that used by the SAS.

Having survived the PRC, he had taken an arduous four-week parachute course in Borneo, then been posted to an operational Boat Section, before completing his specialist training at Royal Marines (RM), Poole, Dorset. Accepted by the SBS, he had been allowed to wear the standard uniform of the Royal Marines and the Royal Marine Commando green beret, but with parachuting wings on the right shoulder and the Swimmer Canoeist badge on the right forearm. He had felt proud to do so.

As a member of 41 Commando SBS, he had taken part in exercises in Hong Kong and Borneo, carried out a tour of duty in the Mediterranean with NATO, and endured special Arctic training at Elvergaardsmoen in northern Norway. Promoted to corporal, he had gone undercover for internal security duties in Northern Ireland, sometimes working hand in glove with the SAS and Army Intelligence. Finally, just a few months ago, he had fought in the brief but bloody Falklands war.

After being promoted to sergeant for his leading role in a daring SBS raid designed to set fire to the oil storage tanks in Port Stanley's harbour installations, he had been posted to the intelligence unit of the Portsmouth Group RM, where the work was interesting enough but not very exciting. Luckily, the SBS was then, in strict secrecy, given important responsibilities in the security of Britain's offshore oil and gas rigs. Using his past experience on the rigs as the trump card in his application for a position in North Sea security, he had been accepted and sent to work under cover on Eagle 3, in the Frigg Field, with false papers stating that he had spent the previous two years working on Charlie 2, in the Beryl Field.

His brief was simple: to ensure that no terrorists infiltrated the rig for the purposes of espionage or sabotage. In order to do this, he went back to work as a tool-pusher and was very good at it.

'A man deep in thought,' someone said. 'I *do* like to see that.'

Turning his head, Masters found himself face to face with Robert Barker, who was leaning on the bar at his left shoulder. Blue-eyed and blond, he was wearing a fur-collared pigskin jacket and scruffy blue jeans. Though he looked much younger than his thirty-eight years, he was in charge of security for British United Oil, the conglomerate for which all these men worked. He was also one of the only two men in the North Sea who knew that Masters was SBS.

'Gin and tonic,' he said to the barman. 'And one for my friend here. The best tool-pusher in the business needs his breakfast.'

'Mine was whisky,' Masters informed him.

'I know that,' Barker said. 'And the barman obviously knows your tastes: he's just poured you a large one.'

Masters grinned as the barman set the drinks on the counter. Barker gave him two pounds, waited for his change, then put the coins in his pocket and tried his gin.

'Nice,' he said. '*Very* nice. Day like this, a man needs it.'

'I thought you'd be in with the PM,' Masters said.

'I was,' Barker told him. 'He's having brandy and crisps. The brandy's a sign that he's an ambitious Prime Minister; the crisps mean he's still one of the lads. It's what's known as good politics.'

Masters grinned again. 'I'm surprised you're not still in there. You're supposed to be our top security man.'

'How can I protect him? He's already surrounded by bodyguards and military police. If they can't do the job, no one can. Anyway, my real job is to protect the Forties Field. Our esteemed PM is spending two days and one night on Bravo 1 and I've had that platform checked from top to bottom. I also have men all over the place.' He sipped his drink. 'I believe you won't be joining us this time.'

'No,' said Masters. 'I'm flying out to Eagle 3 in the Frigg Field to start closing it down. We'll soon be towing it away to another site.'

'Frigg's dried out?'

'Yeah. It was the most used field during the boom years and now the oil's all gone.'

'I would have come across sooner,' Barker said,

abruptly changing the subject, 'but I didn't want to interrupt your conversation with that nice man, McGee.'

'He's a real pain in the arse. But he happens to be a good worker.'

'He's a troublemaker. He backs the unions to the hilt. Two years ago, when we were having all those strikes, McGee was up to his neck in it.'

'So he's a union man. A *lot* of our men are in the union. I don't give a toss as long as they get on with their work. McGee's all right. He's just a bit obsessed. If he catches you at the bar, he's a pain, but he does do his work.'

Barker sighed. 'I suppose you're right. I just can't stand the bastard.'

Masters smiled consolingly. 'You don't have to work with the bastard – and neither do I.'

'I guess that's right,' Barker said.

They touched glasses and drank, then glanced around the crowded lounge bar. To the casual observer the men would have looked like a single group, but the more experienced eye saw segregation. The rig workers, who felt divorced from the outer world, were also divorced from one another by the singular hierarchy of the oilfields. Packed together in the smoky lounge, they had instinctively moved into their own, very separate groups.

The majority were roustabouts, general labourers who worked on the lower decks of the rigs, unloading the supply boats and moving the machinery or steel pipes in and out of the storage space and up to the drilling floor. They did this and every other unskilled job and in general were the lowest-paid men on the rigs.

The second largest group were the roughnecks, men who worked on the drilling floor, usually around the roaring shaft, changing the bits that had broken on rocks 11,000 feet beneath the ocean bed and extending the drills by adding lengths of heavy steel piping. It was skilled, exhausting, dangerous work and the roughnecks were therefore paid more than the roustabouts.

These two very different groups formed the backbone of the rigs, but their jobs usually kept them apart. Working seven days a week, twelve hours a day, they weren't given enough spare time to strike up close friendships with anyone outside their immediate environment.

Even more remote were the key men, the tool-pushers, who kept a tight rein on the roustabouts and roughnecks and were directly responsible only to company supervisors. The tool-pushers were a breed apart; they had total authority over the other men. If their status could be rivalled, only the divers could come close – not because they had authority, but because their high fatality rate placed them near the top of the wage structure. The divers were the most insular; their odd way of life made them so.

During their time on the rigs they would either be diving or suffering the harrowing isolation of decompression. It was a bizarre way of life – like that of an astronaut. Either under the sea or in a decompression chamber, enduring the danger and monotony of relentless saturation diving, they would not be in physical touch with their fellow human beings for the whole of their two weeks on board. So they were strangers, hardly known to the other men; and in this lounge, in the grey haze of cigarette smoke, they remained a group well apart.

Listening to the murmuring, the sudden outbursts of laughter, the rattling of beer cans and scuffling of restless feet, Masters felt that he had truly come home. The fragments of conversation he overheard were a mixture of the profane and the technological, bringing back the feel and taste of a world that was as far removed from the normal world as was the moon from the earth.

'. . . still drilling for Complex, but expect to complete the current and final hole shortly. Then the rig'll be towed to Hamburg for the demob of diving equipment and a lengthy refit. Then God knows where else . . .'

'. . . "rig workers' widows", they call them. They say they never see their men. The divorce rate's going up and there's far too much booze going down. That's why *my* marriage is doomed . . .'

'. . . definitely a hell of an improvement. Unscrambled speech facilities from the diver back to the bellman; processed speech side-tone speaker for clear speech between diver and bellman; diver tape connections plus tape connections for playback in all chambers; and a good ten hours' life in the power pack . . .'

'. . . it can't go on much longer. She keeps coming to the boarding house. Says I picked her up in the Granada in Peterhead and then got her pregnant. Lying cow! I don't even know her name . . .'

'. . . wind a hundred and fucking thirty, waves ninety foot high. Fucking tanker crashed into the platform and all hell broke loose. Five of the crew were killed, a two-mile slick on the sea, then the bloody well-head exploded and I blacked out and woke up in the knacker's yard. What the fuck am I doing here?'

'. . . Sidko 803 just returned to Rover Oil after drilling a well for BP. Now on permanent contract to Rover since BP no longer seem interested in the rig. Meanwhile, Beta 45 is in the Netherlands having its Comex 1000 system replaced and will soon be operating for . . .'

'. . . a hell of a storm. Dumb bastard fell down the moonpool. Another hit in the face with a bolt from the shaft and a load fell on the crane-driver's cab. They tried to burn through the metal. The storm blew up again. The crane broke loose and was swept into the sea. Four degrees in there, it was . . .'

'. . . I can't go home again. It's all over for good this time. She said it was the North Sea or her, so I picked the North Sea . . .'

Masters listened to the words and heard a familiar refrain. It made him think of the Royal Marine Commandos, the weapons and the boats, the exercises and the undercover activities in Belfast. It was a world in which men without women looked to hard work for comfort. It was an unstated machismo code, removing a man from the normal, and it gave rise to a feeling of freedom that was not quite definable. The North Sea held that attraction. The oil rigs were a world apart. They encouraged fierce competition and a chauvinistic pride that had long since disappeared from onshore life. Masters liked this male world, with its constant action. He'd been married, but was divorced three years later because he couldn't stay at home for long. Masters wanted his freedom, as did a lot of the rig workers. The men who drilled the North Sea, who braved the wind and freezing rain, the dizzying heights, the constant danger, were pioneers of the most ordinary cut, but they *did* stand apart.

'I think the Prime Minister's leaving,' Barker said. 'Let's take a look.'

Glancing up, Masters saw the other men turning instinctively toward the windows that overlooked the landing pads. Following Barker, he pushed through to the front and looked out at the silent helicopters. The rain was still pouring. The wind blew it across the airstrip. The sky was dark and the greyness was foreboding, the view chilly and desolate.

Farther along the airstrip, military policemen were emerging from the sandbagged entrance to the VIP lounge. Bulky in boots and helmets, carrying 9mm Sterling Light Automatic Rifles, they emerged in two lines that formed a grim, protective path for the Prime Minister. Beyond them were two aircraft hangars, rain pouring down their walls; on top of the hangars were more Army marksmen, scanning the heliport.

The Prime Minister emerged, wearing a black overcoat. A man in a dark-grey suit was holding an umbrella over his head while other men in similar suits poured out around him, their hands under their jackets, resting on their Brownings.

Masters watched them carefully. The whole scene was depressing. The men moving towards the airstrip through the rain and howling wind looked like Mafia hit men. There was no ceremony here; simply a watchful, nervous advance. The MPs, holding their sub-machine-guns at the ready, fanned out towards the nearest Wessex while the Prime Minister and his entourage hurried between them, all with heads bowed.

'It's still filthy weather,' Barker said. 'That's a pretty strong wind out there.'

'It must be dying,' Masters replied. 'Almost certainly it's passed over the rigs. They wouldn't let the PM take off otherwise. We'll probably all take off soon.'

'A lot of armour,' Barker observed. 'I never thought I'd see the day. There are enough weapons and ammunition in this heliport to start a bloody war.'

'He needs it,' Masters said. 'The assassination list is growing. It's even been rumoured that a bomb was found in the House of Commons. This whole country's a war zone.'

'Happy days,' Barker said.

Masters looked at the distant hangars and saw the glint of binoculars, the barrel of a machine-gun moving from side to side in a slow, searching motion. Smiling tightly, shaking his head in disbelief, he returned his thoughtful gaze to the helicopters. The Prime Minister was entering the nearest one in the row, being helped up by a bodyguard. He disappeared inside, and his entourage followed him. The military police formed a cordon around the chopper as it roared into life. The rotor blades whipped up the wind as they blurred and merged into a single line. The military police stood beneath them with their uniforms flapping furiously and their weapons together covering every direction.

The Wessex carrying the Prime Minister roared louder, shook and rose a little, turned towards the east, climbed higher and disappeared through the low clouds.

The men around Masters relaxed, then returned to their chairs. Their conversation became louder and more ebullient, as if a crisis had passed. Masters remained at the window, still standing beside Barker. McGee came up to stand between them and gaze out at the cloudy grey sky.

'He's left,' Masters said.

'Sure, I saw that,' McGee said. 'Now maybe we can all get out of here and back to work.'

'It won't be long,' Masters said.

2

The Prime Minister gazed through the window of the helicopter and saw, far below him, through the haze of thinning cloud, the choppy grey desolation of the North Sea. It made him shiver. He felt cold and slightly unreal. The sea stretched out as far as the eye could see and then was lost in drifting clouds.

'It looks terribly cold down there,' he said. 'I would not like to work there.'

'No, Prime Minister,' replied the Under-Secretary of the Department of Energy. 'Neither would I.'

The PM chuckled and gave a fleeting, sardonic smile. He had a florid, well-fleshed, stubborn face with cold blue eyes and grey hair. The Under-Secretary, beside him, had the appearance of a young executive; unlike the PM he had not come up the hard way and the differences between them often showed. Now the PM sighed, keeping his gaze on the North Sea, and his large body shifted uneasily as the clouds drifted past him.

'Well,' he said, 'it's not a job for the likes of me.

It's a job for the sort of man my father was. It must be a rough life.'

Opening his briefcase, the Under-Secretary glanced up in surprise. His accent, unlike the PM's, was public-school.

'You sound almost nostalgic, Prime Minister. That world died a long time ago.'

'Did it? I'm not so sure of that. Those lads aren't paid as much as they're worth and both of us know it.'

'I thought they were paid quite well.'

'You think the miners get paid well?'

'Don't they?'

'The pay's good, but it's not enough for what we ask them to do. And I believe the North Sea's worse than the mines. The fatality rate is high. In fact, according to my reports, the chances of death are ten times as great as in mining.'

'And fifty times as great as in general industry, Prime Minister.'

'Precisely.'

The PM sounded annoyed and the Under-Secretary, smiling slightly, removed some papers from his briefcase. The PM turned his head, saw the papers, and returned his gaze to the sea below.

'Where are the guards?' he asked.

'Up at the front.'

'SAS?'

'SBS – Special Boat Squadron.'

'In case we go down?'

'Yes, Prime Minister.'

The PM grinned sardonically, still studying the restless sea a long way below him. 'I've got to stay on the rig until tomorrow night?'

'Yes, Prime Minister.'

'I hope I'm not seasick.'

'You won't be. You'll be staying on the concrete platform, not on a rig.'

'I thought they were *all* rigs.'

'No, they're not. It's the rig that makes one seasick. A rig is used for test drilling – to check if there's oil in a given spot. Most of the rigs are semi-submersible, with the greater portion of their weight below water, usually in the shape of enormous pontoons and held down by fourteen-ton anchors. They are, in a sense, like floating factories and they *do* pitch and sway just like ships. But the platforms are different. Once a rig finds an oilfield, a platform is sent out to replace it. The rig drills to find oil; the platform houses the production machinery when they actually start bringing the oil up. Made of concrete, the platform's main deck is about the size of Trafalgar Square, and its legs are planted firmly on the seabed. It's more an island than a mere floating factory and it probably doesn't sway as much as high-rise flats. We're going to the new Forties Field platform, the largest in the North Sea. All the oil from the other fields now flows through the Forties and goes back through a single pipeline to Peterhead.' The Under-Secretary paused to give the Prime Minister time to take in this information. 'This platform is really huge. It's almost a self-contained refinery. We won't feel a tremor and I really don't think you'll be seasick.'

The PM nodded, his gaze still fixed on the grey sheet of cold, deadly water. The Wessex roared and shuddered. There was still a wind outside. Inside there were forty-four seats with not one of them vacant. The PM sighed, feeling tired and edgy. The last three years had been terrible, a general election was being demanded, and the importance of this trip weighed heavily upon him, making him nervous.

'What do you think?' he asked abruptly.

'About the oil companies?'

'Yes.'

'I think we'll have to tread with care. They're not easy to deal with.'

'No. They're not easy to deal with. I sometimes wonder who really runs the country – us or the conglomerates.'

The Under-Secretary smiled, knowing what the PM meant. He gazed at the reports in his hand but learnt little from them.

'They're a problem,' he agreed. 'They're almost beyond jurisdiction. We have to think of the voters, British interests, the long term, but the conglomerates are nearly all multinational and don't recognize boundaries. They're not tied to any single country. They simply trade among themselves. If they have a problem with one country, they move their assets to another and there's always one that will offer a tax haven. That's why we're in trouble. They're not willing to pay our taxes. Now they've practically stopped work in the North Sea and instead have turned their attention to the Middle East, where they enjoy tax-free profits beyond belief.'

'Those are *British* companies.'

'No, Prime Minister, they're not. They're multinationals with their roots overseas; the so-called British companies are merely their subsidiaries. As for the *British* companies, they're simply sitting on their oil, claiming they can't afford to invest any more and patiently waiting for us to give in and lower the current oil tax.'

'Bastards,' the Prime Minister said flatly.

'Exactly,' the Under-Secretary said. 'But we no longer have a choice; we have to negotiate with them.'

The PM shuddered again. He had been feeling older recently. He sometimes felt that he had been at this game too long; that he could no longer handle it. There were no simple answers, the ground was shifting all the time, and the politician had to share all his decisions with the unions and businessmen.

Who indeed ran the country? It was a question he often asked himself. There were forces beyond the reach of mere governments that could make and break policies. The government was no more than a mouthpiece, an imperfect focus for public attention. Behind the scenes, in private boardrooms and in far-away continents, the real decision-makers ruled the world.

'How far out is the Forties Field?' he asked, keen to change the subject.

'Just over a hundred miles.'

'It's not near Shetland, then?'

'No. Frigg and Beryl are near Shetland; about halfway between Shetland and Norway.'

'Still, it'll be cold there.'

'Yes, Prime Minister.'

'I hope they don't get any gales.'

'Unfortunately, they get a lot. They even get gales in summer. Work on the rigs is totally subject to weather and the North Sea is terrible in that respect. It makes things costly, destroying rigs, wrecking schedules. Supply boats often toss at anchor for days, sometimes weeks, just waiting until unloading can start. They often can't tow rigs away, men are frequently swept overboard, and rigs are sometimes blown off their sites and have to be towed back. So yes, they get gales all right.'

The PM shifted uneasily in the seat and massaged his ruddy chin with his right hand.

'The Scots won't like it,' he said, returning to the first, uncomfortable subject. 'They'll say we're giving their oil away to make a quick profit. They're getting close to a majority, they're demanding independence, and they'll want the oil to be there when they get it.'

'*If* they get it, Prime Minister.'

'I don't think we can discount the possibility, though it may take a long time. Meanwhile, we've the Irish to contend with. What about them?'

'You mean their threats against the oil rigs?'

'Precisely.'

'The rumours that the IRA are planning to hijack the rigs and hold the British government to ransom remain just that: rumours. So far we have no cause to think otherwise.'

'But what if they *did* do what they threatened and captured the oil rigs? How would that effect us?'

'Frankly, Prime Minister, it would be a catastrophe. With the economy on the verge of collapse, only North Sea oil revenue can possibly save it. The Irish Troubles continue, our unemployment is shockingly high, overseas investors are pulling out with increasing frequency, and the possibility of economic collapse has become public knowledge. That's why we so desperately need the oil revenue: it's all we have left. If the rigs were to be taken over or, even worse, destroyed, our economy would collapse overnight.'

'Wonderful,' the PM said drily. 'I trust we've taken the necessary safeguards.'

'Yes, Prime Minister. Naturally. There's at least one top security man on every rig and platform. Each rig and platform also has an SBS intelligence man operating under cover as a rig worker. On shore, both the SBS and the SAS are on constant alert, ready to be flown in at thirty minutes' notice. Even if these measures fail and one of the rigs or platforms is somehow captured, it will be an isolated incident that can't affect the other rigs and platforms. By this I mean that no group can steal the entire oilfield network, which is what they'd have to do in order to hold us to ransom. For instance, if a bunch of terrorists capture a rig, we'll simply leave them there until they give in, letting them starve to death if necessary. Meanwhile the other rigs, being many, sometimes hundreds, of miles apart, will keep operating. In other words, individual rigs or platforms may be endangered, but the oilfields are safe.'

'Let's hope so,' the PM said.

'We're going down,' the Under-Secretary noted. 'We must have reached the Forties.'

Glancing out through the window, the PM saw the bleak, wind-whipped sea. There was a derrick on a platform far below, looking terribly desolate. Then the helicopter dropped lower. He saw a second rig, then a third. One of the rigs was burning off its waste gas and the smoke billowed sideways. The helicopter dropped lower. The rigs started looking bigger. He saw a square-shaped concrete platform with huge legs and crossbeams and a couple of frail-looking derricks. The platform didn't move as the sea poured between its legs. The helicopter continued its descent, and the platform grew wider and taller, taking on shape and detail.

It was huge, like a giant Meccano set. The towering derricks and cranes, steel catwalks and metal tanks, piles of crates and a plethora of prefabricated buildings impressed the PM; he felt an unaccustomed, childlike awe. The helicopter dropped lower, to below the tallest derrick . . . and then suddenly the massive platform was spread out to his right like some monolith from an unknown world.

The legs were incredibly wide and webbed with thick steel beams. The sea surged up to smash against the legs, then fell back and rushed in again. The PM held his breath. He saw the helicopter pad. Circled in blue and white, it was on the edge of the platform, and loomed nearly 200 feet above the sea, just above the main deck. The helicopter dropped towards it. The steel-webbed derricks grew taller. The PM glanced up, but he couldn't see the tops of the derricks, so he looked down again. The landing pad rushed up towards him with the sea far below it. The monstrous steel maze swung around him in a grey haze, then suddenly it was towering above him, reaching up to the stormy sky.

The PM licked his lips. The helicopter roared even louder. It bumped on to the landing pad and bounced a few times, then finally came to a shuddering rest. Its engine died and the spinning rotor blades separated. Staring out in a daze, the PM saw a huge factory where men hung from metal girders, clambered up swaying ladders, crossed catwalks swept by spray, crawled along lengths of steel pipes that swayed dangerously above the roaring waves. Then the PM looked down. He saw the sea far below. An enormous concrete leg plunged towards it and made him feel dizzy.

'Home and dry,' someone said cheerily.

3

The rotors of the Wessex were still spinning when Tony Masters jumped out of the helicopter and stood on the landing pad of Eagle 3, Frigg Field. The wind whipped his face and he breathed the fresh, freezing sea air. When a man in red overalls waved at him, he grinned and waved back. The chopper's engine tapered off and the rotors finally stopped spinning. Two men in yellow overalls placed blocks around the wheels as the pilot jumped down behind Masters. The pilot combed his brown hair, chewed gum and grinned at nothing in particular as he gazed about him.

Masters looked at the floating factory that soared up to the grey sky and heard the savage roaring of the drilling shaft. Too big to be imagined, the rig never failed to impress him. It was a factory built for giants and the men were like ants beneath the huge structures. They were working on the muddy deck, which was a maze of cranes and loading bays, countless lamps and antennae, three-ton pipes and Portakabins. Though a quarter of a mile wide, the deck rose and fell constantly. Beneath it there were two other floors; beneath those, the massive legs.

'Shall I get them out?' the pilot, Jack Schulman, asked.

Masters nodded and glanced down at the sea way below him. It was grey and quite rough, washing around the pontoon legs, stretching out to the distant horizon, now obscured in a dismal haze. This was a semi-submersible rig. It had four main pontoon legs, thirty feet wide and nearly three hundred feet long, which plunged eighty feet beneath the sea to the massive pontoons. The pontoon legs were hollow and webbed with steel ladders. The pontoons themselves were filled with water and attached to the seabed with huge anchor chains.

'All right!' Schulman bawled. 'Shake your asses!'

Glancing over his shoulder, Masters saw the first of the replacement crew clambering down out of the Wessex. Beyond the helicopter, stretching out to the horizon, was the featureless grey mass of the North Sea. The chopper seemed to rise and fall. The deck was swaying to and fro. The men were clambering down and piling up their luggage on the vibrating landing pad. In fact, the whole rig was vibrating. The central shaft continued roaring. The jib of a distant crane swung out over the sea and its thick chain rattled over the side.

Masters shivered and clapped his hands. The

wind was constant and always icy. Eagle 3 was two hundred miles north of Aberdeen, halfway between the Shetlands and Norway. Originally its oil had been piped down through Beryl to the Orkneys, but threats from the IRA had put a stop to that and now it went on through Beryl to the Forties Field, where about now the Prime Minister would be landing.

'OK,' Masters said to the men grouped around the Wessex. 'Sort out your gear, then follow that man in yellow overalls – that's Jim Webb, by the way – down to your quarters. Let me remind you new men to watch your step. Don't trip on anything, don't fall off the edge, and *don't* let the wind blow you away.' Some of the men laughed at that, but they stopped when Masters stared coldly at them. 'I'm not kidding,' he said. 'These rigs are extremely dangerous. The decks are slippery with mud and oil, machinery often breaks loose, and the wind can unexpectedly turn fierce and blow men off the catwalks. The sea's two hundred feet below. The water temperature's five degrees Celsius. So if you don't break your neck when you fall, you'll freeze to death in minutes. OK, let's get moving.'

The men sorted out their gear and followed Jim Webb to the steps that led down from the landing pad to the deck below. The deck was swaying, dipping towards the sea and back up, the waves growling and smashing against the pontoon legs and sending spray fanning into the air. Masters looked at the derrick. Grey clouds drifted above it. It was a hundred and fifty feet tall, its tapering legs webbed with steel, and its square base rested firmly on the roof of the semi-enclosed drilling deck. The drill shaft was rotating, making a Godalmighty roaring. Around the shaft, on the edge of the immense deck, cranes shrieked and turned back and forth.

'You gonna sign for this lot, Masters?'

Schulman, chewing gum, was standing beside the tool-pusher and holding out the passenger list. When Masters signed it, Schulman winked and spat out his gum. He put his hand in his pocket, pulled out another stick, unwrapped it, slid it between his teeth and started chewing again.

'Why did you bring those new kids?' he asked. 'I heard this rig's closing down.'

'It is. We're towing it away next week. The work on board will be light and we can teach the new ones easier that way.'

'Hi-ho,' Schulman said in his broad Montana accent. 'I have another load to go back. What time are they leaving?'

'About an hour,' Masters told him. 'One, maybe two. I've got to check the new ones in before I can check out the old. So just hang on to your balls and we'll get there.'

'Fireball Masters,' Schulman said. 'Read you

loud and clear, chief.' He grinned as he chewed. After glancing at the stormy sea far below, he zipped up his bright-red flying jacket. 'A nice place to work,' he said, shivering in the wind. 'It sure beats air-conditioning.'

Masters grinned at him. 'You're getting soft, Jack. It's the curse of being born an American; your bones have gone soft.'

'Oh, yeah,' Schulman replied. 'Don't I know it? Now you, Masters, you're just a goddamn monster. You've got no sensitivity.'

'I eat a healthy breakfast,' Masters said. 'I try not to masturbate. I'm a clean-living, all-British lad, and I work for my tuppence.'

'How'd you get to be a tool-pusher?'

'I worked for my tuppence.'

'Come *on*, Tone! Most of the tool-pushers are American, so how did you get the job?'

'I honestly can't remember.'

'Bullshit! You're snowing me. Anyway, my friend, you sure climbed fast. You must've been pretty good. The oil companies don't normally think so highly of Limey rig workers. Yeah, you must've been sharp.'

'Thank you, Jack, for those kind words.'

The pilot grinned. 'You going down now?'

'Yeah.'

'I'll come down for a beer.'

Masters picked up his rucksack and they both

walked away from the helicopter. Located above the main deck, the landing pad was joined to it by a steep catwalk. Beneath the catwalk was nothing but a dizzying plunge to the water. Stopping halfway across, Masters looked out over the sea. On the horizon was a rig, barely distinguishable except for the dark smoke from waste gas coiling skyward. Masters looked down and saw the huge, slanting leg. Hollow supports, a yard thick, formed a web beneath the decks and angled down about a hundred and forty feet to join the pontoon legs. The sea smashed against the legs, making a hollow drumming sound. The shifting shadow of the rig turned the grey water black and made it look even more frightening.

'Hey, Masters, what the fuck are you doing? Planning a swim?'

Already on the deck, Schulman was waving up at Masters. He looked small and he was shouting against the noise as the wind beat at him. Masters waved and clambered down, keeping his hand on the railing. He stepped on to the deck with great care, seeing patches of oil and mud.

'These rigs are fucking filthy, man,' Schulman said. 'I don't know how you can work here.'

They started across the open deck. The oil and mud had made it slippery. From the centre of the deck, to their right, came the roar of the drilling room. They passed stacks of iron piping, then went under a raised crane which was rumbling fifty feet above their heads on a broad, round steel base. Masters stopped to glance up. The crane was picking up some large wooden crates with men standing on top of them and holding on to the thick chain of the jib. The crane whined and turned around, swinging the men out on the crates. They swung out beyond the deck, high above the sea, shouting instructions as the crates were lowered to the supply boat below.

'Goddamn roustabouts,' Schulman growled.

'Yeah,' replied Masters. 'They're obviously taking off the heavier equipment before the tow starts.'

They started walking again. When a yellow fork-lift trundled past them, the driver shouted a greeting and waved at Masters. Masters waved back as he passed some cursing roustabouts. They were leaning on a spanner that was bigger than a man, straining to disconnect two massive pipes, forty-five feet long and each weighing three tons. The men cursed and strained. The wind lashed across the deck, which constantly vibrated, swayed from side to side, and gave off an insane metallic shrieking and the roar of the drilling shaft. The sea smashed relentlessly against the hollow pontoon legs and made them reverberate.

Schulman reached one of the modules, opened the door and bowed to Masters. The tool-pusher grinned and stepped in, followed by the American. They heard a deep, muffled rumbling.

'Just show me the bar,' Schulman said. 'I could do with a drink.'

Masters unzipped his jacket. 'No spirits allowed,' he said. 'We *do* permit two cans of beer a day. You can take it or leave it.'

Schulman grinned and chewed his gum. 'Fucking hot in here. Yeah, I'll take you up on that offer. It's the beer I came down for.'

They were in a narrow, low-ceilinged, brightly lit corridor. It was just like a ship, with many steps, steel doors, and passages leading off in several directions. It was one of the many prefabricated buildings known as modules. Erected after the rig had been towed to its site, they could easily be dismantled and offloaded.

'It's a morgue,' Schulman said.

'The living quarters and operations rooms,' Masters informed him.

'Christ, I feel buried here.'

Masters led the pilot along the corridor, turned the corner at the end, then went along another corridor, its steel walls painted white, and disappeared through an open door. Schulman followed him into a cluttered office module. It had a single porthole, through which the hazy horizon could be seen. Another white-painted wall was occupied by a large map of the North Sea, while a third was covered with various nautical charts and graphs. A heavy, suntanned man was sitting behind the desk. Schulman recognized a redneck when he saw one and knew this Yank was a redneck.

'How are you, Tone?' the man drawled. 'You bin gettin' your rocks off?'

'Dipped it once or twice,' Masters replied. 'Academic interest, mainly.'

'Jesus,' the redneck said, 'you goddamn Brits. Always quick with the come-back.' He scratched his nose and stared at Schulman. 'Who the hell's that?' he asked Masters. 'Looks like Jack Nicholson.'

'First name's right,' Schulman informed him. 'Jack Schulman. I'm the pilot who's taking your old crew back. When do we leave?'

The man yawned and stretched. After rubbing his face with his hands, he stood up and gazed through the porthole.

'They're already waiting in the canteen,' he said. 'They've been cleared to leave.'

'Any problems in my absence?' Masters asked.

'No problems. Apart from the fact that most Brits are lazy cunts, it's all been hunky-dory on Eagle 3.' Grinning, the redneck turned back to face Masters. He was wearing grey trousers and a shirt that advertised Twentieth Century Oil. 'We're offloading the heavy gear and extracting the blow-back preventer. We'll soon be putting the locks on the cranes and then it's all set to go. It'll look like a ghost ship.'

He yawned again and rubbed his eyes. Schulman noticed that his shoes were covered in oil and a thin, slimy mud.

'Are you going back?' Masters asked him.

'Yeah, I'm goin' back. I'm having two weeks onshore and then I'm taking over a rig in the Forties.'

'There'll be a lot of work there shortly.'

'There hasn't been in the past. That fucking government of yours has killed it off and we're not playing ball.'

'That's going to change,' Masters informed him. 'The Prime Minister's there right now. I think he's going to reduce the oil tax. If he does, we'll start drilling.'

'I hope so,' the redneck drawled. 'I sure as hell hope so. I don't want to be pensioned off.' He grinned again at Masters. 'So,' he said, 'I better get ready to leave. Go and get your new boys organized – and send mine up to the chopper.'

Masters and Schulman left the cabin, and made their way down a flight of steel stairs and into the canteen. It was a functional, brightly lit room with white tables and blue-leatherette chairs. The replacement crew were eating T-bone steaks with chips and mushrooms. The departing crew were drinking at the bar. Since hard liquor wasn't allowed on the rigs, they were all guzzling beer.

'Hey, Masters!' one of them shouted across the room. 'When the fuck are we leaving?'

'Leaving?' Masters replied dourly. 'You want to leave? I just don't understand that.'

Most of the men laughed. 'I want the night-life of Aberdeen,' one of them said. 'I'm in need of a quick thrill.' More laughter followed. 'Two weeks on shore, that's all,' someone else said. 'What's the delay?'

Masters grinned and put his hands up as if holding them at bay. 'Take it easy,' he said. 'The chopper's being refuelled right now and when that's done you can go.' The men at the bar cheered. 'OK,' Masters said when the cheering had died away. 'I want you to wait in the recreation room. You can take your beer with you. We'll call you when we're ready to leave. That's it. On your way.'

The men cheered again, traded ribald remarks, slapped each other on the back, then picked up their luggage and filed out of the canteen.

'Right,' Masters said, remaining standing to address the men still at the tables, 'put your knives and forks down and listen. You regular crew members know what I'm going to say, but you'll just have to bear with me. You new men, please note these facts. Most of you have probably worked in a factory before and an oil rig resembles a factory. But that resemblance is deceptive. An oil rig is very different. For one thing, it floats. That means it's always rolling. The decks are slippery and it's easy to lose your footing and slide right off the edge. It's a two-hundred-foot drop. If you survive the fall, you won't survive the sea, so try not to fall. A rig is also exposed. An average North Sea wind can be something like fifty miles an hour and it often reaches a hundred and sometimes a hundred and fifty. We get waves the size of your average office block. They wreck machinery and swallow men. Even a modest gale can cause chains to snap and then all hell breaks loose. Watch out for flying bolts. Beware of sliding equipment. It's easy to get crushed between crates when they slide on the decks. And be careful on the catwalks. Keep your hands on the railings. When a man gets too cocky he gets careless and that's something he can't afford. Men have been swept off the catwalks. They've fallen down the moonpool. They've been hit by flying bolts, crushed between machines, and killed by equipment falling from cranes or the platforms above them. Believe me, all this happens.'

The men, he noticed, were all listening carefully, impressed by the sound of his voice and his air of authority. He had picked up this skill in the SBS and he was now grateful for it.

'About your work,' he continued. 'It's two weeks on and two weeks off. What you do on shore is your own business, but on the rig you'll obey all the rules. Work on the rig goes on all around the clock in two shifts. You work twelve hours a day, seven days a week. You sleep four to a room, but since you all work in shifts, there'll only be two of you sleeping at any one time. Work is hard on the rigs and you'll find that you need your sleep, so you won't want to be disturbed by the other two men. Bear this in mind if you have to go to your room, and try not to disturb the ones sleeping. If you do and a man complains you'll be dismissed and that's that. You have a recreation room with a film on every evening. You're only allowed to smoke in off-duty space and off-duty time; and the only alcohol permitted is your free allowance of two cans of beer a day. Anyone caught breaking these rules will be flown back on the next available chopper with no chance to appeal.'

Masters stared at the new intake, his face firm and uncompromising, his hands on his hips, his long legs outstretched.

'Another point to remember,' he continued. 'Most of these rigs are hired from drilling companies and are indirectly under their supervision. Now although you men are employed by the oil company, you'll find yourselves dealing with men employed by the drilling company, a geological company, repair and maintenance companies, and a catering company. Don't mess with any of these people. Avoid all disputes with them. If you've any complaints go direct to your foreman and let him investigate the matter. Anyone breaking this rule, whether for good reasons or bad, will end up on the first chopper back to Aberdeen.'

He turned to the wall behind him and picked up the telephone. 'Hello, Segal? This is Masters. Get yourself down to the canteen. I've got some new men here.' He put the receiver back on its hook and then turned to the men again. 'You'll find a guide to the rig on your beds. Study it carefully, have a good look around, then report to the foreman named at the top of the guide. His location will be marked on the scale drawing. He'll tell you when and where you'll be starting. Once you've started, make sure you do what you're told and don't piss around. If you cause any trouble, you'll be dismissed – and I'm notoriously deaf to excuses.'

A man entered the canteen. He was wearing overalls and boots, his brown hair was dishevelled, and he was covered from top to bottom in mud and oil. He grinned and nodded at Masters, waving a grimy hand, then glanced at the new men.

'I've just completed the briefing,' Masters said, 'so you can show them down to their quarters, then tell Delaney you've got them.'

'Right, chief,' the man said.

The men were led out of the canteen and Masters and Schulman went to the bar. Masters asked for two beers, snapped the lids on both cans, then pushed one of the cans across to the American.

'There,' he said, 'have some vitamins.'

Schulman rolled his eyes and drank some beer. He wiped his lips with the back of his left hand and grunted with pleasure.

'That was a pretty good speech, Tone,' he said. 'I could feel my flesh creeping.'

Masters grinned. 'I'm glad it got through to *someone*. It's a pity you can't practise what I preach. Why not stay for a fortnight?'

'No thanks, man. I feel safer in my chopper. The only thing you've got to offer is beer and that ain't enough.'

'I'd keep you busy,' Masters promised.

'I bet you would,' Schulman replied. 'You'd run my ass ragged and then send me back home in a pine box. Thanks, but no thanks.'

Masters drank some more beer, then glanced around the almost empty canteen. It wasn't very different from the canteens in the various SBS bases he had passed through. That was why he felt so at home.

'What about those guys I'm taking back?' Schulman asked. 'Do I go get them now?'

'No, not yet. I've got to check a few things first. Once the men know they're shore-bound they're inclined to get careless and leave cock-ups that can cause a lot of damage. I want a quick look round first. I want to check that none of the bastards have fouled up in their urge to take off.'

'And what if someone has?'

'Then you'll be taking him back to Aberdeen and leaving him there. I won't want him back.'

'You're a tough nut, Tone.'

'Which is why your American friends appreciate me. Now drink up and let's go.'

They finished their drinks and left the canteen, with Masters leading the way down more steel steps and along narrow corridors, passing storerooms, administration modules, living accommodation and the radio shack. All the corridors were brightly lit, all the ceilings were low, and the many portholes overlooked the heaving sea and its murky horizon. There was a constant bass rumbling that grew louder as they descended more steps. Suddenly it turned into a shocking roar that shattered the senses.

They were on the drilling floor. A massive derrick towered above them. The drilling floor was walled in, but it was open to the sky, and there was a large, square-shaped hole in the deck: the 'moonpool'. The sea was two hundred feet below it, and enormous lengths of piping plunged down through the hole over twice that distance to the seabed. The central shaft was roaring and spinning. Men worked all around it, wearing overalls and helmets, every one of them filthy with oil. The central shaft kept roaring, making the whole deck vibrate. Other men were balanced on girders directly over the sea, tied securely to the structure with rope.

Schulman wanted to cover his ears. Instead he glanced down the moonpool. He saw the linked pipes running down and disappearing into the dark sea. That sight almost made him dizzy. It wasn't like being in the helicopter. When he saw the men above, tied to the structure with rope, hanging over that terrifying abyss, he had to admire them.

'What are they doing?' he asked.

'Removing the blow-back preventer,' Masters replied. 'It's a twenty-ton cube, but it's down four hundred feet and that makes it weigh four hundred tons. They're bringing it up, but they have to do it in forty-five-foot sections. They have to disconnect each pipe as it comes up and it's a hell of a job.'

The roaring stopped abruptly and the shaft whined to a standstill. On the girders, the men fixed huge clamps to the pipe and then attached thick chains to the clamps. The chains rattled and banged as the clamps made a dreadful screeching sound. The men were fixing large handles to the clamps as Masters walked from the hut.

Schulman followed him out and felt the blast of an icy wind. They were now on the main deck with its network of huge oil tanks and catwalks and thick, silver-painted flow-pipes. The derrick soared above the deck. Low clouds drifted over it. There were three platforms inside the derrick and the highest was the smallest. More men were working up there, looking minute and defenceless. The wind was howling between the girders of the derrick and making their overalls flap ceaselessly. Schulman glanced across the deck and saw more stacked pipes and oil tanks. Like everything else here, they were immense, soaring high above him. He followed Masters across the deck. A crane clanked and whined above them, swinging a stack of large wooden crates out over the sea with men hanging from the chains, giving the crane-driver hand signals.

Nearing the edge of the main deck, Masters waved Schulman forward. They both stopped when they were close to the rim, then Schulman looked down. He sucked in his breath automatically, then grabbed the railing beside him. The wind was beating at him, trying to push him off the edge, making him feel very vulnerable. The sea was very far below and he was looking down at a supply ship which, though immense, looked like a toy. Schulman felt a bit dizzy. It wasn't like being in the helicopter. The massive legs of the rig, running outwards and down, emphasized that dreadful plunge to the sea and made his head reel.

The crane was lowering the wooden crates, which were swinging to and fro. They swung under the decks and out again, each time dropping lower, with the roustabouts still balanced on them. Looking like ants on the chains, the men were now about a hundred feet down, still shouting and waving.

Schulman had to feel respect. He also felt a childish pride. His gaze fell upon the void between the men and the sea, then he saw the waves washing over the long, bobbing bulk of the loading ship, and that made him feel strange again. He turned away from those frightful depths. There was a sudden, savage roaring from the drilling hut and it gave him a shock. The enormous derrick towered over him.

Having just walked off the deck, Masters was framed by the sea and the sky as the wind howled about him. Then Schulman saw the platform thrusting out from the main deck. It was looming out over the sea and Masters stood on its far edge, at a bottle-shaped metal tank with a diving bell on the top. The diving bell was clamped on to the tank and the tank had round windows. It was a decompression chamber. Masters was at one of the windows. He gestured at someone inside, then put his thumb up. Schulman was loath to join him. He felt queasy at the very thought of it. He didn't want to go out there and be picked up by the wind and hurled down a couple of hundred feet to the sea. He was too young to die.

Another man walked past Schulman, off the deck and across the platform to Masters. He was wearing a white helmet and his overalls were smeared with oil. He grinned and shouted at Masters, glanced up and gesticulated. Schulman heard the appalling din of a crane, then saw a chain swinging into view. It stopped above Masters's head, above the decompression chamber. When the tool-pusher waved, two roustabouts rushed forward and clambered up the sides of the diving bell. There was a huge clamp on the chain, like a monstrous metal claw; it closed around the steel ring at the top of the diving bell and the roustabouts tightened screws all around it. Masters waved, left the platform and walked back up to Schulman. The men on top of the decompression chamber were checking the diving bell as the tool-pusher bellowed his instructions.

'It's the divers,' Masters explained. 'They're on saturation diving. We're going to lower them down there again, to check out the drilling point. They go down in the bell.'

'How deep?' Schulman asked.

'Four hundred feet.'

'Jesus,' Schulman hissed. 'How do they stand it?'

'It's a tough job,' Masters replied, meaning it, having himself gone down in a decompression chamber as part of his SBS training. 'That chamber's only ten foot long and there's six men inside it.'

'How long have they been in there?'

'Two weeks,' Masters told him. 'There's six

bunks in there. The men go down, the bell's hauled up when they're finished, it's attached to the top of the decompression chamber again, and then they go straight into the chamber.'

'You mean they *live* in that fucking thing for two weeks?'

'That's right. In the old days they would dive, undergo decompression, have a long break and then go down again. It was known as bounce diving. But now we can't afford that. We just don't have the time. Now we do saturation diving, which is what these men specialize in. The diver comes up and stays in the chamber until he needs to go down again. Since he doesn't step out into normal pressure at all, he doesn't have to be completely decompressed before he goes down again. He eats and sleeps in there. Food is sent in through the airlock. The pressure turns his voice girlish and the helium destroys his sense of taste. He lives and works there for a fortnight, then spends another week there decompressing. It's a hell of a life.'

Schulman looked back at the platform. The roustabouts were still on top of the decompression chamber, surrounding the diving bell. One of them put his thumb up. Masters waved them down, and they slid off the side of the metal chamber and hurried back to the main deck. The tool-pusher looked through a window, then grinned and jerked his own thumb up. He walked away from the platform and glanced up, then waved his right hand.

The crane whined into life, its winch clattering noisily. The chain went taut as it picked up the diving bell, which swung from side to side over the decompression chamber, dangling in the grey void of the sky with the sea far below. It dropped towards the water, bouncing gently against the platform. It had half disappeared when the sea started roaring.

'Jesus Christ!' Masters whispered.

The roaring started far below, then spread out and reverberated. The men all rushed automatically to the platform and grabbed hold of the railing. Suddenly, the whole deck tilted. The roar of the sea became much louder. They saw the waves leaping up and curving back down, to smash again and again over the loading ship. Then the roaring became an explosion, with water geysering up and outward. It was exploding out from under a pontoon leg and turning the sea wild.

Schulman couldn't believe it. The deck tilted to the left. The whole rig shook and he heard the exploding sea and saw a white wall of water. The water exploded upwards, a hundred feet high. It spread out like a great fan and crashed down on top of the loading ship, completely submerging it. Schulman glanced around at Masters and saw his wide eyes, his knuckles white on the railing, which slanted down alarmingly to the left. The whole deck was slipping. Then it jumped up and fell again. It was a quarter of a mile long and yet it was tilting and screeching insanely. Schulman saw the diving bell swinging out and in again. It crashed into the platform with a dreadful bang. Then Schulman saw the sea and the sky and found himself on his back.

'The diving bell! Get it in!'

Schulman felt himself sliding, heading feet first towards the edge. He couldn't breathe and his heart was racing wildly as he clawed at thin air. His hand found something solid, his fist closed around a chain. His head was spinning and the roaring was in his ears, though he could hear Masters shouting. Schulman swallowed hard and blinked, then gazed down at his own body. His feet were dangling over the edge of the deck and beyond the narrow platform tilted downwards. There the decompression chamber was nearly on its side, hanging out over the sea. He heard the shriek of tortured metal, the snapping of bolts, and saw the chamber's clamps splitting open. Men were shouting on all sides. He glanced down at the bell, which was swinging out from the tilting side. Masters was looking back up over his shoulder, bawling instructions at someone. The crane was winching up, but the bell swung out and in again and smashed against the deck.

'Jesus Christ! The crane's going!' Schulman yelled.

Hanging down the tilting side, the American rolled on to his belly. He pulled himself toward the crates piled high above him and heard the shriek of bending metal and the heavy rattling of chains. He pulled himself to his feet, and saw men running in all directions. Looking up, he saw the crane way above, slowly turning and tilting. It was making a fearsome sound, being torn from its support. The huge support was leaning far to the right with the crane sliding off it. Schulman couldn't believe it. The crane was fifty feet up. It was monstrous, a huge contraption and its jib, about to crash to the deck. Men bellowed and scattered. Metal shrieked as the crane broke loose. It seemed to hang in the air, the jib buckled and broke apart, then the whole mass of metal and chains exploded over the deck.

Someone screamed and Schulman blinked and saw the spinning bell. The chain snapped and the bell disappeared as it plunged to the sea. Then the noise became overpowering. The falling crane had smashed through the deck. A huge chain whipped through the air and the jib fell apart and enormous, jagged pieces of steel pipe started bouncing and clattering. These rolled off the edge of the deck and plunged towards the sea, smashing on their way down into wooden crates, which exploded and were torn from their moorings and crushed men as they plummeted into the water.

Schulman heard the dreadful screams. The deck shuddered beneath him. He looked up and heard the derrick groaning and saw its frame bending. 'Oh, my God!' he cried out.

'Schulman, move!' Masters bawled. Something grabbed Schulman, tearing him from the crates and pushing him forcefully forward. He knew it wasn't Masters, but he didn't stop to look back. Racing away from the derrick, he ran straight for the landing pad, hearing bawling and fearsome metallic screeching, and seeing chaos on all sides.

Something heavy crashed into the American, almost making his head explode. Recovering, he looked about him and saw enormous metal pipes breaking loose and rolling over the deck. They made a dreadful din, sweeping men and crates aside. Then Schulman glanced up and saw the towering derrick breaking apart and collapsing.

It was a terrible sight. The webbed beams were snapping free, bending and flying out and falling down and crashing into the drilling room. Schulman heard the demoniac noise, punctuated by the screams of the dying men. The derrick platforms fell apart and dropped down between the legs, then the legs themselves buckled and broke as the massive structure collapsed. Schulman looked up in awe. The spectacle froze him where he stood. There was an inferno of clanging steel and splintering wood and screaming men. Then the roof of the drilling room caved in and the noise grew even louder.

'On your feet! Get going!'

Galvanized by Masters's voice, Schulman started running, heading for the helicopter pad now sloping towards the sea. A sudden panic seized him. The helicopter had started moving. It was sliding towards the edge of the landing pad while slowly turning around. Schulman sobbed, but kept running. He didn't look back for Masters. He heard screams and passed other fleeing men, then saw a huge tank collapsing. It smashed through its supports and hit the deck with a fearsome sound. Though forty feet wide, the tank rolled rapidly across the deck to crush two men and crash into the modules and sweep the structures over the side.

Schulman didn't stop to help. He saw the helicopter slipping. A large wooden crate was racing towards him, shaking and screeching. It hit a tank and fell apart, the wood exploding in all directions. The yellow fork-lift inside it spun round and crashed into a catwalk, tearing it from its moorings. The catwalk buckled down the middle, bounced up in the air, rolled shrieking across the careering fork-lift and was finally dragged along with it. Schulman glimpsed waving arms and heard a terrible, dying scream. A decapitated body was mangled up in the spinning catwalk, limbs flailing in a gruesome dance as it went over the side.

But Schulman kept running up the sloping deck. Seeing the helicopter slipping towards the sea, he wanted to scream. Another roar, another crash. More explosions and colliding pipes. He heard bawling and saw shadowy, running figures as he reached the catwalk. The landing pad was tilting badly, its nearside swinging upwards, tearing the catwalk out of the deck and making its bolts snap. Without thinking, Schulman leapt forward to grab hold of the railing. Glancing down, he saw the sickening drop to the sea. Then Masters slapped his back and bawled something. The catwalk shuddered and its steel frame shrieked and bent as Schulman started his climb.

'It's broken loose!' Masters bellowed.

Schulman dived at the landing pad, hit the deck and rolled over. He heard the mangling of metal as the catwalk tore loose, then felt something fall across him and roll off. Blinking, he saw Masters sprawling beside him, then clambering back to his feet with great agility and rushing forward again.

The American sprang to his feet as the catwalk disappeared. The whole rig was now tilting towards the sea. Turning towards the landing pad, Schulman saw Masters at the helicopter, which was sliding dangerously close to the edge as he tugged its door open. Masters hauled himself up and Schulman raced up behind him. As Masters disappeared inside, the pilot hauled himself in and scrambled past him like a madman to get at the controls.

Schulman hardly knew what he was doing, but his training saw him through. The engines roared into life and the props picked up speed. Glanced out, he saw the deck veering down, the edge curving away from him. He worked the controls, felt a feverish, fearful clarity, then glanced down at the sea far below, the upturned loading ship and the drowning men.

Schulman tried to control the helicopter, but it swung towards the edge. The deck disappeared beneath him and he felt his stomach lurch. The helicopter dropped into space, fell a little, then rose again.

'Jesus Christ!' Masters groaned.

They climbed to eight hundred feet and hovered there to survey the wreckage. The huge rig was sinking down at the north-east corner, slipping into the sea, the massive deck a hideous mess of tangled steel and broken crates. A deluge of men and equipment was pouring over the sides. The corner of the rig sank, the sea boiling and swirling around it. The rest of the deck was pointing at the sky, swaying to and fro, before sinking slowly. Two pontoon legs surfaced, rising up three hundred feet in the air, and then slid under the water. The water churned and closed over them. A black hole materialized and turned into a whirlpool that imprisoned the men and machinery and sucked them all down. It was a ghastly, silent spectacle; a dark, eerie dream. The whirlpool swirled and sucked everything down and then folded in on itself.

Eventually the sea settled. It was calm and utterly desolate. Schulman looked down and saw nothing but those grey Arctic wastes.

'Head for the Forties Field,' Masters said.

4

The first interruption came in the middle of the Prime Minister's opening remarks. Keith Turner, sitting at the long table in the boardroom of Bravo 1, looked exasperated as he picked up the telephone. 'Excuse me, Prime Minister,' he said. 'I have to leave this line open.' He put the receiver to his ear and saw the Prime Minister watching him. He had never met the PM before, and found him intimidating.

There was some static on the line and Turner, the general supervisor of all the North Sea oil rigs, flushed with annoyance. He had told them specifically not to call him unless it was urgent. Now he heard the radio operator and it was clear that he was upset. 'I think you better get here right away. Eagle 3's in bad trouble,' the man said. Turner coughed into his fist and glanced apologetically around him. The PM had his chin in his hands and was staring straight at him.

'Trouble?' Turner asked. 'What kind of trouble?'

The boardroom was crowded. It overlooked the Forties Field. There were isolated oil rigs in the distance, and Turner couldn't stop staring at them. They suddenly filled his whole consciousness. The PM and his executives and the oil men and the secretaries – all disappeared from his vision and his thoughts as his heart started racing.

The operator's voice was high-pitched, almost hysterical. The man was babbling about a message from Eagle 3 and Turner sensed it was serious. He mumbled something to the operator, put the phone down, then glanced at the men all around him and shook imperceptibly.

'Excuse me, gentlemen,' he said, 'but I have to leave. We have an emergency.'

'Emergency?' someone repeated. It was Sir Reginald McMillan, the Chairman of British United Oil, and he was drumming his fingers. 'What *kind* of emergency?'

'I'm not sure, sir,' Turner said, standing up and tugging at his neat black beard. 'We've just had a call from Eagle 3 and I'll have to attend to it.'

He didn't wait to discuss it further. He wasn't too sure of what he'd heard. Smiling nervously, he rushed from the boardroom and headed straight for the radio shack. It took him quite a while to get there. Bravo 1 was immense; it was a platform with five drilling units and numerous decks. Turner hurried across the catwalks, feeling a warm, southerly wind. He saw the sea far below, all around him, and it gave him no comfort.

Could Eagle 3 really be sinking? The question rang in his head as he raced across a deck and wove his way between fork-lifts and modules. He felt the pounding of his heart and felt distinctly unreal. When he saw the antennae rising above the radio shack, he thought of the gibbering operator and felt even more concerned. Is Masters all right? he wondered, anxious about his SBS man. Then he opened the door of the radio shack and hurried inside.

The first thing that struck him when he entered was how pale the operator looked. The man was trying to contact Eagle 3. He was cursing as he looked up at Turner and took off his earphones.

'I can't get a response,' he said.

The radio shack was small and cluttered, uncomfortably hot and badly lit. The operator had his sleeves rolled up and was spattered with oil.

'They said they were *sinking*?' Turner queried, still not able to grasp it.

'That's right,' the operator replied. 'That guy on Eagle 3, he was practically screaming and he said they were sinking. There was a hell of a lot of static. His radio wasn't working properly. I asked for confirmation, but he just went demented. Repeated that they were sinking. Said they were going down fast. I tried to get some more details, but the line just went dead and I haven't been able to get them back since.'

'You didn't get any other calls?'

'No, chief, not one.'

Turner bit his lower lip and glanced anxiously about him. This was something he didn't want to accept; it just didn't seem possible. How could it sink so suddenly? What the hell had gone wrong? A rig didn't just sink in a matter of minutes . . . Turner tugged at his black beard, his broad bulk trembling slightly, then he blinked and looked down at the operator, trying to order his thoughts.

'Any other calls from Eagle 3 this morning? Any messages at all?'

'No. We've been keeping the lines clear. All the rigs had instructions not to call except in an emergency.'

'No message from Masters?'

'Not a thing, chief. The first call I got was from Eagle 3 – and he said they were sinking.'

'I don't believe it,' Turner said. 'An accident, yes, I can accept that; but I can't see it sinking.'

'It sounded like it,' the operator said. 'That fucking guy was hysterical. And his radio was really in a mess, even before it went off. Since then, nothing, and that can't be a good sign.'

'Bloody hell,' Turner said. He reached for a telephone, punched out a number, and glanced distractedly out of the open door at the sea. 'Hello,

Jackson? Turner here. I want a helicopter over the Frigg Field to survey Eagle 3 . . . No, not from here. That would take too long. What's the closest rig in the Beryl Field?' He drummed his fingers on the desk, then nodded and put the phone down. 'OK,' he said to the operator. 'Ring Charlie 2. Tell them to get their chopper to Eagle 3 and check out what's happening.'

The operator nodded and put on his earphones. Turner walked out of the radio shack and looked up at the sky, wondering what the hell was happening out there. The afternoon light was hazy. The southerly wind was turning cold. He suddenly remembered the conference in the boardroom and his stomach churned.

Could the rig have gone down? The possibility was enough to make him shiver with a fearful fatigue. He wouldn't tell anyone yet. He would keep it quiet until he knew. The very thought of having to announce such a catastrophe was beyond his imagining.

The operator came to the doorway to stare at him with wide, disbelieving eyes.

'I can't get them,' he said.

'What?'

'I can't get them. I can't get in touch with Charlie 2.'

'What the hell do you mean?'

'I can't get them to reply. Their line's open,

but there's no answer. They're just not replying.'

Turner could hardly believe his ears. He glanced out at the murky sea. When he turned back, he saw that the operator was scared and confused.

'You mean there's no one at their radio? The operator isn't there? Are you trying to say there's no one on duty?'

The operator threw up his hands. 'I just can't get a reply. I'm saying that the line's definitely open, but they just won't reply.'

'This is crazy!' Turner exploded.

'Yeah, it's crazy. I know.'

'For Christ's sake, keep on trying,' Turner said. 'What the hell's going on?'

The operator disappeared and Turner paced up and down beneath the modules that had been piled upon modules as this platform had grown bigger. He was dwarfed by its immensity. The five derricks towered above him. The grey sky loured beyond them, the sea was all around them and the silence of the platform was eerie. None of the drills was in operation; they hadn't been working for weeks. Nevertheless, the enormous platform was busy, working as a refinery. Men were hurrying across the catwalks. Cranes and fork-lifts were in action. New buildings were still being erected. Turner looked all around him, surveying his vast domain. He pondered the riddle of Eagle 3 and Charlie 2 and it didn't make sense.

He went back to the radio shack. 'What the fuck's going on?' he snapped, more to himself than to the operator, who lifted his left hand and waved him into silence, then said: 'OK. Roger and out.' The operator switched to Receive, placed his earphones on the table, swivelled around in his chair and stared straight at Turner.

'Charlie 2?' Turner asked.

'No. That was Masters.'

'Eagle 3?'

'No. In a chopper. He says he's coming in now.'

Feeling confused and fearful, Turner fiddled with his beard and glanced through the open door. There was no sign of the helicopter. Sighing, he turned back to the operator and noticed again how pale he looked.

'Did he say anything other than that?' he asked.

'Yes,' the operator replied. 'He asked if you were here.'

'Did he say anything about Eagle 3?'

'He said to tell you to be here.'

That wasn't like Masters. It sounded like a command. Turner cursed and paced back and forth, trying to order his thoughts.

'What about Charlie 2?' he asked.

'There's still no reply.'

'What's going on?' Turner asked, his tone more resigned now. 'I don't get the connection.'

He left the radio shack, climbed down a steel ladder, then crossed the deck between towering blocks of modules, and skirted around the soaring steel derricks. The wind was growing colder and the sea rose and fell. He passed some men on an enormous pile of pipes, then walked beneath a raised crane. Turner felt his heart pounding. He didn't like to feel this nervous. He reached the end of the deck, climbed up another ladder, then mounted the steel catwalk to the landing pad.

The Bravo 1 helicopter was parked there, beside an empty space. Turner went to the phone in a booth near the landing pads. He rang a tool-pusher, Dwight Bascombe, and told him to send up two roustabouts. Having done so, he put the phone back on its cradle and walked to the empty landing pad. He looked up at the sky and saw the Eagle 3 helicopter descending.

Turner cursed and paced the deck, keeping his eye on the helicopter. The two roustabouts came up the catwalk, wearing bright yellow overalls. They nodded at Turner, then glanced up at the sky. The Wessex Mk 3 was dropping towards them, sounding muffled and distant. The roustabouts went to work, unlocking the holding clamps. When they were finished, they stepped back beside Turner and, like him, looked up at the approaching helicopter.

It was roaring right above them now, its props whipping the wind about them. They held on to the railings of the catwalk and watched it come down. It landed with some precision, bouncing only a little. Its engines stopped and the props turned more slowly and then the side door opened.

Masters emerged first. Schulman followed him too quickly. The broken features of the tool-pusher's face were like granite and his brown hair was windswept. He hurried towards Turner with the pilot close behind him, letting the other passengers disembark by themselves, most looking dazed. Turner noticed that Schulman was drained of colour and looked scared. The roustabouts went to work, blocking and clamping the chopper's wheels. Masters walked up to Turner and stared at him with bright, anguished eyes.

'Eagle 3 has gone down,' he said.

Turner didn't know what to say. It seemed incomprehensible. He swallowed and then glanced at Schulman, who seemed physically ill. There was shock and disbelief on the American's face and he was visibly shaking. Then Turner stared hard at Masters, who nodded and turned to Schulman. He told him to go down to the bar and get himself a stiff drink. The pilot did what he was told, turning away without a word. They watched him go along the sloping catwalk and enter one of the modules. Then Masters went to the phone and rang through to the doctor. He told him to go down to the bar and take a look at Schulman. When he had done so, he hung up the phone and turned back to Turner.

'What happened?' Turner asked.

'It went down,' Masters replied. He took Turner by the elbow and led him away from the listening roustabouts. They stopped beneath the catwalk, above the murmuring of the sea. Masters ran his fingers through his short brown hair and glanced sharply about him. 'We were bombed,' he said quietly.

Turner felt a little dazed. He also felt a creeping chill. He was trying hard not to think of the Prime Minister and of what he might have to tell him.

'Jesus,' Turner said.

'Yeah,' replied Masters. 'Some bastard planted a bomb in the north-east pontoon leg.'

'A bomb?'

'You've got it – a bomb. It blew a hole in the leg, the platform tilted, and the whole rig went crazy.'

'It's totally gone?' Turner asked.

'Yep. The whole rig fell apart and then it sank and took everything with it.'

'No survivors?'

'Apart from the few in the helicopter, no. No other survivors.'

'My God,' Turner said. He looked at the other man's eyes, which were glinting with shock and anger. They kept flitting back and forth around the deck, as if searching for clues. 'Who the hell . . . ?'

'I don't know,' Masters said. 'I've considered various possibilities, but most don't make sense.'

'It had to be someone on the rig.'

'You're pretty smart,' Masters said.

'A fanatic. Someone who didn't care if he went down with the rig. Some dumb bastard who wants to be a martyr.'

'Maybe,' Masters said. 'But he didn't have to go down with it. He might have used a long-delay timer. He didn't have to be there himself.'

'*Why?*' Turner asked.

'The Prime Minister,' Masters suggested. 'The time and dates can't have been accidental. It's just too close for comfort.'

'But why Eagle 3? It's a hundred and fifty miles north.'

'I know. It doesn't add up. There must be something else coming.'

Turner glanced around him, drawn by the sea's murmuring. He tried to focus on the roustabouts and roughnecks swarming over the platform.

'They're still in conference?' Masters asked.

'Jesus Christ, don't remind me.'

'Do they know?'

'No, they don't. They know there's an emergency, but they don't know what it is and I doubt whether they suspect the extent of it.'

'What about the radio operator?'

'Well, he knows it went down. He knows that, but he doesn't know what happened. Your man didn't get that far.'

'OK,' Masters said. 'We better make him stay quiet. We can say there's been a very bad accident. We needn't say what it was.'

'A bomb,' Turner said distractedly. 'Jesus Christ. Do you think it's us next?'

'I doubt it,' Masters said. 'I mean, I really can't believe it. This whole platform was checked from top to bottom – by your men *and* the SBS. Our divers were down there today. We've got cameras on the seabed. We've X-rayed every crate and every pipe, and the boardroom's well guarded. No, I don't think it will be here. I don't believe so. But I still can't work it out.'

'Why Eagle 3?' Turner asked for the second time. 'They must have known it was closing down. Why the hell would they plant a bomb on Eagle 3? They must be out of their minds.'

'I can't figure it out,' Masters said, staring at the ground.

'Charlie 2,' Turner recalled. 'When we heard what had happened, we tried to get in touch, but they simply wouldn't answer our calls.'

Masters jerked his head up and stared hard at Turner. 'You received no reply from Charlie 2? You think *they* might have sunk as well?'

'No,' Turner replied. 'The line was clearly open. Their radio was definitely turned on.' He shrugged. 'They just wouldn't respond.'

'Oh, my God,' Masters said.

He hurried away. Turner blinked and rushed after him. They walked across the main deck, past the stacked pipes and crates, beneath the cranes, around the derricks and modules, to a vertical ladder, which Masters climbed with practised ease. Turner followed and stood beside him on the platform, where the wind moaned about them. Masters massaged his forehead, blinked, rubbed his eyes, looked briefly at the leaden sky and the sea, then studied the radio shack.

'Let's keep it quiet for now,' he said. 'The last thing we want is panic. Let's just say there was a very bad accident and we're working it out.'

'An explosion,' Turner suggested. 'We'll say the well-head exploded. We'll say a pile of oil drums went up with it and caused complete chaos.'

'Charlie 2,' Masters said. 'There must be a connection. They wouldn't leave the radio open. They wouldn't just walk away.'

'Jesus Christ,' Turner whispered.

'It's on the pipeline,' Masters said. 'The main pipe runs from Frigg down to Beryl and then on to the Forties.'

'You mean terrorists?'

'Yes.'

'Jesus Christ, that's impossible!'

'There's no security on Beryl or Frigg. The security's here.'

'The *Prime Minister's* here!'

'That's correct: he's right here.'

'Then why Beryl? Why Frigg? I don't get it. It doesn't add up.'

'It just might,' Masters said, glancing intently around him. 'There's a floating refinery on Beryl and the pipe runs to here.'

'Then why Frigg?' Turner asked.

'The Frigg supply runs through Beryl. The oil extracted from Frigg goes to Beryl and then on to here.'

'But Frigg's drying up.'

'That's right, it's drying up.'

'Then why would they want to cut off Eagle 3 if the field's drying up?'

'I don't know,' Masters said.

He started walking again, heading for the radio shack. When he entered, Turner followed him in and the operator looked up, surprised. He was very pale. Staring at Masters, he opened his mouth to speak, then nervously cleared his throat.

'I've got Charlie 2,' he said. 'They want to speak to you, Masters. I asked for the message and they wouldn't give it. Instead, they told me to find you.'

'There's been an accident,' Masters told him.

'They sounded weird, chief. It wasn't the usual guy – it was McGee, and he sounded really strange.'

'What did he say?' Masters asked.

'Nothing,' the operator replied, glancing from Masters to Turner, clearly confused. 'He just said: "Go and get Masters." What's happening out there?'

'There's been an accident,' Turner lied. 'An explosion on Frigg. We're still trying to find out what caused it, so we want it kept quiet.'

The operator looked relieved. Shaking his head, he offered a tentative grin, then slowly stood up.

'Oh,' he said. 'I see. I mean, I thought it was just me. I thought maybe I'd done something wrong and I just couldn't work it out.'

'It's classified,' Masters told him. 'Accidents like this always are. We have to check it out thoroughly and put in a report. It has to be strictly confidential.'

'I understand, chief.'

'Make sure you do,' Masters warned him. 'If I hear the slightest word from the crew, you'll be out of a job.'

The operator licked his lips and nodded.

'Go outside,' Turner told him. 'Close the door when you leave. Stay out there and don't let anyone in. Is that understood?'

'Yes, chief,' the operator said, then hurried out of the radio shack. When the door was closed, Masters sat at the table and put on the earphones.

'Bravo 1 to Charlie 2,' Masters said. 'Are you receiving me?'

Turner heard the crackling radio. He couldn't hear what was being said. He heard Masters, but he couldn't hear Charlie 2 – only the static.

'Bravo 1,' Masters said. 'Yes, it's Masters. Let me speak to McGee.'

Turner paced up and down, feeling dazed and ill. He was nervous and he looked down at Masters with a singular sympathy. Masters listened for a long time. His hands were steady on the table. He had large hands and long, calloused fingers which didn't move once. Turner found the shack stifling. He paced up and down the short, narrow room and tried to empty his mind. Then he heard Masters curse and saw him put the earphones down. The tool-pusher swivelled around in his chair and looked at Turner with piercing eyes.

'It's McGee,' Masters said. 'He's got a terrorist group on board. He says they've also got a plutonium bomb on board – and they're willing to use it.'

'Jesus Christ!' Turner groaned. 'Oh, my God! What the hell do they want?'

'They want the Prime Minister.'

5

Masters and Turner were both sitting by the radio when Robert Barker entered the shack. He saw the sweat on Turner's forehead and the tension on the tool-pusher's face. He had not seen Masters so tense before, so he knew it was bad.

'OK,' Barker said, 'what's the emergency?'

'It's bad,' Masters said.

'I gathered that, Tone. I'm supposed to be protecting the Prime Minister, so what the hell is it?'

'We were bombed,' Masters said. 'Eagle 3 has been sunk. Now a bunch of terrorists has taken over Charlie 2 and they've got a plutonium bomb.'

Barker was silent for a moment, trying to take in this ghastly tale. He didn't have to ask if it was true; he could tell by looking at the two men's faces.

'Bombed?' he asked nevertheless, needing confirmation. 'How the hell did they do it?'

'They bombed one of the legs of a pontoon and the whole rig went down.'

'Oh, my God.'

'It's the IRA,' Masters explained. 'There's a

foreman on Charlie 2 called McGee and the cunt's a terrorist.'

Suddenly, Barker felt claustrophobic. The radio shack wasn't well lit and it felt like a Turkish bath. He glanced from Masters to Turner and saw the sweat on the latter's forehead. The supervisor was drumming his fingertips on the table, staring at the radio.

'Why Eagle 3?' Barker asked.

'I don't know yet,' Masters said. 'I didn't get a chance to ask that question. They want the Prime Minister.'

'The Prime Minister,' Barker repeated flatly.

'That's right: the PM. They say they'll blow up Charlie 2 – and if they have to, they'll do it – if we don't let them speak to the PM. They've got a plutonium bomb on board. McGee said they would use it. I don't know how they managed it, but they've taken over the whole of Charlie 2.'

'You mean they've hijacked the rig?'

'Looks like it.'

'How many?'

'I don't know.'

'There's eighty men on that rig.'

'I know. I don't know how they did it, but they've certainly taken it.'

Barker whistled, patted his blond hair and shook his head from side to side.

'God,' he said, 'this is bad. It's fucking disastrous.

If they say they're willing to go down with Charlie 2, then they probably mean it. Fucking IRA lunatics!'

'It's McGee,' Masters said. 'He seems to be the leader. He said: "This is an official announcement from the IRA. We've hijacked your rig." He didn't bother explaining any more. He just said he wanted to speak to the Prime Minister, but he'd speak to you first.'

'Bastard,' Barker said.

'He's not kidding,' Masters told him. 'He could be bluffing, but he certainly isn't kidding – and he *did* blow up Eagle 3. They probably used a long-delay timer with the primer on Charlie 2.'

'Some of the crew,' Barker suggested. 'The rig workers aren't checked out. I've been wanting to run checks on them for years, but the bigwigs wouldn't let me.'

'They will in future,' Turner said.

'Fucking great,' Barker responded. 'In the meantime it costs us two rigs and now they want the PM.'

'That's right,' Masters said.

'It's impossible,' Turner said. 'We can't even let him know this has happened. We can't let the word out.'

'It'll get out,' Barker insisted.

'Not immediately,' Turner replied. 'The PM's in conference and we'll let him stay there until we manage to sort this mess out. We can't tell him till then.'

Barker looked at the floor. 'Let me get this straight. The terrorists have bombed Eagle 3. They've taken over Charlie 2. We don't know how, but they've managed to gain control and now they've got a plutonium bomb. Where the hell did they get the bomb? How on earth did they take the rig? There's eighty men in that crew and you don't buy plutonium bombs for peanuts. Have they got any proof?'

'I don't know,' Masters said. 'McGee wouldn't discuss it with me. He just said he wasn't kidding, that he wanted the PM, and that he was willing to speak to you first.'

'The PM's impossible.'

'That's what he wants, Barker.'

'It's not feasible,' Barker said. 'He must be bluffing. He's just trying it on.'

'Maybe,' Turner said.

'Maybe not,' Masters said. 'But the only way we're going to find out is to get on that radio.'

Barker glanced up and smiled, chuckled sardonically, shook his head, then paced up and down the cramped hut, pursing his lips. He stopped after a short while.

'OK, I'll talk. Let's hear what they have to say. We'll hold them off as long as we can and keep the PM out of it.' He studied the radio. 'Has that got an open line?' Turner nodded and reached out and flicked a switch. 'Now we'll all hear,' he said. Barker nodded and said: 'That's what I want.'

Turner leant forward and spoke into the microphone, keeping his voice low and level. 'Bravo 1 to Charlie 2. Bravo 1 to Charlie 2. Are you receiving me?' There was the crackling of static, swelling up and fading out. 'Charlie 2 to Bravo 1, we're receiving. We don't want you, Turner. We want Barker.' Turner couldn't help grinning at Barker as he got out of the chair. Barker distractedly smoothed his hair as he sat down at the microphone.

'OK,' he said, 'it's Barker. Put McGee on.'

There was silence for a moment, apart from the crackling static. Barker placed his elbow on the table and rested his chin in his cupped hands. Turner moved sideways to stand close by Masters. Their eyes met, then they both stared at the radio, feeling tense and defeated.

'Barker?' a voice on the radio asked.

'Yes, this is Barker.'

'This is McGee. I'm speaking on behalf of the Irish Republican Army. I'm officially notifying you that we've requisitioned Charlie 2 on behalf of the IRA for the . . .'

'Cut the shit,' Barker interjected. 'What do you want?'

'Our demands will only be given to the Prime Minister. We won't settle for less.'

'You can't speak to the Prime Minister. It's impossible and you know it. There's no way I'm going to bring him into this and that's all there is to it.'

'You'll give us what we want,' McGee said, 'or suffer the consequences.'

'Which are?'

'We've captured Charlie 2. We've got a plutonium bomb on board. We won't hesitate to set the bomb off if we don't get satisfaction. Don't attempt to attack the rig. If we see any ships or helicopters, we'll set the bomb off.'

'Do that and you'll blow yourselves up as well.'

'We don't care, Barker. We're willing to go down with the rig. And you all know enough about the IRA to know we mean what we say.'

'I don't believe you,' Barker said. 'You couldn't find a plutonium bomb. If you did, you couldn't transport it to the rig without being detected. I think you're bluffing.'

'Eagle 3 was no bluff. It was a demonstration and warning. It was a much smaller bomb on Eagle 3, but this one is the real thing. We didn't find it – we made it. They're surprisingly easy to make. The finished product is only thirty-six inches long and it doesn't weigh much. It was easy getting it on the rig. In fact, it's been on board for months. It only weighs half a ton and it was put in a packing crate and shipped out from Aberdeen with the regular equipment. I'm the foreman on this rig. Your tool-pushers are all my mates. We shipped it in with the regular supplies and now it's all set to blow.'

'I don't believe you,' Barker said.

'You don't have to,' McGee replied. 'We've left the proof for you to find. Get your onshore security team to check out the Aberdeen heliport. Tell them to check the toilets, third one from the door, and look behind the cistern. I left a brown envelope there. It contains full details of the design and construction of the bomb. Ask them to check it out. They'll soon confirm that it's authentic. When they ring you back with that confirmation we'll be able to deal.'

Barker studied the microphone. He covered his face with his right hand. After rubbing his eyes, he glanced at Masters and shook his head in despair.

'OK,' he said finally. 'We'll check it out.'

'You have one hour,' McGee told him. 'I won't give you any longer. If I don't hear back in that time I'm gonna blow up this rig. You know what that means, Barker. The blast will destroy the whole of Beryl, wiping it out completely. It'll also cause a lot of damage to the Forties Field. And the supply pipes will go with it. You'll lose two-thirds of the North Sea oil. There'll be enough contamination to ensure you can't work this sea for years. Think about that while you're waiting.'

Masters glanced at Turner. The supervisor was

visibly shaken, leaning against the door of the radio shack, wiping sweat from his brow. Masters then studied his friend Robert Barker. The chief security man of British United Oil was tapping the table gently with his fingertips as he stared at the radio.

'How many men have you got?' Barker asked.

'Sixty,' McGee replied. 'They were all regular crew members. We've been working on this plan for eighteen months, so we'd plenty of time. Your chief tool-pusher's my man. He's been with us from the start. He's the man who hires and fires and he's gradually been replacing your men with ours, as well as a lot of Scottish nationalists who're helping us out for their own ends.'

'I don't think you could have managed that,' Barker said, though he didn't sound hopeful.

'Rig workers aren't asked questions. As well you know, Barker, any man who's willing to work on a rig will be hired without question. You never approved of it. Too bad your superiors didn't listen. It's taken us eighteen months and we had to use the Scots, but now we've got sixty of our own men on board and we've executed most of the remaining crew.'

'You bastard,' Barker said.

'We spared two,' McGee said. 'I thought you might want a few witnesses, so there's two still alive. One's John Griffith, your geologist. He's standing right beside me now. You want proof, so I'm gonna put him on and you can ask what you like.'

Masters felt himself burning with a murderous rage. He smacked his fist against his hand and turned away to stare out through the window. The afternoon light was dull. The North Sea was calm. It stretched out to the horizon, towards the Beryl Field, then was lost in a misty haze. Masters turned back again when he heard the voice of Griffith coming over the radio.

'Barker?'

'Yes, Griffith.'

'It's true, Barker. All true. They've got about sixty men on this rig and they've taken it over.' Griffith's voice was shaky and high-pitched. 'They killed the remaining crew. Took them up on deck and shot them. They just shot them and threw them over the side and they made us two watch it.' Griffith stopped and seemed to sob. They heard him trying to control himself. Masters clenched his fists and stared at the radio, wanting to smash it. 'They're serious,' Griffith continued. 'They mean every word they say. They spared me and Sutton, but they killed all the others and dumped them into the sea. Oh, dear God, I just don't . . .'

Barker lowered his head. They all listened to Griffith sobbing. Masters clenched his fists and Turner turned away, looking like death warmed up.

'Bastards!' he whispered. Griffith's sobbing faded out as McGee started talking again.

'Is that enough for you, Barker? Are you satisfied? Or do you want to hear more?'

'No, that's enough. I don't want to hear any more.'

'You have one hour,' McGee repeated, then he cut the connection.

Barker turned off his receiver, pushed back his chair, and stood up, deep in thought.

'Well?' Masters asked. 'Do I call in the SBS and try to take that rig back?'

'Not yet,' Barker said. 'Not if they've got a plutonium bomb on board. I can't believe they've made a working nuclear bomb, but we'll have to find out first. I'll ring Andy Blackburn. He's the best man I have. I'll tell him not to use the local police, but to use our own security men instead. We have to keep this thing private. We don't want the regular Army or police involved. If word got out that a bunch of terrorists had managed to do all this, the repercussions internationally would be disastrous. Jesus, it's so *stupid*! We've no security on these damn rigs. We've actually *hired* sixty terrorists over the past eighteen months and I don't think we could ever live that down. We *can't* let the news out. We've got to solve it on our own. We've got to check if that bloody bomb works and then take it from there. I'll ring Andy right now.'

Barker picked up the telephone and rang the heliport. He spoke to Andy Blackburn, told him what to look for, then told him not to ask any questions and to keep his mouth shut. Masters stood there and listened. Barker gave nothing away. Masters gazed out the window and tried hard to control his boiling rage. His hands opened and closed, clutched the air and released it. He looked out at the sea and thought of Griffith and Sutton on that rig. The terrorists had sunk Eagle 3. Most of the crew had gone down with it. The terrorists had murdered twenty men on Charlie 2 and thrown them over the side. Masters felt like exploding, like smashing the radio shack. He heard Barker speaking into the phone, sounding calm and collected. Then Barker rang off. He turned around to face Turner. The bearded supervisor was chewing a matchstick and sweating profusely.

'OK,' Barker said, 'he's going to check. In the meantime, we wait.'

6

Convinced that the situation should be kept secret as long as possible, Turner decided to return to the boardroom. Walking across the main deck, seeing the rig workers all around him, he felt himself succumbing to panic. The terrorists had a plutonium bomb. They could obliterate the Beryl Field. The bomb could also devastate the Forties Field and set them back a good ten years. The results would be catastrophic. The whole of Britain could collapse. When he pictured the faces in the boardroom, Turner felt like a drowning man.

He reached the end of the deck, started climbing the steel steps, and saw dull clouds passing slowly over the sea as if nothing had changed.

Turner didn't want to do it. The thought of the boardroom made him ill. He would have to go in there and lie, and the thought made his heart pound. He wished that Masters was there with him. The SBS trooper had the strength he needed. But what would happen when Blackburn called? What could they do if the bomb worked? Turner desperately tried to find a way out as he climbed the ladder.

He reached the upper deck, opened the door of the nearest module, stepped inside and closed the door behind him, then took a deep breath and walked on.

Not believing he could face the meeting, he was trembling when he reached the boardroom. The guard opened the door and Turner felt himself smiling, putting on a casual mask as he walked in. Then the panic disappeared. It simply fell away from him. He walked over to the table, sat down in his chair and gazed calmly around him.

'Sorry, gentlemen,' he heard himself saying. 'A spot of bother on the Frigg Field.'

The Prime Minister, who had been talking, went quiet and glanced up. Turner noticed that his eyes were very blue, with a cold, hard intelligence.

'Oh?' the PM said. 'I'm sorry to hear that. Anything serious?'

'We're not sure yet,' Turner replied. 'We think a well-head exploded. We don't know how much damage it caused, but we're having it checked out.'

Tapping a pencil on the table, Sir Reginald McMillan stared at him. He was slim, grey-haired and distinguished, with a pale, remote face. 'An explosion?' he asked.

'Yes, sir,' Turner said.

'Dearie me. What rig was this?'

'Eagle 3,' Turner said.

Sir Reginald glanced at the PM. Clearly the news hadn't pleased him. Sir Reginald turned his pencil over and started doodling, then looked over at Turner. 'What happened?' he asked.

'We don't know, sir. They're still trying to sort it out. Apparently some oil drums exploded, which has made it all the worse. We're waiting for further news and they're ringing us back as soon as possible. I've left Masters in charge, but I'll probably have to go up there again. I hope you'll excuse me.'

'Of course,' Sir Reginald said. 'Who's this Masters?'

Turner hesitated. Apart from Robert Barker, he was the only man in the company who knew that Tony Masters was one of the many SBS men working under cover on the oil rigs. He wasn't sure that the PM knew about the SBS involvement; if he didn't, he might be outraged to learn about it by accident. Discretion being the better part of valour, Turner decided to keep his mouth shut on this particular issue.

'A top tool-pusher,' he said. 'He's one of our best men. He's handled situations like this before and knows what he's doing.'

Sir Reginald sighed, trying to hide his annoyance. Such accidents could happen, but it was dreadful to have one at a time like this. He glanced at the PM and saw those blue eyes staring at him with a mixture of accusation and pleasure. Of course, the PM would try to use the accident as a stick to beat the oil companies with. Any suggestion of negligence would strengthen his government's bargaining position.

'An explosion?' the PM asked like a perfect innocent. 'Is this sort of thing common?'

'No, Prime Minister,' Turner said. 'It does happen, but very seldom. The North Sea's very deep and the pressure is tremendous and that obviously leads to the unexpected. It's happened before and it'll happen again, but it's by no means common.'

'I see,' the PM said.

'It's in the Frigg Field,' Sir Reginald explained. 'Luckily the explosion was on Eagle 3, which is closing down anyway.'

'Closing down?' the PM asked.

'Yes, Prime Minister, closing down. Eagle 3 was drying up and was due to be towed away to another field. The blow-up therefore won't be as bad as it might have been, since to all intents and purposes the rig was closed. Had she been operating it might well have been worse.'

'That *was* lucky,' the PM said brightly.

'Yes, Prime Minister, very lucky. That no oil was coming out of Eagle 3 was very lucky indeed.'

Sir Reginald's smile was not returned by the PM. Instead, the PM glanced in turn at each of the other men, who were all sleek and well-fed. These were the oil magnates, representing the conglomerates. They headed individual companies that were part of larger companies and the source of their power was elusive. They were an international crew, living in boardrooms and hotels, reporting behind closed doors to unknown superiors, not intimidated by politicians or the rule of law. The PM didn't like them because they had rendered his government impotent. He could never forget that fact.

'Anyone hurt?' he asked.

'We don't know yet,' Turner replied. 'I would anticipate casualties, but we won't know until they ring back.'

'They seem slow,' the Under-Secretary said.

'They're fighting the fire,' Turner told him.

'I trust we'll receive a full report.'

'Of course, sir. That's our policy.'

The Under-Secretary smiled thinly. He sensed that Turner was being too calm. He knew that accidents on the rigs were handled by the oil companies and that the reports were written up by their own men. The Under-Secretary did not approve. He knew the reports could not be trusted. He felt that the Department of Energy should be called in at such times to conduct an independent investigation. He had been fighting for this for years, but it was a fight he hadn't won. The oil companies had resisted all attempts to uncover their skeletons.

'What's happening now?' he asked.

'We're simply waiting,' Turner replied. 'I've left Masters in the radio shack with instructions to call me.'

'Excellent,' Paul Dalton said, smiling encouragingly at Turner. He was a rough-looking, suntanned American with a shock of red hair. 'I've met Masters and think he's a good man – completely trustworthy. The guy has an air of authority.'

Knowing that this 'air of authority' had been instilled by the SBS, Turner was relieved to receive Dalton's support, which would, he hoped, deflect any further questions about Masters. Dalton was one of the American top dogs, so his word carried weight here. He had worked his way up the hard way, first as a roustabout, as a roughneck and tool-pusher, then as head of security for American oil companies in Saudi Arabia and New Mexico. Now he was one of the most powerful men in the business, a top-flight executive who worked for most of the conglomerates, the kind who made lesser men uneasy, particularly because they didn't know his specific function nor precisely for whom he was working. They only knew that he was free to roam the world at will, dropping in on any oilfield, company office or headquarters, and that he did so with alarming frequency. Where Dalton went, heads invariably rolled, which made him all the more frightening. His presence at this top-level conference had put them all, even the PM, on their toes.

'Masters is good,' Dalton insisted. 'He's really good. I don't doubt we can trust him.'

'I agree,' Turner said. 'He's been through this kind of thing before and knows how to deal with it. He also knows what to do when the rig calls: he'll send someone to fetch me.'

'Will they need help?' Sir Reginald asked, meaning the men on the rig he thought was only damaged.

'We won't know until they call back,' Turner said. 'In the meantime, we'll sit tight.'

'Fine by me,' Dalton said.

'Most unfortunate,' Sir Reginald murmured.

'So,' the PM said firmly, trying to avoid Dalton's steely gaze, 'let's get back to business.'

The conference continued with voices arguing back and forth as the smoke from cigars and cigarettes drifted over their heads. Turner heard himself talking, but hardly knew what he was saying, being too busy looking through the portholes at the rigs in the distance. Was the Forties Field safe? Could Barker be sure of his security? Could they be certain there wasn't a terrorist right here in their midst? Should he not say to hell with it all and call in Masters's fellow SBS men? Turner heard the PM's voice, then Sir Reginald and then himself. His own voice seemed to come from far away, though it sounded surprisingly calm and reassuring. Turner gazed through the portholes. Rigs were smoking on the horizon. They were miles apart and looked very small, isolated, defenceless . . . Turner shivered. He tried to focus on the conference. He thought bitterly of the terrorists on Charlie 2 and he wished that the phone would ring.

When it rang, he felt paralysed.

7

Robert Barker knew the news wasn't good when he saw Turner's face. Turner was back in the radio shack, standing opposite Masters. Neither of them looked happy. When Barker entered, Turner looked out the window and Masters offered a tight smile.

'Well?' Barker asked.

'Blackburn thinks the bomb would work,' Masters told him. 'He found the photos and technical data behind the cistern in the toilet of the heliport, as McGee had said he would. He took them to the Aberdeen munitions lab of British United Oil. They phoned him five minutes ago and said they thought it would work.'

'Are they certain?' Barker asked.

'They can't be, but they're pretty sure. It's about the size of a tea chest, it weighs approximately a quarter of a ton, it's got everything it needs, all the pieces are in the right place, and with a minimum of luck it would work.'

'Jesus!' Turner gasped. He was looking out at the darkening Forties Field.

'OK,' Barker said. 'It's a workable design for a plutonium bomb, but that doesn't mean the bastards could actually make it. They're terrorists, not scientists. They're a bunch of killers. To design a bomb like this is one thing; to actually make it is another. Where did they get the materials? How did they put it all together? And how the hell would they manage to test it? The drawings by themselves don't mean they've got one.'

'You'd be surprised,' Masters said, thinking of the many extraordinary explosive devices created secretly in RM Commando demolition establishments. 'According to Blackburn, they're relatively easy to make, not that expensive, and becoming more common every day. He says that schoolkids have made them. He says that all the materials can be bought in the open market and that a large bomb, a workable one, is not out of the question. The plans McGee left were perfect. The lab thought the bomb could work. True, we don't know if he's actually made it, but we'd be safest to assume that he has.'

Barker smacked his forehead, then shook his head in disbelief. He walked to the door of the hut and then came back again.

'We have to know for sure,' he said. 'We have to know if they have a bomb on that rig or if they're trying to bullshit us.'

'Blackburn's on to it,' Masters said. 'He's trying

to find out right now. He's going to check out McGee's movements over the past few months and try to come up with more concrete information. In the meantime, we'll have to accept that they might have that bomb.'

'Which means that even your SBS commandos can't make an assault on that rig.'

'Unfortunately not,' Masters said.

'Let's talk to McGee,' Barker suggested. 'Try to sound him out. To stretch it out a bit longer and give Blackburn more time.' He looked at Turner, who nodded and stepped aside. Barker sat at the radio and switched it on, engaging the open line. An unfamiliar voice asked him who he was and he said tersely: 'Barker. Now get me McGee.' After a long silence they heard the crackling of static, a snatch of laughter in the background, then someone coughing.

'Is that Barker?' McGee asked.

'Yes, McGee, this is Barker. You told me to call you back in an hour, so I'm calling you back.'

'I'm glad you listened,' McGee said. 'It shows common sense. I didn't like the thought of what would happen if you didn't show that.'

'How are Griffith and Sutton doing?'

'The prisoners of war are doing fine.'

'They're not prisoners of war, they're fucking hostages, so let's cut the horse-shit.'

McGee chuckled. 'Sure, you're a sharp one,

Barker. You can call them what you like, but we've got them and that's all that matters.' Barker didn't reply. There was a very long silence. 'So,' McGee said eventually, 'I take it you know our bomb works and we can get down to brass tacks.'

'It might work and it might not,' Barker replied. 'We want proof that you have it.'

'Eagle 3 was your proof.'

'That blast didn't come from an A-bomb, so don't pretend otherwise.'

'It doesn't matter,' McGee said. 'It was proof of our intentions. Proof that we could smuggle a bomb on board and that we mean what we say. You know we're not bluffing, Barker. Sure you're shit-scared and sweatin'. If you really want proof, try to take back this rig or simply refuse to meet our demands. You know what would happen then. If our bomb goes off, you're finished. It'll wipe out Beryl, devastate half of the Forties, and destroy the main pipeline to the refineries. That's over half of Britain's oil. We'll wipe the North Sea off the map. Think about that if you've got any idea that we're trying to bluff you.'

The radio shack was quiet but for the crackling static. It was growing dark outside and they heard the sea washing around the rig. Resting his chin in his hands, Barker stared blankly at the radio. He seemed pale and the shadows fell over him, rendering him ghostlike.

'What do you want?' he asked.

'The Prime Minister,' McGee replied.

'You want me to let you talk to the Prime Minister?'

'No,' McGee said. 'More than that.'

Barker almost stopped breathing. He leant back in his chair. After stretching his hands out on the table, he studied his fingernails. He didn't move for a long time and there was no sound from the radio. Barker finally sat forward again to speak into the microphone.

'You mean in person?' he asked.

'Ackaye. I mean in person.'

'And where do you plan to have this great meeting?'

'On Charlie 2,' McGee said.

Masters clenched his fists. He was thinking of the SBS assault squadrons presently on hold at the RM Commando base at Achnacarry. He was frustrated because he desperately wanted to call them out to deal with the terrorists, though that didn't seem likely. Opening his clenched fists, he glanced through the window. Shadows swooped across the sea. He saw the afternoon becoming evening, heard the wind, felt the deepening cold.

'You're kidding,' Barker said.

'Sure, I'm not,' McGee replied.

'You know we'd never fly the PM over there.'

'Sure, you've no choice,' McGee said.

Barker listened to the static like a man in a trance. The demands were impossible. The alternative was unthinkable. He glanced despairingly at Masters and Turner, then tried as best he could to fill the silence.

'I can't do that,' he said.

'You're going to have to,' McGee replied. 'I want the Prime Minister. I want him here by 1900 hours. Fifteen minutes after that, if he isn't here, I'll set the bomb off.'

'You'll go up with it,' Barker reminded him.

'You've already said that,' McGee responded. 'And I'm saying again, we don't mind. We're all committed to taking this to the limit if necessary. We're prepared to die for it.'

'Why do you want the Prime Minister?'

'I want to give him our demands.'

'Why not let me pass them on?'

'I want him as collateral.'

'Collateral?'

'That's right, Barker, our collateral. We need a guarantee as big as our demands, so we want the Prime Minister.'

'What the hell are you trying to pull, McGee? I want to know your demands.'

'You won't be told,' McGee said. 'I'll only inform the Prime Minister. He's the only man who's got the authority to get us what we want.'

'You might kill him,' Barker said.

'Ackaye, I might do that.'

'Then you know we can't possibly agree.'

'Sure, you will. You've no choice.'

Barker broke all the rules by lighting a cigarette. He inhaled and leant back in the chair and gazed up at the ceiling. Masters studied his face, which seemed thin and very pale. There were beads of sweat shining on his forehead, just beneath the hairline. It was quiet in the module, and they were all aware of the murmuring sea. Turner tugged at his beard and glanced at Masters, shook his head and looked down again. The tool-pusher remained standing, opening and shutting his large hands. Barker sat up, leant forward again, and looked straight at the radio.

'No arguments,' McGee said. 'No delays and no tricks. If anything comes anywhere near this rig, the whole thing'll go up in smoke. We want the Prime Minister. We want him at 1900 hours. We want him to arrive by helicopter with no cops or soldiers. You and Masters can come with him. I want Masters to fly the chopper. If we find another pilot on board, he'll be executed. You'll land at 1900 hours. We'll give you fifteen minutes' leeway. If you're not here by 1915 we'll blow the whole rig to hell.'

'I refuse,' Barker said.

'You can't refuse and you know it.'

'I won't do it.'

'I don't care,' McGee said. 'Sure, it's your choice, boyo.'

Barker opened his mouth to speak, but the line went dead on him. He sank back in the chair and fumbled for another cigarette.

'Jesus Christ,' he said quietly.

Masters looked out of the window at the darkening sea. Bravo 1 wasn't drilling, but he could hear the isolated roar of a fork-lift, the shouting of men. The radio continued crackling, though Charlie 2 was not receiving. Barker sat before the radio and stared at it while smoking his cigarette. Masters studied him and then looked at Turner.

'We can't,' Turner said. 'It's out of the question. We can't possibly give this news to the PM. It's too much to ask.'

'What else is there?' Barker asked him. 'The decision isn't ours to make. We can't take a chance on that bomb. We'll have to let *him* decide.'

'Let's go,' Masters said.

8

Each man in the boardroom looked about him as if suffering from shock. The news seemed so preposterous that they couldn't quite take it in, but gradually, in the grim silence following Turner's level recital, the awful reality sank in. Sir Reginald McMillan glanced at the Prime Minister, but could not meet his gaze. The PM's bright-blue gaze swept the table, then returned to the general supervisor.

'Well,' the PM said, 'that's quite a tale.'

'Yes, sir, I'm afraid so.'

'Nineteen hundred hours?'

'Yes, Prime Minister . . .'

'Then we have ninety minutes.'

Turner glanced at Masters and Barker. They were standing at the head of the long table, their eyes wandering back and forth. Sir Reginald glanced at Dalton. The American was smoking a cigarette and studying the others around the table with a steady, unblinking gaze. His eyes finally came to rest on the Prime Minister, whose bulky frame filled the chair. The PM was flicking the ash off his cigar and looking up at Turner.

'You can't do it,' Sir Reginald said. 'We can't let you go over there. We can't hand the Prime Minister of the United Kingdom to a bunch of murderous terrorists. It's completely out of the question.'

'I agree,' Dalton said. 'The request is just crazy. I'm all for trying to meet their demands, but I stop short at this.'

'Ludicrous,' Sir Reginald said. 'They must be utterly insane. I simply won't accept this.'

The PM leant forward in his chair. His florid, fleshy, stubborn face held a shrewd native cunning.

'Yes,' he said, 'it *is* ludicrous. That's *exactly* what it is. Now, what *I* want to know is how it happened. That really does interest me.' He turned his blue eyes on Barker, picked up his cigar, inhaled and blew the smoke into the air, then sat back and waited.

'It seems irrelevant . . .' Sir Reginald began defensively.

'It's not irrelevant,' the PM told him.

'Correct,' Dalton said. 'It's not irrelevant. It's a goddamn disgrace!'

The PM looked at Barker. 'So? I'm being asked to fly out to that rig and I want to know why.'

Barker sighed and shrugged his shoulders in defeat. 'Well,' he confessed, 'it seems we simply hired them as legitimate workers. We've been doing so for a long time.'

There was silence in the boardroom. Sir Reginald kept his head down. The PM breathed evenly in his chair and kept his eyes fixed on Barker. 'You *hired* them?' he asked.

'So it seems, sir. They signed up just like all the others and were shipped out the normal way.'

'Sixty terrorists,' the PM said.

'Yes, sir, that's the figure.'

'You're trying to tell me you signed on sixty terrorists without checking them out?'

'Not all at once, sir. They signed on over eighteen months. They came out of the dole queues and factories just like all the others.'

'I appreciate that, Mr Barker. I'm well aware of that fact. What I want to know is how a terrorist can get a job on an oil rig.'

'You don't check them out?' Dalton asked.

'No, we don't,' Barker confessed. 'There are so many unemployed, we don't bother checking credentials, so we don't know too much about their past.'

'This is incredible,' the PM said. 'It's utterly scandalous. Any fool, any madman can get a job on the oil rigs.'

'It's not *that* bad,' Sir Reginald said.

'It's bloody scandalous,' the PM told him. 'These

oil rigs are the life-blood of this country and you don't check who works on them.'

'I didn't realize,' Sir Reginald said. 'I must say, it *is* appalling. I shall, of course, order an investigation and demand a complete report.'

'It's Barker's bag,' Dalton said. 'He's in charge of security. I'd like to know how the hell he got his job if this is in any way typical.'

'I won't take that,' Barker said. 'I don't work in the employment office. My job is security on the rigs. I can't check out who's being hired.'

'So no one does,' Dalton said.

'I've been wanting checks for years,' Barker said, glancing at Sir Reginald. 'An inspection of my files will confirm that. My requests were denied.'

The PM glared at Sir Reginald. 'This is scandalous,' he repeated. 'You won't let the government touch the oilfields and this is what happens.'

They all glared at one another. The air was smoky and stank of brandy. Through the windows they could see the falling darkness, the lights winking on.

'Eightly minutes,' Masters said. 'We have exactly eighty minutes. I think we should be talking about Charlie 2. I think we'll have to decide.'

They all stared at Masters, surprised. The silence lasted a long time. 'Just who the hell *are* you?' Dalton finally asked him. 'And don't try telling us you're just a tool-pusher. That wouldn't get you into this boardroom with Messrs Turner and Barker. You're security, aren't you?'

Masters glanced from Barker to Turner, not sure what to say. Turner coughed into his fist and then reluctantly confessed: 'This man is a sergeant with the SBS – the Special Boat Squadron of the Royal Marine Commando. The SBS and the SAS have been given certain responsibilities regarding security in the oilfields. Sergeant Masters, though a former tool-pusher, is presently here on behalf of the SBS, acting under cover.'

There was another long silence while everyone took this in. The PM, who was furious, fought to control himself, though he couldn't help glaring at Sir Reginald. The latter's hands were folded in his lap and he kept staring at them. Eventually, when the tension became unbearable, the PM cleared his throat and said: 'This is neither the time nor the place to ask why I wasn't informed about this . . .'

'Neither was I,' Dalton interjected.

'And nor was I,' the Under-Secretary added.

'. . . though the matter will certainly not be forgotten,' the PM continued icily. 'But for now, given the urgency of our situation, let us stick to the issue in hand. And regarding that, as our SBS sergeant has informed us, we have to decide.'

'Decide what?' Sir Reginald asked, feigning outrage to cover his embarrassment. 'There's simply nothing *to* decide. Our Prime Minister isn't going on that rig and that's all there is to it.'

'I agree,' Dalton said.

'They have an A-bomb,' Masters reminded them.

'Correction,' Dalton said. 'We don't know that. We don't know that they have it.' He turned to the PM. 'We'll recapture the rig. We've no choice but to try it. We can't let you go to the terrorists. We don't know their intentions.'

'And the bomb?' the Under-Secretary asked. 'What happens about that? They've said they'll set it off if we attack. They might actually do so.'

'I think they would,' Masters said. 'I'm pretty certain they would. I don't think they'd be shy.'

The PM rubbed his forehead, stubbed out his cigar, clasped his hands under his chin, then gazed left and right. He avoided Sir Reginald, looked carefully at Masters, and finally his gaze came to rest on Dalton, who was pursing his lips.

'We're still assuming they have that bomb,' the American said. 'However, the fact that they had a photograph and a workable design doesn't mean they've managed to make the thing.'

'That's true,' Sir Reginald said. 'It seems a bit far-fetched to me. I don't think it's all that easy for amateurs to make an A-bomb. I find it hard to accept.'

'It's been known, sir,' Masters said. 'Our onshore men think it's possible. They say the materials can be bought on the open market and that the making of the actual bomb is relatively easy.'

'That's preposterous!' Sir Reginald snapped.

'No, it's not,' Dalton said. 'There's kids making them in their backyards in the States. They're pretty crude, but they would work.'

'It would help if we had proof,' Masters said. 'And Andrew Blackburn of our onshore security is trying to find it.'

'*He'll* be lucky,' Sir Reginald said.

The emergency telephone rang. Every head in the room turned towards Barker as he picked it up. There was a tense, lingering silence. Barker covered one ear. He nodded and then lowered the phone and looked at each man in turn.

'It's Blackburn,' he told them. 'They're putting him through now. I think he should talk on the open line to let us all hear this.'

'I don't think . . .' Sir Reginald began.

'I certainly do,' the PM interjected. 'I think we should *all* be kept informed from this moment on.'

Barker glanced at Sir Reginald. The Chairman nodded reluctantly. Barker pressed a button on the telephone and they all heard a soft, hissing sound.

'Blackburn?'

'Yes, Barker. We've managed to check out this McGee. It wasn't very difficult at all. He didn't cover his tracks.'

'Good,' Barker said. 'Go ahead.'

'Is this line scrambled?'

'Yes, Andy, go on.'

'Good. I think it's all pretty dodgy.'

Blackburn was silent for a moment, obviously checking his notes. Those waiting studied the speakers on the boardroom walls, most too breathless to speak.

'McGee lived in a boarding house,' Blackburn said eventually. 'In George Street in Aberdeen. He's been using the same place for the past two years, every time he's on shore. A pretty normal boarding house. A typical rig worker's place. McGee used to have a lot of friends in, but apart from that the landlord had no complaints. We searched his room. He hadn't attempted to hide anything. The search revealed correspondence between himself and various known members of the IRA. McGee was clearly quite high up. The correspondence covered a lot. Plans for bombings and assassinations and hijackings, most of which, as the records now reveal, were accomplished successfully.'

Sir Reginald coughed into his fist. The PM glared at him. Sir Reginald offered a smile that was rejected, so he studied the floor.

'Also found,' Blackburn continued, 'was a notebook with some odd addresses, including one for a closed-down car repair place. I only mention this because it ties in with the fact that we also found invoices from various specialist libraries and bookshops, all of which were unusual. Included were the National Technical Information Service of the US Department of Commerce; the US Atomic Energy Commission; the Science Reference Library in Chancery Lane, London; and the Office of Technical Services. A subsequent search of the closed repair shop revealed various books – all openly available from the sources I've just named and all filled with unclassified and declassified – but extremely dangerous – information. Among these books were both volumes of *The Plutonium Handbook*; another book called *The Science of High Explosives* – this one written by Melvin Cook, Professor of Metallurgy and director of the Explosives Research Group of the University of Utah – and, finally, the *Source Book on Atomic Energy* and the *Los Alamos Primer*. This last book consists of notes made during the production of the first A-bomb in Los Alamos, New Mexico, and is published openly by the US Atomic Energy Commission.'

'Did you say "published openly"?' Sir Reginald asked.

'That's right,' Blackburn replied, failing to use the proper form of address because he didn't know to whom he was talking. 'These are treated as information libraries. This information, which our own experts have confirmed is extremely dangerous, is, as I said, either unclassified or declassified and therefore freely available to the general public. You just walk in and pay for the books and that's all there is to it.'

'That's scandalous!' Sir Reginald exclaimed.

The PM glared at him. Embarrassed, Sir Reginald coughed noisily again and gazed at the speakers.

'Anyway,' Blackburn continued, 'this is particularly interesting. Also found in that supposedly closed workshop were traces of plutonium oxide – which I'm told can be converted easily into concentrated plutonium nitrate; an electrical induction furnace; a sealed glove-box of the type used to avoid contamination; high-temperature crucibles; hydrofluoric acid, oxalic acid, metallic calcium, crystalline iodine, quartz glassware, and a cylinder of argon and nitric acid – all available on the open market; all ingredients for a workable plutonium bomb.'

Blackburn let his words sink in. None of the men in the boardroom spoke. Finally, after what seemed like a long time, Barker asked him a question.

'What does all this mean?' he said. 'That they could make it?'

'Yes,' replied Blackburn. 'All the information needed to put those materials together into a working bomb can be found in the books I've just named – and the bomb could be made in a car workshop or something even less grand. According to our lab boys, any particularly complicated calculations could be done simply by using hired computer time with any legitimate computer firm. The computer operator, probably innocent, would be shown nothing other than a set of partial differential equations and a written request for a particular programme to be run. He or she therefore wouldn't have a clue what it was for. Also, suitable explosive lenses are now commercially available just about anywhere; and the initiator and other materials can be bought over the counter from any firm supplying university labs. In short, your terrorists appear to have made their plutonium bomb.'

Dalton gave a low whistle. Turner wiped sweat from his brow. The PM was immobile, staring up at the loudspeakers as if not believing his ears. Masters looked at each man in turn and sensed the fear grow in all of them.

'OK,' Barker said. 'So they made their bomb. But could they test it without setting it off?'

'Dead easy,' Blackburn said. 'Piece of pie, really. They only have to test the detonating circuits for simultaneity – and the equipment for this is also available on the open market. Apart from ordinary metering equipment, it would consist of a double-beam oscilloscope with long-stay traces, a pulse-height analyser, and an accurate recording digital timer – all on sale commercially. My lab boys tell me that they've previously come across arming devices made from cooker timers and second-hand servo-motors; and that the detonation circuits can actually be linked to a device known to every telephone engineer – an arrangement that allows detonation of the bomb by phone on any line using STD codes. So they could have – and probably have – tested their bomb.'

Turner sat in a chair and covered his face with his hands. The PM watched him, then glanced at Sir Reginald, who seized this opportunity to wriggle out of his own guilt by launching an attack on the Under-Secretary.

'I can't believe it,' the Chairman said. 'I cannot believe my own ears. I am informed that the materials and the instructions for a workable atom bomb are freely available to the general public. I find this whole thing appalling.'

The Under-Secretary refused to rise to the bait.

'Any more?' Barker asked.

'A bit,' Blackburn said. 'We tried tracing the people detailed in McGee's notebook and we managed to find some. A few are in prison, others have disappeared, and a fair amount are working on the oil rigs. I assume that's your problem.'

Turner uncovered his face to look across at Sir Reginald, who was leaning back in his chair, staring up at the ceiling. He had almost stopped breathing.

'Yes,' Barker said, 'that's our problem. It's a very big problem. I'm classifying this whole item top secret and I want it to stay that way.'

'Right,' Blackburn said.

'Put a seal across it.'

'Will do,' Blackburn said. 'Have no fear. Is there anything else?'

'No, nothing else.'

'Best of luck,' Blackburn said.

The line went dead. Barker switched off the phone, turned away and stared into space, then shrugged his shoulders.

They all sat for a while in silence. The sea was a remote, rhythmic murmuring all around the platform. It was now dark outside and the platform's lights were blazing, throwing shadows across the tiered decks and reflecting off the antennae.

'So,' the Under-Secretary said. 'They probably have a working bomb. They may use it, but they may just be bluffing and there's one way to find out. Are we willing to take that risk? Can we afford to do so? All in all, I don't think we can risk it. There's too much at stake here.'

'And if we don't?' the PM asked. 'If we wait until seven-fifteen? What happens if we wait and the bomb goes off? Can we possibly live with that?'

'It's your life at stake, Prime Minister. We don't know what they want. Those men are assassins – they've killed before and they will again – and of all the political figures in this country, you're the biggest prize there is. I don't think you should do it. You shouldn't take that chance. I think we should recapture that rig before they set the bomb off.'

'That's impossible,' Masters said.

'Why?' the Under-Secretary asked.

'All the rigs have radar. That means we can't use boats. They've got cameras and sonic beams beneath the water, so we can't use submersibles. There's no way we can surprise them. It's out of the question. We either sit here and pray that they're bluffing or we do as they say.'

'I see,' the Under-Secretary said to the others around the table. 'Our SBS colleague wants to risk the Prime Minister. He's willing to risk our Prime Minister's life on a mere speculation.'

'They're not bluffing,' Masters insisted.

'We don't know that,' Sir Reginald said.

'So what if they're not bluffing?' the PM asked. 'I don't think we can risk that.'

'You're the head of the British government,' the Under-Secretary said. 'You can't give yourself up to the terrorists on the chance that they'll spare you.'

'Is there a choice?' the PM asked. 'I can't see that there is. A bomb like that will finish off the North Sea, not to mention the UK. So I *don't* think there's a choice. I side with Sergeant Masters. We'll just have to see what they want and hope it isn't my neck.'

'Once you're there, there's not a thing we can do,' the Under-Secretary said, 'and they can do what they want. They could kill you and *still* set the bomb off – or set it off while you're on the rig.'

'True enough,' Masters said, 'but we still don't have a choice. And at least, if we can get on that rig, we have the chance to do something.'

'*Do* something, Sergeant?'

'That's right, sir – do something. It's a long shot, but at least we'll be aboard and that counts for something. I might be able to get away. I don't know how, but it's possible. I might be able to disappear long enough to find out where the bomb is. If I do, I can disarm it. I know enough about those things to do that. I can ensure that it won't work and then we'll take it from there.'

'They'll kill you,' Dalton said.

'At least they won't have their bomb. And if they don't have their bomb, then the only thing they have is the rig.'

'They'll kill you,' Dalton insisted. 'You *and* the Prime Minister. If you take their bomb apart, they're going to kill you. I'm certain of that.'

'It's our only chance,' Masters said. 'Our only possible hope. It's a long shot, but it's the only one we've got, so we might as well take it.'

'It's suicide,' the Under-Secretary insisted. 'There's no other word for it.'

'It's a chance,' Masters said.

The PM stared at him. It was a hard and searching look. His penetrating blue eyes were set in a rough worker's face. He saw that Masters was looking back. There was no sign of intimidation. He saw intelligence and a growing frustration and a fierce, controlled anger. There was no other option. While they talked the bomb was ticking away and the future was shrinking. The PM didn't like it. He didn't really want to do it. He studied Masters and wondered what would happen if they sat it out. The bomb might go off. The oilfields would be destroyed. His own future and the future of Britain would go down with the rigs. There could be no doubt about it. The PM studied the SBS sergeant and saw his one hope on earth. 'We've no choice,' he said.

9

The black sky was all around them. Below was nothing but darkness. The RN Dragonfly helicopter rose and fell on the wind as it headed for the Beryl Field, powered by its single Pratt & Whitney R-985 450-hp engine. Masters was at the controls with Barker beside him. The Prime Minister, seated close behind them, coughed lightly to clear his throat.

Masters glanced down at the sea and saw a dark, vitreous void. He didn't like to look down – it was the black void of a dream. They were fifteen hundred feet above the sea but couldn't see a thing. Masters felt very strange, slightly high, his nerves tingling. Excitement was mixed up with his natural fear and clinging sense of disbelief.

He was a Royal Marine Commando, a member of the SBS, trained rigorously at the Amphibious School of the Royal Marines at Eastney and elsewhere in a remarkably wide variety of specialist activities, including offensive demolitions, close-quarter combat (CQB), firing rifles and automatic weapons from the hip, stalking, fighting in densely wooded country and on the streets, abseiling, navigation, assault-opposed landings, elementary bridging, the use of assault boats and scaling ladders, tactical manoeuvres involving endurance, living on concentrated rations, ambushes, night operations, general boating, parachuting and flying single-pilot aircraft and helicopters – all that and he was still nervous, not because of the nature of this operation, but because he was now in charge of the fate of the British Prime Minister.

Luckily, if he survived this op, he would no longer be alone. Just before flying from Bravo 1 with the PM, he had been ordered by the latter to obtain proper authorization from his CO to make this flight and engage with the terrorists. Shocked by what he had been told, the CO, Lieutenant-Colonel Ben Edwards, had insisted on flying out to Bravo 1 to confer with the others in the boardroom and personally supervise all further SBS activity in the matter, including, if necessary, a full rescue assault against Charlie 2. On hold with his SBS squadron in the old Commando Basic Training Centre at Achnacarry, near the foot of Ben Nevis, Lieutenant-Colonel Edwards had decided to fly with one of his most experienced officers, Captain Rudolph 'Rudy' Pancroft, to Bravo 1 even as Masters was *en route* to Charlie 2. By the time Masters returned from Charlie 2 – if he returned – his two superiors would be relocated on Bravo 1. This thought gave him some comfort.

Masters looked down again and saw blackness everywhere. There was no moon, but he did see the clouds as deeper stains on the darkness. He shivered a little, his excitement warring with fear, as the Dragonfly dropped into an air pocket, shook violently, then picked up speed again and flew on.

'Are we close?' the PM asked.

'Yes, Prime Minister,' Masters replied. 'We should be seeing their lights any minute now. We'll be descending soon.'

'What time is it?'

'Eighteen-fifty hours,' Barker informed him.

'Ten minutes,' the Prime Minister said. 'I trust they'll be amenable now.'

Masters didn't reply. His brain was racing with possibilities. He wondered where he would be held, where the bomb was hidden, if he could make his escape and stay out of sight long enough. It wouldn't take long to dismantle; the time spent would be in locating it. He had to elude his captors long enough to find and destroy the bomb. And what if he succeeded? Would that help in the long run? He tried to think of a way of escaping but couldn't come up with one. After all, he had the Prime Minister and Barker to think about as well. He couldn't simply disarm the bomb and run away, leaving them trapped with the terrorists. His mind was racing, yet his eyes scanned the dark sky systematically. Looking down, he saw distant, winking lights and knew they were close.

'That's it,' Barker hissed.

'Yeah, I can see it.'

'I feel trapped,' Barker said. 'Utterly useless. What can we do down there?'

Masters looked ahead and saw the distant lights approaching, pinpoints growing bigger in the darkness to become stars in space, then lamps floating on high. There was something chilling in that sight, something unreal and frightening. Suddenly, he felt all alone, floating free in the cosmos. He blinked and swallowed, torn between dread and excitement, then gave in to a cold, competitive rage against the men on that rig. He had to beat them somehow, deprive them of victory. His own future, and that of his country, both hung in the balance.

'I'm starting the descent now,' he said.

'I'm glad,' the PM replied gamely. 'I want to get this over and done with. I don't like not knowing.'

The distant lights were approaching rapidly. Moonlight fell on the water. The Dragonfly, shaking a little, dropped lower and Masters saw Charlie 2. It was a pyramid of lights that rendered the rig invisible. The lights seemed to be floating in the dark sky above the moon's reflection in the water.

That water was almost black – a bottomless well. The lights of Charlie 2 shone above it, danced and leapt in the lapping waves. Masters tried to concentrate, taking the helicopter lower. He had a vision of the lights of Manhattan, sweeping out, soaring skywards. It was a beautiful sight that made him catch his breath. He looked down and saw the silhouetted derricks, the black mat of the platform.

'There they are,' he said. 'The bastards are waiting down there for us. Now let's find out what's happening.'

He turned the Dragonfly around and started descending towards the rig, heading for the circle of lights on the edge of the platform. Now he could see the whole rig, the towering derricks and tiered modules, a patchwork of shadow and light, stark black and white brilliance. There were dots in that mosaic, moving back and forth, gradually taking shape and becoming the human beings surrounding the landing pad. The Dragonfly shuddered as it dropped below the lights. Far below, beneath the illuminated landing pad, was the dark, surging sea. The helicopter descended vertically until the derricks towered above it. Dropping lower, it touched lightly on the deck and finally came to a halt.

Masters switched off the engine and waited patiently until the props had stopped rotating and the slipstream had subsided.

'Here we go,' Barker said.

The men moving in on all sides were wearing overalls and were armed with 5.56mm Heckler & Koch MP5 sub-machine-guns, 7.6mm Kalashnikov AK47 semi-automatic assault rifles, and a variety of handguns, including the 9mm Glock 17 semi-automatic and the .455-inch Webley Mark 6. The lights washed across their faces, rendering them ghostly white and featureless. They closed in, surrounding the Dragonfly, as Masters moved towards the door. The PM hesitated when he saw those floodlit faces. Beyond them were the blazing lights of the derricks and the stark, jet-black shadows.

Masters smiled reassuringly at the PM, then unlocked the door. After sliding the door open, he threw out the short ladder and made his way down, followed by Barker. A cold air rushed into the helicopter as the PM stood up, bit his lower lip, then moved to the exit and stared down at the brightly lit landing pad. The terrorists were keeping Masters and Barker covered, but otherwise they seemed calm. The PM took a deep breath and made his way down the ladder until he stood between Masters and Barker.

'So,' Masters asked, 'where's McGee?'

One of the terrorists stepped forward and grabbed Masters by the shoulder, jerked him around, threw him against the side of the helicopter and then roughly kicked his legs apart. Masters offered no resistance. The terrorist ran his hands up and down the SBS man's body, then stepped back and motioned to Barker.

'Your turn,' he said.

Barker faced the Dragonfly, putting his hands above his head and spreading his legs. The terrorist frisked him expertly, then stepped back and nodded at the Prime Minister.

'You, too,' he said quietly.

The PM straightened his broad shoulders and stared straight at the terrorist. 'I am the Prime Minister of the United Kingdom,' he declared. 'I do not carry weapons.'

The terrorist raised his MP5 sub-machine-gun and aimed it at the PM. 'I don't give a fuck,' the terrorist said. 'Put your hands on that chopper.'

The PM bristled, but did as he was told. The terrorist frisked him and then stepped away, saying: 'Right, turn around.' The three men did as they were told, facing the circle of armed terrorists. The wind moaned and stark shadows formed a web on the steel of the platform.

'Where's McGee?' Masters asked again.

'In the radio shack,' replied the terrorist who had frisked them.

'I know where it is,' Masters said. 'Are we going there now?'

'Right now. After you.'

The terrorist motioned with his MP5, the surrounding men parted to form a pathway, and Masters, followed by the PM and Barker, headed for the catwalk. The PM glanced left and right and saw the weapons pointing at him. He felt a tension that wasn't quite fear – more a heightened awareness. Some armed terrorists went on ahead while others fell in behind. Masters mounted the catwalk, Barker close behind, and then the PM also stepped forward and felt the blast of an icy wind. Following Barker across the catwalk, he glanced down and felt dizzy. The surging sea way below was a dark pit flecked with silvery lights. The PM took a deep breath and gripped the railing tighter. There was nothing on either side but the sea and the sky, both black, both offering lonesome sounds: splashing water, the moaning wind. The PM stopped once. He was prodded with a gun barrel. Advancing again, he walked carefully down the catwalk, eventually finding himself standing on the main deck, beside Masters and Barker.

'Keep going,' the leading terrorist said. 'You're not here for the scenery.'

The gunmen formed a circle around them as they crossed the main deck. There were more terrorists standing along the modules, looking on with great interest, some laughing, others shouting derisory remarks. The PM kept his dignity, not responding in any way, following the others past huge oil tanks and derricks, under cranes and catwalks. The deck was slippery under foot, filmed with mud and oil, and they walked either through the dazzling brilliance of the floodlights or through a stark, blinding blackness. It was very quiet here. The drilling floor had been silenced. They heard the wind, the sea, their boots banging on metal.

They came to a steel ladder leading up to another deck. The terrorists in front climbed up, Masters and Barker followed, and then the PM, breathing heavily. It was a vertical climb and he wasn't used to such exercise; when he reached the top he found himself gasping, felt the strain in his muscles. Barker was grinning at him, at once amused and admiring. Masters was intently studying their surroundings, fixing them in his memory. Following the SBS man's gaze, the PM saw the radio shack. The front door was open, light was flooding out, and a man was silhouetted in the doorway, surrounded by armed guards.

'Is that McGee?' the PM asked.

'Yes,' Masters replied.

'Obviously he has a flair for theatrics,' the PM said.

They walked across the deck and stepped into the light. McGee, unarmed, was in the doorway, a grin on his face.

'Have you come?' he said to Masters, using that oddity of speech peculiar to Ulster.

'Yes. Here we are.'

'Did I surprise you?'

'Yes, McGee, you surprised me. I would never have guessed.'

McGee's grin was not good-humoured. His brown eyes, bright and hard, turned from Masters to Barker to finally settle on the PM, whom he studied for some time. The PM was unflinching. McGee turned away and motioned the three men inside. Brushing past him, they entered the radio shack, which was small, bright and sweltering. McGee stepped in after them, flanked by two armed guards. One of them closed the door, the other moved up beside him, and both of them levelled their MP5s at the three visitors. McGee grinned, sat down by the radio and looked up at his hostages.

'Sure, I thought I'd make this radio shack my HQ,' he explained. 'Particularly when we'd so much to talk about.'

No one smiled. 'All right,' Barker said. 'You've got us here, so just tell us one thing. Is there really a bomb?'

'Ackaye,' McGee replied.

'Where?'

'Where do you think? Inside one of the pontoon legs – just like the first one.'

'Which leg?' Masters asked.

'Don't be daft, Tone. Do you think I'd be

dumb enough to tell you? Ask me something else, like.'

'Would you really use it?' the PM asked.

'Ackaye, Prime Minister.'

'You must be mad,' Barker told him.

'No, I'm not. And you damn well know it.'

McGee stopped grinning, looked at each of them in turn, then settled his gaze on Masters.

'Tell us about the bomb,' Masters said.

'Sure, Tone, why not?' McGee grinned again. 'It's about the size of a tea chest and weighs . . .'

'We already know that,' Masters interrupted.

'Right,' McGee said, grinning even more broadly, though with no sign of humour. 'It was shipped in in separate parts in various supply crates, over a period of time, and the parts were hidden in the rig's regular storage space. A lot of my men were on the night shift and often had to check the pontoon legs; so bit by bit they took the parts down into the pontoon leg and gradually reassembled the bomb down there. It's now resting on a girder halfway down – and it's all primed to go.'

He grinned at the three of them. They all looked at him in silence. The floor was undulating from side to side, very slowly, hypnotically. Eventually the PM coughed into his fist, clearing his throat.

'What are your demands?' he asked quietly.

'I speak for the IRA,' McGee responded portentously. 'I want you to understand that. These demands are on behalf of the Irish . . .'

'I don't wish to hear your nonsense,' the PM snapped. 'I just want your demands.'

'We want one million pounds sterling. Then we want four of our men out of the Maze prison. It's as simple as that.'

'What men?' the PM asked.

'You mean you agree to the money?'

'I haven't said that,' the PM replied firmly. 'Now who are these men?'

'Seamus McGrath, John Houlihan, Kevin Trainor and Shaun McGurk – the four best men we've got.'

'That's rather a large demand,' the PM said after a lengthy pause. 'I seriously doubt that I could order their release.'

'Sure you can, Prime Minister. You can dream up an excuse. They're political prisoners, there's already doubt that you can hold them long, but we want them to be pardoned and set free before this week's out. We won't settle for less.'

'That's impossible,' the PM said.

'Sure, nothing's impossible, Prime Minister. We don't care how you explain it to the public; we just want them pardoned.'

'I can't do it,' the PM said.

'Yes, you can,' McGee insisted. 'They're in the

Maze awaiting trial, their guilt hasn't been proven yet, so you can say that the evidence against them was all circumstantial and wouldn't have held up in court.'

'That will make fools of our intelligence people.'

'That's part of our general plan.'

'And the million pounds? You want us to give you a million pounds so you can finance more terror?'

'Ackaye, that's right, Prime Minister. That's just what we want, like.'

The PM stared at him with cold rage in his eyes, then scratched his chin and studied the floor, clearly deep in thought. Eventually raising his eyes again, he said: 'Then what? You've already done all the damage you can. I can't see us recovering from the public knowledge that all this has happened.'

'That's correct,' Barker interjected. 'You've done too much damage already. We'll lose international confidence when this gets out and that will finish the North Sea.'

'It won't be public,' McGee explained. 'It doesn't have to be known. Sure, if you give us what we want, we'll pull out and keep quiet about it. Then you people put out a statement. You say the loss of Eagle 3 was due to a serious earthquake on the seabed that caused damage as far away as Charlie 2. You say most of the crew on Charlie 2 were killed and will have to be replaced. Naturally, we'll be gone. You then bring the new crew in. They'll take over without knowing what's gone on – nor will anyone else.'

'To your advantage,' the PM said.

'Ackaye, Prime Minister. Sure we'll stay quiet as long as our men stay out of the Maze. We'll only talk if you try to drag them back in or otherwise harm them.'

The PM was thoughtful, pursing his lips and tapping his chin with his fingertips as the hut swayed from side to side.

Eventually, to break the silence, Robert Barker said: 'So what if we agree? What guarantee do we have that the Prime Minister will then be released and that the bomb won't be set off?'

'Now why would we do that? We'd be cutting our own throats. Why destroy British oilfields and kill the Prime Minister, turning public sympathy against us, when we've got everything we need with minimum damage? We rely on public support as much as you do and we don't want to lose it.'

'So why demand the PM's presence here in the first place?'

'Because there's something I have to tell you in his presence – and you're not going to like it.' He glanced at each of them in turn, grim-faced now. After checking the guard by the door, he turned back to them. 'The IRA couldn't have financed an operation this big on its own. No, we were approached by the spokesman for some overseas backers who wanted us to assassinate the Prime Minister.' McGee's thin smile at this point was not returned by the PM. 'We only had one meeting with this single representative and he didn't say who the others were. He only described them as a group with unlimited funds. But since he specifically wanted the assassination to take place during the PM's visit to the oilfields, I think it's safe to assume that they've some interests here.'

Masters felt a sudden chill sliding down his spine. He was shocked by this fresh revelation, the thickening plot, and felt that he, an SBS commando, a good marine, was out of his depths in this murky world of conspiracy.

'This unknown group,' McGee continued, 'wanted the assassination to look like the act of a local terrorist group. For reasons not explained they didn't want it to be connected to anyone outside the United Kingdom. They wanted us to do the job. We also had to take the blame. In return, they would finance the hijack operation and pay a separate fee of two million pounds.'

Barker glanced at his granite-faced Prime Minister, then lowered his gaze to the floor. Masters knew he was shocked.

'As I said before,' McGee continued, 'it's not in our interest to lose public sympathy by assassinating the Prime Minister – but we needed the money and we *did* want our men out of the Maze.

So we accepted the job, receiving full finance for the hijack and with the first half of the two million to be paid to our representatives in Aberdeen the minute you all stepped aboard this rig. The other million was to be paid when we killed the Prime Minister.'

'I don't get it,' Barker said. 'How would these men, your backers, know that the Prime Minister had boarded this rig? Would they take your word for it?'

'Of course not. They'd know because one of them – and I honestly don't know who – is one of the men who took part in your conference back on Bravo 1. He'll know the Prime Minister's here. He'll know everything that's happened. He'll be contacting the mainland right now, to arrange for the first million to be handed over. When my man rings to say that's been done, I'm to kill the Prime Minister . . . begging your pardon, sir!'

The PM responded with a flat gaze. 'But you won't kill me,' he said.

'No,' McGee replied. 'And I've already told you why. I don't know who these men are, but alienating the British public is something we wouldn't do for their benefit. They offered two million pounds. We want you to offer more. Their first million plus your million makes two million – the original fee – but we also want our men out of the Maze and that's really the capper.'

There was silence for a long time while they tried to digest the facts. Masters, Barker and the PM were all thinking of Bravo 1 and the unknown traitor in their midst. Which one of them was it? What was his motivation? Who on earth could have set all this up while pretending to be one of their own? Barker looked stunned and drained. Masters was still and self-contained. The Prime Minister, by contrast, was shocked and outraged, his icy-blue eyes bright with a burning anger.

'I won't agree,' he said harshly. 'The price is too high. I will not release your murderous friends from the Maze just to watch them organize more terrorism. Nor will I give you the money. I won't finance the IRA. To capitulate will merely be a sign that you can get away with this again. No, I won't do it. Nothing you say will make me do it. There are limits and I think you've just reached them. You won't go any further.'

'That I will,' McGee promised.

'I don't think so, McGee. You said yourself that you depend on public opinion, so I don't think you'll risk turning it against you. You won't do what you're threatening.'

The second he finished speaking, he realized how wrong he was. He looked into the growing rage in McGee's eyes and saw the truth of fanaticism. McGee was pushing his chair back, standing up, his eyes widening. He grabbed the PM by the collar to tug him forward and breathe right in his face.

'Sure, I'll do it,' McGee snapped. 'Believe me, mister, I'll do it! I'll do anything that puts you bastards down, even if I go with you!' He pushed the PM aside, snatched a pistol from the table, then violently kicked the door open and stepped out of the hut. 'Bring the bastards out here!' he bawled.

One of the guards grabbed the PM and threw him out through the door. When he nodded curtly at Masters and Barker, both men left the radio shack, stepping into the light beaming out from the doorway and further dazzled by the lights shining down from the derricks and modules. Temporarily blinded, they blinked and then saw the two survivors: Griffith and Sutton, the geologist and the driller, both on their hands and knees on the deck, surrounded by gunmen. Sutton had been badly beaten; his face was bruised and he was weeping. Griffith, kneeling beside him, was untouched, but his eyes shone with fear.

McGee didn't waste any time. He grabbed Griffith by the hair, jerked his head back, placed the barrel of the pistol against his head and then glanced around wildly at the PM. The latter tried to step forward, but two of the guards stopped him, then twisted his arms behind his back and held him there while he looked on in horror.

'No!' the PM cried out. 'No! For God's sake, you can't . . .'

His voice was cut off by the gunshot. Griffith's head exploded. His body jerked like a puppet on a string and then collapsed to the deck.

'Do you believe me?' McGee hissed.

He spun around and grabbed Sutton and jerked his head back. Sutton shrieked and the Prime Minister cried 'No!' and then the gun fired again. Sutton convulsed and collapsed. His body shuddered and then was still. The blood dribbled from the shadows where his head was to touch the PM's boots. The Prime Minister started sagging, but the guards pulled him back up. He shook his head from side to side as if dazed, then started shaking all over. McGee walked up to him, his eyes bright and obsessed, and waved his gun in the PM's face as if wanting to hit him.

'Do you believe me?' he hissed again. 'Well? Is that enough for your conscience?'

The Prime Minister did not reply, but simply gasped and shook his head. Barker bit his lower lip and Masters clenched both his fists as the two bodies were thrown overboard. They didn't hear the splash: the sea was too far below. They glanced down and saw the blood on the deck, seeping out of the shadows. The PM shuddered and Barker bit his lip again. Masters opened his clenched fists and spread his fingers as he fought to control himself.

The huge derricks soared above him, their lights merging with the stars. Masters dropped his gaze only when he was prodded, none too gently, at gunpoint, back into the hut.

The PM was in a chair, covering his face with his hands, shuddering. Barker was standing beside him, clearly as shocked but trying to hide it. Masters, turning away in embarrassment, came face to face with McGee.

'You have one hour to decide,' McGee said, before slamming the door shut.

10

The Prime Minister raised his head and looked at them with shocked eyes. He shuddered and then controlled himself and sat up in the chair. Covering his face with his hands again, he took deep, even breaths, then removed his hands from his face, placed them lightly on his knees and stared at them as if praying for clemency.

'My fault,' he said softly. 'So stupid. God forgive me for that.'

'It wasn't your fault,' Masters said. 'I think he wanted to do it anyway. He wanted to put on a show and he used you for that.'

The PM shook his head. 'I can't believe it, Sergeant . . . Like animals . . . They were shot down like animals. One always thinks men can't do that.'

'They can do it,' Masters told him. 'They've been doing it for centuries. Let's forget it. Let's talk about something else. We've got one hour to stop it.'

'Stop it?' Barker said. 'How the hell can we stop

it? We're locked in and they won't let us out. We just say yes or no.'

'Wrong,' Masters said. 'McGee made one mistake. Of all the places on the rig to lock us up, he picked the wrong one.'

Barker looked sharply at him, then glanced around the radio shack. The single window had a solid metal covering which the terrorists had locked.

'We can get *out*?' Barker asked.

'That's right,' Masters said. 'But what happens then, I don't know.'

He glanced at the PM, who was still taking deep breaths. The PM's eyes were clearer now, and he seemed to be calming down.

'Are you all right, sir?' Masters asked.

'Yes, I'm all right. I don't feel good, but that can be lived with. Apart from that, I'm OK.'

'They forgot something,' Masters told him. 'They probably don't even know about it. This hut has a trapdoor in the floor, practically under your feet.'

The PM glanced down and saw nothing but solid steel. He looked between his legs, under the console, and saw a steel plate. It had an embedded handle.

'That's it,' Masters confirmed. 'It leads down to the drilling floor. This hut's above one corner of that floor, well away from the moonpool. The corner's packed with large crates, filled with spare parts and antennae. If anything goes wrong with the communications unit, the spare parts are passed up through the trapdoor. We can get down to that floor. The packing crates will give us cover. That corner of the floor rests on top of a pontoon leg and an exit door leads out to the catwalk. Ladders run down the pontoon legs – straight down to the sea. I know that there's a supply barge anchored beside the rig and since they always unload from this side that's where it'll be. We can climb down the pontoon leg. There'll be no one on the barge. If we go down the inside of the leg there's no way we'll be seen.'

'And once there?' Barker asked. 'What happens then? Do we just hide and wait?'

'No,' Masters said. 'We don't have to do that. The barges are towed out by small boats, so we'll take one of those. They're not fast, but they'll do. We'll have to time it pretty well. McGee's left the radio open to let us ring Bravo 1 because he thinks we can't get away anyhow. So we *will* ring Bravo 1. We'll ask for a helicopter to pick us up. It's not much, but it's something.'

'We can't just leave,' the PM said. 'I don't think we should do that.'

'The bomb,' Barker explained.

'That's right,' Masters said. 'We have to disarm the bomb and kill their radar and cameras. If we manage that, we can return. Launch an assault against the rig. With their cameras and sonic beams out of action, we can come under the sea and get to the rig before they see us. In short, we have to leave them paralysed until we come back.'

'It's impossible,' Barker said. 'It can't be done. We don't know where the bomb is.'

'I think I do,' Masters told him. 'McGee said a bit too much. He said the bomb was inside a pontoon leg – halfway down a pontoon leg.'

'You're going to search for it?' Barker asked.

'That's right,' Masters said. 'The support legs are hollow, they're laced with steel ladders, and if I don't find the bomb in the first leg, I'll climb through to the next.'

'You haven't time,' Barker said. 'The four main legs are a quarter of a mile apart. You haven't time to check all of them.'

'I won't have to,' Masters said. 'At least I might, but I doubt it. I think the bomb is on this side of the rig and probably right there below us. McGee's made this hut his base. He wants to be near the radio. I suspect he'd automatically place the bomb in the leg nearest to him. There's another reason for him to do that. The offloading is done this side. When McGee brought the bomb aboard, whether it was well hidden or not, I think he would have wanted it stored in the nearest available spot. The closest spot is beneath this hut; it's the first storage space you come to. Christ, come to think of it, he said the bomb was packed with some radio spares

– and all the radio spares are stored beneath this hut. That's where the bomb is – I'm almost certain of it. It's in the pontoon leg directly below us.'

Barker gave a low whistle. 'If you're right,' he said, 'that just leaves the radar and cameras. How the hell can you kill them?'

'I'm not sure,' Masters confessed. 'But if I cannibalize the plutonium bomb, I might be able to make some more modest explosives. I suspect the terrorist bomb is an implosion-type weapon, which means that the plutonium metal core is surrounded by a large quantity of ordinary, conventional explosive, such as dynamite.'

'*Sticks* of dynamite?' said Barker.

'Yes. And if it's that kind of bomb – and I think it has to be – I'll use the dynamite on the antennae and the drilling room.'

'You'll never get there,' Barker said. 'The terrorists are bound to see you.'

'I'm not sure that they will,' Masters replied. 'There are sixty terrorists aboard and they all arrived separately over the last eighteen months. They all worked with the regular crew and they all worked in shifts. Given the size of this rig and the nature of shift work, I think it's safe to assume that one half has never seen the other half. A lot are probably meeting for the first time. Some probably haven't even met yet. I'm in overalls and I look just like the rest, so they probably won't give me a second glance. True, McGee knows me and a lot of the men outside have seen me; but I think those men are all stationed on this deck, so if I can manage to keep out of McGee's way I'll have a fairly good chance.'

The SBS man's grey eyes shone with a hard, driving light as they focused steadily, relentlessly, on Barker. The Prime Minister was standing up. He wasn't shaking any more. The colour had returned to his face and he gave a small smile.

'I don't believe this,' he said.

Masters grinned. 'It's a long shot,' he confessed. 'But we don't really have another choice, so I think we should try it.'

'Yes,' the PM said, 'so do I.'

'There's no time,' Barker said. 'We've only fifty minutes left. That gives us time to get off this rig. There's no time for the rest of it.'

'You want to leave them with the bomb?'

'No, I don't. I just think fifty minutes is too short. There's no way you can do it.'

'If the bomb's below I can.'

'It might not be below. It might be in the leg at the other end. It might be right over the other side.'

'At least we can try.'

'I agree,' the PM said. 'But what happens if we don't get off in time?'

'Then both of you leave me,' said Masters.

The PM looked at Barker, who shrugged and

turned away. He stared at the bolted steel door and then turned back again.

'If you don't get off, they're going to find you,' said Barker.

'Not before I get their bomb.'

'Then they'll kill you. They'll definitely do that. They won't like what you've done.'

'It's the only way.'

'No. Let's call their bluff.'

'No, we can't call their bluff. You know they're not bluffing.'

Barker looked at the floor, his shoulders slumped in fatigue and dread, but he soon regained control of himself and gave Masters a painful grin. 'OK,' he said. 'Let's go.'

'Can you work the radio?' Masters asked.

'Of course,' Barker replied.

'Good. Get in touch with Bravo 1 while I remove the trapdoor. Tell them we want a helicopter. Say we want it right now. Tell them to make sure that they fly by the chart route and that they stay at low altitude all the way. We'll be in a small boat. We'll be five miles north-east of the rig. Tell them to keep their eyes peeled because we'll want picking up. They should have the harness ready. They should search around in that area. When we see them, we'll send up a flare and they can come down and get us.'

'I've got it,' Barker said. 'Now what about this

radio? I think we should knock this out as well, once we've used it ourselves.'

'No,' Masters said. 'They can't detect us with a radio. And we'll still need communication with the terrorists when we get back to Bravo 1.'

'*If* we get back,' Barker said.

'Yes, *if* we get back.'

They went to work. Barker turned on the radio. Masters crawled under the operator's console and reached out to the steel plate. It had a small handle set flush with the steel plate. Masters raised the handle and the plate came out with a harsh, grating sound. He laid it aside. The PM glanced at the hole it left. There was no sound of movement, so clearly the noise hadn't been heard out there.

Meanwhile Barker was on the radio, getting in touch with Bravo 1. He had the volume turned down low and the other two heard him whispering into the microphone. Masters crawled from under the console, stood up, wiped his hands on his overalls and then grinned at the PM. The latter was watching Barker, listening to what he was saying; Barker was talking in nautical terms and arranging the pick-up. After finishing, he turned off the radio and told the other two: 'It's all set.'

Masters went to the table, picked up a box of matches, and put them in the pocket of his overalls.

'Right,' he said to the Prime Minister. 'Please

listen carefully, sir. Barker here knows the rig well, so he's going to guide you. You'll go down through that hole. There's a steel ladder below it and it goes down twenty feet. I want you to go down carefully and wait at the bottom. You should be hidden by the crates. Barker's going first, so he'll already be down there and he'll guide you the rest of the way. It's pretty simple – but dangerous. There's a door right by the ladder. It leads to the outside of the rig just beneath the main deck. That ladder drops to a catwalk that's on top of the pontoon leg, running down two hundred feet to the loading barge. Don't look down or you'll get dizzy. And don't let go for a second. You'll be hanging on the outside of the pontoon leg and the wind there is rough. The deck stretches out above you. That means the terrorists won't see you. They might see you when you jump on the loading barge, but I think it's too dark. You'll both wait for me there. Give me forty minutes from now. If, by that time, I don't show up, just get in a small boat. Barker knows how to use them. He'll take you out to where the helicopter should be hovering, and they'll pick you both up.'

'Fine,' the PM said unconvincingly, taking a deep breath and letting it out slowly. 'So what about you?'

'If I don't show up, I've been caught. You'll find out soon enough. The terrorists are bound to ring Bravo 1 and give you the good news.'

'And what do we do then?'

'You can go back to square one. You can either give in to their demands or let them blow up the rig.'

The PM stared at him and was aware only or his grey, driven eyes. He looked at Barker, who just nodded, and they went to the console. Barker crawled under first, then slithered down through the opening. He kicked at air until his feet found the ladder, then his head and hands disappeared. The PM smiled bleakly, then knelt on the floor. He crawled under the console, put his legs through the hole, found the ladder and started lowering himself down. He glanced back up at Masters, who was waiting to follow him. The PM, knowing he might not see him again, grinned at him and waved. 'Good luck,' he said, then dropped down through the hole.

Masters waited for a moment, gazing around the radio shack, listening carefully at the door, then went to the console and disappeared into the darkness below.

11

Standing on the ladder just beneath the radio shack, Masters pulled the steel cover back over the hole. It dropped back into place and he checked that it was secure. There was a good chance that when McGee entered the hut he wouldn't notice the trapdoor. Then Masters looked around and saw the ceiling of the drilling floor. He was twenty feet above the floor, just above the packing crates, and he looked beyond them at the large, cluttered workshop, the pipes and chains of the moonpool. It was very quiet out there, with no work going on. He saw some terrorists wandering lazily to and fro, holding MP5 sub-machine-guns in their hands, though not at the ready. They seemed very far away and their conversation echoed dully. The lights blazed and the machinery cast great shadows that swallowed whole areas.

As Masters climbed down the ladder, the drilling floor disappeared. The packing crates were piled high above his head when he stood on the lower floor. The floor rose and fell, swaying gently from side to side. The Prime Minister was about five feet away, standing close to the wall. There was a steel door beside him, and the handle squeaked when Barker turned it. Barker winced and glanced over his shoulder and nodded at Masters, who nodded back, gesturing for him to continue. Barker carefully pulled the large handle down until it locked into place. The sound of the lock echoed, seeming louder than it was. Masters turned away to peer through the packing crates at the vast, silent drilling floor.

None of the terrorists had heard the sound. They continued wandering back and forth, moving in and out of the shadows, talking lazily, bored by their vigil.

Masters turned back to Barker as he was pulling the door open. He stepped outside and waved to the PM, who hesitated, then followed him. Masters waited till they had gone, then checked the drilling floor again. There was no sign that anyone had noticed their activity, so he walked through the door.

He was slapped by an icy wind, which beat and moaned around him. He was on the catwalk of a circular deck that was thirty feet wide. It was the top of a pontoon leg, and the main deck loomed above it. The leg plunged two hundred feet to the sea, where reflected lights slid over the waves. The catwalk was dark and the surrounding night was black with clouds. The wind moaned and rushed in from the sea and he heard the waves hammering, smashing against the pontoon leg. Masters turned back and closed the door behind him, making sure it was locked.

'I can't do it,' the PM said, looking down through the catwalk. He was staring at the ladder that was fixed to the huge leg and dropped vertically to the sea way below. It was exposed to the beating wind. He would have to climb down that two hundred feet and he just couldn't face it.

'Don't look,' Masters whispered. 'Just forget it. Just get on and climb down.'

The wind howled around the catwalk, beating and tugging at the Prime Minister. Gripping the railing and shivering with cold, he was looking down fearfully at Barker, now already on the ladder, hanging in an all-enveloping darkness with nothing below him.

'Go down!' Masters snapped.

He grabbed the PM's shoulder, shook him roughly and pushed him down. The PM trembled visibly, licked his lips and then murmured: 'Oh, God!' He turned his back to the sea, gripped the railing even tighter, put his right foot on the step just above Barker's head and followed him as he started his descent.

Masters watched them go down, which they did very slowly, hanging in a black, howling void without shape or dimension. The sea wasn't really visible: the darkness just fell down and deepened. The silvery-grey head of the PM was bobbing in the middle of nothing. The wind howled around the ladder, and Masters heard it rattling. He looked down and saw the grey head disappearing, watched it melting in darkness.

Masters dropped to one knee, kneeling in front of another trapdoor. He grabbed the handle, pulled up the steel plate and looked into a black, seemingly bottomless pit. There were rumblings in that darkness and the noise reverberated. The pit, which was the interior of the huge pontoon leg, was circular and thirty feet in diameter.

Masters lowered himself in and the icy air clamped around him. His right foot kicked the side and found the ladder, then his other foot followed. He climbed down a few rungs, then reached out for a switch. When he turned the lights on, he looked down and saw the dizzying depths.

The pontoons were filled with water which rose halfway up the leg, splashing up and down as the tapering leg swayed from side to side. The circular wall was webbed with ladders that ran down into the water, tapering off into single lines before they finally disappeared.

Feeling dizzy and claustrophobic, Masters almost stopped breathing. The water outside the leg made a hollow, drumming sound; the water inside, in that shadowed pit below, splashed and sent up its echoes. Masters looked to his right and saw a black, three-foot hole. It was the entrance to one of the support legs and it echoed as well.

He looked into the support leg and saw the glint of steel through darkness. The knowledge that he would have to crawl down there made him feel queasy. Reaching up above his head, he pulled down the steel cover. It clanged shut and the noise reverberated up and down the main leg.

Masters started his descent, moving slowly and carefully, hearing the echo of his footsteps on the ladder, watching the wall rise above him. He didn't look up – only left and right. He closed his eye when he passed the dimmed lamps, and moved through shadow and light. The leg was swaying from side to side. The curved walls creaked and shuddered. The waves outside the leg pounded dully; the water inside was splashing.

Masters kept going down, passing girders that formed shelves around the wall, red with rust, strewn with debris. The divers often came down here, leaving plastic cups and bits of wire. Masters felt a brief annoyance when he saw this, but he kept going down.

He kept looking from left to right. He was convinced the bomb was here. He was sweating fifty feet above the water when he finally saw it.

The bomb was resting on a narrow girder that

circled around the wall, about two feet away from Masters's head. As Masters had expected, it was the size of a tea chest, had a slotted iron frame, and was attached to the base of the girder with two cast-iron clamps.

There was no dynamite.

Masters cursed his own ignorance. Of course there wouldn't be dynamite. The plutonium metal core would be surrounded by TNT and packed tight inside the sealed explosive shell. Masters swore again, his voice echoing and returning. He gripped the ladder as it swayed from side to side, as the shadows fell over him. Still, he had found the bomb. Now at least he could dismantle it. Reaching out, he nearly fell off the ladder, so he grabbed it again.

Cursing, he just hung there. The ladder swayed with the pontoon leg. The shadows darted up and down the rusted steel, changed their shapes, crept around him. He remained on the ladder, hearing the water far below, recalling that the men who worked here were normally tied on with safety straps. But he had no safety straps; he had nothing to hold him on. He would have to climb up on that girder and do it from there.

Masters briefly closed his eyes and pressed his forehead against the ladder. As he felt it swaying gently from side to side, he heard the water below. He didn't want to look down. That vertical tunnel was terrifying. It plunged down to the water, which now looked much darker than the sea. Masters opened his eyes and felt the sweat on his brow. He heard the rumbling of the sea all around him as he moved up the ladder.

He climbed on to the girder, which was eighteen inches wide. On his knees, he pressed himself against the wall and tried not to look down. The glint of water caught his gaze. His eyes were drawn against their will. He looked down past the bomb, down that spiralling fifty feet, and saw the round pool of water far below, very black, deadly cold. Masters knew how cold it was and that he couldn't survive in it. If he fell, and if he couldn't find a ladder, he would freeze to death in five minutes.

He fixed his eyes on the bomb.

Disarming it was easy. He was surprised at his own skill. It was a skill that he had picked up in the Royal Marine Commando Munitions School, though not during work on live plutonium bombs. Still, he managed to do it, as the basic principles were the same, requiring only his pocket screwdriver and past experience. He pulled the connecting wires loose, unscrewed the explosive lenses, then dropped the separate pieces into the water fifty feet below. When he had finished, he loosened the clamps and tried to push the bomb off the ledge. But he couldn't budge it an inch – it was too heavy to move. Smacking it with the palm of his hand in frustration, he decided to leave it.

According to his watch he had nineteen minutes left. He felt a cold, sneaking panic that made him crawl back up the ladder. Reaching out with one hand, he grabbed the ladder and swung back down, kicked out with his feet and found the rungs and then hauled himself up.

He felt better as he ascended and saw the roof of the leg above him. It was swaying from side to side and creaking loudly, but this didn't concern him now. He kept going up, feeling a warming exultation; it was born of his need to escape from this chill prison. This mood carried him upward, rekindling his fire. Then he reached the narrow entrance to the support leg and his panic returned.

The support leg was three feet wide and merely part of an immense steel web. The support legs criss-crossed beneath the decks and ran down to the pontoons. Masters had to go down there, but he really didn't want to do it. Instead, he wanted to climb out of this leg and breathe the fresh air. Yet he had to cross the rig in order to reach the drilling room, located in a module on the drilling floor, just beyond the moonpool. As he couldn't get to the drilling floor, he simply had to go under it. He could do so by going down this support leg until it joined with another. That was sixty feet down. From there he could climb the other leg. That second leg, also sixty feet long, would bring him out on to the lower deck, not too far from the drilling room.

Masters clung to the ladder, looking down the support leg. It was narrow and its ladder fell steeply and disappeared into darkness.

Not having a choice, he started down the support leg, his footsteps echoing as he stepped on each rung, his own breathing amplified. It seemed to take a long time. In fact, it took no time at all. Conscious only of the ringing of his steel-tipped boots, he soon started climbing. The climbing was worse. He kept straining to see the top. Looking up, he heard increasing noise, a dull cacophony of movement. It was the rattling of chains and the clanging of pipes: the general background noise of a rig that was no longer working. The noises made Masters dwell on the world outside; they made him think of the terrorists on the deck and of the time he had left. Yet he finally reached the top. There was a catwalk and a door. Opening the door carefully, he looked out and was blinded by light.

He was on the storage deck and its wall lamps were blazing, illuminating the crates and throwing great shadows across the floor. Masters glanced left and right, but saw no sign of movement, so he stepped out and walked across the steel deck until he came to another door. He opened this and walked through, then climbed up another ladder. There was a low, narrow corridor at the top, leading out to the drilling floor. Masters didn't go out there, but instead turned left near the exit. He went straight up another steel ladder and walked into a module, located just above the drilling deck. Looking down, he could see the terrorists, wandering back and forth past the moonpool, talking and laughing. The deck was cluttered with equipment, the bright light cast stark shadows, and the men were all carrying their weapons in a careless manner.

Masters entered another corridor, which was bright and low-ceilinged. A man stepped out of a doorway just ahead and nodded curtly and brushed past. Masters walked to that doorway, heard the sound of a TV monitor, looked in and saw a man in a chair, looking up at the screen. The cameras were searching the seabed, scanning over the anchor chains. The bottom was four hundred feet down and the whole view was murky. The man had his back to Masters, his feet up on the desk, and seemed bored as he coughed into his clenched fist and gazed at the monitor. His weapon was leaning against the desk – an MAS Combat Rifle. There was a pile of hand-grenades on the table close by the terrorist's booted feet. Masters glanced at the floor and saw some magazines for the gun. The man coughed again into his clenched fist, clearing phlegm from his throat.

Masters walked up behind him, moving swiftly

and silently, to bring the edge of his calloused palm down on the terrorist's neck, at the side of the throat. The man didn't cry out; he simply grunted and slumped forward. Masters confirmed that he was dead, then closed the door. The monitor above the dead man was still showing the murky seabed.

Looking out through the window at the floor twelve feet below, Masters saw the terrorists gathered around the moonpool, smoking and drinking beer, leaving their weapons scattered carelessly on the deck nearby. They appeared to be having a break and Masters didn't like that.

He turned off the monitor, then switched off its power supply. Opening a box in the wall, he found the fuses amid a tangle of wiring. He pulled out some of the wires, quickly tied them together, then pushed them back against the wall and closed the box. The monitor was dead. The terrorists, finding it that way, would turn on its power supply. That's all Masters needed: the crossed wires would do the rest. The whole system would ignite and burn out beyond hope of repair.

A corpse would cause panic, so Masters had to move the dead man. He wanted the terrorists to find the room empty and think the man had just bunked off. But first he checked the grenades, which were not hand-grenades, but ones for use with the launcher that was attached to the barrel of the combat rifle. It was just what he needed.

Masters put on the belt to which the grenades were clipped. Opening the door, he glanced out and saw no sign of movement. Satisfied, he went back to the dead man, pulled him from the chair, and dragged him laboriously out into the corridor, where he hauled him along to the next door, a small storage room. After hurriedly bundling the corpse into that room, Masters returned to the drilling room, where he picked up the combat rifle and then casually walked out.

According to his watch, he had just under ten minutes left. He climbed down the steel ladder and turned left and walked on to the drilling deck.

The terrorists he had seen were still lounging around the moonpool, but others were wandering to and fro, in and out of the shadows. Masters simply started walking. It was a trick he had learnt somewhere. He knew that a total lack of self-consciousness could make people ignore you. He advanced across the drilling floor. A few passing men nodded. They glanced at him and looked away, as if they hadn't really seen him. He kept walking across the deck, passing through shadow and light, then climbed up steel steps and walked out of the drilling hut, emerging into the cold air of the main deck.

The derricks towered above him. The lights

tapered up into nothing. Floodlights beamed down on the deck, illuminating the terrorists. They were wandering back and forth, carrying AK47 assault rifles and MP5 sub-machine-guns, walking under the massive cranes, past the stacked pipes, with the darkness beyond them. Ignoring them, Masters made his way to the end of the deck until he was parallel to the radio shack. The same two guards were still standing outside the door, looking bored and lethargic.

Masters checked the time: he had five minutes left. He started walking along the edge of the deck, towards the radio shack. The sea murmured far below and the wind howled across him, but he made it to the hut and then slipped in behind it. It was very dark in there. He glimpsed the corner of the rig. Glancing down, he saw the huge pontoon leg, disappearing in darkness. He thought of Barker and the Prime Minister, silently praying that they had made it. They should both be down there in the barge, checking the time. Masters looked up again, beyond the roof of the radio shack; he saw the radar antennae thrusting skyward, halfway down the deck.

Breathing deeply, he put his arm through the sling of the rifle, then carefully climbed the ladder right in front of him. He reached the roof of the radio shack, slithered across it on his belly, only stopping when he reached the far edge and could see the whole deck. There he made himself comfortable, but remained on his belly. He pulled the rifle off his shoulder, checked the magazine, ensured that the grenade-launcher was working, then took the safety-catch off. The guards below made no sound. Masters looked along the deck, where the radar antennae were being bent by the wind.

He had one minute left. Still on his belly, he adopted the firing position and took aim with the combat rifle. The two guards were still below him, but the others were far away. Masters aimed at the guard to his left and then fired the first shot.

There was a crack; it was not very loud at all. The guard jerked violently, staggered in a circle, then went down. The other guard dropped to his knees, turning around, raising his weapon, looking shadowy and unreal in the gloom as Masters aimed for his chest. The rifle cracked again in his ear. The guard's arms flew out sideways. He spun away but had not yet hit the deck when Masters rolled from the edge.

He heard shouts and running feet, then the roar of many guns. Knowing they were confused, he reset his rifle and fixed a grenade to the barrel-mounted launcher. The running feet were approaching. A machine-gun stuttered. Still on his belly, he twisted to the side and aimed his rifle at the radar antennae. He didn't have much time. The shouting and shooting were spreading. He took aim at the base of the antennae and fired the grenade. It seemed to take a long time. Shadowy figures advanced towards him. Guns flashed and then he saw the flaring, silvery-white explosion, followed instantly by a roaring and the screeching of scorched, buckling metal.

He didn't wait to check the damage, but instead attached a second grenade, took aim and squeezed the trigger. He felt the recoil as the butt punched his shoulder. The second blast seemed even louder, with metal shrieking over the explosion as the antennae burned, buckled and twisted in searing white heat.

Masters put another grenade in the launcher and fired it at the terrorists. It exploded in the darkness, flared up and faded away. The antennae swayed to and fro, then caved in before the wind and crashed down over the deck and the running men. Steel exploded in all directions, a shower of sparks shot skyward, as Masters slithered back across the flat roof and climbed down to the deck.

He was behind the radio shack, on the corner of the rig, and looking down he thought he saw the sea below, a black mat in the void. The wind was pushing him against the wall as he fought his way to the catwalk. He saw a steel ladder that ran down past the decks to the top of the pontoon leg. Starting the climb down, he heard gunshots and shouting. He also heard the door of the radio shack banging against the wall, followed by McGee's voice bawling angrily.

Masters had no time to deal with McGee, so he kept climbing down. The wind howled and tried to sweep him from the rungs, but he didn't dare stop.

He finally reached the pontoon leg, where the wind howled dementedly, but he found the hole in the catwalk, put his feet on the ladder, and started to descend once more. It took a very long time. He passed under the lower deck. Looking through the silvery web of the supporting legs, he saw the darkness beyond. The wind here was fierce, howling under the rig. He glanced up and saw searchlights beaming down, raking the sea below.

Masters clambered down as fast as possible, hearing the firing of guns above his head, very high up and muffled. Then he heard the clang of boots above. There was shouting and the ladder vibrated and he knew they were following him. He climbed down even faster, forgetting the wind and the dreadful height, hearing the smashing of the sea against the legs, a dull metallic cacophony. The men above were shouting. That made him move faster. He climbed down and heard the roaring of a motor launch and knew that Barker was leaving.

He started yelling crazily, letting Barker know who he was, as the rifle slung over his shoulder pummelled his ribs.

Masters jumped from the ladder and fell down through darkness. He landed on the barge and rolled over and crashed into some crates. Barker called out his name, not sure what was happening. Masters jumped up and stumbled across the deck, hitting boxes and cables.

Suddenly, he saw Barker, not too far away, silhouetted against the cloudy night, at the prow of the loading barge. He lurched towards him, but he disappeared from view, then Masters reached the prow and saw the boat below him. Barker was at the wheel. The Prime Minister was waving at him. The sea was rough and the engine was roaring as Masters jumped down, almost hitting the PM, before crashing into the cabin wall. Barker ceded his place at the wheel to the SBS man and the engine roared louder as the boat moved off.

They saw the rig high above them, and searchlights beaming down on the water, then heard the gunfire. Wood splintered all around them. Barker screamed and threw his hands up. Masters saw his eyes, in them an awful incomprehension, before he jerked back and appeared to somersault and went over the side.

There was no point in stopping.

12

The small boat's motor roared against the wind. The sea was rough and it sloshed across the deck and drenched Masters as he struggled with the wheel. He heard the louder roar of the guns as the terrorists fired from the loading barge. They were shouting and then another engine growled into life, which meant they were following him. He glanced back over his shoulder and saw the Prime Minister at the stern, fully exposed to the gunfire, gazing into the water.

'Get down!' Masters shouted. 'Get your head down! They're trying to kill you!'

An automatic rifle cracked and he heard the bullets whipping past him. Fragments of wood exploded off the prow of the boat and as Masters dropped low the wheel started spinning. Cursing, he glanced up and saw the rig soaring above him, its many lights blazing out of the darkness. Glancing back, he saw that the PM was crouching low, peering from the stern of the boat, trying to see the men following them.

'Keep down!' Masters bawled.

'What about Barker?' the PM shouted back. 'I can see him! He's floating out there in the water! I'm sure I can see him!'

The boat had gone into a spin with waves sloshing across the deck, then it rose and plunged down into the waves, almost submerged. Masters jumped up, reaching for the runaway wheel. The terrorists' guns barked and more splinters of wood flew about him as he yanked the wheel back. The boat started straightening out, heading away from the oil rig. He heard the terrorists' launch ploughing through the waves as more bullets whipped past him.

'What about Barker?' the PM shouted above the roar of the motor and the sea.

'It's too late!' Masters yelled back.

'We can't just leave him!'

'There's no choice! Keep your head down, sir!'

Masters gave the engine full throttle, and the launch nosed up and plunged back down through the spray and waves. The PM yelped with shock as he stumbled back to Masters; soaked to the skin, he was looking down at himself as if not quite believing it. 'It's freezing cold!' he shouted. Masters didn't respond. He was gripping the wheel and heading into the darkness, the rough sea and the cutting wind. As the boat rose and fell the PM held on to the side. From behind they heard the rumble of the other boat and the shouts of the terrorists.

'They're following us!' the PM shouted.

'I know that!'

'Is there anything I can do to help?'

'Just keep your head down!'

Sub-machine-guns snapped behind them and bullets whined past on both sides. The PM dropped low behind Masters and mumbled something inaudible. Glancing back over his shoulder, Masters was temporarily blinded by a searchlight that passed across the boat, wavered, then came back towards him. He glanced down. The PM was crouched low. Masters grabbed him by the shoulders and tugged him up and placed his hands on the wheel.

'Hold her steady!' Masters shouted. 'Don't let the wheel move! Don't let the boat change direction!'

The PM's eyes widened, staring at Masters as if stunned, but he grabbed the wheel and looked straight ahead at the dark, surging sea. Masters unslung his combat rifle, then he heard the snap of automatic fire from behind him and dropped to the deck. The sea growled and washed over him as he crawled to the stern. There he looked up just as the searchlight found him, filling the launch with a dazzling light. The PM was exposed, so there really wasn't time to spare. Masters set the weapon on automatic fire, then aimed directly at the source of the blinding light. He could hardly keep his eyes open and the boat was pitching wildly, but he fired a short burst, a second, then a third, and was blessed with the distant sound of smashing glass as the darkness rushed back in.

He had knocked out their searchlight, but this respite was all too brief. He knew that the terrorist boat would have flares and emergency lights. Still growling behind him, banging noisily through the waves, it was starting to catch up. Masters hurried back along the boat to find the PM still holding the steering wheel. When the PM saw Masters, he gave a shy smile, as if embarrassed to be there.

'I'm no good at this,' he said.

'You're doing fine, sir.'

'I don't think I'll ever forget this experience.'

'I'm sure you won't, sir.' Masters took over the steering wheel once more. 'Can you fire a rifle?' he asked.

'No,' the PM replied. 'I'm no good at that either.'

The wind howled about them, the boat bucked and plunged back down, and the water sloshed across the deck to their rear and poured back out again. Masters held a steady course and knew just where he was going. Glancing briefly over his shoulder, he saw the lights of the distant rig, soaring up to the black sky, a diamond web illuminating the darkness. The other boat was closing the gap all the time, growing larger, a black shape on the light-flecked waves. Masters heard the men shouting and saw lamps flickering on, then another powerful light beamed down on the water and started inching towards him. Suddenly, the boat was looming large to the stern, cutting around Masters to run parallel to him.

'They've caught up!' the PM called out.

'Not for long,' Masters rasped, reaching down to grab a rope from the deck and lash the steering wheel to its support. 'Get into the cabin!' he shouted, but the PM just stared at him. The guns roared and Masters grabbed the PM and threw him down to the deck. 'In the cabin!' he bellowed. 'Get in the cabin! Move!' The terrorists' guns roared and again wood fragmented all around Masters, so he grabbed the PM by the shoulders and threw him bodily towards the steps. The PM crawled forward and made his way down the steps. Masters glanced at the wheel and saw that the rope was holding it steady. Reassured, he crawled forward as a stream of bullets stitched the whole boat, causing large chunks of wood as well as splinters to fly through the air.

He went to the starboard side, huddled up there and waited, listening to the rumbling of the other boat as it attempted to come close enough for the terrorists to board him. The terrorists were excited, shouting a lot as they fired their weapons. Masters heard their boat crashing through the waves, coming closer each second. Still, he didn't move. The sea hissed as it poured over him. The guns roared and bullets riddled the deck near the stern and made streams of water shoot upwards either side of the boat. Masters cursed: they were punctured below the water-line. He could tell by the noise that the other boat was coming in broadside. It was practically on top of him and would ram him any moment now.

Masters unclipped an American M26 hand-grenade, pulled the pin out, then jumped up and threw it. The other boat filled his whole vision. He saw the crazed eyes of his pursuers. They seemed startled as the grenade sailed through the air and he dropped low again. The grenade exploded with a deafening, staccato roar. He heard shrieks and the sound of tumbling bodies as he stood up again. He fired his combat rifle, still set on automatic, without looking. White flames were daggering up from the other boat, silhouetting the spinning, staggering men. Masters kept firing in short bursts, spraying the deck from prow to stern. Men screamed and tumbled over the sides or threw themselves to the deck.

The boat was pulling away from him, obviously out of control, with yellow flames licking over the wheel-house, turning blue, edged with black smoke. The grenade had ignited their spare petrol and the flames hissed and crackled.

A silhouette was jerking frantically by the smoking wheel-house – on fire, screaming dreadfully. Masters fired a burst at him and the burning man fell. A light winked and Masters dropped to the deck and heard the roar of the gun. He crawled back to the wheel-house, reached up and untied the rope. Opening the engine, he let the boat rush forward, then turned it to starboard.

The Prime Minister reappeared, looking up from the wheel-house steps. Masters told him to stay there, but the PM ignored him and clambered up the steps to crouch beside him. They both looked back and saw that the burning boat was falling well behind them, the flames clawing at the darkness and casting shadows on the sea's glowing surface. Human screams rose up from the water near where the blazing launch was drifting, out of control. Their own boat was now circling around it, cutting across to its starboard side.

The PM glanced at Masters, wondering what he was doing. Looking back, he saw the flames of the burning boat, which was turning and bobbing, moving across on their right, drifting very close to them. An inflatable dinghy had been thrown over the side, into the sea, and some terrorists clambered down on a rope ladder and fell into the dinghy. More screaming came from the deck – someone burning to death. The terrorists in the dinghy started rowing as the yellow flames licked out over them.

'Take the wheel,' Masters said.

The Prime Minister took the wheel, hardly thinking, just watching. Masters had turned the engine off and the little launch was just drifting. The PM held it steady as Masters picked up his rifle and aimed it at the terrorists in the dinghy. 'No, Masters!' the PM shouted. 'For God's sake, you can't . . .' But Masters was ignoring him and taking careful, deliberate aim. The PM released the wheel and rushed at Masters and tried pushing the gun up. Masters cursed, grabbed his shoulder and threw him aside. 'Damn it, let me go!' he said harshly. 'I won't let them go back!'

The PM stood where he was, shocked by Masters's venom. He glanced across the choppy, freezing sea at the men in the dinghy. Then Masters fired. It was a short, decisive burst. Someone screamed and a man threw up his hands and splashed over the side. Masters lowered the weapon. Air hissed out of the dinghy. The men shouted and waved their arms wildly as the dinghy collapsed. The PM closed his eyes, listening to their frightened screaming. Opening his eyes, he saw them splashing in the water and swimming frantically towards him. Masters went back to the wheel-house and turned the motor on. The launch growled and the water boiled around it as it moved away from the swimming men. Their cries for help were loud and clear. The PM was in shock. Masters steered a wide arc around the burning vessel and headed into the darkness.

Looking back, the PM saw the other launch sinking slowly. He heard the pleas of the men in the water, first receding, then fading out completely as the darkness took over.

'They'll freeze to death,' the PM said.

'That's right,' Masters said. 'But at least they won't go back to that bastard McGee and help him tomorrow.'

He headed out to sea, keeping the launch on an even course, while the PM lowered himself to the deck, stunned and exhausted. The darkness was all around him, having swallowed the terrorists' boat; the lights of the rig had long since vanished and the moon hid behind the clouds. Drenched and extremely cold, shocked by what he had witnessed, the PM gave in to a fear that he could scarcely control.

Masters's ruthlessness had startled him. He understood it, but it had unnerved him. Knowing that Masters was a sergeant in the legendary SBS, he also knew just how well he had been trained and how courageous he had to be. Masters lived in another world, one in which violent death was the norm; he had been trained to use his wits and not give in to doubt; and to kill without hesitation when he deemed it necessary. Now, with all the skills at his command, he would ensure, even at the cost of the lives of the terrorists, that he, his Prime Minister, would be returned safe and sound.

In Masters's view, the PM knew, the terrorists burnt alive, drowned or frozen to death in the sea behind him had merely received their just rewards. This knowledge was what frightened the PM, but he could not avoid the truth. The others had died that he might live and he and Masters both knew it.

They soon heard the rescue helicopter. It was flying from east to west just ahead at a very low altitude. Masters immediately stopped the boat, then went back to the stern. The deck had been shot full of holes and the water was pouring in.

'We were lucky,' he said. 'Another ten minutes and we'd have sunk. We'd have frozen to death just like that lot.'

He threw the anchor overboard and returned to the wheel-house, where he rummaged about on the floor, then stood up with a flare gun, which he aimed at the sky. There was a short, dull explosion. The flare burst in the sky high above, streaking the darkness with green and purple light. Masters fired a second signal and the coloured streaks formed an umbrella, racing outward, then curving back down to fade above the dark sea.

The Dragonfly's pilot saw the flares and descended to approach. Soon the helicopter was hovering just above the boat, its props causing a whirlwind.

A searchlight cut through the darkness as the helicopter hovered thirty feet above them, swaying dangerously in the wind, its engine making a deafening noise. The spinning props whipped the air and made the sea swirl and roar, the waves rushing across the deck of the launch to drench the PM and Masters. They held on to the sides, blinking against the powerful light. Falling out of the Dragonfly, the abseil harness blew out wildly on the fierce wind. The PM looked up and saw the wildly swinging harness, then looked higher at the bottom of the helicopter and felt his head spinning. Masters was shouting and waving at him, trying to give him instructions. The PM glanced down and saw the water creeping over his ankles.

'. . . boat's going down!' Masters was shouting. 'We've no time to lose!'

When the PM reached out for the harness, it flew away from his grasp. The helicopter continued roaring above him, the waves rushed in to drench him. Masters reached for the harness and caught it, then waved at the PM, who stepped forward, gripping the side of the boat. The boat was rocking in the violent, surging water, sinking down at the stern. Masters indicated the harness, holding it up to the PM. He saw two loops for his arms, and an encircling belt, so he held his arms out. The boat rocked and he nearly fell. Masters was speaking, still trying to give instructions, but the

PM couldn't hear a word. Masters attached the harness to him, tightening the belt around him, as the wind continued howling about them.

The SBS sergeant stepped back and waved at the helicopter. The PM felt the pounding of his heart, an absurd, childish dread. The cable above him went taut and he sucked his breath in. He was picked up and flew out on the wind and then was swinging in mid-air.

The PM gripped the straps, gasped for breath and closed his eyes. His stomach heaved and he suddenly felt hollow, so he opened his eyes again. He heard the roar of the helicopter, felt himself swinging freely, and glanced down to see the sea far below, its dark waves flattening out. He kept swinging back and forth as he was winched up on the cable. The roaring of the helicopter increased and the wind beat more fiercely.

The PM swung in space, seeing dark sky and the sea, feeling the wind and tasting the salt in the air before being jerked up and in. Strong hands grabbed his shoulders and dragged him in farther, until he saw the cluttered interior of the helicopter and a pair of wide, staring eyes. Seeing these, the PM realized who he was: that he *was* the Prime Minister. He said his thanks to the nervous eyes, smiling kindly as he did so. Grateful, the young, wide-eyed Royal Navy loadmaster unclipped the harness, took it off the

PM, then threw it back out again and watched it fall to the sea.

The PM looked down and saw the dark sea. The boat below seemed too small to be real and its stern was sinking under the water. Masters stood on the prow, which was pointing at the sky. He swayed to and fro as if about to fall, then reached up to the harness. The sea washed across the boat, engulfing most of it. The prow suddenly lurched up and fell back and Masters jumped into space, swinging away from the sinking boat as it disappeared beneath the waves. Masters dangled momentarily in the harness and then started ascending.

It seemed to take a long time. The wind howled through the Dragonfly. Masters floated far below in the darkness, moving up, coming closer. Then his head appeared through the floor. The loadmaster hauled him in. Masters turned around and looked back through the doorway at the black void below. There was no sign of the boat. The sea was merging with the darkness. Masters gasped and rolled on to his back and just lay there and smiled.

'Now we've got them,' he said.

13

'The situation is this,' Masters said to his CO, Lieutenant-Colonel Edwards, and Captain Pancroft. 'The terrorist bomb is now inoperative. We've knocked out their radar. That means we can get close to the rig without being detected. I suggest that we do so and that we do it this morning, while it's dark, before the dawn breaks.'

'Right,' Captain Pancroft said keenly. 'First light is always the best time. Catch the buggers napping.'

Masters grinned at Rudy Pancroft. He admired him greatly. Captain Pancroft had often been referred to as a legend in his own lifetime for his sterling work with the anti-smuggling patrols in Hong Kong, his surveillance activities in the 'bandit country' of Northern Ireland and, in particular, his heroic performances during the war in the Falklands, which had ended only a few months earlier. He was a good man to know.

'I agree,' Lieutenant-Colonel Edwards said. 'The sooner we clear this mess up the better. So let's be getting on with it.'

The two officers wore the full Royal Marines uniform, including the Commando green beret, plus parachuting wings and a badge denoting that they were Swimmer Canoeists. Both also had numerous military awards stitched to their tunics. Compared with them, the other men in the boardroom of Bravo 1 looked almost anaemic.

Masters was standing at one end of the table, wearing spotless overalls. The Prime Minister was sitting at his right hand, in a new, dark-grey suit with white shirt and silk tie. The rest of the men looked tired and pale from lack of sleep and anxiety. Turner played nervously with his beard; Sir Reginald McMillan kept drumming his fingertips on the table; and only Dalton, the American troubleshooter, had managed to retain his sardonic, hard-edged pragmatism.

Turner glanced at the two immaculate RM officers and said: 'I'm still worried. Who the hell backed the terrorists? You say they've got a man aboard this rig. Which one of us is it?'

'It doesn't matter,' Sir Reginald said. 'We can sort that out later. What matters at the moment is Charlie 2. We have to get that rig back.'

'I disagree,' Dalton said. 'I think Turner has a point. If McGee says their man's aboard this rig, then that man could be dangerous. McGee said he was one of us. He's right here in this boardroom. If, as McGee said, he has a radio, he could contact the terrorists. If he did, we couldn't take them by surprise; they'd just be sitting there waiting. I don't think the SBS can launch a successful assault if the terrorists know they're on the way.'

There were twelve men around the table and they stared at one another, all of them suddenly uncomfortable, self-conscious and edgy.

'One of us?' a Frenchman asked.

'That's right,' Masters replied. 'They definitely said that the man was in this boardroom, so it could be me . . . you . . . *anyone*. We've no way of knowing.'

There was another lengthy silence. The men fidgeted, coughed, or stared at the table. The Under-Secretary put his chin in his hands and looked extremely annoyed.

'Incredible!' he exclaimed. 'Becoming more so every minute. This whole situation defies belief and it's truly quite sickening. First the terrorists sink a rig, then they take over another. Now we find that one of our own senior executives has ordered the assassination of the Prime Minister. I find this whole thing appalling.'

Sir Reginald sighed. 'We've been through all this before. Let's stick to the issue at hand and sort this mess out.'

'It's *your* mess,' the Under-Secretary told him. 'And it's a disgusting mess. The lack of security throughout your organization is utterly scandalous.'

'I agree,' the PM said. 'I'm still appalled by the whole affair. If word of this ever gets out, the repercussions will be devastating to us all.'

'We'd be a laughing-stock,' the Under-Secretary said.

'Precisely,' the PM replied. 'Worse still: confidence in the viability of the North Sea would be lost internationally.'

'That's true enough,' Dalton said. 'My side would definitely pull out. I don't see any Americans staying in the North Sea if this mess is made known to them.'

They all slumped back into a silence that was filled with nervous coughing. More cigarettes and cigars were lit and their smoke turned the air blue.

'He has a radio,' Turner reminded them. 'Whoever he is, he has a radio. We better search every cabin in the rig and make sure we find it.'

'No,' Lieutenant-Colonel Edwards said. 'I don't think so. For one thing, he's possibly got rid of the radio already, to avoid being caught; for another, such a search is bound to arouse the suspicions of your crew. You want this kept as quiet as possible. If, as McGee says, the man is here in this boardroom, then let's just make sure he stays here. We'll attack the rig immediately. It'll all be over by first light. Until then, don't let anyone other than the SBS leave this boardroom. That should solve *that* particular problem.'

The CO glanced around the table. Most of the men seemed to be in agreement. The PM could not resist a slight smile when he gazed at Sir Reginald.

'And what then?' Dalton asked. 'We still have to find out who he is. If he can pull this stunt, he'll pull others and that isn't acceptable.'

'I think you should leave that problem until tomorrow,' Captain Pancroft said. 'Right now, the major concern is the recapture of the rig held by the terrorists.'

'I agree,' the PM said. 'We must get the terrorists off Charlie 2 and then hush this thing up. That's our prime concern.'

'But why attack?' Turner asked. 'I don't see the point. An assault like that requires a lot of men – and a lot will be killed. Why not just sit tight? The terrorists have lost their bomb. Why attack when we can just leave them there until their food runs out?

'It would take too long,' Masters said. 'Fresh supplies went out to Charlie 2 yesterday. That gives them four normal weeks, which they could stretch out much longer.'

'So what?' Turner responded. 'I say sweat them out.'

'No,' Dalton said. 'I back Masters in this. If we

let them sit on Charlie 2 for four weeks, they'll start using their radio. They'll talk to the press – to the whole damn media. Before we know it, the entire world will know about it. We have to prevent that.'

'The media will learn about it anyway,' Turner insisted. 'If we capture the terrorists, they'll talk. You can't keep a thing like this quiet. It's too big for secrecy.'

'I disagree,' the American said. 'Nothing's too big for silence. If the terrorists are captured, they'll be rushed straight into prison and allowed no access to the press. This is, after all, a matter of national security. On those grounds we can ensure that the trial takes place behind closed doors. The oil companies will then agree their own version of events, the terrorists will each be given twenty years to life, and by the time the dumb bastards are released this episode will be ancient history. And by then the North Sea will be drained dry of oil and we'll be drilling elsewhere.'

'That's important,' the Under-Secretary said. 'A total lock-up is vital. The only people who know about this affair are the terrorists and us, so we've got to make sure it remains that way.'

'The terrorists' backers know,' Turner reminded him.

'They won't talk,' Masters said. 'As McGee

kindly informed me: they can't ever discuss this affair without giving themselves away.'

'McGee really screwed them,' Dalton said.

'That's right,' Masters replied. 'He screwed them and now they have to sit tight and keep their mouths shut.'

'So,' the Prime Minister said. 'We attack them immediately. We launch a full-scale assault and get them off that rig, and then throw them in jail and forget about them.'

'Correct,' Dalton said. 'McGee's given us our story. We say it was an earthquake on the seabed. We put that out as our press release.'

'It's rather risky,' Sir Reginald said. 'We'll have to use a lot of men. I can't see how we're going to keep it quiet with so many men knowing.'

'*SBS* men,' Lieutenant-Colonel Edwards emphasized. 'My men always operate in strict secrecy and they *never* talk afterwards.'

'So,' Dalton said, 'we use the SBS to recapture the rig, then we put out our own press release and replace the whole crew with new men who don't know what's been happening. I think that solves the problem.'

He smiled and glanced around him, receiving nods of agreement from everyone except Masters, who was looking out through the nearest porthole at the dark Forties Field. He was recalling Barker standing up in the motor launch, his eyes widening with stunned disbelief as he went over the stern. Now Barker was dead and drifting somewhere out there; he was at the bottom of the sea with the other dead, rig workers and terrorists alike, and those bastards on Charlie 2 were responsible. Masters glanced at the Under-Secretary and saw his handsome, shocked face. He knew that the civil servant wasn't shocked by the body count; that his hatred of the oil companies had totally erased the dead from his thoughts. He was a political animal and this was all politics. In the end, it was *always* politics. Masters knew it and felt deep revulsion, but he had to live with it. He still had a job to do.

'All right,' the PM said gravely, after considerable thought. 'I authorize the assault.'

The wave of relief that passed around the table was jarred when the red telephone rang. Looking startled, Turner picked it up.

'I've got Charlie 2 on the line,' the operator informed him. 'They want to speak to the boardroom.'

Turner frowned. 'Anyone special?'

'No. It's their leader, McGee. He just wants the boardroom.'

Turner visibly trembled and focused on the floor. 'All right,' he said, sounding defeated as he switched to the open line. 'Tell him I'm here.'

McGee came on the phone, clearly angry, his voice hoarse. 'OK,' he said, 'you bastards fixed my bomb, but I'm not finished yet. Let me speak to Masters.'

There was a brief, tingling silence as Turner stood there with the receiver in his hand, not knowing what to do. Eventually, after nods of permission from the PM and Sir Reginald, he handed the phone to Masters.

'This is Masters speaking.'

'You're a smart bastard, Masters.'

'Thanks for the compliment,' Masters said. 'Now what do want?'

'I want your hide,' McGee said.

'You're not going to get it.'

'I just might. Sure, I'm not finished yet. I've something else up my sleeve.'

Masters glanced at the others around the table and saw the return of their fear. 'What's that, then?' he asked the terrorist leader.

'You think I'm dumb, Masters? You think you've fucking beat me? Well, don't think too soon.'

'What do you want?' Masters repeated.

'I want what I've always wanted. I want a million in cash and my four comrades out of the Maze.'

'You're too late,' Masters told him. 'You've nothing left to offer. You can't even bargain with your bomb. I took that away from you.'

'Ackaye, you did. But that doesn't mean I'm sitting here stranded. Not by a long chalk.'

'No?'

'No. Sure, if you weren't so fucking dumb you'd have guessed. I can still sink this rig.'

Masters glanced around the boardroom. The men sitting at the table leant forward, looking tense and confused.

'We came prepared,' McGee said. 'We've got plastic explosives. We can't blow up the whole of the Forties, but we can still sink this rig. I'll blow a pontoon leg off, Masters, and you know what that means. This whole fucking rig'll go down – and that isn't good news.'

Turner groaned audibly and covered his face with his hands. The other men looked at each other, some turning pale, but Dalton stood up, walked deliberately around the table, then stood beside Masters and studied him with eyes slightly narrowed.

'Plastic explosives?' Masters asked.

'Right,' McGee confirmed. 'Enough to blow a hole in one pontoon leg and sink the whole rig. And that, Masters, is what I'm gonna do if we don't agree right now.'

When Masters glanced at Dalton, the American shrugged and nodded, telling him to agree.

'All right,' Masters said. 'How do we do it?'

The PM stared disbelievingly at Dalton, who shrugged again, then raised his hands in the air in a gesture of resignation. Turner groaned, his head still in his hands, and Sir Reginald sighed.

'You've got till dawn,' McGee said. 'I don't need the Prime Minister. I've already stolen a million from our backers; I'll take the rest from you bastards. You'll deliver the cash by dawn. By helicopter. You'll personally fly the chopper, Masters, and then we'll have words. That leaves my four men in the Maze. I want them out by six a.m. tomorrow. I expect one of them to ring me as soon as they're all free and I also want the pardons announced in the evening papers in England.'

'And then?'

'We'll leave. Flying out by helicopter. We'll land on a private airstrip and then disappear and we'll keep our mouths shut as long as we're free and untouched. If you touch any of us, we'll talk; if you don't, we'll keep quiet.'

'Anything else?' Masters asked.

'No,' McGee said. 'You've got till dawn to fly here with the cash; if you don't, this rig sinks. And don't try a sneak attack. That wouldn't please me at all. At the first sign of an assault, we'll blow up the pontoon leg. That's all there is to it.'

There was a long silence. Masters sucked in his breath and then let it out again. His gaze came to rest on the portholes, on the darkness beyond. He coughed and took another deep breath and then let it out slowly.

'Agreed,' he said. 'Dawn.'

McGee rang off and Masters put the phone

down, then he scanned the many faces around the table. The PM leaned forward, scratching his chin, looking at the SBS man as if trying to take his measure. Masters offered a slight smile.

'Yes?' the PM asked.

'No,' Lieutenant-Colonel Edwards replied on Masters's behalf. 'We're going to take that rig back tonight. We'll start the whole thing right now.'

'We can't do that,' Sir Reginald insisted. 'We all heard what the man said. The minute he sniffs an attack, he'll blow a hole in that leg.'

'What does that mean?' the Under-Secretary asked.

'The rig will sink,' Turner explained.

'Can we afford to lose another one?' the PM asked. 'Can we sacrifice that much?'

'No,' Sir Reginald replied. 'I really don't think we can. Charlie 2 is the most important of all the rigs and we can't let it go.'

'Why the most important?' asked the Under-Secretary.

'It's a refinery,' Turner explained. 'It's a floating refinery, controlling the flow of all oil north of the Beryl Field.'

'I don't understand,' the Under-Secretary said. 'It's only one rig. Surely a single rig is disposable.'

'One more rig we can afford,' Turner said. 'But not Charlie 2.'

'Why?' the Under-Secretary persisted.

Turner stood up and went to the large map of the North Sea that was pinned to a blackboard. He placed his index finger on the Forties Field, moved it north to the Beryl Field, then moved it farther north until it passed Eagle 3 and came to rest well above the Frigg Field.

'More than half our oil – by which I mean the oil in the British sector – now flows from a single undersea pipeline linking the five major oilfields to Peterhead. As you can see, that single pipeline connects every major field north of the Forties Field. The oil from *all* the fields north of the Frigg Field flows down through Frigg, from there down to Beryl, through Beryl to here, and then on from here back to Peterhead. In this link-up, Charlie 2 acts as a refinery, controlling the speed of the oil flow. If McGee blows a hole in that leg, Charlie 2 will certainly sink – but to sink, it first has to topple over. That would almost certainly tear out the extractor pipes, which in turn would split the main pipes. We'd lose the oil then. The pipes would just break apart. The oil would pour into the sea and miles of pipe would be lost. We wouldn't be able to repair that damage – at least not for a long time – and in the meantime, all the oil north of here would be lost for good. That amounts to almost half our total output.'

'You mean *Britain's* output,' the Prime Minister emphasized.

'Yes, sir, Britain's output.'

'And what if we can't avoid this?' the PM asked. 'Just how bad would this be in general economic terms?'

'*Very* bad,' said the Under-Secretary, now on more familiar ground. 'Oil is our primary machine-driving fuel. We also need it for power stations and domestic fuel. It's also the raw material for all kinds of substances, such as plastics, and without it the petrochemical industry would die. As of this moment, Britain is dependent on oil for almost two-thirds of its fuel needs. To lose over half now, for the length of time envisaged by Mr Turner, would almost certainly be catastrophic.'

'All right, Mr Turner,' the PM said. 'Just how long *would* it take to repair the damage?'

'One to two years,' Turner replied, 'depending on weather conditions and always assuming that the damage *could* be repaired.'

'Also,' Sir Reginald cut in, 'since government taxation and British organized labour forced us to have the rigs made in France and Norway, rather than at home, those two countries, seeing our predicament – and being already annoyed by our ongoing concentration on US and Middle East markets – would doubtless get their own back by charging the earth for future rigs and by enticing foreign investors to deal only with them. In short, Prime Minister, it would be disastrous.'

The PM knotted his hands, cracked his knuckles, flexed his fingers, then glared at the Chairman.

'Laying the blame on this government,' he replied icily, 'is scarcely appropriate.'

'So,' Lieutenant-Colonel Edwards said, to avoid a lengthy debate. 'We attack them tonight.'

'If we attack them,' Sir Reginald responded stubbornly, 'they will sink Charlie 2.'

'No,' Masters said, 'they won't sink it. They'll just blow a hole in it.'

'And that won't sink it?' the PM asked.

'Not immediately,' Turner explained. 'It would take at least twenty minutes. It depends how big the hole is, but the SBS would have *some* time.'

'That's right,' Masters said. 'And the terrorists won't know we're coming. They won't know until we're actually on that rig, which gives us a head start.'

'The submersibles,' Captain Pancroft suggested.

'Exactly,' Lieutenant-Colonel Edwards said. 'We'll use our miniature submarines. They normally carry two men, but we can squeeze three men in each and still leave just enough room for the weapons. We'll leave from Peterhead. The boats will take us close to Charlie 2. About five miles from Charlie 2 we'll dive in the submersibles, travel to the rig, and surface right beneath the main deck. We can climb up the ladders. The terrorists won't be expecting us. A lot of the terrorists will be asleep, which is to our advantage. Another advantage is the weather. There's a storm due in three hours. If that makes our climbing difficult, it's also certain to make the terrorists more lethargic. So, we get on board. The first wave attacks the terrorists. While they're doing so, the second wave enters the damaged pontoon leg – we can assume the terrorists will have blown that hole in it by then – and blocks the hole up before the rig sinks. Once that's done, they return to the rig and help the other SBS troops mop up the terrorists.'

'This all sounds terribly efficient,' Sir Reginald said. 'But are you sure the terrorists won't see you approaching, even though you're submerged?'

'I don't think so,' Masters said, glancing at his CO and answering the question for him. 'I knocked out their radar and their undersea cameras, so they won't see us coming in. They might see us on the ladders, but that's a chance we'll have to take. Even if they *do* see us there, at least we can fight our way up. Obviously they'll blow that hole in the pontoon leg as soon as they see us, but we'll still have that twenty minutes left. If we manage to get down that leg in time, we should save the rig.'

'But the rig will still be damaged,' Sir Reginald insisted. 'It will be severely damaged by all the fighting.'

'That's true,' Masters replied. 'I'm afraid we'll have to accept that. But at least if we can keep it afloat, we'll be able to repair the damage that's been done. Besides, according to the story you're going to put out in your press release, that rig's supposed to have been damaged by an earthquake under the seabed – so I think it should look that way.'

'Good point,' Dalton said. 'As soon as the press release goes out, we'll see planes flying over. The media will want photos. They'll want to see a damaged rig. So *let* the terrorists knock the hell out of Charlie 2; it fits in with our story.'

The PM sat back to gaze at each of them in turn. Placing his hands flat on the table, he shook his head in amazement. 'I don't believe this,' he murmured.

'Let's do it,' Lieutenant-Colonel Edwards said. 'We have to hit that rig while it's dark and it's two o'clock now.'

'I agree,' Dalton said, pushing his chair back and rising to his feet. 'Let's get going. We've no time to waste.' Everyone stared at him in surprise. 'I'm going as well,' he explained. 'I want to have a talk with that McGee. I want to know who his backer is.'

'You can't go,' the Under-Secretary told him. 'The man who backed the terrorists is right here in this boardroom. We must all stay here until the SBS complete their attack. That's what was agreed.'

'With all due respect,' Turner replied, 'it hardly seems likely that Dalton would be that man since the survival of the rigs is in his own interests and those of his company.'

'I agree,' Lieutenant-Colonel Edwards said. 'If he wants to come, let him. Mr Dalton's not only widely experienced at counter-terrorism on behalf of the oil companies; he was also in the US Special Forces SEAL unit – the Amphibious Sea Air Land unit – which indeed is where he and I first met. So if he wants to come along, I have no objections.'

They all stared at the PM, who shrugged wearily and said: 'I agree.'

'Good,' Dalton said.

Silence reigned over the boardroom for what seemed like a long time, though it was, in fact, only a matter of seconds. There were rumblings outside, distant shouting and muffled banging; as usual, work was continuing throughout the night, conducted by roughnecks and roustabouts, oblivious to what was happening inside.

Masters glanced at his watch, then at the Prime Minister. He was held by the sharpness of the blue eyes in that flushed, knowing face.

'I'll stay here,' the PM said, addressing Lieutenant-Colonel Edwards. 'The rest of us will all stay here until it's over. I'll personally ensure that no one leaves this room until you give us a call.'

Edwards nodded, then smiled at Masters. Turner stood up and yawned and stretched himself as if no longer nervous. Masters glanced around the room.

It was bright and filled with smoke. The realization that it was two in the morning suddenly made him feel tired. He shook his head and rubbed his eyes, feeling slightly unreal. Opening his eyes, he saw Dalton grinning like a schoolboy as he walked to the door. Turner opened the door to let the American walk out. He was followed by the two SBS officers. Masters glanced this way and that, at the men around the table. Every one of them looked guilty as he walked from the room.

14

Walking with the others across the enormous platform, feeling the cold wind at his face, seeing the lights of the derricks tapering up to the dark sky, where the clouds formed a low, oppressive ceiling, Masters experienced a feeling of elation, a fresh surge of energy. He walked quickly and impatiently, between Edwards and Pancroft, just behind the enthusiastic Dalton, who appeared to be leading them. The American cut around the cranes and stacks of wooden crates, exposing them to an even stronger wind and the sound of the pounding sea. Reaching the end of the deck, he led the way up a steel ladder, then diagonally across a smaller deck to the cramped radio shack. The door was closed, but Dalton opened it and walked in, followed by the others. The operator looked up in surprise.

'Mr Dalton!' he exclaimed, fazed by the sudden appearance of the feared but respected figure.

'Take a break, kid,' Dalton said. 'Close the door after you.'

'Sorry?' said the operator.

'I want you to leave,' Dalton said.

'I'm not supposed to do that, Mr Dalton. You know I can't.'

Masters walked up and jerked his thumb towards the door. The operator, recognizing him as a top tool-pusher, stood up, looking very confused, and walked to the door. He left, but then stuck his head back in.

'Do I wait here?' he asked.

'That's right,' Masters said. 'Just wait there. When we want you, we'll call you.'

'Righto, chief!' the operator said chirpily, then stepped out and closed the door.

Masters sat at the radio, contacted onshore security, and told them to put Blackburn on as quickly as possible. The line was crackling with static. The storm was obviously brewing. After what seemed like a very long time, Blackburn came on the line.

'Masters?' Blackburn asked.

'Yes,' Masters said.

'What's up?' Blackburn asked. 'I was sleeping. This better be good.'

'It's an emergency, Andy. Can you connect us from here on a scrambled line to the SBS on hold at the old training centre at Achnacarry?'

'Sorry, Tone. I'd need higher authority for that. What the hell's going on?'

Dalton moved up behind Masters and leaned

down to the microphone. 'This is Paul Dalton,' he said. 'I'm your higher authority.'

'I'm sorry, sir, but I can't accept that. As far as I'm concerned, you could be anyone. Do you have your ID?'

'Good man,' Dalton said, then he recited the lengthy, confidential personal number by which he could be identified over the phone. There was a pause while Blackburn checked it in his pocketbook of ID numbers, then he said: 'Fine, sir. Go ahead.'

'I'm going to put the Commanding Officer of the SBS squadron at Achnacarry on the line. Lieutenant-Colonel Edwards. I want you to put him though to his second in command at Achnacarry. Understood?'

'Yes, sir, I've got it. Just bear with me a minute or so and I'll make the connection.'

'Scrambled.'

'Yes, sir.'

The radio emitted static that crackled loudly and faded out as Masters stood up and gave the chair to his CO. Lieutenant-Colonel Edwards sat patiently in front of the radio, listening to the rise and fall of the static until another voice came on the line: 'Lieutenant-Colonel Edwards?'

'Yes, this is Edwards. Please identify yourself.'

'Major Laurence Lockyard speaking.'

Edwards chuckled. 'That voice couldn't belong to anyone else, Major. You just sound a bit sleepy.'

'I'm in my pyjamas, boss, and was having a good sleep. What's up out there?'

'This is confidential, Laurence. I want a seal placed across it.'

'I didn't think you'd be using this line, boss, if that wasn't the case. So what's the situation?'

'Emergency. Action immediate. An oil rig has been seized by a large group of terrorists – sixty men – and we're going to launch an assault to take it back. It has to be before first light.'

'Read you loud and clear, boss.'

'The requirement is for five submersible-carrying boats to leave Peterhead as soon as you can get your men there. The lead boat, *Victory*, will carry four submersibles and the remaining four vessels will carry two each, making a total of twelve. The boats will sail directly to the Beryl Field. I want thirty-two battle-experienced SBS Marine Commandos to go with the twelve submersibles, with myself and three others, all here, making up a total compliment of thirty-six men. The men are to be equipped with full combat packs, including Sterling sub-machine-guns and Armalite rifles with M203 grenade-launchers. Six of the men will work as a maintenance team equipped with spare plates for the pontoon leg and emergency wet-welding equipment. Have you got that so far?'

'Yes, boss, I've got it.'

'Good.' Edwards coughed into his clenched fist,

clearing his throat, then continued in his clipped, precise manner: 'I want the boats to leave as soon as your men reach the secured dock at Peterhead. You will fly there by helicopter. The British United Oil security chief, Andy Blackburn, will be there to greet you and see you into the dock. Once the boats leave, I want them to sail with all due haste. The RV is five miles east of Charlie 2 on a grid reference being sent through on a burst transmission when Mr Blackburn informs us of your arrival at the Peterhead dock. Once at the RV, you will anchor and await my arrival. Launch the submersibles while you're waiting. We'll put three, repeat *three*, men plus weapons in each. You can tell them that they're going to make an assault against Charlie 2 and that I'll be giving them further instructions when I arrive. Place the maintenance team on hold. I'll be set down by chopper on *Victory* and will want to have a word with them, so don't let them get into their submersibles until I arrive. Is all that understood?'

'Understood, boss.'

'Can you give me an estimate for arrival time at the RV?'

There was a pause while Major Lockyard calculated the time required to gather the men together, get them into the helicopters, flying them from Achnacarry to Peterhead, transfer them to the boats, then carry them on the boats to the RV. Eventually, having completed his calculations, Lockyard said: 'About four hours.'

'That's too long,' Edwards told him.

'There's a limit to how fast those submersible-carriers can go. And, of course, there's the unpredictability of the weather. I can't promise a faster time than that.'

'It's too long,' Edwards insisted.

They all heard Lockyard sigh. 'How soon?'

'Three hours maximum,' Edwards said. 'I can't launch the assault later than 0600 hours, so that will give me four hours to co-ordinate everything.'

'I'll need at least an hour to get the men together,' Lockyard insisted, 'and get them into those choppers.'

'Cut that time down by half. You can make it in thirty minutes. Once you get to the docks, Blackburn will clear the way and ensure that you save another thirty minutes in getting to, and into, the boats. The journey from Peterhead to the Beryl Field should take no more than two hours. One and two makes three.'

This time they heard Major Lockyard chuckling. 'Right, boss, I'm convinced. We'll be at the RV in three hours. Anything else?'

'No.'

'Roger. Over.'

'Over and out.'

The radio went dead and a happier Lieutenant-Colonel Edwards sat back in the chair. 'So what about a helicopter?' he asked.

'I'll attend to it,' Masters said. He picked up a telephone and called the surgery of Bravo 1, then asked for Dr Seymour. When the doctor came on, Masters said: 'How's that American kid?'

'Schulman? He's OK, but he's sleeping.'

'Where?'

'In the surgery.'

'Drugged?'

'No, just sleepy. He had a couple of beers and fell asleep, so I just let him lie there.'

'Wake him up,' Masters said. 'Send him up to the bar. Tell him to be there in half an hour. I want to talk to him.'

'Will do,' Dr Seymour said.

Masters put the phone back in its cradle, then yawned and stretched himself.

'The good sergeant is tired,' Captain Pancroft said with a grin. 'We should put him to beddy-byes.'

'Instead of dragging him along on this mission,' the CO said sardonically. 'It's bound to be too much for him.'

'Do you think you can make it, Sergeant Masters?' Pancroft asked.

'I always finish what I start,' Masters informed him. 'It's the SBS way.'

'Good man,' Edwards said. 'Now let's get out of here.'

They all left the radio shack and found the operator standing outside. He was shivering and flapping his arms vigorously against the cold.

'Can I go in now?' he asked.

'You can go in,' Masters told him. 'But don't let anyone – and I mean *anyone* – make a call out. I don't care who it is.'

'I don't think I can argue with . . .'

'I'll authorize that,' Dalton said. 'Any arguments, use my name. And if anyone *does* comes to make a call, I want to know who they are.'

'Right, chief,' the operator said, then went into the hut and closed the door.

Dalton led the way across the deck and back down the ladder. The wind was growing stronger, moaning around the derricks, and the great platform was a patchwork of bright lights, white spaces and shadows. Walking across the main deck, they were surrounded by men still working, climbing up and down ladders, crossing catwalks, carrying crates and huge pipes. Dalton climbed another ladder, followed by Masters, then Edwards and Pancroft. They all entered the modules, made their way along narrow corridors, went down more steps and then found themselves in the canteen, also used as the bar. Some of the shift workers were eating, cutting into thick steaks with piles of chips. The three SBS men leant against the counter while Dalton ordered them coffees, just like one of the boys.

'When do we leave?' he asked, turning around to face Edwards.

'As soon as we can,' the CO replied.

'Just as soon as Schulman gets his chopper going,' Masters clarified. 'It won't do any harm to be early.'

'Do you think the boats will make it, Tone?'

'Yes, Paul, I do. That storm isn't due until 0600, so we should have a smooth trip. But the storm'll be rough. It won't make the climb easy. On the other hand, it'll put the terrorists off their guard. They won't expect us to arrive in such weather, so that could be a help.'

'Thirty-six men,' Pancroft said. 'Against sixty terrorists. I don't see that as good odds.'

'Shame on you,' Edwards admonished him. 'I'd have thought they were terrific odds for us. Not even two terrorists to each SBS man. Hardly worth another thought, Captain.'

'To hell with it,' Masters said, taking note of Pancroft's grin, but deciding to be serious all the same. 'We're just going to have to risk it. Besides, half the terrorists will be asleep. We can hit them really hard before they even get their eyes open. That should bring their numbers down, even the odds a little, and with the storm and the element of surprise they'll be pretty confused.'

'I hope so,' Pancroft said.

'What the hell!' Edwards exclaimed with a cheerful grin. 'It's all up for grabs now.'

They glanced repeatedly at their watches while drinking their coffee. The roustabouts and roughnecks at the tables were still eating, drinking, smoking and talking a lot. Masters was thinking how unreal it all was. Everything had taken place in twelve hours and these men had continued working right through it. They still didn't know about it and probably never would. They would read about an earthquake beneath the seabed that destroyed one oil rig, badly damaged another and killed many rig workers, and they would simply see it as part of the job, par for the course in the North Sea. Masters shook his head at the thought.

The four men had just finished their coffee and were returning their cups when Jack Schulman walked up to them.

'Hi,' said the helicopter pilot, grinning wryly at Masters, but looking curiously at Dalton and the two Royal Marine Commando officers with him.

'You look tired,' Masters told him.

'I *am* tired,' Schulman said. 'I'm fucking beat, so what the hell did you want me for?'

'We need you,' Masters said.

'At *this* hour?'

'At this hour.'

'Don't tell me another goddamn rig's sunk. I still haven't recovered from the last one.'

'No,' Masters said. 'It's nothing like that. We just want you to fly us out to Beryl. We have to fly there immediately.'

'Charlie 2?'

'Five miles east.'

'What the hell's there?'

'You'll find out soon enough,' Masters told him. 'Now go and get ready.'

Schulman, who still believed that Masters was a top tool-pusher, looked at the Royal Marine Commandos standing on either side of Dalton, but didn't ask what they were doing there. 'I don't believe this,' he said.

'You better believe it, Jack.'

'It's two-thirty in the morning, for Chrissakes. What the fuck's going on?'

'It's an emergency,' Masters said.

'Jesus Christ, not another.'

'The same one, in a sense,' Masters lied. 'Eagle 3 was the victim of an earthquake on the seabed. The bottom split open right beneath it, then that crack spread as far as the Beryl Field.'

'That's what sank Eagle 3?'

'That's what sank it,' Masters said firmly.

'And now the earthquake's gone as far as the Beryl Field?'

'Yep.'

'Here,' Dalton said. 'Have a coffee, kid. It might wake you up a bit.'

'Gee, thanks a lot, chief.' Schulman took the coffee, drank some, then wiped his lips with his hand. 'So what's happening out there in Beryl?'

'It's Charlie 2,' Masters told him. 'It's been badly damaged, so we're mounting a rescue operation.'

'From five miles east?' Schulman asked.

'That's right,' Masters said. 'We don't want to land the chopper because the rig might be sinking, so we're planning to move in slowly by boat.'

'I'm supposed to drop you on the boat?'

'In a nutshell,' Masters said. 'You drop us and then you fly back here and wait for our call.'

'If you get aboard I'll pick you up?'

'If we save the rig you'll pick us up.'

'So what if you don't save the rig?'

'Then we might go down with it.'

Schulman glanced at the men eating, as if yearning for steak and chips. 'OK,' he said, turning back to Masters, 'what time do we leave? I could do with a hearty meal.'

'We leave yesterday,' Masters said. 'We're a day late already. I want you to go straight up to the flight deck and call us here when you're ready.'

'Jesus!' Schulman groaned.

'Have a sandwich,' Captain Pancroft suggested.

'Thanks,' Schulman said. 'That's a thought. I mean, I like the high life.'

He grabbed a sandwich from the counter, jammed it into his mouth, started chewing and waved a hand in farewell as he walked out of the canteen. Dalton ordered more coffees and the man was quick in getting them. Dalton passed the cups around and they all sipped their coffee.

'You're pretty smart,' Dalton said.

'I hope so,' Masters replied.

'I know that's how you made it to the SBS, but you should come work for me. The pay's an awful lot better.'

'Don't tempt him, Paul,' Edwards said. 'We need him more than you do – and you'd just spoil him rotten.'

Pancroft looked at his watch. '0245 hours,' he said. 'Those boats should have set out from Peterhead by now. They'll be well on their way.'

'I hope so,' Dalton said.

'They'll be moving,' Edwards said. 'Major Lockyard is a very good man. He knows what he's doing.'

'I don't like it,' Pancroft said. 'I want to get out of here. I wish that young Yank pilot would get moving and pick up the telephone.'

'You take the maintenance men,' Edwards told him. 'You know all about that business. When we reach the deck, go straight to that pontoon leg and get them to fix up the hole.'

'I may not get there,' Pancroft replied.

'You'll be protected,' Masters assured him. 'I'll make sure you're covered all the way. I'll make sure you get there.'

'I want McGee,' Dalton said quietly.

'So do I,' Masters told him.

'I want him alive,' Dalton said. 'I want to talk to that bastard.'

'Who backed him?' Pancroft asked. 'I'd really like to know that. McGee . . . he must know.'

'That's right,' Dalton said. 'McGee knows. And we'll make sure he tells us.'

The telephone ran and the man behind the counter picked it up. He was hot and wiped sweat from his forehead as he put the phone down.

'The helicopter pad,' he said to Masters. 'They want you all up there.'

They left the canteen and climbed to the flight deck. The lights on the structures beamed down, cutting swathes through the darkness. Masters heard the wind moaning mournfully through the derricks; it was stronger than it had been before and that made him feel good. They all crossed the catwalk, where the wind was even stronger; it came from the north and blew straight across them, sweeping south. The sea was very far below, but obscured by the darkness; they could hear it smashing into the concrete legs as they passed over open space. Then they were on the landing pad, where the Dragonfly was already roaring, its rotors whipping the air about them as they hurried towards it. They bent low beneath the rotors, leaning into the slipstream. Two men in yellow overalls were pulling the blocks away from the wheels as the wind howled about them.

'You going as well, chief?' one of them asked Dalton.

'Yep.'

'You better get that suit off and put on some overalls,' the man said.

'I thought you'd never ask,' Dalton replied.

The man grinned and jerked his thumb towards the hut at the edge of the landing pad. As Edwards and Pancroft clambered up into the helicopter, Dalton hurried to the hut, remained inside for a few minutes, then emerged wearing a pair of orange overalls. To Masters's surprise, he also had a 9mm Browning High Power handgun holstered at the hip.

'I always carry one,' he explained without being asked. 'Even when I'm wearing my nice grey suit. It comes with the territory.'

Masters nodded and stood aside to let Dalton climb into the Dragonfly. When the American had done so, Masters followed him.

With its narrow fuselage, the Dragonfly wasn't

really suitable for four passengers, the pilot and a loadmaster, but they gamely squeezed in. As Schulman made his way to the pilot's cabin in the nose, the loadmaster slid the side door closed, then indicated that they should strap themselves in. Then, with Schulman at the controls, the Dragonfly roared even louder, shuddered violently, bounced a little and lifted off the ground. The deck fell far below them, a deeper darkness closed in, and then the Dragonfly lurched in the wind and headed towards the Beryl Field.

Masters looked out at the sky to see the moon lighting up the huge clouds. Glancing to his right, he saw the winking lights of Maureen, though he couldn't discern the oil rig itself. The Dragonfly rose and fell, roaring, shuddering, and swaying, fighting against the wind that was blowing fiercely down from the north, between Shetland and Norway. Masters was pleased to feel its buffeting; it was just what he wanted. Let the sea rise up and smash the whole bloody rig; let it provide the SBS with cover and distract the terrorists.

Schulman chewed gum ceaselessly and glanced keenly around him. Masters grinned at the sight of him, strangely comforted by the younger man's presence. He closed his eyes, put his head back on the seat and tried to let the time pass.

'What time is it?' Dalton asked.

'0430 hours,' Pancroft told him.

'What time do you think we'll get there?'

'About 0500 hours,' the captain said.

The time seemed to pass slowly. The helicopter bucked and roared, battered by the wind. Masters opened his eyes and glanced left to see lights far below. They were the lights of the Piper Field, winking fitfully in the darkness. Although Masters couldn't see the oil rigs, he knew the work was still going on there, twenty-four hours a day. He shifted uncomfortably in his narrow seat, watching the lights moving backwards, falling behind until nothing was left but darkness.

'What time is it?' Dalton asked again.

'0440 hours,' Pancroft told him.

'Jesus Christ,' Dalton said, 'we're in a black hole, with time running backwards.'

'We're nearly halfway there,' Schulman informed him.

'Good,' Dalton replied.

'It's a bitch of a night,' the pilot said. 'There's a storm coming up.'

They said nothing after that, concentrating on the sky outside, seeing only the moonlight rippling and gliding over clouds that were black painted on blackness. Schulman chewed his gum. Pancroft checked his watch. Dalton was lost deep in thought, his face hidden in shadow. The Dragonfly kept going, its roar filling their heads, shuddering and bucking more with each mile, battling against the growing wind. Masters emptied his mind. It was a trick he had learnt somewhere. He went down through himself to find peace, then slowly surfaced again. Opening his eyes, he glanced down and saw more lights, winking in the blackness far below.

'Beryl,' Schulman announced.

'Just keep going,' Masters told him.

'The rig's still afloat,' Schulman observed. 'You want me to take you lower to have a look?'

'No,' Edwards said. 'We have other fish to fry.'

They flew over Charlie 2, recognizable by its lights. Slowly those lights passed below and behind them and then the darkness returned. Schulman studied his chart, looking for the RV, then snapped his fingers and said: 'Here we go!' as he began his descent. They dropped to a thousand feet, passing through some thin clouds. Looking down, they saw nothing but darkness, a black abyss streaked with grey light. Schulman flew back and forth, circling around the void. He was looking for the lights of the boats, but so far there was nothing.

'We're too early,' Masters explained.

'I gathered that,' Schulman replied.

'Head direct for Lerwick,' Edwards said. 'We're bound to pass over them.'

The pilot did as he was told, keeping at low altitude. The Dragonfly rocked crazily, shuddered rapidly, then steadied again. Masters checked the sea below, but it was still lost in darkness. The clouds above had cut off the moonlight, and that would help the assault. Still, he kept looking, wanting to see those damn lights. If the lights didn't appear pretty soon, they'd be too far away. The Dragonfly growled and shook. A black mass passed overhead. The helicopter was fighting the wind and flying under the clouds. Another five minutes passed and then finally, far below and just ahead, they saw the moving lights of the SBS boats.

'There they are,' Schulman said.

'Thank Christ for that,' said Pancroft. 'I thought they might still be in Peterhead, bottled up by the storm.'

'I'm going down,' Schulman told them.

'Right,' Edwards said. 'Get down there and drop us on *Victory*. That should be the lead boat.'

As the Dragonfly dropped lower, the lights ahead raced towards them. The lights were like candles in a black room, appearing to float in space. Then they grew larger, illuminating the ploughing boats. There were five boats and they formed a large triangle with its tip pointing towards the Beryl Field. Schulman dropped lower, coming down over the lead boat. The Dragonfly dipped forward, rocking lightly, shuddering, but continuing its oblique, almost vertical descent until the boats could be made out in detail. Dimmed lights illuminated the sunken decks and their off-white submersibles.

'The first boat?' Schulman checked.

'The first one,' Edwards confirmed.

'OK,' Schulman said. 'We're right on top of it. I'm going down now.'

The Dragonfly started falling, in a perpendicular descent. As it did so it rocked wildly, shuddered more violently, and roared even louder against the howling wind. Masters looked down on *Victory*. The deck was expanding dramatically right below him, a pattern of dim light and shadow, rising up, then falling back again. As the Dragonfly hovered over the deck, swaying dangerously in the wind, the sea was whipped up by the slipstream and sloshed over the vessel. The waves were ribbons of black and white, forming circles around the boat. The circles rushed in to explode and soar skyward and then sweep out again. The submersible-carrier had dropped anchor and the Dragonfly stayed right above it, hovering about thirty feet above the deck, hammered by the fierce wind.

'Right, men,' Edwards said. 'Let's get down on that boat.'

Everyone except Schulman unclipped their safety belts and gathered around the sliding door in the side, where already the loadmaster was working at the lowering harness of the rescue winch. Satisfied, he slid the heavy door open, to let in a freezing wind that howled and pummelled at those gathered near the opening.

With a wave of his right hand the loadmaster indicated that the CO should put on the canvas harness. Experienced at this, Edwards did as he was told. He then sat in the doorway, his legs dangling over the side, and carefully let himself slide out. The straps went taut above him and then he was winched down, with the loadmaster controlling his rate of descent and Edwards controlling his own position in the battering slipstream.

Masters leant forward to look down. He saw Edwards swinging out on the slipstream, then back in the other direction in a dangerous arc. Nevertheless, he was going down, veering this way and that, bobbing up and down, spinning, but gradually shrinking as he descended over the boat. The wet deck dipped and climbed. The deck hands were looking up. Edwards swung right above them, still spinning in the slipstream. When he had dropped low enough, two pairs of hands reached up to pull him aboard.

Dalton went next, spiralling down into the darkness. He too was tossed to and fro by the wind, but he kept dropping steadily. Masters looked down as Dalton was grabbed and pulled aboard, the American releasing the straps and tugging three times to inform the loadmaster. The latter winched the harness back up, helped Pancroft into it, and lowered him down the same way. Then Masters put the harness on, sat in the wind-blown doorway, and heard the voice of his young friend Schulman.

'Don't get too wet down there!' Schulman called out. 'Don't go for a swim! Give me a call if you get back in one piece and I'll buy you a beer. *Adiós* and good luck!'

Masters dropped into space. The wind howled and picked him up and threw him sideways and then the straps took control of him. He dangled high above the boat, above the black sea and white foam, aware only of pale faces staring up from the darkness, squinting against the wind and spray as they checked his position. Then he was lowered down, swinging in and out on the wind, spinning, dizzy, fighting for breath, his head tight and filled with noise: the roaring helicopter, the howling wind, the squeaking winch, the pounding, splashing waves and the bawling of many men. The descent seemed to take a long time – as if time had stood still – but eventually two pairs of hands grabbed him and pulled him down to the boat.

He rolled across the deck, then stood shakily and released the harness. Looking up and blinking, rubbing salt water from his eyes, he saw Lieutenant-Colonel Edwards, Captain Pancroft, Dalton and a lot of soaked, grinning deck hands. The harness was winched up and pulled into the Dragonfly. The side door was slid shut. The helicopter ascended vertically, hovered shuddering for a moment, then headed back the way it had come, disappearing in darkness.

'Home and dry,' Lieutenant-Colonel Edwards said with a grin.

'Hardly dry,' Masters said.

15

Victory was tossing from side to side. The sea roared and smashed over it. The other submersible-carriers had stopped also and were widely spread out in a triangular formation, rising up and falling on the high waves. Masters fought to keep his balance as the icy spray showered over him. Looking around, he saw the lights of the other boats illuminating the water. The wind howled and made the sea hiss and swirl and then explode into fine white spray.

'That sea's rough,' Dalton said.

'It's only just starting,' Masters told him. 'I wouldn't like to see it in an hour. Those waves will be murder.'

The men on deck were a combination of Royal Navy sailors, divers and SBS Marine Commandos, all wearing wet suits. Lieutenant-Colonel Edwards and Captain Pancroft were already donning wet suits while talking to the CO's second in command, Major Laurence Lockyard, who had come from Peterhead on *Victory*. Six other men were on the lower deck at the stern, clambering over the four pinioned submersibles. The stern was open to the sea. A steel frame formed a bridge. The submersibles were connected to the frame, all set to be lowered. The stern rose and fell to let more waves wash over it. The men at the submersibles were in wet suits as black as the night.

'Are those the maintenance men?' Edwards asked Major Lockyard.

'Yes, boss. They've already put their kit and explosives in the submersibles, but they're waiting to talk to you.'

'Good,' Edwards said. He zipped up his wet suit and was starting forward when he was approached by a Royal Navy officer wearing a soaked gabardine raincoat over his uniform.

'Lieutenant-Colonel Edwards?'

'Yes.'

'I'm the captain of *Victory*. Lieutenant Commander William Sandison. Apart from being told to rendezvous here, I'm still a bit in the dark.'

'I want us dropped off in the submersibles at a given location, then your boats can return to Peterhead. You don't need to know any more than that. Where are we, precisely?'

'Ten miles east of Charlie 2. You said five, but you arrived too early. We only stopped to let you aboard. Shall I start up again?'

'Will the submersibles go that far?'

'A lot farther than that if you want.'

'Excellent. You can drop us off right now.'

Victory rose and fell, then a roaring wave drenched them. The water swept noisily around their feet and then poured out through drainage holes on both sides. Masters, slipping into his wet suit, as was Dalton, looked at the other four boats in the triangular formation. The reflections of their lights were dancing in the hollows between the waves, racing to and fro like flying saucers, gliding like fireflies.

'Are the men in the other boats ready?' Edwards asked Lockyard.

'They should be,' Lockyard replied. 'They won't be in the submersibles right now, but that can soon be arranged.'

'Weapons?'

'Full kit. L34A1s and Armalites with M203s, as requested. They're also equipped with Brownings, number 80 white-phosphorus incendiary grenades, a variety of plastic explosives, and abseiling equipment.'

'Our kit and weapons?'

'Already in the submersibles.'

'Instructions?'

'I deliberately left those vague, but told the men you would be filling them in when we left for the Beryl Field.'

'What do they know about Charlie 2?'

'Only that it's been captured and that they have to get it back. They know commencement time is 0600 hours, but they don't know much else.'

The CO looked at his watch. It was 0530 hours. They would have to leave very soon.

'Are they in contact?' he asked.

'All communications systems are open,' Lockyard informed him. 'Just give me the word.'

'Right,' Edwards said. 'I want the men in the submersibles as of right now. I want the submersibles launched straight away.'

'How do you do that?' Dalton asked Masters as Edwards went off to have words with the six-man maintenance team, now waiting patiently on top of a submersible on the low stern deck.

'It's pretty simple, though easier in better weather,' Masters told him. 'A large lift-line picks the submersible up off the deck and lowers it to just above the water. A diver stands on the casing and disconnects the lift-line to let the submersible half sink in the sea. It's held up by a tow-rope. We tow it out to its diving position and then, when it's all set to go, the diver disconnects the tow-rope. You sink to whatever depth you require and then switch on the engines. It's as simple as that.'

'What kind of submersibles are they?'

'Vickers Pisces III,' Masters said. 'Battery-operated.'

'Communications?'

'Marconi Modular systems with thruster control circuits, sub to sub. No interference at all.'

'So the boats pull away, we float on the end of tow-ropes, the CO gives his instructions while we're drifting and then we cast off.'

'Very good, Mr Dalton.'

Dalton grinned. 'Will we get there in half an hour?'

'Those little buggers are fast,' Masters said.

'I certainly hope so.'

They had to wait for five minutes until the CO returned from the lower deck. 'Right,' he said crisply. 'I've just given the maintenance team their instructions regarding the plugging of the hole blown in the pontoon leg by the terrorists, should such be the case. They're dividing into three teams, taking three of the four submersibles. You, Rudy,' he said to Captain Pancroft, 'will join the first team, then take command of all the teams once the assault begins. You, Mr Dalton, will be in the second and are responsible for yourself once aboard the rig.'

'That's as it should be,' Dalton said.

'I'll take the third submersible,' the CO continued. 'Major Lockyard will cross by motor launch to boat two, *Nelson*, and you, Sergeant Masters, will leave from this boat in the fourth submersible. Any questions, gentlemen?'

All the men grouped around the CO shook

their heads. The CO glanced at the other boats. The wind howled and the sea was roaring, with the waves curling higher each minute, exploding over the deck. The CO studied the sky. It was black and forbidding. Glancing across at the other four boats, he saw their lights through glistening showers of spray.

'I'll contact the others from *Nelson*,' Lockyard said, 'and order them into the submersibles. I'll have them all over the side fifteen minutes from now.'

The CO checked the time. 'Good. Let us drift for five minutes. That will give me enough time to brief the men. We can all cast off then.'

Lockyard nodded and went to the starboard side to catch the small launch that would take him to *Nelson*. The others made their way to the stern, being careful and holding firmly to the railings. The sea was roaring all around them, sweeping noisily across the deck, pouring over the other side or through the drainage holes while the ship rose and fell and plunged through more oncoming waves. They finally reached the submersibles. The maintenance men were already boarding. The launching deck resembled a cross-Channel ferry and the wind howled icily across it. The ship was rolling from side to side, the sea roared and flooded the deck, but the submersibles were pinioned firmly to their stays and, though drenched, seemed secure.

Twenty feet long and eleven feet high, the

miniature submarines looked like huge insects perched on skis. The ports comprised three round windows and had reinforced lights above them. On each side there were propellers. They had no rudders, but were steered simply by increasing the drive on the relevant propeller. Squat legs joined up to the skids, which were to allow movement on the seabed. Beneath the ports, at the base of the prow, was the manipulator assembly, or CAMS (Cybernetic Anthropomorphous Machine System): a set of robotic steel arms used for remote-control work on the seabed. It was those windows on the nose of the submersibles, Masters realized, combined with the skids, that made them look like giant insects.

As Edwards, Pancroft and Dalton were clambering into their respective submersibles, *Josephine*, *Huk* and *Genesis*, Masters looked up at the two muscular SBS corporals waiting on top of the fourth submersible, *Trinity*. Wind-blown and drenched, they had bandoliers of white-phosphorus incendiary grenades strung around their wet suits. The grenades were all wrapped tightly in cling film to protect them from the water. Masters didn't know the men. Both were specialists with all kinds of boats and in another squadron.

'Who's in charge?' Masters asked.

'I am,' one of the men, a blond giant, said.

'Do you know what you're here for?'

'No, Sarge.'

'It's terrorists,' Masters said. 'They've taken over Charlie 2 and threatened to blow a hole in a pontoon leg if we attack. Unfortunately, we have no choice, so we're going to attack. The job of this team is to mend the leg before the rig sinks.'

'We'll have to fight our way to it.'

'Correct,' Masters said. 'We three can take care of the fighting while Captain Pancroft leads the men down the pontoon leg. That's it. Let's go.'

Without a word, the second corporal clambered into the submersible and Masters followed him in, first grabbing hold of its curved metal 'sail' to haul himself up. Once on top, he had to fight to keep his balance, since the boat was now rocking heavily. Waiting for the first man to lower himself down the hatch, Masters glanced at the boat's low, open stern and saw a powerful wave breaking over it, filling the air with a fountain of hissing spray. The corporal dropped through the hatch, then disappeared completely, so Masters swung his legs over, sat briefly on the edge of the steel sail, then carefully lowered himself down.

He landed on a wooden deck. Beneath the deck were pipes and pumps. The interior of the submersible was small and very cramped, with curved walls of steel and a low ceiling. Masters had to stoop low. The hatch was directly above his head. He saw two curved wooden benches around the side of the sphere, facing the three ports at the front. There was more equipment beneath the benches, there were controls on all sides, and every available space in the sphere was covered with gauges and valves.

The corporal was at the pilot's console, sitting on a low wooden bench. When a pair of big, soaked boots dropped down just above Masters's head, he had to quickly move back. Bumping his head on the low ceiling, he cursed and sat on the bench. The blond giant had just dropped on to the wooden deck and was shutting the hatch. He grunted as he turned the locking wheel, which made a harsh, grating sound. The noise reverberated around the small sphere and then the wheel clicked shut. The blond giant muttered something and knelt between the benches. He seemed ridiculously large in that enclosed space, grinning at Masters.

'They're pretty small,' he said.

'Too small,' Masters replied.

'I don't like to be underwater in these fuckers. At least not for long.'

Suddenly, the submersible started shaking and giving off reverberating metallic sounds. Startled, Masters glanced up, then he recognized the sound of clanging chains.

'It's the diver,' the blond giant explained. 'He's standing on top of the submersible. He'll stay there while we're lowered over the stern and then he'll disconnect the lift-line. The boat will pull away from us and we'll float out on the tow-rope. Then, when we're ready to cast off, he'll disconnect that as well.'

The man's voice had an echo, as did every sound inside the sphere. The lights were on and they shone down the curved walls, gleaming off pipes and valves. Masters didn't feel claustrophobic – he'd been well trained for this – but he certainly felt the urge to get out and back into the open air. Trying to distract himself, he glanced around the cramped sphere. The corporal-pilot was facing the pilot's console, checking gauges and dials. Masters glanced at his watch. It was 0540 hours. They would reach the rig shortly after 0600 hours, which is when it would all start.

The submersible started vibrating, shaking violently, breaking loose, then it jumped up and swung from side to side as if hanging in space. That's exactly what was happening: it was swinging over the launching deck. It had been picked up by the lift-line and was now swinging over the stormy sea. Masters held on to the bench, feeling a bit disorientated. The submersible shook with a dreadful clanging sound, then suddenly dropped like a stone, going down very fast. There was a crashing sound as the dropping motion stopped abruptly, followed by a reverberating drumming sound as the submersible bounced up and down and finally settled again, rocking lightly from side to side.

'We're drifting out,' the corporal said. 'The boat's pulling away. When we stop drifting out, the tow-rope's tight. We get the CO's speech then.'

Masters gazed through a porthole. The sea fell away into darkness. The waves rolled up and rushed down to form a tunnel, then raced up again. The sea was extremely rough, and it was like being on a big dipper. Masters felt his stomach heave as they climbed up and then plunged down again.

Outside the porthole was a whirlpool of water; rushing forward, it smashed noisily against the port, swirled around wildly as if in a washing machine, then fell away to reveal the dark sky, drifting clouds, a few stars. This movement was continuous and soon became sickening, with the submersible leaning over dramatically, then straightening again.

Masters crawled away from the porthole and sat on the wooden bench, but instantly was almost thrown sideways by another violent motion. He heard the drumming of the sea against the hull, then the sphere settled down.

Turned on by the corporal, the radio was crackling. The voice of Lieutenant Commander Sandison came through the speaker, distorted and unreal. '*Victory* to *Josephine*. *Victory* to *Josephine*. You are now in position to tow-drift. We will launch in five minutes.'

'*Josephine* to *Victory*. *Josephine* to *Victory*. Message received. Roger and out.'

The corporal turned around. He had left the radio open. Waving his right hand at the console, he nodded to Masters.

'The CO should come on any minute now, then we'll be taking off. The CO's in *Josephine*.'

'*Josephine* to all subs. *Josephine* to all subs,' came over the radio. 'This is your Commanding Officer speaking. We are now in tow-drift and will be casting off as soon as I finish speaking. We will be heading for Charlie 2. That rig has been hijacked. The crew have all been murdered and sixty terrorists are now aboard. We have to rout the terrorists and take the rig back. We are not concerned with damage to the rig, nor with the lives of the terrorists. Once aboard you will shoot to kill. You will board by climbing the pontoon legs. Your orders are to commence firing as soon as you reach the deck or as soon as the enemy fires. We are casting off now. We will submerge to three hundred feet. We will follow the chart route to Charlie 2 and surface under the main deck. The pilots will open the hatches and check with the other pilots. No one is to move to the ladders until all hatches are open. There's to be no noise down there. The assault commences when *Josephine* signals. At the signal you will advance to the ladders with weapons ready to fire. Select the ladder closest to you. Shoot on sight of the enemy. Don't stop until the whole rig is cleared and every terrorist is either dead or captured. Over and out.'

When the static rushed back in the corporal turned the volume down. He turned the volume back up a few seconds later, when the CO came back on line.

'Instructions for *Auk, Huk* and *Genesis*. Repeat: instructions for *Auk, Huk* and *Genesis*. You are not to engage the enemy unless absolutely necessary. Your mission is to get to the damaged pontoon leg. You will stay with the crew of *Trinity*, who will give you cover. You will descend into the damaged pontoon leg and repair it as best you can. Take full diving kit and wet-welding equipment. As you also have to carry the replacement plates for the pontoon leg, the only weapons you can carry are your Brownings. Repeat: stick with *Trinity*. Your mission is to fix that damaged leg. I want no deviations.'

Masters checked his watch. It was 0550 hours. They would get to Charlie 2 by 0630. It would still be dark then.

'We're casting off now,' the CO announced over the radio. 'Good luck to all of you. Over and out.'

When the corporal switched off the radio, Masters stared around the sphere. The walls curved upward to meet above his head where a bright light was blazing. They were covered in gauges, the benches hid more equipment, and the spaces between the floorboards of the deck were filled with steel pipes and pumps. Masters blinked a few times, heard the drumming of the sea, looked at the three small, round windows and saw the dark waves outside. Then he heard the diver's footsteps as he walked along the hull. There was a dull metallic sound from the stern as the tow-rope dropped off. This was followed by splashing and a scraping along the hull. The diver's face, grotesque in his oxygen mask, appeared at the window. He stuck up one thumb. The pilot waved back. A white foam bubbled over the window as the diver swam off.

The pilot switched on the engines, which made a bass humming sound. When he switched on the outside lamps their light beamed into the dark waves. The pilot opened the vents and water hissed into the tanks; the sea rose up above the three portholes and gradually covered them. The submersible sank steadily, vibrating and humming deeply. Masters went to a porthole and looked out and saw the murky, deceptive depths. The beams of light cut about six or seven feet through the gloom. It was not very far; beyond the lights was total darkness. The only matter lit up by the dulled beams of the lamps was a drifting, grey-green mass.

The depth gauge registered a hundred feet, inched

around to two hundred, and after what seemed like a long time finally registered three hundred. The pilot closed the vents, then turned on the radio. He checked that the other submersibles were all down and then turned the propellers on.

The submersible moved forward, its lights cutting through the murk. The vessel vibrated slightly, making a bass humming sound, and the hands on all the gauges were quivering, recording their progress. The pilot switched on the sonar set. After studying the small screen, he checked the gyro compass and settled back, keeping his eye on the lights through the windows.

'What's your name?' Masters asked him.

'Walters. Roy Walters.'

'And you?' Masters asked the blond giant.

'Ralph Hubbert.'

Masters couldn't stand upright, could scarcely move his arms; it was more comfortable sitting, so he sat there and studied the weapons. There were L34A1 Sterling 9mm sub-machine-guns and twenty-round magazines, all wrapped in specially reinforced cling film. He also saw a pile of white-phosphorus grenades, some police clubs, sets of handcuffs, and, to his relief, a couple of Browning 9mm High Power handguns, also wrapped in cling film, as were the holsters.

'We've been well equipped,' he said, picking up a holstered Browning and strapping it, still wrapped in its cling film, around the waist of his wet suit.

'That's what you wanted, wasn't it?' Hubbert said.

'That's right,' replied Masters. 'I got just what I wanted.'

Hubbert grinned laconically. He was sitting on the bench facing Masters, his blond head almost scraping the convex ceiling, his large hands on his thick thighs.

'You think we'll get them?' he asked.

'We've *got* to get them,' Masters told him.

'They're a tough nut to crack,' Hubbert said. 'The IRA, they're all psychos.'

'You think so?' Masters asked.

'Yeah, I think so. They're all psychos and fucking suicidal. It's part of their rules.'

'You've been in Northern Ireland?'

'Nah,' Hubbert said. 'I haven't fought them, but I've read all about them and they're all mad as hatters.'

Masters said nothing.

The voyage seemed to take for ever. They were gliding through silence. The submersible was vibrating and humming, but it moved forward smoothly. Masters went up to the front, where he heard the pinging of the sonar; he saw the pinpoints of light on the screen and the beams of light outside, cutting through the dark sea. The darkness parted where the light shone, then spread its wings around them. The beams lit up translucent fish through the murk. Masters could almost hear the silence out there, feel the cold of the sunless depths. He sat beside the pilot, who was still watching the gyro compass. The needle of the compass was quivering, but moved very little.

'How long?' Masters asked.

'About ten minutes,' Walters said. 'We'll have to start surfacing in five minutes. I think the sea's pretty rough.'

'How rough?' Masters asked.

'Bloody rough, Sarge. Those waves might be fifty foot high. I can't be sure, but they could be.'

'The rig?' Masters asked.

'The rig's out,' Walters said. 'If we try to get under that bloody rig, we'll be smashed to pieces.'

'We'll have to surface,' Masters said.

'That's right: we'll have to surface. We'll have to come up well away from the rig and then put on our diving masks.'

'That's not practical, Corporal.'

'Yes, it is, Sarge. We'll keep our weapons in cling film, put them in a sealed bag, then drag the buggers behind us in the bag. No problem at all.'

'What about the replacement plates? That crew can't drag them through the water – they're too heavy.'

'No,' Walters said, 'they won't be able to take the plates with them – but they *will* be able to take the welding equipment and that could be enough. Failing that, though it'll take a bit more time, they'll find plates on the rig.'

Masters swallowed hard as he thought of fifty-foot waves, imagining the men swimming through the water, beneath the sea's killing surface. They would come up under the pontoons, at the base of their huge legs. They would climb the pontoon ladders to the surface and the waves would then find them. In waves like that, the men would have to be strong. Doubtless more than one man would be lost before he reached the top deck.

'OK,' Masters said, 'I take your point. So let's see if the CO agrees. Give me that microphone.'

When Walters handed him the microphone, Masters contacted *Josephine*. He asked for the CO and, when he got him, relayed the corporal's theory to him. To his credit, Lieutenant-Colonel Edwards instantly agreed, saying he would instruct the other submersibles to surface right now, on the present grid reference.

'Thank Corporal Walters for me,' he added. 'He must be a bright boy. Over and out.'

Masters handed the microphone back to Walters. 'You're a bright boy,' he said.

'Can we surface right now?' Walters asked, as if not quite believing in his own wisdom.

'Right now,' Masters said.

Walters opened the tanks and the deep humming changed pitch slightly. Masters heard the tanks ejecting their water and then the craft started rising.

'Bless us all,' Walters said.

Hubbert slid off the bench, pulled some rubber bags from out under it, and passed one each to Masters and Walters. Each man then placed his weapons and other kit in his rubber bag, zipped it up, sealed it with water-resistant tape, then slung it on to his back and tightened the shoulder straps.

'Well,' Masters said, 'it's a start.'

As it rose slowly from the depths, the submersible started to rock from side to side. Hubbert sat on the bench beside Masters and gripped the arm-rest. Masters glanced through the portholes and saw light outside. The separate beams of light were rising up and down, splaying wide, disappearing. The submersible kept rising, rocking more as it neared the surface, and Masters heard the drumming noise from outside as the waves grew in strength.

'Right,' Hubbert said. 'Here we go. Help me on with the cylinders.'

After putting on his flippers, he knelt by the bench and told Masters to hold up the heavy oxygen cylinders. When Masters had done this, Hubbert put his hands backwards through the straps, then humped the cylinders on to his broad back. Masters then buckled the straps around his chest and Hubbert put on his oxygen mask. When he had finished, he nodded at Masters and held up his thumb.

The submersible was still rising and rocking more rapidly; it was coming to the surface and it was stormy up there. Masters put on his flippers and picked up his oxygen cylinders, but Hubbert stepped forward, walking awkwardly on his own flippers, and helped Masters put on his cylinders. Masters then covered his face with the oxygen mask, instantly feeling hot and suffocated, as well as half blind. He clipped the breathing tube in and turned around to look at Hubbert. They gazed at one another through their masks, then turned on the oxygen.

The submersible was still lurching badly from side to side. Masters turned around and blinked through his mask and saw Walters sitting at the console, putting on his flippers. When he had done so, he stood up and reached for his cylinders. Hubbert helped him to put them on, though both were shaken by the submersible, which was rocking more violently all the time as it rose to the surface. Masters watched the two men. They both moved in total silence. The only sound Masters heard was his own breathing, the rhythmic hiss of the oxygen. Finally Walters was ready, and pressed his hands against the wall. Hubbert followed his example, so Masters did the same and then waited.

The submersible broke the surface. It soared up and crashed back down. It was swept along the trough between waves and then hurled up again. Masters timed the rise and fall, bracing himself beneath the hatch. The submersible raced along the next trough and Masters reached up above him. He turned the wheel very hard, wrenching with all his might. The submersible reached the crest of a wave and started racing back down again. Masters wrenched the hatch open, grabbed the handles on both sides, held on as the submersible plummeted down and spun around and rushed sideways. It ascended again, climbing a huge wave; and Masters took a deep breath and jerked his arms and pulled himself up.

He flopped over the curved steel sail. A monstrous wave towered above him. It roared and then curled above his head, before exploding all over him. Masters clung to the sail as the water swirled around him. When it poured back down the sides of the submersible, the wind started beating. The noise was incredible – Masters heard it through his mask. He glanced up and saw the sea's rise and fall, the huge waves heaving skyward. Masters clambered over the sail and took the grip in one hand. He reached down with his other hand to let Hubbert reach up and take hold of it. Masters started pulling.

A wave picked the submersible up. Masters felt the wind and heard the roaring wave and saw a valley of darkness. The water down there was black. It poured away and swept up again. Masters held the grip tight as the submersible plunged down and then was borne up on another high wave. He tried not to look around him, tried ignoring the roaring sea. Taking a deep breath, he pulled Hubbert up and knew that Walters was pushing him. Hubbert flopped across the sail, wriggled around and lay flat out. He took hold of the other grip, then he and Masters started reaching down for Walters. The sea roared and swept across them, sweeping Hubbert off the hull; then the submersible rose high on a great wave and Masters flew into empty space.

He didn't know what was happening, but saw distant lights spinning, a huge wall of darkness rising high to block out the sea and sky. Then there was the void, streams of light through a blackness, and he kept spinning, turning rapidly upside down, bereft of any sense of direction. His head broke the surface as he rose on a roaring wave. He saw the lights of the rig straight ahead, soaring up to the sky. It didn't seem real, was too fierce to be real. He was carried through the air, felt the wind, and then was hurled down again.

At that moment Masters sensed that he wouldn't come back up. He saw a submersible spinning around not far away, then dark forms in the monstrous waves. Masters blinked and glanced below. He saw a black, concave void. He was plunging rapidly towards it and it roared and then swallowed him whole.

16

Masters didn't rise up again. He kicked out with his flippers and went down, gliding through the dark, silent depths to where the waves could not reach him. A grey-green murk filled his vision, he felt as light as a feather, and he went down, levelled out and kicked his legs, heading straight for the rig.

There were other men around him in the calm and quiet, looking like strange, primordial fish, but kicking their legs and blowing bubbles, dragging bags on long chains. Masters was thrilled to see them, and proud too.

He saw the shadows increasing in number in the murk all around him, and coming closer. A lot of the men had obviously made it. That was due to their training. They were now swimming expertly all around him and still had their weapons, some in waterproof bags strapped to their shoulders, others in bags that they towed behind them on short, lightweight chains. Masters kicked harder and glided forward, hearing a hissing in his ears. It was the soft, rhythmic hissing of the oxygen, which was all he could hear. He glanced left and right, seeing streams of small bubbles, streaming back and upwards in silence, a dance of air and trapped light.

Masters felt divorced from his own body; apart from his own steady breathing, he could not hear a sound. The gloom ahead was unrelieved. Beyond it was total darkness which swallowed up the men ahead, the drifting bags, the kicking flippers. Masters headed straight for it, but it always moved on; the gloom parted and swept by on either side and the darkness receded. Nevertheless, he swam towards it, mesmerized by the silence. He started dreaming, drifting out of himself . . . and then he saw something moving.

Masters swam forward cautiously and approached shadowy figures. He saw a black wall that was darker than the depths, and the shadows were touching it. Masters swam on, gratefully breathing the oxygen, and the black wall became the immense bulk of the round pontoon.

He went into that darkness. The other men were spiralling above him, below him, beside him, vague figures drifting up and down languidly. Masters swam even closer until the pontoon curved above him. He went under it and swam around it and then went up towards the surface. He saw the base of the pontoon leg, still obscured by the murk. At least thirty feet wide, it dwarfed the swimming men, soaring above them to disappear into darkness. Masters swam close and touched it. A pair of flippers kicked above him. He glanced up and saw the bottom of the ladder, stopping short at the pontoon.

Masters took hold of a rung and started pulling himself up. It was difficult, so he took off his flippers and used his bare feet. The water was so icy his feet started turning numb within seconds; even so, other men were doing the same and discarded flippers drifted down past him.

Masters pulled himself up, trying not to go too fast. He knew that he would have to be holding the ladder when he broke through the surface. He kept moving upwards and saw the kicking feet above him; the water, cold and black, moved around him, filled with bubbles of trapped light. Masters heard his own harsh breathing, felt the tugging of the sea. The darkness weakened and let in some light and then the black became grey. Masters felt a sudden tension, but it passed away as he kept rising. He felt the swirling of that grey, icy mass and then he broke through the surface.

The noise exploded around him. He gripped the rung of the ladder. The sea roared and swept between the pontoon legs and then roared out again. Masters clung to the ladder, seeing men on the other pontoon legs. There were also men on the thinner support legs criss-crossing above him. The noise was appalling. The sea roared and hammered the great pontoon legs, exploding and shooting upwards and outwards, then pouring back down the support legs.

Masters gripped the ladder tightly as waves roared and swept across him. He was punched by the fist of a giant and nearly torn from the ladder. He clung desperately to the rung and watched the men on the support legs; they had jumars – metal clamps – attached to their belts and were fixing them to the rungs of the ladders. The jumars kept them from falling off, leaving their hands free for manoeuvring. Clamped tight to the rungs of the ladders, the men were helping each other. The sea roared and exploded, echoing under the deck above.

The men were now opening their waterproof bags and taking out their weapons. They slung the Sterlings across their backs, and clipped grenades to their webbed belts. The spare magazines were in small, waterproof bags that hung from loops around their necks. Masters climbed up the ladder, then stretched out on a support leg. He took a jumar that was chained to his waist belt and clamped it over a rung. The sea roared and swept across him, almost tearing him from the leg. Though only six inches long, the chain on the jumar kept him from being swept away. The sea came in once more, its white foam streaked with black, roaring up and clawing frantically at the men and then rushing back out again.

With their weapons at the ready, the men were starting the real climb, snapping the jumars open and clambering up the ladders and then locking the jumars around the nearest rung when they had to rest or use their hands for something else. The sea roared and swept across them, making some of them disappear. The sea rushed away and took the men with it, leaving no trace at all. The other men kept climbing, only stopping to help each other. Masters saw them disappearing in the darkness, climbing up to the main deck.

Suddenly kicked on the shoulder, he glanced along the support leg. The sea roared and poured across him to drench him, then he saw a pale face. Captain Pancroft was shouting at him, pointing at his back, telling him to remove his sub-machine-gun from his waterproof bag and have it ready for use when they boarded. He did as he was told, removing the weapon from the bag, slinging it across his shoulder, then attaching the spare magazines to his webbing – all while lying stretched out on the support leg, whipped by wind and lashed by rain. When he had finished, he waved to Pancroft, then snapped the jumar open. The demented sea rushed at him, making him cling to the support leg. The sea pummelled him and poured all around him and then fell away. He slithered back down the leg to reach the main pontoon leg, stretching out with one hand and taking hold and then swinging across. He landed on the other ladder as the waves roared in. Fifty feet high, they towered darkly abovc Masters, and made an indescribable noise as they exploded around him. He clung to the ladder, feeling the jolting along his arms, as the waves howled past and rushed beneath the rig and poured out through the other side.

Masters started climbing, but he had to rest often. When he did so, he used the jumar, snapping it over the nearest rung. The other men were all around him, above him and below him, clambering up the ladders of the pontoon legs, stretching along the support legs. They were vague in the gloom, but clearly fighting the fierce sea, using the short breaks between incoming waves to climb higher. Sometimes they failed, clamping themselves on too late; when this happened the waves smashing down upon them bore them away. Yet the other men kept climbing, advancing up into the gloom. They were swallowed by the darkness beneath the deck that loomed high above Masters.

He, too, kept climbing, fighting the wind and fierce sea. Though now well above the waves, he still felt the icy sting of the spray. The men above were near the deck, disappearing into darkness. Masters wondered if the first men were aboard, and if so, what was happening. The storm had grown extremely violent, making the rig sway and creak, and Masters hoped that the terrorists would be indoors, hiding from its fury. He kept climbing the ladder, the wind howling and teasing at him. The waves thundered below and the spray geysered up to him and drenched him.

Glancing back down the leg he saw men on the support legs, throwing off their cylinders and masks, unwrapping weapons and magazines. He also saw the snarling waves crashing over the swarming men, then rushing away, allowing the men to keep moving upwards, dark ants on a silvery web. Some crawled along the support legs; others climbed the great pontoon legs. They all climbed out of that roaring dark pit to clamber up the steel ladders.

Masters looked up again, to where the bottom of the main deck was spread out directly above him. Very close to him, it was swaying up and down, its bolts and nuts squealing in protest. Then Masters heard gunfire. It was coming from the main deck. It was the sound of Sterling sub-machine-guns, dominating the howling wind.

Masters reached the catwalk. It was dark and the wind howled across it, making it shudder and rattle. The sound of gunfire was now louder, rising above the howling wind, and the catwalk was moving up and down as the massive deck heaved. Masters reached up through the hatchway, grabbed the handles on either side, took a deep breath and pulled himself up and then rolled on the deck.

The wind beat about him, the sea roared and hissed below, and he glanced down to see foam-capped waves, climbing high, smashing in. More shots rang out. There was a muffled, deep explosion. Masters felt the blast jolting up his legs as he grabbed for the railing. He glanced down the pontoon leg. The sea was boiling around it. Someone screamed and was grabbed by a white claw and dragged into the darkness. The whole leg shook visibly, then the massive platform tilted. The seething water fell back and gave way to monstrous waves. Masters realized that the explosives had gone off in the pontoon leg and that he was now standing right on top of it as the water poured into it.

Cursing, shaking his head, he ran along the catwalk. He removed his Sterling from his shoulder as he ran, and managed to snap in a magazine just before he arrived at a ladder that climbed the wall of a module. He clambered up the ladder, using only his free hand; he reached the top and went through an open door where a bright light washed over him. He was on the drilling floor, right behind the stacked crates. The noise of gunfire echoed noisily and he saw other SBS men in wet suits. They were kneeling behind the crates, firing into the drilling room, and Masters looked beyond the crates and saw the terrorists, racing back and forth, shouting. They seemed small and distant. The drilling floor was very bright, its light falling across the crates and machines, casting large, bizarre shadows.

Masters knelt beside his friends and released the safety-catch on his Sterling. There was a roaring from the far side of the deck and wood splintered near his face. He and the others returned fire and the noise was harsh, almost deafening. A terrorist screamed and threw up his arms, then turned away and collapsed.

'Masters!' someone bawled. 'Over here!'

Jerking his head around, Masters saw Pancroft kneeling near the door. The captain still had his oxygen cylinders and breathing mask on, the latter strapped to his belt. Masters ran over to him as the guns roared right behind Pancroft. Dropping to a crouching position, Masters moved up beside him.

'They've blown the leg right beneath us,' Pancroft told him. 'That saves us a journey.'

'I know,' Masters replied. 'Where are the maintenance men?'

'Four are still making their way up to the deck, but I've got the first two just outside. That's all we need, Tone.'

The guns continued firing, someone screamed and fell down, and more SBS men were rushing through the open door, crouching low, weapons ready. Masters glanced back at the crates to see an SBS commando hurling a smoke grenade; he jumped up and his arm swung in a blur, then he dropped low again. The grenade flew far out above the drilling floor, seemed to hover there eternally, then dropped languidly towards the drilling room. The explosion came immediately, a cataclysmic roaring, with pieces of debris flying out on billowing smoke and men screaming inside.

'. . . the leg!' Pancroft was shouting as the smoke from the grenade thinned out. 'We've got to repair that pontoon leg! Come on, Sergeant! Let's go!'

Masters looked past the crates at the massive drilling floor, where SBS men were running, dropping low, then jumping up again. They were firing on the move and their fire was being returned. A terrorist hand-grenade exploded with a mighty roar and blew apart a large wooden crate. The smoke cleared to reveal a man writhing on the deck, screaming dementedly, his hands clawing at his lacerated, bleeding stomach. As he was wearing a wet suit, he had to be an SBS man, so another SBS man rushed up to him, intending to help him. A hail of bullets cut him down. His weapon clattered to the deck as he shuddered violently and then fell and rolled over, staring up at the sky. An SBS grenade exploded very close to the moonpool. Metal shrieked and a standpipe buckled and crashed down on some terrorists. Instantly, the SBS men in wet suits ran forward, firing from the hip, their guns roaring on both sides as the shouting of the men echoed noisily.

'Now!' Pancroft yelled, slapping Masters on the shoulder. They both jumped up and rushed through the doorway and felt the blast of the wind. Masters ran along the catwalk and saw the floor-hatch opening. The head of a terrorist emerged and the man looked up, startled. Masters glimpsed the wide eyes, that brief, scalding panic, then kicked the man's head, which jerked back and thumped on the catwalk. The terrorist vomited and dropped back through the hatch, leaving blood on the catwalk.

Masters dropped to his knees and looked down the pontoon leg. Something splashed far below – the body of the man he'd kicked – and then he saw another face staring up at him. The man was hanging from the ladder. The water boiled far below him. He glanced up and shouted 'No!' and Masters fired and saw blood and stripped bone. The man's face split in two, his hands slid from the ladder, his body curved back like a bowstring and his arms wildly waved, then he plunged down the dark, hollow leg and splashed into the water. Masters had another look. There was no sign of other terrorists. He glanced up and saw Pancroft with two SBS corporals, both wearing full diving kit.

'We're OK,' Masters told them. 'I know this rig well. There are spare plates on the catwalk in the leg. I don't think there's a problem.'

'Good,' Pancroft replied. 'These men have the welding kit and tools, so let's get the hell down there.'

Pancroft shuffled across the catwalk, his flippers around his neck. He untied them and put them on his feet and then untied the oxygen mask. The catwalk rose and fell, the wind howled, the sea roared. They heard the sound of gunfire from inside and then heard more above them. Pancroft put on his oxygen mask and waved at the two corporals. Encased in full diving equipment, they moved forward awkwardly. One of them had the welding kit in the bag on his back; the other was holding a battery-operated electric hammer and other bits of equipment.

Suddenly, the rig tilted farther and the pontoon leg sank lower. Thus reminded that time was running out, Pancroft sat on the edge of the hatch and then slid down and disappeared.

The second man took the same position. Masters heard a sound behind him. Turning to face the door, he saw a silhouette framed in light . . . and the barrel of an MP5 pointing straight at him. Masters fired first, moving his Sterling submachine-sun left to right, and as the weapon roared the terrorist shuddered wildly and fell back through the doorway. Another terrorist appeared. Masters shot him and he fell. Masters tugged a grenade from his belt and then ran to the door. After throwing in the grenade, he flattened himself against the wall; the grenade exploded and the steel wall vibrated. Masters rushed in.

One man was sliding down the crates, leaving a trail of blood behind him; another was rolling on the floor with his tattered clothes smoking; and the third was staggering blindly in circles, screaming in agony and fear, covering his blinded eyes with his bloody hands.

Masters's Sterling spat fire and he felt the backblast. The three men convulsed in a hail of bullets, then collapsed and were still.

Rushing back out to the hatchway in the catwalk, Masters looked in and saw the three SBS men on the ladder, climbing down towards the water. That water was far below them, over a hundred feet down, boiling up and sinking repeatedly, rushing in from outside and pouring out again. Masters closed the trapdoor, then checked the wind and sea. The storm was not as strong as it had been; it was gradually fading. He looked all around him, seeing grey light in the darkness, then turned away and went back through the doorway and into the drilling hall.

The dead men lay at his feet. Blood streaked the crates; Masters walked past these and looked out at the vast drilling floor. The SBS were still fighting and had reached the moonpool, where they were hiding behind the stacked pipes and chains, firing up at the drilling room. Masters ran across the floor, his bare feet slipping in mud; he was drenched and felt very cold, though there was sweat on his brow. The guns roared and bullets whistled, ricocheting on all sides. He kept running and on reaching a fork-lift dropped low behind it.

Bullets whipped past his head and a grenade exploded. Glass shattered and he heard a piercing scream that made him glance towards the moon-pool. His mates were stretched out around it, hiding behind what they could find, shouting at each other and waving arms and firing up at the drilling room. Masters looked at the room and saw terrorists at the windows. The glass was shattered and the terrorists were firing down at the men in wet suits. Then a grenade sailed towards the window and fell among the terrorists. When it erupted in a blinding flash of light, more shards of glass rained down.

The SBS men darted forward. A terrorist flopped through the smashed window. The SBS men raced across the floor, firing on the move, then ran up the stairs and turned a sharp corner, disappearing from view. Masters jumped up and ran, then saw a terrorist at the window, taking aim with an AK47, its barrel pointing at him. Before the terrorist could fire, someone shot him from behind. The terrorist was punched forward, over the window frame, then slid off and plunged screaming to the drilling floor. Relieved, Masters ran up the steps and turned into the drilling room. The other SBS troops were there, examining their own handiwork. The room was wrecked and the terrorists, all dead, were drenched in blood.

'Anyone seen Dalton?' Masters asked.

'Who's Dalton?' came the reply. 'If he's in a wet suit he's one of us. If not, he's in trouble.'

Masters left the drilling room and hurried along a narrow corridor; the lights were bright and the ceiling was low and he felt his eyes stinging. It was quiet in the corridor. Now the gunfire sounded distant. He kept walking and turned a sharp corner and then came to more steps. Catching a glimpse of blue overalls, he raised his weapon and fired a short burst. The overalls flapped like a wind-blown flag and then the man in them started falling. His weapon clattered down the steps and he pitched forward and followed it. His head thumped on a step and split open as his body flipped over. His boots banged on the floor, his spine cracked on another step, and then he sprawled there, propped up by the steps, as Masters jumped over him.

Masters raced up to the main deck and stepped out into the wind. He noticed that the storm had abated, though the wind was still icy. The sound of gunfire was loud here; it ricocheted and reverberated. There were men running this way and that, through shadow and light. A grenade exploded, its flash illuminating the darkness. Silhouetted figures spun in white light and crashed back down through boiling smoke.

The immense deck was tilting. It was covered in mud and oil. The guns roared and men shouted as they ran to and fro, exposed in bright lights, lost in shadows, skidding over the deck.

Masters glimpsed the sea far below the tilting deck, brief flashes of white through the gloom, a black void turning grey. Then he heard a shocking noise, felt fierce heat, was rendered breathless. Snatched up by a giant hand, he was smashed against a wall, blacked out for a moment, then awakened lying flat on his back. Looking straight up, he saw a towering derrick with lights blazing on its platforms. There was a scream and then he saw a man fall from a platform and plunge down through the moonpool to the sea.

Masters jumped up and advanced, still gripping his Sterling, glancing sideways at the base of the platform and expecting to die. He saw terrorists huddled up within the web of the girders, firing down from the roof of the drilling floor, their guns winking and chattering. Masters ran across the deck, trying to avoid the hail of bullets. A man in overalls jumped out from behind a wooden crate, aiming at him with a Glock 17 semi-automatic pistol.

The terrorist didn't have time to shoot: Masters just bowled right into him. They both tumbled to the deck and rolled over, one on top of the other. The man straightened up, still trying to aim his handgun, but Masters kicked his kneecap and he collapsed, his head thumping the steel deck. Then Masters jumped up. The man was rolling away from him. Masters took a step forward and kicked him in the ribs and on the head. The terrorist grunted and shuddered. Masters kicked his head again. There was a muffled snapping sound and the man twitched convulsively, then froze. Masters picked up his weapon as splinters of wood from the crates beside him exploded just above him. He turned away and ran as fast as he could toward the nearest derrick.

The other SBS troops were scattered widely around the deck, firing up at the derrick. The base of the derrick rested on the roof of the drilling room and the terrorists were firing down from there. The SBS troops were trying to storm it, rushing forward and dropping low. A CS gas grenade had fallen near the room and its smoke spiralled skyward. The sky itself was turning grey, drifting beyond the tall derrick, as the guns roared, a hand-grenade exploded and some SBS men screamed and fell.

Masters saw Corporal Hubbert pointing up at the shooting terrorists, drenched like the rest of the SBS men, his pale face now flushed. Masters crouched low and ran, but skidded crazily in the mud; he fell down and slithered over the deck and then crawled up to Hubbert. The blond giant stared at him. He seemed startled, but then he grinned as he poked a finger in his right ear, turned it like a corkscrew and gently smacked his own head.

'I'm half deaf!' he bawled.

'What happened to Walters?' Masters bawled back.

'I don't know! I haven't seen him since the climb! I don't think he made it!'

There was another loud explosion. Lumps of metal flew through the air, and a man's head bounced across the deck, pumping blood. Then Masters saw the body. It was standing beside some gas pipes, dressed in a shredded SBS wet suit, also pumping blood from its headless neck. One hand flapped in the air, the legs shook and then the body collapsed. Another explosion was followed by flying shrapnel. The guns of both sides roared in a dreadful cacophony.

'Those bastards!' Hubbert bawled. 'They're holed up in that bloody roof! There's nowhere they can go, so they're staying there and cutting us to pieces!' Suddenly, he stood up, fully exposed to the terrorists; he glanced at the men all around him and waved his sub-machine-gun. 'The hell with it!' he bawled. 'Let's get them! Wipe out the bastards!'

The men cheered and jumped up and started running across the deck. The guns of the terrorists cut some down, but those left kept on going. Masters found himself near the drilling room, where he heard screams and saw terrorists convulsing as they collapsed and rolled over. A grenade exploded and tore the running men apart; another flew down from the roof of the drilling room to add its deafening explosion to the general bedlam. Glancing up, Masters saw the terrorists firing from the roof. Simultaneously a hail of bullets thudded into the deck behind him and ricocheted off the nearby modules. A grenade exploded above him, searing the gloom with jagged white light; there was screaming and a man somersaulted as he plunged to the deck.

Then Masters saw Hubbert: he was on a ladder, clambering up the side of the drilling room, his weapon dangling from his free hand. Masters followed without thinking, but the corporal's huge frame disappeared above him. Still climbing, Masters felt almost numb from the roaring and shouting. Reaching the roof, he saw a group of armed terrorists crouching around the hole in the drilling shaft. A lot of them fell when the SBS troops fired at them. A few screamed and staggered back against the shaft and plunged down the moonpool.

Masters saw sticks of dynamite piled up around one leg, with the wire from a timing device running behind a module.

'Get down!' he bawled.

He threw himself down, slithered back towards the ladder, grabbed the top rung and tugged himself over the edge of the deck and managed to place his feet on a lower rung, holding his weapon in one hand. His whole head seemed to explode, he saw white light and flames, then he dropped through a deafening cacophony, crushing pressure and fierce heat. The sky above seemed to split, there was a rainfall of debris – scorched nuts and bolts, buckled pieces of metal sheeting, dust and cement – and Masters crawled across the deck on his hands and knees, shook his head, then fell face down. The thunder imprisoned him. He was pummelled and scorched. He shook his head again, heard a ringing in his ears, then blinked repeatedly and glanced sideways. The deck was spinning around him, smoke billowed across the modules, and he rolled on to his back and looked up wide-eyed as the whole derrick fell.

Bent by the explosions, the legs were buckling and breaking apart; the tiered platforms started shrieking and tearing loose, then they plunged down the centre. The roof of the drilling room caved in, men and machinery poured down through it, and black smoke billowed up from a wall of flame to form a great mushroom. Finally, the derrick fell, toppling over to the right, exploding in a mass of wood and steel, then crashing over the main deck. Many men screamed as the massive girders fell, bounced over the deck, smashed through men and modules, then flew off the edge of the deck, to plunge into the sea.

Masters scrambled to his feet, feeling dizzy and unreal. He turned around and picked up his Sterling. Then he saw the blond giant.

Hubbert was crawling towards him. His hair had been burnt off. His face was blistered and his wet suit was in tatters and appeared to be smouldering. He crawled right up to Masters and stared at him with dazed eyes. He raised one limp hand in greeting or farewell, then coughed blood and died.

Masters felt a searing rage. He cursed and looked all around him. He saw the dawn light pouring over the sea – but he did not see McGee. Now he wanted McGee; wanted justice for all the dead. He stepped forward and stumbled over another dead man. He cursed again and walked on.

The air was filled with smoke, guns were firing from all sides, and he heard the clatter of booted feet across the catwalks, along with more shouting and screaming. One terrorist flopped across a railing; another swung his legs up; a third cried out in agony as he fell through the air and thumped on to the deck. Masters just kept walking, his nose filled with smoke and cordite. There was a flash and then he heard the explosion and dropped to the deck. The blast pummelled his body; he felt scorched

17

Masters and Turner, both wearing British United Oil overalls, stood on a catwalk on Bravo 1 and looked out at the Forties Field. The sea was quite calm, the sky was grey and cloudy as usual, and the distant rigs, scattered along the horizon, seemed fragile and lonesome.

As one they glanced down at the landing pad just beneath them. They heard the roar of the Wessex Mk 3 transport helicopter, watched its rotors spinning, and then saw the armed SBS bodyguards emerging from the nearby module. The guards fanned out across the deck, forming a path to the helicopter, their green berets worn proudly on their heads, weapons at the ready. The Prime Minister emerged soon after, walking between the watchful guards, bent against the strong wind and shivering visibly. His silvery-grey hair was ruffled and he was slightly stooped, clearly weary, but when he reached the helicopter and was standing on the top step, he turned back and waved up at the catwalk. Masters and Turner waved back. The

PM studied them for what seemed like a long time, then he turned away and entered the Wessex.

'He's bloody angry,' Turner said. 'It was our mess and yet it trapped him. He had to give us our reduction in oil tax and he won't like us for it.'

'I'm surprised,' Masters replied. 'I thought he had you by the short and curlies. I thought he could have used this whole mess against you and made you settle for less.'

'It doesn't work that way, Tone. You can't fight the oil companies. With the loss of Eagle 3 and the virtual destruction of Charlie 2, Sir Reginald threw up his hands and said we couldn't go on. The PM was flabbergasted. He couldn't believe what he was hearing. But Sir Reginald just looked him in the eye and pointed out what our losses were. He mentioned the cost of rebuilding the rigs, said how long it would take to do it, suggested that British United couldn't possibly survive all that without a substantial reduction in oil tax. The PM was outraged and said the Chairman was blackmailing him. He said the government couldn't pay for the mistakes of incompetent oil companies. Sir Reginald just smiled at him. It was a hell of a smile. He said that the oil companies couldn't afford to return to drilling if they weren't given a reduction in tax to offset their losses. He also told the PM that if the oil companies stopped drilling, the press would want to know why and then word of the terrorist outrage would be bound to slip out. He then pointed out what that would mean: an international loss of confidence in the North Sea in particular and the UK in general. The PM surrendered – and British United Oil is back in business, bigger than ever.'

Masters smiled and glanced down at the landing pad. The Under-Secretary was entering the Wessex, stooping low at the door. The SBS guards followed him in, moving backwards up the steps, their weapons at the ready. The last guard vanished into the helicopter and the loadmaster slid the door shut.

Masters smiled to himself. Though he was now back as an undercover man on Bravo 1, acting as a tool-pusher – just as other SBS men were on other rigs – he knew that if anyone asked about SBS involvement in the North Sea they would be given an official denial. SBS involvement in the North Sea, though vital and ongoing, retained its top secret classification.

'You were right,' Turner said. 'The man behind the hijack was Dalton. It was him all along. Andy Blackburn phoned through with the proof. He'd questioned some of the people listed in McGee's address book and they confirmed that McGee had been seeing Dalton. They first met in the Middle East, when Dalton was negotiating on behalf of the oil companies and McGee was buying weapons for the IRA. They met later in Paris and it's believed they sealed the agreement there.'

'I don't understand,' Masters said. 'That means one of your overseas backers was behind the whole thing.'

'Correct,' Turner replied. 'It certainly seems that way. We can assume that someone in the conglomerate instigated the whole operation.'

'Why would they do that? It doesn't make sense.'

'Yes, it does, my friend. It certainly does if you think in international terms. The conglomerate must have known that if the British government reduced North Sea oil taxes, all the revenue they were giving to their overseas interests would have been diverted into Britain. The conglomerate knew that it was exorbitant British taxes that had forced the subsidiaries to cut back on drilling and invest their capital in the conglomerate's tax-free havens. It was therefore in their own interests to get rid of the Prime Minister, discredit the British oilfields, and ensure that future British oil revenue continued to be dependent on the conglomerate's tax-free – therefore more lucrative – overseas markets.'

'But it backfired,' Masters said.

'Yes. Because of McGee. They didn't think for a minute that the Irishman would stop short at killing a British Prime Minister. They also forgot that it wasn't in the IRA's own interests to instigate the destruction of North Sea oil revenue. Fanatics or not, the IRA are, in their own bloody way, fighting for an Ireland which, though independent, would still require the benefits of North Sea oil. If McGee hadn't wanted that, if he had assassinated the Prime Minister, the North Sea would now be finished and the UK would be forced to buy from elsewhere. As it stands, by what's almost pure chance we've been given the winning hand.'

They looked down at the landing pad, where the Wessex was ready to take off. Its spinning rotors had created a slipstream that lashed at the roustabouts. The landing pad vibrated, roughnecks pulled the blocks away, and the helicopter roared even louder and lifted awkwardly off the deck. It hovered a few seconds, framed by sea and sky, then swayed a little and began its ascent. It climbed steadily, hovered again above the derricks, then turned away like a huge, crippled bird and flew towards the mainland.

'So,' Masters asked, 'what do we do?'

'We do nothing,' Turner said.

Startled, Masters stared at him. 'What the hell do you mean, Keith? You're not trying to find the men behind Dalton? Is *that* what you're saying?'

'Yes, Tone, that's what I'm saying.' Turner tugged at his beard, ran his fingers through his hair, gazed out across the desolate sea and then shrugged forlornly. 'What can we do? Not a damn thing! Dalton was with the conglomerate for years and he knew lots of powerful men. Which one of them gave the order? Which company stood to gain most? Was it the Americans or the Germans or the French or our Middle Eastern friends? We'll never find out. The conglomerate's too big to investigate. Like most of the conglomerates, it's a multinational affair, divorced from any single jurisdiction and removed from morality. And what if we mentioned Dalton? Or accused the conglomerate in general? We'd just receive a faultlessly worded missive denying all knowledge of Dalton's political, financial or criminal activities. They've got us whipped, Tone. There's not a thing we can do about it. We'll just have to get on with our jobs and forget that this ever happened. There's no evidence for their guilt, no authority that can find the truth. The politicians no longer rule the world – the multinationals do.'

Masters sighed, glanced up at the cloudy sky and saw the Wessex, a tiny speck in the distance, flying over another rig before disappearing beyond the horizon as if it had never been.

It's been like a dream, he thought. It might never have happened. Twenty-four hours have passed and apart from the many men dead and wounded, nothing has changed.

Sergeant Masters, SBS, sighed again as he gazed across the sea to the distant horizon. 'Well,' he said, 'at least for the moment Britain still has its oil.'

'Thanks to the SBS,' Turner replied. 'Let's hope it stays that way.'

PRESS RELEASE BRITISH UNITED OIL
DATE: 20 August 1982

UNCLASSIFIED

1. On 18 August 1982, at approximately 1830 hours, an earth tremor travelling from north to south along the bed of the North Sea caused extensive damage to some of British United Oil's major oilfields. Shock waves from the tremor caused extreme turbulence on the sea's surface with winds of approximately 150 miles per hour and waves as high as 120 feet. As a result, Eagle 3, the main semi-submersible rig on the Frigg Field, was sunk with all hands. The tremor then travelled on a south-westerly course until it reached the Beryl Field where, before dissipating, it caused considerable damage to the main rig, Charlie 2, and led to the unfortunate deaths of twenty crew members who were trapped beneath a collapsed section of the drilling floor.

2. As Eagle 3 (Frigg Field) was being prepared for

shut-down and towing to another site, no plans for its reconstruction are envisaged.

3. Charlie 2 (Beryl Field) has been shut down temporarily for extensive repairs and the surviving crew members repatriated for medical examination and subsequent transfer to other rigs.

4. As many of the crew members are suffering from severe trauma it is felt by this Company that their names should be withheld from the media and general public. Private settlement of compensation for the dependants of the deceased is currently being negotiated.

5. A full investigation into the nature of the earth tremor has been ordered and a complete, top-classified report will be submitted in due course to the Under-Secretary of the Department of Energy. For reasons of internal security British United Oil has agreed with the Department of Energy that no further information regarding this matter should be released.

MARINE B: SBS

THE AEGEAN CAMPAIGN

Ian Blake

Prelude

August 1943

The British Chiefs of Staff committee listened to the Prime Minister with a mixture of resignation and indignation. After more than three years at the helm the old man was still at it with his impossible schemes. Impossible on this occasion because their great American allies were not interested.

The First Sea Lord reminded the meeting that the navy's strength had been shifted from the eastern Mediterranean for the proposed invasion of the Italian mainland; the Chief of the Imperial General Staff remarked on the burden of the British commitment to the Italian campaign; the Chief of Air Staff just took his pipe from his mouth and shook his head.

Operation Accolade, however many attractions it may have had, was now impossible.

Churchill glared at them through his cigar smoke. The heat of a Canadian summer's day had not improved his temper and the Quebec Conference was turning out to be a wearing, knock-down affair. It had taken much argument before the Americans had finally agreed to increased British participation in the Pacific War and their scepticism of Churchill's policy of bringing Turkey into the conflict and striking at the guts of Germany through the Balkans, had remained undiminished.

The previous day at the conference the British contingent had raised the advantages of snatching the Italian-occupied Dodecanese Islands from under the noses of the Germans in order to encourage Turkish entry into the war. But the Americans had remained adamant: if the British wanted to pursue such a policy they could not stop them. But no help was to be expected from them, and there was to be no draining of resources from the great undertakings the Allies had jointly set in motion elsewhere.

In short, paddle your own canoe up shit creek. It had not been either a friendly or a successful session.

'Come, gentlemen,' said Churchill, 'we must have a special force capability in the Middle East which could move swiftly into these islands until regular troops can be sent to garrison them. The Italians are about to surrender. They are not going to oppose us. I need not remind you how great the rewards will be if Turkey – to whom the islands once belonged – can at last be brought into the war.'

The Chief of the Imperial General Staff reluctantly opened the file in front of him. As always, the brief given to him was meticulous in its detail and range. It covered every possibility, every Churchillian vagary.

'There is, Prime Minister. It is a unit called the Special Boat Squadron.'

There was a satisfied grunt. 'Good!' At last, the Prime Minister felt he was getting somewhere.

'It will need to be Special.' His joke fell flat. 'Who commands this body of men?'

The Chief of the Imperial General Staff glanced

again at his brief. 'An ex-SAS officer, Prime Minister. Named Jarrett.'

Another grunt of satisfaction. As an ex-First Lord of the Admiralty during the First World War as well as the Second, the Prime Minister knew the man's father well. The provenance of a good fighting man was as important as it was for a painting.

'And how do we transport Jarrett and his men?'

The bulldog face now fixed itself on the First Sea Lord, who pressed the tips of his fingers together and pursed his lips. He did not need to open the briefing file in front of him: he knew every word. Nevertheless, he hesitated. Should he argue, or should he not? His duty got the better of his common sense.

'I must protest, Prime Minister. Alone, we simply do not have the resources. The reaction of the Italian garrisons will be unpredictable and they have airfields on Rhodes which the Germans may well seize. They also have others on Crete. Our nearest airfield is on Cyprus. Air and ground reinforcements are easily available to the Germans from Athens and Crete. Most importantly, without air supremacy what naval forces we have will be in jeopardy.'

The other two Chiefs of Staff murmured their agreement. Regrettable as it was, without American support nothing could be done.

Churchill ignored them, and barked: 'What naval forces would be available?'

The First Sea Lord resigned himself. He had done his best. 'Currently perhaps half a dozen destroyers, nothing more.'

'But these could be reinforced when the opportunity arose?'

'Naturally, Prime Minister. But . . .'

'And there are coastal forces?'

The First Sea Lord nodded. In this mood he knew there was nothing that would stop Churchill. *He* certainly couldn't.

'Anything else?'

It was like squeezing blood from a stone, but the First Sea Lord said reluctantly: 'The Flag Officer Levant and Eastern Mediterranean informs me that in pursuance of your policy for capturing the Dodecanese – and in particular Rhodes – he has already formed a small naval raiding force. It is similar to one which has been mounting clandestine operations into these islands for some months and is therefore familiar with the area.'

'Its name?'

'It's called the Levant Schooner Flotilla, Prime Minister.'

'And this could transport special troops to the islands at short notice?'

The Admiral's sigh was audible. 'Yes, Prime Minister.'

The cherubic face beamed. 'There we are, then, gentlemen. Accolade can proceed. Another problem solved.'

And a larger one created.

1

The only sound was the slight slap of water on the canvas sides of the cockle as it slid up the dark tunnel of river. The paddles dipped silently. They left – for a second or two – small phosphorescent pools that glittered in the blackness, tell-tale signs for any alert German sentry.

It was like being moved inexorably into a cone of perpetual and impenetrable night. It pressed in on either side, squeezing the cockle forwards into a cul-de-sac, a trap from where it would be impossible to turn back, to even move.

He could feel the tingling sweat on his forehead, and beads of it ran from under his arms down his side. It was not the sweat of exertion but of fear, of knowing what would happen, of knowing there was nothing he could do about it.

Then, on cue, it did. The searchlight, the screaming siren, the shouts of '*Hände hoch! Hände hoch!*' and the high, frantic chatter of a machine-gun. Splinters flew up from the plywood deck of the cockle and he felt one pierce his cheek. Bullets struck the blade of his paddle and spun it out of his hand.

The cockle tilted and as it did so he saw fleetingly, but with awful clarity in the blinding light of the searchlight Matt's blackened face as the force of the bullets twisted his body round towards him: the dead eyes, the open mouth with its shattered teeth, the two small black holes in the forehead already seeping blood.

Then he was in the water under the cockle, and the water and the cockle and the darkness bore down hard on his chest with suffocating force. He thrashed out with his arms, but he seemed paralysed, already dead.

It was cold. Icy cold.

Sergeant Colin 'Tiger' Tiller, Royal Marines, woke, as he always did from this recurring nightmare, to find himself on the floor. He was bathed in sweat. He lay there for a moment, as he always did, taking in the fact that he wasn't dead, that he was lying on a cold stone floor in Eastney Barracks, Portsmouth, very much alive.

But Matt's face was still there in his mind's eye. He cursed silently and wondered if the nightmare would ever stop haunting him, would ever lessen in intensity with time. How could the unconscious retain such details so vividly? He didn't know and the surgeon commander, the only person he had ever told about his recurring nightmare, hadn't known either. The mind, the surgeon commander had said kindly, was still largely an unknown area to medical science. Otherwise, he had said cheerfully, Tiller was in good shape considering the prolonged ordeal he had been through. The nightmare would fade with time, he had said reassuringly. But it hadn't.

Tiller got up from the floor, staggered to the wash-basin, and slopped cold water into his face. Dawn was breaking, but the early-morning light of a late-summer day was only just beginning to show behind the blacked-out barracks window. Tiller shivered and threw a blanket over his bare shoulders, and sat on the bed. Another hour to go before reveille, but he wasn't about to go to sleep again.

He lit a cigarette and inhaled deeply. Slowly the intensity of the dream faded. He wondered if the inner trembling he felt showed outwardly. He held his hands out in front of him and was relieved to see they were as steady as a rock. He showered and dressed, had another cigarette, and walked over to the sergeants' mess for breakfast.

A squad of new recruits was already on the parade ground in front of the officers' mess. They looked a right shower, but he knew that within days they would be marching as one man, and within weeks efficient, self-contained, fighting units. The Corps, as the Royal Marines was called by everyone in it, did that to you. Tiller didn't know quite how it did it, but it did. Perhaps it was a mixture of fostering a man's pride in himself before taking him to what he thought was the limit of his endurance, and then deliberately pushing him beyond it. Whatever it was it worked.

In the sergeants' mess the buff envelope he had been expecting was waiting in his pigeon-hole. He tore it open and read through it as he sipped his tea.

'Movement order?' his mate, Ken 'Curly' Watson, asked.

Tiller nodded. He had been expecting it for days, ever since his CO, Major Henry 'Blondie' Tasler, had called him into his office and had said that Combined Operations had asked for a volunteer from the unit for special duties in the Middle East. The ideal candidate would be a senior NCO, a canoeist with operational experience who was trained in the latest explosives techniques.

'You seem to fit the bill, Tiger,' Major Tasler had said to Tiller. 'That is, if you can tear yourself away from the delights of Pompey,' and he had treated the sergeant to that wry smile of his.

The difference in rank between a major and a sergeant is large at the best of times. In the Marines it was a yawning chasm, but that did not stop the two having a healthy respect for one another based on knowing each other's strengths and weaknesses, and on appreciating the former while making allowances for the latter. They had fought together in that shambles of a campaign in Norway in 1940, where they had come to rely on each another totally, and had taken part together in the raid up the Gironde. So when the Royal Marines Office at the Admiralty had announced that volunteers were wanted for hazardous service, and that men were wanted who were 'eager to engage the enemy' and were 'free of strong family ties', Tiller had guessed that Tasler had been mixed up in it somewhere.

But before Tiller had even had time to respond to the call Tasler had approached him about volunteering. Right up his street, Tasler had assured him, though he couldn't tell him what it was about, of course. Because they knew each other so well Tiller also knew exactly to what – or rather to whom – the major was referring when he had asked his question about Tiller being able to drag himself away. He had been 'free of strong family ties' when he had first joined Tasler's unit, and had been determined to remain so. But somehow, he wasn't sure how, it had become increasingly difficult to stay that way . . .

Nothing, of course, had actually been said. But Tasler had not looked surprised when Tiller had replied immediately that he would go. Nor could the major keep his face entirely straight when Tiller had added fervently: 'Thank you, sir.'

But Tiller now read the movement order again with mixed feelings. Even in wartime, Pompey wasn't a bad place to be and being part of Tasler's secret organization made life more than usually interesting. Besides it was his home town, where he had grown up.

However, the hard fact was that, apart from the raid up the Gironde – the scene of Tiger's persistent nightmare – he had not seen any action since joining Tasler's organization, which had been formed to find different methods of raiding enemy shipping in harbour. There had been no more operations, just constant rumours of them. So the truth was – and he and Tasler both knew it – that, his little local personal difficulties apart, Tiller had been bored out of his frigging mind for some months and had been only too glad to volunteer. It was, after all, pointless knowing everything there was to know about explosives unless you could put that knowledge to good use.

But Athlit in Palestine? And this so-called Special Boat Squadron? What the hell was that? He shrugged. They were flying him out, so it must be operational, must be urgent. He felt a tremor of excitement run through him as he passed the movement order to Curly.

Curly and he had grown up together as kids, had both sat at the feet of Tiger's grandad, who told them tales of the action he had seen with the Marines in Burma and west Africa, and then in the Boer War. Curly knew all about the various special forces units that were fighting their own individual campaigns in the Middle East and the Mediterranean because, for a short while, he had served with the Special Boat Service under its founder, Major Roger Courtney.

'Is this the same outfit?' Tiller asked.

Curly scratched his head and said: 'Don't think so, as a lot of them were wiped out in a raid on Rhodes. We seem to have been trying to lay our hands on that place for most of the war. The rest were absorbed into Colonel Stirling's unit after Major Courtney came back here to form a second section. That's why I left. I like water, not the fucking desert. Remember the old ditty your grandad used to sing to us, Tiger?

> When years ago I listed, lads,
> To serve our gracious Queen,
> The Sergeant made me understand
> I was a Royal Marine.
> He said they sometimes served on ships
> And sometimes served on shore,
> But never said I should wear spurs
> And be in the Camel Corps.'

They both laughed. Tiller's grandad had been quite a character. He liked to entertain visitors by strumming on his banjo and singing various ditties he had picked up. It had been Tiller's grandad who had encouraged them both to join the Corps. Their dads had been pleased enough. But they hadn't shown it, of course – just said: 'You could do worse.'

As the great depression of the 1930s was then at its height – the Jarrow hunger march was splashed across all the newspapers – both young men knew they could have done a lot worse. It was Tiller's grandad who had sneaked them both into the pub to celebrate, though the landlord must have known neither of them was yet eighteen, and, to the embarrassment of the two young men, had entertained the saloon bar with a rendition of a poem by Rudyard Kipling.

'Do you remember when he took us to the local?' Tiller said to Curly. 'Thought I'd sink through the bleeding floor.'

'Two pints of beer, mate, and you were almost stretched out on it,' Curly replied with a chuckle. 'But he was that proud of you, Tiger, and of the Corps. What was that ditty he stood up and quoted about the Corps?'

Tiller knew it by heart, of course, for his grandfather had made him learn it all.

> ''E isn't one o' the reg'lar Line, nor 'e isn't one of the crew.
> 'E's a kind of giddy Harumfrodite – soldier an' sailor, too!
> For there isn't a job on the top o' the earth the beggar don't know,
> For you can leave 'im at night on a bald man's 'ead to paddle 'is own canoe –
> 'E's a sort of bloomin' cosmopolouse – soldier an' sailor, too.'

'That's the one.' Curly laughed and then indicated the movement order. 'Well, looks like you'll be paddling *your* own canoe again before long, mate.'

Tiller nodded but his mind was still back with his grandad and the time when he had been a raw recruit. His first months in the Corps all seemed a long time ago now, but he remembered how its rituals, its history, its traditions, had swallowed him whole. He had slept, eaten, and drunk it, and had loved every waking moment of it. A King's Badge man – first in his passing-out squad – and a crack shot who had represented the Corps at Bisley, he was, from the start, marked out for promotion.

In any other regiment – and that included those poofters in the Guards – he'd be a sergeant-major by now. But the wheels of the Corps ground slowly. NCOs, the corporals and sergeants, and colour-sergeants, were the backbone of the Corps and the Corps knew it. However good a man was, however thorough his training – and by Christ it was thorough – he still needed time to mature to become the kind of leader the Corps required – no, demanded.

Yes, the wheels ground slowly. And they ground very small. Tiller had never forgotten, as a small boy, the sight of his father on the parade ground, the scarlet sash of a colour-sergeant across his chest, the glitter of his medals and his buttons and his cap badge, the precision with which he had moved, the band thumping out the regimental march of the Corps, 'A Life on the Ocean Wave'.

Tiller knew he was as steeped in the traditions of the Royal Marines as a pickled onion was in vinegar, with their centuries-old connection with the Royal Navy. *Per Mare per Terram* was their motto, 'By land, by sea', and they were, as every recruit had drummed into him, the country's sheet anchor. That was how some admiring monarch – Tiller had forgotten which one – had described them, and they had battle honours that went back to the capture of Gibraltar in 1704.

Some of the young wartime conscripts – the HOs

or 'Hostilities Only' – had thought tradition and discipline, and the spit and polish that went with it, was all so much crap. But Tiller knew better. In battle a man had to rely on others and that reliance came from the parade ground.

'I must say I'd like to know more about this frigging outfit I've volunteered for,' Tiller said, his mind snapping back to the present.

'Can't help you there, Tiger. But I was told by my brother, who was in Cairo earlier this year, that Colonel Stirling's unit – the Special Air Service, it's called, or something like that – was split up after the colonel was captured. Perhaps it's an offshoot of that mob.'

Tiller had vaguely heard of Stirling and his recently formed Special Air Service. The SAS's desert exploits sounded like *Boys' Own Paper* stuff to him – not the kind of fighting the Corps went in for. The Marines had a long tradition of amphibious raiding and a Royal Marine Commando had already been formed, and had taken part in the Dieppe raid the previous year. But a few men dashing around the desert in jeeps fitted neither of these categories and Tiller looked sceptically on anything the Corps wasn't involved in as probably not worth pursuing.

Which was why he had been – he had to admit it now – very doubtful at first about Tasler's organization and schemes, though anything the major normally said or did was all right with Tiller. Indeed he would have followed that resourceful Royal Marines officer to the end of the earth if necessary. Still, he remembered thinking at the time that if the Chief of Combined Operations, Vice-Admiral Lord Louis Mountbatten, had backed Tasler's ideas, then who was he, a mere sergeant, to have his doubts?

'Sally'll take it hard, you know.'

Tiller nodded. 'I know.'

Curly grinned. 'I'll look after her.'

'I bet you bloody will, you randy sod,' said Tiller, who knew Curly to be happily married with two kids and a third on the way. Now that was the perfect example of what was meant by having 'strong family ties' and Tiller was having none of it.

He got up, folded the movement order, and put it in his pocket. 'I'd better get my kit ready and say my farewells to the lads. I'm being picked up first thing tomorrow morning.'

'Rather you than me,' Curly said, but Tiller could detect the envy in his voice.

'Yeah, I suppose so,' he said. 'So long.'

He extended his hand. Curly shook it and said: 'Don't do anything I wouldn't do. The brothels there are notorious for some interesting strains of clap.'

Tiller walked out to the barracks and turned left along the coast road to Southsea. The rest of the mob had local billets since they had the same status as commandos. But Tiller had preferred to sleep at the barracks at Eastney, where he could keep his nightmare to himself.

The unit's training headquarters were two Nissen huts on the sea front. One was used as a lecture room, the other for stores. They were situated right under one of the forts which had been built in Napoleonic times to guard the Solent. Called, for some reason Tiller had never discovered, Lumps Fort, it lay at one end of the six-mile boom which had been erected to protect Portsmouth harbour from torpedo attacks by submarines or from surface attack by small craft. Two other forts had been built in the Solent at around the same time as Lumps. They, too, were now part of Portsmouth's defences, for the boom, which stretched to Seaview on the Isle of Wight, was not only joined to them but they were bristling with anti-aircraft guns.

Behind the Nissen huts was Southsea Corporation's Canoe Lake, which in peacetime had attracted the many day trippers and holidaymakers who came to the seaside resort during the summer months. Tiller remembered splashing around in it as a small kid. Now it was deserted and drained, with only a puddle of rainwater in its middle. One of the concrete sides, Tiller noticed, was badly cracked, perhaps caused by a bomb a 'tip-and-run' German aircraft had dropped nearby a couple of months back.

Tiller skirted it and made for Dolphin Court, a block of flats which overlooked the lake and the Solent. The block had been taken over by the Admiralty. Flat 24 had originally housed the Development Centre of Combined Operations. But the Centre had been absorbed into the Combined Operations Experimental Establishment and its staff relocated to north Devon or somewhere, and Tasler, who had been an early member of the Centre, had requisitioned the flat for his unit.

Tiller showed his pass to the naval sentry and, ignoring the lift, climbed the stairs three at a time. It was all part of the fitness regime Tasler had imposed and which was second nature to Tiller now.

The door of the flat was open but Tiller knocked before entering. A pretty Wren petty officer, the unit's clerk, looked up from her typewriter. 'He's waiting for you, Sergeant.'

'Thank you, Maggie, and how are you this sunny morning?'

'Just fine,' the young woman said, and, fluttering her long eyelashes in mock coquetry, added: 'As if you cared.'

Tiller leant on her desk and looked deep into her amazingly blue eyes. 'Oh, but I do, Maggie, I do.'

But the Wren's pretty face was deliberately expressionless now. She simply nodded towards the inner office. 'You're lucky. He's in a good mood. So you'd better go in before the wind changes.'

Tiller pursed his lips and blew her a kiss. Maggie was a good sort who knew never to take anyone, or anything, too seriously. He turned and strode towards Tasler's inner sanctum while the Wren studied Tiller's straight back and broad shoulders, and renewed her resolve. Men like Tiger, her instincts told her, made wonderful lovers but they were not husband material. And she knew, with more than a twinge of regret, that much as she desired the former her nature and upbringing dictated she acquire a reasonable specimen of the latter.

The door had on it a neat sign reading 'Major H.G. Tasler DSO OBE RM, Commanding Officer, Royal Marines Boom Patrol Detachment'.

'Come,' Tasler called out in response to Tiller's knock. Tiller closed the door behind him, stiffened to attention, and saluted. Even after all these years he still counted to himself 'up, one, two, three, down' as his hand, palm outwards, came up to his beret before snapping down to his side.

Tasler sat at his desk surrounded by trays of paper.

He was a man in his late twenties with red-gold hair, most of which he had lost, and a flowing moustache. He was studying a plan of a small craft which he thrust towards Tiller. 'Morning, Tiger. Beautiful day. What do you think of this?' He handed Tiller the plan. 'We're calling it the Sleeping Beauty.'

'The motor submersible canoe,' Tiller read aloud. 'So here it is at last, sir.'

'The first is just about to be delivered for trials,' said Tasler. 'I'm sorry you won't be here to try it out. I assume your movement order has arrived?'

'Yes, sir. This morning.'

Tasler snorted. 'About time, too. We'd better start the rigmarole for signing you off the unit's strength. But before you go I want to show you something else. Maggie!'

The Wren appeared at the door.

'Sergeant Tiller's leaving us, Maggie, so get the necessary bumf ready for me, will you. I won't be long.'

The Wren's blue eyes rested on Tiller for a moment, but the twinge of regret she felt again did not show in them for an instant.

'The best of luck, Sergeant,' she said. She didn't ask where he was going. No one in the unit was ever asked that.

'Thanks, Maggie,' Tiller said. 'Perhaps you'll stop refusing to come out with me when I come back a hero.'

'I doubt it, Sergeant. I very much doubt it.'

The two men doubled down the stairs and out into the summer sunshine.

'I think that girl's saving herself for her knight in shining armour, sir,' Tiller said.

'I think it's just,' Tasler replied with a grin, 'that at a very young age her mother must have warned her about men like you.'

Half the unit's complement of thirty-four men were attending a navigation lecture in one of the Nissen huts. The other half were training on the beach. The boat-house, where the cockles were kept, was on the road along the sea front. Beyond the road was a sea defence wall with a drop of five feet to the beach. It was another of Tasler's rules that although there were steps down to the beach these were never to be used. Whatever a man was carrying he had to go via the wall not the steps.

As they approached the boat-house Tiller could see that an instructor was supervising a race between three teams of two men each to get their cockle from the boat-house, across the road, down the wall, across the beach and into the sea. The teams then had to paddle round a buoy some three hundred yards from the beach, return, run up the beach with the cockle, heave it over the wall and across the road, and set it back on its cradle in the boat-house. Another three teams were practising how to push their cockles down the beach with their paddles and then into the water, the most effective way, it had been found, of launching a cockle with its crew in rough seas. Others were doing their daily feet-hardening exercises, which entailed running up and down the pebble beach in bare feet or jumping on to the pebbles from the wall. One whole section of ten men would be aboard *Celtic*, an old Thames barge moored in Chichester harbour. Sections were rotated a week at a time to practise, among other routines, shallow-water diving in the DSEA Sladen diving suit and, the most unpopular exercise of all, crawling across the mud-flats at low tide.

But the most effective exercise Tasler had developed was for his canoeists to sneak up on, and board, the official boom patrol boats before their crews were aware what was happening. It was like a game of grandmother's footsteps at sea and some of the canoeists had become very good at it. Favourite targets were the patrol boats which were dispatched to keep the Solent clear while the anti-aircraft batteries on shore and on the forts practised shooting. These patrol boats were sometimes manned by Wrens and in the summer, when they thought they were safe from prying eyes, they were often tempted to strip to their undies and sunbathe.

Tiller had met Sally that way. She had been lying on her back on the deck when he had silently levered himself aboard. She had been modestly attired in nothing more than a small towel draped across her middle. Her scream must have been heard in Southampton.

Tiller smiled to himself now when he remembered the heated conversation that had followed. Perhaps it was the manner of their first meeting that had persuaded her to try and make an honest man of him.

Yes, it was time to move on.

'They all look ready for action, sir,' said Tiller.

A shadow passed over Tasler's face. 'So am I, Tiger, so am I. But whatever plans we put up, there seems to be a good reason for not going ahead with them. As you know, we were going to have a crack at going up the Gironde again, but in the end the good and the great decided against it. I certainly wouldn't let you be leaving us if there had been any chance of us being able to have another go. That is, presuming you would have wanted to have another try?'

Tasler looked at Tiller enquiringly.

'I'm sure I would have, sir,' Tiller replied. Like falling off a horse, he knew the best possible way of combating fear was to remount as quickly as possible. Now he would have to find another way of eradicating his nightmare.

'Well, "if ifs and ands were pots and pans",' Tasler quoted cheerfully. 'It didn't happen so we must get on and hope something else crops up.'

As they walked back past the two Nissen huts the major said: 'This is what I wanted to show you.'

They entered the store hut and walked to the back of it. Tasler threw back a canvas cover and displayed the captured Italian explosive motor boat.

'The Eyeties officially call them *Motoscafi di Turismo modifacti*, or MTMs,' said Tasler, 'though the pilot who we captured said they were generally known as *barchini esplosivi* or *barchini* for short.'

Tiller whistled. 'So that's what it looks like. It's bigger than I had imagined.'

'Eighteen feet. Vosper's have finished with it as ours is now well developed, so I am sending it to *Celtic* for the lads to practise on.'

So this, Tiller thought, was what the unit's secret weapon was being modelled on; the weapon which had always been referred to as a boom patrol boat to cover up its real identity. It had been the hub of Tasler's activities, the original reason for the formation of his unit. Yet no one had yet had a chance to see even the Italian version of it.

'It looks fast, sir.'

'It's powered by an Alfa Romeo engine which can crank out 120hp. Vosper's got over thirty-five knots out of it.'

Tiller studied the craft intently, astonished by its compactness and the audacity of those who had operated it. He touched a hinged rectangle of wood attached to the boat's counter right behind where the driver sat, and looked quizzically at Tasler.

'That's the flutterboard,' said Tasler. 'It's attached by a line to the driver's wrist. When he wants to bale out he pulls this lever here and the flutterboard drops into the water. The driver can climb on to it to escape the concussion of the explosion when the boat hits its target. It can also be used as a surfboard.'

'Ingenious.'

'Very. The Italians aren't half as daft as some people make out.'

'And this is the detonating device?' Tiller pointed to the bumper-car rim around the bows of the boat.

'That's it. This one had 500lb of TNT in its bows. It was meant to be detonated by a hydrostatic fuse, but something went wrong with it and it ran up on to the beach with the driver. Suda Bay in Crete that was, in April '41. But others managed to cripple a tanker and damage the cruiser *York*. Gave everyone a nasty shock, I can tell you.'

'Is that how we're going to use them?'

Tasler shook his head. 'We're going to drop them by parachute near their targets, complete with driver.'

Tiller whistled quietly again. So that was why they had all been put through a parachute course earlier that year.

The two men walked out into the sunshine and back

to Dolphin Court, where Tasler shook Tiller's hand. 'Good luck.'

'I reckon I'm leaving just when things are beginning to happen, sir.'

'Let's hope so,' Tasler replied, but he sounded doubtful. 'Anyway, I look upon you as the unit's standard-bearer in the eastern Mediterranean. Not enough of the high-ups know what we're about or what we're capable of. Show 'em what we can do, Tiger. I'm relying on you.'

2

The roar of the Halifax bomber's engines made it impossible to hear anything, and the fuselage vibrated and bucked. The dispatchman touched the shoulder of the young army officer sitting nonchalantly on the bench reading a book. For the first time the dispatchman noticed the officer's sand-coloured beret with its unusual winged badge. He had no idea what it signified, and it was now too late to find out. Anyway, on this type of mission it was better not to ask too many questions.

The officer looked up and the dispatchman gestured to the officer's beret and then to the pudding-basin-shaped paratroop helmet lying next to him. The officer nodded and smiled, and reached for the helmet. He took off his beret and tucked it under the epaulette of his left shoulder, which had a single crown stitched to it.

Christ, thought the dispatchman, if majors are *that* young nowadays the British Army must have suffered heavy losses among its officers. Or perhaps, he corrected himself, this chap's just brilliant. He looked the studious type. The dispatchman glanced at the dog-eared service-issue paperback the major was reading, its cheap paper already greying and frayed. *The Aeneid*, it was called. The title meant nothing to the dispatchman.

He held up five fingers.

The major buckled the chin strap of the parachute helmet, and nodded.

Five minutes, the dispatchman mouthed, just to make sure.

The major nodded again, moved his beret from his shoulder to a pocket of his battledress trousers and buttoned it up. Then he leant across to the two figures lying on the floor of the Halifax, and shook each in turn.

One was the major's wireless operator, a sergeant, the other his Italian interpreter, an elderly English captain. Both buckled on their gear and donned their helmets. The sergeant put his helmet on with practised ease, but the captain initially put his on back to front. The major grinned at him encouragingly. The captain smiled grimly and allowed the major to adjust his chin strap.

'It's easy!' the major shouted above the roar of the engines, but the captain shook his head, not in disagreement but because he couldn't hear.

The dispatchman was back now. He held up two fingers and indicated that they should attach their static lines to the wire running along the bomber's roof.

Parachutists dropped from Halifax bombers usually had to exit from a hole in the fuselage floor. But this one, part of a Special Duties squadron based in the Middle East, had been specially converted by having a door cut into its side. But it did not run to such refinements as red and green lights to indicate when the parachutist had to jump.

The dispatchman opened the door and it swung inwards and clipped itself open. The rush of night air and the increased noise made all three men gasp and lower their heads.

Below them the major could see flickers of light and it took him a few moments to realize they were being fired on from the ground.

The dispatchman had decided the wireless operator should jump first, then the elderly captain, and finally the major. That way the captain would be able to see the sergeant jumping and his parachute opening. This would encourage him to follow. If it didn't, then the captain knew he had the major behind him, which should be encouragement enough to jump. In parachuting, pride usually conquered fear.

Thirty seconds, the dispatchman mouthed, and the wireless operator, his set strapped to his back, took his position by the door, gripping each side of the opening. The dispatchman banged the operator's shoulder and the operator was gone, and seconds later the captain saw the operator's parachute bloom. It did nothing to alleviate the dryness of his mouth or the thought that he must have been stark raving mad to volunteer for such a mission.

He gripped the sides of the door as he had seen the operator do. He had seen the signal the operator had been given to jump, and expected the same slap on the shoulder. But the dispatchman knew his job and wasn't taking any risks. With just the right amount of force he ejected the captain by pushing him between the shoulders and watched until his parachute opened. Poor bugger, he thought, he was much too old to be jumping.

The dispatchman saw the young major watching him with a grin on his face. The dispatchman grinned back and gestured him forward, waited the obligatory amount of time, then raised his hand.

But the major was gone. Even above the roar of the engines and the rush of air the dispatchman was sure he heard the major whoop with joy as he jumped. Well, it took all sorts. He unclipped the door and swung it closed.

'Chums away, sir,' he told the pilot through the intercom. The crew of aircraft on Special Operations always called their human cargo 'chums'.

Without replying, the pilot put the Halifax into a steep, climbing turn. Whoever was firing at him must be pissed as a newt, but he wasn't taking any chances.

The major had indeed whooped, but with relief not joy. The spread wings on his battledress showed that he had passed the parachute course, but he never much liked the sensation of jumping into space. But doing so from an aircraft was infinitely easier than from a balloon, which was what the first training jump was usually from. That was gut-wrenching. And once the parachute was open after jumping from an aircraft there was that blissful, transient feeling of being suspended in time as well as space.

The major looked down and saw that the sporadic flashes, now accompanied by a high-pitched crackle, were still coming from the ground. At first they seemed to be firing at the diminishing sound of the Halifax grinding its way back to Cyprus and he thought what silly sods they were wasting their ammunition like that. Then he realized they were firing at him too, and the tracer bullets were arching into the sky either side of him. He searched for any sign of the ground and as he did so remembered how he had last visited Rhodes. It had been by boat from Brindisi. He'd been an archaeology student then. It was only five years ago but it seemed a lifetime away. Perhaps the Italian professor of archaeology who had so courteously taken him under his wing on Rhodes was now in charge of those taking a pot-shot at him as he swung helplessly above them.

He suddenly saw the ground appear out of the dark. It seemed to be coming up towards him at an alarming rate. It always did. He flexed his legs. There was no time to pick a landing place. It looked horribly rocky. The shock of landing jarred right through him, even though he rolled as he had been taught. A rock hit him under the ribs and knocked the wind out of him. A gust caught his parachute and pulled him like an express train through some gorse. He struggled to release it and just managed to do so before it threatened to throw him against a rocky outcrop. The parachute collapsed and the major staggered to his feet and began winding it rapidly towards him. It was only then that he realized that it was blowing half a gale. The met people had got it wrong. Again. There was little chance they had landed in the right place in such a wind.

The major finished winding in the parachute, took off his helmet, put the helmet into the parachute and pushed the bundle out of sight under a gorse bush. He put on his beret and then checked his equipment: water bottle, commando knife, silenced Sten gun with extra 9mm ammunition, pistol, rucksack with rations, night binoculars, and lastly the letter. Nothing missing.

A gust of wind brought with it the staccato sound of semi-automatic weapons. What the hell were they firing at now? He tried to identify the sound: German Schmeisser or Italian Breda, but it was too indistinct and sporadic to be certain. The major decided they – whoever they were – must be firing at his two companions. But it was also possible, perhaps more likely, that they were firing at each other. He had been warned that the Germans and Italians might clash when the surrender of Italy became known.

He began making his way cautiously towards the sound of the battle. The ground was very broken and steep. Twice he stumbled and fell. After ten minutes or so he came to a crest. He flung himself down and crawled cautiously up to it so that he was not silhouetted against the night sky. Now he could see tracer flying in all directions and a flare spluttered upwards, burst, and lit the ground with an eerie light before extinguishing itself. Someone seemed to be putting up a hell of a fight. He started to shift forward when his ankle was gripped in a vice. His hand went for his knife but then relaxed when a voice hissed urgently: 'Major Jarrett, sir. It's me. Kesterton.'

'What the hell's going on?' Jarrett whispered to his wireless operator. Whoever was firing was obviously not doing so at Kesterton. 'Are they firing at Dolby?'

'I don't know, sir. If they're Eyeties they're probably firing at one another. Regular Guy Fawkes night, it is.'

As the major's eyes became accustomed to scanning the area he could see figures moving. They seemed to be approaching the ridge where the two men were lying. Jarrett knew there were only about 10,000 Germans on Rhodes while the Italians had a garrison of 35,000. Perhaps the Italians had decided to make a pre-emptive strike at their former allies.

He trained his binoculars on the moving figures but they were still too far away. He passed them to Kesterton. 'Krauts?'

Kesterton peered through the glasses. 'I don't know, sir,' he said doubtfully. 'Could be. It's mostly rifle fire now, though they were firing something much heavier earlier on.'

It mattered to Jarrett who it was. It mattered a lot. He fingered the letter in his pocket. It was addressed to Admiral Campioni, the Italian governor of the Dodecanese, who was based on Rhodes, and was signed by General Maitland Wilson, Commander-in-Chief Middle East. It was couched in diplomatic terms and expressed the wish of the British for the Italian garrison to co-operate with incoming British forces. It flattered Admiral Campioni no end. It was not the kind of document Jarrett would like the Germans to find on him, especially if there happened to be any Gestapo on the island. The Gestapo shot parachutists out of hand and probably had a more lingering and painful death in store for those who were trying to suborn the Führer's former allies.

But what really mattered was that, once the Germans got a whiff of what the British were planning to do, they could decide to take over the islands themselves, and Jarrett's orders were precisely to prevent that happening. Campioni would have to do without his letter. He explained the situation briefly to Kesterton and could hear the surprise in the operator's voice.

'You're going to eat it, sir?'

'Well, I can't burn it, can I?' Jarrett said irritably. 'And there's nowhere to hide it.'

But it was the Italians who found them an hour later. By then Jarrett had laboriously swallowed the letter and was badly in need of the Chianti bottle that an unshaven but friendly *carabinieri* corporal offered him.

Admiral Campioni surveyed his visitors cautiously. If they were who they said they were things might be looking up. The one now lying on a stretcher with a broken leg spoke good Italian and certainly knew more about the surrender of Italy than he did. Campioni had only been told about the armistice the previous day – by the wife of a German officer who had just happened to be passing by – and this information had been followed by an agreement with the commander of Sturmdivision Rhodos, General Klemann, that both commanders would not move their troops.

The agreement had suited Campioni as he had no transport. But the Germans had then promptly broken it by sending patrols to take over the three Italian airfields at Marizza, Calato and Cattavia. It was, Campioni thought gloomily, typical of how his country – of which he was inordinately fond – had fought and lost the war. No proper communications, treacherous allies, and a lot of promises, all broken.

He wiped his heavily gold-braided sleeve across his brow and began reading the teleprinter message his aide had brought. It came from Cairo and was in Italian, and confirmed the names and ranks of the three Englishmen, and the purpose of their visit. Campioni smiled. Major the Earl Jarrett. If the

British were prepared to risk an English milord – and one whose father Campioni had much admired – on such a mission then they must be serious. Things were definitely looking up.

'Of course,' Campioni said to Dolby. 'If we were to be supported by a British armoured division and if an airborne brigade were to be dropped within, say, the next twenty-four hours on the airfields then we would be in a position to go on the offensive against the Germans.'

Campioni's staff officers clustered around him and nodded their agreement. Jarrett looked quizzically at Dolby. 'Well?'

'He wants the whole damned 8th Army air-dropped here this evening,' the interpreter said wearily. 'And I daresay he's going to want Monty in command of it. Under him, of course.'

Despite the morphine injection the Italian doctor had given him, Dolby's leg hurt abominably. But he felt the shock he was suffering was more from being within an ace of being shot by the *carabiniere* who had found him. Only some quick talking had saved him.

'You're joking,' said Jarrett.

'Am I? You had better believe it, George,' Dolby said, then turned to Campioni. 'You have many more troops than the Germans. Are such strong reinforcements necessary?'

Dolby hoped he was implying that the reinforcements were all lined up, ready to go if Campioni really needed them. So far as he knew there was half a battalion of the Buffs on Cyprus, and most of them were on leave.

'Oh, but certainly. And we would also, of course, need strong logistical support and good air cover.

Then we have a famous victory. We would wipe those damned Germans right off the island.'

The Admiral's staff looked as if they were about to applaud his brave speech.

'He does want the 8th Army,' Dolby told Jarrett. '*And* he wants the bloody Desert Air Force as well.'

'To avoid the – ah, unfortunate – reception you received this morning,' Campioni said to Dolby. 'I would like to inform our batteries as to when and where these reinforcements are arriving. Will it be at dawn or afterwards?'

'What's more, he seems to think they're already on their way.'

Jarrett's face was a mask. 'What can we tell him?' he asked Dolby.

A spasm of pain crossed the interpreter's face. 'How many men do we have available, George?' he asked curiously.

'About fifty,' said Jarrett.

'Well, I won't tell him that,' said Dolby firmly. 'I'll let him down as gently as possible.'

Jarrett did not try to follow the rapid flow of Italian that passed between the two men but the result was obvious. Campioni's expression changed from amiability to irritation to petulance. Watching the Italian admiral reminded Jarrett of the story that had lately been circulating in Cairo. When Stalin was told by Churchill during a conference in Moscow that the Pope would not approve of some action the Allies were about to embark upon the great leader of the Soviet people had leant forward and asked: 'And how many divisions does the Pope have?'

Jarrett did not have any divisions either – just a wireless operator, an elderly captain with a broken leg, and a lot of promises. His knew his advance party of fifty men would have already left their base and would at this moment be landing on Castelrosso, a small Italian-held island between Cyprus and Rhodes which was to be their base for operations in the rest of the Dodecanese. An infantry battalion on Malta was being readied to follow but that could not arrive for another six days.

'Remind him that his king has ordered all Italian commanders to defend Italian land.'

Dolby did so but it did not go down well. Campioni simply shrugged and spread his hands open; his staff looked glum. In his mind Jarrett dwelt fleetingly, and adversely, on the fighting qualities of Italian troops generally and of Italian admirals in particular.

Beads of sweat glinted on Campioni's forehead. His fingers picked at the resplendent gold braid on his sleeve. An awkward silence descended which was broken only by yet another member of the Admiral's staff who entered the room and whispered in his ear. Campioni produced a handkerchief so seeped in eau-de-Cologne that Jarrett caught a whiff of it ten feet away. He dabbed his forehead and spoke imploringly to Dolby. It was a long, involved explanation.

'He says General Klemann wants to confer with him,' Dolby explained when the tirade had ceased. 'As soon as possible. We have to go. He'll fly me out in a seaplane immediately, while it's still dark. He'll arrange for you and Kesterton to be taken off by torpedo boat this evening. In the meantime you must put on civilian clothes and keep out of the way while this is being arranged. Under no circumstances must the Germans know we've been here.'

Dolby waited for Jarrett to absorb this information, before adding needlessly: 'He's running scared.'

3

'We don't stand on ceremony in the SBS,' said Captain Magnus Larssen of L Detachment, SBS. 'The chaps just call me skipper.'

Tiller studied Larssen discreetly. He was fresh-faced, fair-haired and looked appallingly young. But Tiller discerned there was something razor-sharp about him, too. Touch him and you'd cut your finger.

Tiller's salute snapped up and down. He registered Larssen's Scandinavian accent, the absence of any badges of rank on his blue shirt, the fact that his feet, clad in disgracefully dirty desert boots, were propped on the ramshackle table which he presumably used as his desk.

'Yes*sir*,' Tiller replied loudly. Marines didn't call officers by their nicknames. Especially scruffy army officers without pips on their shoulders, especially foreign-sounding officers, especially ones who had crossbows hanging on their walls. What was he, frigging William Tell or something?

Larssen's eyes, a piercing, very pale blue, caught Tiller's and bored into him. Tiller grinned lamely.

'Good,' said Larssen briskly, leaning forward to shake his hand. It was, Tiller couldn't help noticing, like shaking a piece of particularly tough leather and the grip was vice-like.

'So that's settled, then. Sit down, Sergeant. Let's have a gossip.'

Gossip? Tiller gingerly lowered his six-foot frame on to the edge of a rather rickety chair.

'So,' Larssen said softly. 'You are Sergeant Tiller. I call you Tiger, is that right?'

Tiller nodded. He stifled the 'yessir' that was on his tongue, but he couldn't bring himself to call this extraordinary individual 'skipper'. He had too many other unusual things to get used to.

Tiller took off his beret and wiped his face. The tiny island of Castelrosso seemed hotter than Hades, hotter even than Athlit had been, and the crumbling house that Larssen had requisitioned as headquarters for L Detachment was like an oven.

'I'm glad you catch up with us at last,' said Larssen. 'We were ordered to move quickly.'

Tiller had been travelling non-stop for five days. It felt like five years. At Athlit no one appeared to know where his detachment had vanished to, so they had sent him to the 'Killer School' for a refresher course while they tried to find out. The school was in the old police station in Jerusalem and was run by a major who wore two pearl-handled revolvers. Until he had shot the ace of diamonds out of a playing card at twenty paces with one of them Tiller had thought him a bit of a comedian.

When they still hadn't been able to find his detachment they had sent him to Haifa on an aircraft identification course – why he never knew – but before he had had time to savour the delights of the city he had been bundled on to a plane bound for Akrotiri airbase in Cyprus, so he hadn't even had time to collect all his new kit.

His one evening in Limassol had proved entertaining but abortive as, for some reason, the Turkish belly dancer had proved unresponsive to his approaches. Perhaps he was losing his touch. Then at dawn he had been flown to Castelrosso by a jovial RAF type in a captured Italian Cato floatplane which, with its load of ammunition and food supplies for the SBS, had seemed inordinately reluctant to become unstuck from the waters of Limassol harbour.

'Underpowered,' the RAF pilot had shouted cheerfully at him as they had bucked across the waves. 'Bloody useless, really. Like everything Italian. Still, it's better than warming a chair in some Cairo office.'

Tiller, who would not have minded being in Cairo at that particular moment, had shut his eyes. A fortune-teller Sally had taken him to had predicted he would have a watery grave, but he had never supposed his coffin would be a clapped-out Italian seaplane. He had never been more glad to step on to terra firma after the two-hour flight, even if it was a bare, hot, miserable rock like Castelrosso.

'You know anything about the SBS, Tiger?'

'Not much, sir. You were part of the SAS at one time?'

The forbidden sin had slipped out. Larssen scowled but let it pass. 'That's right. We were D Squadron SAS. In April, after Colonel Stirling was captured, we became SBS – Special Boat Squadron. Full establishment is three detachments each of seventy men and seven officers, but we are still recruiting. We're part of what is known as Raiding Forces, controlled operationally by GHQ, Cairo. A few of the men served with Courtney in the Special

Boat Service, but they've spent a couple of years attacking Kraut airfields in the desert, and have probably forgotten everything they learned. Anyway, techniques and equipment have changed. You will have to instruct Corporal Barnesworth, the man we have given you as your swimmer.'

'Here?' Tiller asked. He had already met Billy Barnesworth and had taken an immediate liking to the lugubrious, powerfully built guardsman.

'Yes, here. We are ready to move but the navy takes a little longer to get ready. We'll be here for a couple of days at least.'

A couple of days! He hoped Billy was a quick learner. To help him get the picture of how he might be used he asked what the SBS did exactly.

'We were formed for raiding operations in the eastern Mediterranean. Quick in-and-out affairs to harass the enemy. Blow up a few ammunition dumps, cut a few throats. What Mr Churchill calls a "butcher and bolt" policy. You get the idea?'

A jolt of excitement ran through Tiller. 'Sure,' he said.

'So we've been training in Palestine for the past few months to mount that sort of operation. But instead of jeeps taking us to our targets, as the Long Range Desert Group took the SAS, we have caiques of the Levant Schooner Flotilla doing the same job.'

Larssen pronounced the word 'kayik'. Tiller shifted uncomfortably in his seat. He felt he was getting out of his depth, but Larssen quickly came to the rescue. 'Caiques are the locally built sailing vessels for fishing and inter-island trade. They vary in size but the Flotilla's are mostly between ten and thirty tons. They're armed and have engines, but to the

Krauts and Eyeties they look Greek or Turkish. Very useful.'

'Useful?' Tiller queried.

'They just run up a Greek or Turkish flag. Then they are left alone. Very useful.'

And illegal, Tiller guessed.

'You look doubtful, Tiger?'

'Is that allowed?' Tiller asked uncomfortably. Tasler had made his men learn all about the Hague Convention, which laid down the rules of warfare, in the hope that if they were captured they could argue their case with their captors. A fat lot of good it had done Dick and Terry: the Germans had shot them out of hand.

Larssen's eyes opened wide and then he burst out laughing. 'No, of course it's not. The caiques also hide out along the Turkish mainland when necessary. That's illegal, too, as Turkey is neutral. Does that worry you?'

Tiller shook his head. It didn't worry him at all, but it confirmed his opinion that he had joined an unusual unit.

Larssen looked at the latest addition to his detachment with approval. He liked Tiller's open face, his determined jaw, his movements, deft for such a large man. He could be a very useful addition. But Larssen wondered if Tiller would fit into the Special Boat Squadron, whose unofficial motto 'Sink or swim' reflected not only the operational medium in which they were going to work but the individual nature of the way the unit operated. There was no one to tell an SBS man what to do. It was up to him. Individual initiative, it was called, and if he was unlucky, well, he sank alone.

Tiller, with his dark, short-cropped hair and immaculate uniform, looked to Larssen like one of the thin red line the British Army was so proud of. Brave, no doubt, and superbly trained to obey orders unquestioningly, but did he have the ability to act and think on his own? Larssen knew the task of the SBS wasn't going to be about charging the enemy trenches with bayonets fixed, of bravery over and above the course of duty in the face of the enemy. On the contrary the SBS had to make sure the enemy was facing the other way so that they could be outmanoeuvred, bypassed, or simply stabbed in the back. The SBS was all about silent infiltration of the enemy's position, not of storming it with banners flying, amid blood and guts.

How was he, Larssen, going to convey such a concept to this immaculately turned-out Marine who had obviously had centuries of tradition and discipline drummed into him?

'I'd remove all that shiny brass if I were you,' Larssen said in a friendly way. 'We don't have the spit and polish in this detachment.'

Tiller looked awkwardly down at the glistening globe and laurel badge in his blue beret, the gleaming brass of his belt, and the brilliant shine on his boots.

'At Athlit there was only sand,' Larssen explained. 'Can't parade on sand. So we didn't try.'

He leant forward. 'The first thing we always ask volunteers is whether they will jump. But I see you have already jumped.'

'Jumped?'

'A parachute course.'

Tiller grinned. 'Oh, yes, that. I did it at Ringway.'

He now saw that Larssen wore the spread wings of a parachutist over his left breast pocket.

Larssen grinned back at him. 'It's a good way of sorting out the sheep from the goats. If anyone refuses we RTU them immediately. Not, I suspect, that we're going to be doing any parachuting for the time being.'

'So we're here to raid?' Tiller asked.

'Castelrosso is our forward base,' Larssen said. 'But God knows what we're doing here.' He glanced at his watch. 'The boss will tell us soon enough. Any other questions?'

Tiller hesitated. 'Yes. What's the crossbow for?'

Larssen glanced up at the wall behind him. 'You have never used one? It is a wonderful weapon. Accurate, without noise, kills a man instantly if you hit him in the right spot.'

Tiller was intrigued. 'You've used it in action?'

Larssen just grinned.

'If it's so effective, why aren't all the special forces issued with them?'

Larssen sighed. 'Ah, rules and regulations. Nothing but damned rules and regulations. They were used by the Carlists in the Spanish Civil War, you know. They killed quite a few Republicans on night raids using bows and arrows. I recommended to the bigwigs in London that they were used. You know what they told me? I couldn't use it because it was an inhuman weapon.'

He bent forward again and his voice suddenly changed from being light-hearted, flippant, to one of great intensity. His blue eyes were like ice. 'I tell you, Tiger, me, I have only one rule of warfare. You kill the other man before he kills you. You have killed a man, yes?'

Tiller shook his head. Larssen said softly. 'But you know all the different ways because you went to the Killer School. But did they tell you where not to knife a German?'

'No. I wasn't there long.'

'I tell you. With the German army uniform the water bottle is worn so that it protects the kidneys. Also, the braces, where they cross over, they protect the vulnerable part of the spine. So don't try either place. Go for the subclavian artery. Here.'

Larssen pointed to his collar-bone. 'You pull the man's chin sideways and put the knife in here. He is unconscious in three seconds, dead in four. Silently. He drowns in his own blood. So when I can I use my knife. It's quick and silent – and not classed as an inhuman weapon.' He laughed lightly. 'Tell me, what is a human weapon?'

He did not seem to expect an answer to that conundrum. Instead, he swung his feet from the table and stood up with a speed that surprised Tiller. 'Come, I show you around before the boss's briefing.'

'Right, gentlemen.' The thickset, donnish figure rapped the stick he was going to use as a map pointer lightly on the table before him. 'I've not had time to meet any newcomers yet, so I'd better introduce myself. I'm your CO. Jarrett's the name.'

Corporal Billy Barnesworth leant over and whispered in Tiller's ear: 'Major the Earl of, Sarge. Just in case you didn't know.'

Tiller didn't, but he was already sure he had joined a unit unlike any other. He was far from certain he was going to enjoy it. Captain Larssen's appearance and demeanour had rather shaken him. His detachment officer had looked and talked – and no doubt behaved – more like a brigand than an officer of His Majesty's armed forces. Billy was one of the few survivors in the Middle East of the Special Boat Service. He had informed Tiller he had been a professional swimmer before the war, but it hadn't been Billy who had told Tiller that the guardsman was so at home in the water that he could eat bananas and drink beer while submerged. Quite how he managed this Tiller had yet to find out.

It was Billy who had also told him about Larssen, that he was a Danish merchant seaman who had escaped from his country to fight the Germans. 'Don't ask him why he hates the Germans so much,' Barnesworth had advised him. 'Otherwise he'll give you a twenty-minute lecture on how the Danes lost Schleswig-Holstein to Germany in the Middle Ages. Just take it from me that he does.'

Barnesworth had added that, because of his knowledge of the sea, Larssen had somehow become involved in the pinprick cross-Channel raids during the early years of the war. He had been picked to ferry ashore members of the Small Scale Raiding Force on a Channel Islands raid in 1941 and had distinguished himself by covering the raiders as they had re-embarked. He had been commissioned more or less on the spot and had been in the special forces ever since. A good man, Barnesworth had said, but a bit of a head case. 'He's had no military training whatsoever.'

Tiller had looked dumbfounded. 'None?'

'None. He couldn't march to save his life. But he knows more about weapons than anyone I've ever known. He's apparently killed more Germans than the rest of us put together.'

'Never been on a parade ground?'

'Never. But he's already got the Military Cross and bar. Not bad, eh, for someone who doesn't know what "port arms" means?'

Tiller had looked surprised. 'But he wasn't wearing any ribbons.'

'Nah,' Billy had replied casually. 'Our Magnus doesn't bother about things like that.'

Jarrett tapped the map. 'Here's our objective. Or rather, here they are: the Dodecanese islands. Not far from the Turkish coast, as you can see. The population's nearly all Greek, but the Italians were given the islands in 1919 after the Great War and they garrison them. However, Jerry has also set up shop on some of the strategically more important ones.'

He paused and a voice interjected from his audience: 'We can take care of them, sir. No problem.'

Jarrett smiled. 'Possibly. But as there are only about fifty of us at the moment I don't propose a confrontation. No, our task is to secure the other islands and to persuade the Italians to help us defend them. We also have to mount reconnaissance patrols and set up a communications network to prepare the way for army units who will be sent in as proper garrisons. We'll be ferried around by courtesy of the Levant Schooner Flotilla. Since they brought you here, they don't need any further introduction from me. If the Italians co-operate I'm sure we can thwart any attempt by Jerry to take over the islands should he try to do so.'

'But why should the Eyeties help us, sir?' asked a voice from the audience.

'We don't want them on *our* side, for Gawd's sake,' said another man. 'They're much more useful to us fighting with the Germans.'

There was ribald laughter. Jarrett smiled and raised his pointer, but silence had fallen before it ever touched the table. 'Anyone heard of the 10th Light Flotilla?'

No one had.

'An Italian unit. Its men blew holes in our only two battleships in the Mediterranean a couple of years ago. Right under our noses in Alexandria harbour. It was the Italians who invented – and used – midget submarines in the Great War. And it was an Italian who first sunk a warship with explosives by swimming into the harbour where it was anchored. Don't knock them. They can be as brave – and as foolhardy – as any of you lot. We are going to need them to secure these islands against the Krauts.'

There was a murmur of appreciation as this sank in. Jarrett decided not to dwell on the cowardice of Admiral Campioni, who earlier that morning had surrendered his 35,000 men to 10,000 Germans without firing a shot. Instead he just said briskly: 'The bad news is that my mission to Rhodes failed. We have just heard that the island is now in German hands. This means that unless we can retake it quickly they will have three airfields at their disposal, though I doubt if they have either the aircraft or the fuel to make maximum use of them immediately.'

Jarrett paused while this piece of unpleasant news was digested. It was received in glum silence. Raiding airfields in enemy territory was what those present knew and did best, but obviously that was not what their CO had in mind now.

'We have every reason to believe the Germans may try and seize the other islands, too, if they think they can get away with it,' Jarrett continued. 'So the good news is that my orders still stand. I therefore propose to send out preliminary patrols of three or four men to find out the disposition of the Italian garrisons. I shall be going to Leros in the north. We will land a couple of you on Stampalia, the most westerly of the group, to act as an observation post, and Captain Larssen will go to Simi, in the south. He will support any of the nearby islands which may have Italian garrisons on them. These patrols will sail tonight at dusk. The remainder of you will stand by to be ferried wherever you're needed. You'll be reinforced by some members of the Greek Sacred Squadron, who should arrive tonight.'

Tiller glanced at Barnesworth, who whispered: 'Fancy name for a handful of Greek bandits Colonel Stirling picked up somewhere. They're part of Raiding Forces now.'

'Those of you who were with us in the desert will also be pleased to hear that our friends from the Long Range Desert Group, fresh from their Mountain Warfare course in the Lebanon, will also be joining us,' Jarrett announced. 'They will be working in the more northerly of the Dodecanese. Oh, yes, there's just one more thing I should mention. Just to complicate things the Greeks, as you probably know, have several different guerrilla organizations. Andartes, we call them. The two main ones are ELAS – pro-Communist, anti-royalist – and EDES, which is apparently working with the objective of restoring the King of the Hellenes to his throne. The Allies have been trying to work with both, but they're at each other's throats as much as they are at those of the occupying forces. We have no idea which group might be working in the Dodecanese, or even if there are any there at all. Now, any questions?'

'What's the chance of a good scrap, sir?' a voice asked from the back.

Jarrett smiled. 'Pretty high, I'd say. Though quite who we'll be fighting is another matter.'

4

They spent several more days hanging around waiting for their final orders. The time dragged and Tiller remembered the saying that war was ninety-nine per cent boredom and one per cent sheer terror.

The island was a miserably poor place, its inhabitants thin and ragged and dirty. The children, especially, were pathetic to look at, their stomachs distended by starvation. It seemed to Tiller that even at the best of times the island's occupants must have had great difficulty scraping an existence from the rocky ground. Most of the buildings clustered around the harbour were in a terrible state of repair and some seemed little better than ruins. Only the church on the hillside, newly painted, looked untouched by the war and the poverty.

The Italian garrison of thirty or so members of the *Fascisti*, who had surrendered after firing a few desultory shots, had made themselves scarce. The Greek inhabitants hated these blackshirts, that much was obvious, and already one of them had been found in an alley with his throat cut.

The detachment's orders eventually came late on the third day and the word was passed round for the patrols to muster on the harbour quay. To pass the time, and because it came to him automatically, Tiller was cleaning his gear when Barnesworth came to tell him that at last they were on the move. He watched Tiller with amusement.

'I'm a guardsman, Tiger, but I've learnt there are better things to do in life.'

Tiller breathed heavily on his cap badge and buffed it vigorously. 'Just habit, I suppose.'

When they arrived at the quay the rest of the detachment was viewing the motley collection of vessels tied up along the harbour quay with misgiving.

'Jesus!' one of the men exploded, running his eye over them. 'What's this, the local fishing fleet?'

Tiller's only experience of serving with the Royal Navy afloat had been a pre-war two-year stint aboard the battleship HMS *Ramilles*, and the submarine which had taken him to the mouth of the Gironde. On the battleship he had served as part of the gunnery team for X turret, the traditional one reserved for the Royal Marine detachment aboard a warship. It was this time that had started his interest in explosives, but it had left him with no abiding love of the senior service or of life afloat.

The submariners, on the other hand, had been a friendly lot and he had had nothing but admiration for the way they taken the raiders to the correct release point in as accurate a piece of dead reckoning as he had ever witnessed. And they had stayed on the surface, refusing to panic when the steady throb of an E-boat had been heard in the distance. As cool as cucumbers they had been. He had appreciated that, had known then that they would be waiting for him when he returned. He often wondered how long they had waited. He bet it was longer than their orders had stipulated.

He strolled over to a leading seaman who had a

sheaf of papers in his hand and was obviously going to help organize the embarkation.

'What's this lot, then, Killick? The Dunkirk Veterans' Association?'

The man grinned and said: 'I suppose you're used to serving aboard nothing smaller than a battleship, Sarge? This is the cream of His Majesty's Mediterranean Fleet. As fine a squadron as ever flew the white ensign.'

'Spare me the Nelson touch,' Tiller groaned. 'What the hell are they?'

'That's an ML, a Fairmile Motor Launch. A hundred and twelve foot long. They can do about sixteen knots in a seaway, so they are nothing like as fast as MTBs. Silent engines, they've got some of them.'

'What are they?' Tiller queried.

'The engines' exhaust pipes are below the water, not above it. Now, those two are Motor Torpedo Boats, one's a Thornycroft, the other a Vosper. The Vosper's got three Packard engines that give her a speed of thirty-four knots or more, but the Thornycroft . . .'

Tiller interrupted him firmly. 'I meant those.'

He pointed at half a dozen or so curious wooden vessels, some with one mast, others with two. They lay tied-up neatly alongside each other and moved in unison in the gentle swell caused by the arrival of an RAF high-speed launch. At a convenient extremity each flew a white ensign which flapped sporadically in the light evening breeze.

'Oh, those,' said the seaman offhandedly. 'They're the Levant Schooner Flotilla. Powered with Matilda tank engines and whatever sail they can hoist, and armed with anything the crews have been able to lay their hands on.'

'Rather them than me,' said Tiller, who didn't immediately associate this tatty collection with Larssen's more romantic description of the Flotilla's vessels. 'I wouldn't fancy sailing in a beer puddle aboard any of that lot.'

'Don't malign them, Sarge. They're your principal means of transport from now on.'

'Good grief,' muttered Barnesworth, who was standing beside Tiller.

'So *that's* a caique,' said Tiller. 'I didn't know they'd be quite so small. They all look different, too.'

'Each island that builds them has its own design,' the leading seaman said. 'They're constructed to ride out the *meltemi*, so they must be seaworthy.'

'*Meltemi*?' said Barnesworth.

The leading seaman looked at the two SBS men with amusement. 'Well, if you two gents haven't heard of the *meltemi* I won't spoil your holiday cruise. Now, if I could have your names, I'll tell you which of these luxury vessels you're sailing in.'

When they told him he looked down his list and then assigned them to LS8, the most outboard of the group which were tied up alongside each other. From the quay it also looked one of the smallest. They picked their way gingerly across the decks of the other caiques, stepping between piles of stores, ammunition boxes, and the usual clutter found aboard a sailing vessel. When they eventually arrived they found Larssen already aboard, smoking a pipe and gazing up at the hills behind the port, which were etched out by the last rays of the setting sun. He pointed to the ruins of an ancient fortress on one of the summits. 'A Crusader castle,' he said. 'The Knights of St John held this island until 1440.'

Tiller and Barnesworth glanced at each other. 'Is that right, skipper?' they replied in unison. They had quickly learnt during the course of the last few days that when their detachment commander was spouting history it was best to sound interested, but not to prolong the conversation by asking questions they didn't want to know the answer to.

LS8 still smelt of fish but her captain, wearing a bushy black beard which hid his schoolboy face, showed them over her with ill-concealed pride. He introduced himself as Andrew Maygan. The two interlinked wavy gold stripes on the epaulettes of his service shirt showed him to be a lieutenant in the Royal Naval Volunteer Reserve, the 'Wavy Navy' as it was called.

'Either of you know anything about sailing?' he asked.

They said they didn't.

'You'll soon pick it up,' Maygan said cheerfully. 'Just keep your heads out of the way of the boom – this chunk of wood here that the mainsail's attached to – because it will crack them open if you don't.'

Tiller knew that many RNVR officers were drawn from the ranks of knowledgeable amateur yachtsmen and this gave him some cause for comfort. LS8 might be flying the white ensign but she was more like a yacht than a warship. She certainly wasn't like anything Tiller had come across in his days with the Royal Navy where quarterdecks were scrubbed white and brass glistened like gold. He reckoned no regular naval officer would be seen dead aboard this crate. Which was just as well. What was that jibe about the three most useless things to have aboard a sailing boat? Oh, yes: an umbrella, a cuckoo clock and a naval officer.

'Bit cramped, I'm afraid,' Maygan said, 'but you'll only be aboard overnight. We want to get to Simi before dawn.'

The two SBS men peered into the caique's small hold, which was filled with jerrycans, food cartons, ammunition boxes and assorted weaponry. Tiller checked that his crate of plastic explosive and limpet mines was among them and noted the wireless set screwed to the bulkhead. No doubt its aerial ran up inside the mast.

'I haven't seen a set like that before,' he said to Maygan.

'The Kittyhawk fighter-bombers they were fitted in have been re-equipped with the latest VHF sets, so we managed to scrounge them from the Yanks. Ideal for what we want.'

The deck was equally cramped. The sail, rolled loosely around its boom, took up a good deal of room. There were two small anchors lashed astern of the small cockpit and two larger ones in the bows, their warps coiled neatly on the deck. 'You've got enough anchors,' Tiller remarked.

'Our engine's got no reverse,' Maygan said cheerfully. 'We've got to stop somehow.'

In front of the mast, shrouded, was a gun set on a bipod. Maygan lifted its cover and Tiller noticed that, unlike any British weapon, its magazine was mounted on the left side. He had never seen anything quite like it.

'A Solothurn,' Maygan explained. 'Swiss-made 20mm semi-automatic anti-tank rifle. The Eyeties used them against our tanks in the desert. Against any armour except sardine tins it's pretty useless, but it would give most things afloat around here a fright.'

The Matilda engine started with a roar that sent a belch of black smoke from the exhaust in the stern.

'What *are* we likely to meet?' Billy asked.

'Nothing, I hope, now that the Eyeties have surrendered. But they have a number of MAS boats – small torpedo boats – which Jerry may well have purloined. The Germans have several armed schooners for supplying their outlying garrisons and a Siebel ferry or two. They're nothing more than floating platforms really,' he added when the SBS men looked blank. 'But they're heavily armed with AA weapons. Their main armaments are two 105mm guns which could blast us out of the water in thirty seconds flat. L-boats we call them and I don't go anywhere near them. Anyway, we're not here to sink the opposition. Our job's to keep out of sight – or be sufficiently well disguised to pass as a local caique – so that we can land you blokes and take you off again, if necessary, without Jerry knowing what we're up to until it's too late.'

The seaman deck-hand and the caique's engineer, who had been introduced to them as Sandy Griffiths and Jock Bryson, started casting off from the caique LS8 was moored alongside. Then Maygan took the tiller to steer LS8 out of harbour.

'We avoid open water if we can,' he said, 'so we'll be going into Turkish waters and following the coast.'

Once out of the harbour he held the tiller between his knees, opened a chart he had under his arm, and showed the SBS team where he proposed to go by tracing the Turkish coastline with his finger.

'It's here, where we have to leave the coastline to cross to Simi, that it could be a bit dodgy. Jerry may have air patrols out now that he has control of the Rhodes airfields. But hopefully we'll be crossing while it's still dark.'

Griffiths appeared from the hold and the SBS men noticed that he and Bryson were now wearing civilian clothing: old caps, baggy trousers and threadbare jackets.

'Hoist the Turkish ensign, sir?' said Griffiths.

Maygan nodded and they watched the white ensign being hauled down and be replaced by a red Turkish flag with its crescent and star.

'We call ourselves filibusters,' Maygan said. 'Now you know why.'

'Filibusters?'

'Irregulars. Pirates, really. If their lordships at the Admiralty knew we were sailing in neutral waters under a foreign flag – especially a neutral one – we'd be hung, drawn and quartered.'

Out of the shelter of the harbour the caique bucked and rolled and its hull and rigging creaked under the strain of being pushed through the waves at eight knots. The Matilda engine, Bryson explained, was far too powerful for the size of the caique, but at least it was quiet because it was running at quarter throttle.

Maygan steered LS8 north-east towards the nearby Turkish mainland and then turned north-west to clear the headland that protected the harbour. Once past it they saw the sun dip into the sea on their port side. Ahead lay what, to them, seemed to be pitch-darkness, but as their eyes slowly adjusted to it they could see the first stars pricking the sky and could just make out the outline of a headland. Even at this distance it looked high and forbidding.

The hump of Castelrosso dropped quickly astern and gradually merged with the sea. The caique jerked and plunged and a cascade of spray swept over them. The helmsman swore loudly as some of it hit him.

'Quite a swell on,' said Maygan.

'What's the *meltemi*?' Barnesworth asked Griffiths.

'No need to worry about that tonight,' Griffiths replied. 'I'd get your heads down while you can.'

'Where?' Tiller asked.

Griffiths pointed to the rolled sail. 'It's as dry a place as anywhere.'

The sail smelt of tar and canvas, and was, after they had managed to wedge themselves between the boom and the cockle that had been brought aboard, surprisingly comfortable. Tiller stretched out, his unloaded Sten gun cradled in his arm, his beret a thin pillow between his head and the fish-impregnated deck.

LS8 rose and fell beneath them and the Matilda engine thumped away comfortingly in their ears.

The nightmare was taking a slightly different form when Tiller was suddenly awake, instantly alert. He sat up and slid the magazine into the Sten. It was an automatic reaction to an unknown situation but he could not instantly discern what was the matter, only that something was. Then he realized it was the silence that had woken him. The caique's movement had changed. With the engine stopped it was wallowing motionless in the sea.

Tiller levered himself out of the sail and on to his feet, and walked aft. Maygan, now also dressed in civilian clothes, was handing an adjustable spanner to Bryson, who was crouched over the engine, which lay below the cockpit floor. Larssen was holding a shaded torch.

'You know anything about engines?' Maygan asked him. Tiller shook his head.

Larssen chuckled. 'Tiger doesn't mend them. He blows them up, don't you, Tiger?'

'I wish someone had blown up the tank this fucking engine was in,' Bryson grumbled into the engine space. 'It's always been dodgy. I told them so in Beirut.'

Maygan glanced anxiously at his watch. Its luminous dial showed it was 0230. The cliffs of the Turkish coast looked close, very close. For a quarter of an hour Bryson laboured in silence except for the occasional expletive.

Then Maygan said: 'I think we'd better hoist the sail. At least we'll be able to stand off from the shore and not get taken too far off our course by the current.'

Tiller hadn't been aware of any breeze but once the mainsail and foresail were hoisted they filled at once and the caique stopped wallowing. It surged forward and the motion, Tiller noticed, was quite different under sail than it had been under power. Instead of punching into the waves the caique moved over them with an easy, rhythmic motion.

Maygan and Larssen spread the chart across their knees and studied it with the torch. 'There's a Turkish coastguard station on Cape Alupo,' said Maygan. 'I had hoped to get past there while it was still dark.'

'Trouble?' Larssen enquired.

'You never know. Nine times out of ten they'd never look at you twice. Nothing we can do about it anyway, except keep you lot in the hold. Might make sense to lie up in the daytime somewhere in the Gulf of Doris and cross to Simi tonight. We've got camouflage nets. No one would spot us, not even from the air.'

'My orders are Simi today, Andrew,' Larssen said. 'We've got to get to the Italian garrison before Jerry does.'

'Well, I'm game if you are,' said Maygan.

An hour later the engine broke into a healthy roar and Cape Alupo was passed just as the sun had begun to burn the night mist off the sea. The ensign was dipped to the coastguard station but there was no reply and half an hour later they changed course for Simi and the island's main port, where the Italian commandant had his headquarters.

Tea had just been brewed and some bread and jam distributed when Griffiths, who had been acting as lookout, shouted: 'Aircraft, port quarter, sir. Looks like a flying boat.'

Maygan threw his tea into the sea and snapped: 'I want all SBS below. Now.'

'Shall I man the gun, sir?' Griffiths asked.

'No, just make sure it's covered with the foresail. And make sure that canoe's out of sight under the mainsail.'

'Aye, aye, sir.'

'Jock, can we increase speed without shaking the hull to bits?'

'I doubt it, sir.'

'Well, try.'

'Aye, aye, sir.'

The orders had been issued crisply and were being obeyed with an easy assurance. As he crouched in the tiny hold Tiller decided that perhaps the three men on deck did know about white-honed decks and shining brass, after all.

'Put those binoculars away, Griffiths,' he heard Maygan tell the deck-hand. 'If the sun catches the lenses it'll be an open invitation for him to blast us out of the water. The wages of Turkish fishermen don't run to binoculars.'

They could all hear the aircraft now. It seemed to be moving very slowly and quite high. Every now and again it dipped its wings as if the pilot wanted to have a better look at what was below him. It moved north of LS8, circled and came lazily back to them.

'Wave!' Maygan ordered his crew as the aircraft passed astern of them. The aircraft, its Luftwaffe crosses plainly visible on its wings and fuselage, wiggled its wings in acknowledgement.

It flew south and then banked and headed back towards them. 'Never seen one like that before,' Maygan said. 'Any of you know anything about German aircraft?' he shouted down into the hold.

'A bit,' said Tiller.

'Be careful, but poke your head out and see if you can recognize it.'

Tiller stuck his head out and saw the aircraft approaching from astern. He shaded his eyes from the sun. 'Your beret, man!' Maygan shouted. 'Take your beret off.'

Larssen, standing behind Tiller, grabbed it from his head as the aircraft passed overhead. It was much lower this time. Then it swung round and came at them at masthead height. Its engines thundered and they could see the pilot leaning out to have a closer look. This time he didn't wave back.

Tiller poked his head up after it had passed and said: 'A Blohm and Voss, would be my guess.'

They waited for it to turn and come back again. If it did they knew the pilot would be making up his mind what to do. It was probably a forbidden area for

Turkish fishermen or the pilot had divined the caique was not all that it appeared to be. He was probably radioing his base for instructions before returning to rake them with his machine-guns.

'There's a Bren down there somewhere,' Maygan shouted into the hold. 'Get it ready. We may need it.'

The aircraft banked and flew off at a right angle. It was worse for those below because they could not see what was happening – just hear the dwindling sound of the engines.

'Is it going?' Larssen asked.

'He'll be back,' said Maygan grimly. 'He's turning now.'

This time, when he turned the pilot dived steeply and came straight at them towards their port side. Now he was flying below the height of the mast.

'Bloody show-off,' Maygan shouted.

The noise of the engines increased as Barnesworth passed up the Bren light machine-gun to Larssen, who sat crouched in the entrance to the hold. He covered the weapon with the corner of a tarpaulin and brought its muzzle level with the approaching aircraft.

'I reckon I could take him, Andrew,' he yelled.

'No! Hold your fire!' Maygan shouted. 'Wave, for Christ's sake, wave.'

He took off his ancient cloth cap, stood on the caique's counter, and waved his cap above his head. When the German opened fire he knew he would be the first to be hit. But then he could have overruled Larssen. LS8 was his command and now he was going to lose her. At that moment he was more angry than afraid. The sound of the German's engines filled the caique's small hold.

'What's he going to do?' Barnesworth snarled. 'Sink us by ramming us?'

But at the last split second the pilot drew back his joystick and missed the mast by a matter of feet. The whole hull of the caique shuddered.

'Fucking hell!' shouted Maygan. He was frightened now. The shock wave of the passing aircraft had nearly thrown him into the water. 'Fucking silly bugger!'

The aircraft was already half a mile away and was beginning to climb. They all knew that if he came back again it would be to sink them. The aircraft began to bank.

'Here he comes again!' Maygan shouted. 'Flat on the deck this time, lads. And I want Lanchester up here too.'

But then the aircraft straightened out and headed off in the direction of Rhodes. It steadily dwindled into the distance and soon all that was left was a dot in the sky and the faint vibrations of its engines in the early-morning air.

'Christ,' said Maygan. 'I have a feeling that was a bloody close call.'

Larssen handed Tiller back his beret and pointed at the badge. 'The sun must have caught this. Now you know why no spit and polish, Tiger. You can have my spare beret. And I have an SAS badge somewhere. All cloth, no brass. But you bloody sew it on yourself.'

Tiller grinned and retrieved his headgear. He removed the gleaming badge of the globe and laurel and put it in his pocket. This simple action seemed to him an acceptance of this strange new life.

Larssen slapped him on the back. 'That's a start,

Tiger. But it's up here,' he said, pointing to his head with a forefinger. 'That's where it really counts. But it's a start.'

Maygan had his log open on his knees. He licked the end of his pencil. 'How do you spell Blohm and Voss?' he asked.

Maygan would have liked to hug the eastern shore of Simi until they had reached the far end, where the port of Simi lay in the deep natural harbour of Yalo Bay. He knew the garrison was a small one, perhaps no more than fifty Italians, but Jarrett had told him there was no knowing how they would react. And somewhere – no one quite knew where – there was at least one gun battery. Having nearly lost his command already once that day Maygan explained that he wanted to keep out of the range of any guns for as long as possible, or at least not sail up their muzzles.

He spread out the chart and showed Larssen his proposed course. 'We could put into Marathonda or Nano Bay, but I wouldn't like to approach the shore any further north as at least one of the batteries is bound to be sited close to Simi.'

'What is the safest from your point of view?' Larssen asked.

'Put into Marathonda Bay.'

'And how do we get to the port?'

Maygan shrugged. 'Hijack some donkeys, I suppose. It's about five or six miles as the crow flies across the hills. Probably twice that if you find and follow the track which connects Panormiti Bay with the port.'

'And the quickest way?' asked Larssen.

'Sail into Simi flying the white ensign and our best uniforms, and hope for the best.'

'I prefer the quickest,' Larssen said immediately. 'Are you game?'

Maygan hesitated. 'I'll keep offshore until we reach the port and then sail straight in. That way we won't suddenly appear, which might make them shoot first and ask questions afterwards.'

'They'll be trigger-happy, that's certain,' said Larssen.

The caique worked its way steadily up the island's coast, but no one aboard saw any sign of life on the rocky shore. Behind the arid littoral the mountainous interior looked bare of vegetation. The heat shimmered on the water and contorted the rugged coastline. They passed Pethi Bay and turned north-westwards towards the tiny island of Nimos, which lay just beyond Simi. Gradually the large expanse of Yalo Bay opened up before them.

'I can see the port, sir,' Griffiths, who had the binoculars, shouted from the bows.

'We'll stand on for another ten minutes,' Maygan called out, 'and then head inshore. Hoist the white ensign.'

Maygan tossed his cloth cap into the cockpit and donned his service one. Off came the baggy trousers and on went the regulation navy shorts. Off came the seaman's vest and on went the regulation white naval shirt with the lieutenant's ranks in gold braid on the epaulettes. Both officers also buckled on their holsters. Pistols would be of little use in the situation they now found themselves in, but they were a kind of symbol of authority.

After ten minutes Maygan turned the caique into the bay and headed for the port. He cut the engine right back, and then put it in neutral so that LS8 was just moving gently through the calm water.

'Any shipping?' Maygan called out to Griffiths.

'Nothing that I can see, sir.'

'Keep a sharp lookout.'

'Aye, aye, sir.'

They left behind the headlands that protected the bay and could soon discern with the naked eye the buildings clustered around the port. Rows of multi-coloured houses were built on the steep hillsides that surrounded the port, which was dominated by an old castle. Atop this flew a very large but indistinguishable flag which flapped lazily in the light breeze.

They strained their eyes and ears, looking for movement or for the sound of the alarm being raised. But all they could hear was the chuckle of water under the caique's bows.

'Do you know, I think we've made it, gentlemen,' Maygan said. 'They're going to welcome us with open arms.'

As he spoke there was a large splash a long way astern of them and then they all heard the dull crack of a distant gun.

Maygan swore loudly.

The second shot was close enough for them to hear the curious whirr the shell made as it passed over them.

'Where is it, Griffiths?' Maygan shouted.

The deck-hand pointed and said: 'On that point there, sir.'

Sure enough, with the third shot they saw the flash.

'That's incredibly bad shooting,' said Larssen coolly.

'Perhaps they don't want to hit us?' Maygan suggested. 'Perhaps they're just firing warning shots across our bows to make us stop.'

'Then why are the shells all falling astern?' Larssen replied scornfully.

'Well, they're wasting valuable ammunition we might want,' Maygan argued. 'We might as well stop and see what happens.'

He put the engine in neutral and the caique slowly lost way and came to a halt. It bobbed up and down in the flat calm water. There was hardly any wind now and Maygan had the ensign hauled down and draped over the side where those manning the battery could see it. The battery fell silent, and they waited for the Italians' next move.

This came quite quickly, for they saw a motor launch leave the port and make its way towards them. It circled them warily and then came to a halt about 300 yards from them. In the bows a naval rating manned a machine-gun, which he pointed straight at them, and flying from the stern was a disproportionately large Italian flag with the emblem of the Italian royal house at its centre.

But what drew the immediate attention of the men aboard the caique was the figure seated in the centre of the launch. He was dressed from top to toe in pure white. A cascade of gold-braided tassles flowed from one shoulder and a parasol of delicate hue protected him from the sun.

'Cor,' said Barnesworth in mock awe. 'King Kong himself.'

A more modestly dressed officer stood up and bellowed through a loud-hailer: 'You spik English?'

'We are English,' Maygan shouted back. He pointed

at the white ensign. 'Royal Navy. Special Operations.'

'What you want?'

'We have come to talk with your commandant. We come as allies.'

The two figures conversed, then the man with the loud-hailer called out: 'Please. Follow us.'

Those in the launch obviously weren't completely convinced of the caique's identity for the machine-gunner was ordered to move with his weapon to the stern, where, to the amusement of those aboard the caique, the large flag kept winding itself around his head.

'Should I man the Solothurn, sir?' Griffiths asked. 'I can load it, but keep it under the foresail.'

Maygan nodded, and said: 'And let's have the Bren where we can get at it quickly.'

Larssen also slid up a Lanchester carbine he had found in the hold. He pushed it into a position where the folded mainsail prevented it being seen from the launch. He sighted down the barrel carefully.

'If you keep them slightly on your starboard bow as you're doing now I can take the machine-gunner,' he said to Maygan quietly. 'Then I'll puncture the elegant bastard under the umbrella.'

'Good. If it's a trap we can always turn and make a run for it. That battery couldn't hit a battleship at a hundred yards.'

'Oh, no, Andrew,' Larssen said softly. 'I think we run nowhere. Look at that.'

From behind the stone pier of the inner harbour a low, grey silhouette slid into view. It turned towards them and they could hear the powerful grumble of its engines as it picked up speed.

'Shit, eh,' Larssen whistled admiringly. 'That's some boat. What is it?'

'A *Motoscafo Anti-sommergibile* or MAS boat,' said Maygan, who had been chosen for the mission because of his smattering of Italian. 'A smaller equivalent of our MTBs.'

'We captured one earlier this summer,' Bryson said. 'They've got three Isotta-Fraschini engines and go like greased lightning, but are hopeless in any sort of a sea.'

They watched the MAS boat approach. It had a very low freeboard and seemed excessively narrow for its length, but it looked fast. Very fast. It had two torpedo tubes which were positioned either side of its bows and between them was mounted a dual-purpose machine-gun. Two members of the crew stood by it.

'Boy,' Larssen breathed, watching the white feather of water growing under the MAS boat's curved bows. That's a forty-knot boat, I reckon.'

'Nearer fifty actually,' Maygan corrected him. 'At least that's their design speed.'

The MAS boat surged forward effortlessly and circled astern of them. Maygan saw with some relief that the two-man crew of its main armament, twin 20mm Bredas positioned aft of its bridge, kept their weapon trained fore and aft. But the trap, if it was a trap, was now closed.

But, having shown its turn of speed, the MAS boat turned back and came alongside the caique. Abruptly, its engines were cut and the sleek grey hull stalled in the water. It had an open, streamlined, aluminium bridge on which a naval officer was sitting on a stool. He wore not a cap but a leather helmet rather like those worn by racing drivers of the day.

He stepped down from the stool, took off his helmet, and came down on to the deck. He leant on the rails of his elegant craft and called across to the caique. 'British navy?'

'That's right,' Maygan shouted back.

'Your ship's name?'

'LS8 of Levant Schooner Flotilla. Special Operations. *Buon giorno.*'

'*Buon giorno, Capitano.*' The officer smiled broadly as he snapped to attention and saluted. 'Welcome to Simi.'

Maygan returned the salute. 'Thank you. *Grazie.*'

'When you get into harbour you come aboard, *sì*? I want to welcome you.' The officer made the gesture of lifting a glass to his lips.

'Thank you,' said Maygan with more feeling.

'Pink gin. It's good?'

'That'll do nicely,' said Maygan.

'*Arrivederci.*'

The officer saluted again, returned to his bridge and his stool, and the MAS boat surged forward.

'He seems friendly enough,' said Maygan. 'I wonder how he knows about pink gin.'

Larssen grunted. Jarrett had told him how complicated the situation was, how nothing would be what it seemed, and he remained sceptical. Put in its simplest terms, Jarrett had explained, the Italian *Fascisti* still supported the Germans, whereas the non-fascist Italians certainly didn't. The non-fascists loathed the Germans and Mussolini's jackbooted supporters in equal measure, but were scared of both. Most Greeks loathed all Italians and all Germans and were scared of neither, but only the Andartes had arms. And then there were the fascist Greeks, the collaborators. Who were on which islands and in what strength remained a mystery, as did the allegiance of the various groups to the Allied cause. It was, Jarrett had told Larssen, a bit of a hornets' nest.

He could say that again.

A group of civilians had gathered at the end of the breakwater as they passed into the inner harbour.

'*Yasus*!' Larssen called out, using the only word of Greek he knew.

The civilians waved frantically. '*Yasus! Anglika! Yasus!*'

They waved and called, thin, ragged figures alive with delight. They ran along the breakwater, ignoring the MAS boat, which was returning to its berth there. They waved and shouted as they went, and then the crew of the caique saw that small groups of other locals were beginning to gather on the quay that ran the length of the tiny port.

'Unload the Solothurn, Griffiths,' Maygan ordered. 'Make sure it's covered up.'

'Aye, aye, sir.'

'All other arms in the hold. If it's a trap, there's nothing we can do about it now. I'm not going to risk hurting the locals in a running gun battle.'

They watched the launch go alongside the quay and tie up. The elegant figure in white stepped out from under the parasol and on to the quay. They could see him flicking dust off his uniform and pulling his skin-tight jacket straight.

'What the hell's he got on his head, sir?' Bryson asked.

'Looks like ostrich plumes to me,' said Maygan.

'Jesus,' Bryson said quietly.

The other officer aboard the launch jumped ashore

and indicated to those aboard the caique that they should berth alongside the quay next to the launch.

'Here we go, lads. Mooring warps ready fore and aft.'

Tiller watched with admiration as Maygan manoeuvred the clumsy vessel. It came alongside with hardly a bump.

'Cut the engine, Bryson.'

The crowd surged forward and began to clap and call out their welcome.

Many eager hands grabbed the mooring warps and stretched out to greet the caique's crew. Thin, lined faces, nut-brown from the sun and wreathed in smiles, clustered round. A bunch of green grapes and a bottle was handed through the crowd and passed to those on deck.

'Drink, drink, drink,' the crowd demanded.

Maygan raised the bottle and drank deeply. It was retsina, very harsh and dry but welcome nonetheless. Everyone in turn on the caique took a swig and each time the crowd cheered its approval. The babble was tremendous but then half a dozen soldiers wearing the curious cocked hats of the Italian *carabinieri* pushed their way through the crowd to make a path for the two officers in their white uniforms. The crowd muttered among themselves and stepped back reluctantly. One or two even resisted the soldiers' advance but were shoved aside by their rifle butts.

The soldiers looked nervous, the Italian officers even more so. They approached the caique and halted, then both gave the fascist salute, the right arm outstretched at forty-five degrees, the open palm of the hand held outwards.

No one on the caique moved. The muttering in the

crowd stopped. The silence was broken when one old man at the front hawked noisily and then spat into the water. Another copied him but he spat on the ground. Maygan could see that some of the saliva had splashed on to the shiny black knee-boots of one of the officers, who pretended not to notice. The tension between the two groups was unmistakable.

'There's going to be trouble,' Maygan said to Larssen quietly. 'I think we've got to do something. Quickly.'

Larssen swung himself up on to the bulwarks and grabbed the rigging to steady himself.

'Does anyone here speak English?' he addressed the crowd. A tough-looking man with greying hair and a lined face burnt almost black with the sun pushed forward. He wore a large knife on his belt and his right hand lay loosely on its hilt as he spoke. 'My name is Christophou, Angelios Christophou. My family are fishermen. We have lived here many generations. The British navy is welcome.'

They shook hands and the crowd murmured appreciatively. It had not gone unnoticed that the British visitors had refused to acknowledge the Italians' salute.

Larssen quickly explained that they were the advance guard of a larger British force, that the British were old friends and allies of the Greeks, that he understood how the local people felt, but that there must be no trouble, and that they must all disperse to their homes.

'Tonight we celebrate,' he ended. 'But now we have business to discuss.'

He gestured towards the Italian officers. The fisherman nodded and turned and addressed the crowd.

When he had finished someone shouted something from the back. The crowd tittered and the fisherman grinned. 'He wants to know if you have come to hang all the Italians. He will help you. He has some good strong rope.'

Larssen thought of telling them that the Italians had to be their allies if the islands were to be kept free of Germans. But he looked at their faces and thought better of it. That would have to wait.

'No hanging, no shooting, no fighting,' Larssen announced firmly and loudly. 'Any of you making trouble will be answerable to me.'

Larssen pointed his finger at random into the crowd and then at his chest. He saw that they knew what he meant before Christophou had even translated his words, and that they didn't like it. They had scores to settle and the sooner they started settling them the happier they would be.

It looked like being an impasse. But then in one of those gestures that only a natural diplomat can plan Larssen took a small Greek flag out of his pocket, knotted it to a halyard, and hoisted it to the masthead. They went wild with delight, shouting at Christophou to translate their demands. Christophou grabbed his arm.

'They do what you say. But tonight you come to the taverna. Tonight at nine o'clock. We celebrate. They want your promise.'

Larssen pointed to his watch and then to the taverna, and then lifted an imaginary glass to his lips. They cheered.

'Nine o'clock,' he shouted, and they cheered some more when they knew they had his promise. But it was not quite over yet, for each of the male inhabitants insisted on hugging each of the crew and pumping his hand before they would leave. Even so, within twenty minutes the quay was deserted except for the *carabinieri* leaning on their rifles and the two dejected officers wilting in the heat.

'And who,' said Larssen pointing at them, 'exactly are you two comedians?'

5

'*Prego*? Comedians?' The more plainly dressed of the two Italian army officers looked perplexed; his elegant companion impatient.

An hour previously the SBS patrol had received a hostile reception from the Italian garrison. Now the SBS men realized that their erstwhile enemies were in more imminent danger than they were. If the nearby Germans didn't get them the local Greeks certainly would. And if the two standing before them were typical examples of those defending the Dodecanese, there didn't seem much hope of keeping the Germans at bay if they chose to come.

'*Prego?*' the Italian officer said again.

'Who are you?' Larssen repeated.

The officer drew himself up and his chest swelled beneath his exquisitely cut uniform. He was a young man with an oversized moustache the ends of which he tended to bite when he was nervous. 'I am Giuseppe Antonio Giuliano Perquesta, lieutenant in the army of His Majesty King Victor Emmanuel, and until recently a troop commander in the Cavour armoured division. Now I am the interpreter on the staff of His Excellency Colonel Ardetti, the island's commandant. At your service, *signore*.'

'And him?'

'The colonel's aide-de-camp, *signore*. Captain Salvini.'

At the sound of his name the captain bowed stiffly. His ostrich feathers made his head look top-heavy. He was dark and swarthy, with narrow eyes and twitchy hands. Larssen didn't like the look of him at all.

'Look Giuseppe,' Larssen said firmly. 'Firstly, no more of this.' Larssen waved his arm above his head in a parody of a fascist salute. 'Understood?'

The lieutenant nodded and grinned his agreement, but Salvini looked glum.

'Secondly, we come as friends and liberators, not as conquerors. That applies to you as much as to the islanders. We come as advisers. You understand me?'

'*Sì, capisco, signore*. I quite understand.'

'My first piece of advice is don't annoy the locals. Your men should keep out of their way.'

'I understand, *signore*. But of course that is a matter for the commandant. He sends you his friendly greetings.'

'He has a damned funny way of doing it,' Maygan interrupted crossly. 'It's bloody lucky your gunners can't shoot straight.'

Perquesta smoothed his moustache in embarrassment. '*Scusi, signore*. It was a mistake. Everyone is – how do you say? – very nervous. At any moment we expect the Germans. They demand we still fight on their side. The commandant has already had a radio message from General Klemann on Rhodes. The general is a hard man.'

It dawned on Larssen as he watched Salvini's expression that it had not been a mistake at all. If the Italian garrison resisted any English intrusion the Germans could hardly accuse them of treachery. On the other hand the Italians would not want to damage, much less sink, a Royal Navy ship in case the British appeared in force. Which was why the battery had made quite sure it had not hit the caique. And doubtless there were warring factions among the Italians themselves – probably represented by the two men standing in front of him.

Perquesta could see Larssen disbelieved him. He tugged nervously at the scarlet cravat around his neck. 'The commandant would like to meet you to hear what the British propose. May I take you to him?'

Larssen told him to stay where he was and took Tiller and Barnesworth to the other side of the caique.

'We've got to do some swift talking,' he said. 'We'll go armed to show we mean business, and we're going to have to smarten ourselves up.' He rubbed his chin. 'I'd better shave.'

'I could put on my cap badge again, skipper,' Tiller said with a grin. He had found that Larssen's nickname came easily to him now.

'Good idea,' said Larssen seriously. 'Clandestine warfare is one thing, diplomacy quite another. We're going to have to get used to wearing several hats.'

'I volunteered for the SBS to fight, skipper, not pander to a lot of comic-opera characters,' Barnesworth grumbled.

'You'll get your fighting, Billy,' Larssen promised. 'I'll see to that. Now let's get this ship looking like a fishing boat. That damned Jerry plane might still be nosing around.'

The commandant's headquarters was in the Crusaders' castle that was perched above the port. It took them some time to climb the steep track to it but, as Perquesta explained apologetically, the garrison had no transport. The commandant's office was like a hothouse. A dowdy grey-haired figure, Colonel Ardetti stood up behind his desk and pumped their hands while Salvini, bareheaded now, stood silently and moodily behind him. The colonel talked in rapid Italian which was accompanied by expressive gestures with his hands.

His duty, he said through Perquesta, was to defend Italian soil. If the British would help him, so much the better. The aide-de-camp bent and whispered something in his ear. The colonel's face darkened, but he nodded his agreement. However, he continued, it was not as simple as that. The armistice was by no means clear. The loyalty of the armed forces was divided. There were other ways of defending the integrity of Italian territory besides fighting over it.

He shrugged apologetically, spread his hands out, and then shrugged again. What can I do? his expression said; my hands are tied.

'But the commandant does agree that the garrison must not clash with the civilian population,' Perquesta said. 'His excellency says it is a delicate situation. But he will give orders at once for all patrols to be withdrawn and for his troops to be confined to their barracks. Maintaining law and order on the island is now in British hands. Once that has been established, gentlemen, perhaps you would care to have further discussions early tomorrow?'

'First round to Salvini,' Larssen muttered to Tiller as they left. 'He's a Fascist if ever I saw one. I think we must knock the colonel off the fence he's sitting on.'

'And how do we do that, skipper?' Barnesworth asked.

'We visit our Italian naval friend. He might be prepared to declare his hand.'

They returned to the caique, which now had a large fishing net 'drying' halfway up its mast, collected Maygan and then walked along to the stone pier where the MAS boat was moored. The sentry at the gangplank saluted smartly and her captain appeared at the rails.

'Welcome, welcome,' he called down. 'Come aboard.'

He took them below to the tiny ward-room under the bridge and mixed the two officers a pink gin each, expertly swirling the Angostura bitters around the glass before adding a generous measure of gin and a touch of bottled water. Tiller and Barnesworth opted for the local ouzo.

The Italian then introduced himself as Lieutenant Commander Balbao. 'Cheers, as you say. The British Navy's favourite drink, eh?'

'You speak good English,' Larssen said.

'I attended a staff course at your Royal Naval College at Greenwich before the war. What a place, eh? That painted hall. Never shall I forget those guest dinners.'

He stood up and raised his glass in imitation of the senior naval officer who presided on such occasions. 'I give you the toast, gentlemen: Admiral Nelson.' He sat down, happy that he had remembered the occasion so well. 'And I found the sweetest girl, a real English rose.' He kissed his fingers.

'We need help, Commander,' Larssen said.

'Then you come to the right place,' said Balbao, suddenly serious. 'You have already talked to the commandant here, yes?'

Larssen nodded cautiously. Balbao twiddled his

glass, drained it, mixed himself another pink gin, and glanced at each of them in turn. Then he seemed to make up his mind. 'What can I do for you?'

'You are under the commandant's orders?'

Balbao shook his head. 'My superior is Admiral Maschinni on Leros. I answer to him and him only. But naturally my task is to liaise with the army garrisons.'

'And where do you stand, Commander?' Larssen asked quietly. Balbao knew exactly what he meant.

'I hate fascism. I hope that someone strings up that jackal Mussolini. But I am proud of my country, gentlemen. Italy will rise again.'

'You are on our side, then?'

'Of course.'

'And you'll fight alongside us if necessary?'

'Admiral Maschinni has already given orders to defend Italian territory,' Balbao said cautiously.

It was the reply of a diplomat. Balbao knew it and the tone of his voice changed to one of anger. 'I have no love of the Germans. But what is more important to me is the honour of the Italian Navy. We are an honourable service with a brave past. But never were we allowed to fight. We were always told to avoid it. Run here, run there. Always away from your navy. You understand?'

Larssen and Maygan nodded in agreement.

'I have no respect for those who commanded our navy. You know what our great poet D'Annunzio said that MAS stood for? For *Memento Audare Semper* – Remember always to dare. But never, never were we allowed to dare.'

Maygan and Larssen listened respectfully and later Larssen was to say that the Italian had 'a buzz in his bonnet, yes?' Then they led him to the problem in hand by asking how they could best get the commandant on to the British side.

Balbao sighed. 'That is another matter. Ardetti, you understand, is not a young man. He wants to get home alive to his wife and children in Genoa. He is much swayed by possible retaliation from the Germans and there are committed Fascists among his staff.'

'Salvini, for instance?'

The Italian nodded, and added: 'And some of the men. They are not to be trusted. If I were you I'd lock them up.'

'But we can trust the local people?' Larssen asked.

The Italian shrugged. 'At a time like this, who can tell? Why do you ask?'

'We must visit the smaller islands around here,' Larssen explained. 'We therefore need someone with local knowledge. Unless of course . . .'

He looked at Balbao hopefully, but the Italian shook his head ruefully. 'I would like to help but it is not possible. I do not have the fuel. I left harbour today because I, too, must be seen to be supporting the commandant. Every move I make is noted.'

'There is no fuel on the island?' Maygan said in astonishment.

'There is some fuel, but it is under the commandant's control. I only have what is in my tanks. Enough to get us back to Leros. No more.'

'Ammunition?' Larssen asked.

'Plenty of ammunition. Plenty of food.' Balbao lifted his glass and grinned. 'Plenty of drink. But no fuel.'

'Well, it won't run on gin, I can tell you that,'

Maygan said to Larssen as the captain ushered the SBS party back on deck.

'It needs high-octane petrol. Aviation fuel,' Balbao said. 'If you can find me fuel, I can help you.'

The local taverna, a crumbling building on the quay, was packed when the SBS party arrived, and a small crowd had also gathered outside it. A path to the bar was cleared for them and they were slapped heartily on the back as they walked along it. Inside the bare wooden tables were packed with locals.

'*Yasus! Yasus!*' they called out, lifting their glasses. 'You are welcome here.'

Angelios Christophou stepped forward from the crowd of men at the bar and gripped their hands. It reminded Tiller of when, as a small boy, he had got his fingers caught in his mother's wringer. A table was dragged out from the back for them and a bottle of retsina and some glasses placed on it. An ancient radio on a shelf behind the bar blared out martial music. Christophou gestured to it in disgust. 'Music, music, but they tell us nothing. What is happening, my friends? Italy has surrendered, but no one knows anything else.'

He poured out the retsina and pushed the glasses brimming with the clear liquid towards his guests. 'We drink to the Allies, and to give thanks for the defeat of the Italian fascist scum.'

Larssen glanced at Maygan and knew they were both thinking the same thing: it was going to be difficult to persuade the islanders that Italy was no longer the enemy.

'We know no more than you do,' Maygan said. 'Except that the Germans may want these islands. Once they have had time to organize themselves they might try and occupy them. They have already taken over from the Italians on Rhodes. We have come to stop them if they try.'

Christophou was instantly alert. 'The Germans?' He uttered the word 'Germans' with unmistakable venom. 'Why should they come here?'

Larssen pointed in the direction of the mainland. 'Turkey. They want her to stay out of the war.'

Christophou spat on the floor. 'Bah! the Turks.'

'He doesn't seem to like anyone very much,' Tiller murmured to Barnesworth.

'I'm glad he's on our side,' Barnesworth replied softly. 'I wonder if there are any more like him.'

Both SBS men had already glanced around the taverna to see what local manpower might be available to help defend the island, and had come to the same conclusion that there would be none. There were no young men in the taverna, nor any women come to that, though they had seen plenty of children around the port, thin and in tattered clothing.

All the men they had seen looked over fifty, and many appeared much older. Grand-looking fellows, some of them were, with their long moustaches and dark, piercing eyes. But many appeared to be victims of the islanders' traditional method of making a living, sponge-diving, for both SBS men recognized the symptoms of diver's palsy among some of them and noticed in others the swollen joints caused by nitrogen saturation.

'They must be keeping the womenfolk out of sight,' said Barnesworth, nudging Tiller. 'They saw you coming, Tiger.'

The more they looked around them the more obvious it was that the islanders were living on the brink of starvation. Compared with the smooth, well-fed faces of the Italian garrison, the islanders were in a pitiful state.

'We eat,' Christophou announced. 'Then we drink some more.'

He clapped his hands. Tiller made as if to protest, but Larssen shook his head at him. 'You don't refuse a Greek's hospitality even if you know what he is offering you has meant sending his children to bed supperless.'

The first woman that they saw now appeared from behind a black curtain at the back of the taverna. Her tray was loaded with bread and olives and a plate of cheese. Behind her a girl, her eyes cast down in embarrassment, brought a large plate of salted fish.

'My mother,' Christophou announced proudly. The old woman nodded and smiled, and shook each hand in turn, but her eyes were sad and cast down.

'And this is my daughter, Angelika. My mother speaks no English but Angelika speaks it well. She is clever, aren't you, Angelika?'

The girl looked as if she wished the floor would swallow her up. Tiller caught her eye and smiled encouragingly. 'This food' – he gestured at the table – 'you are very kind.'

She recognized at once that he was trying to make it easier for her and he was rewarded with a quick glance of gratitude.

'It is nothing,' she said softly in clear English. 'You must excuse me', and before her father could stop her she had slipped away behind the curtain.

Christophou growled in disgust. 'Clever she may be, but stubborn, too. That is what is wrong with giving women education. It gives them minds of their own.

She would not stay in Athens when the war started. She insisted she came here, and I must say she has been very useful. She is strong and without the young men we need every pair of hands we can find aboard the fishing boat.'

'Where are your young men?' Tiller asked.

'Many were drafted into the Italian army or navy,' Christophou answered, 'but those who escaped are in the mountains.'

'Here?'

Christophou shook his head. 'On the bigger islands. That is the trouble. We can't stop the Germans from coming to Simi or prevent the Italians from staying.'

Larssen leant forward and said: 'We can't stop the Italians from staying either, Angelios. That is something that will be settled when the war is over. But we can stop the Germans coming. To do it we need the Italians to help us, at least until we can bring our own troops to the islands.'

Christophou absorbed this information without changing his expression and Tiller realized that he had underestimated the Greek, that Christophou had already arrived at that equation himself.

'And us?' he asked. 'You mean you want no trouble between us and the Italian pigs?'

'Exactly.'

Christophou stroked the stubble on his chin. 'That is a hard thing to ask. We are Greeks. The Italians have no right to be here. For most of my life they have suppressed us. They have starved us. Many of us have been beaten by them.' He shook his head angrily, remembering the injustices. 'How can I tell the people here not to take revenge? Many are already sharpening their knives.'

'We understand,' said Larssen. 'But that has to be settled after the war.'

Christophou thought for a moment and then shouted across the taverna to a tall, swarthy Greek, who stood up and joined them. He solemnly shook hands all round, and accepted a glass of retsina but refused the food. Christophou talked rapidly to him in Greek. The man argued, then shrugged his shoulders, and eventually nodded.

'Dimitri is the mayor here. He will see there is no trouble. But can you get us food? Our children are hungry.'

'In the morning I am seeing Colonel Ardetti,' said Larssen. The Dane had seen the condition of the children on Castelrosso and on Simi, and it angered him. 'I promise you that he will release some food.'

Dimitri shot a sentence in Greek at Christophou and lifted his glass in turn to the SBS men, who reciprocated. 'He says we help the English by not cutting any Italian throats. But is there no other way we can help?'

Larssen hesitated. He was reluctant to involve the islanders, but their local knowledge was needed if he was to fulfil his mission. 'There is. Tomorrow more of my men will come. Not many, but enough. They will stay and organize the island's defences while we visit the other islands around here. Piscopi, Calchi, then Alemnia. To do that we need the help of a pilot – someone who knows the area well.'

Christophou translated rapidly into Greek. Dimitri nodded, and pointed to Christophou, who spread out his hands in a gesture of modesty which he obviously did not feel. 'Dimitri says I am the right man.'

'You agree to go?' Larssen asked. 'It could be dangerous.'

'Dangerous? Bah! You know the old way we use here to get to the sponges? Just as we did in the time of the ancient Greeks. A rope is attached to us and we sink to the bottom by holding a heavy stone. Like this.' He clasped an imaginary rock to his chest. 'We had . . .'

He gestured to show his eyes were covered.

'Face masks.'

'Yes. Nothing more. Then we use – how do you say? – a kind of fork to take the sponge from the bottom. As a boy that was how we did it. Don't talk to me about danger.'

'Shit,' Barnesworth said admiringly under his breath.

Tiller's professional interest was aroused. 'But you've got diving equipment now?'

'Of course. Diving suits and boats with air pumps. Off the North African coast that is the only way because the sponges are in very deep water. Now that can be dangerous, yes?'

Tiller remembered a time, in Chichester harbour, when the Davis submarine escape apparatus he was testing malfunctioned. They had got him up just in time. He nodded sympathetically.

'But we sail in my boat, not yours. Many Turkish caiques visit Simi, but not so many sail west of here. Everyone knows my boat. No one will be suspicious.'

Larssen nodded. 'That makes sense. Agreed, Andrew?'

Maygan nodded. The arrangement suited him well. He didn't fancy putting his caique in the hands of a pilot of unknown skill. Anyway, Bryson needed time to strip the Matilda engine to find the cause of the trouble that had been plaguing it.

They agreed that only one guard was needed. Tiller took the first watch. He sat next to the covered Solothurn, his back propped against the mast, his Sten across his knees. The taverna shut soon after they left and the few flickering oil lamps in the houses around the quay were extinguished one by one. A dog howled in the distance. The night was moonless but the glittering stars seemed to illuminate the quay with a pale light. The water slapped lazily against the side of the caique, which moved uneasily when the wind gusted in occasionally from the sea. Tiller saw a cat move swiftly between two houses, but no other movement.

His thoughts strayed to Angelika. Had that look contained anything except polite gratitude? He guessed not but the two hours' watch was passed pleasantly enough speculating about the shy Greek girl and the nature of her stubbornness.

When his watch was up he leant over and shook Griffiths awake, handed him the Sten gun, pulled part of the mainsail over him, and slept without the nightmare recurring. He was woken at first light when Bryson prodded him with the butt of the Lanchester. 'Tea's brewed, Sarge. Captain Larssen says he wants to go to the castle in ten minutes.'

As soon as they were ushered into Colonel Ardetti's presence it became apparent that the Italians had had at least a partial change of heart. Perquesta told them that Admiral Maschinni had radioed the previous evening to say that Jarrett and his party had arrived on Leros, and had told Ardetti he was to co-operate with the SBS.

The SBS men sat down with the Italians, who showed them the plans of the island's defences. On paper these appeared adequate but on closer questioning Ardetti admitted he was short of ammunition and that not all the gun positions were manned. The ground, he said, was too rocky to dig slit trenches, so stone sangars had been built instead. These overlooked likely landing places, but they provided inadequate protection against anything except small-arms fire and virtually none against air attack.

There were no landlines between the outposts on the island and no central reserve force to reinforce any of them. Even if there had been there was no method of transporting them as Simi had no roads.

Larssen then inspected the outposts on the island's only vehicle, a tractor. At the end of it he advised the colonel to withdraw all his troops from the other parts of the island and concentrate them around the port. 'And make them dig slit trenches,' he added. 'The ground's not too rocky. They just need to expend a bit of sweat.'

Many of the garrison, Larssen had noticed, were fat, others were well past their prime. Their morale was suspect – some saluted Ardetti half-heartedly, others ignored him – and their weapons were hopelessly antiquated. They were all equipped with the outdated 6mm Mannlicher-Carcano rifle, which had remained practically unchanged from when it had been first manufactured in 1889 as a copy of the bolt-action Mauser.

Even the garrison's light machine-guns were the 1930 model 6.5mm air-cooled Breda, which had all sorts of design problems. Larssen remembered the comments of his instructor on the foreign weapons training course he had attended outside Haifa. If something looked right it generally was right: the Breda looked wrong, was wrong, and invariably went wrong.

The two coastal batteries were in no better shape than the garrison's personal weapons. Both had been sited incorrectly and were short of ammunition. The one that had fired at the caique had just half a dozen rounds of 75mm ammunition left. Most seriously, there were no anti-aircraft guns. If the Germans came Larssen knew it would only be the bravery of the garrison that stopped them, not the weight of the defenders' fire-power.

Ardetti, who looked pale and rather shaken by his excursion round the island, turned even paler when Larssen told him, through Perquesta, what he expected from the garrison.

'Naturally, we will support the British force here,' Ardetti replied. 'But as you can see my garrison cannot prevent the Germans from taking the island if they want to. We shall need a brigade of good troops here, supported by artillery, of course. When can we expect such a force?'

'Some reinforcements will be arriving this evening, after dark,' Larssen told him.

Ardetti's face lit up when Perquesta translated this. 'Good, good. A battalion perhaps?'

Larssen looked at him. 'No. Four of my men.'

Perquesta's jaw dropped. 'Four?'

'Four,' Larssen repeated, and held up four fingers.

Perquesta wrung his hands as he translated. The colonel just shook his head. Salvini smirked. 'They don't seem to have much faith in us, skipper,' Tiller remarked.

'I'll boot their arses from here to Cairo,' Larssen said in a sudden flash of temper. 'They'll fight whether they want to or not. I'll see to that. You make your colonel understand that,' he snarled at Perquesta.

The Italian lieutenant bit the edges of his moustache and nodded, but Larssen had now worked himself up into a fury.

'I want work on the trenches started now and I shall inspect them this evening. I want them manned at all times. I want flour and pasta released to the local population. Now. And I want fuel for cooking and for the MAS boat.'

Ardetti's Italian was so rapid when Perquesta told him this that Perquesta had trouble in translating the torrent. 'He says the garrison is short of food. They now only have one cooked meal a day. The other two meals are cold. The fuel they need for cooking and for refrigeration and . . .'

'And for what?' Larssen snarled.

Perquesta hesitated. 'For heating, *signore*. The colonel says the castle is damp. It has to be dried out as he suffers from rheumatism.'

'Then the colonel is relieved of his duties and is, as of now, officially on sick leave,' Larssen snapped. 'You, Perquesta, will take immediate command.'

'But *signore*,' Perquesta protested. 'Captain Salvini is of senior rank to me.'

Larssen turned to Salvini, who flinched under the Dane's hostile stare. 'Tell our friend here that I don't like his politics or his face. So I do not propose to put the garrison under his command. However, I won't lock him up so long as he behaves himself. I want from him a complete list of stores and fuel held by the garrison to be delivered to me on the caique immediately. Is that understood?'

Salvini, who obviously understood some English, nodded before Perquesta had finished translating. He looked glummer than ever.

'I shall be assigning one of my men to conduct a daily routine of physical exercises for the garrison which will include all officers,' Larssen added. 'The first of these will be held in exactly two hours. Captain Salvini is personally answerable to me that these orders are carried out. You, Lieutenant Perquesta, can get on and lick this garrison into some sort of shape. We may not have much time.'

'You can't do that, skipper,' Tiller said admiringly as the SBS party descended the hill to the quay, 'you don't have the authority.'

'Just watch me, Tiger,' Larssen retorted. 'Just watch me. Our job is to keep the Krauts out and that's exactly what we're going to do.'

Salvini, realizing Larssen meant business, had a list of stores and fuel brought to the caique within the hour and an hour after that Barnesworth was putting the garrison through a series of physical jerks and making them negotiate an improvised assault course.

As soon as it was dark Christophou's caique came alongside LS8, and arms and ammunition and equipment were passed over. Tiller felt a flicker of disappointment when he realized that Angelika was not aboard. Instead there was a slip of a youth whom Christophou introduced to them as Giorgiou. The youngster smiled shyly, and did what Christophou required of him with a practised ease that came with utter familiarity, but uttered not a word to anyone.

The Italians, Christophou explained, had taken away both Giorgiou's parents to the mainland. They had been betrayed by a collaborator on another island who had accused them of being Andartes. Since then Giorgiou had said very little. In his few unoccupied moments aboard the caique he sharpened his knife on a whetstone and tested its sharpness with his thumb.

Soon after midnight another caique from the flotilla came alongside, having lain up under camouflage nets on the Turkish coast during the day. It offloaded Corporal Ted Warrington, two other SBS men, and a member of the Greek Sacred Squadron, and then set sail for Kos, where it was to meet up with Jarrett.

Larssen briefed the SBS men to help the Italians organize the garrison's defences along the lines he had recommended, and ensure his orders regarding the food and fuel were carried out. He then assigned the Greek Sacred Squadron officer, a young lieutenant called Kristos, to the job of making sure the local population kept the peace.

Before dawn broke, borne on a light wind that eddied off the hills, Christophou's caique left the port with Larssen, Tiller, and Barnesworth aboard. Their first stop was at Piscopi, south-west of Simi. Piscopi, Christophou told them, meant 'lookout', as men in olden times had been sent there from Rhodes to watch for Turkish shipping. It was about the same size as Simi – some eight miles long – and was well named, for the high ground dominated the surrounding waters. But it was not as strategically placed, for it did not bar the passage of shipping southwards along the Turkish coast, as Simi did. The Italians had therefore only garrisoned it with a dozen *carabinieri*, who seemed to have become quite accepted by the population. One had even married a local girl.

A local Greek spoke a smattering of Italian and through him Larssen impressed the corporal in charge with the importance of radioing Simi if the Germans arrived. The caique then sailed south-east under a clear blue sky and reached Calchi that evening. As they were uncertain whether the Germans had already occupied the island from Rhodes – only a few miles to the south-east – Christophou landed the SBS men outside the port.

This proved to be a wise precaution for they were soon met by a young Greek who had obviously run from a nearby lookout to greet them. Breathlessly he introduced himself as Demetrios and in broken English explained that ten Germans had arrived in a motor launch from Rhodes earlier in the day and had requisitioned a house near the quay. Soon afterwards, the boy had gone on to explain contemptuously, the small Italian garrison had melted into the hills without firing a shot. After patrolling through the port the Germans had retired to the house with food and wine they had demanded from the locals.

Larssen sat Demetrios down and had him sketch out on the ground the exact location of the house the Germans had commandeered, and where they had moored their launch. The boy told them there was a sentry outside the house and they had also put one to guard the boat.

With a twig the boy then traced in the dust a route the SBS patrol could take that would bring them to the back of the house without being seen. Larssen pointed to Demetrios and then to the route. The boy grinned and nodded.

'Good, we have a guide,' said Larssen. 'What do you think, boys?'

'I could take the sentry guarding the launch, skipper,' Tiller volunteered, 'while you and Billy knock off the one outside the house. Then you can both get into position at the front and back of the house while I'll chuck in one of those Eyetie grenades you're so fond of, skipper. They'll come out like scalded cats and you can finish them off.'

At Simi they had found a box of Italian grenades, and Larssen, who had used them before, had brought them along.

'No. I don't want too much shooting in the streets. Locals might get hurt.'

'Set the house alight,' Barnesworth suggested. 'Burn the buggers.'

'And probably half the port,' said Larssen. 'It would also almost certainly alert the Krauts on Rhodes and we want to be well clear before they send anyone to investigate what's happened to their patrol. No, that's not the answer. I think we dispose of the launch's sentry first, then kill the other sentry, and then finish off the others inside the house. That way there'll be not much noise.'

The other two nodded. It made sense.

Demetrios led them at a brisk pace until they arrived at a high wall that ran alongside the quay. The boy signalled to them that the sentry guarding the launch was on the other side of the wall, and that further along there was a break in it. They moved forward cautiously on their rubber-soled commando boots, stopping to listen every few yards. Soon they heard the sentry's boots scraping on the stone quay. Then a match was scratched and the faint flare as it lit showed that the German was some thirty feet from them on the other side of the wall.

Larssen took out from his holster the special .22-calibre pistol all SBS men were issued with, screwed on the silencer, and tapped Tiller on the arm to show he was ready. Tiller and Barnesworth moved silently along the wall until they came to the break that Demetrios had indicated. They went through it and crouched by an upturned boat.

At first they could only see the glow of the sentry's cigarette, but then they saw his silhouette. Tiller was relieved to see he was wearing a desert-type forage cap. It would have been more difficult to break his neck if he had been wearing a helmet. They waited what seemed an age. Then they saw the glow of the sentry's cigarette butt as it arced through the air into the harbour, heard the clatter as he picked up his weapon and the bright ring of his boots on the stone as he approached them.

The SBS men shrank back behind the counter of the upturned boat until the sentry was just beyond them. Tiller made no sound and the sentry neither saw nor heard anything until Tiller's forearm tightened around his windpipe and turned his brief cry to a subdued gurgle. But then the German twisted round with a desperation born of terror and for a heart-stopping second Tiller realized that his grip had slipped and that he was not going to be able to break the man's neck cleanly.

Suddenly the sentry went limp and Tiller lowered him gently to the ground.

'A strong fellow,' Barnesworth whispered. 'But not strong enough.'

He wiped his knife clean on the German's uniform before sheathing it. 'Shove him under the boat.'

'Thanks, Billy.'

'Think nothing of it, mate. Now where's this fucking launch?'

They found it further down the quay, a wooden motor boat painted white with a swastika flag fluttering at its stern. Tiller lowered himself into it and opened the seacocks, then climbed back on to the quay. He watched the water rising rapidly up to and then over the thwarts, and then severed its mooring lines. It sank quickly and quietly. If the Germans wanted it they would have to send a diver down to get it.

They rejoined Larssen and Demetrios, and gave Larssen the thumbs up. Larssen indicated to Demetrios to lead the way to the house. It was a small, two-storey villa, somebody's holiday home in peacetime. Larssen moved quietly around it while the others waited nearby in the shadows. He returned with a grin on his face, the cheese wire with its wooden handles at either end still dangling from his hand.

'The sentry was sitting near the back door,' he whispered. 'Very easy. Let's go. I take the first floor. You two clear the ground floor. You' – he pointed at Demetrios – 'wait here.'

The sentry lay where he had dropped. Even in the half light Tiller could see his face was puffy and black. His eyeballs were almost out of their sockets and his tongue stuck out. There must be more pleasant ways of dying, Tiller decided, than being garrotted.

The back door was unlocked. They eased their way

in and found themselves in a passage that led straight through the house to the front door. On either side were two rooms, their doors shut. Larssen indicated that Tiller take one and Barnesworth the other, then pointed upstairs and held up his hand with the fingers spread apart, and then bunched them three times.

Tiller and Barnesworth nodded. They'd give him fifteen seconds after he had reached the first floor before opening fire.

They watched Larssen move silently down the corridor and listened for any sounds. Through the doors they heard snoring but otherwise the house was as silent as a tomb.

As Larssen reached the stairs Tiller took one of the scarlet-painted grenades from his pocket. Larssen had told him they were only made of tin, and were nothing like as lethal as a British No. 36 grenade, the so-called Mills bomb. But they made a hell of a bang and, unlike the British grenade, you could follow up behind it immediately without worrying about being hit by fragments. He just hoped Larssen was right.

Fifteen . . . ten . . . five . . . Tiller pulled the pin from the grenade, kicked the door in, tossed the grenade into the room, and followed in behind the explosion.

There was a scream and a guttural curse, but at first Tiller could see little through the smoke. Then he saw something move in the far corner and remembered the advice of the instructor at the Killer School: 'Shoot the man who moves first, as he's the one who's recovered first', and gave the lurching figure a short, measured burst. The man jerked and then slid gently down the wall as the Sten's 9mm bullets thudded home.

Then Tiller turned and shot a man who was still

on the floor groping for his rifle. The third one had received the full force of the grenade and wasn't moving.

It was over in seconds. Tiller cautiously inspected the three bodies by kicking them over on to their backs. They were all dead. The room stank of vomit. Obviously the soldiers, confident that they were safe, had drunk their fill of the local ouzo.

Next door Barnesworth had killed four others with his grenade and precise, conservative bursts from his Sten. That left one upstairs somewhere.

The two men took the stairs in quick bounds and found Larssen on the landing.

'No one up here,' he hissed. 'Were they all downstairs?'

Tiller shook his head. 'Only seven.'

'Shit!'

They stood stock-still alert for any movement in the house. They could not hear anything, but Larssen's instincts told him the German was there. Somewhere.

'The lavatory,' Barnesworth suddenly whispered. 'It must be downstairs.'

He thrust his Sten at Tiller, drew his pistol, and in two quick movements jumped down the stairs and vaulted the banisters. He landed in the correct crouching position in the passage below, his pistol held out in front of him in both hands.

Bending double saved him as the first burst from the German's Schmeisser almost took off his beret.

The German was a big fellow. His bulk filled the passage, blocking out the little light that there was. He was stark naked, and he came at Barnesworth at full tilt, screaming obscenities.

Barnesworth rolled sideways just before the second burst from the Schmeisser ripped by him, and then carefully and clinically shot the German through the head. Barnesworth had never believed the cliché of a single bullet stopping a man dead in his tracks, but then he had never shot anyone at quite such short range.

The German's head went back, his knees buckled, and down he came, his forward momentum reversed by the impact of the bullet.

'Timberrr!' Tiller called softly from the stairs as the man pitched forward.

'Christ,' said Barnesworth with feeling. 'I know how those big-game hunters feel now. That was close.'

'Well-trained bugger, wasn't he?' said Larssen admiringly. 'Taking his gun with him to have a pee. But next time shoot for the middle, Billy. The head is too small a target.'

6

They left it to Demetrios, to whom they awarded the German rations they found in the house, to explain to the locals what had happened. To avoid any possible reprisals, they were to clean up the house, dispose of the bodies, and to tell any other Germans who might appear that the first patrol had moved inland to find the Italian garrison. A battalion of men could vanish without trace in such wild country.

Before leaving they threw all the Germans' weapons into the harbour. To leave them would be too great a temptation for the locals, whose hatred of the Germans, so Demetrios told them, was matched only by their wholehearted contempt for the Italians. In the early-morning light they also looked to see if the launch was visible, but it lay safely out of sight in ten fathoms of murky water.

The sun was well up as they got back to the bay. In their absence Christophou had moored the caique by a stern warp to a tree. Its bows were held from swinging on to the rocky shore by an anchor whose warp was strained and taut. Demetrios bade them an emotional farewell.

The wind had freshened in the night and was now blowing strongly from the north-west and the water, even in the sheltered bay, was flecked with white.

Christophou, who had always been quite imperturbable, seemed agitated. 'This is a dangerous place when the *meltemi* blows. We must leave at once. There is a good anchorage at Alemnia for sheltering from a northerly gale.'

Tiller listened to the wind as it shrieked through the rigging and watched the waves pounding the shore.

'So this is the *meltemi*,' he said to Barnesworth. 'No wonder they didn't want to tell us about it.'

It seemed inconceivable to him that there could be gales in such tranquil waters, and when the sky was such a vivid blue, but there was a faint chill in the air and the boat moved uneasily under their feet. Giorgiou released the stern rope while Tiller hauled in on the anchor warp and Larssen and Barnesworth hoisted the sails. The mainsail canvas cracked noisily as it ran up the mast and the foresail slammed to and fro until its sheets were hauled tight and it filled with wind.

Outside the bay the waves had begun to build. They ran with white crests off which the wind whipped spray that stung the eyes of those aboard the caique and soaked their clothing. The caique's timbers groaned as it forged through the water and every now and again water slopped over the bows and ran down the scuppers.

'Should we reef?' Larssen asked.

Christophou shook his head and pointed ahead. 'Once we get beyond that headland we will be more sheltered.'

He grinned at Barnesworth, who had gone very pale. 'If you want to be sick, my friend, be sick over that side. Otherwise it all blows back into your face.'

'I know how to be fucking sick on a fucking boat,' said Barnesworth, and was.

'I didn't know you suffered from *mal de mer*, Billy,' said Larssen with mock horror. 'You should have stayed in the Guards.'

'I like being in or under the bleeding water,' said Barnesworth, 'not on it. At least not in a tub like this.'

The wind continued to rise, but once beyond the headland the caique moved more easily through the choppy water and, with the wind now on its quarter, it sailed close to its maximum speed of six or seven knots.

Alemnia, at first an indistinct hump on the horizon, grew rapidly bigger and an hour after leaving Calchi they were entering the tiny island's one good natural harbour. There were a scattering of cottages at the inner extreme of the large inlet, two churches, and a castle ruin atop a hill, but no sign of life.

The beach shelved so steeply that Christophou was able to throw out a stern anchor and run the caique gently on to the sand. The SBS patrol, their Stens at the ready, jumped off the caique's bow and looked around them. The door of one of the cottages banged in the wind. Nearby was a flag-pole with a tattered Italian flag fluttering halfway up it.

They searched the houses. They were all empty except for one whose occupants lay dead on the earth floor. A horde of flies buzzed over the bodies. There was only one man – the rest were women or children. Larssen slammed the door shut, his face aflame with anger.

Behind the last house was a crude stone wall, perhaps the beginning of some unfinished building. By it lay five bodies dressed in Italian army uniform. Their hands were tied behind their backs with wire. Larssen turned them face up with the toe of his boot.

'Executed,' he said. 'They must have been propped against the wall and shot.'

When they returned to the beach Christophou was talking to an old priest whose grey beard reached to his chest.

'Does he know what happened?' Larssen asked.

'The Germans came,' Christophou said with a shrug. Whatever the Germans did came as no surprise to him. 'He hid in a tomb. He heard firing. The Germans searched the church but didn't find him. He saw them go.'

'How did they go?' Larssen asked, his fury unabated. 'What were they in? How many of them were there?'

It took time for Christophou to extract the answers from the old priest, who was still visibly upset, but eventually Christophou was able to say: 'He thinks there were ten of them. In a white launch. It had a flag at the back.'

'If I'd known about this,' said Barnesworth. 'I'd have shot that bastard a lot lower down than his head.'

'Tell the priest that justice has been done,' Larssen told Christophou. 'That they are all dead.'

They found spades and a pickaxe and dug eleven graves by the beach. The two babies they laid to rest with their mothers. The priest said a few words over each of the graves and they found some driftwood and made crosses for each mound of earth.

When they had finished they searched the area for arms or supplies. They found some Chianti, which they drank, but the Germans had destroyed or taken everything else. The priest wrung their hands and blessed them as they climbed aboard the caique from the beach. As they hauled in on the stern anchor and the caique's bow slid off the sand he called out to them.

'What'd he say?' Tiller asked.

'He says war is a terrible thing,' said Christophou. 'But you have behaved honourably. He says: God speed.'

It was open water between Alemnia and Simi and Christophou took the precaution of reefing, but even with its sail area reduced the caique seemed to be more under the water than riding on it. The wind continued to rise and it chopped up the sea into vicious steep-sided waves that threatened to sweep the deck from stern to stem. Each time this looked inevitable the caique's counter managed to lift itself above the foaming water at the last moment, the bow would dip, the old sail would shake itself like a dog, and the caique would plunge forward, spray cascading over the deck.

Barnesworth retched occasionally over the side, and looked miserable. Giorgiou, impervious to the water cascading over him, sat propped against the mast, ready to lower the sail if necessary. He stropped his knife with quiet intensity. Larssen, brought up on the waters of the Skaggerak, was in his element.

Tiller, experiencing the power of the wind and the sea at close quarters for the first time, was surprised at the noise the storm generated. The wind shrieked through the rigging, a loose halyard banged with fearful force against the mast, the hull shuddered and groaned like a dying man, and below in the hold something rolled and clanged. How everything held together was a miracle, but Christophou, who was having to use all his strength to control the caique with the long, curved tiller, seemed quite unconcerned.

'The *meltemi* comes out of a clear sky,' he shouted at the SBS men above the racket. 'Brrm, just like that. This one is not too bad. By this evening it will be flat calm.'

'Is there no warning?'

'None. It blows from between north-east and north-west during the summer months. August is the worst month. If you are in harbour and it starts to blow hard you must stay there. If you are at sea run for shelter quickly. If there is no shelter make for open water, drop your sails, and run before the wind. If the storm is very bad you throw out warps to slow you down. I have known boats to be blown halfway to Cyprus by the *meltemi*.'

Larssen noted this information; there might be a time when he would need it.

As if on cue, the wind began to die as they approached Simi and its last puff bore them into the port as the sun dipped behind the mountainous interior.

Warrington, like Barnesworth, a Special Boat Service survivor from the days of Roger Courtney and Stirling's D Squadron, was on the quay to greet them.

'The major was on the blower earlier today, skipper,' he said to Larssen. 'He asked that you stand by the set at 2000 hours.'

'Thanks, Ted. All quiet here?'

'Lieutenant Kristos has the locals under his thumb, but the Eyeties seem to blow hot and cold. No sign of any Krauts yet.'

The garrison had begun to dig slit trenches and some food had been delivered to the village from the castle. But no fuel had been sent to the MAS boat, which was still moored at the far end of the quay.

The radio in LS8 came to life at exactly 2000. 'Sunray calling LS8. How do you hear me? Over.'

'Strength 8, Sunray. Loud and clear,' Griffiths replied and handed Larssen the microphone.

'Sunray minor here. Over.'

'I am on Epsilon, repeat Epsilon.' Larssen glanced at the code-book on his knees which the SBS patrols had devised for communicating unimportant tactical information to one another. Alpha was Simi, Omega was Rhodes, Epsilon was Samos, north of the Dodecanese. What the hell was Jarrett doing there?

'Roger, Sunray. Over.'

'Beta, Gamma and Delta all secured, and will be replaced shortly. I am still negotiating here. Accolade going to plan, especially on Beta. Over.'

That meant SBS patrols had established control on Kos, Kalimnos and Leros, and that they would be relieved by army units, probably the battalion of the Durham Light Infantry that had been dispatched from Malta. It also meant that the single airfield on Kos was fit to receive the seven South African Air Force Spitfires earmarked for the islands. That was a big bonus. Without any air cover the whole enterprise was in jeopardy.

'Good going, Sunray. But why Epsilon?'

'Our friends require our presence. We have reasons to believe that Epsilon may receive visitors. Any sign of them around you?'

Larssen briefed Jarrett on the situation on Piscopi, Calchi and Alemnia, and expressed his doubts about the garrison on Simi. Jarrett advised further pressure on the Italians as 'visitors' had to be expected eventually.

'Intelligence sources indicate preparations around Athens and on Crete. You can take it our friends will arrive. So you have my authority to use whatever persuasion you think best on our friends. Alpha is essential as a base for you. But minimum force. We have enough problems without creating more. Is that understood? Over.'

Jarrett then said his operator was going to send a coded message by the one-time pad method, and Larssen handed the microphone back to Griffiths. Decipherment was Griffiths's business, not his.

Jarrett's operator gave Griffiths the number of the top sheet of the one-time pad and then switched to Morse code. Griffiths took down the encoded message – a string of meaningless letters and numbers – and then translated these from the top sheet of the one-time pad. Then he ripped off the sheet from the pad and put a match to it before dropping the charred remains overboard. The one-time pad was the most secure method of transmitting signals in code. It was also very slow and laborious.

Larssen waited with ill-disguised impatience while Griffiths went methodically about his task of decipherment. Eventually Griffiths handed Larssen the message on a piece of signals paper and logged that he had received it in his book. Jarrett's message said that he had been ordered to send a patrol to Rhodes as quickly as possible to find out if the Germans were reinforcing the island. A co-ordinate was given where the patrol should land to reconnoitre Marizza airfield in the north-west corner, and the following evening the patrol would be met there by Andartes, who would hand over what they knew about German reinforcements elsewhere on the island.

Larssen swore under his breath as he read the signal. He could hardly ask Christophou to go on such a potentially dangerous mission, the MAS boat still had no fuel, and the engine of LS8 was spread out on its deck.

But then he read: 'T-class submarine will be with you by midnight tomorrow. Acknowledge. Jarrett.' Well, that settled who the patrol would consist of: it was a job for the cockle and its crew.

Larssen decided that Jarrett's orders gave him a free hand with the garrison. 'Minimum force' was, in the circumstances, a conveniently vague phrase. It was time to get some action from the Italians. But when Tiller and Barnesworth went with him next morning to confront them Larssen sensed that Salvini knew the Germans were going to try and pre-empt British occupation of the Dodecanese, for he was wary and certainly in no mood to be helpful. He said, through Perquesta, that the garrison had spared as much food as it could for the local population.

'Crap,' Larssen snapped. 'There wasn't even enough for the kids.'

Salvini shrugged as Perquesta translated and Larssen's quick temper nearly got the better of him. Instead he pointed at Salvini's prominent stomach and said to Perquesta in as level a voice as he could manage: 'Tell the captain that being so overweight is unhealthy. I am recommending a diet for him.'

Perquesta nibbled at his moustache. 'A diet, *signore*?'

'That's right. I shall make sure he eats only what the children eat.'

'But how? . . .'

'An enforced diet, if necessary. Do I make myself clear?'

He did, and Salvini was quick to take the hint.

'The captain says that the food that was delivered was only a first consignment. Naturally, more is being sent today.'

'Naturally. Please congratulate the captain on his generosity and common sense. Now there is the little matter of fuel for the MAS boat.'

Salvini appeared to consider himself on firmer ground with the fuel. It was, he said, regrettable that none had yet been delivered to the MAS boat but he had to have the permission of his superiors on Leros and so far he had been unable to contact them by radio.

'So how long will it be?' Larssen snapped.

Not long, Salvini promised.

'What do you reckon Salvini's word is worth, skipper?' Tiller asked as they made a quick tour of the garrison's new defences with Perquesta.

'Not a row of beans,' said Larssen. 'But I want food for those kids first. We don't know for sure if Balbao will help us. We know the locals will. Remember the garrison outnumbers us by ten to one.'

'Make it fifty to one and I'd still fancy our chances,' said Barnesworth, looking at the men who were manning the slit trenches. He turned to Perquesta. 'When did these men last see any action?'

'Some fought in Abyssinia,' Perquesta said.

'Abyssinia!' Larssen exploded. 'Christ, that was eight years ago.'

'They are middle-aged,' Perquesta admitted, 'and the fire has gone from their bellies. They are confused, too. Whose side are they meant to be on? They are in no man's land and they are afraid they will be shot at from both sides. When are your reinforcements coming, Captain? What is needed is a show of strength.'

'Soon,' said Larssen. 'In the meantime the garrison has an obligation to defend Italian soil. They must understand that.'

Perquesta shook his head. 'They know it. They also know – because the population never lets them forget it – that these islands are not Italian.'

The transport turned out to be one of the T-class submarines the British had handed over to the Royal Hellenic Navy. The *Papankolis* had been diverted at the last minute while on passage from Alexandria to its operational area off Salonika. Its recognition signal had been radioed to the SBS men an hour before it arrived and the Italians were warned of its arrival.

Few submariners, Larssen knew from experience, liked being involved in clandestine operations. These were risky enough for those going on them, but they were even more risky for the submarine and its crew. Submarines needed deep water for safety, and depth was not to be had near any coastline. Caught on the surface, a submarine had little chance against air attack and was horribly vulnerable to fast surface forces. Coldly calculated, it meant risking a highly trained crew and a vessel worth God knows what to get two men ashore in a flimsy canvas contraption on a mission that could be, and often was, a wild-goose chase.

Commanders-in-chief valued their submarines, and did not risk them lightly. When an admiral reluctantly agreed – and it was always reluctantly – to assign one to a clandestine mission his staff tended to choose one that had some connection with the operation it had been ordered to mount.

However, the Greek CO of the *Papankolis* saw no connection at all. As far as he was concerned he was wasting valuable time and valuable fuel which he could have spent sinking German shipping off Salonika.

He told Tiller and Barnesworth all this in no uncertain terms after they had paddled the cockle out to the submarine to where it lay off the port. They must understand, he said, that if they did not return to the rendezvous on time the following night he could not wait for them.

They supervised the stowing of the cockle, watching to make sure the fragile craft was not damaged in any way. The sixteen-foot cockle they had brought with them from Castelrosso was of the collapsible kind, an improved version of the Mark II that Tiller had used on the Gironde raid the previous year. It had a plywood deck and bottom but canvas sides and by hinging forward the struts that kept the deck in place they were able to concertina the whole structure to a compact depth which enabled it to fit down the torpedo hatch.

The submarine submerged and ran at periscope depth.

In Christophou's caique the voyage of twenty miles or so had taken much of the day. In the submarine it took under two hours. When it surfaced they could see from its bridge the hump of Alemnia on the horizon on their starboard side.

The white-flecked waves had gone now, for the *meltemi* had long since blown itself out and had been replaced by a gentle offshore breeze which hardly ruffled the water. The captain of the *Papankolis* kept the profile of his submarine as low as possible and its decks were almost awash as the crew opened the torpedo hatch to bring out the cockle.

The north-west coast of Rhodes, where the Marizza airfield lay, loomed straight ahead in the darkness. Tiller remembered the massacre on Alemnia and regretted he was only on a reconnaissance patrol. He was itching to use his explosives, but Larssen had expressly forbidden any attacks on the airfield. Information was what was needed. Any attack would lessen the chances of the two men returning with it and could jeopardize the safety of the submarine when it returned to pick them up the following night.

'Are you going to use RG equipment?' the captain asked, referring to the infrared lamps with their invisible beams of light which canoeists sometimes used to rendezvous with a submarine.

Tiller shook his head. 'No. We now use what we call the bongle', and he explained how it worked.

'Good. The Mountain will come to Mahomet, then. Make sure you're at least three miles offshore. Good luck.'

The cockle was carefully extracted from the hatch by two of the submarine's crew and laid on the deck. Their faces blacked with camouflage cream, and dressed from head to foot in their rubberized paddler's suits with rope-soled boots, the two SBS men carefully checked for a final time that everything was in place.

They moved the cockle under the barrel of the submarine's four-inch gun. Beneath the barrel was clamped a steel girder, rather as a bayonet was to a rifle. They placed the craft gently into a specially designed sling and attached it to a rope tackle which hung down from the end of the steel girder. Then they climbed carefully into the two circular cockpits, Tiller in front, Barnesworth behind him, and two members of the submarine's crew then hauled in on the tackle and lifted the cockle from the deck. The gun was elevated slightly, and then swivelled sideways before the craft was lowered carefully into the water so that it floated alongside the slowly moving submarine.

'Don't keep the warps too taut,' Tiller called up to the crew. In the choppy water this could have caused the cockle to hit the sides of the submarine and capsize. They unshipped their double paddles, ensured they were properly locked in the middle so that the blades at either end were at right angles to each other, and then with fierce, quick strokes moved the cockle away.

Dispatching the SBS team was a vulnerable moment for everyone involved. Tiller knew this and he had been trained to leave the submarine's side with the utmost speed. He was pleased to see how quickly Barnesworth acted, too.

The submarine, which had remained with its deck nearly awash throughout the launching, now began sliding silently into the depths. The water boiled for a moment around the top of its conning tower and then it was gone.

The submarine had submerged slowly but its bulk created a wash that made the cockle yaw violently. Tiller flicked his paddle expertly into the water to steady it while Barnesworth took a bearing with the hand compass on a prominent headland off the port bow and then on Alemnia, now hardly visible on the horizon on the starboard side. He jotted the two bearings on a slate and then tapped Tiller twice on the shoulder to indicate that he was ready.

Tiller adjusted the grid of the P8 compass – which was fixed to the cockle in front of Tiller – to 160 degrees and then propelled the cockle forward with steady, powerful strokes. By locking the blades of the paddles at right angles the two men were able to 'feather' the blade that was in the air. This kept down wind resistance and gave the craft a lower silhouette.

If the submarine had dropped them in the right place this would bring them to a beach just three miles from Marizza airfield. It was always a big 'if'. After an hour they stopped for a few minutes to take new bearings and to rest, and to subdue the hallucinations that commonly haunted canoeists at night. Then they struck out for the shore again and within an hour they had reached the right spot. Silently Tiller thanked the Greek captain. He might have been a dour bastard but his navigation had been superb.

They stayed offshore for a short while, scanning the beach and its surroundings for any movement. They saw nothing, and could only smell the fresh scent of sage wafted on the breeze. They then unlocked their double paddles, stowed the female half, and manoeuvred the cockle closer to the shore using the single paddles. This gave them a much lower profile and a completely silent approach.

They were only too aware that a sharp rock could wreck the operation, and approached the beach with great caution. When the cockle was fifty yards from it Barnesworth shipped his single paddle, leant back and extracted his legs from beneath the canvas cover. He lifted himself up carefully, straddled his cockpit, and then expertly flipped himself over and into the water before swimming to the bow and guiding it on to the beach. The craft grounded gently and Tiller extracted himself with a quick, practised movement.

Both men now worked in silent unison, for their training had made it second nature to them. They lifted the cockle, ran up the beach with it, and hid it among rocks. Tiller stripped off his paddler's suit and donned shorts, SAS beret and a service shirt with his sergeant's stripes on both sleeves. If the Germans found them the fact that they were in uniform might save them from execution, but Tiller knew all about Hitler's Commando Order and would not have put his back pay on their surviving if they were captured.

So far as intelligence knew there were no Gestapo on Rhodes, just regular Wehrmacht troops, but the orders were for all 'saboteurs' to be handed over to the Gestapo for 'questioning'. All those undertaking special operations were under no illusion that this encounter invariably meant a bullet in the back of the head. Only recently Tiller had heard that the French resistance had reported back that this had been the fate of two of the canoeists on the Gironde raid.

Barnesworth returned to the water's edge and eradicated any footmarks with a rake he had designed for the purpose. Then, as Barnesworth stripped and changed, Tiller extracted their haversacks, Stens, revolvers, rations and water bottles from the cockle before camouflaging it with netting. With a brief nod to his companion, Tiller turned inland, his pocket compass in his hand.

The ground was rocky at first but then became flat and fertile. There were plenty of olive trees and the occasional scrub but nothing that would hinder their approach to the airfield. It would take them, Tiller calculated, not much more than an hour to reach it. That would give them plenty of time to find a convenient observation point before dawn broke. A game-bird bursting from under their feet with a clatter of wings gave them an unpleasant shock, but otherwise they neither heard nor saw anything. They might as well have been on the moon. After an hour Tiller beckoned his companion.

'It's in a shallow valley under that mountain,' he said in an undertone, 'so it should be over the next brow, I reckon.'

Barnesworth nodded. Close to the crest they dropped down on all fours and wriggled forward.

The airfield was bigger than they had anticipated. It was surrounded by wire and there was a cluster of huts at the far end. At one time it must have been a civilian strip, for there were a couple of hangars and a petrol pump. At first they could not see any aircraft but as their eyes became accustomed to the dark they could see the outlines of two parked on one side of the field.

'Eyetie bombers,' Tiller whispered. He lowered his night binoculars. 'Reckon this is as good a place for a hide as any.'

They found a rock behind which they could observe the airfield, ran a small camouflage net over the dip in the ground behind it and stuck dried grass, twigs, and small branches in the netting, and then settled down in the dip. It just held the two of them and was swelteringly hot when the sun came up.

For several hours nothing much happened. They saw guards patrolling the perimeter, but no sign of any aircraft apart from the two triple-engined Savoia-Marchetti bombers. Tiller scrutinized each part of the airfield with great care while Barnesworth drew a diagram of it in his notebook, divided it into nine squares, and gave each square a letter of the alphabet. Methodically, Tiller described what he saw in each. When he got to 'G' he muttered: 'Eh, what have we here?'

It was, Tiller guessed after studying it carefully, an ammunition dump of some kind, but it was well screened by netting. He handed the binoculars to Barnesworth, who said: 'Bombs. Those are bombs. Hundreds of them. What load can those Eyetie bombers carry?'

'About 1500 kilogrammes each – no more. Perhaps less.'

'It would take them months to get rid of that lot, then.'

'So there must be others around.'

'There are,' said Barnesworth, looking skyward. 'Can't you hear them?'

Tiller listened intently, and soon caught the beat of aircraft engines. Then he saw the first. It was flying directly towards him and as it grew larger its gull-shaped wings and fixed undercarriage made its identification simple. Behind the first was another and another.

'Stukas,' he said.

'Even I recognize that bastard,' said Barnesworth softly. 'Once seen, never forgotten. Ever been bombed by one?'

Tiller shook his head. He had only seen the German Ju87 dive-bomber in action on the newsreels. Even in the cinema the scream of the aircraft as it descended on its target almost vertically had been impressive. But it was, he knew, a slow and, by now, obsolete fighting machine. If they managed to base Hurricanes on Leros the Stukas wouldn't stand a chance.

The first one swept overhead, circled behind them and came into land. It taxied to the other end of the field and up to the bomb dump, where it was soon joined by the other two. They watched as the crew clambered down from the aircraft and disappeared into one of the huts. Soon afterwards a lorry approached and disgorged what must have been the German ground crews. With them were two fuel lorries which moved along the line of aircraft and then the SBS men saw the German armourers fitting bombs to the Stukas' bomb racks under their fuselages, and then priming them. They wondered uneasily what the planes' first target was going to be.

Two hours later, as the sun was low in the sky, three more Stukas came in and the operation of fuelling and arming was repeated. Then the ground crews departed in the lorry, though some stayed behind as guards. Two had Alsatians on leashes and the two SBS men watched them release the dogs outside the perimeter wire. The animals began to quarter the ground systematically and the whistles of their handlers drifted up to the two men in their hide. Both knew that a man could pass within ten yards of them and suspect nothing, but a trained dog could pick up their scent from five times that distance. At least they had taken the elementary precaution of building their hide downwind.

The sun seemed to sink very slowly. The guards' shouts of encouragement to the dogs were wafted clearly to the two men on a breeze which stirred the dried grasses in front of their hide.

The dogs barked occasionally as they criss-crossed the ground outside the perimeter, slowly working their way towards the crest. But they were still half a mile away when darkness closed in and their handlers recalled them.

Cautiously the two men folded the netting and eradicated any sign of their presence, then withdrew from the crest. They followed the reverse compass bearing and were at the beach in just over an hour. At exactly the right time three bearded figures emerged out of the darkness, shook their hands, thrust an envelope into Tiller's hand, and vanished into the night.

They changed back into their paddle suits, launched the cockle into the calm water and an hour later reached the approximate point where the submarine had dropped them.

Barnesworth now set up the 'bongle' by lowering its rod into the water and propping the box containing the hammer on to the side of the canoe. Then he began cranking the handle – coffee-grinding, it was called – which governed the hammer hitting the rod. Tiller wondered at the ingeniousness of whoever had invented this simple device. It radiated sound waves of a recognized pitch which the submarine's hydrophones could pick up and home in on. No longer did canoeists have to try and find the submarine; instead the submarine came to the cockle.

Half an hour later the submarine rose slowly from the depths. The SBS men paddled quickly over to it and were hauled aboard by the same method as they had been launched the previous night.

The captain was in the conning tower scanning the horizon with night binoculars. 'Your little gadget is very effective,' he said with grudging approval as they passed him to go below. In the mess deck, hot cocoa was thrust into their hands. It was gratefully received for, despite their paddlers' suits, the cold had begun seeping into them as they waited for the submarine.

The effect of the benzedrine tablets they had taken before leaving the beach now began to wear off. They both slumped on to bunks and fell asleep at once, only to be woken, or so it seemed, as soon as they had closed their eyes.

'No time to go into the bay,' said the Greek captain as they joined him in the conning tower. 'You boys will have to paddle a little bit further.'

It was a lot further but they made it as the first sliver of light began to show over the mainland. Lieutenant Kosti was there to greet them with a warm handshake, and within a few minutes Larssen had joined them. Tiller turned to him wearily, handed him the envelope, and said: 'I think you'd better get everyone prepared for air raids, skipper.'

7

In the following days they did what they could to prepare for the Stukas, and warned the other islands that they might be raided. But it seemed extremely unlikely that Simi would be the Germans' target for they still did not appear to know that the SBS were on the island.

Nevertheless, as a precaution, both the caique and the MAS boat were moved out of the port. The caique was moored under a cliff, where its netting made it virtually invisible from the air, and the MAS boat was anchored in a small bay and crudely, but effectively, camouflaged. Those inhabitants with cellars were advised to turn them into shelters and those without were warned to be prepared to move into the hills.

Though Simi was not yet a target, one morning Larssen told his men that once the Germans knew the SBS were there it would be vulnerable to a landing by German troops. 'So we cannot allow the Germans to take over the outlying islands from which they might possibly launch an attack on us here. The Italian garrison on Piscopi have just radioed the castle that a German patrol has landed on the far side of the island from their headquarters. It will take some time for the Germans to get to them but they need to be reinforced. Quickly. I want you, Tiger, to take Billy and four men to Piscopi with additional arms and stores for the garrison, and make sure the Krauts are driven off.'

'Who will take us? One of the Schooner Flotilla?'

Larssen shook his head. 'It would take too long. I have spoken to Balbao. He will take you and pick you up.'

'But he still has no fuel,' Tiller objected.

'We're going up to the castle now,' Larssen replied grimly. 'No more shilly-shallying with our Italian friends. We get the fuel. Now.'

Salvini, when they arrived at Colonel Ardetti's office in the castle, blustered and prevaricated. He had, he said, still not received permission to release the fuel. When Perquesta translated this Larssen unslung his Sten and said: 'Tell Captain Salvini that if he does not produce the fuel – now – I shall take it myself.'

Salvini's expression darkened and he almost spat out his reply.

'He asks how you propose to do this,' Perquesta said. He looked distinctly uncomfortable at being the go-between.

Larssen smiled pleasantly at Salvini and said to Perquesta: 'Tell him I shoot him first. Then I shoot whoever else stops me,' and he lifted the barrel of his Sten a few inches. It was a small gesture but an unambiguous one. In the silence that followed, one of the SBS men could be heard putting the garrison through its daily exercises.

'Your pistol, please,' Larssen said, nodding at the holster strapped to Salvini's thick, glossy leather belt. Salvini's hand lingered momentarily over the holster but the butt of his pistol was covered by a leather flap which was buttoned to the holster. He would have been dead before he had even undone the flap.

Instead he shrugged, undid his belt, and dropped it and the holster on to the colonel's desk, then snapped something at Perquesta.

'Captain Salvini says that he will lay a formal complaint before the Italian Armistice Commission.'

'Fuck the Italian Armistice Commission,' said Larssen pleasantly.

'*Prego, signore?*'

'It doesn't matter. Captain Salvini and I understand one another.'

Larssen nodded to one of the SBS men. 'Take him down to the port and lock him up somewhere that's safe from the locals. I want him on the next boat out of here.'

Tiller stepped forward, undid the flap of Salvini's holster and withdrew the pistol. He slid the magazine from the butt, flicked the cartridges on to the table with his thumb, and pocketed them before returning the pistol to its holster. It would make a nice souvenir.

Larssen turned to Perquesta: 'Where do you keep your fuel?'

Perquesta took them out of the castle and up a path which led towards the hills. Around a corner they found a steel door let into the hillside which was surrounded by barbed wire and guarded by two Italians with sub-machine-guns.

Perquesta went up to them and when they shook their heads he started arguing. The guards continued to shake their heads.

'What's the matter?' Larssen said impatiently.

'They let no one in without a pass from Captain Salvini. He gave them the strictest orders.'

Larssen joined Perquesta and said: 'Tell them Salvini has been arrested. By me.'

This did not go down well with the guards, who shifted uneasily and looked at one another. One of them began to slide his weapon off his shoulder.

What Larssen did next was so quick and effortless that Tiller, standing only a few yards away, did not immediately grasp what had happened. The Dane stepped forward and in two swift movements struck one man on the side of the jaw and then rammed the same fist into the stomach of the second. As the second guard doubled up Larssen hit him accurately, though not too hard, on the back of his neck with the side of his other hand.

'Very neat, skipper,' said Tiller, surveying the two men sprawled on the ground.

'These help,' said Larssen removing the brass knuckledusters from his right hand and sliding them into his pocket. 'Not according to the Geneva Convention, Tiger. No spit and polish. Just wham, bang. You disapprove, eh? Not cricket.'

'It worked,' said Tiller. 'That's what counts.'

'Eh, Tiger, we make a pirate of you yet,' Larssen slapped him delightedly on the back.

The hands of the two unconscious guards were bound with their belts and with a short burst from his Sten Larssen smashed the lock on the gate of the compound. But the steel door was a much more formidible barrier and when they could not find the key on the guards Tiller fetched some explosive. He returned with a yellowish lump of material which had the consistency of plasticine and was the size of a large orange. He moulded it round a small metal cone, attached it with tape to the keyhole and took out a pencil fuse from a container which looked like a small cigar tin.

'Ten minutes is the shortest time delay I've got,' he said.

'We can wait,' said Larssen. 'Just don't blow up the fuel as well.'

'Come on, skipper,' said Barnesworth reprovingly. 'Tiger does this sort of thing in his sleep.'

Tiller removed the coloured safety strip from the five-inch fuse, stuck it in the plastic explosive, squeezed the fuse's soft copper tube to activate it, and retired to a safe distance.

Perquesta, who had watched Tiller prepare the charge in puzzled amazement, said as they waited: 'That is explosive? Never have I seen explosive like that.'

'It's RDX,' Tiller explained. 'Research Development Explosive. What you call T4. Mix it with beeswax or oil and it becomes malleable. Plastic explosive, we call it.'

What he didn't tell Perquesta, because the lieutenant seemed to have an excitable nature, was that the main ingredient of RDX was hexamine, an unstable combination of ammonia and formaldehyde. To stabilize it another explosive like amatol or TNT had to be mixed with it.

'But why the cone?' Perquesta asked.

'It concentrates the shock waves of the explosion into a very small area. Increases the power of the explosive by up to 15 times. Shaped charges, they're called.'

The explosion, when it came, was violent and effective. Larssen inspected the result approvingly. 'Good stuff, plastic explosive, but that wasn't ten minutes, Tiger.'

'So far the boffins haven't been able to come up with

a pencil fuse that isn't affected by the temperature,' Tiller replied. 'It's a hot day so it works quicker than it should. And vice versa. I reckon you could wait for ever at the North Pole.'

Perquesta was told to fetch the tractor, and its trailer, while Larssen investigated the fuel store. It was almost empty but there were a dozen large drums of high octane petrol in one corner and these, along with the half-conscious guards, were loaded on to the trailer.

'We'll take the fuel,' Larssen told Perquesta. 'You take the guards. Let your doctor look at them and then lock them up. They're Fascists and I've had enough of Salvini and his followers. We'll be back in an hour. I want every soldier not manning a gun position to be on parade in the castle quadrangle. I'm going to tell them exactly where they stand and what they must do.'

Balbao greeted them when they reached the quay with the drums of fuel. There was enough in them, he said, to take them to Piscopi and back and there would be plenty to spare 'just in case'.

Larssen asked him if he knew the waters around Piscopi.

Balbao shook his head. 'We take a local man. No problem.'

Tiller suggested Christophou, and Balbao agreed. The drums were left on the quay for the crew and the SBS men to take aboard, and Larssen and Tiller returned to the castle in the tractor. Perquesta had rounded up all the men not on duty and had paraded them in the quadrangle.

Larssen, when he addressed them through Perquesta, said he would not tolerate Fascists any longer. They would be locked up. Those not locked up would fight for the Allies and on Simi the Allies meant him. Perquesta, a fine officer, would lead them and he, Captain Larssen, would ensure they had help from his men and food and ammunition from the British Navy. God Save King Victor Emmanuel.

His address was received in stoic but friendly silence.

'Are you going in the diplomatic corps after the war, skipper?' Tiller asked with a grin as they returned to the port.

'No bloody fear,' retorted Larssen. 'I think big-game hunting is what I do. I shall be well trained for it, yes? I have the right instincts. Now you go and talk to our friend Christophou.'

But when Tiller went to the taverna Christophou was not there and when he told Angelika what he wanted him for she said her father would not be able to go. Tiller was puzzled.

'Why not?' he asked.

'Here we all seem friendly to you. But some of us are not. There is at least one collaborator here who serves the Italians, the fascist cause.'

'Are you sure?'

Angelika nodded. 'Since he took you the other day my father has been threatened. If he helps again his boat may be tampered with, perhaps sunk. He may even be killed.'

'So he is not prepared to help?'

Angelika hesitated and said: 'Yes, of course he will help if you ask him. But please do not ask him. He is not a young man any longer. It is too dangerous for him. Choose someone else.'

'But who?'

Angelika blushed. 'Ask me.'

Tiller's expression made her laugh. 'I know these islands like – how do you say? – the back of my hand.'

Tiller congratulated her on her English and asked where she had learnt it. 'At college. Then I worked for a tourist firm in Athens. Showing the English around the Parthenon and other places. I also speak Italian. Well? You will take me?'

'It might be risky,' Tiller protested. 'And might not collaborators threaten you?'

'If they found out, yes. But I make sure they do not find out. If anyone asks, my mother will say I am ill.'

'I think she fancies you, Tiger,' Larssen said when Tiller told him about Angelika. 'Still, we don't want to cause trouble for Christophou and there's no time to find anyone else. I don't see what else we can do.'

Larssen looked at Balbao, who shrugged and nodded reluctantly. Women were never popular aboard a ship – they were thought to bring bad luck – but he couldn't see any alternative either. 'So long as she knows her job,' Balbao said.

As soon as darkness fell Angelika, dressed in her father's clothes and cloth cap, came aboard, asked for the MAS boat's charts of the area and went below to study them. An hour later, after all the patrol's equipment, which included a swimmer's suit for Barnesworth, had been loaded, along with stores and arms for the Piscopi garrison, the MAS boat left the quay and headed out to sea.

'Get your heads down while you can, boys,' Tiller told his men. 'You might not be getting much kip for the next day or two. I'll stay on the bridge.'

To conserve fuel and prevent a tell-tale white bow wave, which could betray its presence to a German sea patrol, the MAS boat used only one of its engines. Even so Simi quickly became a thin, dark ribbon on the sea behind them. Balbao searched the horizon ahead with his night binoculars. Angelika stood near him on the open bridge, a chart in her hand. Her presence made Tiller wonder why it was some women looked even more attractive in men's clothes than they did in their own.

After an hour one of the crew brought them mugs of ersatz coffee. Tiller found it almost undrinkable but the night was chilly and it warmed his insides.

Balbao and Angelika spoke in rapid Italian and then the girl tapped Tiller lightly on the arm. 'You need to go alongside?'

Tiller nodded. 'We need to get the stores ashore quickly.'

'There is only one place. Here.' She shone a shaded torch on the chart and indicated with her forefinger a promontory to the north of the bay. 'The commander wants to go alongside the quay. It's all right for a small caique like my father's, but it is too shallow for an MAS boat.'

'It is deep enough where you want to go?'

'Yes. But it is just a flat rock which sticks out into the water. It can only be done in fine weather when the sea is calm.'

'And it will stay calm?'

Angelika nodded. 'No *meltemi* tonight.'

'What do you think, Commander?' Tiller asked Balbao.

'We see,' said Balbao enigmatically. Out of earshot of Angelika he added: 'Our pilot is pretty, Sergeant. But how can we be sure she knows what she is doing?'

Piscopi was now large on the horizon ahead. Balbao cut back the MAS boat's speed until it was only just making way through the oil-calm water. As the boat approached Livadia Bay, where the Italian garrison had its headquarters, the crew took up their action stations.

Tiller went below and woke his men but told them to stay where they were for the moment as there was very little room on deck. But he told Barnesworth to put on his surface swimmer's suit and then took him back to the bridge.

'This man's an expert swimmer,' Tiller said to Balbao. 'He can swim ashore and test the depth by the quay and the jetty. You won't even need to stop. Just make a pass close to it. While he's measuring you can look at the rock.'

'How will he measure it?' Balbao asked. Barnesworth produced his beach gradient reel from a pocket of his suit. Balbao examined it curiously.

'A fishing reel?'

'Very nearly,' said Barnesworth. 'Except the line on it is marked with split lead pellets so I can read off the depth in the dark or under water. It's designed for COPP parties to gauge beach gradients.'

'COPP?' Balbao queried.

'Combined Operations Pilotage Parties,' said Barnesworth. 'They're the lads who go ashore to recce prospective beaches before an amphibious landing. But it's easily adaptable to measure the depth of water. I just insert a crampon somewhere at water level, hook on the line and take the reel to the bottom. The lead pellets will tell me how much line has been unwound. If there's nowhere to use a crampon I just use a float. Very simple really. But if it's as shallow as our pilot says it is I won't need it.'

The explanation convinced Balbao and they crept slowly into the bay. There was no sign of life anywhere. If any of the garrison were still around they must have been fast asleep.

'Wait till you see us come back,' Tiller said to Barnesworth as he waited in the stern with him. 'Then signal us. A series of "R"s will do. But don't start swimming until I reply with a series of "O"s. You never know, there might well be some Jerry-manned MAS boats around that look like this one.'

'The captain, he say now,' said one of the crew emerging out of the dark.

'Good luck,' said Tiller.

Barnesworth lowered himself into the water from the ladder, held on for a second and then dropped. With strong powerful strokes he swam away from the MAS boat to clear its propellers, and in moments had vanished into the dark. The MAS boat increased speed slightly and turned back out to sea.

Tiller returned to the bridge with some misgivings. He did not like putting himself and his team in the hands of a former enemy and a Greek girl about whom he knew next to nothing. Still, there was nothing he could do about it now. As a precaution, he called the SBS party up from below and told them to find what cover they could on the deck. At least they would not be trapped below if something went wrong.

With Angelika giving instructions, the MAS boat turned to port. Once out of the bay Balbao turned it north and then circled slowly near the promontory that Angelika had pointed out on the chart. The large slab of rock was just where she said it would be and, with the wind blowing offshore, Balbao readily agreed it would be possible to go alongside it – provided there was enough water.

'There is,' Angelika said confidently.

They returned to the position where Barnesworth had left them and after a couple of minutes his shaded torch began flashing the agreed signal. Tiller replied and ten minutes later, like a seal surfacing for air, Barnesworth bobbed up by the counter and climbed aboard by the ladder.

'Five feet,' he said when he reached the bridge.

'Not enough,' Balbao admitted.

'Any sign of life?' Tiller asked. Barnesworth shook his head. 'I reckon the garrison have taken to the hills along with all the locals.'

The MAS boat crept back to the flat rock and everything was rapidly unloaded on to it. Balbao had to return while it was still dark and once all the stores were ashore he manoeuvred the MAS boat expertly away from the rock, and with a wave headed back to Simi. Tiller fancied that Angelika waved, too, but he could not be sure.

Two of the SBS men went ahead and scoured the buildings around Livadia Bay. To their surprise the *carabinieri* were still there, their inactivity accounted for by the number of empty Chianti bottles that lay strewn around their quarters. The SBS men brought some of them back to the rock and with their help the stores and extra arms were quickly moved into the bay.

The small garrison appeared cheered by the arrival

of the SBS. Tiller found the scruffy, balding corporal who was in charge. He looked old enough to be Tiller's father, and had that worn-down look all of the SBS had seen on the faces of Italian troops, the look of men who had been beaten and had had enough of fighting. All they wanted to do, their expressions said, was survive and go home to their families. If only life were that easy, Tiller thought grimly.

It turned out that, when pressed, the corporal spoke broken English, which, perhaps cannily, he had not revealed on the previous occasion. From him it soon became clear not only that the locals had fled into the hills when they heard the Germans were coming but that the garrison was expecting to be evacuated before they arrived. When it sunk in they might have to stay and fight they looked appalled.

Tiller and Barnesworth started by checking the Italians' equipment. They soon found that, as with all the Italian troops they had encountered so far, the garrison had inferior weapons and had little ammunition. Some of their rifles were so rusty they looked dangerous and these were replaced with the Lee Enfield rifles the SBS had brought with them – the standard British infantryman's weapon – and boxes of .303 ammunition were handed out. Tiller also made sure the Italians knew how to use the twin 6.5mm Breda light machine-guns he had brought along, and then he heated up enough tinned stew for everyone. It always helped to go into battle on a full stomach and the Italians looked half-starved.

At daylight Tiller inspected the defensive positions of the *carabinieri* and put the garrison to work to improve them. He tried to discover more about the Germans who had landed, but the corporal did not know even how many there were. He had received only one message from the lookout at Monastery Point, on the other side of the island, who had seen them land in Kamara Bay.

'He say many, many. Then the telephone not work any more.' Why it had stopped working, the corporal did not know either.

Tiller's questions were answered later that morning when the lookout arrived. On seeing the Germans land he had immediately abandoned his post, commandeered a donkey and ridden to Livadia Bay during the night. There were, he said, about twenty of them.

'They arrived on a barge which went away,' the corporal was able to add. 'It had plenty guns.'

'Sounds like a Siebel ferry,' said Barnesworth. 'Hope it doesn't turn up here.'

'How long before the Germans arrive?' Tiller said. The Italian corporal sketched the shape of the island with a twig and indicated that the patrol had gone clockwise round the island.

'Soon if they march quick.'

'The Krauts march quick,' said Barnesworth. 'You can be sure of that. Do we lay a nice little ambush for them north of here, Tiger?'

'You bet we do, Billy.'

'We leave?' the corporal asked eagerly. 'Twenty, too many Germans. Yes?'

'Twenty Germans not too many,' said Tiller, giving the Italian a friendly slap on the back. 'Not too many at all.'

'But we can do without the bleeding Luftwaffe,' said Barnesworth suddenly. 'Can you hear that, Tiger?'

It was the Blohm and Voss again. It circled once above them and then dropped a cloud of leaflets before flying off. The leaflet was in such rudimentary Italian that one of the SBS men was able to translate it without difficulty. It exhorted the Italians to support their old allies by refusing to join the British.

'Very artistic,' said Tiller, looking at the cartoon which accompanied the message. It was an ugly, slobbering bulldog which vaguely resembled Churchill and was wearing a helmet painted with the Union Jack. Its front feet were planted firmly on a valiant-looking Italian soldier shaped like Italy. Its hind feet were on the Dodecanese. The Italian was being handed a bayonet by a smiling, shining Wehrmacht soldier which the Italian was about to plunge into the bulldog's throat.

Tiller watched the Italians carefully as they studied this crude piece of propaganda. They read it impassively, but Tiller could see it had some effect. One of the Italians slowly unslung his rifle and propped it against the nearest wall.

The corporal ripped one of the sheets in two and spoke to the garrison sharply. Most of them threw the sheets away, but one slipped off his rifle and dropped it to the ground. Another folded the piece of paper carefully and put it in his pocket. Both gestures were unmistakable.

The corporal snarled and ranted. One of the soldiers reluctantly picked up his weapon, but the other refused. He was not defying authority, but every inch of him seemed to spell defeat. He'd had enough and nothing the corporal said would move him.

Then the corporal grabbed one of the sheets from the ground, dropped his trousers, and wiped his behind with it. This brought a snigger from his audience and a roar of approval when he held up the paper, smelt it, and let it drop from his thumb and forefinger with an expression of total disgust.

'Quite the little actor,' Barnesworth murmured to Tiller.

Reluctantly, the second soldier picked up his rifle and slung it back on his shoulder with an embarrassed smile. The corporal then looked at the man who had pocketed the pamphlet. The man extracted it and let it drop to the ground.

'Giovanni might have some spunk after all,' said Barnesworth. He had christened the corporal Giovanni because the Italian looked the archetypal ice-cream vendor.

'We'll soon see,' said Tiller. 'I want you to remain here, Billy, with Tranter and Simmonds and seven of these characters. The Krauts aren't going to oblige us by all of them walking into here in single file together. They're going to come from at least two directions. I'll need you to protect my back.'

Barnesworth nodded his agreement.

'I'll take the other two blokes to man the Bren. I'll also take Giovanni and one of the Bredas. He can choose which four men he wants to have with him.'

Tiller signalled the corporal to join him and sketched his plan out in the dirt. He indicated where he intended to set up the ambush to the corporal and made him understand what he intended to do. The corporal nodded. Tiller told him to choose four men and then, nodding meaningfully, put his left hand on his right bicep and flexed the muscle. Giovanni grinned. He knew exactly what Tiller meant.

He called out four names and harangued them briefly. One of them was the man who had refused to pick up his rifle.

'These good men,' he said.

To Tiller they looked no different from the others. They were unshaven, their uniforms were torn and dirty, their boots worn out. One wore plimsolls. He indicated the one who had dropped his weapon and asked if he was any good.

'My cousin,' the corporal replied.

'Christ!' said Barnesworth. 'They're worse than the bloody Mafia.'

'They probably *are* the Mafia,' Tiller said. 'Make sure he doesn't shoot you in the back, Sarge.'

'I'll keep him in front of me,' Tiller promised.

The ambush site was about a mile along the path towards the promontory. It was even better than Tiller had remembered it because the ground on either side trapped the path into a narrow defile.

Tiller placed the Bren at the start of the ambush area, knowing the two SBS men manning it would not open fire until the trap had been closed, and the less reliable Breda with its less reliable crew at the far end to seal off any escape. He then distributed the Italians along the rest of the path.

'Tell them that as they are firing from above, they must aim low,' he told the corporal, indicating his legs. In the heat of a fire-fight it was an error even the most experienced infantryman could make. Giovanni understood.

'They must not fire until I say so.' Again the Italian nodded.

The grenades, the more powerful Mills bombs, were primed and distributed, and the ambushers settled down to wait.

The Germans, when they came, could be heard a

long way off, shouting gutturally to one another and crashing through the undergrowth.

'Must think they're on a fucking Sunday picnic,' one of the SBS men muttered to Tiller as he pulled back the cocking handle on the Bren. Tiller suddenly felt the adrenalin pounding through him and he gripped the man's arm so that he looked at Tiller in astonishment.

'What is it, Sarge?' he whispered.

Tiller cursed himself under his breath. The skipper was right: he was too conventional, did not use his instincts to keep one step ahead. One day it could be the death of him – and of those with him.

'They're doing that deliberately,' he whispered.

The SBS man thought about it. He had fought against the Germans in the desert, knew they were wily adversaries. It made sense. 'They could be, at that, Sarge.'

'Take the Bren and go back to Billy,' Tiller whispered. 'Tell him most of them must be coming his way. Take all the Eyeties with you except Giovanni and his cousin, and the Breda team. Make it snappy.'

The two SBS men slipped away. Giovanni and his cousin looked too nervous to hold a gun, much less fire it straight. The shouting and the trampling was closer now. Tiller cocked his silenced Sten, gripped the thick canvas handguard around the barrel, and edged closer to the path, gesturing for the two Italians to follow him.

Suddenly three Germans appeared out of the undergrowth about a hundred yards from Tiller. He held them in his sights. He was in trouble if there were more, he thought. They were making no attempt to keep quiet, but were pushing their way through the bushes, and calling out to one another.

Tiller watched the bushes behind them. There could only be three of them, he decided. He could cope with that. He looked across at Giovanni and his cousin and indicated that he would do the shooting.

The Germans were big, blond fellows, clean, well fed and well armed, but they were very young. And much too sure of themselves.

They entered the cut without a second glance, carrying their rifles at the trail, and when they were ten yards from him Tiller stood up and fired three single shots from the Sten.

The shots made less sound than a champagne cork. The first hit the leading German in the throat before he even saw Tiller. His rifle clattered to the ground and his hands flew up to the wound as he spun round.

The second German saw Tiller just as the SBS sergeant carefully squeezed the trigger again. The bullet ripped into the soldier's chest and knocked him backwards. His legs buckled under him and he pitched forward on to the first German sprawled across the path. He was dead before he hit the ground but through some physiological quirk he retained his grip on his rifle.

Only the last German had time to do anything. He dropped down on one knee and levelled his rifle. Fleetingly, as he shot the man between his eyes, Tiller admired the speed with which the German had moved, but even with such quick reactions he had had no chance to take proper aim.

Out of the corner of his eye Tiller saw the Italians rise from cover. He waved them down impatiently and then dropped into a crouching position to listen.

A lizard crossed the path, paused enquiringly, and then scuttled into the undergrowth. The first German made a strangled gurgling sound, drummed his heels on the ground, and died. Apart from that all Tiller could hear was the buzzing of the flies which were already beginning to gather over the blood and brains seeping on to the path.

For several minutes Tiller stayed crouched by the path watching the cloud of flies. Then he rose, indicated to the Italians they were to stay where they were, went back to the two men manning the Breda, and beckoned them to follow him.

'The other Germans must have gone inland,' he said to Giovanni, indicating with his hand. 'We'll take them from behind.'

The Italians followed Tiller back down the path. As they skirted the dead Germans, Tiller was drawn to the open, staring eyes of the one he'd shot in the throat. He looked away quickly.

They headed inland. Away from the beach the ground was rocky and steep. Apart from a few stunted bushes it was almost bare of cover, but a deep gully, which carried a stream to the sea during the wet season, gave them what was needed. Even so, they had to move carefully, one at a time.

Eventually they were able to work their way round until they were directly inland from the bay. They could see the Germans now, large dots spread out across the hillside. They were moving slowly down towards the garrison's defensive positions. There was a crackle of shots and the dots dropped to ground and returned the fire. Tiller wormed his way forward until he found a good position from which the Breda could enfilade the line of advancing

Germans and he indicated it to the two Italians manning the gun.

Suddenly there was a puff of smoke from the hillside and the whoomph-crack of a mortar bomb. Shit, thought Tiller. He had not reckoned with the Germans having a mortar. They had, he knew, a reputation for using them with devastating accuracy.

'I'm going to have to take that out,' he said to Giovanni. He pointed to the German position and slit his throat with his forefinger. Giovanni nodded. 'You stay here. Fire when you know I have taken out the mortar,' he said, and he made the gesture of firing. 'Understood?' Giovanni grimaced.

Tiller worked his way up the hillside, round behind the mortar team, and then crawled forward until he was close enough to be able to throw a grenade.

There were two Germans working methodically from a small dip in the ground which made them invisible to those defending the bay. One was feeding high-explosive bombs down the mortar's barrel, from which they were ejected with a subdued crump. Tiller watched two bombs as they whirred through the air and exploded on the hillside below.

The other member of the mortar team was breaking open a wooden box full of smoke bombs and piling them beside the mortar. Tiller guessed the mortar crew was just softening up the garrison's positions before laying smoke to screen the attackers when they made their final dash forward.

Tiller crawled forward, extracted the pin from the No. 36 grenade with his teeth and lobbed it into the dip. He had primed it with an five-second fuse rather than the normal seven-second one, so it exploded with a jarring thud almost as soon as it hit the ground.

There was a terrible scream from one of the Germans; the other, holding his leg, started scrambling up the hill. Tiller lifted his Sten and fired twice; the soldier staggered and fell.

That was five of the bastards, Tiller thought. Another fifteen to go. He heard the enemy commander shouting orders in the distance and tried to pinpoint his position. He had obviously decided to attack anyway, for the patrol rose in line, from what cover they had been able to find, and began advancing on the garrison's positions.

The Germans were well beyond the range of Tiller's Sten, so he scrambled to the mortar position and snatched up one of the dead men's rifles. He thought of using the mortar, but decided it would take too long to realign it. He took careful aim at the nearest German, who was about 200 yards below him and to his right. He squeezed the rifle's trigger, and the soldier pitched forward, though whether he had been hit, or had just tripped, Tiller couldn't tell.

Then the Breda opened up below him and to his left. It was in a perfect enfilading position and three of the enemy were hit with its first burst. The figures on the hill hesitated; some went on; others dropped to the ground. A whistle blew and the German commander began shouting his orders above the firing before a brief burst from one of the garrison's Brens forced him to the ground.

It did not surprise Tiller that Barnesworth, following the adage of reinforcing success, should now mount a counter-attack on the enemy's right flank. Billy knew his stuff. What did surprise him was that Giovanni and his cousin, who must have followed him round, now rose from cover below him and charged the left end of the German line. He could hear the two men screaming what must have been Italian obscenities as they ran forward and he gave them what cover he could with his rifle until they disappeared over a ridge to his right.

Then another Bren opened up on the Germans' right flank. That was too much for the attackers and within a minute a white handkerchief appeared on the end of a rifle barrel and then another and another, and the shooting petered out.

Tiller worked his way cautiously forward. From the garrison's defensive position someone shouted, '*Hände hoch! Hände hoch!*'

Slowly, cautiously, the Germans rose from the ground, holding their hands well above their heads. Tiller watched them carefully, alert for any trick. He counted nine of them. '*Kommen Sie hier!*' the linguist shouted. '*Schnell! Schnell!*'

But the Germans were reluctant to come quickly, or indeed to come at all. They stood on the hillside as if rooted to the spot, perhaps awaiting instructions from their commander. But it was the Bren to the right of them which eventually gave them their orders, because a burst was fired from it over their heads. The closest broke into a shuffling run and the others followed suit.

Tiller worked his way back down the hillside, collected the Breda team and the two Italians – all of them now grinning from ear to ear – and made his way down to the bay. Barnesworth greeted him enthusiastically. 'Good going, Tiger. That mortar was causing us real problems. I liked the way you sent those Eyeties in as well.'

'Not my doing,' said Tiller. 'They did it on their

own initiative. Talk about Charge of the bloody Light Brigade.'

'Good Christ!' said Billy. 'Whatever next. How did you guess what the Krauts were up to?'

'I nearly didn't,' said Tiller sourly.

'Well, if you hadn't sent back that Bren and those extra men I . . .'

'If, if, if, Billy.' Tiller felt the tension snap something inside him. Barnesworth looked at his friend understandingly.

'Two Eyeties dead,' he said after a pause. 'A mortar bomb got them in their slit trench.'

Tiller, quite irrationally, felt furious. 'If they'd dug the fucking slit trench properly, with a parapet, they'd have been all right. Fucking no-hopers.'

Barnesworth paused and said gently: 'No, it landed right in the trench, Tiger. They didn't stand a chance.'

Tiller wiped his face. The fury left him as quickly as it had built up, and he said tiredly: 'You're right. Sorry, mate. Any other casualties?'

'Couple of mortar-bomb fragments, a bullet through the arm, nothing serious. One of the Eyeties was advancing in the wrong direction and got a fragment in his arse. He won't be sitting down for a while. But most of them behaved pretty well.'

'And the Krauts?'

'We found eight dead on the hill, including the mortarmen. A couple more have a hole or two in them. They'll survive if the Eyeties don't slit their throats.'

'There are three down the track,' Tiller said. He remembered the cloud of flies and added: 'We'd better bury them quick.'

The Italians were talking excitedly among themselves.

'Good, good, eh?' the corporal said enthusiastically to Tiller.

'Very good,' said Tiller. 'You're a brave man, Giovanni. All your men, brave men.' The corporal saw that Tiller meant it. His effusive gratitute at being so praised was almost embarrassing. Poor bastard, Tiller thought, the Krauts when they came would not call him brave – they'd just shoot him. If he was lucky.

Balbao arrived late at the rendezvous, having been delayed from leaving Simi when naval intelligence in Alexandria put out an alert that two Italian destroyers, now in German hands, were heading towards the islands from Crete.

He brought a sick-berth attendant with him, one of a trickle of key personnel arriving on Simi as the British effort to reinforce the islands gathered momentum. The man treated the wounded, who were then, with the prisoners and the SBS men, loaded aboard at the jetty, while more stores for the diminished garrison were brought ashore. But it was dawn before the MAS boat was ready to make its daylight dash to Simi.

Giovanni wrung Tiller's hand in farewell. 'Italians fight good, eh?'

'Very good, Giovanni, very good. Good luck, mate.'

Tiller knew he would need it. They were all going to need it.

The MAS boat's crew had just cast off when one of the crew shouted out a warning and pointed seawards.

In the exhilaration of victory Tiller had quite forgotten about the Siebel ferry and when he saw it clawing its way awkwardly around the next headland to the north he could not immediately think what it was. Balbao ordered full speed ahead and the MAS boat leapt forward as the gun crews scrambled to man their weapons.

The Siebel ferry fired first. It began pumping 105mm shells at the MAS boat as the latter picked up speed and made for the open sea. But the German gunners underestimated the astonishing acceleration of their target and the shells fell well astern. The MAS boat's twin 20mm Bredas returned the fire and Tiller could see in the half light of dawn that the arcing tracer was hitting the target.

The Siebel was well armed but it was very slow and made an easy target. The MAS boat was now making thirty knots and the German gunners had little chance of hitting it. Balbao made a run parallel with the ferry which allowed his gunners to rake it from stem to stern. Then a shell from the Bredas hit a fuel tank on the Siebel and the German vessel suddenly blew up in a sheet of flame.

Balbao slowed and manoeuvred towards the Siebel, but by the time the MAS boat arrived there was no sign of it. A large patch of oil, some of it still alight, with pieces of charred, unidentifiable wreckage floating in it, was all that remained.

8

Tiller woke with a start. There was no moon; it was still very dark. A soft breeze sighed through the caique's rigging. Occasionally it gusted more strongly for a moment, snapping a halyard against the wooden mast, making the caique's hull creak against the quayside.

The SBS had set up its headquarters in the port and a more powerful radio than the Kittyhawk in the caique had been installed there. An empty house on the quay had also been acquired as sleeping quarters, but Tiller preferred to stay on the caique, where he could keep his nightmare to himself.

He stood up and and stretched himself and Griffiths, who was on guard, called out to him: 'I'm brewing up, Sarge. Like a cuppa?'

Griffiths handed up the steaming mug and Tiller wrapped his hands around it. With autumn on the way the air had a definite nip in it. He wondered as he sipped the strong, sweet tea if Giovanni and his garrison on Piscopi would survive. The SBS had given the Italians what stores they could spare, had even left one of their precious Brens behind.

The defeat of the German patrol had certainly given the morale of the Italians a lift, he decided, not only because their former, and intensely disliked, allies, had been beaten – and had shown themselves to be beatable – but because the tiny garrison had survived its baptism of fire. The male sex was pretty basic, Tiller realized now. Only two things concerned them: that they could screw and that they weren't cowards – and they frequently needed proof of both.

Tiller had no doubt now that if the Germans returned to Piscopi the garrison would fight. Tiller had told them that if they didn't he would come back and shoot them himself. He had come to like, almost respect, those dark, scruffy men. They weren't, he knew now, as bad soldiers as their army's reputation had led him to believe. Given the right leadership, they could be tough and resilient. He remembered Giovanni's wild, whooping cries as he had charged forward on the hillside waving his gun above his head, and grinned to himself. It had been quite a sight.

'Heard you had quite a time of it on Piscopi the other day,' Griffiths said as if reading the SBS man's thoughts. 'Those Jerries you brought back with you seemed fucking fed up with life. I suppose they thought they'd just come to beat up a few Eyeties. Hadn't reckoned on you lot.'

Tiller flung the dregs of his tea into the water. 'It's just been patrols we've encountered so far,' he said. 'Reckon they'll be moving in with more fire-power soon.'

'Larssen has got the Eyeties here running around like scared rabbits,' Griffiths said cheerfully. 'When the Krauts come, we'll be ready for them.'

'Let's hope so.'

Tiller shaved, fried himself two eggs, lit a cigarette, and was watching the sun rise over the mainland when Larssen appeared on the quay.

'We've just heard from our observation post on

Stampalia that an RAF crew have been stranded there. Engine failure apparently and they had to ditch. Several of them are hurt, so they need taking off quickly. I don't want to ask Balbao as I want to conserve what fuel he has, but Andrew's back from Leros and he said he'd pick them up in the caique. But he needs one of us to go with him. Fancy a few days at sea?'

'Sure, skipper,' said Tiller, flicking his cigarette stub into the harbour. 'Better than sitting here waiting for the Krauts to come.'

'Good,' Larssen said, and then added mischievously: 'Andrew's going to need to take that girl with him, so you should have an enjoyable trip, Tiger. You know how romantic the sea can be.'

'You tell me, skipper,' said Tiller, surprised at the embarrassment he felt. 'You were in the merchant navy.'

'Ah, but only cargo ships. Never aboard liners. Too bad. Anyway, work before women, Tiger, work before women.' And with those few words of advice Larssen turned away.

'Work before women' was one of Larssen's catchphrases. It was, Tiller decided, just another way of issuing the old warning to keep your eye on the ball and not be distracted. Larssen stopped and turned round.

'Oh, Tiger?'

'Skipper?'

'I think you did a good job on Piscopi. Well done.'

'Thanks, skipper. But they almost foxed me.'

'Almost. But they didn't, did they? I begin to think I was wrong about you.'

'In what way?'

'Spit and polish, Tiger, spit and polish. A good man, I said to myself when we first met – no doubt about that. Disciplined. Well trained. All that. Just who we need if we're in a tight spot to blow something up for us. But can I make him into a pirate? I asked myself. Is he a brigand at heart. Can he think on his feet. I looked at you that first day, Tiger, with your brass belt and shiny cap badge, and I must say I had my doubts.'

Tiller glanced down at his dirt-encrusted boots and the shirt and shorts he hadn't changed for a week, and grinned. It seemed a far cry from the immaculate lines of Marines drawn up in perfect order on the parade ground at Eastney, and said so.

'I wouldn't know one end of a parade ground from another,' Larssen said. 'But you have made me think it is not a total waste of time.'

'Any news of what's happening?'

'I think it's a matter of who builds up the most forces the quickest. The boss did a good job paving the way for the army, which now has three battalions in place, one each on Kos, Samos and Leros. But it's going to be a hard job keeping them supplied. And us for that matter. Every day there seem to be more attacks by the Luftwaffe. Yesterday they sank two of our destroyers at Leros. I'd say it's touch and go at the moment. But at least they still don't seem to know we're here on Simi.'

At dusk that evening an SBS medical orderly boarded the caique with three stretchers and his medical equipment. Kristos had imposed a curfew on the port to curb the hotheads among the locals, so Angelika had no difficulty in slipping aboard unnoticed soon afterwards. Half an hour later the caique motored out of the harbour flying the Turkish ensign at the truck of her mast.

Naval intelligence at Beirut had passed on to the SBS the information that, according to the Andartes' report Tiller had brought back from Rhodes, the Germans were indeed rapidly building up reinforcements and supplies on the island, and were also increasing their air and sea patrols among the other islands. There was, therefore, an increased risk of encountering an armed schooner or caique, so the Solothurn was loaded and a spare magazine placed beside it under the foresail. Griffiths propped himself against the mast ready to man it at a moment's notice; the others had their Lanchester carbines and Stens out of sight but close at hand.

The cockle had been removed and the three stretchers had been lashed to the deck in its place under the folds of the mainsail. There was, too, extra water, drums of fuel, and ammunition. Angelika acknowledged Tiller's presence with an impassive nod and a brief smile before settling herself beside Maygan in the cockpit. They spread out a local chart on their knees to estimate the best course for the caique to take to their destination.

Stampalia was the most westerly of the Dodecanese and lay some seventy miles from Simi. To reach it, Maygan and Angelika decided the safest route was to sail north towards the finger of Turkish coastline that stuck out into the Aegean and helped to form the Gulf of Doris. Though the Germans as well as the British infringed Turkish neutral waters, it made sense to keep as close as possible to the Turkish coastline and to make as much of the open-sea crossing as possible during the hours of darkness.

As Simi and the tiny island of Nimos to the immediate north of it dropped slowly astern the Matilda engine throbbed and burbled with a smooth power that kept a little smile of satisfaction on Stoker Bryson's face. The medic cut up a watermelon and passed slices around. The short crossing of the gulf to the Turkish mainland took less than an hour, but it seemed much longer as they scanned the night horizon and listened for the sound of marine engines.

Halfway across they fancied they did hear the faint, powerful throb of what was probably an E-boat. But they saw nothing and it soon faded, and once they were well within Turkish waters, the tension lessened. Maygan altered course to motor westwards and soon afterwards entered the bay he had decided to lay up in during daylight hours.

Once they were safely moored and the camouflage netting had been erected Griffiths brewed some tea and issued corned-beef sandwiches before they settled down to wait, and to sleep if they could. Dawn came red and glowing behind the barren mountains. They waited all day and watched the sun creep around in a deep-blue sky until, by evening, it began to sink behind the volcanic island of Nisiros, and the much smaller islands of Yali and Yassi to the north of it. No garrisons, German or Italian, had been reported on Nisiros and there was no sign of life on it when, after darkness fell, they steered between the islands.

'How the hell do you find your way around at night when there aren't any lighthouses or buoys,' Tiller asked Maygan, for the young lieutenant now seemed to have perfected a method of sailing among the islands on moonless nights to drop off SBS reconnaissance patrols or supplies for those manning lookout posts.

'By silhouette,' Maygan replied. 'You start off on a certain course knowing that you'll come to a rock or an island. That's your point of departure. You then alter course until the silhouette of one mountain or island can be seen between the gap of other mountains or islands. Or the end of one island overlaps the end of another. That's your transit. You know you're on the correct course for wherever you want to go. You can only do it in fine weather, of course, and I still need someone who knows the area to pilot me into some of the harbours or creeks. The charts we're using are hopelessly out of date.'

He showed Tiller what he meant by lining up the southern tip of Nisiros with the tiny island of Kandhilousa, which lay beyond it. As long as the outline of Kandhilousa was kept on their starboard bow they were safe from the rocks that extended from Cape Lutros, the southernmost point of Nisiros. But once the cape was abeam they changed course to keep Kandhilousa on their port bow.

Once clear of the rugged coastlines and the numerous tiny islets west of Nisiros, Maygan altered course slightly to the south to bring the caique into the tiny port of Maltezana, their agreed rendezvous with the SBS men on the island, which lay towards the northern end of Stampalia.

During the night the wind increased suddenly – the beginnings of a late *meltemi*, Angelika said – and sent spray flying across the deck, and by the early morning they were all cold and wet. At dawn they could see Stampalia ahead, its twin mountain peaks making it look at first like two separate islands. With Angelika issuing directions Maygan steered the caique towards Maltezana, threading it between several rugged islands that guarded its entrance. The foreshore was surprisingly green, a pleasant contrast from the barren hills behind, and the earth was tinged with red. Once in the bay they were sheltered from the *meltemi*.

The quay was empty except for the SBS lance-corporal waiting for them. He had brought the two uninjured members of the RAF crew to the port, but reported that the other two were quite badly hurt, so he had thought it best not to move them.

The stretchers and stores were unloaded and the Solothurn was stripped and dried and thoroughly oiled before being replaced on its bipod. Then Tiller, Bryson and the medic, guided by the SBS man, set off with two stretchers for Panormos, on the other side of the island, where the lookout post had been established. They crossed the narrow isthmus and then followed the coastline until they came to a small bay.

Overlooking the bay and with a view of a great sweep of the Aegean was a small wooden hut which the SBS men had reinforced with rocks inside. Below the horizon to the south-west was German-occupied Crete; to the north-west, beyond the scattered islands of the western Aegean, was German-occupied Greece.

'Seen much?' Tiller asked the lance-corporal, Paddy Donington, while the medic attended the two injured RAF men, who lay in one corner.

'You bet. Especially during the last couple of days. Aircraft mostly, making for Rhodes, but small shipping, too. Schooners, the occasional Siebel ferry, that sort of thing. Something big's building, I reckon. Surprised you risked it.'

'Cairo want the crew back,' said Tiller laconically. 'They're far more valuable than any of us lot.'

The medic got to his feet and came over to Tiller. He looked grave. 'I've given one a shot of morphine. He's got a broken leg. He'll be all right. But the other chap's in a bad way. No good moving him. He wouldn't last the trek back to the port, far less the boat trip to Simi.'

Tiller walked across to the dying man. He was no more than a kid. 'What's the matter with him?'

'Internal injuries probably. It's difficult to say.'

Tiller glanced at his watch. There wasn't much time. They had to sail at dusk. 'How long do you reckon?'

The medic knew what he meant. 'Impossible to say. An hour, a day – who knows?'

Tiller was wondering what to do when Donington approached him and drew him aside. 'Dave's been keeping an eye on a schooner coming in this direction from the north-west. He's had it under observation for an hour or more. It's not on the usual course for Rhodes. It could be coming here.' Tiller followed Donington along a coastal path to the ruins of what must have once been a watchtower. The SBS man, Dave Shawn, crouching among the rubble, handed Tiller his binoculars and pointed out to sea. 'That's it,' he said.

Tiller focused the binoculars on the boat. It was large, with two masts, the shorter foremast identifying it as being a schooner. But it was now under power and was butting its way at about five knots through the waves being thrown up by the *meltemi*.

'Schooner,' Shawn said. 'Looks as if it's got a trehandiri rig.'

'What the fuck's that?' said Tiller.

'The sails are hoisted on a gaff that sticks out in front of the mast as well as behind. Rather like an Arab dhow. We call it a lugger rig. The Germans use them quite a bit.'

Tiller could see four men on deck; as he scrutinized them four more came up from below. Even at the distance of some miles, there was no mistaking what they were.

'You're sure it's heading here?'

'Looks like it,' said Donington. 'Shipping for Rhodes usually passes well to the north or south.'

'How long have we got before they arrive?'

'If they're making for Maltezana – which is the likeliest place they would land – at least three hours. Perhaps more.'

They returned to the hut and Donington cranked on the landline telephone to contact Maltezana to warn them to expect visitors. Tiller collected Bryson and Donington, told the medic to stay with the RAF men and Dave, and set off for Maltezana.

Maygan, when he heard that the German schooner might be making for the port, said: 'We've got the element of surprise. We'll wait for it by the next headland and blow it out of the water.'

'What with?' Tiller asked.

'The Solothurn, of course.'

Tiller looked at the curious weapon doubtfully. 'Has anyone ever fired it?' he asked.

'I have,' said Griffiths. 'It kicks like a mule.'

'I don't propose to sit here and wait for them,' said Maygan. Tiller knew Maygan was right. The only advantage they had was surprise. He hesitated nonetheless. He did not fancy putting his life in the hands of an amateur yachtsman who had, so far as he knew, no experience of battle.

Maygan misinterpreted his reluctance. 'Come on, Tiger. There's only eight of them.'

'I only *saw* eight,' Tiller corrected him and, unwillingly, took the plunge. 'You're right, of course.'

'Good. Find a spot where we'll see them before they see us and lie up there under our camouflage net. They won't know what hit them.'

It was putting all their eggs in one basket, a bad principle at the best of times.

'How about leaving Paddy ashore?' Tiller suggested. 'He could act as lookout, warn us when they're coming in case we don't hear their engine, and he could put down some useful covering fire.'

'Good idea,' said Maygan warmly. 'Griffiths will man the Solothurn, you and Jock can have the Bren, and Donington can stay ashore. He can have a Lanchester.'

'If you don't mind, I'd prefer my Lee Enfield, sir,' said the lance-corporal politely. 'It might have a slower rate of fire but it's a bloody sight more accurate when it comes to trying to hit anything over a couple of hundred yards.'

'Fine,' said Maygan. 'Now let's look at the chart and see if we can pick a good spot.'

In the heat of the moment they had forgotten Angelika. She was sitting on a rock about a hundred yards from them, gazing out to sea, her chin cupped in her hands, the chart on her lap.

'Shit,' said Maygan. 'What are we going to do with her?'

'She can't come with us,' said Tiller immediately.

'She's safer ashore,' Maygan agreed. Tiller walked over to her and asked Angelika for the chart.

'What's happening?' she asked.

When Tiller explained the situation she agreed to stay hidden ashore provided she was given a pistol. Tiller shook his head. 'You mustn't resist if anything goes wrong. They won't know you're not a local.'

She looked at him almost contemptuously. 'They'll find out if they want to. And they will want to.'

Tiller hesitated.

'I only want a pistol so that I can shoot myself,' Angelika said fiercely. 'Have you any idea what the Germans do to anyone they suspect of being an Andarte, as you call them? What do you think they would do if they caught me?'

Tiller sank down on his haunches and looked into her face.

'Look,' he said, 'I'll give you mine if you want. But I'll never forgive you if you use it.'

For a moment she looked at him in puzzlement, and then she laughed. 'You English. Such a funny sense of humour.'

'Promise me you'll hide,' said Tiller. 'If things go wrong make your way across the island to the observation hut. It's here.' He pointed to the chart. 'They'll look after you.'

He took his Colt 9mm pistol out of its holster, extracted the clip of cartridges from the butt, and then showed her how the weapon worked before handing it to her. She weighed it in her hand and then snapped the clip of cartridges back into the butt and applied the safety-catch. From the way she did it Tiller knew she had handled a pistol before, and said so. But she just looked at him and smiled thinly, and said: 'I'll hide. I promise.'

Maygan spread the chart on a rock and pointed to a small promontory just north of the port. 'That looks perfect.'

Donington looked over Maygan's shoulder. 'Looks fine to me,' he agreed. 'I'll see you there, Sarge.' He hoisted his rifle on to his shoulder, and set off.

The promontory proved an ideal hiding-place for the caique, as there was an overhanging cliff with a tiny shelving beach inland of it. They put warps ashore, shrouded the caique in the camouflage netting, and then took up their firing positions.

Griffiths swivelled the Solothurn on its bipod ready for it to fire over the starboard bow; the Bren was set up in the cockpit, where it could fire through one of the brass bushes which had been specially let into the caique's high gunwales for just such a purpose. The range, they agreed, would probably be about 300 yards if the Germans came round the headland on course for Maltezana. At that distance even the Solothurn could hardly miss.

Soon after the caique was in position Donington appeared on the beach and called out that he had found a good concealed position from which to fire and that he could see the German schooner about a mile up the coast. She seemed to be keeping close inshore. 'Perfect,' said Maygan. 'Griffiths, fire into her engine space first and then riddle her below the water-line. Tiger, I want you to take out the helmsman and then keep the deck clear of Krauts. I'll fire first.'

Tiller nodded, flipped up the rear sights of the Bren, slid the catch to automatic, and cocked the mechanism. The pistol grip, which he held in his right hand, felt slippery with sweat, but the butt, guided by his left, nuzzled comfortably into his shoulder as he squinted down the sights.

Bryson crouched next to Tiller, his Lanchester carbine to hand, and piled up some spare magazines for the Bren.

It seemed to take an age before they first heard the faint but slow, steady thump of the schooner's diesel. It became gradually louder but then began to fade, and it took Tiller a moment to realize that the sound of it was being screened by the promontory so that he saw the schooner before he heard its engine again.

The schooner was coming on the exact course they had calculated, but it was much bigger than it had looked from the observation post. It must have been at least eighty feet long, and the pronounced curve of its hull gave it a distinctly Arab appearance. Its hull was white, or had been once, and it had a high, ornate stem which protruded above the gunwale. Sheltering behind this were two Germans with a Spandau machine-gun fixed on a bipod. Three more were standing around the foremast with Schmeisser sub-machine-guns hanging from their shoulders. In the stern the helmsman was standing on a kind of platform so that he could see his way ahead. Both his hands were on the large, curved tiller.

All of the Germans were staring ahead, except one in the cockpit, who was shading his eyes and looking behind him at the headland.

Tiller watched this man carefully as he scanned in from the headland until he was looking directly at the caique. Then the man's gaze shifted beyond the caique and into the bay behind it, and Tiller marvelled at the skill of the chief camouflage officer of the 9th Army who had devised the netting and specially coloured scrim. The man was a genius.

But the caique's netting was to disguise the caique from the air, not at close quarters from the sea, and something in the strange outline under the cliff must have alerted the German, for his gaze shifted back again to it. He lifted the binoculars slung around his neck and was focusing them on the caique when Maygan shot him with his Lanchester.

Almost simultaneously Griffiths fired his first round from the semi-automatic Solothurn. The kick was so violent that the caique rolled and bounced, but this did not prevent Tiller killing the helmsman with a short, sharp burst from the Bren.

He then swivelled the light machine-gun to the other end of the schooner and fired a more prolonged burst at the Spandau crew. As he did so he heard Bryson's Lanchester bark twice, three times, and then the Solothurn fired again.

At first the schooner seemed quite unaffected and sailed serenely on, though no one was at the helm. Then gradually she began to yaw. The Solothurn fired again, shaking the caique, and the schooner's engine faltered and then stopped, and slowly she lost way.

It was difficult for Tiller to find a target now, as the Germans on the deck had thrown themselves flat and those below had obviously thought it wiser to remain there. But Donington had a better view and his rifle cracked a number of times somewhere on the headland above the caique. The schooner was drifting very slowly now and was visibly lower in the water, but Griffiths kept pumping 20mm shells into her hull.

One of the Germans, braver – or more foolish –

than the others, opened fire from behind the foremast, but the Schmeisser's bullets sang harmlessly over the caique and a burst from the Bren tumbled him into the water.

The schooner drifted to a halt and a lick of flame came out of the main cabin. Griffiths stopped firing. They watched as the schooner began settling by the stern; the sea had already started flooding into its cockpit before the two remaining Germans burst out of a forward hatch and flung themselves into the water.

Tiller watched them dog-paddling towards the caique and was wondering how they would be able to find room for two prisoners as well as the RAF crew when the schooner blew itself apart with a muffled crump that shook the caique from stem to stern. Waves created by the detonation hammered against its side and bits of debris, thrown high in the air, started cascading into the water all around them. Then there was a large gout of steam and what remained of the schooner slid quickly into the water.

'I suppose, we'd better pick up those Krauts,' Maygan said.

'No point,' replied Tiller. He knew what happened to anyone caught in the water near an underwater explosion – their vulnerable stomachs would have been split open like gutted fish. 'They'll be very dead.'

Griffiths came aft, grinning from ear to ear. 'I said it would work, Sarge,' he said elatedly to Tiller. 'Cuckoo clocks aren't the only things the Swiss make well.'

Cuckoo clocks reminded Tiller of his long-cherished opinion of naval officers. Perhaps some of them weren't so bad, he thought now. Maygan had certainly acted with cool courage throughout the whole brief fire-fight. He already had his log out and was jotting down details before he forgot them.

'Did you see the schooner's name?' he asked, but no one had.

'You sank her too quickly, sir,' said Griffiths.

'She was a trehandiri, that's all I know,' said Tiller.

'A *what*?'

'Local craft. Lugger rig. I would've thought you would've known that, sir,' Tiller said with a grin.

'I didn't know you're an expert at recognizing boats as well as aircraft, Tiger. What do you think she was carrying to make an explosion like that?'

'Mines probably.'

The SBS men received a great reception when they returned to Livadia Bay. During the caique's absence a radio message had come through telling them to withdraw the observation post from the island and everyone guessed that indeed something big was brewing.

Bryson went to fetch the medic and arrived in time to help bury one of the RAF crewmen, who had died soon after Tiller had seen him, and to bring the other down on a stretcher. By the time LS8 left Stampalia it had been dark for two hours. The caique's deck was crowded but the weather was calm. The stretcher case was wrapped in a tarpaulin, and the others huddled together around him. Angelika remained in the cockpit with Maygan and Griffiths, who took turns to steer. Bryson opened up the Matilda engine more than he should have, making the caique roll and butt its way through the glassy water.

Nisiros was sighted an hour before dawn and as the first rays of the sun broke over the horizon ahead of them the rumble of guns and then the sound of aircraft wafted across to them from Kos, which lay on the horizon to the north.

Tiller scanned the sky with his binoculars and pointed. 'There. Look.'

Stukas were bombing the island and the rumble of the explosions floated faintly across the sea like thunder. Then bigger aircraft, which Tiller identified as Ju52 transports, appeared from the north-west and suddenly parachutes began to blossom beneath them. Above the transports flew Me109 fighters. There was no sign of any British aircraft.

'Can we go any faster, Jock?' Maygan asked, but the stoker shook his head. 'I think she's almost falling to bits as it is, sir,' he replied.

They all watched the invasion of Kos in shocked silence until the Turkish coastline blocked the faint sounds of battle from their ears as well as the island from their view.

At midday Maygan made the caique's routine position report to Simi on the radio and was told to go to Kos and collect Jarrett. But Simi did not know where Jarrett exactly was on the island as the message had been garbled.

Maygan and Tiller were just discussing the dilemma this put them in – the injured RAF man needed urgent medical attention – when ahead of them they saw another caique moving along the coast towards them under sail.

Griffiths dashed forwards to man the Solothurn and Tiller brought the Bren up from the hold before watching the slow progress of the approaching caique through his binoculars. It was about the same size as LS8 and looked genuine enough.

'What do you think, Tiger?'

'It could be a local Greek one.'

He handed the binoculars to Angelika, who confirmed that it was.

'I am going to unload our passengers,' said Maygan, 'and then make for Kos.'

Tiller nodded his agreement. When the Greek caique was within hailing distance Angelika shouted across to it. At first the crew seemed reluctant to comply but when Griffiths unveiled the Solothurn from under the foresail they quickly came to a stop.

'They come from Kalimnos,' Angelika said. 'They're genuine.'

'Tell them,' said Maygan, 'we'll pay them to take a wounded man and his friends to Simi.'

Angelika shouted again and then said to Maygan: 'They don't want money. They do it anyway.'

The Greek caique came alongside LS8 and the wounded man was carefully transferred. Then the others crossed, and Maygan indicated that Angelika should join them, but she did not move.

'You know Kos?' she asked him.

Maygan shook his head and said: 'No, but it's only over there. I can hardly miss it.'

'I know Kos. I know every rock and every bay. It is not an easy island to navigate.'

Maygan glanced at Tiller, who shrugged. What the hell, he thought, if she knows how to handle a pistol it is not as if she is some sweet innocent caught up in a war she didn't understand.

For a while, they watched the Greek caique sail back along the coast before turning about themselves.

'We'll stay by the coast after rounding the point,' said Angelika. 'Then we'll cut across to the port of Kos.'

'Is there nothing nearer?' Maygan asked, looking at the chart. Angelika pointed a slim finger. 'There's Kamares Bay. It is where ships used to go in before the war to load the ore that is mined above the port. But communications with the rest of the island are bad. The port of Kos is better.'

Once they had rounded Cape Krio and began crossing the Gulf of Kos the sound of battle, faint at first, became more distinct.

'If they take Kos,' said Maygan, 'Simi will be the meat in the sandwich between Kos and Rhodes.'

'Or the thorn in their side,' said Tiller. 'If we hold Simi their flank will be exposed.'

The port of Kos was dominated by a castle built to the south of the entry to the port. As they approached its entrance they could see a tattered Union Jack flying from its highest point.

'Hoist the white ensign,' Maygan told Griffiths. 'I don't want some trigger-happy gunner putting a hole in us.'

But the gunners had other, more important, targets, for as the caique sailed past the imposing stone walls of the fortress two Stukas came screaming almost vertically out of the sky, dropped their bombs, pulled out of their dive, banked, then disappeared to the north pursued by Bofors fire from the castle.

The double boom of the bombs was followed by clouds of dust from pulverized masonry.

'Get the Bren up here,' Maygan shouted to Tiller. 'If those bastards come back we can have a go at them.'

Inland from the port they could hear the chatter of machine-gun fire and the occasional report of something heavier being fired. Perhaps, Tiller thought, the Fallschirmjäger, the paratroops, had parachuted in some light mountain guns, a daunting prospect.

The island's defenders had obviously received some warning of the attack, because the port had been almost cleared of shipping. A wrecked landing-craft lay half sunk at one end; at the other a Tribal-class destroyer was just casting off its warps from the quay. As it passed LS8 Maygan ordered Griffiths to dip the caique's white ensign. After a prolonged pause, during which they could see a naval officer on the destroyer's open bridge studying them with interest, the destroyer replied by dipping hers.

Tiller could see from the officer's three straight gold stripes on the epaulettes of his white service shirt and the 'scrambled eggs' on the peak of his cap that he was a commander in the Royal Navy. He leant over the side of the destroyer's bridge and shouted down: 'Who the hell are you?'

'Levant Schooner Flotilla, sir,' Maygan shouted back.

'Never heard of you,' the commander replied, and moved back to the centre of his bridge.

'That's fame for you,' said Maygan to the others with a grin.

They came alongside the part of the quay the destroyer had just vacated and were met by an army major and two military policemen. The major looked harassed.

'I'm the port evacuation officer,' he said. 'What exactly do you think you're up to? We happen to be in the middle of fighting off an invasion and you come motoring in here as if you were on holiday. You're bloody lucky those Stukas didn't get you. Who are you anyway?'

'Levant Schooner Flotilla, sir,' Maygan said reeling off a casual salute.

'Never heard of you,' said the major testily, returning the salute by raising his cane in the direction of his cap. Maygan caught Tiller's eye and Tiller found it hard to suppress a smile.

'Special Operations,' added Maygan by way of explanation.

The major's expression softened slightly. 'Ah, I see. And whose orders are you under and who are these men with you?'

He looked hard at Angelika, who turned quickly away.

'Special Boat Squadron, sir,' said Tiller, saluting smartly. 'Orders to contact Major Jarrett immediately. Do you happen to know where he is?'

'Jarrett, eh?'

The name worked like a password, for the major turned to the military policemen and said: 'Show them the way to Major Jarrett's HQ as soon as they're ready.'

He turned back to Maygan and added: 'Good luck. You're going to need it.'

The deserted streets were littered with rubble, as the Stukas had been giving the port their attention ever since the German invasion had been launched. Maygan and Tiller picked their way through it behind the two military policemen.

'Where have the locals gone?' Maygan asked one of them.

'Most of them took to the hills before it started,'

he replied. 'They seemed to know what was going to happen almost before we did. Some are probably hiding in their cellars – those that have got them, that is. Here you are, sir.'

Jarrett's HQ was an old stone warehouse on the outskirts of the port. A sack covered the gap where the door had been. Tiller pulled it to one side and entered, and Maygan followed him. On the left a radio operator was working on his Morse key with his headphones. Next to him Jarrett sat on a packing case reading a signal. He looked up when Tiller entered and acknowledged his salute.

'Where the hell have you been?' he asked irritably.

'We got here as quickly as we could,' said Maygan. 'We were taking back an injured man from Stampalia when we got your message. What's happening?'

Jarrett stood up and pointed to the map of Kos pinned on the wall behind him. 'They've put two battalions ashore, one at Cape Foca, here, the other further west, and at another two points. There are also about two hundred parachutists from the Brandenburgers around Antimachia airfield. Here.'

'Brandenburgers?'

'Brandenburg Regiment. Special service troops. Kraut equivalent of Commandos. I have about twenty men up there, trying to stop them from taking it, but we've now had orders to pull out.'

'Are we going to stop them here, sir?' Tiller asked.

Jarrett shrugged. 'It doesn't look like it. We tried to organize the garrison and put some heart into them. But frankly it's a shambles and the trouble is we've got no air support. The few Spits which we had here were shot up before they even got into the air and the

Beaufighters they send from Cyprus just get chased away by the Me109s.'

The radio operator handed Jarrett another signal, which he read before crumpling it up and letting it drop to the floor.

'They've taken the airfield.' He shook his head and then added wearily: 'We need as many Flotilla caiques and boats to get here as quickly as possible to take us off. How many do you think are available right now?'

Maygan thought. 'Four caiques at the last count. Unless we've lost any in the last forty-eight hours. There are a couple of MLs as well, but they're at Castelrosso. That's about it.'

'It'll have to be enough, then,' said Jarrett. 'Andrew, I want you to take my HQ staff and myself to Leros. Right away. Tiger, I want you stay here and wait for the others to arrive from Antimachia, tell them what's happening, and then make sure they know where the caiques are. I'd already given Bob Baring orders to withdraw before the airfield fell. He knows we're withdrawing to Leros. Andrew will pick you up and take you back to Simi tomorrow. Let's go.'

As dusk fell Tiller watched LS8, its decks crowded with Jarrett's HQ staff, leave Kos harbour. An hour later, two of the caiques arrived from Leros and a third, which had been at Levita, crept in at midnight. They had all been working in the more northerly of the Dodecanese, setting up SBS observation posts on the smaller islands and taking reconnaissance patrols of the Long Range Desert Group to the bigger ones. Tiller estimated how many passengers each could take, told them what was happening, and then returned to Jarrett's HQ.

Shortly afterwards the first group of men from Bob Baring's detachment arrived. By now the perimeter of troops around the port was under heavy pressure and mortar bombs were falling among the buildings. The general opinion was that the Germans would launch an attack at dawn.

Baring and Tiller divided the SBS men between the caiques, which then sailed for Portolago, the principal harbour of Leros. Tiller, guessing that the perimeter would not hold when the German attack came, went with the last caique and at Portolago met up with Maygan, who told him that Kos had fallen.

9

With Kos lost, the caiques of the Levant Schooner Flotilla worked at night between the island and Leros to rescue as many of the British garrison as they could. The SBS landed patrols to scour the island to find any soldiers who had evaded capture and had them taken by the caiques to safety on Leros. But after a week no more could be found, the operation was abandoned, and LS8 sailed for Simi.

During the first night the *meltemi* blew and its autumn chill swept over the caique as it crept southwards around the Turkish coastline. Across the strait which divided Kos from the mainland they could see that part of the port of Kos was still smouldering, and Tiller wondered how many British soldiers had been lost on the island by the dramatic collapse of its defences.

Just before dawn they found shelter in a narrow, uninhabited Turkish bay which was sheltered from the fierce and persistent wind by a small island to the north of it. The camouflage netting was erected and the day spent sleeping. At dusk they set off again under a cloudy sky which threatened rain.

Soon after rounding Cape Krio the Matilda engine gave up again and nothing Bryson did could coax it to restart. They were forced to hoist the sails, which, with the wind on the starboard quarter, gave the caique a soaring, bouncing motion that curdled their empty stomachs.

When dawn broke the sky was grey and they approached the port of Simi in a rainstorm. Then the wind dropped and they sat in the bay with rain tipping down on top of them until eventually Larssen sent out the Italian garrison's launch to tow them in.

Larssen greeted them with the news that intelligence in Cairo had just intercepted German signals which indicated that they had decided to occupy Simi. He also said that the fall of Kos had unnerved the Italian garrison to such an extent that some of them had abandoned their uniforms and weapons, and had taken to the hills in civilian clothes.

'They know what happens to them when the Krauts come here,' he said to Tiller and drew his right forefinger across his throat. Tiller noticed that Larssen said 'when' not 'if'.

In the days that followed the Blohm and Voss twice circled Simi port and once an Me109 flew straight and low down the length of the bay. Then at dawn one morning the Italian observation post at the southern end of Simi called excitedly on their landline that they could see two or three ships approaching. As the light improved they identified one of them as a large caique. It was flying the Kriegsmarine ensign and its deck was crowded with soldiers. Following it was a small landing-craft, also crowded with soldiers, and a sleek speedboat which in peacetime must have taken tourists on day trips round the smaller islands, or perhaps had been the valued property of a local tycoon.

Larssen ordered Tiller and Barnesworth to round up as many of the garrison as were left. The two SBS men searched the castle, which was now suddenly empty and deserted, and it was not until they began combing through the outbuildings that they came across about twenty men huddled together.

Tiller bawled at them to get to their feet as the Germans were on their way, a fact that the Italians, judging by the expressions on their faces, already knew. As they reluctantly began to gather their equipment, Perquesta appeared and began to harangue them in rapid Italian.

'Tell them,' Tiller told Perquesta, 'that for them the war is not over. They are going to fight the invaders of their territory and they are going to fight bravely.'

This was received in sceptical silence.

'Tell them that I shall see that they fight bravely because I shall be right behind them. Tell them that when they attack the Germans some of them may die. But if they don't attack when ordered they will die for sure. Because I shall be behind them and will shoot anyone who does not obey.'

Perquesta looked at Tiller open-mouthed. '*Signore*, you cannot do that,' he stuttered. 'The Geneva Convention . . . It does not . . .'

'Fuck the Geneva Convention,' said Tiller. '*This* is my Geneva Convention.' He tapped his Sten gun. Perquesta swallowed hard. His translation had a marked effect on the garrison.

'I think they think you mean it, Tiger,' said Barnesworth.

'I fucking do,' said Tiller and realized that in the last few weeks he had learnt a lot from Larssen. He turned to Perquesta and saluted him smartly. 'Right, sir. Let's have them outside with weapons loaded.'

Led by Perquesta, the garrison marched in silence

down to where Larssen and the other SBS men awaited them. The German patrol, Larssen told them, was coming in to Pethi Bay, just south of Simi port, according to the Italian lookout post there. 'You and Billy come with me and this mob,' he said to Tiller. 'I want Ted Warrington and the rest of the boys as a second line of defence just outside the port.'

They trudged up the barren hillside that divided the two bays and along the top of which stood a line of old windmills. Just before they reached the skyline Larssen ordered them to halt while he went forward to reconnoitre. He came back with a grin on his face.

'There's about twenty of them,' he said. 'They're only just beginning to climb the path to the port. I can't see if they've got any mortars but apart from one Spandau, they're only armed with rifles and Schmeissers. From the way they're carrying them, they don't seem to be expecting much opposition. We'll move up to the crest, rake them with fire, then charge them with fixed bayonets.'

'Bayonets?' Perquesta looked appalled.

'Yes, bayonets. Tell your men to fix bayonets, Lieutenant.'

The SBS team watched with grim amusement as the Italians drew their bayonets and clipped them on their rifles.

'If the Krauts don't die from bayonet wounds, they'll die from tetanus,' Barnesworth said. 'Some of those bayonets haven't been out of their scabbards since the war started.'

The garrison were now ordered to spread across the hillside, with Barnesworth and Tiller covering them from the more vulnerable right flank. They moved up to the crest and when Larssen gave the order they opened fire on the German patrol below them.

To the surprise of the SBS the garrison gave a good account of themselves at first and several Germans fell. But once the enemy had gone to ground and began returning fire the Italians seemed to lose heart.

It was then that Larssen leapt to his feet and ordered the garrison to charge.

Luckily the German machine-gunner was too eager and the first burst from his Spandau was too high. But it was enough to make most of the Italians scramble back over the crest. Tiller wondered if Larssen would ever even get them on their feet again. He wished he had Giovanni and his cousin with him. They would have shown this lot what to do. He wormed his way over to Larssen, who had also been forced to take cover after the abortive bayonet charge. 'Do we wait for them to come to us, skipper, or do you and I and Billy go and get them?'

Larssen rubbed the stubble on his chin. 'There's not much cover up here. If they've got a mortar it will be a blood-bath, and anyway the Eyeties will just run for it. At least they haven't done that yet. You and Billy take some of them and try and get round the Krauts' flank. Then I can charge them while you give me covering fire.'

'Worth a try, I suppose.'

Tiller collected some of the more willing Italians, and under cover of the crest began making his way cautiously to the right. After a while he moved forward to reconnoitre and saw, about 500 yards away on the next headland, the remains of an old stone building. The ground sloped away sharply in front of it down into Pethi Bay, which he could now see from where he was lying. The ground in front of him was a series of small ridges which sloped more gradually towards the bay. He could see one or two enemy soldiers moving in and out of the stone building and wondered how many more of them there were. He could also see the top of the mast of the German caique at anchor in the bay and hoped he would get a chance to sink it. In the meantime there was the German patrol to dispose of.

Tiller gestured for Barnesworth to come forward and handed him the binoculars. 'That stone building. What are they up to?'

'Bringing up stores from the ships,' Barnesworth said. 'They must think they've come to stay. How much further to go, do you reckon?'

'Another hundred yards or so. Then we should be able to enfilade the patrol.'

Tiller signalled for the Italians to follow him and when he saw the patrol scattered across the hillside below him ordered them to open fire. The Germans scattered but there was nowhere for them to go except back to the beach and when they saw Larssen charging down the hillside driving the Italians in front of him most of them turned and ran back towards the bay. They were followed by concentrated fire from Tiller's group of Italians, who were visibly excited at seeing them on the run.

'Now what, skipper?' Tiller said when he met up with Larssen.

'There are more of them than I thought,' the Dane admitted.

'There are more of us than *they* thought, skipper,' Barnesworth said.

'But most of our men won't budge,' Larssen said in

disgust. 'I think we have to try another tack. We've got the caique and the MAS boat. We attack them from the sea. If we sank their ships they'd be cut off. You keep the bastards' heads down, Billy. Any of your Eyeties still in the fight?'

'One or two,' said Barnesworth. 'They saw the Krauts running. That cheered them up.'

'I'll send Kristos up to you with any extra men he can find. Tiger, you and I will take the caique round to the bay. I want Ted and the others aboard the MAS boat. If the Kraut boats come out, all well and good. If not we'll go in and get them.'

Despite Bryson's efforts LS8's engine was still not functioning. But the weather had cleared now and a 'soldier's breeze', as Maygan called it, was blowing off the Turkish coast, the perfect direction if they had to enter Pethi Bay. An Italian Breda was added to the caique to supplement the Solothurn and Bren, and the sails were hoisted.

'When was the last time the Royal Navy fought a battle at sea under sail,' Maygan wondered aloud. 'We're making history, lads.'

'Tell me, Andrew, what's a soldier's breeze?' Larssen asked curiously.

'One that even a soldier could sail in, of course.'

Balbao was to take the MAS boat in a wide circle so as to approach Pethi Bay from the east. Hopefully this, and the fact that it was flying an Italian ensign, might confuse the invading force and perhaps even make them hesitate to open fire on it. The caique had to tack out of the bay. This took a while and the sun was low in the sky by the time they passed the headland which protected the northern end of Pethi Bay.

Occasionally the faint sound of firing drifted across the caique from the hillside.

Gradually the bay began opening up in front of them and after a while the ruined stone building on the far side of the bay came into view.

The caique was flying the Turkish ensign, which Maygan hoped might baffle the Germans temporarily. But as soon as it was spotted a warning burst was fired over it from the Spandau which had been set up in the stone building. When the caique ignored this another burst cut up the water ahead of it.

By this time those aboard LS8 could see the German caique at anchor. Beyond it the landing-craft and the speedboat had been beached.

'See to that Spandau, Griffiths,' Maygan shouted and the leading seaman whipped the cover off the Solothurn and began pumping shots at the ruined building while Tiller and Warrington opened fire on the caique.

'Hoist the white ensign,' Maygan ordered Bryson. It was already attached to its halyard and seconds later it was fluttering at the truck of the mast.

Figures began running from the stone building down towards the bay. Bullets from the Spandau kicked up the water around the caique and the caique shivered as the Solothurn fired back. Tiller could see bits flying off the German caique as the Bren and the Breda raked its decks. Beyond it he could see the heavy machine-gun aboard the landing-craft being swivelled towards them.

Tiller lifted the sights of the Breda a couple of notches and fired a short burst at the landing-craft. The man pedalling the machine-gun mounting around fell backwards but another immediately took his place.

'Put the Kraut caique between us and that machine-gun,' Larssen shouted at Maygan. Maygan nodded and altered course.

But the German caique had been cut loose from its anchor and its engine started, and it began to move slowly across the bay as it continued to be hit by the fire from LS8.

Larssen tried to drop its helmsman with a burst from the Bren but the man's position was well protected by sandbags. Slowly, inexorably, the German caique swung towards the entrance to the bay.

Tiller squeezed the trigger of the Breda, but nothing happened and he knew at once that its complicated blow-back system had jammed. Cursing everything Italian, he picked up a Lanchester just as the heavy machine-gun on the landing-craft opened up.

The first burst went high and wide, and spattered into the cliff behind the British caique. But Tiller knew – they all knew – that their old wooden hull would not be able to absorb many of the enemy gun's heavy-calibre bullets.

Maygan changed course towards the German caique in another attempt to put it between the machine-gun and themselves but the distance was too great now. The second burst from the machine-gun shredded the caique's mainsail and smashed the gaff. The heavy wooden spar crashed down on to the deck in pieces and then fell into the water, pulling the tattered remains of the mainsail with it. The wreckage slowed the caique and, powered only by its foresail, it began to lose way.

'Cut that mainsail loose!' Maygan shouted, but

Griffiths was already leaning over the side, sawing at the ropes that still held the gaff and mainsail to the mast.

Tiller waited for the next burst, which, he knew, would rip into the hull, for even in the gathering dusk the machine-gunner could not miss his target as it was now broadside on to him.

Then behind him Tiller heard the throaty roar of the MAS boat's engines and the distinctive bof-bof-bof of its twin Bredas opening up. Balbao's gunners were using tracer and Tiller could see it arcing past the caique and on to the landing-craft.

The machine-gun stopped firing and there was a dramatic whoomph of flame as the landing-craft suddenly caught fire, and the gunners on the MAS boat turned their attention to the ruined stoned building, pumping shell after shell into it.

Germans were running everywhere and Barnesworth and his men were trying to pick them off in the gathering gloom. The German caique was now motoring away as fast as possible but the MAS boat simply blew it apart with the Bredas. Bits of planking and wooden coaming flew everywhere and the crew jumped into the water. The caique's engine stopped and without anyone at the helm an inshore current caught the drifting hulk and grounded it on an outcrop of rocks below the next headland.

This only left the speedboat, but that never even got under way, for Griffiths holed it with a shot from the Solothurn and sent the men in it tumbling into the shallow water and wading for the shore.

Suddenly it was quite dark except for the area around the burning landing-craft. A red Very light curved into the sky. Gradually the shooting above the bay petered out.

Balbao came alongside. 'Are you all right?' he asked.

Maygan gave the thumbs up and said: 'Can you give us a tow back?'

'No problem,' Balbao shouted back, elated by the success of the operation. 'Always a pleasure to help the Royal Navy.'

A line snaked to the caique from the stern of the MAS boat. Griffiths caught it deftly and tied it round the bottom of the mast.

Now that the fight was over Tiller found himself in a fury with the Breda which had let him down. He picked it up and threw it overboard.

Kristos was on the quay to greet them and to tell them that the seaborne attack had resulted in the rest of the Germans being routed, for the Italians, heartened by witnessing it, had held their ground well when the Germans tried to break through their cordon. It had given way in the end but the German survivors, more intent on survival than on driving home any kind of attack on the port, had simply dispersed into the night. They were probably making for the hills, Larssen added, in the hope that they would be able to hide out there until they were rescued. If they met any local people who might be sheltering up there he doubted if they would ever come down again.

The next day Maygan sent Tiller and Griffiths in the garrison launch to see what could be salvaged from the German caique and to bring back the damaged speedboat. They found the caique hard aground on the rocks. On searching it they found nothing of more interest than two dead Germans and a bottle of schnapps. They took the schnapps, and the caique's sails and gaff, weighted the dead Germans and dropped them overboard to the accompaniment of a perfunctory burial ceremony, and then went to look for the speedboat.

Up on the hillside above the bay they could see a party of Italians with picks and shovels scouring the ground for dead Germans to bury. The speedboat was lying in shallow water. Except for the shell hole from the Solothurn, it seemed undamaged. They bailed it out, plugged the hole, and towed it back to the port.

Bryson, who had just finished repairing the caique's engine, inspected the trophy with interest. 'The Eyeties can certainly build them fast,' he said. He checked that the speedboat's engine was still in working order. 'That's an Alfa Romeo unit which can develop God-knows-what horsepower. I reckon it's probably got a top speed of fifty knots or more.' He wiped his hands on a rag and looked suitably impressed.

Larssen, however, remained quite unmoved. 'It's no bloody use to us, is it?'

Tiller looked with fascination at the sleek craft with its long, curved counter and pointed bow, and asked: 'How fast did you say, Bill?'

'I reckon fifty knots. In flat water, that is. If it went at that speed in any kind of a sea it would sink like a stone. It beats me why the Krauts brought it along.'

'For reconnoitring the island, perhaps,' said Larssen. 'Get rid of it.'

'Eh, wait a tick, skipper,' Tiller interjected. 'You never know. It might come in handy.'

Larssen shrugged. 'All right, but get it out of sight. I

suspect from now on we'll be attracting the attention of the Stukas.'

Many of the local people had vanished before the Germans had even landed. Now they began returning to the port.

'How did the locals know?' Larssen asked Angelika when he and Tiller visited the taverna.

'It was an instinct,' she answered. 'The people here have lived with the war for a long time. They have learnt what to do to avoid being killed.'

'Where did they go?'

'Into the mountains. There is water there, and some food has been stored in a safe place. It is a way of avoiding reprisals. They did it for centuries when the Turks ruled the islands. The Turks sent out search parties but they never found anyone. Nor did the Italians. How could you find anyone in those mountains? Impossible!'

'There are Andartes up there?' Larssen asked casually.

Angelika hesitated. 'Perhaps.'

'Which ones?'

The girl's face was expressionless.

'ELAS or EDES? Which ones?' said Larssen.

Angelika wiped the palms of her hands on her apron. 'Perhaps I can find out for you,' she said quietly. 'Now please excuse me. There are other customers I must serve.'

'When the Germans come again,' Larssen said, 'they will come in strength. We will need all the help we can get.'

Angelika inclined her head. 'I understand.'

'We want to know how many of them there are and whether they need arms or ammunition,' Larssen said urgently, putting his hand on the girl's sleeve. 'Above all, we need to know if they are prepared to help us. Or if they only care about who is in power after the war. Are they politicians or fighting men, Angelika?'

The girl did not attempt to pull back from him, but for a moment, when her eyes met Larssen's, Tiller felt that perhaps the Dane had met his match. Then, just as quickly, the flash of anger at Larssen touching her was gone and she dropped her gaze.

'Please. I must go,' she said quietly. 'I'll try and find out for you.'

Larssen removed his hand. She glanced at Tiller and then turned on her heel and disappeared behind the black curtain.

Larssen gave a grunt of disgust and reached for his glass. 'I sometimes wonder if your little navigator has not got other allegiances, Tiger. I see what her father meant by being stubborn. She has quite a temper, yes?'

'She's a looker,' said Barnesworth admiringly. 'I'd never really noticed her before. Bloody good navigator, though,' he added as an afterthought.

'Perhaps we didn't tackle her the right way,' said Tiller. 'You know how touchy the Greeks can be.'

Larssen grunted again. 'You better see what you can get out of her,' he said to Tiller.

'Me?' said Tiller, alarmed. 'She's like a clam with me. Doesn't even want to pass the time of day.'

'See what you can do, Tiger. It's important. I think maybe somewhere she has a soft spot for you.'

The fall of Kos drove a wedge into the British presence on the islands, isolating the garrisons of Leros and Samos. It brought an end to any Allied fighter presence and the Luftwaffe now turned its attention to softening up the British garrison on Leros and preventing supplies from reaching it. Five weeks later it fell too, isolating the last and strongest British garrison, on Samos.

German air patrols were now so effective and so frequent that it became virtually impossible for the larger British warships to pass north-westwards between Rhodes and the Turkish mainland. But coastal forces, and the Flotilla's caiques, were still managing to get through to Simi and Samos with supplies by hugging the Turkish coastline and lying up under camouflage nets during the day.

'I've just heard the boss and his team are now on Samos,' Larssen told his patrol after Leros fell. 'But he told me the situation is serious. The bigwigs are determined to hold on because they still want Rhodes. Badly. Everyone else seems to think our position is untenable. Our job is to show them that it's not. The Krauts know we're here now, but they're too busy further north to do anything much about us – except to send in Stukas occasionally. For the time being we stay here. But we may soon have to move, perhaps to the Turkish mainland.'

There was a murmur of surprise.

'There's something else,' Larssen said after a pause. 'Naval intelligence has just reported that the two destroyers which were seen making in this direction last month are in Rhodes port. They can't do much damage there but they may be planning to move to Portolago now that Leros is in German hands. At the moment they are not fully operational and Rhodes has no proper dockyard for them. Portolago, as you know, was the Italians' main base in the area. It has all the facilities the destroyers need. I don't need to tell you the serious implications it would have if two such comparatively powerful vessels were at large in the area.'

'Reckon Griffiths's Solothurn wouldn't make much impression on them,' Barnesworth remarked lugubriously. Tiller noticed he had lately taken to sucking his teeth, an irritating habit.

'You're right there, Billy,' said Maygan. 'And frankly, the navy's now got nothing in the area that could touch them, especially once they've had their boilers cleaned and are fully fuelled and armed.'

There was a moment's silence as everyone digested this. Then Larssen, in his casual way, dropped his bombshell. 'We're being asked if there is anything we can do about them.'

'Jeesus!' Tiller groaned.

'What the hell are we supposed to do, skipper?' said Barnesworth. 'Motor out in the caique and wave them down when they pass here, and ask them to let us scuttle them?'

Larssen grinned his boyish grin. 'I hope we can think of something better than that, Billy. RAF Akrotiri managed to get some air reconnaissance photographs for us of where they are lying in Rhodes port. One of their air-sea rescue launches will deliver them to us after dark tonight.'

'There's the MAS boat,' Tiller said doubtfully. 'But what chance would that have against two destroyers even if they aren't fully operational.'

'None,' Maygan confirmed. 'But I have no doubt our Italian friends would have a go if asked.'

'Our best chance is to get them when they're in

harbour,' said Larssen. 'We can't risk waiting until they arrive in Leros. Anyway, they may not even go there. We've got to try and get them before they leave.'

'Do we know when they're leaving, skipper?' Tiller asked.

'Intelligence reckons we've got a minimum of forty-eight hours, perhaps seventy-two. But no more.'

The air reconnaissance photographs arrived that night, as promised. Larssen spread them out on the table. The vertical shots clearly showed the layout of the port's three harbours. Looking from seaward Mandraki, the smallest, was the right-hand one. Behind it lay the modern town. Next was Emborikos, where the two destroyers were moored. Behind it lay the old walled city of Rhodes, with the castle in one corner. Next to Emborikos was Akandia, the commercial harbour, with its long pier. In peacetime it was used by local ferries as well as merchant ships. The deep waters of Emborikos harbour showed up clearly on the photographs in contrast to the shallows of Akandia harbour, inshore from the pier.

Larssen arranged the relevant shots of Emborikos harbour together and began scrutinizing them closely with stereoscopic magnifiers. 'Whoever took these deserves a medal,' he said. 'Just have a look at that.'

He passed the magnifiers and photographs to Maygan, who peered at them with the viewing device. Every detail of the harbour leapt out at him with amazing three-dimensional clarity.

'How the hell do you chaps do it?' he asked the flight sergeant who had brought the photographs from Cyprus.

'It's simple enough, sir. The camera is set automatically to take a succession of photographs which each have a sixty per cent overlap with the previous print. Because of the forward movement of the aircraft each photograph is taken at a slightly difficult angle from its predecessor. As you can see, if you put two successive ones together, and view the overlap through the magnifiers, a three-dimensional effect is achieved. It usually shows up the details on the photograph with great clarity.'

'It certainly does,' said Maygan.

Even objects on the decks of the two destroyers, which were tied up alongside one another at the central quay, were crystal-clear. A man on the bridge of one could be seen shading his eyes as he looked up at the passing aircraft. Half a dozen more men had been frozen by the camera as they scrambled for what must have been the destroyer's anti-aircraft armament placed either side of its after funnel.

'The oblique ones might be more useful to you, sir,' said the flight sergeant, handing Larssen another bundle.

'How the hell did the pilot get away with it?' Larssen wondered aloud as he viewed the oblique photographs. 'He must have come in at about a hundred feet to get these.'

'The Yanks have lent us a couple of photo-recce P-38s, sir. They go like the clappers.'

Lightnings, Tiller knew, lived up to their name. Even so, he thought as he viewed the entrance to the harbour through the magnifiers, the pilot must have had tremendous guts to get that low.

The obliques were even more impressive than the vertical shots, for the harbour entrance was shown more or less as it would appear to anyone approaching from the sea. The outline of the outboard destroyer was plainly visible, though only part of the bow of the inboard one could be seen. Both had their identity numbers on their bows.

Tiller read them out: 'TA-14 and TA-17.' He looked enquiringly at the flight sergeant.

'TA is the designation the Krauts have given to destroyers they have taken over from other navies,' said the flight sergeant. 'As you know, these were Italian.'

'Do we know anything about them?' Larssen asked.

The flight sergeant handed him a sheet of paper.

'It's all on there, sir.' He glanced at his watch. 'If you'll excuse me, sir, I should go now. My skipper's not too keen to be around here at daylight. He doesn't want a Kraut bomb to spoil his deck.'

'Neither of them is new,' said Larssen, scanning the sheet of paper after the flight sergeant had left. 'The smaller one is the *San Martino*, one of the Generali class. She was built in 1920. Zoelly turbines, maximum thirty-two knots, crew of 105. The other is the *Turbine*, the first of the Turbine class. Slightly bigger and more powerful. She was built in 1927. Crew of 142, maximum speed of thirty-six knots. Both of them are around 1000 tons displacement.'

These statistics were digested in silence. Then Maygan broke it. 'And their armaments?' he asked quietly.

'The main armament of the *Turbine* is four 4.7-inch guns. She also has four 37mm and two 13mm AA guns. The *San Martino* has four four-inch and two three-inch guns, and some anti-aircraft machine-guns. And they both have torpedo tubes, of course.'

Outside they could hear the growl of the air-sea rescue launch's engines as it pulled away from the quay. The group listened to them fade away before anyone spoke.

'Shit,' said Maygan half under his breath.

Larssen scanned their despondent faces and said cheerfully: 'Now we stop arseholing around. We have a proper job to do. Tiger?'

Tiller studied the photographs carefully through the stereoscopic magnifiers once more before replying: 'There are two obvious ways of approaching the targets, by sea and by land.'

'I agree,' said Larssen. 'We must consider both. Perhaps we should try both.'

'It would take longer overland, skipper,' said Tiller. 'If we landed where we did before it is about a twenty-mile trek.'

'Can't we land closer to the port?'

'Probably, but we don't know, do we? And we have no way of reconnoitring first.'

Time spent in reconnaissance is never wasted, Tiller reminded himself. If only they had known, he and Barnesworth could have recced the area when they had landed on Rhodes.

'And by sea?'

Tiller bent over the oblique photographs with the magnifiers.

'There doesn't appear to be a boom,' he said, 'but the entrance is very narrow. No more than a couple of hundred yards, I'd say. I don't see how we could get into the harbour without being spotted. Look, you can see there are observation posts on the end of the quay on the left and on the sea wall jutting out towards the quay from the right. There also seems to be quite a high wall round the harbour. It is bound to be patrolled and anyone looking down on the harbour must have a good chance of seeing anything moving. If the destroyers were berthed on the left side, or even anchored behind the sea wall, it might be worth trying. But where they are now means we would have to go right into the harbour. Virtually impossible to do it undetected, I'd say.'

He handed Larssen the photographs and the magnifiers. Larssen's fingers drummed on the table as he studied the harbour. 'So,' he said finally. 'We must go overland, and to save time we must land close by. Six of us will go, working in independent teams of two. The MAS boat can take us and we can be ferried ashore in its dinghy.'

'How will it pick us up, skipper?' Warrington asked. 'It's short of fuel, isn't it?'

Larssen grinned. 'It won't, Ted. We'll have to make our own way back.'

No one seemed to find that a particularly daunting prospect.

'But to make such an operation viable we need to know two things,' said Larssen. 'Where it is possible to land, and if there is someone who can guide us through the town and down to the port.'

'The Andartes,' said Tiller immediately.

'Exactly. But only Cairo has contact with them and there may not be time. I'll go and talk to Balbao. Tiger, you go and find our little navigator.'

Tiller nodded reluctantly. He had not seen Angelika or her father since Larssen had asked for information about the local Andartes. They had simply vanished and Tiller had to admit to himself that he had not made any effort to find out what had happened to them.

'She has to be found,' said Larssen. 'She is the only person who may help or will know anyone locally who could. Billy, you start getting the gear together. Two limpet mines and a silent Sten for each team. Swimmer's suits under fatigues for everyone. We might not sink the sods but we can blow some holes in them and make them stay in harbour. Tiger, meet me on the MAS boat in half an hour. We do not have much time.'

10

Tiller found Larssen with Balbao in the cramped ward-room of the MAS boat. Between them was a half-empty bottle of Chianti. Both were looking grim.

'Cairo is out of contact with the Andartes,' Larssen said. 'I hope you've had better luck.'

Tiller shook his head.

The locals had told Kristos that Angelika's father had taken her away, no one could say where. When pressed by Tiller for an explanation Kristos added that Christophou had apparently removed his daughter 'to safety'. Because they feared air raids? Tiller had asked. Kristos had said no. Then was it because of collaborators? But Kristos had said there were no collaborators on Simi, which came as a surprise to Tiller after what Angelika had said and he realized later that he should have left it at that. Instead he pressed Kristos to tell him the reason the locals had given. The Greeks, Kristos had explained with a laugh, always guarded their womenfolk closely, and he had given Tiller a friendly, knowing slap on the back. Tiller had got the message.

'I think her father's taken her into the mountains,' he said.

'Many think we will be bombed soon,' Balbao commented. Tiller said nothing.

'And Rhodes?'

'Kristos talked to Dimitri, the mayor. But no one knows that coast, apparently. Kristos said he might just as well have been talking about China.'

Larssen slammed down his empty glass. 'There's no way we can rely on an overland attack, then. We must attack from the sea. But how?'

Balbao pushed the Chianti bottle towards Tiller, but Tiller shook his head. He was going to need to think clearly. In the ensuing gloomy silence an idea suddenly sparked in Tiller's mind.

'The torpedoes, skipper, the MAS boat's torpedoes! They would run through the harbour entrance and Emborikos is deeper than the other two harbours. Deep enough for a torpedo to run right up to the quay.'

Why hadn't he thought of it before! He reached for the Chianti, poured himself a glass, downed it in one go, and reached for the bottle again.

'Yes, have another, Tiger,' said Larssen quietly, 'you're going to need it.'

Tiller's hand stayed on the bottle. 'Why's that, skipper?'

'I'm sorry,' said Balbao. 'But when the armistice was announced the admiral made us neutralize all offensive weapons. All our torpedoes had their propellers and gyros removed at Leros before we came here. Our guns we kept so that we could defend ourselves if necessary. But our torpedoes are no good.'

Larssen slipped the bottle from Tiller's unresisting hand and stood up. 'I think we go and tell the others that we must find another way.'

They walked back around the bay and past the

speedboat which was hidden in a small creek. Suddenly Tiller stopped and grasped Larssen's arm.

'The MAS boat's torpedoes, skipper. It's still got them?'

'Why? Nothing can be done with them, Tiger.'

'Hold it there, skipper.' Tiller returned to the MAS boat and asked Balbao if the nineteen-inch Fiume torpedoes were still in their tubes. Balbao said they were.

'And they still have their warheads?'

'Of course,' said Balbao.

'What's in them?'

'In them?' Balbao looked bewildered.

'What explosive does your navy use in its torpedoes?' Tiller asked, suppressing his impatience with difficulty.

'What you call Torpex. What else would it be?'

'How much is in each torpedo?'

'Two hundred and fifty kilograms.'

That was more than enough. 'And would you agree to have it taken out of the warheads?'

Balbao stared at Tiller. 'What are you planning, Sergeant?'

When Tiller explained his scheme, Balbao's face lit up. 'I used to be a member of the 10th Light Flotilla. They were the only part of the navy which did anything.'

'And I want the exploder mechanisms as well.'

'It can be done.'

'Torpex?' Larssen queried when Tiller explained that he had asked Balbao to extract the explosive warhead from the torpedoes.

'It's a mixture of RDX, TNT and powdered aluminium, skipper. Half as powerful again as TNT on its own.'

'So you want to make up a special charge? Aren't your limpet mines good enough?'

'I've got a better idea. This is what we're going to sink those destroyers with.' Tiller pointed down at the speedboat.

Larssen stared down at the sleek mahogany hull shrouded beneath its camouflage netting. 'But it's a plaything, Tiger, just a holiday boat.'

'But it's fast, skipper, very fast.'

He went on to explain about the work that was being carried out by the Royal Marine Boom Patrol Detachment, and how its boom patrol boat was modelled on the Italians' explosive motor boat, or EMB.

'If Jock is as good a mechanic as the lieutenant says he is we can turn this boat into a *barchino*.'

The others were waiting for them when they returned to the SBS headquarters. Larssen explained the situation and then let Tiller describe his plan. The others listened in stunned silence.

When Tiller had finished, Warrington said: 'Are you seriously telling us you intend to turn this speedboat into an EMB by packing its bows with Torpex from the MAS boat's torpedoes? And then you intend to drive it up to the harbour and let it rip, and then bale out?'

Tiller nodded.

Larssen looked at the caique's stoker. 'Jock? It's possible?'

Bryson scratched his cheek, his Scottish caution making him consider the matter carefully. 'Aye, it's possible all right. There's no problem with the explosive charge. The difficulty is making the boat run straight after Tiger's left it.'

'Sounds fucking suicidal to me,' Warrington said.

'It's been done,' Tiller reminded him.

'Where?'

'Suda Bay, April 1941. The Eyeties used EMBs to wreck the cruiser *York* and a tanker.'

'And the drivers survived?'

'They did.'

Warrington shook his head in wonderment. 'Rather you than me, Tiger.'

'You say there are three methods of detonating the explosive?' Larssen said.

'That's right. Impact, hydrostatic, and with time fuses. The last isn't an option in this case as the exact time it would take the boat to reach the target is too imprecise to calculate.'

'What did the Eyeties use at Suda Bay?'

'Hydrostatic. That's how depth-charges are detonated. When the pressure of the water reaches a certain amount per square inch it triggers the detonator mechanism. In the case of the EMB an impact fuse detaches the bow containing the explosive when the vessel hits its target. The bow sinks under the target and is then detonated by the hydrostatic fuse.'

'Very inventive, the Italians,' Barnesworth commented. 'They can't fight, but they're inventive, I'll give them that.'

'It's the most effective way of sinking a target,' Tiller said, 'but I don't have any hydrostatic fuses. It might be possible to make one, but then we'd have to fashion a method of detaching the motor boat's bows when it hits the target. We haven't got the time and it's much too complicated.'

'That leaves an impact fuse,' Larssen said.

'It's the simplest method and a torpedo's fuse

mechanism can easily be adapted to explode the charge when it strikes the target.'

'But you can only hit the outboard destroyer,' Barnesworth objected.

'But if we hit it with the explosives from two torpedoes it could take the other with it if we're lucky.'

'And how do you escape?'

'Swim to a predesignated place where Billy can pick me up in the cockle which the MAS boat will carry to the area. We can then rendezvous with the MAS boat. We'll be back here before any Kraut will have woken up to what's happening. There will be such chaos in the harbour that it will take them ages to work out what occurred.' There was a pause while everyone digested what Tiller was proposing, and then Maygan said: 'It's either the most fiendishly clever plan I've ever heard anyone come up with – or it's the daftest, as well as the quickest, method of getting a posthumous VC. I'm not sure which. I'll have to sleep on it before I make up my mind.'

'No time for that, Andrew,' retorted Larssen. 'Anyone got a better idea?'

No one had.

'Right,' said Larssen. 'What do you need, Tiger?'

'Once we've made the necessary alterations I must find out how the speedboat steers on its own with its rudder locked. I'll need the caique to help me.'

'Can't do it here,' said Maygan firmly. 'Too risky. We'll tow the boat across to the mainland tomorrow night. I know just the spot there. Totally deserted.'

Larssen stood up. 'Let's get the boat out of the water and under cover where we can work on it.'

Using a block and tackle set up on the caique's boom, they lifted the boat out of the water and on to an old wagon they had found and pushed it to a nearby warehouse, where Griffiths and Bryson could work without being disturbed or seen. While they started work Maygan and Tiller walked to the MAS boat to join Larssen and Balbao, who were poring over a chart of the waters off northern Rhodes.

'We can take the boat and the cockle quite close to the port,' the Italian said, 'and then wait for the cockle down the coast. Around here.'

He pointed to the chart.

'Provided the weather is good, there should be no problem. There might be a local current, but we'll just have to risk that.'

'How close do you need to get to the destroyers?' Larssen asked Tiller.

'The closer the better.'

'And how do you get close without being seen or heard?'

Tiller shrugged. 'That's a risk I'll have to take.'

'Jock said the speedboat's engine at low speed would be very quiet,' said Maygan. 'But that once you open its throttle it will make a hell of a racket. I think Magnus has put his finger on what is the weak link in the plan. What we need is a diversion.'

'I go along with that,' said Tiller. 'Would the RAF be willing to mount a night raid?'

'No bombers closer than Cairo,' Larssen was thinking aloud. 'They might agree to send out a couple of Beaufighters from Cyprus. But their range is limited and they wouldn't be able to stay long. It would need split-second timing for them to be over the port at just the right moment. If they arrived too soon they'd just wake up the defences; if they arrived too late we'd be risking two valuable aircraft and their crews for nothing. No, I think we're going to have to do without the RAF.'

'The navy?' Tiller suggested, but Larssen simply said: 'Why do you think we're sitting here, thinking up a crazy plan to get you killed, Tiger?'

'I could take the caique and we could shoot up Mandraki harbour with the Solothurn,' Maygan said eagerly.

'It needs something like that,' Larssen admitted. 'But I don't think the Solothurn is exactly going to cause any panic ashore.'

Tiller snapped his fingers. 'I've got it, skipper. We could put a couple of limpet mines on the garrison launch and send that towards the shore unmanned. We'll put a time fuse in it so that it goes up just as I'm ready to send the speedboat in.'

Larssen looked doubtful. 'It could just alert the defenders. There's no guarantee it will cause a diversion.'

'I could shell the harbour,' suggested Balbao, but Larssen and Maygan vetoed the idea immediately on the grounds that the MAS boat was more valuable as a means of escape than as a diversion.

In the end a compromise was reached and it was agreed that the garrison launch would be used and that the MAS boat would only open fire if something went wrong with using the launch as a diversion.

When they returned to the warehouse Griffiths had already fashioned a flutterboard which, when a catch was released, slid along rails and off the speedboat's counter. Bryson's task, of making a control for the boat's throttle which would work from the flutterboard, was more complicated, but he had no doubts that he could do it.

Tiller had to devise a means whereby the Torpex would be exploded when the boat hit its target. The simplest solution was to insert a detonator mechanism from one of the torpedoes into the bow of the boat. But Tiller soon decided that it was expecting too much for the boat to hit its target with such accuracy. It was much more likely to hit on one side of the bow or the other. So he decided to fit the same kind of bumper as he had seen on the EMB at Southsea. Any pressure on the bumper would trigger the torpedo's detonator mechanism.

The next evening the speedboat, with its deadly cargo, was put back in the water. It floated bow down, but when Tiller climbed on to the flutterboard it came back on to an even keel, though it was noticeably lower in the water.

That night Maygan towed the speedboat across to the mainland and at dawn the next day Tiller began by testing how straight the boat ran at different speeds without any manual adjustment to the steering wheel to keep it on course. In the flat water of the Turkish bay it held a straight course with very little assistance up to about twenty knots, but beyond that speed it needed an increasingly firm hand on the wheel.

Tiller then tied the wheel with the rudder amidships and let the boat rip. This time it ran smoothly and straight up to about thirty-five knots, but if he increased the speed beyond that it began to yaw.

Next he tested how far it would run in a straight line at different speeds as he had to calculate at what distance from the target he would be able to leave the boat to run on its own. The closer he got to the harbour mouth the more likely he was to be spotted, but the closer he got the more likely he was to hit his target. He had calculated from the chart that the harbour was about 200 yards long and that the pierhead on its left, which included the quay for steamers, was another hundred.

On the other side, to seaward of the sea wall, was the pierhead of Mandraki harbour. He just hoped it did not have guards patrolling it as he would have to get very close to it before baling out. This meant that altogether the boat would have to run for a minimum of 400 yards on its own, much further, he knew, than the Italians had run at Suda Bay.

Maygan marked off this distance with two buoys and after experimenting Tiller found the speed at which the boat ran rock steady for this distance was about thirty knots. So, he calculated, it would take the boat about thirty seconds to reach its target. Tiller knew the German defences would be trying to locate the speedboat and sink it immediately he opened up its engine. But it would take time to focus their searchlights and aim their weapons – not easy to do on an object travelling at thirty knots over water on a dark night.

'Looks remarkably steady,' said Maygan when Tiller returned to the caique. 'Mind you, I still think it's a crackpot idea.'

He insisted that Tiller practise controlling the speedboat from its counter and then, while Maygan was aboard, sliding into the water with the flutterboard. The speedboat's propeller was fixed forward of the counter, so Tiller found there was no danger of being hit by it as he dropped off the counter into the water. He also found that Griffiths had given him an unexpected bonus by shaping the board so that it was quite easy to propel through the water with his hands and by kicking gently with his feet.

What would have been useful would have been those swim fins for his feet which had been captured from the Italians and which Tasler had been experimenting with. Combined Operations calculated they increased both a swimmer's power and endurance by a hundred per cent. But even without these aids Tiller found he was able to progress at a reasonable speed.

Once darkness had fallen they returned to Simi. While they had been away Bryson had altered the steering of the garrison launch so that it could be clamped using the same method as Bryson had devised for the speedboat. But as accuracy was unimportant it was decided that there was no need to test it.

By noon everything had been prepared and Tiller and the others, who had been working throughout the night, got a few hours' sleep before having a meal. As soon as darkness fell they boarded the MAS boat, and the cockle and the speedboat were hoisted aboard. The launch was too big to be stowed on deck and was towed astern.

The night seemed ideal for the operation. It was overcast, very dark, and with practically no wind. The MAS boat cut its speed to ten knots both to conserve fuel and to prevent the launch from yawing too wildly on the end of its painter. Halfway across a bottle of brandy was passed round and Tiller changed into his surface-swimmer's suit and Barnesworth into his paddler's suit.

It was the first time Tiller had worn the suit since he had arrived in the region and he checked it carefully before he donned it, making sure there were no holes in the rubberized fabric and that the urination valve and the mouth-inflated rubber stole, used for buoyancy, worked properly. He carried his commando knife in a sheath attached to his belt, but was otherwise unarmed. Also hooked to the belt was a signalling torch and a small watertight flask filled with brandy. Barnesworth had the cockle fully equipped with food and water and two silent Stens.

The MAS boat arrived off Rhodes port before midnight and eased its way inshore with its engines hardly ticking over. The island was just a hump in front of them. They could hear nothing and the port was so efficiently blacked out that they could not see anything either. When they were about five miles offshore Balbao brought the MAS boat to a standstill, and the cockle, with Barnesworth aboard, and the speedboat, were lowered into the water.

Barnesworth paddled off without pausing as he needed to be in position well before the attack was launched. The cockle was quickly swallowed up in the dark and Tiller, who was watching it, was relieved that it faded out of sight so swiftly. Poor visibility was a bonus he had not expected. He clambered down into the speedboat carefully and started its engine with the MAS boat between him and the shore.

Luckily, there was a slight offshore breeze which would help carry away the sound of his engine. Alongside him Larssen was making last-minute adjustments to the launch.

'When you're in position, you flash the letter "R" and I'll release the launch,' Larssen said and then repeated his instructions. He knew that apprehension and the cold did terrible things to the memory; he always believed that operational instructions could not be repeated too often. Tiller nodded.

'When you signal I'll put a five-minute time pencil in the limpet mines,' Larssen said. 'That should give you plenty of time.'

They made sure their watches were synchronized. Then Larssen leant across and gripped Tiller's hand. 'Good luck. See you in a couple of hours.'

'Thanks, skipper.'

Larssen let go the warps holding the speedboat and Tiller slipped its engine into gear and edged it round the stationary MAS boat.

Griffiths had fixed a compass in the speedboat's cockpit and Tiller steered due south by it. He strained his eyes into the blackness, and kept the revs of the engine right down so that the speedboat crept forward with hardly any way on it.

At first he encountered a slight swell but as the boat edged towards the land the sea became quite flat. Slowly his eyesight became used to the dark and gradually, very gradually, the island began to take shape in front of him, and after about twenty minutes he could make out the outlines of the port.

Soon Tiller was inshore of Cape Zonari, the most northerly part of the island, which lay to starboard of him, and he turned and flashed an 'R' with his shaded torch out to sea. He repeated the signal twice more, noted the time on the slate he carried, and then turned his attention once more to the shore.

Almost immediately he saw the outline of the castle against the night sky and realized he was too far to the right of Emborikos harbour. That meant there was more of a lateral inshore current than Balbao had thought.

Swearing under his breath, he began edging the speedboat to port and after a few minutes saw the two piers that made the entrance to Mandraki harbour. He was now heading south-east and for a moment he slipped the engine into neutral so that he could orientate himself.

As he peered intently into the dark he could just discern the stone sea wall that jutted out into Emborikos harbour. He engaged the engine at minimum revs and slowly the mouth of the harbour began to open up.

When he calculated he was on the correct course he swung the boat around until its bow was pointing straight into the harbour. The compass was now indicating due south.

He glanced at his watch and was alarmed to see that he only had ninety seconds left before the launch was due to explode.

He made sure the speedboat was on course, locked the wheel, wriggled stomach downwards on to the flutterboard behind him, and grasped the throttle extension. By pulling the wire out to its fullest extent and winding it round a cleat, he would jam the engine at three-quarters throttle, which would give it the required speed of thirty knots.

Lying flat, Tiller thought he could just make out the outline of the outboard destroyer against the light-coloured buildings around the quay. He looked around him and saw that he was now just inshore of the right-hand pier of Mandraki harbour. There was no movement from on shore, no light of any kind. The only sound was the faint barking of a dog and the mutter of the speedboat's engine.

He glanced at his watch and swore. The pencil fuse was either not going to work or had been retarded by the cold and he began calculating how long he could wait. The speedboat was only just making headway and the offshore breeze helping to hold it back, but it was still creeping closer to the harbour.

He'd give it ten seconds and he began counting under his breath. 'Seven . . . six . . . five . . .'

There was a huge bang to the right of him as the two limpet mines ripped the launch apart and flames lit up the night sky. The sound of the explosions reverberated on to the island and back out to sea again.

Immediately, several searchlights were switched on, a klaxon cranked itself up and then began to wail, and parachute flares blossomed in the night sky. He hadn't reckoned on those.

Tiller pulled steadily on the throttle wire until it had reached its maximum extent and felt the boat leap into life under him. It was still running true. He wound the wire around the cleat, hit the catch that released the flutterboard, and felt himself sliding backwards down the speedboat's reverse sheer counter.

The flutterboard took most of the impact on to the water, but the wash from the speedboat hit him full in the face and made him splutter and gasp. Then, using both his arms in a butterfly stroke and kicking hard with his feet, he began moving the board sideways as fast as he could. He concentrated on getting a rhythm going, but the board kept jagging into the water and slowing him down, though he did not dare abandon it.

He was vaguely aware that some guns had begun firing and more than once a searchlight lit up the sea around him before moving on. But the loudest noise was the rasping sound of his breath as he strained to move the board through the water and the slap of the water on his face, and when the explosion came the water in his ears made it seem a million miles away.

It would, he knew, take the shock from the explosion about thirty seconds to reach him and he felt the primeval instinct for survival flood adrenalin through his body. With every muscle he strained to move the flutterboard faster, but when it came the shock wave merely lifted the flutterboard slightly from the surface of the water.

Tiller stopped swimming, lowered his body into the water and just hung on to the flutterboard with his hands. To his surprise he was further to the left of the harbour than he had thought possible and supposed there must be an inshore current running counter to the main one further out.

The harbour entrance was behind him now and he could not see if the speedboat had hit its target. What he could see by the beams of the searchlights sweeping across the harbour was a rising column of smoke and a lurid glow where the destroyers were moored. He felt a great elation surge through him.

Suddenly he could hear voices borne to him by the offshore breeze and a torch was flashed from the end of the pier. Instinctively, he sank lower into the water. He could see now that it was not a torch but some kind of portable searchlight, small but powerful. Its operator began scanning the water around the end of the pier while another German soldier shouted instructions at him. A third held a rifle or sub-machine-gun at the ready.

The current was slowly carrying him sideways, away from the pier, but he was still well within the range of the searchlight. He allowed the flutterboard to drift away from him, let the air out of his rubber stole, and began to swim slowly towards the left-hand pier of Akandia harbour. But he kept glancing over his shoulder and when the searchlight began sweeping towards him he would sink gently under the water.

Once the soldier in charge started shouting and the soldier with the gun opened fire. Tiller could tell from its rapid, distinctive sound that he was using a Schmeisser. He thought that perhaps they had seen his flutterboard, but he couldn't tell for sure.

The outline of the pier and the soldiers remained quite distinct because of the fire in the harbour beyond it, but after a few minutes Tiller knew he was out of range of the searchlight and concentrated on what lay ahead of him.

It looked as if he was about halfway across Akandia harbour and swimming straight for the end of the harbour's left-hand pier. On the far side of the pier Barnesworth would be lying up in the cockle.

But if the Germans were sending search parties on to the end of each pier, Tiller realized, he would either have to swim well out to sea before approaching the other side or swim right up to the pier and move round it right under the feet of the search party. He remembered Tasler saying that anyone searching for someone often failed to look under their noses, so he chose the latter option and hoped Tasler was right.

Despite the kapok lining of his suit he was starting to feel the cold. He began swimming slightly to the right so that he would reach the pier about fifty yards before the end of it. As he approached he heard a vehicle draw up and more shouting. Three or four figures began running along the pier. He trod water and once they had passed him swam strongly until he reached the pier.

It was made of stone and it took him a moment to find a good handhold. He kept his head low in the water and looked around him. The wall of the pier was about thirty feet high and rose vertically from the water. Inshore of him were wharves. Most of these were deserted except for one or two caiques. On the seaward side there was just the sheer face of the stone pier at the end of which he could just see the glass revolving top of an unlit lighthouse.

Luckily, the end of the pier seemed to have a stone lip on it which made it more difficult for anyone looking down to see what was underneath at sea level. Cautiously he began pulling himself along the stone wall with his hands, stopping every few yards to look and listen.

As he approached the end of the pier a searchlight on it began playing on the surrounding water. At first it flicked here and there, but then began to quarter the area methodically. When Tiller noticed that even when fully depressed it could not shine within a hundred feet of the pier he pressed on as quickly as he dared.

He reached the end of the pier and began alternatively swimming under water and just floating on the surface head down, propelling himself slowly forward by pushing with his hands on the stone wall beneath the surface. Once the slop of the water on the pier tore his grip from the stonework and he felt himself being drawn seawards by an undertow. It took a lot of control not to look up but instead to turn his body back towards the pier until he felt the stonework again.

He allowed his body to sink and then he turned on his back and surfaced. Staring up at the end of the pier, he saw two helmeted heads leaning over the lip of the end of the pier and looking directly down at him. He froze, his left hand grasping a piece of protruding stone below the water.

He thought for a terrible moment that his blackened face might have been washed clean and the men were wondering what the pale, oval shape below them might be.

He could not hear them, but he could see the glow of two cigarettes. Then one butt spiralled its way down towards him and fizzed out in the water next to his head. Then the other arced out and fell some yards away, and the two smokers disappeared.

He sank down again, turned over, and began to feel his way along the outside of the pier. He had agreed with Barnesworth that it would be impossible to say exactly where the cockle should lie up as they had no means of knowing what, if any, shelter there would be for it.

It looked at first as if there was none, but then he saw that a narrow wooden jetty ran alongside the wall. It was supported on the seaward side by wooden piles and was about ten feet above the water. He supposed it was for a ship waiting for a berth on the inner side of the pier. It looked an ideal hiding-place and he approached it quickly, anxious now to get out of the water, which was chilling him to the marrow.

Under the jetty he could not see anything. He thought of calling out but decided the risk was too great. He felt his way along, but he could not see the cockle, and his heart sank when he saw he had almost reached the far end of the jetty. Billy had obviously not made it. Perhaps he had been caught or, more likely, lost his way.

Tiller came to the last diagonal wooden support for the jetty floor above him and heaved himself partly out of the water so that he could lean on it and consider his options. It would be impossible to swim to the MAS boat. If exhaustion didn't get him the cold would. He could wait in the hope that Barnesworth would turn up or the MAS boat might conceivably come and search for him. Or he could try and find some sort of boat and make his escape that way.

He was just deciding that the last option seemed to be the most practicable when he felt something cold and hard pressed up against the base of his skull, and an arm snake round his throat.

'*Du bist ein Tiger, bitte?*' a voice said quietly in his ear.

'For Christ's sake, Billy,' Tiller croaked.

Barnesworth's arm relaxed from around Tiller's throat and he returned his pistol to its holster.

'Just had to make sure, Tiger,' he whispered. 'You've stirred up a fucking hornets' nest, I can tell you.'

'Did I hit the bleeders?' Tiller asked eagerly.

'How the fuck should I know?' said Barnesworth. 'I've been clinging to the arse side of this jetty for the last forty minutes. You took your time, mate. Let's go.'

He swung from one support to another and then lowered himself gently into the front cockpit of the cockle, which lay right under the stone wall. Tiller followed him in the water and climbed into the rear cockpit from the craft's stern. He reached for the flask still attached to his belt, took a good swig of brandy, and passed it to Barnesworth.

'What now?' he whispered in Barnesworth's ear. 'Do we wait for things to quieten down, or what?'

Barnesworth turned and held up his arm with his

luminous watch on his wrist turned towards his companion.

'No time,' he whispered back. 'The sky's clear now and the moon is due up in an hour. With any luck, they'll be concentrating their searches around the harbour, not in this direction. Let's go.'

Using single paddles they emerged cautiously from under the jetty and when they had ensured the coast was clear put as much water as they could between the pier and themselves by steering eastwards.

When the darkness had swallowed up the pier they stopped to turn their single paddles into doubles. Searchlights were still playing on the water outside the port and something still seemed to be on fire in Emborikos harbour. However, they did not linger, but paddled on a course of 160 degrees by the compass as fast as they could.

The cold that Tiller had felt was now replaced by a warm glow and a feeling of intense exhilaration, and he dug his paddles into the water with zest. After an hour they could see ahead of them the promontory off which the MAS boat would be waiting for them.

When they were abeam of the headland they turned due east and began signalling out to sea with the shaded torch, and after half an hour they saw the outline of the MAS boat on their starboard side. They stopped paddling and guided it to them with the torch, and minutes later eager hands were hauling them aboard.

11

'I want to put you up for the DCM,' Maygan said enthusiastically. 'If you hadn't made it back, I'd have had a crack at getting you a posthumous VC.'

'It was a damned good try, Tiger,' Larssen said.

'Thanks, skipper,' said Tiller wearily. His sleep had been continually interrupted throughout the day by the Stukas which had started systematically grinding the port into rubble. The Germans had guessed from where the raid had been mounted and were exacting what retribution they could.

He had also just heard from Larssen that the Germans, who had been taking over the smaller islands one by one, had moved nearer to Simi by overrunning Piscopi. Tiller hated to think what might have happened to Giovanni and his Mafia there.

'What do you think went wrong, skipper?'

'Wrong?' Larssen queried. 'I'd hardly call it that. You blew half the bloody quay away.'

'But missed the destroyers,' said Tiller quietly. He had always known there must have been only a small chance of success, but the disappointment he felt was sharp.

'But according to photo recce they haven't moved,' said Maygan. 'You may have stopped them from sailing. They could be damaged in some way.'

'The lads did an incredible job on that speedboat,'

said Tiller. 'Everything worked. I can't understand it. The boat was running absolutely true.'

'A bit of flotsam in the harbour probably,' said Larssen. 'The boat only needed to touch something floating in the water to make it deviate from its course. It's bad luck, but there you are.'

'What now, skipper?'

Larssen rubbed his stubble. 'Beirut's just informed us that the navy's trying to get enough ships together to take the garrison off Samos. It looks as if the Krauts are going to try and land there soon. Beirut wants to know what we're going to do because our friend the Flag Officer Levant and Eastern Mediterranean is not going to risk any more ships to rescue the garrison if there are two destroyers on the loose. The odds against them would be stacked much too high. So if we fail, 5000 troops on Samos go into the bag.'

A silence fell while this review of the situation was assimilated.

'What a fuck-up,' said Tiller eventually. 'Whose idea was this mission, anyway?'

'Ours not to reason why, Tiger,' Larssen said.

'Ours just to do and die,' Maygan finished off the famous couplet with relish.

'On the positive side Cairo has agreed to increase the number of photo-recce flights over the port of Rhodes,' said Larssen. 'The Germans have nothing that can touch the Lightning, so it can operate with impunity. Also, my guess is – and it's only a guess – that Cairo is now giving higher priority to deciphering Kriegsmarine signals between Athens and Rhodes. Certainly the time-lag between transmission and us receiving the deciphers has decreased dramatically.'

The esoteric world of signals intelligence, run from

a building in the Cairo suburb of Heliopolis, was way above the heads of anyone present. Nevertheless, enough was known by any alert officer serving in the Middle East for Maygan to suck in his breath and say: 'Jesus! If they're doing that they're pulling out all the stops.'

'I think a lot is riding on all this,' said Larssen. 'Much more than the loss of a few destroyers and 5000 men. Don't ask me what it is because I don't know. It's just an impression I get and it's getting stronger.'

Above them there was the crump of bombs exploding and dust from the cellar roof cascaded down on them. Larssen shook it off the chart that was opened in front of him and said: 'So when the destroyers sail what course will they take? Andrew?'

'If I were them I'd take the shortest course consistent with safety,' said Maygan, following his suggested route on the chart with his forefinger. 'Which means passing Simi and sailing between Piscopi and Nisiros and then passing the western end of Kos. That's about 120 miles. Even steaming at reduced speed, they could do that in a night without trouble. That's the safest and quickest route.'

Larssen nodded his agreement. 'So how close will they come to Simi?'

Maygan bent over the chart and used a pencil and parallel rulers to draw the destroyers' most likely course from Rhodes. He then stretched the two points of his compass between the course and Simi and measured off the distance from the side of the chart.

'It depends. If they head for the western end of

Kos the most direct route would take them between Simi and Seskli. Seskli is that small island off Simi's southern coast.'

'Would they do that?'

Maygan shook his head. 'Unlikely. Not at night. They'd leave Seskli to starboard, though by how much it's impossible to say. The water's deep there so they could pass close by it if they wanted to. I'd say they'd come within a few miles of Simi. Perhaps only a mile from Seskli.'

'And how long would it take them to get there from Rhodes?'

'It shouldn't take them more than a couple of hours at the outside.'

'Two hours! Is that all?'

''Fraid so. If we want to mount some kind of attack on them as they pass Seskli, we'd have to go and wait for them by the island.'

'We've got nothing to mount an attack on them with,' protested Tiller. 'The speedboat's gone, the launch has gone. We can't use the caique as we'll need that if we have to attack the destroyers at Leros.'

'There's the MAS boat,' said Maygan.

'But that's only got its twin Bredas and a machine-gun,' Larssen pointed out. 'That won't stop them. Anyway, it's hardly got any fuel left.'

'If it's going to attack them off Seskli, it won't need much, will it?' said Maygan quietly. Larssen looked at Maygan hard and drummed his fingers on the upturned wooden crate which was acting as a table. 'What you're suggesting is that . . .'

'It rams one of them,' Maygan said. 'It's not going to be any use to us without fuel. It's an outside chance but one we shouldn't miss.'

'It's a viable option?'

'Certainly,' said Maygan. 'The MAS boat could run rings round the destroyers and neither of them is particularly big. Thousand-tonners, aren't they. If you hit one of them in the right place, in the engine space, say, you'd certainly cripple it.'

'And who's going to man the MAS boat?' Kristos asked.

'We will, of course,' said Larssen briskly. 'You couldn't expect the Eyeties to do it. Why should they?'

'Balbao may not like having his command taken from him,' Maygan suggested.

Larssen stood up, buckled on his belt and pistol holster and said briskly: 'Too bad. He won't have any choice, will he? Let's go and pay him a visit.'

Balbao seemed more amused than annoyed when Larssen told him what he proposed to do. He could see that the SBS party had no alternative to using the desperate methods they were proposing, but tried to persuade them there was no way they could put them into action.

'You've handled an MAS boat?' he asked Maygan, who shook his head.

'And you, Captain?'

'In the merchant navy we handled anything and everything,' Larssen said. 'A couple of years ago I skippered a tug to tow out a German liner from a neutral port.'

'And who will man the guns?'

'Our chaps. They have been taught how to fire German weapons and Italian ones.'

'And the engines?'

'Bryson,' said Maygan immediately.

Balbao nodded. 'A good man, but the Isotta-Fraschinis in this boat are pretty temperamental. They should have been overhauled months ago.'

He paused and looked at them, and then shook his head. 'I'm sorry, gentlemen. I cannot agree.'

'You have no option, Commander.' Larssen's hand dropped casually on to the butt of his pistol.

'Oh, but I have, Captain. All my crew have been instructed how to – how do you say? – scuttle the boat if it is necessary. We have a drill, you know, on when to carry this out.'

Larssen's hand dropped away. 'And what drill is that?'

Balbao laughed. 'Come, come, Captain. You don't expect me to tell you that.'

Stalemate, Tiller thought to himself. He could see Larssen was getting very angry. Balbao leant forward. 'May I make a suggestion?'

Larssen nodded.

'I skipper the boat, you man the guns. I see if my chief engineer will come, too. He loves those engines like babies. I don't think he allows anyone else to touch them. You understand?'

Larssen looked at Maygan, who shrugged. It was a gesture of resignation more than approval, but Larssen said: 'If we accept your conditions, how do I know you'll carry out my orders?'

Balbao smiled. 'You don't.'

'It's a high-risk operation,' Larssen warned him.

Balbao brushed Larssen's comment aside with a weary wave of his hand. 'The boat has an emergency steering position in the stern. If we are going to ram one of the destroyers, we'll use that for the final run in. We'll dump the Carley floats over the stern and jump after them and the lieutenant can pick us up in the caique. You must remember I was once a member of the 10th Light Flotilla. I am used to performing such antics.'

'This will delay our move, skipper,' Tiller said as they left the MAS boat. The bombing and the fall of Piscopi had made Simi untenable as a base for the SBS and orders had come through that Larssen was to move his team to the Turkish mainland as soon as possible. A rudimentary headquarters had been set up for them aboard a schooner which had been moved by stages from Castelrosso. It was in an isolated bay which provided good cover and was rarely visited by the Turkish coastguard. And when they did come they only came to collect their bribes.

'If this op goes wrong there won't be anything left to move,' Larssen replied.

The Stukas came over again at first light and more houses in the port crumbled to dust.

At midday a high-priority signal came on the radio from Cairo, informing the SBS men that the destroyers would sail that night at an unspecified time. Their destination was Portolago, Leros.

At dusk the MAS boat and the caique emerged from their hiding-places and went alongside the quay. Tiller, Larssen, Simmonds and Warrington, all wearing shallow-diving suits to protect them from the cold when they abandoned ship, went aboard the MAS boat and the Italian crew filed ashore. Barnesworth went with Maygan in the caique. The caique would stay out of the way behind Seskli; the MAS boat would lie in wait on the island's seaward side. It wasn't much of a plan, but they agreed it was the best available.

They were in position by ten that night. When the destroyers had not appeared by midnight they began to think that they must have taken another course, or had been prevented from sailing for some reason. But ten minutes later Balbao nudged Larssen, handed him his night-glasses, and pointed southwards.

Larssen adjusted the binoculars and scanned the inky black horizon. At first he could see nothing, then slowly, gradually, two indistinct objects began to form in the lenses. He handed back the glasses to Balbao. 'That must be them,' he agreed.

Balbao ordered slow ahead and the MAS boat crept out from under the lee of the island.

'Would they have radar?' Larssen asked.

Balbao shook his head. 'Remind me to tell you the sorry story of radar and the Italian Navy some time.'

He ordered an increase in the MAS boat's speed and told Larssen that he planned to get as close as possible to the destroyers without being detected and then, and only then, open fire on them. He would run the MAS boat parallel with the two warships, swing round the stern of the second one, and then choose which one to ram.

After a few minutes it was possible to see the two shapes without the night-glasses. It was soon apparent from the changing angle of approach that they were moving at about fifteen knots, and were moving slightly away from the MAS boat.

Their speed and course made Balbao decide it would be better to approach them from behind and swing round ahead of them. The MAS boat's engines throbbed powerfully and it was less than a mile away when a shaded signalling lamp from the leading destroyer started to flick out a message to the MAS boat.

'He wants to know who we are,' chuckled Balbao. 'We'll soon let him know.'

When the signal was ignored the destroyer opened fire with a single shot from its aft four-inch gun. The shell whirred overhead and fell into the water beyond the MAS boat. Calmly, Balbao ordered full speed ahead and the MAS boat leapt forward, its hull vibrating, its engines gurgling and thrumming. A second shell fell short and when a third narrowly missed the MAS boat Balbao shouted 'fire, fire, fire,' into the intercom which connected the bridge with the twin Bredas' crew.

The 20mm tracer arced towards the second destroyer and tiny fireballs danced on its upperworks. A fourth salvo from the destroyer's stern four-inch gun went high over the MAS boat and Tiller, who was working the forward machine-gun with Larssen, realized the MAS boat was now so close to the destroyers that their gun crews could not depress the main armament sufficiently to hit it.

Then the MAS boat was running parallel with the second destroyer and its Breda was raking its deck and bridge. Larssen and Tiller opened up with the machine-gun on the destroyer's open gun position on a circular platform behind its second funnel. They could see the gun crew, who were running to close up with their weapon, scatter and fall.

Then, in a surge of speed that Tiller calculated must have exceeded forty knots, the MAS boat began drawing ahead of the destroyers. He managed to get in one final burst, at the destroyer's bridge, and saw its glass screen shatter.

'Taking target on starboard, repeat starboard, side,' Balbao shouted into the intercom and the Breda's crew began frantically peddling the guns from port to starboard as the MAS boat swerved across the path of the second destroyer and through the wake of the first.

Larssen and Tiller swung the machine-gun round and opened fire, spraying the first destroyer's superstructure with bullets. Then the twin Bredas opened up, too, and Tiller could see that the 20mm shells were causing some damage.

After a few seconds Balbao brought the MAS boat round to starboard so that it was running parallel with the target and 200 yards from it. Again they saw the sparks as the Bredas' shells smashed into the destroyer at what was virtually point-blank range.

Balbao now slowed to the speed of the leading destroyer so that the Bredas could rake it from stern to stem. Then he increased speed again and, once it was ahead of the destroyer, swung the MAS boat away to port.

A parachute flare blossomed in the sky and lit the ink-black waters with a pale glow. But the MAS boat, now streaking away at right angles from the leading destroyer, was out of the circle of light that it created before the destroyer's guns could be brought to bear on it.

'Now what?' Larssen shouted into the intercom. 'They'll be ready for us the next time. We won't get away with that again.'

Balbao shouted back: 'I shall make a run at them so that they will think we are going to use our torpedoes. That will force them to turn this way to make the smallest possible target.'

Another parachute flare lit the sky where the destroyers supposed the MAS boat to be but Balbao had already altered course again. Tiller admired the cool skill with which the Italian was handling the MAS boat and, as he had predicted, the destroyers now both swung to port.

They were now dim outlines again, about two miles distant, moving westwards at about twenty knots, while the MAS boat was moving slowly eastwards.

'I am going to turn to port to ram the nearest destroyer,' Balbao told Larssen through the intercom. 'There is not enough fuel to do anything else. I slow down. Then you abandon ship.'

The SBS men moved aft and when the MAS boat slowed the two Carley floats were thrown overboard and Tiller and the other SBS men followed them, dropping backwards into the foaming wake of the MAS boat. Larssen watched them go before he turned and climbed on to the bridge to join Balbao. He was not about to miss the most exciting part of the action.

Balbao called for full power and told his chief engineer to abandon ship. The seconds ticked away, the destroyers to port of them were approaching fast.

'Time to move to the emergency steering position,' Larssen shouted at Balbao above the sound of the engines. Balbao shouted back: 'You abandon ship. Now.'

'What about you?' Larssen shouted. 'Go aft now.'

'Go!' Balbao shouted. 'I follow you.' He drew himself up and saluted Larssen. '*Memento Audare*

Semper, Captain. Remember always to dare. Now go!'

Larssen ran aft with the chief engineer. They threw over another Carley float and followed it. The water stunned Larssen for a moment, but then he grabbed the Carley float, climbed on to it, and dragged the engineer aboard it, too.

They watched as the MAS boat converged with the approaching destroyers. Another parachute flare lit the water and the nearest destroyer's searchlights flicked on. The MAS boat was caught in a pool of light and both enemy vessels opened up simultaneously with all their armament. Tracer arced across it as it sped unerringly towards the nearest destroyer.

'For Christ's sake, why doesn't he jump?' Larssen bawled, seeing the MAS boat was about to hit its target. 'Jump, you fool, jump.'

The MAS boat was about 200 yards from the nearest destroyer when two four-inch shells hit it above the water-line and there was an ear-splitting explosion. One moment the MAS boat was there, travelling at forty knots in the middle of the pool of light created by the flare and the searchlights, and the next there was just smoke and debris.

The flare dowsed itself in the water and the searchlights swung and scanned the debris, and were then turned off, and the dark shapes of the destroyers quickly faded into the night.

Larssen looked at his wrist compass and then began signalling with his shaded torch towards the island. Half an hour later they saw the outline of the caique approaching them, and they were quickly hauled aboard. Ten minutes later they saw the signals from the other Carley floats and their occupants, too, were hauled aboard.

'What happened?' Maygan asked Larssen as they turned for Simi.

'God knows,' said Larssen tiredly, 'except it didn't work.'

'And Balbao?'

Larssen turned to the Italian engineer. 'Your commander, why didn't he use the emergency steering position?'

The engineer looked at him blankly. 'You must be mistaken, *signore*. There was no emergency steering position.'

The Stukas were back again the following morning, circling round Simi port like vultures. There was very little left for them to destroy, but their shrieking descent on it, followed by the scream of their bombs plummeting down, was slowly wearing down the psychological resistance of the defenders. It was impossible to sleep, or even rest, and the air was filled with dust.

The Italian garrison as well as the local inhabitants had mostly fled by now, and only the bravest attempted to fire on the Stukas as they swooped down out of the sky.

In the cellar of the detachment's headquarters Larssen was using the radio himself to report with an enciphered signal to Beirut that their latest operation had failed. Beirut signalled back their regrets and asked what Larssen proposed to do now. Attack the destroyers at Portolago, replied Larssen, but he had yet to finalize his plans. Keep us informed, Beirut signalled, your operation is being given the highest priority. A photo-reconnaissance flight is being mounted today on Portolago and an ML will bring you the results tonight. Good luck.

Larssen took off the headphones and slammed them down on the table in disgust. 'How like the top brass,' he said irritably. 'They give us impossible jobs to do and then just wish us luck. You'd have thought they could have got rid of the two bloody destroyers themselves. Or found another way of taking off the garrison from Samos. Jesus, are we winning this war or not?'

Above them another bomb exploded, the concussion of it shaking the cellar.

'That's your answer, skipper,' said Tiller grimly.

Larssen sat down and spread out the chart of Leros in front of him. 'What do we know about Portolago?'

'As you can see, it is the most southerly of the three bays on the western side of the island,' said Maygan, 'and is the largest. It runs north-east south-west and is about a mile long. It almost cuts the island in two. Steep hillsides run down to it on either side. Not an easy place to attack.'

'What do you think, Tiger?'

'Looks like a job for Billy and me,' Tiller said evenly, suppressing a surge of excitement. 'Provided, of course, someone can get us there and back.'

'That's not going to be easy,' said Maygan. 'Though I'm sure I could find a way of doing it.'

Larssen shook his head. 'We need you to move everyone to the mainland, Andrew, while we're away. No, we'll see how important the bigwigs really think this operation is. We'll tell them we need the ML for the operation.'

Larssen scribbled a note on a signals pad and handed it to the radio operator who had just come on duty. He enciphered it and then sent it out in Morse. He received a reply almost immediately and handed it to Larssen.

'That's quick,' said Larssen. 'They must mean business.'

The signal confirmed that Larssen could have the motor launch for the operation and that it would be with them before dawn the next morning provided the photo-reconnaissance flight was successful.

The ML arrived that same night, having had a clear run from Paphos. Its captain was a cheerful young RNVR lieutenant, a pre-war sailing friend of Maygan's who knew the Dodecanese well from cruising among them before the war. He handed over a thick brown envelope to Larssen, who sliced it open with his commando knife.

The aerial photographs were clear and detailed, and the analysis of them by the RAF interpretation unit at Akrotiri was especially detailed. The first point Tiller noticed was that a boom protected the harbour mouth. One arm of it extended from two places on the southern headland to a single point about halfway across the harbour. Inshore of this single point they could make out what must have been a boom patrol boat. The other half of the boom extended in a straight line from the northern headland to within about 200 yards of the anchored patrol boat.

'That's not going to be easy to negotiate,' Barnesworth commented.

'Balls, Billy,' Tiller said. He could already feel the adrenalin pumping through him. 'We used to skip over obstacles like that every night in the Solent.'

On the northern side of the harbour and about a thousand yards from the entrance a largish ship was anchored under the lee of the cliffs. The interpretation unit identified this as the German ammunition ship *Anita*, which had just arrived as part of a convoy from Piraeus.

At the far end of the bay was another anchored part of the convoy, identified as a supply ship called the *Carola*, and an F-lighter, a shallow-draft craft similar to a Siebel ferry which was used by the Germans for supplying their garrisons on the islands. Astern of the *Carola* were anchored a variety of small, unidentifiable craft. On the opposite side of the bay to the ammunition ship was the naval base, with a slipway, sheds, floating dock and seaplane hangars. Larssen pointed to the naval base and said: 'There they are.'

The others crowded round. The pilot had taken a series of oblique photographs of the two destroyers as they lay at anchor close to the naval base. The stereoscopic lenses showed up every detail of their superstructure, which looked undamaged despite the hail of fire from the MAS boat's Bredas. As they pored over the photographs another signal came in from Beirut saying that 'operational contingencies' required the detachment to sink the *Anita* and, if possible, *Carola* and the F-lighter, as well as the two destroyers.

'The cockle doesn't normally carry more than eight limpets,' said Tiller. 'This lot will all need three each. That's a hell of a lot of extra weight.'

'You'll be in and out in a couple of hours,' said Larssen. 'You'll just have to leave most of the equipment behind.'

'We won't be able to use the compass with that number aboard,' Tiller objected. 'We won't have time to swing it, and we only have a compass compensator for eight.'

'I'll make sure you're dropped in the right place,' said Denvers, the ML skipper, reassuringly, 'and I'll give you the dead-reckoning course to steer.'

They went through the list of equipment but decided that if the extra limpets had to be carried then everything was expendable except the water, primus and the twenty-four-hour ration packs.

'I don't know why Cairo don't tell us to recapture the island while we're at it,' grumbled Barnesworth.

'They will, Billy, they will,' Larssen said with a grin. 'Just give them time. They probably haven't even realized yet that the Krauts are in residence there. Now, Bob, we want to arrive no later than midnight. Can you do that in one run during the hours of darkness?'

Denvers shook his head. 'I'm driving an ML, remember, not an MTB. We'll have to lie up somewhere for a day along the Turkish coast. On our runs to Samos we've been using a place called Yalikavak. The *meltemi* when it blows from the west makes the anchorage a bit uncomfortable, but the *meltemi* season is over now.'

He pointed on the chart to a small headland on the Turkish mainland north of Kos. 'There's a small fishing village but the locals keep their mouths closed – provided their hands are crossed with silver, of course.'

'Good. We can sail tonight and get there before dawn?'

'No problem.'

'And where do we rendezvous afterwards, skipper?' Tiller asked. 'On Leros somewhere?'

Larssen shook his head. 'The Krauts will be combing the island for you. Kalimnos would be safer. It's only a short distance from Portolago.'

Maygan spread out a large-scale chart of the area. 'Vathi looks suitable. Do you know it, Bob?'

Denvers nodded. 'Dropped anchor there several times before the war. It's rather like a Norwegian fiord. Very deep. It's a bloody tricky area for navigation, especially if you approach it from the south, but I know every inch of it. I could certainly take the ML in far enough to get it out of sight of any Jerry air recce.'

Larssen glanced at his watch. 'We've got about four hours of darkness left. Andrew, bring the caique alongside the quay and unload the cockle. We're going to have to see how it floats with the weight of the extra limpets.'

He looked at Tiller and Barnesworth. 'Have you both got your escape kits? You may need them.' They both pulled their silk-handkerchief maps out of their pockets and held them up.

Barnesworth flourished his SAS beret. 'I've got two hacksaw blades, one on either side. Reckon I could get out of Sing-Sing if I had to.'

'I'll make sure I tack mine in before we go,' said Tiller.

'Good. And you'd better have some money just in case you need to bribe someone.' He unlocked a steel box and produced fifty gold sovereigns which he divided between the two men who put them in a money-belt hidden under their shirts and signed for them.

'I want those back,' said Larssen sternly. 'Otherwise the boss thinks I pinch them.'

The major, Tiller decided, had the measure of Larssen all right.

Half an hour later Tiller and Barnesworth began stowing the limpet mines in the floating cockle and added a half-filled can of water and two twenty-four-hour ration packs. The cockle was now floating very low in the water: they could only hope that the sea approaching Portolago was smooth.

The cockle was lifted gently out of the water and on to the deck of the ML and its crew were handed steaming cups of hot cocoa. Tiller carefully checked the cockle once more to ensure that the limpets were safely and securely stowed.

Tiller had never been aboard an ML before. It was bigger than any of the MTBs he had seen. It was, one of the crew told him, 112 feet long and was powered by two Hall-Scott Defender engines. It was also well armed for a ship of its size, having one three-pounder and several smaller-calibre dual-purpose guns.

Denvers made straight for the Turkish coast from Simi and then worked his way northwards at a steady ten knots while Tiller, Larssen and Barnesworth slept on the deck by the cockle. They reached Yalikavak just as the first glimmer of dawn was appearing behind the mainland mountains.

Tiller could see why it had been chosen as a convenient rendezvous for the Levant Schooner Flotilla and other raiding forces, for the steep cliffs overhanging the bay gave any ships anchored there excellent cover, especially from the air. He thought at first it was empty of any vessels but as the light increased he could see first one camouflaged shape and then a second. One was a caique which belonged to the Flotilla. It had been delivering supplies during the night to one of the isolated groups of men who had escaped from Leros and were now scattered across the Dodecanese. The other was an RAF rescue launch which, because of its speed, was being used as a shuttle for sending in emergency supplies to Samos from Castelrosso and evacuating critically wounded personnel from the beleaguered island.

Denvers moored between them and the ML's camouflage netting was erected. The skipper of the rescue launch, an RAF flight-lieutenant, came aboard and was met with a barrage of questions about the situation on Samos.

'The Luftwaffe's really softening the place up,' he said. 'After the bloody nose you gave the Germans on Simi, and the mauling they received on Leros, they're not going to invade Samos before they're ready. But the Stukas are pounding the place to bits and morale isn't too good. Most of the Eyetie garrison has fled into the hills to escape the bombing and there are not enough of our blokes to stop the Krauts when they do decide to land. They keep asking me when the navy's coming to pick them up. I tell them they're coming and that the navy's never let the army down yet. Remember Dunkirk, I said, and Crete. But I don't know.'

Tiller could hear the doubt in the young flight-lieutenant's voice and could see that beneath his tan his face was haggard and his eyes were bleary from lack of sleep. 'To be frank, I think the navy's chickened out. They've lost too many ships on this caper already,' the officer said with finality.

'Don't you worry, sir, the navy hasn't chickened

out,' Tiller heard himself say. 'It will find a way. It always does.'

The young man's eyes focused wearily on Tiller and a glimmer of a smile lit his face when he saw the 'Royal Marine' flash on Tiller's shoulders. 'Ah, one of His Majesty's Jollies. My brother's one of you lot. I might have known there'd be a bootneck among you pirates. But why the winged device?' He pointed to Tiller's beret. 'Where's the globe and laurel?'

'Seconded,' said Tiller.

'I made him take it off,' said Larssen. 'No blanco and brass in this unit. He's one of us now.'

The flight-lieutenant turned to Larssen and said: 'I don't know what the hell you're up to, Captain, or even who you are, and it's none of my business. But if you've got a bootneck to look after you, you'll be OK. Good luck.'

'I was surprised to hear you sticking up for the senior service, Tiger,' Larssen said mockingly after the rescue launch had creamed out of the bay. 'I didn't think you had much time for it. What was that gag you once told me about naval officers and umbrellas.'

'Yeah, well,' Tiller said awkwardly. 'I suppose, skipper, I have to stand up for the navy when I'm among you lot.' But his surge of loyalty had surprised himself as much as it had Larssen.

'And what did he call you – a Jolly? What is that, for Christ's sake?'

'"'E was scrapin' the paint from off of 'er plates an' I sez to 'im, "oo are you?"'' Tiller quoted instantly. '"Sez 'e, 'I'm a Jolly – 'er Majesty's Jolly – soldier an' sailor too!'"'

'Kipling,' said Denvers at once.

Larssen shook his head in irritation. 'You'll never quite be one of us, will you, Tiger, whatever cap badge you wear?'

Tiller grinned and said prophetically: 'No, skipper, I suppose not. But one day perhaps you lot will be with us.'

The November sun rose over the mountains and at midday its heat began to pierce the ML's camouflage netting. Under it the SBS team checked their weapons and equipment methodically before settling down for a nap and an evening meal.

As the sun was setting a German Arado seaplane passed overhead, searching up and down the coastline for any sign of life. There was a rush for the ML's dual-purpose guns, but the sound of the Arado's engines soon faded into the distance.

At dusk the caique weighed anchor and left the bay, the crew shouting good luck to those aboard the ML. It was a fine night, but the breeze that sprang up and ruffled the waters of the bay had the chill of winter in it.

A silence settled over the ML as they waited to receive the final signal from Beirut. In the tiny wireless cabin the wireless operator – known aboard, as wireless operators were known on every ship, as 'Sparks' – crouched over the radio, which hummed and crackled. Then, three hours after darkness had fallen, the message came through in Morse from Beirut: 'Execute Sunbeam.'

Denvers ordered the ML to weigh anchor and the engines, now in their silent mode, came to life. The netting was wound up and the ML crept out from the shelter of the cliffs.

'Steer two-seven-o,' Denvers instructed the helmsman. On deck Tiller and Barnesworth began blackening each other's face.

12

The ML's silent engines propelled the ship through the water with an almost eerie quietness – very different from the dull roar of the MAS boat.

'A penny for your thoughts, Tiger,' Barnesworth whispered after a while. He was lying next to Tiller on his back, staring up at the night sky. 'Or should I say a drachma.'

'I was just thinking of that crazy Eyetie,' Tiller said. 'What did he think he was up to?'

'Balbao? I don't know. Perhaps he wanted to show how brave the Eyeties could be. Perhaps he hated the Krauts so much he'd take any opportunity to knock a few of them off. Perhaps he thought he'd get away with it. Perhaps he knew that the MAS boat was finished without any fuel and felt that he was finished without the MAS boat. Perhaps it was a bit of each. Why do people act as they do in war? Don't ask me. I just do what I'm told and keep my head down.'

It was a sensible philosophy, Tiller decided, and wished that it was one he was able to follow, but somehow he always seemed to leap in feet first.

Normally, the hours before an operation held no worries for him. He just relaxed, and though the adrenalin would start to pump through him he never got wound up as many people did. But this time he felt distinctly edgy.

'If you ask me,' said Barnesworth, 'all these Mediterranean folk are a bit melodramatic. Know what I mean? That girl, for instance . . .'

'Angelika?'

'Yeah, that's the one. I mean one minute she was all over us, couldn't do enough to help, and the next she's scarpered. Could have left us in a right hole. I thought she took rather a shine to you, Tiger, but that didn't stop her buggering off, did it?'

'She was probably acting on orders.'

'Orders? Whose orders?'

Tiller ducked the question by saying: 'The skipper and I reckon she belongs to one of the Andarte bands.' He wondered if he would ever have a chance to find out.

Barnesworth snorted. 'Fat lot of good they've been. Spend their whole time fighting each other from what I hear. We never found out if there are any on Simi anyway, did we?'

'We didn't hear any more of those Krauts that landed,' Tiller reminded him. 'They may have mopped them up.'

'Perhaps. Perhaps not. I wouldn't have liked to have been a Kraut in those hills with all the locals up there sheltering from the Stukas. The Greeks have a terrible contempt for the Eyeties, but they loathe and detest the Germans. I reckon it was them who finished the Krauts off. Assuming,' he added darkly, 'they have been finished off.'

Denvers's number one, a chubby-faced RNVR sub-lieutenant, came along the deck. 'You two ready? We're nearly there.'

They could see now the most southerly point of Leros to starboard and the larger, higher, land mass of Kalimnos to port. It was time to prime the limpet mines. The sub-lieutenant watched them with interest as they opened the box of pencil fuses and selected the ones coloured for the five-hour time delay.

'How exactly do those fuses work?' he asked.

'When the ampoule of acetone is broken it eats away at a celluloid washer which retains the firing pin,' Tiller explained. 'The thicker the washer the longer the time delay. Quite simple really.'

'But why two fuses?' he asked.

Tiller explained that the sympathetic fuse would detonate a limpet if another limpet attached to the same target went off prematurely. 'The time pencil fuses aren't always one hundred per cent accurate,' he said. 'It depends on the temperature.'

The wireless operator came out of his cramped little cabin and said to them: 'Beirut has just radioed that Leros is partially garrisoned by Brandenburgers. So if any naval guard challenges you just shout out "Brandenburger, Patrola," and they'll probably think you're one of that lot.'

'Thanks, Sparks,' said Tiller. 'We'll keep that in mind. Is there anything else they know about the place?'

'Just that it's swarming with Jerries,' the operator said cheerfully. 'Good luck.'

Denvers scanned the coastline of Leros with his night-glasses. The minutes ticked by, and then he said quietly into the voice pipe: 'Stop engines.'

The hull of the ML stopped vibrating. It lifted and dipped in the slight swell.

'Kill both engines.'

The silence enveloped them. They listened for any sound but could hear nothing except the creak of the ML as it rose and fell on the swell.

'That's it, boys. We're here.'

Helped by the ML's crew, Tiller and Barnesworth silently lowered the cockle into the water, making sure its fragile frame was not knocked against the ML's hull. Denvers watched them from the bridge. When the cockle was afloat he looked at his watch and then stepped on to the deck and said to Tiller quietly: 'You can't see it but we're four miles off the north headland of the harbour entrance. It's due east from here and is very distinctive. You should be able to pick it without difficulty.'

'Any current?' Tiller asked.

Denvers shook his head. 'Not for the next hour or so. Then it will set north-south along the coastline, but it will be less than a knot. Nothing to worry about.'

'Wind?'

'Due south, what there is of it. The forecast is for no more than six to eight knots. Perhaps you should allow a degree or so for it if it pipes up any more than that, but if you're more than two hours on the water the current will offset it.'

'I plan to be over the boom in two hours,' said Tiller. 'And the course for Kalimnos from Portolago?'

'That's trickier.'

'The compass will be working then.'

Tiller turned his back on the shore and shone his dimmed torch on to his chart case. It contained a large-scale chart of the area on which Denvers pointed out his course to him.

'When you come out of the bay steer one-three-five until you pass this headland here. It's not much more than a mile and a half once you've crossed the boom. After you've passed the headland alter course to one-one-zero. That will take you across the straits and bring you to the eastern side of the northern extremity of Kalimnos. That's about two miles.'

On the transparent cover of the chart case Tiller had marked in blue pencil the scale in sea miles and a crude compass rose with magnetic north. With a notched pencil he now measured off one and a half miles from the scale on the chart, kept his thumbnail on the notch, put the pencil against 135 degrees on the compass rose, and moved the pencil down like a parallel ruler until its tip rested against the southern headland of the harbour entrance. He then transferred his thumbnail to the Perspex cover of the chart case, which had been roughened with emery paper so that it would take the pencil's marks, and put a cross where his thumbnail was. Then he did the same again, making a new course of 110 degrees from the cross to the northern headland of Kalimnos.

Denvers, who was looking over his shoulder, nodded. 'That's as near as dammit. You'll need to lie up somewhere on the eastern side of the headland for the day. Then you follow the coast until you reach this small promontory. It's a long haul down to there but Vathi's just beyond it. We'll be waiting for you.' He stuck out his hand. 'See you tomorrow night. Good luck.'

Tiller and Barnesworth lowered themselves carefully into the cockpits of the cockle and Tiller tucked the chart case behind his backrest.

Larssen looked down at them and said quietly: 'Don't do anything I wouldn't do, boys. Remember, work before women, work before women.'

They both gave him the thumbs up.

'Right. Let's go,' said Barnesworth in Tiller's ear and they pushed the cockle away from the ML.

At sea level there was more of a sea running than had been noticeable on the ML and the extra limpets made the cockle ride lower in the water. To add to their problems the wind began to rise beyond what Denvers had predicted, and occasionally it whipped the top off a wave and drifted it into their faces. But the extra-high v-shaped wooden breakwater they had fitted to the craft's bow prevented most of the water from running across its plywood deck.

They used double paddles and soon got a rhythm going which kept them warm. Sometimes they had to turn into a wave to prevent it from swamping them. Neither spoke but each could feel the tension in the other.

After half an hour the land began to take shape ahead of them and after another twenty minutes, when they started to come under its lee, the sea was smoother and the cockle rode more easily. Soon afterwards Tiller was relieved to see the north headland of the entrance to the bay gradually beginning to emerge from the dark.

They rested and Tiller quickly checked the chart to make sure the features he could see dimly ahead were the correct ones. The exertion and tension of keeping the heavily loaded cockle going had made them sweat profusely, and both took greedy swigs of water from the can. They'd have to go easy on that, Tiller reminded himself. There was a long way to go yet and dehydration was debilitating.

He began paddling again and could hear Barnesworth's grunt of disgust behind him for not resting longer. But he wanted to get on with it. He headed directly for the northern headland which guarded the entrance to the harbour. The headland's cliffs were steep and high and in the extra darkness that they provided the two men stopped paddling and turned their double paddles into single ones.

They kept close to the land, which now sloped down to the bay, but not too close in case there were shore patrols. Once they thought they heard boots crunching on gravel and they brought the cockle to a halt and kept their profiles low. When they did not hear the sound again they moved forward, but very slowly.

Tiller knew they must be getting close to the boom but he could not see it. Suddenly he caught the faint tinkle of a warning bell. He stopped paddling, bent forward to lessen his profile, and listened intently. The cockle drifted and again he heard the bell. Was it some kind of alarm system the Germans had rigged up?

His mouth felt dry. He licked his lips and felt the salt on them. Tinkle, tinkle. What the hell was it?

Then he felt Barnesworth prod his back. 'It's only bleeding goats,' he whispered.

The boom, when they reached it, was no obstacle for the cockle, for the technique Tiller had learnt in the Solent worked perfectly. There was no sign of life on the patrol boat, which was anchored by the narrow entrance.

Their first target was the ammunition ship, which

was anchored under the cliffs about halfway along the northern shore. The lack of any tide and the direction of the wind had made her swing on her anchor so that she lay broadside on to the cockle, with her bows pointing into the harbour.

She had a straight single funnel, situated behind the central bridge superstructure, and a prominent poop and forecastle. She looked an ordinary tramp steamer which had seen better days, but was bigger than Tiller had anticipated. Each limpet contained two pounds of explosive which could blow a hole in a ship's side six feet in diameter. This one would definitely need three limpets to make sure she sank. If the ammunition was still aboard, and it was detonated by the limpets, she would certainly sink. In fact, there wouldn't be much left of her.

He turned to port so that the cockle moved right under the cliffs. There was no beach at this point so that they did not have to worry about shore patrols. Approaching the *Anita* from the stern instead of the bow was not the right technique, but it did mean they could carry straight on across the harbour once the limpets had been put in place.

They rested again when they were opposite their target. Tiller turned his head and whispered: 'One by the propellers, then one by the engine space, and the third by the bows. Port side or starboard?'

'It would help if we could see the fucking guard,' Barnesworth grumbled in his ear. 'There must be one.'

Tiller glanced at his watch. 'We can't hang about.'

Barnesworth tapped him on the shoulder. 'There he is.'

They were some 200 yards from the ship but they

both could now see the glow of the guard's cigarette as he stood on the afterdeck looking at the shore.

'Cor, lucky bugger. I could do with a draw,' Barnesworth whispered.

Tiller felt within him the first signs of irritability with his partner and strived to suppress it. Like hallucinations it was something canoeists often encountered and which had to be dealt with rationally. Still, Barnesworth's flippant asides annoyed him and he turned and put his forefinger to his lips. He heard his swimmer grunt, but whether it was with annoyance or acceptance, he could not tell.

The guard flicked his cigarette end into the water, but instead of strolling forward he moved right into the stern of the ship and peered down.

The two SBS men sagged forward on to the plywood deck of their cockle. Tiller grasped the cockle's wooden breakwater in front of him and pressed his head down until his nose was touching the compass.

He felt himself stifling his breathing, but forced himself to suck in deep gulps of air.

Nothing happened and after what seemed an age Tiller cautiously, very gradually, raised his head. The sentry was still there. He seemed to be looking straight at the cockle. He *was* looking straight at the cockle. Tiller did not dare move.

A match flared and Tiller could see the outline of the guard's face and the rifle slung across his back as he lit another cigarette. He flicked the match into the water, and then turned and walked away down the starboard side. Relief surged through Tiller and made him gasp for air.

'Port side,' Billy hissed in his ear.

Both men opened their cockpit covers, and Barnesworth pulled from under the stern a pair of limpet mines attached to their keeper plate, and the magnetic hold-fast. He passed the mines forward to Tiller and undid the line which was wound round the hold-fast.

Tiller put the pair of mines between his feet and pulled out from under the bow the hollow steel rods that made up the placing rod. He carefully connected these, and laid the completed rod, now six feet long, across the cockle's deck. Then he dipped his paddle cautiously into the water and moved the cockle forwards.

Barnesworth prodded Tiller and indicated the ship's Plimsoll line, which was almost level with the water.

'She's still fully loaded,' he breathed into Tiller's ear. Tiller nodded and again indicated that Barnesworth should shut up.

Close to, the ship appeared huge, its steel topsides towering above them. They inched the cockle slowly under the ship's counter, on which was written in large white letters 'Anita Genoa', until they reached a point where the propeller shafts extruded from the hull.

The hull here was dented and rusty. A line of encrusted barnacles and old weed above the faint white band of the Plimsoll line showed that the ship must have been frequently loaded beyond its safety limits. Tiller pointed the weed and barnacles out to Barnesworth, for flaking rust or anything non-ferrous on the steel hull could affect the magnets on the hold-fast as well as on the limpets.

Barnesworth tapped Tiller twice on the shoulder to

indicate that he understood. Tiller lifted the hold-fast and carefully attached it to the ship's side at shoulder level and hung on to the line attached to it.

The hold-fast made what seemed to them a horrendously loud clunk as the magnets connected with the steel, and both men held their breath. When nothing happened Barnesworth tightened the line and drew the cockle closer to the ship's side.

With the hold-fast steadying the cockle, Tiller got on with the delicate task of attaching the limpet mine. He had done it many times before on exercises but he always found it difficult to detach a mine from its retaining plate, so powerful were its magnets and so restricted was the space in which he had to work.

At the third attempt he managed it, but he could feel beads of sweat running down his face. He rested a moment before bringing the mine on to the deck in front of him. He hooked it on to the end of the placing rod, screwed down on the butterfly nut to break the fuse's ampoule of acid, and slowly and very carefully lowered the mine into the water. He kept it well away from the ship's side until his hand holding the rod was just under the surface. Then he moved the mine very slowly towards the ship's side.

When the magnets were close to the steel they battened on to the ship's side with a sudden jerk and another clunk. Again they waited, but when they heard nothing Tiller pushed the rod downwards to disconnect it from the mine and brought the rod back to the surface and stowed it alongside him.

Once Tiller had finished, Barnesworth pulled off the hold-fast and moved the cockle gently forward. When they reached the middle of the ship, where the engine room lay under the central superstructure, they repeated the operation. Then they allowed the cockle to drift forward again until they were near the bow. For a moment they clung to the ship's side while they tried to locate the guard. But all they could hear was the slap of water against the vessel and a wireless somewhere playing music.

Tiller placed the third limpet and then allowed the cockle to drift out beyond the ship's bows. Its stem was straighter than on a modern ship but there was enough overhang to give them some protection from anyone looking casually down from the deck above.

They drifted slowly past the rusty anchor chain, its links dripping with water.

They had assumed the prone position, but felt horribly vulnerable. The minutes ticked by. They were aware that they were gradually drifting away from the ship and when no challenge rang out across the water they cautiously began to paddle out into the middle of the harbour.

It would have been easier to continue up the northern shore to where the F-lighter and the supply ship lay, but Larssen had decided – and Tiller and Barnesworth had agreed with him – that the longer they were in the harbour the greater chance there was of their being discovered, and that the two destroyers therefore had to be dealt with as quickly as possible.

Near the middle of the harbour, which at this point was nearly a mile wide, a patrol boat with a searchlight passed well ahead of them and they stopped and crouched low in the cockle. But the beam did not sweep near them and they waited until the sound of the patrol boat's engine had faded.

It was very dark and although the distance across the harbour was hardly more than half a mile Tiller found it difficult to keep his bearings. He was still searching the horizon ahead when Barnesworth tapped him on the shoulder and whispered: 'There, slightly to starboard.'

Tiller strained his eyes and was just able to make out a long, dark shape. As they got nearer they could see it had two funnels. The forward one was much higher than the aft one.

'That's the *San Martino*,' Barnesworth hissed into his ear. 'The smaller of the two. We'd better sheer off a bit until we can find the *Turbine*.'

They turned the cockle to port and then south again and closed with the shore. But the *Turbine* was not there. They turned west and saw the sharp silhouette of the *San Martino* ahead of them. They rested and had another swig of water, and considered what to do.

The reconnaissance photograph had plainly shown the two destroyers anchored almost side by side at the northern end of the naval base.

'They must have moved her,' Barnesworth whispered.

'That's pretty fucking obvious,' Tiller murmured furiously to himself.

'What shall we do?'

Now Tiller could not restrain the irritation in his whispered reply. 'Deal with this one and then look for the other, of course.'

What did Billy think they should do: paddle home to mummy and complain? He heard Barnesworth suck his teeth and knew his partner was also keeping his temper in check with difficulty.

He indicated that he wanted two pairs of limpet mines and Barnesworth passed them forward. Tiller tugged three of them from their retaining plates and hooked one on to his placing rod.

'Bows, amidships, and on the stern,' Barnesworth whispered. 'Port side to.'

Tiller nodded his agreement and they paddled slowly forward, this time approaching from the correct direction by keeping the destroyer bows on to the cockle. There was no sign of a sentry, though they knew there must be one, if not two. They would be German sailors, too, who were trained to be observant, while the man on the *Anita* had probably been just a civilian member of the crew.

For a moment they hung on to the destroyer's anchor chain, and now they could hear the guttural sounds of a conversation somewhere above them. There was a hoarse laugh which ended in a cough, a burst of music, faint but distinct, and a shaft of light as a bulwark door on the destroyer was opened and then closed with a clang. Somewhere a dog barked.

Tiller froze. If there was a dog on board, that could mean trouble. Dogs had an uncanny way of detecting the unusual which went way beyond their sense of smell and hearing.

He held his hand vertically just above his shoulder to indicate he wanted to wait and heard Barnesworth suck his teeth again. Impatient bastard, Tiller thought.

Again the dog barked. Where was it? Sounds at night and over water were often distorted, and always deceptive.

Tiller felt the pressure of Barnesworth's hand on his shoulder and Barnesworth whispered: 'It's on shore. Forget it.'

Again, Tiller indicated with his hand that he did not want to move until he was sure.

'For fuck's sake,' Barnesworth snarled in his ear. Tiller grasped the anchor chain in case Barnesworth decided to let go of it, and listened intently.

The conversation above them was more animated now, and Tiller thought he heard the chink of glass. At least Barnesworth had chosen the correct side to place the mines, for the conversation, Tiller could tell now, was definitely coming from the starboard side somewhere.

But the dog did not bark again and after a minute of listening to Barnesworth sucking his teeth Tiller reluctantly let go the anchor chain and propelled the cockle towards the sharp bow of the destroyer.

Its sides were clean compared to that of the ammunition ship and looked as if they had been recently repainted. How like the Kraut, Tiller thought with grudging admiration, to make even an out-of-date Eyetie warship spick and span.

He felt the cold, wet steel against his hand as he steadied the cockle for Barnesworth to apply the hold-fast, which, to their relief, made less noise than it had when applied to the ammunition ship. The first and second limpets were secured without a problem, but for some reason the third refused to adhere to the destroyer's stern near the rudder. Tiller swore under his breath, but wherever he moved the placing rod the mine's magnets refused to take.

He could feel Barnesworth's mounting impatience behind him and indicated that they should try the other side. They were moving the cockle cautiously round the stern when a powerful torch was turned on above them. They froze in the lowest position, keeping close to the ship's stern. The torch played on the water, went off, came on again, and then settled directly on them.

Tiller remembered the wireless operator's tip and shouted up, '*Patrola, Brandenburger*', and dug his paddle into the water. There was an indistinct shout from the sentry holding the torch and looking back Tiller could see he was struggling to unsling his rifle from his back. His companion, his rifle already off his shoulder, was running to join him.

With half a dozen vigorous strokes Tiller knew they could put the cockle beyond the range of the torch, and the darkness would almost immediately swallow them up. But if the guards started firing the operation would have to be aborted. It was equally certain that the destroyer's hull would be scraped with a wire hawser as a precaution and all their efforts would have been in vain.

'I'm going to face the fuckers,' he said to Barnesworth and swung the cockle around and stopped.

'*Patrola, Brandenburger*,' he called out again, and waved.

The first sentry was trying to juggle the heavy torch with his rifle and Tiller could see that he now had the barrel on the guard rail aiming straight at them, but he seemed unable to bring the torch's beam on to the cockle.

When Tiller called out, the second sentry pushed the first sentry's rifle sideways along the rail. The first sentry dropped the torch on the deck and while he was bending to pick it up the second sentry called out something in German to them.

Tiller waved again and the second sentry waved back. Tiller turned the cockle away and paddled swiftly into the darkness before the first sentry could focus the beam on them again.

'Jesus H. Christ,' Barnesworth said in his ear when they stopped to rest. 'You've got a nerve. I thought he was going to put one between your eyes.'

'So did I,' whispered Tiller. He could feel he was wet with sweat. He took a gulp of water from the can and then passed it to Barnesworth.

They were now rather too close to the naval base for comfort. They could not see anyone moving among the buildings but they sheered off before paddling parallel with the shore once more. The dog, a lot nearer now, started barking again.

'I told you it was on the shore,' Barnesworth hissed in Tiller's ear. Exuberant with relief, Tiller just turned his head and whispered: 'You've just got big lugs, Billy', and felt the guardsman punch him good-naturedly on the shoulder.

They passed several lighters moored together, and a small coastal patrol vessel of some kind which lay at the end of a long wooden pier. Ahead they could see several motor launches and tugs moored around a large floating jetty. They were considerably bigger than the MAS boat and made tempting targets, but Tiller ignored them. He had a bigger fish to fry – if they could find it.

They were just beginning to despair of ever doing so when a much bigger bulk began to loom out of the darkness ahead of them on their port side.

'That's her,' Barnesworth whispered excitedly.

Even in the dark Tiller could see from the outline of the destroyer that it was the one the MAS boat had tried to ram. They edged closer and made out the lettering 'TA14' on her bow. She was moored alongside the naval base. A large crane overhung her central superstructure and Tiller wondered if the MAS boat had, after all, inflicted some damage on her.

Then, to his consternation, he saw that the destroyer was surrounded on the seaward side by a number of much smaller ships of various sizes, and one was moored right alongside her. Tiller recognized at least two of them as being *Motosiluranti*, or MS boats, the Italian equivalent of the ML. They were larger and more heavily armed than a MAS boat and must have been, Tiller supposed, taken over by the German Navy.

But there was also a large caique, a MAS boat, and one or two others he could not identify. Judging from the activity aboard these ships, it was evident that they had only recently arrived in Portolago or, more likely, were just about to depart.

The SBS men rested and let the cockle drift while they summed up the situation. It did not take long.

'We'll never get through that lot without being spotted,' Barnesworth murmured in Tiller's ear. 'Not in a month of Sundays.'

Tiller knew he was right, for even when the crews went below or ashore a sentry would be left on deck. They might slide past one or two, but even if they managed to squeeze their way past them all they would be totally exposed when they reached the destroyer's side. They had to devise another method, and quickly.

'I'm going to circle round them and come up as near as I can astern of the destroyer,' Tiller whispered. 'Then you're going to have to swim the rest of the way with a couple of limpets and put them on her stern. At least we might be able to damage her steering gear.'

The possibility of using this method of attack had been foreseen, and Barnesworth wore a swimmer's suit and had with him a long length of line. There was nothing moored directly astern of the destroyer, but to approach it the cockle had to keep close to the shore, so that it would be moving right under the noses of any patrol.

Tiller saw that the quay of the naval base jutted out slightly into the water so that they were able to manoeuvre the cockle under it and then pull themselves towards the destroyer by pushing on the wooden beams that supported the quay. It would have been possible to get right up to the destroyer in this manner except that they soon gathered there were several men on sentry duty by the destroyer's stern. They stamped their feet and swore in German and one sent a jet of urine almost into the cockle.

Tiller backed off slightly until he felt a tap on his shoulder and he knew Barnesworth was ready. He steadied the craft while his partner slid from his cockpit and into the water. Then he handed him two limpets on their retaining plate and Barnesworth clipped them to the line. He then handed one end of the line to Tiller and slid away silently into the bay.

The limpets and the line sank beneath the surface but most of their weight was supported by Tiller. Above him he could hear the scuff of the sentries' boots on the quay and the murmur of their conversation, but the destroyer was shrouded in darkness and silence.

After twenty minutes there was a tug on the line

and Tiller began slowly and carefully hauling it in. Moments later Barnesworth's head surfaced by the cockle. He gave the thumbs up and indicated that Tiller should back off down the quay while he hung on to the cockle's bow.

Once they were far enough away from the sentries, Tiller turned the cockle and Barnesworth levered himself back into it.

'A cinch,' he whispered triumphantly. 'I put one close to its depth-charge rack. It should make an almighty bang.'

'Good man,' Tiller replied. 'Let's get the hell out of here.' He glanced at his watch. They had been in the harbour exactly two hours. It seemed like two weeks.

'What about the supply ship and the F-lighter?' Barnesworth asked.

'What about them? They only said 'if possible'. If we hang around any longer the sentry on that first destroyer might find out the Brandenburgers don't have a harbour patrol.'

Barnesworth didn't argue. They dumped the remaining mines and the compass compensator overboard and once across the boom and out of the bay Tiller set a course of one-three-five on the compass grid.

13

Away from the shelter of the bay the sea and the wind increased, and the cockle encountered short, steep waves which threatened to swamp it. Water cascaded over the deck and began finding its way into the craft. It swilled about their feet, and they took it in turns to try and bail it out.

To add to the miserable conditions it started to drizzle and this cut visibility to such an extent that Tiller was concerned about making the passage across the straits between the two islands. The compass seemed to be behaving itself, but compasses, he knew, were never wholly reliable. After half an hour he told Barnesworth to keep the cockle heading into the waves while he consulted the chart with his shaded torch. He stared into the darkness to port and decided, from the vague shape of the land, that he must be opposite the headland where Denvers had told him to alter course. He moved the compass grid to one-one-zero.

'It could be bumpy across the strait,' he shouted over his shoulder. He heard Barnesworth grunt an acknowledgement.

Turning the cockle even slightly side on to the wind and waves made it dip and swing alarmingly. After a quarter of an hour on the new compass bearing the veil of rain lifted momentarily. Kalimnos should now be directly ahead of them but he could not see it, could see nothing but a black void.

Tiller dug in his blades with increased fury, but he was now feeling the extreme fatigue, a reaction that always followed the elation of a mission safely accomplished. And fatigue, he knew, brought with it hallucinations, cramped lower limbs, and intense, irrational anger with the other member of the team.

'We'll rest,' he shouted back to Barnesworth.

'We'd better keep going,' Barnesworth said. 'It'll be light soon.'

'I said we'll rest,' Tiller snapped.

'Eh, take it easy, Tiger.' Tiller felt the friendly pressure of his companion's hand on his shoulder.

He glanced at his watch. He knew Billy was right and that irritated him even more. He also knew that they also had to find a safe hiding-place before the limpets exploded. Once they went off, the whole area – land, sea and air – would be saturated with search parties and if the cockle was caught in daylight in the open sea Tiller knew they would be dead meat.

After five minutes they started again. Pain began to course through Tiller's arms as he dug in his paddles. His legs and thighs started to lose any feeling, and then he felt the first tingling agony of cramp.

The rain started again, heavier than ever, but the sea as they came under the lee of the northern headland of Kalimnos became smoother and the tops of the waves, though breaking occasionally with an alarming hiss, were no longer being whipped off by the wind. But the rain was being driven straight into their faces and Tiller could see nothing but blackness ahead.

It was like the nightmare, paddling into nothingness, going nowhere.

Each stroke was agony now. He kept being aware that his eyes were shut and he forced himself to keep them open by looking at the compass. But after a while the luminous numbers began to spin before his eyes like a roulette wheel. It took a superhuman effort of concentration for him to confirm that they were still on the correct course and not paddling round in circles.

Tiller's mind wandered. He tried to quote *Barrack-Room Ballads* to himself. But its words and rhythm were a jumble and would not come out straight.

''E isn't one o' the reg'lar Line, nor 'e isn't a kind of giddy Harumfrodite – soldier an' sailor, too . . .'

He gave up and his mind wandered back to Barnesworth and why he insisted on making comments in the middle of the operation, but now, when it was safe to shout at the top of their voices, the cat seemed to have got his tongue.

Why didn't he go to the dentist?

Was that Sydney Harbour bridge ahead? Now that was a run ashore he wouldn't forget. What was her name?

He started humming the regimental march, repeating the words a line at a time with each stroke of the paddle:

'A Life on the Ocean Wave,
A home on the rolling deep,
Where the scatter'd waters rave
And the winds their revels keep.'

But he couldn't remember any more so he kept

repeating the first four lines, hoping the next four would come into his mind. But they didn't come and the compass spun before his eyes. What was Billy saying, why did he keep interrupting?

Barnesworth hit Tiller in his back with his fist and screamed: 'For fuck's sake, Tiger. That's land ahead, you silly sod. What do you want to do, end up halfway up a cliff?'

Tiller jerked awake and struggled to refocus his mind and eyes.

Land it was, and very near, so near he could see the waves breaking at the bottom of a cliff face. But it was indistinct, too, blurred by the rain and his own utter weariness. He stopped paddling and watched the cliff get nearer. Like the nightmare there was nothing he could do.

'Back off! Move left!' Barnesworth bawled in his ear. 'Paddle, you bastard, paddle!'

Sluggishly Tiller's mind and muscles responded. He back-paddled and slowly the craft slewed away from the cliff face. A wave slopped across them and the rain hammered down. They must be in some kind of local current, Tiller thought, for something was drawing the cockle towards the shore like a magnet. Ahead he thought he saw the first glimmer of dawn in the sky and then he heard the distant boom of an explosion.

'The limpets,' he shouted exultantly. 'Did you hear the bang?'

'It's the fucking waves hitting the fucking cliffs.' Barnesworth's fury penetrated Tiller's fuddled mind. 'Keep paddling, you silly sod, or we'll hit them, too.'

Resentment welled up in Tiller that he had made

a mistake. He thought vaguely that Barnesworth was having him on, but he had no strength to start an argument. His back ached, and the cramp in his water-soaked legs was gnawing into him. With his last remaining strength he dug his paddles into the water and tried to maintain some kind of rhythm for Barnesworth to follow. His body, accustomed to years of rigorous discipline, responded automatically to what Barnesworth was now yelling in his ear. 'In, out, in, out. Count your strokes, Tiger. Keep it steady. In, out, in, out. We're nearly out of trouble. Just a dozen more strokes. In, out, in, out.'

But his mind kept wandering so that his body seemed a machine quite apart from it. He half saw, half felt the looming presence of the land above him, and the violence of the water around the cockle, and the spray in his face, and heard Barnesworth bawling: 'In, out, in, out, dig deep, you sod.'

Then quite suddenly the water was calm, the cockle upright.

'There's a beach,' Barnesworth shouted. 'We'll go for it. Turn right, Tiger. Right.' The cockle swung, tipped, went too far to the right, then was straightened by Barnesworth. Seconds later they were in shallow water and Barnesworth half fell, half scrambled out of his cockpit. He grabbed the cockle's stern and ran it gently ashore. Tiller dropped his paddle and it floated in the water secured to his wrist by a short piece of line.

Tiller tried to pull himself out of the cockpit but the pain in his legs was excruciating and had seemingly locked them tight.

'Cramp,' he said. 'Sorry. Fucking cramp.'

Barnesworth hauled the cockle's bow on to the

sand and then swung it broadside on to the beach. Then he tipped it sideways and dragged Tiller out of his cockpit. He took a bottle of salt tablets from a pocket in the craft and handed them to Tiller with the can of water. Tiller swilled them down and struggled to his feet. He banged the calves of his legs with his hands and jigged up and down.

'Come on,' said Barnesworth. 'It'll be light soon. We've got to get under cover.'

They drained the cockle of water, picked it up and carried it up the beach. On their right was the rocky cliff top which they had just managed to avoid, but ahead and to their left the land was much lower and flatter. The beach ended in a field of olive trees. They laid the cockle down and began searching for a hiding-place.

There was no shelter around the beach, but when they moved inland they found part of a stone wall which was overhung by an olive tree. They carried the cockle there, covered it with camouflage netting and then went back to the beach to obliterate their footmarks with branches from one of the trees.

It was beginning to get light now. It was a grey, windy morning, but the rain had stopped though the clouds above them were leaden with it. They unearthed the small primus, stewed some tea in the tin mugs they used for bailing, and broke open one of the two ration packs. They devoured the biscuits and then heated a tin of stew in one of the mugs. The stew didn't seem to taste of anything but it was hot and stopped their gnawing hunger. They decided to keep the bar of chocolate until later.

'Fucking cramp,' said Barnesworth sympathetically as Tiller massaged his legs. 'It's the one thing that scares me when I'm swimming. You get stomach cramp at the wrong moment, and you sink like a stone. It's happened to me once, and I tell you, mate, I wouldn't want it to happen again.'

'Dehydration, I should think,' Tiller said. He looked at his watch. 'Those limpets should be going off soon.'

'The wind's in the wrong direction,' said Barnesworth doubtfully. 'We might not hear them.'

'We'll hear them,' Tiller promised. 'Especially if that ammunition ship goes up.'

When they came the explosions were like distant thunder, the last one much louder and longer than the other two.

'She went up all right,' said Tiller.

The two men shook hands.

'Got the sods,' Tiller said. 'Now let's get some shut-eye. I'll take the first watch.'

Barnesworth grinned at him. 'You must be joking. You wouldn't last ninety seconds. You were kipping in the cockle. The Krauts aren't going to find us here. No way. Let's get our heads down while we can.'

Tiller raised himself above the wall and scanned the interior of the island. It was bare and brown and without life of any kind. Kalimnos, they had been told, did not have a garrison and the population had deserted it long ago. Only the local fishermen and the occasional German sea patrol visited it now.

'Yeah, you're right.'

They took out their pistols, took them apart, and dried and oiled them. Then they removed the backrests from the cockle to use as pillows, lay down under the lee of the wall, and pulled part of the camouflage netting over themselves.

The next thing Tiller knew was Barnesworth shaking him vigorously.

'There's a hell of a rumpus going on over there,' he said pointing eastwards across the island. Tiller levered himself up and peered over the wall. There was nothing to see but he could hear the crump of bombs exploding and the steady thump, thump, thump of a heavy automatic weapon. They both knew what was in each other's minds.

'The ML?' Barnesworth queried eventually. Tiller shook his head with a confidence he did not feel. 'More likely they found an MTB sneaking along the Turkish coast.'

The firing and bombing went on for about twenty minutes and then suddenly stopped. It was late afternoon now and the sun had come out. They opened the second ration pack and ate everything in it without bothering to heat it, and when dusk came they carried the cockle down to the water, and launched it. The weather looked as if it was going to remain fine. But it was quite cold, and Tiller was looking forward to a proper meal aboard the ML.

They rounded the north-east tip of Kalimnos without trouble and by midnight were beyond the promontory where Vathi lay. They paddled close to the land but still almost missed the entrance to the bay, so narrow was the entrance. They turned in, narrowly missed two large rocks, and passed into the inlet. Denvers had been right. Without local knowledge it was a dangerous place.

Once inside the water opened up. Along the southern edge was a beach but the rocky shore came right down to the water on the northern side. There, lurking somewhere in the shadows, they hoped the ML would be waiting for them and eventually, around a bend in the bay, they came upon her right under a shallow, overhanging cliff.

'Shit,' said Tiller quietly. The ML had received a direct hit which had broken her in two and she lay in two distinct pieces in the shallows under the cliff.

A wreath of smoke still curled up from the tangled, blackened wreckage that had been her bridge and the barrel of the three-pounder was skewed at an improbable angle as if some giant hand had seized and bent it. The only visible part of the stern section was a half-submerged mangle of twisted steel.

They moved slowly forward through the flotsam and jetsam of any marine casualty of war: life-jackets, charred bits of wood, gratings, books, mattresses, clothes, the shredded remains of the curtains from the tiny ward-room.

Unthinkingly, Tiller poked with his paddle at a floating life-jacket and the body that he suddenly saw was attached to it rolled on to its back. The scorched, unidentifiable face stared up at him out of the dark water with wide-open, reproachful eyes. Tiller withdrew his paddle and the face, with what seemed deliberate slowness, bobbed a moment before turning over and disappearing beneath the surface. The accusing eyes, even under the water, seemed fixed on his face.

'Shit.'

They paddled up to the remains of the ML. Close to, they could smell the stench of burning and heard the gentle hiss of steam escaping from a fractured pipe.

'Nobody could survive that,' said Barnesworth. 'The bomb must have detonated her fuel and spare ammunition.'

They went alongside cautiously and climbed on to the charred and warped deck. They could only recognize Denvers, who lay on the remains of his bridge, from the two intertwined stripes of gold braid on the shoulder of a strip of shirt still attached to the grotesque bundle that had once been a human being.

Under the bridge the wireless room had been crushed almost flat. One of the crew of the three-pounder lay slumped across the breech of the gun, the other two on the deck near it. There was no need to confirm that they were dead.

Larssen and the other crew members, Tiller supposed, must have been caught below or had been blown into the water as there were no other bodies visible. Only one of the .5-inch machine-guns, with its belt of ammunition folded neatly into a box, had miraculously remained untouched by the ferocious blast that had torn the vessel apart.

Tiller worked its cocking mechanism and squinted down the barrel. 'This could be useful.'

'Too heavy to take on the cockle,' Barnesworth observed. They carried it between them and got the weapon and the ammunition box ashore. Then they returned to their craft and paddled in silence to the end of the bay, where the chart had showed them was a beach and a few scattered houses.

Some yards from it the cockle collided with what later they decided must have been a piece of debris from the ML. Tiller felt the cockle lurch and slow as it skewered itself on the half-sunken wreckage, and water began gushing in.

They paddled free of the obstruction and then leapt out as the bow began to dip beneath the surface, and pulled the cockle to the beach and on to the sand.

Barnesworth began rolling it over but Tiller said: 'Leave it. There's no point in fiddling around in the dark. More important to see if there are any survivors.'

They searched the length of the beach and the deserted houses beyond. The water's edge was littered with fragments from the ML, but they found no survivors, only one body lying face down at the far end of the beach. His fingers had dug into the sand, showing that he must have been alive when he had reached the shore.

'We'd better bury him,' said Barnesworth, but Tiller said: 'We'd better not. You know how thorough the Krauts are. They're bound to send a patrol to try and find the ML's code-books. We mustn't show we've been here.'

'They won't find code-books in that wireless room,' Barnesworth said. 'They won't find anything. There's nothing left of it.'

Instead of burying him, they noted the dead man's name from the tags around his neck. Then they carried the damaged cockle under some nearby trees and fetched the machine-gun.

'They'll come by water if they come,' Barnesworth said.

'When they come,' Tiller corrected him. They set the weapon up, using a tree as a makeshift support, so that it was trained down the creek. Then they spread out the camouflage netting, divided a bar of chocolate between them, and lay down.

Tiller wondered where Larssen had died, and how. He had come to like and admire his skipper with his dreadful accent, his skill and enthusiasm for killing Germans, and his brilliant leadership.

He slept, and the submerged face bobbed up and down. Somehow it had acquired two bullet holes in its forehead.

He opened his eyes. Barnesworth was leaning over him and shaking his shoulder. 'Stop hollering, Tiger, for Christ's sake.'

Tiller blinked. The first rays of the early-morning sun were spearing through the trees.

'Who's Mac, for Christ's sake?' Barnesworth asked.

Tiller stood up and shook the sand from his clothing. 'Mac?'

'Yeah, Mac. You were shouting "Mac".'

Tiller stretched. He felt stiff and sore. Perhaps he was getting too old for this kind of lark, he thought. Perhaps he should get a cushy number somewhere as an instructor when they got back. Or perhaps he might be one of those blokes who drummed up recruits by standing up with all his gongs on his chest and saying, ever so modestly of course, how brave he had been and how worthwhile it all was. Perhaps that dreaded phrase 'strong family ties' was not the life sentence he had always thought it.

'I don't know. I used to work with a bloke called Matt. A pre-war Olympic canoeist, he was. Mad as a hatter.'

'Matt, was it? Sounded like "Mac" to me. What happened to him?'

'He's dead,' said Tiller. 'Bought it on some op. What the fuck are we going to do with this cockle, Billy?'

In the pale morning light they turned over the craft and inspected the damage. The canvas hull had been sliced neatly as if with a knife along half its length. So sharp was the object that they'd hit that it had also sliced clean through several of the cockle's ribs, cracking and splintering them. For good measure it had ripped the buoyancy bags in the bows as well.

'That's a write-off,' Tiller declared.

'There's plenty of material around,' Barnesworth said doubtfully. 'We could try and patch it up.'

'It's a write-off,' Tiller repeated. 'There's no way we can fix that. Besides, we left the fucking repair kit behind, didn't we?'

'If we hadn't been forced to carry so many limpets. They don't care, do they? Don't give a shit.'

'Who?'

'Whoever sent us on this bloody lark. Sink this, sink that, and oh, while you're at it, old boy, sink the fucking other as well.'

Barnesworth's rage visibly swelled his face and he kicked the cockle hard.

'Steady on, Billy,' Tiller said gently. 'We'll get out of this. Somehow.'

The cockle was useless but he still didn't like seeing it kicked. Billy's rage seemed to subside but his eyes remained puffy with exhaustion.

'Yeah, I suppose so,' he said, unconvinced. Suddenly there was a sound behind them. Tiller whipped out his pistol and cocked it. The sound came again, a sort of half-gasp, half-cough. Tiller gestured to Barnesworth to back away down the beach so that he could cover him.

When Barnesworth was in position Tiller moved forward. Despite what the Killer School had taught him, he had always thought a pistol was a useless weapon and now he felt naked and vulnerable and just wished he had his Sten. Something else which had been left behind.

Out of the corner of his eye he suddenly saw a slight movement under a bush ahead of him. He drew a bead on it and waited, but it did not move again. Whatever it was it was not very threatening. An animal perhaps?

He kept his pistol pointing at the object, which looked, as he neared it, like a pile of old rags. Then he could see that it must be a survivor from the ML who had managed to drag himself off the beach and under cover.

He hurried forward, and bent over the blackened figure. It was so disfigured and burnt that it took him some moments to recognize the survivor as the ML's wireless operator. Tiller's eyes travelled down the man's body and he saw that one of his legs had been blown off below the knee. Somehow he had made a tourniquet, but the sand was soaked with blood.

'Billy!' Tiller shouted at the top of his voice. 'Get the water and the first-aid kit. Quick.'

The operator opened his eyes and tried to smile. He opened his mouth to say something but nothing came out except a croak.

'You just keep quiet, mate,' Tiller said. 'You'll be all right now, but we've got to do something about your leg.'

He took off his shirt, ripped off one of its sleeves, cut it into two lengths, and replaced the blood-sodden strip of cloth the operator had used as a tourniquet.

As he worked he remembered with a curse that the first-aid kit had been left behind as well. He found two sticks and twisted the strips of shirt around them so that the tourniquet was tight but not too tight.

Barnesworth arrived with the water and Tiller

cradled the wireless operator's head and moistened his lips and tongue. The man coughed as the water reached his throat but it revived him and he opened his eyes. His lips moved and Tiller strained to hear what he was trying to say.

'You got . . . them?'

Tiller nodded. 'Yes, we got them.'

It only then occurred to him that the Germans must have searched not only for them but for the ship which would pick them up. Kalimnos was an obvious place to rendezvous. It must have been simple to have pinpointed the most likely sites. Suddenly, Tiller felt that he was personally responsible for the disaster that had overwhelmed his detachment commander, the ML and its crew, and the dying man whose head he was cradling.

What a fuck-up it all was.

'We only got away with it because of the tip you gave us. You know: "Patrola, Brandenburger". It worked.'

A spasm crossed the man's lips.

'Are the code-books aboard, mate?' Tiller asked urgently.

The operator's head moved fractionally sideways.

'You managed to ditch them in the weighted bag?'

Just a flutter of an eyelid acknowledged that the man had followed the correct procedure. He was trying to say something again, and Tiller leant forward.

'. . . message through,' the operator whispered.

'You got a message through that you were being attacked?'

The man's eyelids flickered to say that he had.

'Beirut acknowledged?'

The eyelids flickered again.

'And Beirut said they'd pass it on to Simi?'

The man's eyelids flickered for a third and final time before his eyes went blank and his head rolled sideways.

Tiller felt the man's jugular vein, lowered his head gently to the ground, and then closed the staring eyes. He made a note of his name from his tags and stood up.

'So the caique will come and fetch us?' Barnesworth asked.

'If it can find its way in,' said Tiller.

They decided to sink the cockle. They weighted it with stones, then waded out into the creek carrying it above their heads. When the water reached their necks they let the cockle slide beneath the surface. Its drab colouring blended exactly with the bottom.

They waded ashore, covered their tracks expertly, gathered the machine-gun and ammunition box, and the water can, and searched for a hiding-place among the cliffs which would also give them a good view of the creek. If the caique came it would come at night but the Germans could come at any time. The sun was high in the sky before they found the right place: a small cave near the cliff top which was reached by a narrow strip of grass.

'They deserve to find us if they come up here,' Barnesworth said.

They took turns to stay on watch, one hour on, one hour off. It was late afternoon before the Germans arrived. But they did not come by sea, as the SBS men had expected. Instead they came again from the sky, but this time it was their old friend the Blohm and Voss.

It circled the remains of the ML and then landed in the bay. Two soldiers climbed out of the cockpit and on to the aircraft's wings. They inflated a rubber dinghy, and paddled towards the remains of the ML and out of sight of the two SBS men hiding above them. The pilot threw out an anchor and then climbed on to the wing of the Blohm and Voss, and lay down.

Barnesworth sucked his teeth. 'He's fucking confident, isn't he?'

Signs of overconfidence was something Larssen had taught them always to watch for in the enemy as well as in themselves. It was, he said, something that could always be exploited. They looked at each other and both knew that the other was thinking of Larssen and what he would have done in the same circumstances, and then they both said together: 'Sink or swim.'

Tiller chuckled. 'Great minds think alike, Billy.'

They knew exactly what they had to do and agreed on the plan with a few brief words. They kept well clear of the ML and the beach, where the soldiers would be concentrating their search, found a place inland where they could cross the creek, moved into the remains of the village and found the ruins of a house which gave them a clear view of the bay and where they could set up the machine-gun.

They could see the rubber dinghy alongside the remains of the ML, but there was no sign of the soldiers. The pilot had stripped off his shirt. The co-pilot, they could see, had chosen to stay in the cockpit with a book. Tiller wondered idly what he could be reading.

The sun had dipped below the trees behind the SBS men before the soldiers emerged from their search. They shouted something to the pilot and lowered themselves into the rubber dinghy. The pilot sat up, put his shirt back on, and waited on the wing to grab the dinghy's painter when it was thrown to him.

'The co-pilot first,' whispered Tiller. 'With any luck, we'll get their wireless at the same time. Then the rubber dinghy. Then the pilot. And make bloody sure that ammunition belt isn't twisted.'

He flicked up the rear sight of the machine-gun. 'Two hundred?'

'I reckon so. Two-fifty, maybe. Don't fucking miss. Those Krauts look well armed.'

Tiller slid the rear sight up a notch, waited until the rubber dinghy was halfway to the seaplane and put a short burst into the cockpit. The co-pilot slumped sideways so that his head was out of the open door. Then Tiller switched to the rubber dinghy and gave its occupants a sustained burst. Out of the corner of his eye he could see the pilot running along the wing towards the open cockpit door. Coolly, he made sure that no one in the rubber dinghy had survived before switching back to the flying boat.

Incongruously, the pilot was tucking in his shirt-tails as he scrambled along. Tiller felt almost sorry for him. He knew what it was like to feel exposed, to expect a bullet in the back at any moment, knowing there was nothing you could do about it – except pray. And Tiller wasn't the praying sort. He wondered, as he squeezed the trigger, if the pilot was.

When the bullets hit, the pilot's arms flailed as if he had slipped on a banana. Then he fell head first into the water with a curious elegance that made Barnesworth comment: 'He could have made a good diver with a bit more practice.'

They watched the water and the flying boat warily. Nothing moved, except for the rubber dinghy, which bobbed up and down on the water as it rapidly deflated.

'What about the flying boat?'

'Leave it,' said Tiller.

They walked back along the beach, found two lengths of timber they could use as crude spades and after taking off their identity tags buried the wireless operator and the crewman in the sand. They marked the graves by binding pieces of stick into the shape of crosses. Then they walked along the path under the cliff, past the ML, and round the bend in the creek to find a position where they would have a clear view of the caique approaching.

It arrived soon after midnight and Tiller flashed the prearranged signal with his shaded torch. They saw it swing towards them and their signal was acknowledged. It came to a stop about 100 yards from them and they could see someone climbing into a dinghy that it had in tow.

'I'm bloody amazed they got into the creek,' said Tiller as they watched the dinghy approaching. 'That entrance is fucking hairy enough in daylight.'

Barnesworth's elbow dug into Tiller's ribs. 'I'll give you just one guess who guided them in, Tiger. Just one guess.'

Epilogue

August 1953

'We've got a few minutes left. Any questions?'

The latest draft of National Service recruits to the Royal Marines at Eastney Barracks shifted uncomfortably in their chairs. They knew they were expected to ask questions on the lecture, but could not think of any.

Then one, slightly older than the rest, and wiser in the ways of distracting a lecturer from the dull subject in hand, asked, as other members of earlier classes had asked before him: 'Will you tell us what was it *really* like, sir?'

'What was what like, lad?'

'That Aegean campaign of yours, sir. When you were in the SBS.'

'No different from many other operations. A right shambles.'

'But weren't the Eyeties on our side by then, sir?' another recruit piped up.

'What of it, lad?'

'Well, weren't they' – the recruit hesitated – 'yellow?'

'No, lad, that was the Japanese.'

The recruits sniggered politely.

'You know what I mean, sir.'

So Regimental Sergeant-Major 'Tiger' Tiller, DCM MM Royal Marines, told the class – as he had been inveigled into telling other classes before them – about Balbao and the last final dash of his MAS boat. And he told them too about Giovanni and his Mafia cousin.

And when the recruit then asked, as recruits before him always had, what kind of fighters the Greeks were, Tiller simply said, as he always said: 'They're fierce. And stubborn. I should know. I'm married to one', which delighted the class because they had been told that that was exactly what he would say.

Finally they asked, as others before them always had, about Tiller's legendary detachment commander, the Dane, a man without any military training who had won two Military Crosses. And Tiller told them about Larssen, and his genius for killing Germans, and what his favourite saying was.

'"Work before women", he always said, and he was bloody right. You idle lot of loafers just remember that. Now don't waste my time any more. Get out of here and on to the parade ground. At the double. I'll give you ninety seconds to get fell in. You're in the Royal Marines, not some bleeding pussyfooting army regiment. And don't you ever forget it.'

MARINE C: SBS

THE FLORIDA RUN

David Monnery

1

Nick Russell idled the engine of the *Foxy Lady* and let the boat drift on the placid water. The sun was dropping towards the horizon, flooding the ocean with gold, and he wanted to savour the moment.

As the edge of the molten disc touched the distant horizon, he half expected to hear a loud hiss and to see a plume of steam rise up towards the high, feathery clouds.

Russell had spent his day off in the usual manner, exploring the coral reefs which surrounded the island of Providenciales. Once he had thought that the sense of wonder would gradually wear off, that not even the reefs could keep their magic for ever, but so far there was no sign of any such diminution. The blends of light and colour and movement and mystery seemed just as potent as on the very first day.

The sun slid from sight, and for a few minutes he just sat there, listening to the gentle lap of the water against the hull, and the occasional sound of a car or boat engine drifting across from the direction of the Leeward Marina. The western sky moved from orange to lime green, as the cirrus clouds overhead turned pink against the darkening sky. Above the island the evening star grew more piercing with each passing second.

Russell sighed with pleasure, and then laughed. He engaged the engine and aimed the boat towards the narrow channel known as the Leeward Going Through, which ran between Little Water and Mangrove Cays to the north-west and Providenciales to the south-east. The latter island was known as Provo to almost everyone who lived on it, but even after seven years Russell felt vaguely uncomfortable with the abbreviation – he had come too close to dying at the hands of its Northern Irish namesakes.

That had been a long time ago, though: nearly fifteen years. It was now almost eight since he had worn a military uniform.

Ahead of the boat a lone pelican flew across the channel, headed north towards Little Water Cay. In the distance the lights of the marina were growing brighter against the gathering darkness. At that moment a car started up the slope away from the mooring area, its headlights shining hopefully up at the sky.

Coming here was the best thing he had ever done, Russell thought, and grinned to himself again. The same thought seemed to pass through his brain at about this stage of each journey home from the reef.

But it was true enough. When Worrell Franklin had come to him with the offer of a job his first inclination had been to dismiss the idea. It had sounded great – living in a tropical island paradise, getting paid good money for doing useful and interesting work, able to indulge in all of the outdoor pleasures he loved – but it had also seemed too good to be true. After eleven years in the Marines, the last six of them as a captain with the Special Boat Squadron, Russell had begun to distrust his own good fortune. He had already survived more close encounters with sudden death than seemed natural, and he found it hard to believe that such a run of luck could last for ever.

Even his first meeting with Franklin had been pure chance. A few days before the Argentinians surrendered in the Falklands, Russell had been leading an SBS reconnaissance patrol in the hills above Port Stanley and had just discovered what seemed like the perfect location for an observation post, when a voice came out of the dawn mist, advising him and his men in a Brixton-accented Spanish to lay down their weapons. The SAS, it turned out, had beaten them to it.

In the event the eight men had shared the cramped hide through the hours of daylight, teaching each other regimental slang, listening to each other fart, and wondering out loud whether their respective superiors would ever acquire the skills needed to organize a piss-up in a brewery.

As leaders of their respective patrols, the two men had talked a great deal through the day, and, somewhat to their mutual surprise, had found that they liked each other. They could hardly have come from more divergent backgrounds: Russell was from a merchant banking family and public school, while Franklin was the son of a London Underground guard who had arrived in Britain from Jamaica in 1957. In fact, Franklin had probably been the first black man with whom Russell had exchanged more than half a dozen sentences. Nowadays it was white friends he could count on the fingers of one hand.

Not that it mattered a damn, but it did say something about the way his life had changed. One of the great things about the clinic where he worked was its melting-pot atmosphere, what with Franklin's African wife and the Chinese herbalist and the Puerto Rican doctor . . .

A noise like serrated metal on wood cut through Russell's reverie.

'Shit!' he growled, and instantly cut the engine. It sounded like the keel had scraped a reef, but that was impossible. The *Foxy Lady* was in the middle of the channel, approaching its southern exit. Russell had been through here a hundred times before. There were no reefs, no shallows.

The noise had sounded nasty enough to cut the boat in two, yet there was no sign of damage inside the hull. He would have to take a look at the outside. And right then, he decided. It might make more sense to wait until he was back at the Caicos Marina, but the water wouldn't be so clear, and the *Foxy Lady* was about the only thing he owned in this world. He wanted to know what the damage was.

His determination was frustrated. He had changed back into his wetsuit before he remembered that he had lost his torch the previous week. It would be too dark to see anything under the boat without one.

He restarted the engine and headed for home. The boat wasn't taking any water, and with any luck the damage was considerably less than he had first feared.

Darkness was falling with its usual tropical efficiency, and as he headed south-west, with Long Bay's four-mile stretch of empty sands away to starboard, the heavenly illuminations were gearing up for the night ahead.

After tying up the boat Russell walked down to the office, which was already closed. Fortunately no one had bothered to lock the door, and after a short search he managed to locate a suitable-looking torch. This in hand, he walked back along the slip, past the row of darkened boats. This was the off-season for tourists and part-time residents, and in any case most of the former kept to the island's north coast, where all the new hotel developments were sprouting.

The boats moored here were mostly owned by full-time residents, and came in all sizes and shapes, from yachts to rowing boats, outboards to racing boats, canoes to converted shrimp boats like Russell's own. The biggest craft by far was the *Tiburón Blanco*, the White Shark, which occupied the two moorings next to Russell's. According to the locals the boat belonged to a Cuban-American gangster who owned one of the restored plantation villas behind Long Bay. Russell had never laid eyes on the man, but he had shared a brief conversation with the boat's captain that morning, an Hispanic with a weathered face, hooked nose and longish hair.

The topic of the conversation had been the twenty-foot submersible which was tethered alongside the boat's starboard side. Russell had never seen one like it, and in his years with the SBS he had come into contact with most of the models used by the NATO navies.

'What's it for?' he had asked the man in the captain's hat.

The man had grinned at him. 'We go treasure hunting,' he had said.

'Anywhere in particular?'

'Yes.'

'But that's a secret, right?'

'*Sí.*' The man was still grinning, but Russell didn't get the feeling that there was much enjoyment behind the facial expression. He had restrained himself from asking about the origins of the submersible, thinking that the man might be in a friendlier frame of mind when he returned that evening.

But there didn't seem to be anyone aboard the *Tiburón Blanco*. Russell shone the torch on the tethered submersible. It was actually a submarine in the true sense of the word, with a dry working interior. The propulsion unit was out of sight, under the water at the end furthest from the dock, but he had the distinct feeling the craft was fast, without having any conscious reason for thinking so.

Large front and side windows offered good visibility, and Russell supposed that for anyone searching through the myriad wrecks which littered the local ocean floor it would prove ideal. It looked smart too – the blue-green paint was obviously recent, as was the outsize figure three which adorned the side between the two panoramic windows.

Why had they bothered to number it? Russell wondered, as he clambered back aboard his own, less elegant craft. After donning and checking the oxygen cylinder he adjusted his goggles and dropped himself backwards over the side and into the harbour waters.

It was dark down below, and the powerful beam of light from the torch only seemed to emphasize how much crap there was in the water. After the crystal clarity of the open ocean the waters of the Caicos Marina felt like a microcosm of humankind's treatment of the environment.

He got down to work, methodically scanning the underside of the *Foxy Lady* from the bow backwards, and soon found what he was looking for – a gouge some eighteen inches long. He ran his finger along inside it, and found the cut wasn't deep. Just a flesh wound, he thought with some satisfaction. It wouldn't be hard to put right.

There was nothing to indicate what had caused it, and he couldn't begin to imagine what that might have been. Nothing floating freely in the water could have inflicted such damage. He would have to ask at the office whether anyone else had hit a non-existent reef.

He swam back up to the surface, clambered aboard

the boat, and changed back out of the wetsuit, feeling a huge sense of relief that no real damage had been done. A celebratory drink was in order, he decided, smiling to himself. And maybe Missie would give him a game of chess on her veranda, a bottle of rum within easy reach.

In the old days they might have ended up in bed, but neither of them had been willing to make the relationship as exclusive as the other claimed to want. And though there wasn't much doubt they had enjoyed sleeping together, in time both had come to realize they were better suited as friends.

But first things first, he thought. Some supper and a pint at Suzie's Bar. He locked up the boat, more out of habit than from any sense that it was really necessary, and walked back up to the rack outside the marina office, where the mountain bike which he had acquired secondhand from a homegoing American exile was waiting for him.

It was about five miles to the bar, most of it along the unpaved track which snaked along Provo's southern coast before turning inland to meet the island's one major road – the two-lane Leeward Highway – about a mile east of Suzie Turn. Russell didn't meet a single soul on the track, and treated himself to a spirited rendition of several sixties classics as he leisurely pedalled away the miles. The sea sparkled to his left, low, scrub-covered slopes to his right, and the Milky Way seemed to be pointing his way home. 'To be a rock and not to roll,' he sang, with every bit as much conviction as Robert Plant, though rather less in the way of attention to hitting the right notes.

The mile stretch along the Leeward Highway was more problematic. Lacking any other road on which to practise potential Grand Prix skills, the islanders had turned the road into a formidable exercise of nerve, particularly for cyclists at night. Two trips into the ditch was about par for this stretch, but tonight Russell's luck was working overtime, and only two cars went by, both in the opposite direction, and both travelling at less than Warp 9.

Suzie's Bar was almost empty. Two Hispanic men were sitting at a table near the bar, and a group of obvious tourists sat at one of the farthest-flung tables beneath the two Cuban pines. As Russell approached the bar one of the latter group headed for the toilet, shouting something over his shoulder in German which made his companions roar with laughter.

Russell climbed on to a stool, remembering what an old Frenchman had told him during the previous tourist season – that these days the Germans were becoming as ubiquitous as the Americans had been ten years before. He'd had a theory about it too. This, he reckoned, was the generation of Germans who had been younger than sixteen at the war's end, and who were now retiring, their pockets bulging with the wealth generated by Germany's postwar success. They were the first guiltless Germans since the thirties, the Frenchman had said, and the richest. They were now showing the world the same arrogance their grandfathers had bestowed upon Europe between the wars.

'Mr Nick, sir,' a voice boomed, interrupting Russell's thoughts.

'Mr Jimmy, sir,' he rejoined, mimicking the barman's mock-Sambo act.

They swapped appreciations of the evening and discussed the dance at Downtown on the coming Saturday while the first pint of draught Guinness was religiously pulled.

'I don't suppose I have to ask whether you been out diving?' Jimmy said.

'Nope.'

'You becoming an addict.'

'I hope so. Jimmy, do you know anything about the people who own the big boat down at the Caicos Marina? They've got a small submarine down there now. A guy who looked like the captain said they were going treasure hunting.'

'It's a Cuban owns it – name of Arcilla. He's not often here though. Lives in Miami, I think. His sister lives here most of the time, though.' He raised his eyebrows. 'I hear she has an appetite.'

'She's fat?'

'Not that kind of appetite,' Jimmy said, moving away down the bar to serve one of the German tourists.

Russell turned round idly on his stool, and found the two Hispanics staring at him. 'Nice evening,' he said.

'*Sí* . . . yes,' one of them said, and turned away. The other said nothing, but his eyes seemed to linger on the Englishman, almost like a challenge.

Russell turned back to the bar, and studied the photomontage of fat, bronzed men standing next to fat, dead fish. He had never been able to take fishing seriously himself. He loved the sea too much to use it as a sports field.

'Like I say,' Jimmy continued, materializing in front of him. 'The sister eats tourists. About one a week I'm told, though I expect she sometimes ups or slows the pace, depending on how tasty she finds a particular specimen.'

There was disapproval behind the leer in Jimmy's voice, which Russell didn't find surprising. Afro-Caribbean men might like lives of sexual adventure for themselves, but they expected women to be monogamous. A female who fucked anyone she felt like fucking was almost too threatening to contemplate. Unless she was doing it for money, of course.

'Have you heard about the treasure hunt?' he asked.

'No, but there's always somebody out there looking for treasure. Funny thing is, it's only the people who already have treasure that can afford to go looking for more.'

More tourists arrived – Americans this time – and Russell called Missie on the phone. She would love to see him, she said, and there was a fish stew cooking in the oven. She would even give him a game of chess, though she thought seven defeats in a row should be enough for any man.

He laughed, waved goodbye to Jimmy, and went back to his bike. An hour later he was being fed ladlefuls of steaming stew in Missie's rambling Blue Hills home. Half bungalow and half shack, it seemed to straddle the centuries. Two of Missie's grown-up sons still lived there, while the other two and her lone daughter were scattered across the western hemisphere. Her husband had been lost off a fishing boat in a storm almost twenty years before.

Supper over, they played chess. Missie won both games, and then the two of them sat in silence looking out to sea, sipping their way through the bottle of rum which Russell had purchased on his way through Downtown. Sitting there, he had the momentary feeling that they were like an old married couple, and wondered how that could be when he was only thirty-seven.

He asked Missie.

'That's the big trouble with you folks,' she said. 'You think if something not moving it must be broken or dead.

Hell, I been sitting here peaceful looking at the sea long as I remember. And I ain't broken or dead.'

After one more drink he climbed, somewhat unsteadily, back on to his bike. The three-mile ride home to the clinic was an exercise in keeping on the road, and this he successfully accomplished, eventually negotiating the open gates of the Caicos Research Clinic and Hospital with all the panache of a lion leaping through a blazing hoop. The front door of his bungalow presented rather more difficulty, but eventually he realized it wasn't locked.

From there to the bedroom it was all downhill, and with one last convulsive surge of energy he managed to remove both his shoes.

Three hours later, when the man draped the cloth soaked in chloroform across his face, he came only briefly back to life, before a new and more terrifying darkness swallowed him up once more.

2

Worrell Franklin could feel the sunlight streaming in through the window without opening his eyes. He lay there contentedly, listening to his wife singing to herself in the shower, thinking about the day ahead. He had two classes to take, and a mountain of paperwork to finish, but even the latter failed to douse his sense of well-being. The new computer didn't exactly turn admin into fun, but sometimes it came close.

The noise of rushing water ceased, and he opened his eyes in time to see Sibou enter the bedroom wrapped in a towel. 'Awake already?' she asked, dropping the towel and drying her legs with it.

She was past forty now, and seemed even more beautiful than when they had met, thirteen years earlier in the Gambia. On the wall behind her, now glowing in the sunlight, there hung the brown batik with the stencilled baobabs which they had bought on the Ile de Gorée, off Dakar, all those years ago, on the very day that they had decided to try to turn a love affair into a lifelong commitment. Since both were committed to their professions – she as an overworked doctor in Africa, he as a member of the SAS – their road had not been an easy one. The long separations had been particularly hard, but ultimately worth it. He had saved her life in the Gambia, but she had made his complete in the years that followed.

'Which day is Winnie arriving?' Sibou asked, breaking the spell.

Franklin lifted himself on to his elbows. 'Next Wednesday.' He had to admit he enjoyed his mother's visits. And if only she would stop trying to set up her own School of Nursing in the middle of theirs he would enjoy them even more.

'Great,' Sibou said. 'I've missed her. Maybe this time you can persuade her to come and live here.'

'She won't leave Everton alone in the big city.'

'Everton's thirty-two, with a new wife and enough money to build himself a fortress.'

Which was true. Franklin's younger brother, who had once seemed so firmly mired in Brixton's angry counter-culture, had managed to climb one of the few greasy poles available to him: he had become a highly successful record producer.

'He's still her little boy,' Franklin told Sibou. 'And she's hoping for grandchildren,' he added, and instantly wished he hadn't.

If there was one cloud in their sky it was Sibou's inability to have children.

This time though she just smiled. 'We've also got the second visit from the adoption agency next week,' she said. 'Winnie may find herself with some grandchildren here.'

He got out of bed and took her in his arms. 'I hope so,' he murmured.

'Me too. Now go take a shower,' she said, pushing him away.

He grinned and did as he was told. When he came out she was gone, probably down to the canteen, where they usually ate breakfast with each other and assorted students and staff. Franklin dressed in his usual T-shirt, shorts and sandals and left the bungalow, pausing outside the front door to yawn and rub the remaining sleep out of his eyes. Then he strolled slowly down the path towards the central area.

The clinic grounds spread over several of the island's acres, and had been laid out, largely at Sibou's direction, on the pattern of a similar establishment in the Gambia. Long, one-storey buildings surrounded a large central square of grass studded with ornamental trees, and behind these to the south and east more scrubland had been cleared for staff bungalows and student dormitories. On the west side of the square lay the buildings of the research wing, which was mostly concerned with seeking a reliable detection test for ciguatera fish poisoning, a Caribbean-wide scourge associated with coral reef-derived toxins. The two long-term wards for TB and Aids patients were on the south side, the canteen, nursing school classrooms and daily clinic on the east. The small admin block was just inside the gates, from which a palm-lined lane led out on to the Leeward Highway.

In the canteen Franklin found Sibou working her way through a bowl of fruit salad as she read a newly arrived patient's history. He went for his usual cornflakes, and sliced a banana on top of them. There were about a dozen students scattered round the room, most of them bent over ring files – Nick Russell was probably giving them a test in their first class of the day.

Franklin wondered where his friend was. Nick was usually in the middle of his third cup of coffee by this time.

Still, the clock said ten to eight, so maybe he was already in the classroom setting up the exam. Franklin turned his thoughts back to the classes he was giving that afternoon. Infectious Diseases had never been one of his favourite subjects, but he enjoyed the Emergencies class.

Half an hour later he was searching for a mislaid computer manual when there was an apologetic knock on his open door. He looked up to see one of the students.

'Nick . . . Mr Russell hasn't come to class,' she told him.

'Oh,' Franklin said, surprised. He looked at his watch, but only from habit. Nick was never late for anything.

He accompanied the student back to the classroom, and found it full of adults doing their best to relive their adolescence. He asked what the subject was for that lesson, and set them some reading. Back outside, he started off down the path in the direction of Nick's bungalow.

He hoped that he wasn't going to find his friend sleeping off a drunken binge. When Nick had first come to work at the clinic Sibou had been worried by his alcohol intake, but had gradually come to accept that it never compromised his work. Franklin didn't want her worst fears coming true at this late date. Particularly since Nick seemed to have cut back substantially over the last couple of years.

His bungalow was the farthest from the central compound, and one of the most attractive, its veranda shaded by a stand of beautiful Cuban pines. The red mountain bike was leaning against the veranda steps, so Nick wasn't out on that. The screen door was shut, the door behind it open. There was no noise coming from inside, no screaming riffs from Nick's beloved Clapton, Hendrix or Page.

Franklin let himself in quietly, more from SAS habit

than any sense that danger was present. The living-room and kitchen doors were open, and both rooms looked as tidy and well organized as usual. The bedroom door was closed. Franklin rapped on it lightly, received no answer, and edged the door open. The room was full of sunshine, the bed half-wrecked but empty, as if someone had got up in a hurry.

Most of all, though, Franklin noticed the smell.

He stood there for a moment, worry lines prominent on his forehead, before walking over to close the window. Nick's incense jar – a souvenir of his Hong Kong days – was on the sill, and maybe that was the source of the familiar odour. He hoped so.

Franklin left the room, closing the door behind him, and walked back through the village of bungalows to the medical treatment block. Sibou was in her office between the two wards, talking to two of the trainee nurses.

'Sorry to interrupt,' Franklin said, 'but I need the doctor for a few minutes.

'What for?' Sibou asked, surprise in her voice. One of the nurses giggled.

'Can you come with me,' Franklin said, 'it's important.'

'What's up?' she asked once they were outside.

'I'll tell you in a minute. First I want your opinion on something.'

She heard the trouble in his voice, and didn't ask any more questions as he led the way back to Russell's bungalow. Once inside he took her into the bedroom and closed the door behind them.

'What's that smell?' he asked.

'Chloroform,' she said immediately.

Franklin sat down on the unmade bed. 'That's what I thought. I just wanted to make sure.'

'But . . . where's Nick?'

'He didn't turn up to teach his first class, so I came looking for him.'

She sat down too. 'You don't think . . . ?'

'Someone drugged him with chloroform and took him away?'

'But that's ridiculous. Why would anyone do that?'

Franklin shrugged. 'God only knows.'

Slightly more than a hundred miles away, Nick Russell was experiencing more than a little difficulty in regaining consciousness. His mind seemed to flicker on and off, like a light with a switch containing a loose connection. And though one voice in his brain was all for trying to keep the light on, others were more interested in losing the headache and the nausea and the vague sense of terror which consciousness seemed to involve.

This battle went on for some time, until the need to throw up forced him into greater wakefulness. Between periods of retching over the side of the bed – an iron cot, he realized, with a thin mattress – he managed to focus his eyes sufficiently to pick out the whitewashed cement-block walls, the small window high up behind the bed, and the bare, white-painted door.

The next thing he noticed was someone coming through the door, carrying a tray. It was a grey-haired black man, and he seemed to be angry about something, though the actual words sounded like gibberish.

No, French. The man was speaking French.

'Where am I?' Russell asked, sounding to himself like a man in a bad movie.

The man either didn't understand him, or didn't care to answer. In fact he was already on his way out of the door. A key clicked loudly in the lock, and then silence enveloped his cell once more.

Worrell Franklin nursed the minivan along the Leeward Highway towards the cluster of new shops and offices which was collectively known as Downtown. The island's only police station was on the other side of this development, only a stone's throw from the newly lengthened airport runway. He wasn't expecting much in the way of help from the local constabulary, but he couldn't think of anywhere else to turn.

Downtown seemed almost deserted, with only a trickle of tourists making use of the banks and new shopping mall. The police station didn't seem much livelier. There was only one officer present – Sergeant Oswald.

Franklin had seen the man before – as he had most of Provo's five thousand inhabitants – but couldn't remember ever talking to him. Over the next couple of hours he came to regret breaking this mutual silence.

Sergeant Oswald, though unimpressed by the short space of time for which Nick Russell had been missing, did agree to visit the scene of the possible abduction. Once there he sniffed appreciatively, and announced that there was definitely a hospital-type smell in the room. 'It is a hospital you have here, Mr Franklin, yes?'

'The smell is of chloroform,' Franklin insisted. By this time the odour was growing decidedly faint.

'It smells like the dentist I once went to,' Oswald decided, before abruptly sinking to his knees and looking under the bed. The missing man was not there. He then looked round the room with a professional air. 'There are no bloodstains, no signs of a struggle. You can think of no reason why anyone should kidnap this man. He has no money, you say?'

'Nothing worth kidnapping him for.'

'That's what I thought. And you say his boat is where it should be . . . ?'

'So the marina man told me on the phone . . .'

Oswald nodded wisely. 'I think you will find he has stayed with some woman friend, and they lose track of the time. It is easy to do when you are young,' he added wistfully.

'And the chloroform?'

Oswald sniffed again. 'I can't smell anything now.'

Franklin couldn't either.

'If he has not returned by tomorrow I will take this further,' the sergeant concluded. 'He was a diver, you say?'

'One of the best.' An SBS Swimmer-Canoeist First Class, no less.

'Even the best sometimes get careless.'

'But . . .' Franklin began, and gave up. He was going to ask how Nick's boat had reached port without him, but decided that there was no point in antagonizing the man at this stage. Maybe there was some less dramatic explanation of the chloroform and the disappearance. Whatever had happened, he had no way of making any sense out of it with the information currently at his disposal. Maybe he could gather some more, and give Oswald's brain something to chew on.

After shepherding the policeman back to his car, and watching it accelerate down the lane to the Leeward Highway like a racing car emerging from the pits, Franklin turned to find Sibou coming towards him, white coat flapping in the warm breeze.

'Well?' she asked anxiously.

'I would have got more joy out of talking to one of the pelicans,' Franklin said.

She sighed. 'I saw who it was. Someone told me he was one of the family appointments during the Saunders administration.'

'A professional blind eye.'

'Something like that.'

Franklin grunted. 'He seemed willing to be helpful. Just not able to be.'

'All he ever has to do is wag a finger at the odd drunken tourist. I doubt if he's ever seen a real crime.'

'He looked under the bed.'

She laughed, but only briefly. 'Something bad really has happened, hasn't it?'

'It looks like it,' Franklin agreed, his face grim. 'I can't see any other explanation. And I don't know what else I can do.'

She put an arm through his, and they stood in silence for a minute.

'Missie,' she said suddenly. 'He often goes to see her after his day out on the reef.'

'She's not on the phone.' Franklin looked at his watch. 'I've got a class in ten minutes . . .'

'I can take an hour off,' Sibou said. 'Give me the keys,' she added, offering up her palm.

Russell's next waking thought was that perhaps he had gone to heaven. A face of such loveliness was leaning over his own, large-eyed, small-nosed, with a mouth that, even pursed with concern, seemed almost angelic. Curls of raven hair were slipping out from their confinement behind the ears. Huge earrings dangled half out of sight.

He became aware of something metal against his skin. It was a stethoscope, not earrings.

'Who are you?' he tried to ask, but only a murmur

seemed to emerge from his lips. He tried 'where am I?' with somewhat better results.

'L'Ile de Tortue,' she said.

It sounded French. He had a memory of something else sounding French.

'What's the matter with me?' he asked slowly.

'They used too much chloroform,' she said in French-accented English.

He closed his eyes. The bike ride home, pissed out of his skull. The shot of terror in the night. Had that been . . . ? He opened his eyes again, struggling to keep the lovely face in focus. 'Where is the . . . the place you said?'

He saw the surprise on her face. 'It is an island near the coast.'

'Which coast?' he enunciated carefully.

'The north coast,' she said patiently. '*De Haïti.*'

'I am in Haiti?'

'*Oui*, yes.'

'And who are you?'

'I am a doctor,' she said, but there was a bitterness in her voice he couldn't begin to understand. 'My name is Alabri, Emelisse Alabri,' she added, in a tone that seemed inexplicably defiant.

'Nick Russell,' he said thickly. 'Who brought me here?'

'No more questions now,' she said, smiling to make up for the curtness in her voice. It was as lovely a smile as he could remember, and it seemed to hang in his mind, before receding slowly into the distance, in a manner which somehow reminded him of the Tardis.

Sibou had seen the look on Franklin's face as she headed out of the clinic gates, and spent the next couple of miles resenting it. Certainly she drove fast, but she had never had a serious accident, unlike her husband, who had driven a rental car into a coconut palm soon after their arrival in the Turks and Caicos. The car's bumper had been bent like a boomerang, its roof severely pitted by the resulting shower of dislodged coconuts. Her worst mishap had been to drive through the clinic's gates while they were still closed, and that could have happened to anyone with as much on their minds as she usually had.

She grinned at herself, and forgave Franklin his scepticism. He was only worried about her, after all.

She turned right on to the Blue Hills turn-off just before Downtown, and a few minutes later was following the road which ran behind the beach north from Thompson Cove Point. Inside the dark line of reef the waters were their usual pristine turquoise; beyond it the ribbon of breakers gave way to the deeper blue of the ocean proper. Every couple of hundred yards a group of white tourists was encamped on the white sand.

Sibou shook her head, and wondered for the hundredth time why the European races were so frightened of being close to each other. Twenty years before, when she had first been a student at St Thomas' Medical School in London, she had gone on to the upper deck of a bus, seen only one passenger, and naturally sat down next to him. He had muttered to himself for a minute, and then got off the bus. Looking back, she had been able to see him waiting for the next one.

She was still smiling at the memory when the first dwellings of Blue Hills loomed into view. This was one of the three pre-tourist settlements on the island, and like the other two it hadn't changed very much. It was more scattered than an English village, more like a random spread of homes on which the road had later been superimposed.

Missie's house was down by the beach. Sibou had been there a couple of times with Franklin, in the days when Nick and Missie were toying with the idea of being a couple. She had liked Missie's no-nonsense personality and felt vaguely guilty for not keeping up the acquaintance over the last few months. She told herself that there was always so much to do at the clinic, and so little time, but knew that was not the real reason. Missie was a mother, and Sibou was still trying to come to terms with the fact that she would never be one.

She left the minivan by the side of the road, and walked down the shaded path towards the house. It was unusually hot, and the moment she emerged from the trees the sun resumed its business of trying to burn a hole through her straw hat.

Missie was on her veranda, kneading Johnnycake dough on a wooden board that was perched across her thighs. She looked just the same as Sibou remembered: a tall, big-boned woman with a long neck and beautiful African head. She was dressed in shorts and a Miami Dolphins T-shirt. Her feet were bare.

Her first reaction to seeing Sibou was a look of surprise, the second a warm smile of welcome. 'Come into the kitchen,' she said, getting up. 'You can pour us some coffee while I finish this.'

Sibou did as she was told while Missie shaped the dough into balls, flattened them out and greased a tray for baking. Once they were in the oven, the two women went back out on to the veranda, where the shade and slight breeze offered some respite from the heat.

Sibou took a deep breath and explained why she was there.

'He sure was drunk when he left here,' Missie said. 'I've still got a headache myself. Maybe he just fell off that bicycle somewhere, and . . .'

'The bicycle came home.'

'That sound bad.'

The two women sat in silence for a moment, looking out to sea. It all seemed completely unreal, Sibou thought.

'He didn't say anything to you?' she asked. 'He wasn't worried about anything?'

'He seem fine. He had a good day on the reef. Hit his boat on something, but he say no real damage. He just the same as ever. He still can't play chess worth a damn.'

'Do you know if he came straight here from the marina?'

'Far as I know. No, wait. He phone from Suzie's, and there was beer on his breath when he come here. He must have stop for a drink on the way.'

Sibou couldn't think of anything else. 'How are you?' she asked Missie.

'I was fine until now.'

They talked for a while about her sons, and the clinic, and Franklin's mother's visit, and the possible adoption. 'You come see me again,' Missie said, 'with some good news, maybe. You can bring your husband if you want to. I happy to see you both, or just you. And I'll keep my ears open for any news of Nick,' she added as Sibou was leaving.

On the drive back down the coast Sibou thought the matter through in her usual logical manner, and realized just how little they had to go on. There was a man missing and a smell of chloroform in his bedroom. They had no idea why anyone should want to abduct him. The whole business seemed as ludicrous as it was chilling.

Back at the clinic she found Franklin in the canteen, nursing a can of Coke. She told him what she had found out, which wasn't very much.

'I'd better check out Suzie's Bar,' was his reaction.

'It won't be open until early evening.'

'Do you know where the guy who runs it lives?'

She shook her head.

He gently squeezed the empty Coke can. 'Well, I guess I'll have to wait.' He smiled ruefully. 'It doesn't feel right, calmly going off to teach an Emergencies class when . . . you know . . . I feel like I should be rushing around, trying to do something.'

'I know. One thing that occurred to me – whoever chloroformed Nick could just as easily have killed him . . .'

'Unless they wanted to kill him somewhere else.'

'Why would they want to do that?'

'Christ knows,' Franklin said, angrily crushing the can. 'Why would anyone want to kill him at all?'

3

Aleksandr Solayev bit down on the Bacon Mega Double Whopper and felt the extra mayo he had ordered dribbling down his fingers and on to the plastic tray. The burger tasted like heaven. He followed it with a handful of French fries, and sat there for a moment, holding the last mouthful between sticky fingers, reluctant to complete the meal. He wondered how the Soviet Union could ever have hoped to win the Cold War.

The last mouthful went down, thrilling his taste buds, and he let the flavours linger on his tongue for a few seconds before reaching out a hand for the triple-thick strawberry shake. It was so thick that he almost pulled a lip muscle trying to suck it up through the straw.

Three children walked past his table, all screaming at the tops of their voices. Their parents followed, apparently oblivious to the noise, and herded the whole brood out of the restaurant, across the parking lot and into a large blue Nissan Maxima. Solayev could still hear the children yelling as the car slipped down the ramp and back on to the interstate.

He belched softly, took another draw on the straw, and examined his surroundings again. The restaurant looked as good as the food tasted. Everything was so pleasant on the eye – the printed menu above the servery, the brightly coloured furnishings, the mosaic floor . . . And all of it bathed in the bright Florida sunshine that came pouring through the panoramic windows. There was nothing drab here, nothing grey, nothing . . . like home.

He smiled at the thought that this place was also called St Petersburg. It was a long way from the one he had been born in.

The shake seemed easier to draw on now. He removed the plastic lid to investigate and discovered that the ice-cream around the edges was melting quicker than that in the centre. He gave the whole thing a stir, and tried again. This time less effort was required. Learning to live in America, Solayev decided, would involve the mastering of many such minor techniques.

He began tidying up his tray, and noticed the three unused ketchup sachets. They must have given him four, he realized. Surely no one could use four. And there had been six napkins – he had counted them. Such plenty. It was incredible.

The previous evening, in the motel outside Orlando, he had worked his way through the channels on the TV in his room. There had been cop shows, quiz shows, comedies, music, sports of every kind, people talking about God, people selling jewellery. It had reminded him of the first time his father had taken him inside the special Party shop in Leningrad – there were just too many riches to absorb in one go.

Like the Florida women. All those young girls in shorts. He had a better idea now of what dogs on heat felt like. Well, now that he had all the money at last, some female companionship was one of the things uppermost in his mind. Once he was down in the Keys his new life could begin in earnest.

But not Key West, he reminded himself. At first he had thought the guy was kidding him – a town full of queers! – but someone else had confirmed the story. And looked at him strangely. There were some things about America he would have a hard time accepting. And this unhealthy tolerance of perverts was definitely one of them.

His straw gurgled and struck air. Solayev thought about ordering another shake, his third of the day, but one glance at his waistline dissuaded him. It was partly the light summer clothes, he thought: in Murmansk everyone had needed to dress like a bear, and he had hardly noticed the growing paunch.

But it was also about being forty-five. He had to be careful of his diet now – there was no point in striking it this lucky and then immediately keeling over with a coronary.

He carried his tray to the disposal bin, tipped its contents away, and looked around for someone to say goodbye to. But the woman he had spoken to earlier was gone. He remembered the feeling in the motel room, the sense that the room was too big for just him, and that watching TV was something you did with others. The old Russian habits would die hard, he thought.

He walked out to the car, carrying the brown leather attaché case, and climbed in behind the wheel. He placed the case on the seat beside him and opened it, not so much to check that the money was still in it – the case had never been out of his sight – but simply to enjoy the view. A quarter of a million dollars looked back at him.

He smiled to himself, re-locked the case, placed it on the floor behind his seat, and started the Toyota's engine. The two years he had spent as a naval attaché in Cuba in the early eighties had certainly paid off, albeit in a way that he would never have imagined in his wildest dreams. Back then Raul Ochoa had always behaved as if the sun shone out of Fidel Castro's arse, and in between chatting up girls at Havana's tourist hotels the two of them had argued about the relative merits of the Cuban and Soviet roads to socialism.

Solayev snorted with amusement as he pulled out on to the interstate and headed south out of St Petersburg. The collapse of the Soviet Union had been the first of several big surprises in recent years, but all the others had paled before the sudden appearance of Raul Ochoa at his apartment in Murmansk. Ochoa had not only known the details of the small submarine research programme he had been running, but had also been able to confirm the rumours of the programme's imminent cancellation. Solayev was apparently about to join the rapidly swelling ranks of the post-Soviet unemployed.

But not necessarily, Ochoa had told him. Solayev's government might not want his submarines, but the Cuban knew someone who did. Not his own government, with whom he had come to a reluctant parting of the ideological ways, but a private businessman.

Ochoa also had a plan for getting both Solayev and the submarines out of Russia. There would be a $250,000 fee for facilitating the export process and instructing the new owners in how to use the craft, and then Solayev could begin a new life in the West. What did he have to lose?

Quite a lot, if the new crime-busting KGB had caught him, but the whole plan had gone like clockwork. In Yeltsin's Russia a few dollars bought a lot of silence.

He was driving out on to what looked like an endless causeway. 'The Sunshine Skyway', a plaque announced. Ahead of him the concrete roadway swept across the bay in a graceful curve on its line of cylindrical pilings. A couple of miles away, somewhere close to the midpoint, a strange-looking bridge reared up against the blue sky.

This is America, he thought. This was something that had been built by people who had confidence in themselves and the world. It was like something out of a science fiction novel. As he neared the bridge it became apparent that it comprised two huge stanchions, which rose soaring out of the centre of the highway, and from which were suspended two vast triangular fans of suspension cable.

The genius of simplicity, Solayev thought, and with all the beauty which that implied. He wanted to stop, but as usual there was nowhere to pull over, so he drove on down the causeway, hoping to find somewhere from which to take a photograph.

He had just sighted the lay-by up ahead when a car cut across in front of him and slowed, siren wailing and red light flashing.

Solayev looked at his speedometer. Perhaps he had been a bit over the limit, but only a bit. Still, what did a twenty-five-dollar fine matter to him?

The police car pulled over into the lay-by and Solayev followed. A flicker of doubt passed through his mind, but was quelled by the sight of the uniformed officers emerging from the car. And in any case, cars seemed to be going past all the time.

Both officers seemed to be Hispanic. One leant nonchalantly against the bonnet of the Toyota while the other asked for his driver's licence.

'Was I going too fast?' Solayev asked, his Russian accent still strong.

The officer continued looking at the licence, as if it fascinated him.

'*Es claro*,' the other man said.

The officer returned the Russian's licence, and pulled the gun from his holster. The last thing Solayev saw was the man's brown finger clenching on the trigger.

It was just after six when Franklin arrived at Suzie's Bar, and Jimmy Durham was still in the process of opening up for the evening.

'Mr Worrell, sir,' Jimmy greeted him sardonically. 'Don't anyone in that clinic of yours know that alcohol is bad for you?'

'Only in large doses. Give me a Pils.'

Jimmy retrieved a bottle from the refrigerator. 'Hot day,' he said cheerfully.

'They're all hot,' Franklin said. He might have been born in Jamaica, but he had left for England before he could walk or talk, and contrary to white public opinion, black people were no more imbued with a tolerance of extreme heat than they were with natural rhythm.

'The trick is to sleep by day,' Jimmy confided, drawing a circle with the drops of beer on the bar.

'Right. Was Nick in here yesterday?'

'Yep. Not for long, though. Why – you checking up on your employees?'

'He's gone missing.'

Jimmy's doodling finger came to a stop. 'What – really missing?'

'Looks like it.' Franklin was reluctant to go into the business of the chloroform, though he had little doubt the story would be all over the island before too many more hours had gone by. 'Did he talk to anyone in here last night?'

'Only me. He was asking about that boat moored

next to his – can't remember the name. The one Fidel Arcilla owns.'

'What was he asking?'

'Just that. Who owned it. Oh, and he said something about a submarine . . .'

'A submarine?'

'A small one. You know, the kind they use for treasure hunting. And research. One of those.'

'This Arcilla involved in treasure hunting?'

'Seems like it.'

'But Nick didn't know about him?'

'Nope. I told him about the man's sister. She picks up tourists for a living, screws each one every which way for a few days and then goes back for another.'

Franklin raised an eyebrow. 'And where do they live?'

'The restored plantation villa at the end of Long Bay – the last one you come to on the road. Or the first one on the path from the Caicos Marina. But the man's hardly ever there – spends his time in Miami, they tell me. Just his sister giving it away like there was no tomorrow.'

Franklin grimaced. 'Is that all?'

Jimmy grinned. 'Yep. Total Recall is my second name. Second and third names, I suppose.'

Franklin took a last satisfying swig from the bottle of Pils, thanked his informant, and walked back across to the minivan. Once behind the wheel he sighed loudly, ran a hand through his hair, and started up the engine. A few minutes later he was pulling on to the track which led down to the Caicos Marina, and listening to the minivan's suspension beginning to complain. It was only a four-mile walk, he decided. And the evening breeze was beginning to blow.

His long strides ate up the ground, and not much

more than forty minutes had gone by when he walked down the final slope to the channel's edge. He and Nick had often gone out diving together in the early days – Nick the teacher and he the pupil – and Franklin knew where the *Foxy Lady* was berthed.

But it was fully dark now, the moon yet to rise, and he had to strain his eyes to be sure he had found the right boat. Having done so, the first thing he noticed was the absence of the boat Nick had mentioned to Jimmy. On one side of the *Foxy Lady* a small yacht was tied, one of its sail cords tapping against an aluminium boom in the breeze. On the other side were two empty berths. Arcilla's boat had gone. Treasure hunting, maybe. With Nick on board, maybe.

Franklin clambered aboard the *Foxy Lady* in search of clues.

He found none. The local ocean charts had been generously augmented with felt-tip, but the markings seemed nothing more than a record of Nick's reef explorations. The small cabin below was locked, but Franklin felt no scruples about breaking in. After all there was no need for any damage – picking locks was one of the few skills he had learned before joining the army, from the least reputable of the five uncles on his mother's side of the family.

But there was nothing inside the cabin either. An old Walkman with a Doors tape in it, a couple of private-eye paperbacks, a copy of *Teach Yourself Chess* and a book of tropical fish, and Nick's diving gear.

Franklin re-locked the door, climbed back on to dry land and walked up to the marina office. The man in charge was closing up. He hadn't seen Nick since the previous morning. And the big boat – he seemed reluctant to mention the owner's name – had left before sunrise that morning. Headed west, he'd been told; aiming to do some treasure hunting with their submarine on the Cay Sal Bank.

Franklin thanked him and walked slowly back down towards Nick's boat, wondering what to do next. Then abruptly he reversed course and walked back up to where the footbridge crossed the channel beside the marina office. On the far side he struck off up the path which ran around the headland towards Long Bay.

He had only been walking ten minutes when he rounded a bend and saw the old plantation house, perched on a slight rise above the beach. There were lights burning in several windows, but he could see no movement.

There were two single-storey buildings behind the main two-storey house, and the property as a whole was surrounded by a high wall, along the top of which Franklin could just make out the glint of razor wire. The only break in these perimeter defences was a pair of colonial-style gates, adorned with post-colonial video surveillance equipment.

The plantation house had verandas on three sides of each storey, and as Franklin watched a woman came out through a door on to the upper deck and stood at the railing, looking out to sea. She seemed to be wearing a T-shirt and tight trousers, but as Franklin soon discovered, the trousers were only in his imagination. As she flicked on the lighter for her cigarette, he could see that she was naked from the waist down.

The flare died away, and he stood there staring at the distant silhouette, thinking that a painter or photographer would find it hard to come up with a purer image of loneliness.

* * *

Nick Russell's watch, which he had forgotten to take off in his drunken stupor the previous night, told him it was seven forty-five. The lack of light from the small window high in the wall told him it was evening. Assuming he hadn't been out for two days, it was the evening after the one he had spent with Missie.

He forced himself into a sitting position, and had the distinct feeling his brain was slopping around inside his head. He held his head in his hands and took several deep breaths.

He was still sitting in that position when the key clicked in the door. He looked up suddenly, hoping to see Emelisse Alabri again, and felt his head swim. When his eyes cleared he found a black man standing over him, a gun sticking out of his waistband.

If I was *compos mentis*, Russell thought, the man would be without the gun by now. But he wasn't. And there would probably be other chances to indulge in empty heroics later.

He grinned, and even that seemed to conjure up a desire for sleep.

'You walk?' the man asked in English with a marked French accent.

'I don't know,' Russell said mildly. 'Are we going for a stroll?'

The man smiled. 'Something like that. The commandant wants to see you.'

'I'll be home all evening.'

The man grasped Russell roughly under the arm and pulled him to his feet. His brain rocked to and fro, and settled down once more. Maybe he was getting the hang of it.

'Enough joking,' the man was saying.

It seemed like good advice. Russell tried a couple of

paces and found he could just about walk. The man prodded him in the direction of the door.

Outside he found a short passageway. To the right were more doors, to the left an opening on to the outside world. The man prodded him again, towards the latter.

He emerged from the doorway into a world not that dissimilar to the ones Hieronymus Bosch had painted several centuries before. It was a darkness split by fires, full of reeling shadows, with hanging bodies swaying in the breeze. Bosch had never made movies, but if he had ever needed a soundtrack then the ominous, overlapping rhythms of different drummers would probably have been just what the doctor ordered.

As his eyes gradually focused, Russell could see that the fires were mostly surrounded by people cooking, the shadows were tall palms waving in the breeze, the hanging bodies long garments drying on a line. The drums, though, still sounded ominous.

'Who are the drummers?' he asked his escort.

'Just voodoo priests,' the man said. He sounded bored by the idea.

There were buildings all around them, Russell realized. In fact the place didn't look that dissimilar to the place where he lived and worked. There were several low buildings grouped in a rough square which could easily be hospital wards. Or barracks, he thought, as they emerged from under a group of palms and a tall watch-tower loomed into view against the night sky. It wore a radar dish on its roof, which made the whole structure look like one of H. G. Wells's Martian war machines balancing a plate on its head.

But if it was a barracks, then who were these people

grouped around the fires? They looked more like refugees than soldiers. And in fact most of them seemed to be not much more than children.

Russell began to feel very tired. 'I can't walk much farther,' he said.

'We are almost there,' the man told him, gesturing towards the building directly ahead of them.

What seemed like an hour later they reached the door. Inside the furnishings were smarter than Russell had expected, and had a distinctly military feel to them. It reminded him of the Admin block back in Poole.

The next thing he knew he was coming back to life in a chair, with a new throbbing pain in his head. Since there didn't seem much profit in anyone hitting him again, he assumed he must have collapsed.

'Mr Russell,' a voice addressed him. With a supreme effort he managed to refocus his eyes. The man who had spoken was sitting opposite him, behind an office desk, leaning back in his chair with hands behind his head, legs stretched out and crossed at the ankle. There was more American than French in his accent, but the face, though African, had a Gallic quality to it. The nose was decidedly Roman, the mouth almost thin-lipped, the hair lustrous and wavy. The eyes, though, were what drew Russell's attention. They seemed to be straining at their sockets, as if eager to leap out and devour the world.

For the first time in an often dangerous life Russell had the sense that he was in the presence of evil.

'Who are you?' he asked quietly. The words seemed to boom inside his head.

The man smiled. 'I am Toussaint Joutard. Colonel Joutard. But . . .'

'Of the Haitian Army?' Russell interrupted him.

Joutard didn't seem to mind. 'I am the leader of an

organization known as the Sons of the Motherland. We work closely with the army, of course. Most of the time we share the same objectives.'

His English was perfect, Russell thought, and said so.

'I lived in America for several years.'

Bully for you, Russell thought. The man was probably another CIA-trained fascist gone bananas in his own country. 'Why have I been brought here?' he asked.

Joutard smiled again, but it wasn't the sort of smile which engendered bonhomie. 'You could say this was a job interview . . .'

'I already have a job.'

'No longer. You will either take the job I am offering you, or you will be killed.' His lips creased in response to some inner amusement. 'Either way I shall make an excellent profit.'

The last sentence passed Russell by. 'What have I done to you?' he asked.

Joutard looked at him for a few seconds. 'You don't know?' He laughed. 'Perhaps you don't. It doesn't really matter any more.' He slapped the desktop suddenly with the palm of his hand, and then seemed to examine the backs of his fingers. 'You are an extremely lucky man, Mr Russell,' he said. 'We lose the services of one of our doctors, and, hey presto, here you are. I'm told you're a paramedic, which I assume is a step up from being a nurse. Well, here you'll take another step up – to doctor.'

'I don't have that sort of training . . .' Russell said.

'You will get it here. A man with your experience will have no difficulty learning the techniques required – the operations performed here are simple enough.' He smiled yet again. 'We're not doing brain surgery yet.'

Russell felt a sinking feeling in his stomach. 'What sort of operations are you talking about?'

Joutard told him.

Russell just shook his head.

'Of course, if you refuse you will be killed and your body harvested. Being British, you might think that seems a jolly noble sort of thing to do. But you must also understand that these operations will be performed with or without you, and that the patients' chances of survival will no doubt worsen dramatically if they are performed by people with inferior skills. So it might be more noble to stay, *n'est-ce pas*? And of course if you accept – not that I imagine such matters interest you – you will earn an extraordinary amount of money in a short space of time.' He paused for effect and then looked up and said: 'So you can either leave the sick to fend for themselves or die a useless death.'

Russell just looked at him.

'I will give you until tomorrow morning to decide which.' His eyes moved across to Russell's escort by the door. 'Take him to the late Dr Barlow's bungalow,' he said. 'And tell Dr Alabri I want to see her.'

Franklin got home soon after ten, and found Sibou waiting anxiously for him.

'Where have you been?' she asked angrily. 'Why didn't you phone?'

'I . . .'

'Your best friend vanishes off the face of the earth, and then you take five hours over a trip to Suzie's and expect me not to worry?'

He reached out for her hand. 'Sorry,' he said.

'So I should think.' She burrowed into his arms, and they held each other tight for a while. Eventually she disentangled herself. 'Where have you been then?' she asked.

He told her what he had learned at Suzie's Bar and the Caicos Marina, and of seeing Arcilla's sister. 'When I got back to the marina I had another talk with the guy there. He told me Arcilla has a private helicopter, and that he heard it taking off in the middle of the night.'

'So Nick could have been taken away by air or by boat.'

'Yep. He could be anywhere by now – the Bahamas, Cuba, Haiti, you name it. And we still haven't got a clue why he was taken.'

'Maybe they needed another diver for this treasure business,' Sibou suggested.

Franklin thought about it. 'You could be right there. Though I don't see why they couldn't just hire one. There's enough of them around.'

'I suppose.'

Franklin sat down on the sofa, laid his back against it and closed his eyes. 'I don't know what else we can do,' he said.

She sat down next to him. 'Put pressure on Oswald,' she said. 'If that doesn't work, go to his superiors on Grand Turk.'

'And if they can't find him?'

'I don't know,' she said. It was too much to accept – that a friend could disappear in such circumstances and that nothing could be done to find him.

The late Dr Barlow's bungalow turned out to be as comfortable as Russell's own on Providenciales. The screening seemed to be in good repair, and the air-conditioner, though somewhat noisy, was an efficient enough cooler. There was a refrigerator in the kitchen, a working shower in the bathroom. The furniture was somewhat sparse, but did include a functioning cassette player. The doctor's tastes had apparently been somewhat different from Russell's – Handel rather than Hendrix.

Having concluded this brief tour, Russell sank back exhausted on to the large bed. He could still hear drumming in the distance, and see the reflected light of the fires dancing in the trees outside. It occurred to him that Colonel Joutard had not bothered to warn him against trying to escape.

From what he could remember the Ile de Tortue – or Tortuga, as the English called it – was several miles off the northern coast of Haiti. In the old days it had been used as a base by French and English buccaneers for raiding the Spanish gold traffic which passed through the nearby Windward Passage. Russell had no idea who lived on the island now, or whether the writ of the Haitian Government – such as it was – extended this far. It seemed much more likely that Joutard had turned the place into a semi-private fiefdom.

Escape should be possible. Russell's expertise as a diver was common knowledge on Providenciales, but his background in the Marines and SBS was known only to very few, and Joutard had given no indication that he was aware of this pre-medical career.

Still, as of that moment he was in no condition to walk round the bungalow, let alone make a break for the Turks and Caicos Islands. He would need to be fully recovered from the effects of the chloroform, and to know a lot more about exactly where he was, before seriously contemplating escape. One such attempt, he suspected, was all he was likely to be allowed.

And in the meantime he had Joutard's offer of

employment to consider. Not that there seemed to be much choice.

He wondered if there was anything to drink anywhere on the premises. Levering himself gingerly off the bed, he was halfway to a promising-looking cabinet when there was a rap on the outside door.

Maybe room service, he thought wryly. He tried to shout 'come in', but could manage little more than a loud croak.

Whoever it was seemed to hear. He heard the door open and close, and there she was standing in the doorway of the room, still wearing the white coat. She looked just as lovely as before. But then she had seemed like a ministering angel; now he knew her to be one of Joutard's 'doctors'. And maybe she had been sent to him as a further inducement to sign on the dotted line.

'I thought I'd better check up on you,' she said.

'I'm OK.'

She walked forward and took hold of his wrist, the way he had seen Ching Ling do with patients back at the clinic.

'You do Chinese medicine?'

She concentrated on his pulses. 'Only a little,' she said, taking the other wrist. 'One of my grandmothers was Chinese.'

That explained her extraordinary face, he thought.

'Your pulses are better,' she said. 'You should be back to normal in a couple of days. But you should be in bed,' she added.

'OK, doc,' he said, expecting her to leave.

But instead she stood there, obviously uncertain about something.

Russell found himself wondering what Joutard had wanted with her.

As usual she seemed to read his mind. 'The colonel wants me to persuade you to work for us,' she said.

'With what?' he asked wryly.

Anger flashed in her eyes. 'By appealing to your better nature,' she said sarcastically.

'Not my nose for profit?' he replied in kind.

'I may be mistaken in your case,' she said slowly, 'but nursing isn't usually the sort of career someone enters with money in mind.'

Russell looked at her. 'I may be mistaken in your case,' he said, 'but I didn't think doctors signed on for Joutard's sort of operation with anything else in mind.'

Her whole body seemed to tense, and for a moment he thought she was going to hit him, but then she let it all out in a long sigh. 'How would you know?' she said, looking at the floor.

'Explain it to me.'

She looked him in the eye, and for a moment he felt uncomfortable, as if she was seeing right through him. 'The world doesn't always work the way you want it to,' she said. 'Especially in Haiti. There are two hundred young people here who have no parents, and no matter what I do they will suffer. But I can lessen that suffering; I can see that they lead a healthy life after they leave here.'

'Are you here willingly?'

She shrugged. 'What does that mean?'

'Could you walk out of this place, and take a boat across the strait, and tell the authorities in Port au Prince what is going on here?'

She sighed again. 'You don't understand. There are no authorities in Port au Prince who would care a damn about what's happening here. And even if there were, do you think Joutard would throw his hands up in the air and promise not to do such things again? Of course not. He'd just find another base, another corrupt government.' She shook her head in exasperation. 'This is the Third World in 1994, for heaven's sake – where have you been?'

Exploring coral reefs, was the answer that came to mind. It didn't seem the sort that would appeal to her.

'I'm sorry,' she said, unexpectedly. 'This is not your country, and you have been brought here against your will. There's no reason why you should want to help me.'

'There's no reason why I should want to help Joutard. Except that he'll kill me if I don't.'

She shrugged. 'I'm sorry. If there's some sort of principle at stake here that you think is worth dying for, then there's nothing more I can say. Except that if you do decide to live, then your skills will make a difference to the children here.'

Russell bit back the retort that was on his tongue. 'There's no principle,' he said. 'Nothing that grand. And I have no desire to die, or to be "harvested". I'll work for Joutard. But I'm not going to kid myself into thinking that I'm doing something that's morally acceptable.'

She smiled for the first time, but Russell found it unsettling rather than comforting, for in it he seemed to see his own pomposity reflected.

'Maybe,' she said. 'But after you've been here a while you may decide that morality is just one more luxury no one can afford.'

4

The clear turquoise waters of the Caicos Bank gave way to the deep blue of the ocean trench which separated South Caicos from the Turk Islands. As usual, the eight-seater plane was full, mostly with men in suits. It was only about eighty miles from Providenciales to Grand Turk, but the three intermediate stopovers stretched the journey time to almost ninety minutes.

The pilot began his descent. Franklin looked down at the sea, wondering why he had bothered to make the trip. As far as he could tell the chances of getting any satisfaction from the commissioner were about as minimal as chances got.

But six whole days had now gone by since Nick's disappearance, and he and Sibou had been unable to think of anything else. Making use of his SAS skills in clandestine observation, Franklin had spent several days and nights practically staking out the Arcilla villa, but had come up empty. The sister – whose name was Tamara – seemed to rise around noon, stare at the sea for most of the afternoon, and go out drinking in the evening, usually at the Club Med-Turkoise bar on Grace Bay. Once she had brought a man home with her, and perhaps had sex with him. If so, the encounter didn't seem to have been mutually satisfactory. He had left at two in the morning, looking angry.

She was presumably in charge of the place, but the

man who did what work there was to be done was a Jamaican named Freddie Bartholomew. He collected supplies, acted as a resident watchdog, and lived in one of the converted outbuildings. He did most of his drinking at home, usually with two other equally underemployed cronies. They looked like the sort of men who would be hired by someone expecting trouble. Two ferocious-looking Rottweilers only emphasized the atmosphere of potential siege.

Arcilla himself had not been seen on the island for at least a couple of weeks. Still, Franklin was convinced that the Cuban was responsible, one way or another, for Nick's disappearance. The problem lay in finding a single shred of evidence to that effect. He had gone back to Oswald and asked him to find some pretext for searching Arcilla's home but, not surprisingly, the policeman had refused. Franklin was told what he already knew – that there were no substantive grounds for obtaining a search warrant, and that where prominent citizens like Arcilla were concerned, Oswald was not going to act without such grounds. He was sorry about Franklin's friend, but there was nothing more he could do. Some crimes just remained unsolved. It was the way of the world.

But it was not the way of his world, Franklin thought, to give up looking for a friend who had inexplicably vanished.

The police station was the taxi's last stop. It lay behind the oldest building on the island, Guinep Lodge, which was being turned into a maritime museum. The adjoining building had not as yet been rebuilt following its torching on the last day of 1985. The unidentified arsonist's intention had probably been the destruction of financial and other records, and the attack had spawned an official British government inquiry. Where the police were at the time had never been established. 'Incorruptible' was not a word which came easily to mind where the local force was concerned. At least not in those days.

Maybe things had changed, Franklin thought, as he pushed through the double doors of the police headquarters. There was no one visible, so he pressed the bell.

The commissioner himself appeared in a doorway.

'Worrell Franklin?' he asked.

Franklin nodded.

'Come through,' Missick said, lifting up the counter.

Franklin took a seat in the man's office, which seemed unusually bare. There were no paintings, photographs or posters – just cream walls, an uncluttered desk and a bookcase full of what looked like bound reports.

'Cigarette?' Missick asked, pushing forward a carved wooden box full of Marlboro Lights.

'No thanks.'

Missick lit one for himself. 'So how can I help you?' he asked, in a tone that suggested help was unlikely to materialize.

Franklin doggedly went through the story of Nick's disappearance, and outlined his suspicions.

'But there is no evidence linking Arcilla to your friend?' Missick asked when he was finished.

'He talked about him that evening.'

'He probably talked about other people too. That hardly counts as evidence.' Missick sucked in his lower lip and blew smoke down towards his desk. 'I'm not saying you are wrong in your suspicions, but . . .' He shrugged. 'It's not only that you have no evidence. You have no motive either.'

Franklin offered the notion that Arcilla needed a diver.

'Divers are ten a penny in the islands. Why would he need to kidnap one?' The commissioner took another drag on the cigarette and waved it around in the air. 'People do not like to think they are mistaken about their friends, but have you considered the possibility that your friend staged this disappearance because he had a better offer from elsewhere? Maybe even an offer from Fidel Arcilla.'

'That's crazy,' Franklin said, his voice rising. 'If Nick had wanted to leave the clinic there was nothing stopping him. And the idea of him spreading chloroform around his room to deceive us is just crazy.'

Missick shrugged again. 'Then I don't know what to suggest. But you must see the situation from our point of view. A man has disappeared. There is no evidence that he was abducted, save perhaps a smell which has long since gone. Assuming he *was* abducted, there is no evidence linking him with Arcilla, save an apparently innocent piece of chit-chat in a bar. And in addition to that I find it very hard to imagine that he is being held captive anywhere in these islands. They are too small and too open and everyone knows what everyone else is doing. If your friend has been abducted, then I think he has passed outside my jurisdiction. Of course, I can pass on his details to my colleagues in the Bahamas and Haiti and the Dominican Republic, but unless he has used his passport to gain entry . . .'

'His passport is still at the clinic.'

Missick shrugged for the third time. Three shrugs and out, Franklin thought to himself. He felt as helpless as he could remember. Only those long-gone Brixton summers spent worrying about his kid brother came even close.

Franklin got to his feet. He had been bound to try, but this trip had been as fruitless as he had expected.

He shook hands with Missick and left. There were two hours to burn before the return flight on the inter-island shuttle, so he decided to go and look for lunch somewhere on Front Street.

In the office he had just left Alden Missick was direct-dialling a number in Miami Beach and asking for '*el jefe*', the boss.

Arcilla came on the line. '*Qué pasa*?' he asked, almost playfully.

'The man from the clinic – the Englishman – he has been here. But I think it was his last throw. I think he has realized that there is nowhere else for him to go.'

There was a short silence at the other end. 'OK. *Es bueno*. But I want you to keep an eye on him, just in case.'

That evening Franklin and Sibou went out for an expensive meal at the Club Med-Turkoise. Tamara Arcilla arrived alone when they were halfway through the entrée, and was given a table no more than ten feet away. It was the first time Franklin had seen her up close, and the first time his wife had set eyes on her.

'She's beautiful enough,' Sibou commented.

'On the outside,' Franklin added.

His wife gave him an amused look. 'You're not comfortable with the idea of a woman just picking up men for sex, are you?'

'Not particularly.'

'But men picking up women for sex is OK?'

'No . . . well . . . it seems more natural that way round. And yes, I know, it shouldn't. But it does.' He stole another glance at the Cuban woman. Probably in her early thirties, she was slim, but not model-slim. There was an Hispanic lushness about her body, from the slightly rounded calves up past the prominent hips, narrow waist and full breasts. Her dark hair tangled down past her face, often hiding one dark eye from view. She was wearing a simple white dress and deep crimson lipstick.

She was beautiful, Franklin agreed. But not happy. She was eating the starter too slowly, drinking the wine too fast.

'If you can tear your eyes away,' Sibou was saying, 'I've had an idea.'

'What?'

'Why not contact your old friends in the SAS?'

'What could they do?'

'I don't know,' Sibou admitted. She wanted to give him some hope, even if it only served to soften the blow. 'I thought there was some unspoken rule about looking after your own,' she said.

'Up to a point, maybe. But it doesn't apply to ex-members of the Regiment. And anyway, Nick was in the SBS, not the SAS.'

'Have you got any contacts there?'

'Not really.' But maybe it wasn't such a bad idea, Franklin thought. The Regimental CO at Hereford, whoever he was, might know someone in the Foreign Office. Might be owed a favour, or something like that. Maybe it was worth a shot . . .

'Look,' Sibou said, 'your mother's arriving tomorrow . . .'

'You're right,' Franklin said with a smile. 'I'll give Joss Wynwood a call when we get home.'

'There's a name from the past,' Sibou murmured.

Wynwood and Franklin had been the two junior members of the three-man SAS team sent to the Gambia in 1981 to help restore President Jawara to power after a left-wing coup. The final act of Franklin's first trip to Africa had been to save a local doctor from being raped and killed by a local psychopath. The same doctor who was now eating a chicken salad across the table from him.

Franklin and Wynwood had seen active service again the following year, as members of a four-man reconnaissance patrol on the Falklands. Both had been present when Nick Russell and his SBS boys had stumbled into their observation post.

Since Franklin's departure from the SAS in 1986 he had only seen Wynwood once, for a short drink in a London pub a couple of years later. Since then they had sent each other the occasional postcard, but that was all. Wynwood was still in the SAS, as far as Franklin knew. His last news of the Welshman, which had come via another old comrade, was of a promotion to senior sergeant of the Counter-Revolutionary Warfare Training Wing.

Back at the clinic an hour or so later, Franklin punched out the number on their bungalow phone, and listened to the ringing at the other end. Sibou had suggested waiting until morning, but there was no knowing where Wynwood would be during the day. At three in the morning he should be in bed.

'Wynwood,' the familiar voice said sleepily. In the background a female voice was asking who it was.

'Joss, it's Worrell Franklin.'

'Well, that's nice. I wait ten years for a call, and here it is – in the middle of the night.'

'It's urgent.'

'I suppose you've run out of Weetabix.'

Franklin grinned. 'Yeah. But that's not the reason for this particular call.'

'Shit. OK, let me take the phone through into the living room, so my friend here can get back to sleep.'

'Your *friend*?'

'We've been very friendly for some time now. We've even been thinking of honeymooning in the Turks and Caicos. At your expense, of course. How's Sibou?'

'Fine. She says hello.'

'OK, I'm stretched out on the sofa now. You can tell me all about it. If I start snoring, shout.'

Franklin took a deep breath. 'You remember Nick Russell?'

'The SBS captain.'

'Yep. He works here, or at least he did. He disappeared a week ago.'

'He what?'

Franklin went through the whole story one more time.

'Sounds bad,' Wynwood said, after he had finished, 'but how can I help?'

'Who's the CO at the moment?'

'Barney Davies still. They're putting him out to pasture soon, which'll be a pity.'

'You like him?'

'Yep. He's got a brain *and* a heart. Rare qualities in an Englishman.'

'Good.' Franklin found himself missing Wynwood's company. It would be great to see him on Provo . . .

'You want me to take this business to him,' the Welshman was concluding.

'I thought it would be worth a shot. Maybe he knows someone useful at the Foreign Office, or he can put some pressure on somewhere else. Maybe MI5, for fuck's sake. This is still British territory, even if the money's all American. London still has the final say, at least theoretically.'

'I'll do what I can, Frankie boyo. Now give me your number so I can get back to you.'

Franklin read out the endless digits. 'Any idea when you can see him?'

'Tomorrow. Or should I say this morning.'

'Thanks, Joss. And I'm glad you've finally found a real friend,' he added sardonically.

Seven hours later Wynwood was rapping on the office door of his Commanding Officer in the Stirling Lines barracks of 22 SAS Regiment. 'Enter!' came the cheerful reply from inside.

Lieutenant-Colonel Barney Davies was sitting behind his desk, a mug of tea in one hand and the *Daily Mirror* open in front of him. To one side sat a plate containing crumbs from a recently devoured rock cake. The CO smiled up at Wynwood, and gestured him into a seat. 'I can't believe these people,' he said, looking down at the paper. 'Isn't there anyone in the royal family who thinks about something other than sex?'

'The Queen Mum,' Wynwood suggested.

'Under forty, I meant.'

'Prince Harry?'

Davies grinned. 'I suppose you're a republican,' he said.

'Certainly not,' Wynwood said. 'If Wales has to be ruled by foreigners, I'd rather it was Germans and Greeks than the English.'

'Figures. So what can I do for you this morning?'

'I've had a distress call from the Caribbean. You remember Worrell Franklin.'

'Of course. It was a real loss to the Regiment when he called it a day.' He grimaced. 'We don't have so many ethnic-minority members we can afford to lose them, particularly when they're that good. And no,' he added, seeing the look on Wynwood's face, 'I don't think of the Welsh as an ethnic minority.'

Wynwood laughed.

'So what sort of distress is Franklin involved in?'

Wynwood told him, and got much the same response from the CO as he himself had given Franklin.

'I'll call a few people, but I don't hold out much hope,' Davies said. 'From what you say it looks as if checking out this Arcilla would involve tracking boats and helicopters across the Caribbean, not to mention investigating his businesses in the States. All of which would add up to a major operation, probably costing millions. No one in Whitehall is going to sanction that sort of expenditure just to find one missing ex-Marine.'

Wynwood looked glum. 'I know,' he said. 'But I can understand how Frankie feels.'

'So can I. I'll do what I can.'

'Thanks, boss.'

Once Wynwood had left, Davies ordered another mug of tea and thumbed through his unofficial list of useful official numbers, and noted several of them down. But the man who should be making most of the calls, Davies decided, was Russell's ex-CO. He called up his opposite number in Poole, the officer currently commanding the Special Boat Squadron of the Royal Marines, Lieutenant-Colonel Neil Colhoun.

The two men had not run into each other for several years, but not from any design. They had first met during planning for the Falklands campaign, and Davies had taken an immediate liking to the Scot, despite his stereotypically dour exterior. The liking had deepened with the discovery that, lurking beneath the forbidding mask, there was a warm and affectionate man with an almost impish sense of humour.

'Barney!' the familiar voice answered. 'So how's the competition doing?' he asked drily. 'Still working on those press releases?'

It was a standing joke among the SBS that their brethren in the SAS were prone to glorying in the spotlight of publicity. Though this, with rare exceptions, was far from the truth, the SBS did tend to be more concerned with preserving their anonymity.

'Paranoia is still rampant in Poole, eh?' Davies riposted.

'Aye. There's a rumour going round that the navy's going to be one of the prizes in the new National Lottery.'

'No one would enter,' Davies said.

Colhoun laughed. 'What do you want?' he asked.

Davies told him about Russell's disappearance and Franklin's call.

'You say Franklin was one of your best,' Colhoun said, all trace of flippancy gone. 'Well, Nick Russell was one of ours. He did a brilliant job in Hong Kong for us. Too good, really. He found something that moved him more than soldiering.'

'What was that?' Davies asked.

'Medicine. At least that's the precise answer. But caring for people in the widest sense. He spent almost two years working undercover in the refugee camps there, both Chinese and Vietnamese. His cover was as a medic, of course, and the cover gradually became more important than what it was covering. Not that he did less than a perfect job in both respects, you understand. But once it was over, it was the caring he missed, not the intelligence work. And when your lad offered him a job which allowed him to do both, and carry on a love affair with the sea, then we'd lost him.'

'Not the sort of man to just walk out on a job.'

'No. So what's next? The Foreign Office, I suppose.' Colhoun sounded about as enthusiastic as Davies felt.

'Brits missing abroad are their responsibility. And if you stress the former-hero angle, and find someone sympathetic, then maybe something will get done.'

'Aye, but what? A polite request to the local police commissioner. This doesn't sound like a situation where doing something will be cheap or easy.'

It was the same conclusion that Davies had reached himself. 'We can only try,' he said.

'For us there is only the trying; the rest is not our business,' Colhoun quoted.

'Bill Shankly?' Davies asked.

'T. S. Eliot.'

'It must be easier to find time to read on boats,' Davies suggested. 'How about we talk again this evening?'

'Fine,' Colhoun said. 'We can share our experiences of rejection.' He put the phone down and looked blankly into space for a moment, thinking about the last time he had seen the missing man. It had been at Russell's farewell party in a Hong Kong restaurant, the night before he flew back to England.

He exhaled noisily, got up and walked across to the window. The autumn sun was shining on Poole harbour, the myriad boats bobbing at anchor in the sluggish sea. In his time as the Commanding Officer of the SBS Neil Colhoun had lost several men, most of them in actions which had never received any publicity. In some cases even their wives had not been told all the circumstances of death.

That was bad enough, but somehow it seemed even

crueller to lose a man in such suspicious circumstances after he had left the SBS. There was no reason why men who had been through all the dangers implicit in such service should expect a quiet life thereafter, but it seemed like a fair arrangement to Colhoun. He went back to his desk and reached for the telephone.

For the next couple of hours he sought out potential sources of support in the Foreign Office, at the Admiralty, in the intelligence services, even at Scotland Yard, restricting himself to people who might be able to exert influence behind the scenes. Those capable of making a public stink – contacts in the press and politics – he decided to keep in reserve.

Everyone he spoke to was sympathetic, although in their voices he could hear echoes of his own pessimism. There was no point in exerting influence for its own sake – it had to be exerted in favour of some sort of action, and there was no chance of the Government sanctioning anything really meaningful. Not for one man.

By lunchtime Colhoun felt thoroughly depressed, and the feeling hung over him for the rest of the working day. It was only once he got back home, and found himself back in the usual mix of family problems – a sick dog, a tap that kept dripping, a son who wasn't doing enough homework – that Nick Russell's disappearance, and his own impotence in the face of it, was edged to the back of his mind.

He and Jenny were just sitting down to watch *Between the Lines* when the telephone rang. The caller announced himself as Robert Jacklin.

'Yes?' Colhoun said in an irritated tone, not recognizing the name.

'Junior Minister at the Foreign Office,' the man said smoothly. 'The problem you called about today . . .'

Colhoun's hopes rose. 'Nick Russell.'

'Yes . . .'

'Have you heard anything?'

'No. But there are . . . well, we would like you to attend a meeting tomorrow morning. Here in London, of course.' He gave Colhoun the time and place, and then abruptly said goodbye.

The SBS boss went back to the TV, wondering what devious reason the Foreign Office might have for actually helping someone.

5

The meeting place turned out to be a typically nondescript conference room somewhere in the bowels of the Whitehall government machine. Though machine was perhaps the wrong word, Colhoun thought, as he took his seat at the polished table with its glasses of water. It was more like an organism. One prone to torpor and sudden bursts of spite.

There were four other persons around the table. All men, of course, now that the Medusa had been exiled to the House of Lords. Robert Jacklin, who had called him the previous evening, was obviously in charge. He was a tall, saturnine man with thinning hair, glasses and a rather oily smile. He was also, as Colhoun had discovered from his morning *Times*, one of the rising stars of the ruling Conservative Party.

Jacklin looked anxiously at his watch and began by introducing the meeting's participants to each other. The two men across the table from Colhoun were Brian Findhorn and Gerald Branson, representing, respectively, MI5 and MI6. Findhorn looked like a TV policeman, Colhoun decided, vaguely harassed, overtired, on the verge of a belligerent outburst. Branson looked a bit like his famous namesake, fresh-faced, ex-public school, with a mouth not quite large enough for his teeth.

Another representative from the Foreign Office occupied the end of the table to Colhoun's right. His name was Hilary Smith, and he didn't look much more than twenty. He was nervously fiddling with the knot of his tie and brushing back an obstinate forelock of blond hair from his blue eyes.

The seat next to Colhoun was empty.

Jacklin looked at his watch again. 'I have another meeting in an hour,' he said, 'so I think we must start . . .'

The door behind him swung open to reveal a large, uniformed man with a mass of dark, tangled hair.

'Sergeant Wynwood?' Jacklin said. 'At last.'

'My train was half an hour late,' Wynwood explained. 'I blame impending privatization,' he added mischievously.

Jacklin had the grace to smile back. 'Maybe we can argue about that another time. Gentlemen,' he said, looking round the table, 'we are here to solve a puzzle, or perhaps just get a clear idea of what the puzzle is. Each of you has one of the pieces.' He smiled at everyone, as if expecting applause.

Colhoun remembered the newspaper article raving over his recent performance at the party conference.

'Sergeant Wynwood,' Jacklin was saying, 'if you could start the ball rolling by telling us what you know of the disappearance in the Turks and Caicos Islands.'

Wynwood went through what Franklin had told him, and as he spoke Smith took minutes in an impressive-looking shorthand. Colhoun wondered when the Foreign Office would discover the cassette recorder. Perhaps as they sat there, Q was inventing one in the basement below, unaware that they were on sale down the road at Dixons.

After Wynwood had finished, Colhoun was asked to give an appreciation of Russell. He did so, thinking that if he had been called all the way to London just for this, he would be exceedingly angry.

Jacklin then turned to the man from MI6. 'Eight days ago,' Branson began, reading from a notebook, 'a man was found murdered in his car in Florida. The car was sitting in a lay-by near Tampa Bay, and the man had been shot once through the forehead. His wallet had been stolen, and the detectives could find no identification. There was no luggage in the boot. There was, however, a novel in German in the man's jacket pocket, and a German–English phrasebook on the seat beside him.'

Branson looked up. 'So, at first glance the victim looked like one more European tourist who had been robbed and killed in friendly Florida. But the police didn't have a name for the victim, and when they tried to trace him through the car registration it turned out the plates had been stolen only the day before in Miami. So they either had a German tourist who was also a car thief, or something more mysterious. They started backtracking the dead man's journey.'

Branson looked around the table, just to make sure everyone was paying attention. Colhoun found that he was enjoying himself.

'There was one other clue,' Branson went on. 'An empty milk-shake container from the Burger King chain. The police started checking out the various franchises up and down the man's probable route, and soon got lucky. The man had stopped in a restaurant only ten miles to the north, and the woman who recognized his picture said he had told her he was a Russian. "From the other St Petersburg," she remembered him saying. And he had been carrying a brown attaché case.

'Now, since the man had eaten lunch there around noon and was travelling south, the police worked on the assumption that he had started out that morning from a point some three or four hours' drive to the north or west, and checked out all the hotels in that area for departing guests with Russian-sounding names. There were seventeen of them to choose from, and the dead man was eventually recognized from his photograph in one of the Disneyworld hotels. The name he had registered under was Aleksandr Tretchkin. According to US Immigration he had first arrived in the US some three weeks earlier.'

Branson paused, took a sip of water from the glass, and went back to the notebook. 'The FBI were called in, and eventually the CIA ran a photograph of the dead man through their computer at Langley and came up with a different name – Aleksandr Solayev. Solayev, it turned out, had been a commander in the Soviet Navy, a former military attaché in Havana, and one of the top names in naval craft design at the Naval Research Academy in Murmansk. He had specialized in miniature submarine and submersible technology.'

Hence the connection, Colhoun thought. This was getting interesting.

'US Immigration had one other useful piece of information,' Branson went on. 'Three days after arriving in the US, Solayev had left again, on an American Airlines flight to Providenciales in the Turks and Caicos Islands. He returned to Miami ten days later.'

Branson closed his notebook with a triumphant flourish.

'And all that from a strawberry milk shake,' Wynwood murmured.

'Your turn, Brian,' Jacklin told the MI5 man.

Findhorn had only a crumpled sheet of paper to compete with Branson's notebook, but in any case he hardly looked at it. 'The address Tretchkin – Solayev – gave the authorities on Provo was Fidel Arcilla's villa on Long Bay, so I think we can assume he had some connection with the submarine which Russell told the barman about. Our best guess is that it's a Soviet craft which the Russian somehow or other procured for Arcilla. Afterwards, either to keep the Russian's mouth shut or simply to avoid payment, Arcilla had him killed.'

'What do we know about this man?' Jacklin asked.

'I'm coming to that. First off, he's a British citizen, even though he was born in Cuba and lives mostly in the States. He became one in 1984, probably with the help of his friends in the Turks and Caicos government, the same ones who were implicated in the 1985 drug business . . .'

'Which business was that?' Colhoun asked. He had a vague memory of some Caribbean politicians being charged with drug smuggling, but no more than that.

'In 1985,' Findhorn said patiently, 'three members of the then government, including the Prime Minister, were arrested during a trip to Miami by the US authorities, and charged with conspiracy to import narcotics into the United States. What they had actually done was receive payment for turning a blind eye to drug runners using the islands as a refuelling stop. A lot of minor officials had also got in on the act, and great chunks of the administration had been compromised. The big three went to jail, and another three ministers were forced to resign the following year, allegedly for various improprieties, but basically for being part of the whole crooked set-up. The islands were governed from Whitehall in all but name for a couple of years, and since then things have slowly got back to normal. The Americans wanted a tougher law-enforcement system worked out between themselves and the locals, but the islanders were still feeling a bit too sensitive for that sort of interference, so the Yanks had to make do with access to local bank records for their drug investigations. Which brings us roughly up to date.' He looked round the table. 'And back to Fidel Arcilla. He was undoubtedly one of those involved in the smuggling operation back in 1985, though no evidence was ever discovered against him.'

'He seems to specialize in leaving no traces,' Wynwood remarked.

'He does. The only evidence was against the original three politicians, and as I said, they went to jail. We managed to get rid of a few more of their cronies by political means, but gangster-businessmen like Arcilla are only susceptible to the law. We had nothing on him, and he had spread enough money around, both in Florida and the islands, to buy himself a lot of useful friends, not to mention legal advice. A few years ago he even sued the Florida Drugs Enforcement Agency office for harassment and won.'

'What's his background?' Colhoun asked.

'We don't know that much. He was born in Cuba in 1959, about three weeks after Castro took the place over. Which is probably why his parents named him Fidel. He left Cuba in 1980, during the Mariel boat-lift, and took up . . .'

'What was the Mariel boat-lift?' Jacklin asked.

'The Americans had been demanding that Castro allow people to emigrate from Cuba, and for about six months he obliged them. He also used the opportunity to get rid of a few thousand convicts and mental patients. Arcilla was one of the convicts and, not surprisingly, it didn't take him long to get involved in the drugs trade.

Within a couple of years he was an important player. The FBI have been sending us information on his activities during the last few years. They want us to put him away.'

Finally Colhoun saw where this was all leading.

'What it all comes down to,' Findhorn concluded, 'is that the Americans smell more trouble. They think Arcilla is probably putting together another major drug operation, and using British territory as a base. They want us to either get in there and sort things out, or let them do it . . .'

'Needless to say, Her Majesty's Government prefers the former option,' Jacklin interjected.

Like Grenada, Colhoun thought sourly. 'I don't suppose you have any information on this Russian submarine's range,' he asked.

'No,' Findhorn and Branson answered simultaneously. 'But we have people looking into it,' Branson said. 'Inside Russia,' he added, as if expecting congratulations.

'Good,' Colhoun said. 'Because generally speaking, such craft have a very short range. Considerably shorter than five hundred miles, which, I believe, is roughly the distance between the Florida Keys and the Caicos Islands.'

'Maybe Arcilla has retired from the drugs business,' Wynwood suggested. 'Maybe he really is going after sea treasure. I should think it's a pretty competitive field, and Arcilla doesn't sound like a good loser. Maybe Nick Russell just saw something he wasn't supposed to.'

'Perhaps,' Jacklin said. 'We just don't know. So our first job is to find out.' He looked round at them all. 'We can't send police down there – it would cause too much of a political stink. If we learned anything from '85 it was that the islanders prefer their own corrupt officials to officials from London.

Whoever we do send will have to be sent undercover. That might sound like a job for intelligence, but in this case we've decided that certain factors make this inadvisable.' Jacklin looked straight at Colhoun. 'Because of the submarine angle, and the probable need for qualified divers, it has been decided that the SBS should handle at least the preliminary portion of the investigation.' He paused, as if he expected Colhoun to say something.

The SBS man simply nodded at him.

'Splendid. I would like a plan of action submitted by the end of the week if that's possible?'

'Certainly.' You can have it tomorrow, Colhoun thought.

'Your primary objective,' Jacklin continued, 'is to find out whether the Turks and Caicos Islands are again being used for drug-trafficking purposes. If you discover the answer to that question is yes, then we can go on from there.'

'I understand,' Colhoun said. He was already turning his mind to the question of whom to send.

'I think the four of us – excluding Sergeant Wynwood here – should meet again at the same time next Monday,' Jacklin concluded. He turned to Wynwood. 'Sergeant, thank you for coming,' he said, and offered his hand with what looked like genuine warmth, before disappearing out the door.

The intelligence men followed him, skipping down the stairs side by side. Colhoun and Wynwood descended at a more leisurely pace.

'You'll probably need an SAS adviser on this trip,' Wynwood suggested.

Colhoun grinned at him. 'And what sort of adviser would that be?'

'Oh, you know. How to do things, when to do them. What to do once you've done them.'

'We do all that ourselves. But I might consider buying you a drink if you're good.'

'I'm good.'

They found a pub just past the National Gallery, in the lanes behind Leicester Square tube. Colhoun asked Wynwood about Franklin, and heard the story of their week together in the Gambia. 'He's a nice man, and a straight one. You remember in the old movies when they say someone's a real white man – well, that's Frankie, except that he's black.'

'And a good soldier.'

'No doubt about that. I think becoming a good soldier was one of the few things he found easy in life.'

'I'll need his phone number on the island,' Colhoun said, 'but if you could call him tonight and let him know . . .' The SBS man stopped to think for a minute, and took a sip on his pint. 'If you told him a couple of your friends were arriving on the island in a few days, and would like to contact him, would he catch on?'

Wynwood looked surprised for a moment, then nodded to himself. 'I suppose the clinic lines might be bugged,' he agreed. 'But don't worry, I'll make sure he gets the message.'

After the two men parted, Neil Colhoun walked up Long Acre to Stanfords map shop. There he purchased the best map and most comprehensive guide to the Turks and Caicos Islands he could find. It might be that official sources would come up with something better, but experience had taught Colhoun not to be optimistic in such matters. On the journey back to Poole he read the guide book and then sat watching Hampshire go by, wondering how many men to send.

By the time the train pulled into Poole Station he had decided on two. It was off-season in the Turks and Caicos, and the resident population of Providenciales was only about five thousand. A larger group of men might be noticeable. And if it turned out that more were needed, then more could always be dispatched.

As for the two, they more or less chose themselves. This was a far from purely military mission, and his men would be up against an enemy whose tentacles stretched through several countries. They would probably not be able to trust the local authorities. What Colhoun needed was a pair of soldier-diver-detectives, men who embodied the highest aspirations of the Special Boat Squadron. 'Not by strength – by guile' was the SBS motto, but sometimes both were needed in equal amounts. On land, at sea and in the deeps.

Back in his office he asked for the service files of Captain Callum Marker and Lieutenant Robert Cafell, albeit more from a desire to be thorough than from any real need. Colhoun knew all his men's military records off by heart, and as much about their personal lives as a commanding officer needed to, given that his was the responsibility for sending them out on such dangerous missions.

The Poole classroom that was used for the film test was, as intended, overheated and lacking any compensatory ventilation. Even Callum Marker was having trouble staying awake, and he, unlike the twenty or so Marines with their eyes glued to the screen, wasn't struggling into the fourth day of the SBS pre-selection course.

On the screen an open lorry was being loaded with green oil drums by three men, while a fourth man sat on the wall to one side, smoking a cigarette. A selection of red, green, yellow and black drums were gathered in the road in front of him. Once the greens were loaded the idle man joined one of the others in beginning to unload them again, while two men rested on the wall. One of these then joined the two workers to load up the red and yellow drums. This accomplished the yellows were removed by all four men and replaced with a mixture of blacks and greens by three of them.

And so on. The suspense was hardly killing, but there was no doubt the film offered a good test, not only of the applicant's powers of observation and concentration, but also of his determination to succeed. These men were midway through their fourteen-day nightmare, and had already yomped through most of Dorset with fifty-five-pound bergens on their backs, spent nights under piles of wet leaves which lacked a Michelin rating, and enjoyed long, kit-encumbered night swims in the waters of Poole Bay. Before entering this classroom none of them had slept for forty-eight hours.

Those who got through the fourteen days would be given a further fifteen weeks of assorted tortures to endure. The lucky ones who graduated would move on to eleven weeks of 'trade' training, which included all the advanced techniques and skills required of a fully-fledged SBS Marine. He would learn signal skills, beach reconnaissance, demolition and sabotage, anti-terrorist drills. He would parachute into Arctic seas. His diving, canoeing and weapon-handling skills would be further honed. And at the end of it all he would graduate as a Swimmer-Canoeist Third Class, and be graciously granted leave to serve an eighteen-month probationary period as a member of the SBS.

After that he would be expected to go for Swimmer-Canoeist Second Class, and then First Class, and then the Senior Command Course.

It was a hell of a long climb, Marker thought, as he watched the sea of blinking eyes and yawning mouths in front of him. Thirteen years earlier he had sat in this same room, watching this same dumb film. A lot had happened in the intervening years, including his ascent of the SBS totem pole. The Falklands, the North Sea oil rigs, Hong Kong. He must have seen a thousand movies. He had met and loved and lost Penny.

He closed his eyes for a second, and heard the rattle of the ancient projector change gear. The film was over. He got up, turned on the lights, and started handing out the question papers.

'I was waiting for the naked lady to leap out of the drum,' a tired voice complained.

Marker smiled. 'I'm sure most of you will spend your lives waiting for a naked lady,' he said sympathetically. He placed the last question paper on the last desk and walked back to the front of the classroom. 'You have fifteen minutes,' he said. 'And remember to put your names on the paper.'

At the end of the allotted time he had to nudge three of the examinees awake. Most of the collected papers were covered with barely legible scrawls.

Marker unloaded the projector as the Marines filed out, en route to a shorter rest period than the one they were expecting. Only about a quarter of these men would be accepted for further training, but there was certainly no shame in not being one of them. Marker remembered a visitor from the SEALs – America's SBS equivalent – who had watched the training programmes slack-jawed in awe.

Maybe they were too hard. Marker himself thought so, and having passed them all he felt able to say so. Good men were having good days and all the luck they needed, while better men were making one mistake and failing.

He locked up the projector in the cupboard, and wondered yet again whether to press for something truly revolutionary like a VCR. But you could hardly move around Poole these days without someone moaning about how tight money was, so it probably wasn't worth the hassle. He reluctantly picked up the pile of exam papers and headed for the door.

Outside the day had greyed over, and the wind was rustling the waters of the harbour. It was going to rain, Marker decided. Maybe he wouldn't go into Bournemouth that evening. Maybe he'd stay at home, cook himself something nice, and watch TV. Sooner or later he had to get used to her not being there.

A couple of buildings down from the projection room, Rob Cafell was sitting at a drawing board, pencil between his teeth, studying the sketches he had made over the last half hour. He was alone in the room, and about the only thing in it which looked even vaguely military. Any unwitting outsider who stumbled in through the door would be forgiven for assuming he was in an art college.

Strictly speaking, Rob Cafell had no right to be there. The room was the preserve of the Marines' Illustrators Branch, whose remit included the supply of maps and plans from aerial photographs, and any three-dimensional models of terrain, installations and vehicles which the Corps might meet in the course of fulfilling its military duties. Few solo activities pleased

Rob Cafell more than drawing maps or making models, but unfortunately officers were barred from the Illustrators – supposedly too busy learning how to command – and the time he spent there could only be his own. He had helped out the regulars often enough on urgent projects for no one to mind his using either the premises or the modelling supplies.

That afternoon he had begun planning a model of the sister freighters recently converted for the shipment of high-grade plutonium from British and French reprocessing plants to Japan. The two vessels had originally been American, but a Belfast shipyard had converted them for their new role, strengthening the hatches and removing cranes, converting a high proportion of previous cargo space into extra fuel capacity, creating more accommodation for armed guards, and upgrading all the ships' electronics. The problem for the modeller, as was usual where asymmetrical craft were concerned, lay in providing a clear enough picture of the ships' innards without destroying all sense of what they looked like from the outside.

There was a very good reason for this particular job – if one of these ships was ever hijacked by terrorists the model's availability for planning purposes would save a considerable amount of time. But Cafell didn't really need the excuse. He loved the whole process, from the research through the planning to the manufacture and the painting – all of it. He had always been good with his hands – it saved him using his brain, his mother had always said – and he had been making models of ships as long as he could remember. Both his parents' house in Plymouth and his own flat in Poole were filled with them. His innocent invitation to 'come up and see my Dreadnought' had long since passed into local legend. And still made him blush whenever he thought about it.

That had been a long time ago, he told himself. Almost ten years. He was over thirty now, and these days felt almost as comfortable with women as he did with men. He had always felt comfortable with his date for the evening, but then Ellen had always been a friend before. It was probably going to be a bit strange for both of them.

He looked up at the clock, and realized he should be on his way. But the sketches caught his eye again, and he started thinking about the problems an assault group would have in surprising terrorists on one of these ships. If the terrorists had any sense at all, it would be bloody difficult. There was every chance the plutonium would end up in the ocean.

Maybe his mum was right, Cafell thought. They should just ditch nuclear power altogether. His dad, who until recently had captained one of the Royal Navy's nuclear submarines, had other ideas.

It was time to go. He packed the sketches away in the drawer he always used, and opened the door just as a young Marine was raising a hand to knock.

'Lieutenant Cafell, sir,' the young man said. 'Lieutenant-Colonel Colhoun wants to see you.'

'Now?'

'Yes, boss.'

Cafell and Marker reached Colhoun's door at almost the same moment.

'Any idea what this is about?' Cafell asked.

Marker shook his head and rapped on the door.

'Yes,' Colhoun said.

Inside they found the CO poring over a map of the

Turks and Caicos. Underneath it was a larger scale map of the seas to the south and south-east of the continental United States. It looked promising, Marker thought.

'I've sent for tea,' Colhoun said, sitting back down in his famously tattered leather chair. At that moment an orderly arrived with three mugs of steaming tea and a plate full of Kit-Kats.

'If only the enlisted men could see this,' Marker said wryly.

Colhoun smiled at him. 'I've got a job for you two,' he said. 'In the sunshine.'

'Sounds ominous,' Marker said, but the sudden sense of inner excitement belied his tone of voice.

'Either of you two remember Nick Russell?' Colhoun asked. 'He left us in '86.'

'Only by reputation,' Cafell said. 'Before my time.'

'I knew him by sight,' Marker said. 'Curly-headed guy with an innocent-looking face, like Rob here.'

'That's Russell,' Colhoun agreed. He reached under the maps and extracted two copies of the minutes of the meeting he had attended that morning, which Hilary Smith had faxed through to him an hour or so earlier.

The two SBS officers started reading, and Colhoun watched their curiosity deepen as the pages turned. The two of then looked so dissimilar, the CO thought, and not just in the obvious sense. Certainly Marker was dark, wiry and brown-eyed, Cafell big, blond and blue-eyed, but that only touched the surface. It was all in the facial expression, Colhoun decided. Next to Cafell's open, trusting face Marker's looked almost haunted. They were almost like Lenny and George from *Of Mice and Men*, he thought, only in their case the differences were those of temperament rather than mental acumen. Both these men were supremely competent.

'Comments?' he asked, once they were both finished.

'Just the two of us?' Marker asked.

'For the moment.'

'So basically, we have to check out this Arcilla's boat, submarine and chopper? If he's running drugs he has to be using one or more of them.'

'Right.'

'But none of them are on the island at the moment.'

'That's true. And it may not be drugs. He could be laundering drug money. He could be hunting for treasure.'

'We might find the *Santa Lucia*,' Cafell suggested.

'The what?'

'It's one of the most famous of the Spanish galleons which have never been found. It was carrying more than ten million in gold when it went down south of the Keys.'

'I might have known you'd be up on this stuff,' Marker murmured. 'We'll be needing a boat of our own, not to mention a submarine and access to either a chopper or a light plane.'

'There's a frigate permanently on patrol in the Caribbean,' Colhoun said, 'and the base in Belize has Kleppers and submersibles. I'll get on to the Admiralty tomorrow, and try and persuade them to do a little chauffeuring for us. If that's not on, then we'll have to fly them out from here somehow. As for a boat, you can hire one on Provo according to this' – he indicated the guide book – 'and hiring one will look less suspicious. It's not going to be easy slipping you a submersible and a couple of canoes without getting the whole island talking.'

'With any luck we won't need them,' Cafell said. 'Look at the range we've got here. It's over five hundred miles to the nearest US coast – they can't be running a small submarine there from the islands.'

'And they sure won't be canoeing that sort of distance,' Marker added thoughtfully. 'What about weaponry?' he asked Colhoun.

'No firearms are allowed on the island. And since you're going in as tourists . . .'

'We'll have to be extremely cunning,' Marker completed the thought.

'We'll get you handguns at least.'

'We'll need a couple of MP5s, a couple of harpoon guns,' Marker insisted. 'And some stun grenades might come in handy. Arcilla and his chums don't sound like nice people.'

Colhoun smiled. 'I'll do what I can,' he promised.

'What about the Yanks?' Cafell asked.

'If the trail leads into their territory – and the way they see it their territory includes just about anything within two hundred miles of their coastline – then we'll have to come to some sort of arrangement with the US Navy, Coast Guard and Customs Service. Shouldn't be a problem – they're the ones who want us to do something about Arcilla.'

'So when do we leave?' Marker asked.

'I don't know yet. There's no great urgency – if Russell's still alive he's not likely to be in imminent danger. But there's no point in hanging around, either. So as soon as everything's in place . . .'

'One thing, boss,' Marker said. 'There's nothing in these minutes about rescuing Nick Russell.'

'I know. If he's still alive, then Russell may have struck it lucky. Because there's no way Whitehall would have agreed to send out a rescue mission just for him. As it is . . .'

'We consider him an SBS priority,' Marker said.

Colhoun nodded. 'Any more questions, gentlemen?'

There were none.

'Well, start clearing your personal decks then. Callum, I'd like a word with you.'

Marker looked surprised but sank back into his seat.

Cafell paused in the doorway. 'Nine o'clock tomorrow morning in the mess?' he asked Marker.

'Fine.'

Cafell shut the door behind him.

Colhoun sighed and looked out of the window. Thanks to the grey sky it was almost dark already. 'I don't want to butt in on your personal business,' he began.

'But you're going to anyway.' Marker smiled. 'That's OK. I've got no secrets from myself.'

'I imagine you're going through a rough time.'

Marker shrugged. 'Sounds about right. Beats being in Rwanda though.'

Colhoun persisted. 'A job like this might be a good way of drawing a line under the past. Or it might be you're not ready to do that, and the past might get in the way of the job.'

Marker raised an eyebrow. 'Did you rehearse that, boss?' he asked.

Colhoun smiled in spite of himself. 'I just want you to think about it for twenty-four hours.'

'OK, but there's no need. I miss my wife, no doubt about that. But it won't get in the way. And I don't think I believe in drawing lines under anything. You can hide the past away, but you can't get rid of it. And if you do hide it away, it just makes it easier to repeat your mistakes.'

Colhoun simply nodded.

Marker smiled at him, got to his feet, and took his leave.

The CO leaned back in his chair, going over his earlier thoughts on his pairing of the two men. With any luck they were not only different, but almost complementary. Two sides of a single coin – probably the best currency he had.

6

The sound of the approaching helicopter jerked Russell out of his doze. He lay there with his eyes closed, trying to bring back the dream. Emelisse Alabri had been walking along the street, looking back over her shoulder as if she thought she was being followed. He supposed it had been himself doing the following. Strangest of all had been the location: the local shopping street in Twickenham, where he had grown up.

The helicopter was landing now, on the area of cleared ground which was otherwise used as a baseball diamond. It was the fifth such arrival in the ten days Russell had been on Tortuga, but he had no idea of who or what was being brought in or taken out. He supposed it might be a good idea to find out, but he seemed unable to shake off the mental lassitude which had afflicted him ever since the chloroforming. The causes of this might well be in part physical, but, even if so, Russell had no doubt they were also partly psychological. The more he found out about his new home, the more despairing he felt.

As yet he had not been obliged to do anything more than familiarize himself with the medical procedures. Emelisse had escorted him around the camp, showing him the dormitories where the orphans slept and the dusty space beneath the coconut palms where they went to school. She had not bothered to point out the security features, but then there had been no need to. The walls were real enough, and so were the Kalashnikov AK47s carried by the T-shirt-wearing guards. The atmosphere was not oppressive – two Kalashnikovs had provided the goalposts for an ongoing game of football – and in a way this made things seem even more depressing. The dreadful normality of the whole place made Russell almost want to cry.

After the camp, the hospital had been a revelation. Here everything – technical equipment, instruments, clothing, furnishings – was spotless and new. Nearly all of it was American-manufactured, and as far as Russell could tell no expense had been spared in procuring the best. Even the small outpatient clinic, where Emelisse did her best to function as a normal doctor, was well equipped, presumably as part of the bargain she had made with Joutard's devil.

The guided tour had taken place during his third day in the camp, and he had not seen much of her since. One day she had come by with some books in French, and pointed out sections which she said he should familiarize himself with. The books had all been printed in Paris, and one bore the inscription 'for Emelisse, with love from Jean-Pierre, August 17, 1983.' Russell had asked her if she had ever been to France; she had told him that was where she had studied medicine. He had wanted to ask her more, but the look in her eyes had not been encouraging.

He tried to remember what she had been wearing in his dream. He had only ever seen her in the white coat, and he didn't think it had been that.

His watch said it was almost five o'clock – another hour and he could go in search of food. He got up and removed the Rachmaninov tape from the cassette recorder, and looked through his deceased predecessor's collection once more. Brahms, he decided. If he stayed *chez Joutard* long enough he might even grow to like the stuff.

It was time he gave some serious thought to getting out of the bloody place. He couldn't believe escape from the camp itself would pose any serious problems, but getting himself beyond Joutard's reach probably would. The first thing he needed was a precise fix on where he was, and work out a few options for . . .

The rap on the outside door was swiftly followed by the appearance of Emelisse in the living-room doorway. 'Time to go,' she said.

'Where?'

She was already halfway out of the door. 'To work,' she said over her shoulder.

He hurried after her. This was the moment he had been dreading. Even if everything went right, and he found he could do what was needed, there was still the overwhelming sense of wrongness. As they walked briskly across the camp towards the hospital he told himself once more that a single kidney operating at fifty per cent of its full capacity could perform all the blood-cleaning operations necessary to a normal healthy adult.

It might be true, but it begged more questions than he had answers for.

He followed Emelisse in through the hospital doors, feeling like he was stepping out of one world and into another. These rooms, with their shiny machines and sterile furnishings and efficient air-conditioning, belonged to the rich man's world. It was only a freak of geography that had placed them here. That and the warped logic of global supply and demand.

Two young Haitian women were already scrubbing up

in the washroom, chattering to each other in a language Russell didn't understand. They couldn't be much older than fourteen, he decided, and the pale-blue smocks they were wearing made them look like boarding-school girls getting ready for bed.

One of the other two doctors – the only other European in the camp, an overweight Frenchman named Bodin – was examining himself in the mirror. Seeing Emelisse appear behind him he muttered something sarcastic under his breath. She ignored him, and he turned to leave, casting red-rimmed eyes in Russell's direction as he did so. The Englishman could smell brandy on the man's breath.

He and Emelisse scrubbed their hands with the iodized soap, tied each other's smocks, and went through into the room set up for surgery. The line of four parallel operating tables made it looked like an updated set for the TV series *MASH*. On three of them naked bodies were laid out on sheets. On the far table the last doctor, a bald, middle-aged Hispanic man with a small thin moustache, was already at work.

'Forty minutes,' he told Emelisse. She nodded. 'We'll start in ten,' she told the others.

'Why not now?' Russell asked.

'So that we all finish at roughly the same time,' she said.

That made sense. Russell looked across the room, and suddenly realized that though the two unattended patients were hooked up to tubes, needles and various monitoring sensors the one on the far end was not.

'What's Calderón doing?' Russell asked Emelisse.

'Harvesting,' she said coldly. 'The boy died a couple of hours ago. The helicopter brought in the body.'

'Harvesting what?' Russell asked.

'Kidneys, corneas and as much bone tissue as he can manage in the time.'

'Why not the heart and the liver?' Russell asked, though he thought he already knew the answer. Somehow it felt better talking than simply watching.

'The time factor, I assume.' She seemed nervous too. 'They wouldn't survive the journey.'

'How long does a heart last?'

'I don't know exactly. Six hours? Something like that.'

'And kidneys?'

'More like thirty-six.'

That made sense, Russell thought. Unless they were flying them into the US, which would surely be too risky. Of course, for all he knew the organs were being supplied to some private clinic on another island.

'Why bone . . .' he started to ask, but his voice dried up. Across the room the Puerto Rican doctor had just lifted the kidneys from the dead boy, still with the main vessels attached, and was carrying them across to the table nearby, where a pan of cold solution was waiting to wash off the blood. He then placed the kidneys in a clear plastic box about ten inches square, one of four in a row which sat on a slightly larger box surrounded in blue casing. These were perfusion machines, whose task was to pump cool preservative through the detached organs until they were transplanted into another patient.

Four boxes for four doctors, Russell thought. If the time factor was tight, then the more operations they could perform simultaneously, the more profit per delivery.

And the more lives could be saved, said another voice inside his head. More people with their sight restored. All

Americans, no doubt. All rich by the world's standards. But human beings nevertheless.

The doors behind swung open, and two trolleys were rolled in, each carrying an unconscious young Haitian. One was a boy, one a girl. Russell guessed they were both about sixteen.

They were transferred on to the operating tables, the cotton shifts they were wearing undone and left hanging down towards the floor.

The Frenchman and one of the nurses took up position on either side of the boy, leaving the girl for Emelisse and the other nurse. Russell stood behind the doctor's shoulder, and set himself to concentrate on something for the first time in ten days. He was about to receive his first and last lesson in safely removing a kidney from a live donor.

Emelisse lost no time, making the major incision with an electric scalpel that cauterized the blood vessels as it cut through the thin layers of fat and muscle. Then she used retractors to ease the kidney into view from its position behind the liver in the abdominal cavity.

So far it all seemed pretty straightforward, Russell thought, and said so.

'It is not a difficult operation,' she said. 'But it does require care. One little mistake and you can traumatize an artery or abrade the renal vein. The patient can die, particularly with the sort of after-care we have here.'

She asked the nurse to wipe her brow, and took a long, searching look at the pulsing kidney and the area around it. 'See here,' she told Russell, 'we have to clamp these, cut through them here and here, cut through the ureter exactly here, lift out the kidney and then suture everything back together again.'

'Just a plumbing problem,' he said, more lightly than he felt.

He watched her do it all. After the kidney had been removed and placed in its clear plastic box she began the delicate work of restoration. She had good hands for such work, he thought. Nimble, steady hands. There was no doubt that it was tiring work, but she only stopped once to flex her fingers before the final stitching together of the original incision.

Glancing across at her, Russell saw the skin stretched tight across her cheek-bones, the lips drawn rigidly together. It was as if she had drained the tension out of her fingers by pouring it into her face.

Midway through the process the nurses had carried out the three boxes and their four kidneys, and as the last stitches were threaded Russell heard the helicopter taking off into the night. He looked down at the face of the unconscious girl and felt as if he was seeing it for the first time.

Emelisse either followed his gaze or read his mind. 'When they remove organs in America the surgeon never sees the donor's face,' she said.

'I think this is better,' Russell said.

She looked at him, and for the first time her expression towards him seemed to soften slightly. Then she turned away and told the nurses to take over. They re-wrapped the girl in her cotton gown and wheeled her away on a trolley to join the boy in the recovery room.

Emelisse and Russell undid each other and washed once more.

'Will you have a drink with me?' he asked.

She shrugged. 'Why not.'

Outside, darkness had long since fallen, but the breeze from the sea had not yet picked up, and the air seemed hot and sticky. A huge yellow moon had just emerged above the palms in front of them, and drums resounded from across the camp.

'I always hated World Music,' Russell murmured.

'They're burying the boy,' she said, starting to walk towards his bungalow. There was nothing accusatory in her tone, but she had a knack of making him feel in the wrong.

'What's left of him,' he said.

'If people have souls, I expect his managed to get wherever it was supposed to go.'

He sighed and changed the subject. 'Why bone tissue?' he asked. 'Is it worth that much?'

'You must be kidding,' she said. 'Fresh powdered bone sells for about $200 a gram. That's four times more than the street value of cocaine.'

'*Powdered* bone?' He suddenly remembered the noise he had heard through the wall during the operations – it had sounded like a coffee grinder. 'What's it used for?'

'Mostly replacing skeletal areas that have had to be removed, usually because they're cancerous. Lengthening deformed spines. Dental work. There are hundreds of uses.'

'How long does it last?'

'I don't know. Long enough, obviously. Calderón has an expensive toy next door for freeze-drying it.'

'What brought him here – just greed?'

'Mostly, but not just. Curiosity. He's a researcher at heart.'

'So was Mengele.'

She sighed. 'Calderón was disbarred in Puerto Rico.'

'What for?'

'He hasn't said. Illegal abortions would be my guess.'

'And Bodin – what's his excuse?'

They had reached his door. He reached to push it open for her, but she beat him to it.

'Take a seat,' he offered, as she walked into the main room ahead of him. 'What would you like to drink? Comrade Joutard has supplied me with rum, whisky and beer. Haitian beer, I'm afraid.'

'Whisky,' she said.

He poured two glasses and took one over to her. She was slumped on the sofa, eyes closed, looking utterly exhausted.

'You need some sleep,' he advised.

She half smiled. 'Tell me something I don't know.'

He sat down opposite her. 'What about Bodin? Where does he come from?'

'Martinique, he says. He's just a pig. I've always had the feeling that he's wanted by the police, but he's never admitted it. He just drinks and lusts after the girls. So far, the boys have been pretty good at protecting them.'

'That reminds me,' Russell said. 'I thought organs for transplants had to be tissue-matched, or the chances of rejection got too high.'

'The ones we send are tissue-matched. All the boys and girls here have been typed. The two we operated on today are good matches for the recipients, whoever they might be.'

'You mean there's a shopping list?'

'You could call it that.'

He stared into his glass for a moment, then raised his head. 'And what about you?' he asked. 'Were you struck off? Are you on the run?'

'You know why I'm here.'

'I don't know how you got here. How come your English is so good? Were you born here?'

'In Port au Prince. My mother was French, my father

is African. Our family wasn't socially acceptable, but we had plenty of money. I went to medical school in Paris, and while I was away my mother died. My father moved to America with my two brothers, and I joined them there. I worked in a Boston hospital for four years.'

'Why did you come back?'

'There's one doctor to every three hundred people in Boston, about one to every six thousand here.'

It was the sort of answer Sibou would have given him. The two of them obviously had more in common than being beautiful. 'So how did you get tied up with Joutard?' he asked.

'That's a long story,' she said, looking at her watch and getting wearily to her feet. 'And maybe I'll tell you it some other time. Right now I should be looking in on the two children.'

'You and Dr Bodin.'

'Dr Bodin is not a great believer in post-operative care.'

'Do you want any help?'

'No. But thanks for the drink.'

The screen door slammed shut behind her. Russell poured himself another glass of Joutard's whisky and sat back down again. The drums seemed to have fallen silent, and the only sounds from outside were the chirping of the crickets and the hum of a distant conversation. He wondered where the helicopter was now, and where it was headed. Somewhere out there four people who spent a lot of their life on dialysis machines were about to get another shot at normality. Two more people would probably get the chance to see again. As for the bone . . . well, that was worth four times its weight in cocaine.

If he tried to escape there was no chance she would

come with him. And if he failed he might well end up on Dr Calderón's table, minus both kidneys and corneas, his bones compacted for transport in a jar.

Russell wondered if they'd play the drums for him. As if in answer, the mesmerizing rhythms started up again somewhere in the darkness outside.

Four days after their summons to the CO's office in Poole, Callum Marker and Rob Cafell found themselves between flights in Miami Airport, with three hours to waste before their connection departed for Providenciales. Cafell had bought himself a paperback history of the SEALs in Vietnam, and was devouring it with his usual single-mindedness, apparently oblivious to the fact that the plastic seat on which he was sitting had been designed by either a Martian or a sadist. Marker, meanwhile, was prowling through the waiting and shopping areas, reminding himself that there were few places on earth he hated more than modern airports.

It was because they were the negation of travel, he thought. He and Cafell had come five thousand miles and everything looked the same, smelt the same. The same products were on sale, even the same foods. 'Home of Whopper values' one sign told him. That just about summed it up.

Cheer up, he told himself – you'll soon be eating conch stew beside the shining sea. At least that was what the brochures had promised them.

The wait seemed endless, but at least the American Airlines flight was called on time. The plane was only two-thirds full, and both men managed to grab window seats, from which they watched Miami Beach and the setting sun fall away behind them. Within a few minutes they were flying over the Bimini Islands, and soon after that the first of the Bahamas. The ocean below seemed crowded with boats.

They flew east into the approaching night. Not much more than an hour later their plane was touching down on the runway of what seemed an almost deserted airport. Marker felt a sense of pleasure walking down the steps on to the tarmac – it was so much nicer than being sucked into a terminal building by one of those telescopic corridors. A hundred yards away the lights of the two-storey terminal building beckoned, but in every other direction there was only darkness. Benidorm it wasn't.

The two men went through passport control, and then collected their luggage before going through customs. The officer simply waved them through, which rather devalued all the effort they had put into creating an inspection-proof hide for the handguns inside their diving gear.

Outside, a line of taxis, and only taxis, was waiting. Marker, who had done some overland travelling in South-east Asia during stints in Hong Kong and Brunei, recognized a monopoly when he saw one, and cheerfully accepted the quoted price for transport to their hotel.

'That's a fortune,' Cafell muttered behind him.

'You want to walk five miles?' Marker asked. They had now been up for about eighteen hours, and he felt exhausted.

'Not a lot.'

'Well, get in then.'

They both got in, leaving the driver muttering about how much gear they had. He then leaned against his bonnet for a while, presumably hoping for more passengers, but eventually accepted that none was coming.

The drive took about twenty minutes, and offered little indication of what the island looked like. They passed through two small shopping centres but the rest was darkness, until the taxi breasted a low hill and a shimmering ocean filled the windscreen. The Coconut Cove Hotel – one of the newest on the island – sprawled along low cliffs above a wide, sandy beach, and a grove of the relevant palms stood just beside the men's allotted cabin.

Inside it the rooms were clean and pleasantly furnished.

'You can have the bedroom,' Marker said. 'I'll take the convertible couch here.'

'You want to watch TV in bed, don't you?'

'Privilege of rank.'

By the time they'd unpacked it was gone eight. They walked up to the hotel restaurant, looked at the menu, and realized that they had already had enough meals that day. A pint in the bar seemed like a better idea, but even that was hard to finish.

'I'm going to call it a day,' Marker decided, with two inches of beer still waiting. 'Gonk is calling,' he added, using the Marine slang for sleep.

'We're not going to call Franklin tonight?' Cafell asked, after looking round to make sure no one was in earshot. Feeling a trifle paranoid, he reminded himself who they were probably up against, and how easy it would be to get seduced by the atmosphere of this place into relaxing their guard.

'We'll call him tomorrow,' Marker said. 'Take the day to get acclimatized, and see him in the evening.'

'I hope he has some ideas,' Cafell said, 'because we haven't.'

'Speak for yourself,' Marker countered with a grin.

'If all else fails we can always use you as bait. You see *Jurassic Park*?'

'No.'

'Well, everyone remembers the goat.'

It was only about five in the morning when Marker woke up. Ten in the morning in England, he reminded himself.

His partner seemed to have adapted more quickly. Marker had to pass through the bedroom on his way to and from the bathroom, but Cafell didn't stir, unless an almost melancholy whistling sound counted as such.

Marker dressed, left a note saying he'd be back by nine and went out. The sun was rising above the island, and he managed to coax one of the kitchen staff into supplying him with a premature cup of coffee. Down by the hotel's small jetty a number of boats were tied up – rowing boats, paddle boats and canoes. They had to be there for the use of guests, Marker told himself. None of the rowing boats had any visible oars, but someone had been carelessly kind enough to leave a paddle in one of the canoes.

Murmuring mental thanks to this unknown benefactor, Marker stepped in and cast off. The water was smooth and, as became increasingly apparent with the brightening light, almost unbelievably clear. Once he was out a couple of hundred yards Marker just let the canoe drift, and watched the sun rise across the low hills of the island, turning the waters to a shade of turquoise which any kingfisher would have envied.

After all the hustle and bustle of the last few days, and particularly the frenetic boredom of ten hours' flying the day before, sitting in the gently bobbing canoe felt like the most relaxing massage for the soul anyone could have devised.

He had always felt calmed by the sea. Calmed and comforted. Often challenged, but never threatened. Ever since he was a small boy Marker had cherished the feeling that the sea was his real home.

He had grown up in north London's Highgate, or at least that was where the house the family called home was situated. Both his parents were actors, and fairly successful ones at that, if almost continuous employment could be so called. Neither was famous, although both by now had the vaguely familiar faces of people who had been playing small parts on TV for the best part of thirty years. During Marker's childhood most of their work had been in the theatre, and he had been packed away to boarding school as soon as he was old enough. His most abiding memories of the time were the long summer holidays spent beside the sea, at the resorts where his parents were appearing. The evenings had been spent backstage, the days with the sea, swimming or sailing with his father.

Public school had been an isolating experience. He was tough enough for the school thugs to give him a wide berth, but uninterested in either academic work or team sports. It was only in the Navy cadets that he discovered challenges of lasting interest, and the school had at least shown the sense to encourage his already prodigious skill as a swimmer and diver.

At fourteen, after seven years at the school, he had been brought back to London by his parents. Their work was now almost exclusively in TV or the capital's theatre, and at last the house in Highgate became something of a home. Marker was sent to the local comprehensive, where he found a world utterly different from any he had previously known. His school work didn't improve much, but he found his new schoolmates a much more interesting bunch than the ones he had left behind. For a time other loves like music and films and girls vied with the sea for his attention, but when it came time to leaving school there was no real conflict in his mind. Marker's ambition was to work at sea, and of all the options he considered, joining the Marines seemed the one with the most potential. And once that was decided, he knew he would settle in the end for nothing less than the best – the SBS.

First, of course, he had needed to make the grade as a Royal Marines officer. Marker could remember the first day as clear as yesterday, clearer in fact. He had arrived at the training centre in South Devon on a sunny September morning, and realized that most of the other young men around him were much more nervous than he was. Even some of the ones who had come straight from university had looked lost and lonely. Not for the first or the last time, Marker had appreciated the edge his childhood had given him when it came to self-reliance.

But, as he had found out much later, there had also been a price. The inner-directedness which made him such a proficient SBS officer also made it hard for him to share his life. In one of their final rows Penny had told him she had only stayed for the sex. Their bed was the only place in which he knew how to give of himself.

She had probably been right, Marker thought, as the canoe drifted slowly out from shore. He had been selfish – there was no doubt of that. She had wanted them to have a child, and he had wanted to wait until they were permanently settled in one place. He hadn't wanted to do to his own children what his parents had done to him.

Penny had understood, but that was all. She hadn't

agreed. And now she was gone. And he was sitting in a canoe on a turquoise sea feeling sorry for himself.

'Fuck a pig,' he muttered to himself, and took charge of the canoe's direction again, turning it in a long arc back towards the shore.

He found Rob Cafell halfway through breakfast, and helped himself from the self-service buffet.

'Cabs offer tours of the island,' Cafell told him, 'or we can hire a four-wheel drive. Some of the roads are not exactly built yet, apparently.'

'Hiring a car sounds better. Can we do it from here?'

'No, but the place is only a mile or so away.'

'Good.' Marker looked at his watch. 'And Franklin should be reachable by then.'

'I'm ready to go.'

'Yeah, yeah,' Marker said, scooping up the last of the tropical fruit salad. 'But you're too good to be true.'

They collected the documents they needed and started up the road which led inland from the cove, declining several offers of a cab. It was hot – probably over twenty-five degrees already, though it was not yet eight-thirty – and there wasn't much in the way of shade. The rolling terrain was covered with vegetation, but mostly in the form of scrub. In the open countryside trees were few and far between.

Leeward Rent-A-Car was situated on the other side of the island's main highway, at its junction with the road from the hotel, and was just opening for business as they arrived. Marker left Cafell and the owner picking a vehicle, and went inside to use the phone. He dialled the clinic's number and asked to speak to the administrative secretary.

'Worrell Franklin speaking.'

'Mr Franklin, the consignment of textbooks you ordered from London has arrived.'

Franklin smiled to himself. 'Great. I'll collect them this afternoon.'

'You know where to come?'

'Yep, thanks.'

'Thank you,' Marker said, and hung up.

Outside, Cafell was signing papers on the bonnet of a four-wheel-drive Subaru.

Within minutes they were on the highway, heading east.

They spent the next four hours exploring the island, from the Leeward Marina opposite Mangrove Cay at one end to the secluded, west-facing beach at the other. They briefly visited a conch farm, the ruins of an old slave plantation and a nature reserve. The only road they didn't venture on to was the one which led down towards Arcilla's house on Long Bay. There was no point in offering the enemy a free memory of their faces until they had a plan of action.

In the afternoon they hired a boat from one of the diving services on Grace Bay and tested their equipment on the undersea wall west of Provo, where the shallow waters of the island shelf abruptly dropped into the thousand-fathom depths of the Caicos Passage. Spectacular formations of rock and coral hung over the edge of the wall, and both men caught glimpses of sharks and rays cruising in the shadows. It all seemed a long way from Poole Bay.

'Some people have to pay for all this,' Cafell said, as they stripped off their wetsuits before taking the boat back in.

For Franklin the day passed by at a snail's pace. He

had only had one class to take, but, much to the amusement of his students, twice found his attention drifting helplessly away from the subject in hand.

Soon after five he left the clinic. The Coconut Cove was only ten minutes away by car, but he had decided on walking, and by a roundabout route at that. It might well be no more than paranoia, but several times over the past week he had felt that he was being followed.

After receiving the welcome but surprising news from Joss Wynwood, Franklin's first reaction had been to sit and wait for the reinforcements to arrive. But this, he had quickly realized, would look suspicious. If he didn't keep up his campaign of harassment against Sergeant Oswald and the authorities, then the opposition might get the idea that he had something else up his sleeve.

Now, striding purposefully down the dirt road which reached the northern coast some two miles west of the Coconut Cove, he was eager to meet the SBS men who had been sent out from England. He still had little idea of what any of them could do to find Russell, but over the past few days he had decided there must be more at stake in this matter than he knew. And that meant that the SBS men should have as much to tell him as he had to tell them. And then maybe between them they could build up a wider picture and come up with a suitable plan of action. He hoped this was true, because the only plan he had managed to formulate on his own was not one with which he felt at all comfortable.

Reaching the beach, Franklin walked down to the sea, took off his shoes and paddled around in the shallow water for several minutes, keeping one eye on the road he had arrived by. No walker appeared, and no car. If he was being followed, then it wasn't with much thoroughness.

Darkness fell as he walked the two-mile stretch of beach, and the lights of the hotel grew brighter with every moment. In the bar he spotted the two men straight away, sitting with their cans of Heineken and reading a week-old *Daily Express*. He would have known them without the prearranged signs, simply from the fact that they both looked so fit.

When they got up to leave he waited a minute, and then followed them out to the beach. Half a mile to the east, when all were sure that they weren't being followed, the two SBS men stopped and waited for Franklin to catch up.

They introduced themselves, and sat down with their backs against the abandoned hulk of a rowing boat. A large and lonely sapodilla tree towered above them, black against the sky. To left and right the empty beach stretched away into the darkness.

After Franklin had confirmed that he had no fresh news of Russell, they briefed him on the wider reasons for their presence.

'Have you been keeping an eye on Arcilla's house?' Marker asked.

'Not really. I've been up there a few times, but I can't spend my life in a hide. I've got a job to do. And my mother's visiting from England,' he added with a rueful grin. 'But we've got some friends up on Long Bay, and the guy at the marina isn't what you'd call close-mouthed. Arcilla's helicopter has made a couple of trips to who knows where; the last one was the day before yesterday. After dark both times, which sounds a bit suspicious. The boat hasn't been back . . .'

'The boat's anchored between Muertos Cays and the Dog Rocks on the Cay Sal Bank,' Cafell told him. 'It's a region of shallows between Cuba and Florida,' he added.

'Since it's one of the prime drop sites for drug planes, the US Coast Guard checked the *Tiburón Blanco* out a few days ago. The identity of the owner didn't exactly inspire confidence, but they can't arrest a boat for sitting in international waters. And unless it's waiting a hell of a long time for a drop, it's probably doing what it says it is – treasure hunting. There are lots of known wrecks there, and quite a few more which no one has ever found. The *Santa Lucia* . . .'

'I don't think Worrell needs a run-down of famous wrecks,' Marker interrupted. 'Has Arcilla been here himself?' he asked Franklin.

'Not as far as I know. And there's no reason to think he's skulking in his villa. His sister's behaviour hasn't changed. Neither has the caretaker's.'

'We're waiting for a complete run-down on Arcilla,' Marker said. 'Maybe that'll give us some ideas. But the way I see it at the moment, the only thing of Arcilla's on this island is his house. We have to get into it, one way or another. The question is how.'

'I've been thinking about that for ten days now,' Franklin said slowly, 'and there's not much doubt what the easiest way into it is. In all the hours I've watched the place I've seen three strangers go through the front gate – and all of them have been picked up by Tamara Arcilla at the Club Med-Turkoise.'

Cafell laughed. 'You're not suggesting one of us gets himself picked up . . .'

Franklin shrugged. 'I don't like it, but . . .

'The things a man must do for his country,' Marker murmured.

'Is she beautiful?' Cafell wanted to know.

'Yes, she is,' Franklin admitted.

'I know we're both devastatingly good-looking,'

Marker said, 'but what makes you think she'd pick one of us out of the crowd?'

'It's the low season,' Franklin said, 'and there's not much of a crowd.'

'I don't know,' Cafell said. It didn't feel right, though he wasn't sure why. James Bond did it all the time, and probably charged condoms to expenses.

Marker was looking out to sea, trying to think of an alternative. 'What about a break-in?' he asked.

'You have a look at the place tomorrow,' Franklin said. 'It wouldn't be difficult to get in, but to search the place thoroughly without getting caught . . . There's always people there. And with the woman, well, there's always the chance she'll let something slip in conversation.'

'Or talk in her sleep,' Cafell offered.

'What's her taste in men?' Marker asked.

'All the ones I've seen her with have been dark.'

'I'm afraid it's up to you then, boss,' Cafell said. 'Of course I'll give you detailed advice . . .'

Marker didn't laugh. He could hear Penny screaming, 'I only stayed with you for the fucking sex.' There had to be some other way to do this.

7

This is not going to work, Marker thought to himself. There had to be about twenty available-looking men spread around the Club Med-Turkoise dining room, and probably the same number again in the bar next door. Knowing Tamara Arcilla's predatory m.o. might give him an edge, but forty to one was still long odds.

He lifted the glass of wine to his lips, took a modest sip, and put it down again. Another couple of drinks and his ability to think straight would follow his inhibitions into limbo-land.

He wondered where the inhibitions came from. Before Penny he had stalked his way through enough parties and pubs in search of women to screw. In Hong Kong he had occasionally gone with a street whore. What was the line from the song? – 'times I was so lonesome I took some comfort there.' Lonesome? Horny, more like it. Sex for its own sake was hardly a crime, and he was only sitting at this table because that was the way Tamara Arcilla seemed to like it.

So why was he agonizing about it? Nick Russell's life might depend on him screwing this woman. Maybe other people's too. He told himself to stop being so bloody moralistic, and took a larger gulp of the claret, just as the waiter appeared at his shoulder suggesting coffee. He raised his head to say yes just in time to see the woman enter.

He immediately knew it was her, and the signal from Franklin, sitting across the room, merely offered confirmation. At least she didn't look like Penny, he thought. Almost the opposite in fact. She had those classic Spanish cheek-bones which in some faces seemed unbearably haughty but which in hers were more than offset by the full lips and tumbling hair. The eyes were deep and dark, but Marker was too far away to read any expression they might hold.

She was wearing a simple red cotton dress which made the most of her figure, and walked with an easy grace. Inside his head Marker heard a familiar schoolboy saying, yeah, I'd like to give her one.

He sugared his black coffee and looked at his watch. According to Franklin she never ate more than a starter, before moving through to the bar.

Marker waited patiently, drinking the coffee more from a sense of duty than pleasure. At first he tried not to stare at her, but then realized that it was hardly a suspicious thing to do – most of the men in the restaurant were finding it hard to keep their eyes off her. Occasionally she would look up and catch someone, and a slight smile would crease her lips. It occurred to Marker that with a brother like Fidel Arcilla she would probably have been allowed little control over her own life. Maybe here, in the choosing of sexual partners, she was exercising the only power she had. Like a female Sultan she was visiting her harem to pick out a man for the night.

Suddenly she was getting to her feet and walking out, hips swinging slightly, the dark hair dancing on her bare shoulders.

Marker followed her out of the restaurant, hoping that she followed her usual pattern and went to the ladies, before gracing the bar with her presence.

She did, and Marker quickly took in the situation at the bar. There were only four stools unoccupied, in two pairs of two. Of the four seats adjoining these, one was occupied by a woman, two by middle-aged Americans and one by a handsome young West Indian. Marker took the seat next to him, and hoped she didn't change her usual habits and take a table.

He ordered a drink and waited, feeling more than a little ridiculous. If she was on a power trip, he told himself, then she would have to choose him. He couldn't afford to show any interest in her until she had made the decision. He took a diving school leaflet out of his pocket and begun to study it.

The scent of her perfume was the first thing he was aware of. It was a subtle, lovely, expensive smell. He looked up to say hello and found her eyes already on him. Franklin had told them of his feeling that she was lonely at best, seriously disturbed at worst, and maybe, Marker thought, he was seeing something that wasn't really there, but in that moment her dark eyes seemed to hold a sort of quiet desperation. A stab of pity went through him, just as the smile lit up her face, and drove the bleakness of the eyes away.

'Hi,' he said, smiled, and went back to his leaflet.

'If you're interested in diving you should try the Laurel Canyon,' she said.

'Oh, where's that?' he asked.

'On the West Wall.'

He half turned back to the leaflet, then looked up again. 'Can I buy you a drink?' he asked, in a tone that was mixed politeness and kindness. His parents would have been proud of him, he thought.

'Thank you,' she said, with another smile.

Marker was finding it hard not to stare at her. Her legs

were crossed and the red dress had ridden up, exposing beautiful brown thighs. When she leant forward to put an elbow on the bar more square inches of brown breast came into view.

'Do you live here?' he asked.

'Uh-huh. I have a house over on Long Bay. How long are you here for?'

'Two weeks. We arrived the day before yesterday.'

'We?'

'A friend and I. A male friend. We belong to the same diving club in England.' Which was almost true, Marker thought.

'I like the English,' she said. 'Mostly because they are not American,' she added, smiling. 'Tell me what you do when you're not diving.'

They talked for the next hour, working their way through several drinks in the process. She talked about the islands, and asked Marker about England and himself, but the occasional attempts he made to get her to talk about herself all fell on stony ground. She never refused, just deftly changed the conversation back to safer territory.

After an hour Marker was beginning not to care. He was not drunk, but neither did he feel any intense urge to organize his thoughts. Most of all he wanted sex with her, wanted it more strongly than he could remember wanting sex with anyone for years, Penny included. And he didn't want to think about why.

It was hard not to, though. He told himself it was a primal urge, and that was all there was to it. It was the same urge which had given him such rock-hard erections looking at *Playboy* centrefolds when he was fourteen. It had nothing to do with love or affection or home or anything like that. He just wanted to fuck her, and not because of any desire to extract information from her. He just wanted to fuck her.

And it seemed she wanted to fuck him.

'I'd like a walk on the beach,' she said abruptly.

'Great idea,' he murmured.

There were a few couples on the beach in front of the hotel, but the two of them hadn't walked more than a hundred yards when the sand stretched away empty into the darkness. She put an arm through his, and he felt a shot of electricity pass through him, then a slowly rising sense of excitement. She leant across to kiss him lightly on the lips, as if she was announcing that he had won that evening's prize.

They walked on in a silence broken only by their feet in the sand and the distant swish of the waves on the reef. After about half a mile she pulled them to a halt, and turned to face him, her back to the sea. 'I feel like a swim,' she said, kicking off her shoes. She slipped her shoulders out of the straps, let the dress fall, and stepped out of it. 'Unhook me,' she said, turning her back to him. He did so, and she dropped the brassière neatly on the dress.

'Aren't you coming?' she asked, pulling down the lacy knickers.

She walked into the sea. Marker watched her for a moment, silhouetted against the sky, and then took off his clothes and followed her in.

She swam well, and they were fifty yards or so out from the shore when he caught her up and roughly pulled her into his arms. The water was only about four feet deep, and they found themselves standing in it. She returned his kiss hungrily, almost too hungrily, and pushed her body hard against his. The stray thought went through his head that if there were perfect relative heights for doing it standing up then his and hers qualified.

'Not here,' she said. She sank back into the water and started swimming back towards the shore. He followed, thinking that a few seconds earlier he had been trying to insert himself, without a condom, into a woman who probably slept with two hundred men a year.

She had more sense. 'If you don't have one I do,' she said.

'I have one,' he said, reaching into his trouser pockets for the packet he had bought earlier that evening.

'Give me,' she said, holding herself against him and kissing him again. 'And lie down on your back.'

He did as he was told, his mind spinning off into the distance as she sat astride his knees and took the condom out of its packet. Then she leant forward and took his penis briefly in her mouth, as if she was lubricating it for him. Marker felt he would come on the spot, and frantically tried using his mind to bring his body under control.

She was easing the condom over his throbbing cock, and then holding it in one hand as she gently lowered herself on to him.

'Don't move,' he groaned, and he thought he saw the glint of teeth in her shadowed face as she smiled. Her head was surrounded by stars, and she begun to hum with pleasure as they lay there locked in a stillness that seemed to have no end.

It was almost one in the morning when Marker let himself back into their cabin at the Coconut Cove. He found Cafell and Franklin watching Robert Mitchum and Jane Russell trade innuendoes in an old movie.

Cafell reached forward and turned the TV off. Marker sat down on the couch and closed his eyes. Either he was getting paranoid, or the looks on the faces of the welcoming committee had rather too accurately reflected the way he was feeling.

'Any luck?' Cafell asked. He could tell Marker was not feeling too good about things, but had no idea what to say to make him feel better.

'I scored, if that's what you mean,' Marker said.

Cafell and Franklin said nothing.

Marker opened his eyes. 'Sorry,' he said. 'No's the answer. I didn't get taken to the house.'

'Then where . . .'

'The beach.'

'It's kind of a traditional place around here,' Franklin said. He and Sibou sometimes went to a secluded beach at the western end of the island. And the very first time they had ever made love had been on the one behind the Atlantic Hotel in the Gambia. The memory still made him smile inside with happiness.

'Did she say anything useful?' Cafell asked.

'Nothing. The woman talks about everything but herself.' Marker got up and went to pour himself a glass of water. 'I didn't want to push too hard,' he added, as much to himself as the others.

'Sure,' Cafell agreed. He couldn't remember seeing Marker like this.

'Did you arrange another . . . ?' Franklin began.

'Date?' Marker laughed. 'Yeah, tomorrow night.' He sat down again. 'Maybe this time I'll get invited home.'

'We can always drop this approach,' Cafell said.

'We haven't got any others,' Marker said flatly.

'OK,' Cafell agreed, 'but . . .' He wanted to ask his partner what it had been like, and wondered if his motives amounted to anything more than mere voyeurism. Then again, talking about it might be the best way of ridding Marker of whatever it was that was troubling him . . .

Maybe later, Cafell decided. 'We got the report on her brother,' he said.

Marker looked a bit more cheerful. 'How did it get here?'

'Would you believe by special plain-clothes courier? A Yank flew over with it from Miami, and pressed it into my grubby hand.'

'What's it say?'

Cafell retrieved it from the table. 'There's not much more in the way of hard fact than we had already, but some of it's interesting. He lived in Cuba until he was twenty-one, and he seems to have had problems with the authorities there from about the age of six. Castro's regime set up political neighbourhood-watch-type things called CDRs – Committees for the Defence of the Revolution? Well, young Arcilla managed one hundred and seventeen black marks on his social-behaviour record before he was fourteen. And of course once he really got into his stride, well, then the real trouble started. Black marketeering, ration swindling, simple theft, and eventually murder. He was sixteen when he knifed a boy who he caught in bed with his sister . . .'

Christ, Marker thought. She would have been twelve.

'He spent four years in prison in Havana,' Cafell continued, 'and then he was one of the thousands of misfits Castro managed to dump on the Americans with the Mariel boat-lift. He got his sister out a year later – no one knows how.'

'What happened to his parents?' Franklin asked.

'No information. I guess they're either dead or still in Cuba. Anyway, Arcilla signed on with one of the Cuban crime factions in Miami, probably just as extra muscle. But he obviously has brains – he also got involved with the largest and most right-wing of the exile organizations . . .'

'And they make the Nazis look like Social Democrats,' Franklin muttered.

'He seems to have used his criminal life to do favours for his political chums, and in return he got both money and a degree of protection.' Cafell looked up. 'Of course it wouldn't say so here, but he may even have been doing jobs for the CIA, which would give him a pretty long rope.'

'Any definite drug connections?' Marker asked.

'I'm getting to that. In 1983 he bought the house here on Provo, and a year later he was given British citizenship. The Americans don't know why . . .'

'Neither did the Foreign Office,' Marker said. 'It must have been some local fix. Makes me wonder why we can't just revoke his citizenship and leave it to the Yanks.'

'That wouldn't help us find Nick,' Franklin said quietly.

'Right,' Marker agreed.

'He was a known associate of the three island politicos who got sent to jail for helping drug smugglers, but not a known *business* associate. There was no proof against him then, and there never has been. He hasn't been arrested since his departure from Cuba. He even survived a heavy tax investigation in 1988. He is suspected of involvement in the drug trade, if only as a money launderer, but that's all it is – suspicion. He's extremely rich and getting richer all the time, but . . .'

'If you're rich you have to work really hard not to get richer,' Marker said gloomily.

'It has to be him, doesn't it,' Cafell said. It was half statement, half plea for reassurance.

'Yeah,' Franklin said quietly.

'Who else?' Marker asked. And the only way to reach the man was through his sister, whose perfume was still lingering in his nostrils.

Despite their late night the vestiges of jet lag ensured that neither Marker nor Cafell found it possible to sleep beyond seven. This was particularly bad news for Marker, whose head seemed to be vibrating in an unpleasant manner. 'You're not doing any diving today,' Cafell told him, but he needn't have bothered: Marker knew from painful experience how dangerous diving with a hangover could be.

So when they took the boat out that morning it was Cafell who ventured down into the magical kingdom of the reef, leaving the senior man to gaze out across the open sea and brood over the happenings of the last twenty-four hours. And the last year.

Before he had met Tamara . . . He smiled to himself. Who was he kidding? He had not *met* her in any significant sense – they had fucked, that was all.

He started again. Before he had *fucked* Tamara he had entertained the thought that, however else the experience would affect him, it might at least drive Penny out of his mind. Draw a line under the past, he thought wryly, remembering what Colhoun had said. Well, the boss had been wrong. Somehow the pain of losing his wife seemed even more intense in the cold light of day.

He didn't know what to do about it, and for someone who had made his living overcoming mental and physical challenges that was a hard thing to admit. He knew that in a way it was just a question of grief – learning to accept the loss from day to day. But when the lost one was dead there was no small voice wondering if she would ever come back to you.

He sighed and tried to turn his mind back to work. If Tamara's past habits were anything to go by there was a good chance he would be invited back to the villa that evening, and he would have to make the most of the opportunity. If he was unable to discover anything either incriminating or worth following up, then there seemed no point in hanging around on the island.

An involuntary pang of regret accompanied this thought.

'Fuck,' he muttered to himself.

Russell lay on his bed, a book face down across his chest, watching a mosquito carefully checking out his screen for a possible entry point. Emelisse had just dropped by with the news he had been dreading for days – in not much more than an hour he would be extracting his first kidney.

He covered his mouth with cupped hands and stared at the ceiling, where faint, flickering shadows from fires outside were dancing. Get a grip, he told himself, and abruptly levered himself into a sitting position on the side of the bed.

A drink was what he wanted. In fact he found it hard to remember wanting one quite so much. He also knew that having one would be the worst thing he could possibly do.

Where had all that training gone, he wondered. The self-discipline, the ability to centre oneself, to feel the stillness spreading out from that centre. In Hong Kong he had studied several of the martial arts, and got more than a little interested in the philosophies which underlay them. In some strange way – which seemed less strange as his knowledge increased – his Marine and SBS training had been the perfect preparation for such studies. After all, lying in an inch of water in a soggy hide above Port Stanley for three days presented a man with a pretty stark choice – he could either go mad or start making use of his inner resources.

Which was exactly what he needed to do now, he decided. But he seemed to have lost the knack, to have allowed his mental muscles to get flabby over the years.

He walked through into the main room. His stomach felt the way it always had as a child sitting in the dentist's waiting room. Then he had tried to distract himself with thoughts of some future treat.

It had never worked.

The only thing in this place which might stop him thinking was Emelisse Alabri. The evening he had witnessed his first operations – the evening she had come to his bungalow for a drink – had marked a watershed in their relationship, and by extension in Russell's attitude towards his captivity. She hadn't suddenly started treating him as a friend, and as often as not her instinctive reaction still seemed suspicious rather than trusting, but since that night he had the feeling she had decided to give him the benefit of the doubt. His offer to help at her clinic had been accepted, and now each morning he assisted her in dressing wounds, taking vital signs and dispensing drugs from the surprisingly well-stocked pharmacy. After the last patient disappeared they would usually drink coffee together and reminisce about their pasts. His, of course, had been offered in a somewhat censored version. She had been surprised, and he thought probably somewhat disappointed, to learn that he had been in the armed forces at all, without him regaling her with tales of life in the SBS.

As for Emelisse, she had brought herself to speak freely about her years in France and America, but her life in Haiti, both as a child and now, was still something she rarely referred to.

Russell was not sure whether he could now consider himself her friend, but she didn't seem to have any others. There didn't seem to be a sexual partner either, and occasionally he had found himself thinking about her in that way. The loveliness which had taken his breath away at their first meeting had become something he almost took for granted, except in those rare moments when something caught her by surprise and she let her guard down. Then he wasn't at all sure how he felt about her. Protective maybe, almost fatherly. And sometimes he had felt the beginnings of a desire which he didn't think had anything to do with sex, but for which he could imagine no other outlet.

As the days went by he had also learnt more about the camp. The three doctors – four, if he counted himself – were left pretty much to their own devices, subject to their all being available at short notice for collective surgery. Otherwise Bodin kept to his bungalow and bottle, Calderón to his laboratory, and Emelisse to her clinic and the orphans. Joutard's thugs were always around, but after a while it was possible to think of them as moving parts of the scenery, with about as much brains as the palm trees.

He had not seen Joutard since their one and only meeting, but occasionally he could hear Elvis Presley's voice coming from the colonel's living quarters. According to Emelisse, Joutard never allowed anyone else to be played on his 'boombox'. This, though bizarre, was almost comforting, rather like the situation as a whole. If it hadn't been for his dread of this particular moment, Russell might have thought he was getting used to his captivity, even accepting it.

Twenty-seven minutes had passed since her visit. He took a deep breath, and left the air-conditioned bungalow for the steamy heat of the Haitian evening. As usual, it was like walking out into an oven.

The drums were silent. Maybe the voodoo gods were having an evening off. The groups of mostly young people sitting outside also seemed subdued, as if they knew something bad was going to happen.

Stop it, Russell told himself. You didn't put yourself in this position. You can only do your best.

He found the other three doctors in the theatre ante-room. Emelisse and Calderón were scrubbing up, Bodin sitting on a chair with his eyes closed. There was no powerful smell of brandy on his breath this time, but the Frenchman was obviously the worse for something.

As before, the unconscious donors were laid out naked on parallel tables. This time there were four of them. The other three doctors took the same tables as before, leaving Russell the one which had previously been unoccupied. He wondered if he should ask to have his name engraved on it.

There were two males and two females, all of them aged between adolescence and young adulthood. The girl Russell was to operate on appeared to have fully developed breasts and hips, and seemed every bit as physically mature as the nurse who would be assisting him. He looked at her, wondering if life in Joutard's orphanage was worth the sacrifice of a kidney. But then if the alternative was prostituting herself for pennies on the streets of Port au Prince maybe it was. That shouldn't be the choice, though.

'I'll do the first incision for you,' Emelisse said, 'and then you're on your own. Any questions, ask me.'

Russell watched while she opened the patient and showed him once more how to expose the kidney. Then she was gone. He looked at the nurse, who gave him an encouraging smile that lacked a couple of front teeth.

He started work with the scalpel, and his brain started rerunning its film of the previous week's operation. Now that the moment was here he felt exactly that sense of inner stillness which he had thought was lost. He remembered the sergeant at Poole telling them: 'You'll never lose this fucking training, so get it right.'

It was easier than he had expected. A couple of times Emelisse appeared at his shoulder, looked, and merely nodded. He took five minutes longer than the others, but as he stitched up the original incision he felt a sense of achievement which ranked with any he had ever known.

They met as arranged in the Club Med-Turkoise bar, and spent another two hours drinking and talking about nothing in particular. Marker had been interested in how different she would be now that they had consummated their acquaintance, and was surprised, at least initially, by the answer. She was exactly the same.

After a while he thought he could see why. Each date had to be a seduction; each time they had to start and end in the same place. It was as if she was condemned to life on an ever-repeating emotional loop.

And of course there were only so many times she could repeat it with each man.

Changing the location would help. Soon after ten she

leaned over and ran a hand up his thigh. 'Would you like to see me home?' she asked.

'I'd love to,' he said, and wished that he didn't mean it quite so much.

She let him drive her dark-green Range Rover, directing him east along the Leeward Highway and then down the long, bumpy and unlit track which ended at the gates to the Arcilla compound. A strong source of light somewhere within was throwing a halo into the sky.

She leant over and sounded the horn as they approached, and they waited. Longer than usual, Marker guessed, as she honked again. Almost immediately the gates swung open for them. Marker noticed the video surveillance cameras and the discreetly positioned electronic sensors.

'Why all the security?' he asked casually. 'Is there a lot of crime on the island?'

He thought he saw a glimmer of a smile before she answered: 'It's just to keep my boyfriends in. They never escape until I want them to.'

It occurred to Marker for one ludicrous moment that Nick Russell was chained up in one of the outhouses as a sex slave. The thought was driven from his mind by the sight of the brilliantly lit helipad on the other side of the compound.

'Do you have a helicopter?' he asked, sounding impressed.

'My brother does. Just pull up here,' she said, indicating the front of the main house. It was an old colonial mansion which had been lovingly restored, with perhaps half a dozen rooms and an all-round veranda on each of its two storeys. Two other, more recent, buildings were connected to the mansion's rear by glassed-in, covered walkways.

Marker could only think of one reason for such an arrangement in such a climate: it offered safe passage between the buildings at night, when guard dogs were loose in the compound.

As if to confirm these suspicions, Tamara looked at her watch before opening the car door.

On the veranda she turned, put her arms around his neck, and kissed him the way she had the night before on the beach, rubbing her pubis against him. He felt a surge of desire, and buried his lips in her neck, even while a voice inside his head was telling him she had stopped here on the veranda, where they were clearly visible from the other buildings, for a purpose.

It doesn't matter, he told himself. Whatever games she was playing had nothing to do with him, or the job he was supposed to be doing.

It was hard to draw the distinction, with her hand inside his trouser pocket, stroking him.

'Let's go inside,' she said finally, and led him in by the hand.

The interior of the villa was decorated in a mixture of modern and classic Spanish colonial styles. It was both tasteful and somehow sterile, like a museum without visitors. There were few signs of ongoing life – no magazines or books or dirty cups or toys. The only thing of interest to Marker was the portrait of Fidel Arcilla above the mantelpiece. He looked like a cross between a political visionary and a captain of industry, which was perhaps the effect intended.

'Who's that?' Marker asked.

'My brother,' she said shortly.

'Oh, does he live here?'

'Only for vacations. He lives in Miami.'

'What does he do?'

'He's a businessman. What do you think of my picture?' she asked, reaching down behind a sofa and lifting up a similar-sized portrait of herself. The artist had rendered the lovely curves of her body with even more generosity than nature, but her face had been painted as that of an innocent child. Marker remembered Oscar Wilde's *The Picture of Dorian Gray*, in which a man's face had retained its innocence through life while his portrait had changed to reflect the ugliness growing in his soul. This seemed like an attempt to do the opposite, to hold on to something in a painting which could not be held on to in life.

The fact that she had pulled it out from behind the sofa suggested that her brother was the one with the fixation. For the second time in their short acquaintance Marker felt moved by a terrible pity.

'It doesn't do you justice,' he told her.

Tamara laughed, put the painting back, and took his hand. 'Do you need another drink?' she asked.

'No . . .'

'Then let me show you my bedroom,' she said.

It was as lovely as she was. The furniture comprised a rocking chair, an old Victorian dressing-table and a large bed without head or tailboards. A wooden fan whirred lazily above. Through the open doors which led out to the veranda Marker could see and hear the ocean.

They undressed each other this time, and stood naked in each other's arms for a long time before taking to the bed. Then, as if to make up for lost time, they made love in what seemed a ferocious haste, coming together in a violent arching of limbs and digging of fingernails. They sat outside on the veranda for a while, and then went back to bed and made love again, this time slowly, lingeringly, savouring each sensation until hunger drove them over the brink once more. For half an hour after that Marker struggled to stay awake, until he was sure she was sleeping soundly. Then he eased himself out of the bed, pulled on his trousers, and started to explore the house.

He quickly realized that his chances of finding anything useful were very slim. For one thing he had no idea what he was looking for; for another he could see no reason why Arcilla should leave anything incriminating in a house he only ever used for vacations. The elaborate security might indicate otherwise, but it could easily reflect nothing more sinister than habit on Arcilla's part.

And there was always the risk of his getting caught. He had decided against wearing a gun on the grounds that Tamara's hands would almost certainly have detected it at some point during the evening, and he was far from certain that his unarmed combat skills would suffice to overcome the combination of Arcilla's thugs, the dogs and the wall. Getting caught might be the quickest way to find out what had happened to Nick Russell, but it didn't seem the most sensible.

Of course they might believe he really was looking for the toilet. And that pigs could fly.

It took him ten minutes to go through all the rooms in the main villa. There was a safe behind the portrait of Arcilla which might contain something useful, but he could only have opened it with some C4 explosive. There was nothing else in the house that seemed even remotely suspicious. To all intents and purposes the place seemed set up as somewhere for the idle rich to idle in, and nothing else.

He went back upstairs to check that Tamara was still sleeping, and then down to the door which led out to the covered walkway. In the dark he could detect no alarm sensors, either around the doorway or inside the walkway, and there was no way he could turn on a light.

'Sink or swim,' he murmured to himself, and started forward. No alarms went off, no men came bursting through doorways waving guns. Marker was almost down at the end when he saw two dogs running towards him across the dark compound. They almost threw themselves at the glass, spattering it with flecks of drool, and then stood staring at him, feet restlessly pawing the ground, teeth bared, eyes full of yellow hatred.

But they didn't bark. They couldn't – someone had seen to that. No one would ever hear these dogs coming. They weren't there to provide warning of intruders, they were there to finish them off.

Marker had never liked dogs much. He took a deep breath, opened the connecting door to the next building, and eased himself through it.

The rooms seemed to house the staff, all of whom seemed to enjoy snoring. One door was open though, revealing an empty bed. Either two of the staff were sleeping together, or one of them was up and about.

Confident that he wouldn't be tripping any alarms, and not wanting to attract the dogs' attention again, he took the next passageway at a faster pace, noticing as he did so the light glimmering from one of the windows in the building he was approaching.

Prudence dictated that he check out that room first. He eased his way silently down the passage until he reached the door which was leaking a ribbon of light. Muted Spanish music was audible inside. Putting his eye to the keyhole, Marker could see the back of a seated man, and beyond him a modern radio transmitter. On the edge of his field of vision a silverish glow suggested video screens, presumably those for monitoring the compound. From the man's posture Marker thought it likely he had allowed himself to doze off, confident that any message from the helicopter would wake him up again.

The SBS man started searching through the other rooms in the building. No one lived here – that was for certain. The floors were mostly bare earth, the walls unpainted plasterboard. Several of the rooms were empty, but the largest contained a neat pile of boxes. Marker investigated the contents, and found tinned food, bottled water and sundry general supplies. On the other side of the same room there was a stack of assorted fuel drums, several of them containing marine oil. Twin doors gave on to the empty helipad.

It was all consistent with a regular airlift to resupply an underwater treasure hunt on the Cay Sal Bank. And there was no sign of drugs or guns or any other contraband which Arcilla might be smuggling into the United States.

Tamara Arcilla had led them nowhere, he thought. In his case, in more ways than one.

The silence was suddenly broken by the distant sound of an incoming voice on the radio. Hoping he might hear something interesting, Marker walked quietly and swiftly back towards the radio room, but the message must have been a short one, and the door swung open when he was only about six feet away from it. He flattened himself against the wall of the passage and prayed the man would walk the other way and not look back.

He did, and disappeared into what Marker remembered was the toilet. The sound of piss hitting water confirmed as much.

Marker backed into one of the empty rooms, waited until the man had resumed his position in the radio room, and then retraced his steps through the walkways and buildings to Tamara Arcilla's bedroom. She was still asleep.

He climbed back in beside her, feeling a sense of emptiness which seemed as apt as it was irrational. She stirred and turned towards him, her face almost angelic in the soft, grey light.

Marker let exhaustion carry him into sleep, but not for long. He lay there listening to the sound of decelerating rotor blades, and realized that it been the helicopter's return which had woken him. His watch said half-past three.

When he woke again the sun was already streaming into the room. A hand encircled his neck and gently pulled him into a sleepy embrace.

8

Russell woke to find her face leaning over his in the darkness, and for a moment he thought time had taken him back to their first meeting. But on this occasion her hand was urgently shaking his shoulder. 'I need your help,' she said, seeing he was awake.

'Why, what . . . ?'

'One of the two girls is critical,' she said.

His heart sank. 'Not mine?' he said stupidly.

'No, not yours,' she said impatiently, as he reached for his shoes. 'That bastard Bodin's.'

One voice in his head was thanking God that he was not responsible while another asked bitterly what difference it made. The girl didn't care, that was for sure.

They walked briskly across the silent compound. The first hint of light seemed to be showing in the eastern sky, which meant it had to be around five-thirty. Russell wondered why she had woken him rather than one of the nurses or the vastly more experienced Calderón.

As so often, she seemed to read his mind. 'The last time this happened we had trouble,' she said. 'A boy died and his brother went berserk. A guard shot and killed him. I don't want any of the kids to know about this until they have to. So you're my stand-in nurse.'

They reached the medical building. The girl was lying wrapped in a sheet on one of the operating tables, hooked up to an intravenous drip. Her pulse was almost non-existent.

'Are you going to open her up again?' Russell asked.

'There must be internal bleeding,' Emelisse said. 'I've got no choice. Go and get scrubbed up while I watch her. And be quick.'

He was back out in a couple of minutes, but it no longer mattered. Emelisse was sitting, hands entwined above her head, on the adjacent table. Her eyes seemed cast in stone.

'Is she dead?' Russell said unnecessarily.

'Yes.' She looked at him for a second, then at the dead girl. 'Can you go and wake Calderón,' she said.

'OK,' he said doubtfully. 'What do I tell him?'

She smiled bitterly. 'That there's a fresh corpse for him to harvest – what else?'

What else indeed. He hovered for a moment in the doorway, not wanting to leave her.

She was unwrapping the sheet.

'What are you going to do?' he asked. It sounded the stupidest of questions.

'I'm going to open her up again and find out how that bastard fucked up,' she said in a brittle conversational voice.

Russell went for Calderón. The birds were singing up a storm in the trees now, and he found the doctor already awake, reading an AMA journal and drinking a cup of freshly brewed coffee. The news of the girl's death produced no obvious reaction, except perhaps a flicker of academic interest.

'What was the cause of death?' he asked, as they walked back across the compound.

'Eme . . . Dr Alabri is finding out,' Russell told him.

This produced a quickening of Calderón's pace.

When they reached the operating room Emelisse was back on the adjoining table. This time Russell thought he detected a watering of the eyes. The dead girl lay open on the operating table. 'Take a look,' she told Calderón. 'The bastard forgot to suture one of the arteries. Or just couldn't be bothered.'

Calderón looked, and nodded. 'I'll talk to him,' he said.

'I should save your breath,' she said. 'He'll probably get a bonus for donating the girl's bones.' And with that she strode out of the operating room, eyes blazing.

At twelve-thirty the next day they were eating lunch on the outside terrace of the Ocean View hotel. Marker watched her pick at her chicken salad, and wondered why his own appetite seemed to have deserted him. In the background he could see Franklin lurking, waiting for his signal.

That morning, after they had made love for the fourth time in ten hours, she had announced that she was flying to Miami that afternoon. She didn't know when she would be returning to Provo. She didn't seem to care either.

His implied dismissal had produced a multitude of conflicting emotions in Marker, uppermost of which were relief and an absurd sense of rejection. He had asked her to have lunch with him in reaction to the latter, and it was only later that he had devised the plan which he and Franklin were now about to put into operation.

She had accepted the invitation, but probably only as a convenient way of filling her time. Now, sitting there in dark glasses, she looked as unapproachable as any film star, and it was almost impossible to imagine that less than six hours earlier he had been engaged in passionately kissing almost every inch of the body encased in the tight black dress.

How could feelings so strong mean so little? Because memory was what preserved the meaning, and someone inside her had decided never to remember.

Marker stared out across the tranquil lagoon, inwardly sighed, and scratched his right ear. Almost immediately Franklin was towering over their table, eyes full of anger. He brought his face down to a position only a couple of feet from hers. 'I know your brother kidnapped my friend,' he told her, his voice low and menacing, 'and I'm going to prove it if it's the last thing I do. He may think he has important friends on Provo, but by the time I'm finished the people who live here will know exactly what he is. And all about his whore of a sister.'

'Hey, mister,' Marker said, getting slowly to his feet. 'You take your mouth somewhere else.' Tamara was silent. She seemed to be almost rigid in her chair.

'Her brother kidnapped my friend,' Franklin repeated belligerently, speaking louder this time. 'Or killed him.'

Marker looked across at her, as if inviting a denial.

She just shook her head and looked down.

'If you're so sure, then take it to the police,' Marker said curtly. There weren't many people on the terrace, but they were all looking in his direction. 'Now get the fuck out of here.'

Franklin looked at him, as if wondering whether to knock him over. 'Her brother has the police in his pocket. And she's probably had them all in her knickers.' He turned back to her. 'You tell him,' he hissed.

She said nothing.

'You enjoy bullying women?' Marker asked, but the big man was already walking away through the tables.

Marker pulled his chair closer to her and sat down. 'What was all that about?' he asked gently.

'I don't know,' she said. A lone tear welled up in her right eye. 'I want to leave,' she said suddenly, and reached for her handbag.

'I'll come to the airport with you,' he said.

'No,' she said, almost violently. 'I don't want you to. Leave me alone.'

There was nothing he could do. She walked briskly off the terrace, her heels clicking on the stone, every eye following her. Marker watched her go, and then went in search of Franklin and Cafell. He found them in a dark corner of the bar, and took a pint over to join them.

'No joy,' he said. 'If she does know anything she's either too scared or too loyal or too crazy to tell anyone. The whole business has been a fucking waste of time.'

'With the emphasis on fucking,' Cafell added slyly.

Marker didn't laugh.

'But we have found out something,' Cafell went on, pulling a crumpled sheet of paper out of his pocket.

'What's that?' Marker asked hopefully.

'It's some intelligence from the Yanks. The helicopter touched down on the floating helipad next to friend Arcilla's boat at 22.58, and lifted off again at 00.24 hours. You said the helicopter arrived back here at around 03.30, which would figure. It's a 520-mile trip, and the 365F Dauphin has a cruising speed of about 184mph. So around three hours for the journey.'

'So?'

'Don't you see. We watched the damn thing leave before you went off to meet the lady. At 18.30.'

'It took four and a half hours to get there and only three to get back . . .'

'Deduction – they must have put down somewhere else. And not for fuel: the Dauphin has an operational range of 547 miles, fully loaded.'

Marker and Franklin looked at him.

'Why would someone supplying a treasure hunt do that?' Cafell insisted. 'They're either stopping to pick something up or drop something off. And since you didn't find anything at the villa, the odds are they're picking something up.'

'From where?'

Cafell pulled a tattered map from his hip pocket and spread it out in front of them. 'That's an interesting question.'

'Give us an interesting answer.'

'OK. Half the Bahamas are between here and the Cal Say Bank, and there's Cuba too.' He pointed them out on the map. 'A stopover on either wouldn't be much of a detour. Of course, Cuba guards its airspace pretty thoroughly, but who knows what connections Arcilla might have there. Castro had one of his own generals shot a few years ago for involvement in the drug trade.' Cafell looked up. 'But I don't think so. My money's on here,' he added, plonking a finger down on the map.

'Haiti?' Marker and Franklin exclaimed in unison. 'Why?' Marker asked.

'It's just a hunch. Maybe they're smuggling voodoo dolls.'

'OK,' Marker agreed. 'But let's assume it's drugs. The chopper leaves here, picks them up – maybe in Haiti, maybe somewhere else – and then delivers them to the *Tiburón Blanco* along with the supplies.'

'It's a perfect cover,' Franklin murmured.

'And that would explain why they do the resup at night,' Marker added. 'If anyone did challenge them they could always dump the drugs in the sea and have a perfectly legitimate reason for being in the area.'

'And they must be using the submarine for the last leg of the journey,' Franklin interjected. 'From what I hear the US Coast Guard and Navy have made it pretty hard for smugglers to gain entry by air or sea. On the surface, that is. Arcilla obviously had the bright idea of going in underwater.'

'You mean, while the submarine's supposed to be down below Arcilla's boat looking for treasure it's really running a shuttle service to Florida?' Cafell asked sceptically. 'You'd think the Americans would have twigged the possibility of something like that when they checked out Arcilla's boat.'

'Maybe our allies have a blind spot,' Marker suggested without much conviction. 'But if they weren't using the submarine, then how . . . ? There's only one way to find out,' he said, 'and that's to check out the boat ourselves.'

'Makes sense,' Cafell agreed.

Franklin looked first at his watch and then at the others. 'I guess this is where I'm sent back to work?'

Marker grinned. 'And your mother. It's been a pleasure working with you – that was some performance you gave us out there on the terrace.'

'You can nominate me for the SBS Oscars when you get home.' He downed the remaining half inch of beer. 'Don't get me wrong – I like what I do here,' Franklin said, 'but occasionally I miss the rush – know what I mean?'

Marker just nodded.

'And if you need any jobs done around here you know where I am.'

'Thanks,' Marker said. 'And if I were you I'd watch your back for a while. I don't think Arcilla is the kind of man who likes being bad-mouthed in public. And to judge by her reaction today I should guess the relationship between the two of them is probably borderline pathological. And we don't want a phone call saying you've disappeared leaving only a whiff of chloroform in the air.'

'I'll be careful,' Franklin said. 'I got too much to lose these days.' He gave them a final smile and strode out of the dark bar, disappearing into the sunlight outside.

'Nice guy,' Cafell murmured.

'Yep.' And a happy one, Marker thought. Franklin had told them that morning that he and Sibou had passed the first hurdle in being accepted as adoptive parents.

'I think it's time we reported in,' Cafell said.

They drove back along the coast to the Coconut Cove. Marker extracted the PRC 319 radio from his luggage and put it on the table. 'So what do we need to tell them?' he asked, reminding himself that their activities to date hardly came under the heading of standard procedure.

'A description of the foreplay,' Cafell suggested.

Marker smiled, but the memories that came to mind were not comforting.

'Just tell them what we have,' Cafell said. 'Or what we suspect. A chopper based here is picking up contraband and delivering it to Arcilla's boat. As far as we know the contraband never touches British soil. OK?'

'Right.'

'We need to investigate the boat. And for that we need a boat of our own – one that's capable of carrying a submersible. And probably US permission to fish in their waters, so to speak.' He looked at Marker. 'Why don't you just let me take care of it?'

Marker grinned at him, picked up the radio and walked outside. He had already earmarked the patch of bare ground in front of the coconut palm grove as a perfect spot. It was only visible from the direction of the beach, and that was empty save for one couple soaking up the sun a hundred yards away.

He hunkered down on the sandy ground and arranged the two tuning antennae, pointing them up into the north-eastern sky and searching out the correct frequency. Then he unfolded the tiny keypad, typed out his identification code, and used the burst-transmission facility to send it. After receiving an acknowledgement he typed out his report and sent it, ending with a request for further instructions at 09.00 hours the following morning.

That should give Colhoun plenty of time, he thought, packing up the set once more. Time to persuade the Foreign Office that the operation should continue despite the slightness of the Provo connection, time to persuade the Admiralty to cough up a submersible, and maybe even time to enlist American help. Not too much help, though. He and Cafell didn't want bit parts in a SEAL operation.

Lieutenant-Colonel Neil Colhoun had just reached home

when the phone rang with the news of Marker's transmission. He listened as the duty officer read it to him, then asked him to go over it again, slowly, as he took notes. Ten minutes later, attempting to decipher his own writing in the 'office' he and Jenny shared, he reached the familiar conclusion that it was time they got a fax machine.

Two things struck him immediately. One, if Marker and Cafell were right in their suppositions then the British connection, though negligible, was also vital. Two, they were no nearer to discovering the current location of Nick Russell or the reason for his disappearance.

The importance of a third point occurred to him. Arcilla's treasure hunt was taking place in international waters. Even if anyone argued with Britain's right to board his boat in search of a missing national, no one would be in a position to do anything about it.

He sat there for a few more moments, rehearsing the arguments he was about to make, and then dialled the first of two London numbers.

Fidel Arcilla leaned back in his chair and stretched his arms above his head. It was gone five in the evening, and he had spent most of a long day on the telephone. The slew of real-estate deals and political courtesy calls had all been necessary, but the excitement such activity had once generated in his breast had long since vanished. Making money was just too easy these days, and Arcilla increasingly found himself drawn into ventures that were unusual and uncertain enough to provide him with the challenge his older concerns lacked.

The article he had just finished reading in *National Geographic* was a clear case in point. He smiled to himself and picked up the internal phone. 'Juan, come up for a moment,' he said in Spanish.

His secretary came through the door a few seconds later. 'Read that,' Arcilla told him, passing over the article.

Juan Lozano sat down in the leather sofa, crossed his legs and began reading. He was a thin, handsome Cuban in his early forties, the son of first-generation exiles. His brain was almost as quick as Arcilla's, but he feared he lacked the same imagination.

'Orchids?' Lozano said, looking up with a smile.

'There is a market.'

'I can see that. When people are prepared to pay $10,000 for one rare flower . . .' He shrugged. 'It's incredible.'

'It's logical. This is why I give contributions to the environmentalists. Every time they pronounce a species endangered the value of a live specimen goes through the roof. It doesn't matter whether it's an orchid or a parrot.'

'You're interested in parrots as well?'

'No, just orchids. There's something classy about orchids.'

'You want me to look into it.'

'Yes. Find out who the players are, and whether the market is as good as the magazine says. Journalists have been known to exaggerate,' he added wryly.

'If you want a real challenge, how about whale smuggling?'

'One day.'

Lozano left, and Arcilla got to his feet. That was enough for one day – there was no point in being a millionaire and working yourself to death.

He walked through into the bedroom and took off

the tie he habitually wore for work, even in his own home. He examined himself in the full-length mirror, and saw much the same man he had seen for fifteen years. He was thirty-five now, and things would soon begin to change – his jawline would slacken, and his shiny black hair would begin to thin. Neither was an appealing prospect.

There was always cosmetic surgery. And there were good political reasons for spending money on the preservation of a youthful image. Look at the Kennedys, he told himself. Neither of them had been as good-looking as he was. It couldn't be many more years now before Castro was finally swept away, and then he would need every card he had to reach the top of the pile.

He walked across to the glass doors which led out to the roof garden. Carmen was stretched out in her bikini beside the pool, reading some romantic junk. He wondered why he didn't like clever women – it was not as though he had ever felt threatened by their intelligence. His sister had been clever as a child, but she didn't have the temperament to feed her intelligence, to make use of it. She was arriving that evening, he remembered.

Carmen's body reminded him of Tamara's. Not that he had seen his sister fully naked for many years. In the year before they had sent him to prison, when he had been sixteen years old and she nearly thirteen, they had enjoyed sex together quite often, but once they were both safe in America she had never let him touch her again. He had accepted it, though sometimes he wondered why. Maybe it had been his age, but there had been an intensity about the times with her which he had rarely found again.

Carmen, on the other hand . . .

'*Jefe*, Freddie is on the line from Provo.'

Arcilla walked back into the office, picked up the phone, and listened to what Bartholomew had to tell him, a look of faint amusement on his face.

'Do you want me to teach the man a lesson?' Bartholomew asked.

'No. Not yet, anyway.' Arcilla had just heard the door slam downstairs. It was probably Tamara. 'I'll get back to you,' he said, and put the phone down.

He went downstairs. Tamara was pouring herself a drink in his den, having already turned on the TV. He turned it off again.

She sat down in the massage chair her brother used to relax himself.

'I've just had Freddie on the phone,' he said. 'What did the man say to you?'

She looked at him coldly. 'You promised me,' she said. 'Nothing on Provo,' you said. 'Nothing.'

'I know. I'm sorry, but it couldn't be avoided. It was a one-off, I promise. Now tell me what he said.'

'He said you kidnapped his friend. Or killed him. Did you?'

'He's working for me now. Is that all?'

She smiled. 'And he called me a whore.'

Arcilla's eyes narrowed. 'Who was the man you were with?' he asked.

'One of my tricks,' she said.

'Tamara!'

'Except that you're the only one who has ever paid me,' she added.

Arcilla couldn't decide whether to hit her or try and offer comfort, so he did neither. 'Who was he?' he asked again.

She shrugged. 'An Englishman.'

'What was his name?'

'Marker.'

'Is that his family name or his given name?'

'I don't know. I never asked.'

'I don't expect you know much about him, do you?'

She smiled at him. 'No, I don't.'

He sighed. 'How long are you staying this time?' he asked.

'A few days, a few weeks . . .'

'I'll see you at dinner,' Arcilla said, and went off in search of Lozano. The secretary was in his office, tidying his desk. Arcilla told him what had happened on Provo.

'The man was just spouting off,' Lozano said quietly. 'His friend has vanished, and there's nothing he can do about it. If you take any action against him that will only add weight to his accusations.'

It was what Arcilla had already decided. 'I agree,' he said, walking across to the open window. Two storeys beneath him Calle Ocho, the main business street of Miami's Little Havana, was already lit up against the night. He remembered seeing the street for the first time, a few days after his arrival from Cuba, and thinking he had found paradise.

'But?' Lozano was asking.

His secretary knew him well. There was something not quite right about this business with Tamara. 'I don't know. Probably nothing.' He looked down at the street again, smiling to himself.

Marker and Cafell had an early-morning swim, took breakfast in the hotel restaurant, and got back to their cabin in time to set up the PRC 319 for the expected transmission from Poole.

'Proceed investigation of Arcilla boat,' the message proper began, once Marker acknowledged he was receiving. 'American help in pipeline. Will RV Miami Airport, off 14.30 departure Providenciales. Tickets waiting at airport. Stated requirement en route from Belize, ETA Florida Straits noon Sunday. Offshore rendezvous necessary. Good luck.'

Marker acknowledged once more, and the operator in Poole signed off.

'The old man's been busy,' he said.

'Good job too,' Cafell said. 'So far all I've done is take a holiday. It's been nice, but . . .'

'I get the drift,' Marker said. All he had done was tangle up his own emotions. 'I don't know about you but I fancy a couple of hours on the reef before we leave.'

'Suits me.'

They took their hired boat out one last time, but instead of exploring the reef they decided, on the recommendation of the marina boss, to visit one of the new wrecks, an eighty-foot cargo carrier which had gone down in sixty feet of water less than ten years before. It had been several years since Marker had explored a wreck, but the experience was much the same as it had ever been. Some men find mountain scenery reminds them of how unimportant their own lives are; Marker felt the same way about underwater wrecks. They were nearly always strangely haunting, as if the sea, having once reasserted its power over those who had been foolish enough to challenge it, had draped the sunken craft with living things in an effort to make it feel more at home.

Marker returned to the surface, feeling more at peace with the world than he had going down.

They returned the boat to the marina, packed and ate lunch in the hotel restaurant, then drove up to the car-hire firm, where Marker managed to convince the owner to collect his car from the airport in return for a small bonus. Once there they picked up their tickets, and Marker read a two-day-old *New York Times* while Cafell ploughed happily on through his Tom Clancy novel.

The flight was uneventful and on time. At Miami Airport they hadn't yet reached Immigration when an Afro-American naval lieutenant pulled them to one side, confirmed who they were from their passports, and told them to accompany him. Several empty corridors, a flight of steps and a ride across the tarmac later, they arrived beside a waiting McDonnell Douglas OH-6A 'Cayuse' helicopter. The officer handed Marker an envelope.

'These are your hotel reservations for tonight . . .' he began.

'Where?' Marker asked. 'Where are we going?'

The American looked at him blankly, then laughed. 'Don't you know? Key West. End of the line. Like I said, these are your hotel reservations. Tomorrow morning at eleven someone will collect you from your rooms and take you to a meeting with Vice-Admiral Baskin. OK?'

Marker put the envelope in his pocket. 'OK. Thanks.'

'My pleasure.'

The pilot was waiting in the cockpit, and they seemed to be in the air before they were settled in their seats.

The flight took less than an hour. First they passed over an endless grid of suburbs, then a vast expanse of bare grassland in which stands of trees stood out like islands. And then they were out across the ocean, with the hundred-mile chain of the Florida Keys marching along to their left, the serene waters of Florida Bay directly beneath them.

The Cayuse touched down on the Key West helipad shortly before five in the afternoon, only thirty yards or so from the car which was waiting to take them to their hotel. As they drove across the island towards the old town area the streets became increasingly distinctive, with beautiful old clapboard houses peeking out from behind an abundance of gorgeous tropical vegetation.

A couple of men walking hand in hand reminded Marker that much of the town's recent notoriety rested on the size of its gay population.

Rather disappointingly, their hotel turned out to be a modern six-storey concrete block wedged between the old town centre and the Coast Guard base. Both were visible from their fourth-storey balcony, as was a crowd of apparent revellers on the sea-front promenade almost directly beneath them. Marker asked the navy driver, who had helped them with the diving gear, what was going on.

'It's just the sunset,' he explained.

'The sunset?' Marker asked disbelievingly. The sun was indeed setting, but presumably it did that every night.

'It's a local thing,' the driver explained. 'Every evening people gather to watch it down there. Locals, tourists, everyone. When I was first posted here I thought they must be nuts. But when you think about it, it's kind of a cool idea.'

Marker and Cafell looked at each other.

'When in Rome,' the driver said. 'Anyway, I'll be back at nine in the morning, OK?'

'Sure, thanks.'

'So shall we go join the sun-worshippers?' Cafell asked once the driver was gone.

'Of course.'

They took the lift down and joined the throng, most of whom seemed to be sipping or gulping cocktails. The sunset was certainly spectacular, and when the last slice of brilliance slipped behind a distant island the crowd burst into applause.

Marker found himself thinking about Tamara Arcilla, and the smell of her hair in his face.

9

Having finished breakfast, Marker and Cafell had almost three hours to kill before their meeting with Vice-Admiral Leo Baskin. As a quick glance through the tourist brochures in the hotel lobby made clear, there were plenty of sights to see in Key West, but none that appealed to both men in equal measure. They agreed to meet back at the hotel ten minutes before the time arranged for their collection.

There was in fact only one place that Marker really wanted to see, and he spent half an hour gradually working his way towards it through the grid of sun-drenched streets. The houses and luxuriant vegetation were a feast for the eyes in themselves, and the rising heat didn't encourage haste. By the time he reached Tennessee Williams's house the sweat was lining his brow.

The playwright's former home was a modest affair, a single-storey white clapboard structure fronted by a white picket fence. The garden hosted several species of palms and palmettos, including a towering fan-shaped Traveler's tree. The house was occupied, and there was no sign or plaque to advertise its famous former owner, only the street number quoted in the guide book.

Marker had loved all the films made from Williams's plays, from the still-famous ones like *A Streetcar Named Desire* and *Cat on a Hot Tin Roof* to those that had been almost forgotten, like the original *Glass Menagerie* with Jane Wyman and the young Kirk Douglas. The man had understood something about people. How something pathetic could also be noble, maybe. He was a merciful writer, Marker decided.

And a gay one, he thought, as he took a different route back towards the town centre. It was ironic that he and the seriously macho Ernest Hemingway should be fêted in the same place.

Hemingway's house was as distinguished as Williams's had been modest: a lovely two-storey mansion in Moorish-Spanish style. And it had been turned into a museum. Marker took the guided tour, and saw six-toed cats, hunting trophies, Papa's taste in furniture, and the study in which he wrote *For Whom the Bell Tolls* and the original *To Have and Have Not*. Marker had read the latter after loving the movie, and had to admit the movie was better.

Not much more than a five-minute walk away Rob Cafell was pursuing his different interests. Having already been round the Key West Lighthouse Museum, and admired the view from the newly restored tower, a hundred and ten feet high, he was now entering the portals of the oldest house in the town, a raised white clapboard building which was home to the Wreckers Museum.

Wrecking, as he had already learnt at the Lighthouse, had once been Key West's main dollar-earner. In the late eighteenth and early nineteenth centuries the poorly charted shallows and reefs of the Florida Straits had claimed ships almost weekly, and fortunes had been made by those able to salvage the cargoes. Not surprisingly the locals had not been enthusiastic lighthouse builders, and when the first major installation had been lost in a hurricane the celebrations had probably been audible in New York.

The museum rooms contained ship models, painting and ordinary household artefacts from that era. In one room a 'House-Wife's Guide' sat on the table, in another an old sailing ship's medicine chest. On the wall of the passageway had been pinned a collage of press cuttings to do with wrecks. Cafell was fascinated by all of it, and was only driven out into the back garden by the promise of more exhibits.

It was a lovely garden in itself, with well-groomed lawn and flower-beds surrounded by a variety of tropical trees. At the bottom a large shelter housed an illuminated map of local wrecks. Cafell pushed one of the buttons, and lit the spot where the *Santa Margarita* had gone down in 1554 with a cargo of gold today worth $17 million.

One day, he thought, he would really like to do some treasure hunting. Not for the treasure, but for the hunting. And the history.

He sat down on a wrought-iron garden seat and admired the garden. His mother would love this, he thought. She had always said the garden kept her sane through her husband's long absences. He thought about his parents, and how hard they were finding the process of adapting to his father's retirement. The old man's only forte these days seemed to be getting in his wife's way. Like she said: 'You would think a man who had spent half his life on submarines would know how to move around in a confined space.'

Cafell smiled to himself. They would be all right once the dust settled.

It was almost ten-thirty. He reluctantly lifted himself

out of the seat and went back inside. After signing the visitor's book and saying goodbye to the museum keeper, he walked slowly back down Duvall Street. The number of gay-looking men was quite noticeable, mostly because they all seemed to want to dress like stereotypes. Cafell was rather glad they did. It made the place seem different. Not better or worse – just different. And he liked that.

Back at the hotel he found Marker changing into a fresh set of clothes, and decided to do the same himself. On their way down to the lobby he wondered out loud whether the Americans would be expecting uniforms.

'Probably,' Marker agreed.

Their chauffeur was early, and by eleven o'clock they were being waved through the gates of the US Navy Trumbo Annexe. The car drove down between a barracks block and a docked frigate before pulling up outside an art deco-style office building. Once inside they were left in a plush waiting area, where they drew enough curious looks to make them feel like goldfish in a bowl.

After about ten minutes a young lieutenant came to deliver them to Vice-Admiral Baskin's office. The latter was not much older than they were – around thirty-eight, Marker guessed – with an open face, blue eyes and close-cropped blond hair. The man with him, a moustachioed Hispanic named Jiménez, wore the uniform of a commander in the US Coast Guard.

They all shook hands.

'So,' Baskin began, 'what can we do for the British SEALs?'

Marker smiled. 'We like to think of the SEALs as the American SBS,' he said.

Baskin grinned back. 'OK, so everyone thinks they're

numero uno. Now, business. Your bosses in London have asked us to fix you guys up with a boat that can tow one of your submersibles. Which is fine – we've got you a real doozy.'

'Great,' Marker said.

'And we reckoned you wouldn't want to be hauling it up and down in the elevator at your hotel, so we've found you somewhere more convenient to stay.' He beamed at them. 'It's kind of suitable, in more ways that one. It's in Marathon, which is on Key Vaca, one of the middle keys, about fifty miles east of here. Closer to where your friend is treasure hunting. The house has cable TV, gym, swimming pool – you name it. There's a dock for the boat. And it's private – the neighbours are a long way off. The place used to belong to one of the Colombian cartels, but it was confiscated when the police busted the small fry whose name was on the deed.'

'Sounds ideal,' Marker agreed.

'That's OK then. Next item. Jorge?'

The Coast Guard man came to life. 'London asked us about a week ago for a discreet check on the Arcilla boat. Because of the discreet tag, we decided not to put it under continuous surveillance, but we've had a surface watch in force on and off for several days and through most of the nights. And we filled that out with aerial and satellite recon, so we don't think we can have missed much. And' – he entwined his fingers in front of his chest – 'it *looks* like they're doing what they claim to be doing.'

'What about the submarine?' Cafell asked.

'It's there. And it stays there . . .'

'Are you sure?'

'It was the first thing we looked for. For the obvious

reasons. We don't know the exact maximum speed it is capable of, but even at twenty knots – which I am sure you will consider outside the range of what is possible . . .'

The SBS men nodded.

'Even at that speed it would need ten hours to make a round trip to either US coastal waters or the Bahamas, and the longest interval between sightings which we have is four hours.' He shrugged. 'So you see . . .'

'Could it be meeting up with another boat?' Cafell asked.

'It could, but what would be the point? Why use a submarine at all if you don't intend to use it where it really matters, in coastal waters?'

The argument seemed unanswerable.

'What about the helicopter?' Marker asked.

'It only paid the one visit, on the Thursday night, which you already know about. It was there for about an hour and a half, sitting on the floating helipad they have out there, unloading supplies and taking on fuel.'

'And then it headed back towards the Turks and Caicos?'

'Yes.'

'A mystery,' Cafell murmured.

'Maybe you boys'll have to pay a visit to Mr Arcilla's boat,' Baskin said with an easy smile.

'Maybe,' Marker agreed. He had the unpleasant feeling that Baskin saw him and Rob as mercenaries on loan from the British government. Well, he would take the goodies that were on offer, and as long as their interests coincided he would play the grateful ally, but should those interests ever diverge then the Americans would find out that the SBS were not for sale. 'One more thing,' he said. 'We were briefed on recent history as far as the local drug traffic's concerned, but if you could give us some idea of the current state of play.'

Baskin deferred to Jiménez, who thought for a moment before speaking. 'It's hard to say,' he admitted. 'Superficially, we're going through a good patch. We're using more aggressive tactics, and the interdiction rate is the highest it's ever been. I'm not saying we manage to check out every boat or plane that enters our waters or airspace, but these days at least the bastards know they're taking a big risk when they try. Of course this has meant a shift in the most-favoured routes, and now more stuff is coming in across the Mexican land border . . .'

'You put a finger in one hole, and the stuff comes out of another one.'

'Something like that.'

'What about the local politics?' Marker asked. 'Haiti, for example.'

'What about it?' Baskin asked defensively.

'Is there any evidence of official involvement in the drug trade – by the military, maybe?'

'None that I'm aware of,' Baskin said. Jiménez just shook his head.

Marker had the feeling he was stepping on toes, though he couldn't see why. For several months the Americans had been threatening to invade Haiti and restore the exiled President Aristide, and the notion that they had no intelligence of what was going on inside the country was ludicrous.

Maybe they knew too much, he realized. Maybe there were political reasons why they needed Haitians whom they knew to be involved in illegal activities. That's all we need, Marker thought – to discover that the CIA are behind Arcilla. He dismissed the thought. The Americans – or at least some of them – definitely wanted Arcilla dealt with.

'Any other questions?' Baskin was asking cheerfully.

Marker looked at Cafell, who shook his head. The four men got to their feet and shook hands again. 'And of course we have a car for you,' was Baskin's parting shot.

The young lieutenant who had escorted them to Baskin's office was waiting outside to show them their new means of transport. As they walked round the back of the building he handed over the keys to the SBS men's new home, car and boat, and a sheet of paper containing names, contact numbers and wavelengths for when the need arose. The car was a bottle-green Nissan Bluebird.

The lieutenant travelled with them as far as the base gate, and told them that if there was anything else they wanted they only had to call and ask.

'This is what I call hospitality,' Cafell said, as he checked one of the maps which had been provided for the quickest route to their hotel. 'And you're supposed to drive on the right,' he reminded Marker, as a taxi went honking past, missing the Nissan's wing by inches.

They picked up their gear at the hotel, and drove east out of Key West along a wide road lined with junk-food outlets, miniature golf courses and discount warehouses. A sign told them it was forty miles to Marathon.

It was a beautiful day, with fluffy white clouds sailing across the sky to their left, and the sun shining down out of a clear blue sky to their right. The prominent mile markers on the single highway were not only there to indicate distances travelled, but also, as Cafell soon discovered, formed the crucial element in any address on the Florida Keys. 'See,' he explained to Marker, 'there's a restaurant advertised here and the address is just "45.3". Everything is on the same highway, for a hundred miles.'

'It's not what you'd call beautiful, is it?' Marker observed.

'According to the guide book it gets better as you travel east,' Cafell told him.

'Good.'

They were traversing the fourth or fifth key by now, and so far the sea had been mostly hidden behind bushes, run-down buildings and the huge concrete poles by the side of the highway which carried both power lines and telephone wires.

Suddenly they were on a long bridge, sweeping out across a wide channel, with panoramic views of the bay and straits to either side. The next key was more the way Marker had imagined them. The highway was lined with palm trees, the neon motel signs adorned with crowns of bougainvillaea and hibiscus. Boats bobbed at anchor behind bait and tackle shops, and there were tantalizing glimpses of white-sand beaches lapped by turquoise water. The only possible catch was evident in one of the neon names – the Hurricane Resort Motel. Marker remembered the hurricane in *Key Largo*, one of his favourite films.

'We're coming to the Seven Mile Bridge,' Cafell said, and a few seconds later they were on it. Double yellow lines divided the road between its beige concrete walls, making it seem like an old-fashioned racing track. A hundred yards or so to the left, the old railway bridge ran a parallel course. The two structures seemed almost to hang in space, somewhere between the sea and the sky.

'Key Vaca's next,' Cafell said. 'Look for 47.7.'

They were hardly off the bridge when the turn-off appeared. It was no more than a rough track, winding down from the highway through a stand of royal palms and past two other entrances before ending at the gates of Buena Vista.

Cafell got out and unlocked the gates for Marker to drive through.

The house was a modern, white-painted, one-storey building with a sun terrace. Steps led through more palms to where a picnic table had been placed near the water's edge. A hammock hung between two of the palms.

Close by, the upright arm of a T-shaped jetty ran some thirty yards out into the Florida Straits. A boat was docked along the cross arm. The sixty-foot cabin cruiser, gleaming white with a pale-blue trim, was named the *Slipstream Queen*. It looked fast, Marker thought.

'It'll have to do,' Cafell said sarcastically.

They went aboard. There were two cabins with four bunks each, a lounge area, galley, small bathroom and ample storage space, most of it filled with fishing tackle. On the bridge they found a folder containing Coast Guard charts of the local waters. The boat manufacturer's manual was also prominently in evidence, but as far as Marker could tell the controls all seemed straightforward.

'I wonder why they bothered with the house,' he murmured.

'There's no TV here,' Cafell told him.

They went back ashore and walked up to the house,

noting the drums of marine fuel which had been stacked in the adjoining garage.

'I don't want to be in Poole when the bill for this lot arrives,' Marker said.

The house offered more of the same: crisp sheets, a full refrigerator and drinks cabinet, a massive stereo TV. The two men opened up a huge bag of corn chips, cracked open cans of cold beer, and took it all out to the terrace, where they lowered themselves into reclining chairs, toasted their allies, and considered the next step.

'I've got a feeling our hosts have fucked up over the submarine business,' Cafell said. 'I mean, they've got boats watching, planes watching, satellites watching – it sounds like a case of too many watchers spoiling the broth to me.'

'Broth?' Marker repeated doubtfully.

Cafell threw a corn chip at him.

'Maybe,' Marker agreed, 'but I wouldn't bet on it. Tomorrow we'll go and have a look for ourselves, unless you can think of a good reason for going out there tonight.'

Cafell considered. 'No,' he said eventually. 'I think we should keep a night visit in reserve. Especially since you forgot to ask the Yanks what sort of warning system the *Tiburón Blanco* has.'

'I didn't forget – I already knew. Franklin told me the boat has radar.'

'Then I think our first approach should be as innocent-looking as we can make it. We should let them see us coming. I can be happily fishing, and you can be doing your camp Humphrey Bogart impersonation on the bridge.'

Marker nodded. 'Two men in a boat,' he said.

'We should get a dog from somewhere,' Cafell decided.

Marker grinned. 'Well, while you're out looking for one I'm going to tell the boss what we're planning. Just in case the opposition doesn't buy our innocent routine, and decides to get nasty when there are no witnesses around.'

'Good point,' Cafell agreed through a mouthful of corn chips. 'And while you're at it, you can ask him where the famous frigate's got to. Tell the boss we've seen *Miami Vice*, we know what we're up against, and two handguns doesn't seem like an adequate arsenal.'

Marker went to collect the radio, set it up on the terrace and sent the report, thinking how strange it felt to be using it in such surroundings. He had typed out messages on windswept Norwegian glaciers and in flooded holes on the sides of Falklands hills, but never before in the shade of palms on a rich man's patio.

When he had finished they took the *Slipstream Queen* a little way out to sea, just to find out how she handled. Like a dream was the answer, and a speedy one at that. After tying up the boat, they took a swim. Then, with the light beginning to fade, they walked back up to the highway, crossed it, and found their way down to the shore of the bay. The sunset was as stunning as it had been the night before, and this time graced by the antics of the local pelican, who flew to and fro along the shore in front of them, as if he was auditioning for a part in a tourist board ad.

Back at the house they tried in vain to find something worth watching on one of the TV's sixty-four channels. They then considered microwaving a couple of the TV dinners from the freezer, before deciding that their culinary expectations had been raised by the days on Provo. Relieved at finding an excuse to indulge their restlessness the two men climbed back into the car and headed east once more, Marker at the wheel and Cafell trying to make sense of the guide book.

The road was reasonably busy, causing Marker to wonder how bad it got during the tourist season.

'Seen the film *The African Queen*?' Marker asked.

Cafell shook his head. Marker looked at him with disbelief. 'You haven't!? Well, you should. It's a classic. Anyway it was a boat. They've got the original here. It's on Key Largo, I think. That's another one you should see. Can you see it in that book of yours?'

Within seconds Cafell had found the place. 'Yeah, it's right by the Holiday Inn. But Key Largo's another thirty miles.'

'We've got all night.'

'I'm hungry.'

'I thought you said it was near a Holiday Inn.'

They arrived a little over half an hour later, and found the original *African Queen* tied up at the dock which ran alongside the restaurant's parking lot. It looked smaller than it had in the film, Marker decided, as he tried to imagine Bogart and Hepburn sitting aboard. There was the boiler Bogart used to kickstart. It was all very strange, looking down at a craft which he had only ever seen in the context of an African river, and which now sat in the shadow of a modern hotel, close by a modern highway.

He couldn't have been more than seven when he had first seen the film. Now, staring down at the boat, he had an almost overwhelming feeling that he had lost something, and that there was no way he would ever get it back. This might be the real *African Queen* in one way, but in another it was no more than an echo of the real thing. The film's final scene on the German boat flashed through his mind, and then his marriage to Penny on that rainy day in Dorchester.

He turned away from the boat. 'Let's eat,' he told the waiting Cafell.

Russell lay awake, listening to the steady hum of the air-conditioner and the random song of the cicadas. It was gone three in the morning, and the excess of booze which had put him out like a light had refused to leave him in this blissful state. His mouth felt like someone had filled it with sand, but he couldn't persuade his legs to go and fetch him a long, non-alcoholic drink.

He was feeling sorry for himself. And sorry for himself that he was feeling sorry for himself.

A racking cough erupted in his throat, and finally forced him up off the bed and into the kitchen. He took the half jug of fresh mango juice out of the fridge and drank straight from it. It was far too sweet, but it soothed his throat. Russell wiped his lips with the back of his hand and sat down in the nearest chair.

Another month of this, he thought, and I'll be drinking as much as that bastard Bodin. And probably forgetting to suture some kid's artery.

There was no getting round it – he had to get out of this place. Up until the previous Friday he had been doing a fair job of convincing himself that he had a duty to stay and help Emelisse. An attempted escape, he had kept telling himself, would be selfish as well as dangerous.

The girl's death had not destroyed the argument, but it had certainly weakened it. If he could get away, and expose this place for what it was, there would be an outcry. It wouldn't matter a damn how many influential friends Joutard had in Port au Prince – someone would close him down. And there would be no more teenagers dying on Bodin's operating table.

That was the optimistic view. Russell took another swig of the mango juice, and stared at the wall. A pessimist might predict that Joutard would react to the threat of imminent closure by liquidating all his human assets in one fell swoop. And become the first millionaire bone salesman.

Russell looked at the floor. He couldn't make a break for it without offering to take her along, even though he was ninety-nine per cent certain she would refuse. 'No, make that a hundred per cent,' he murmured out loud. She couldn't leave her orphans to the mercy of Joutard, Calderón and Bodin.

So how could he? 'Self-preservation,' he told the floor. If he didn't escape, then sooner or later he was going to die here. And so, in all likelihood, were the others. If for some reason the boom came down on the enterprise there was no way Joutard was going to be handing out fat redundancy cheques and gold watches for devoted service. In fact the logical way to close this business down was to sell off first the patients and then the doctors, organ by organ, bone by bone. Two birds with one scalpel – they would be making money out of destroying evidence.

No, he was going to get out, or at least have a shot at it. But he wouldn't tell her yet, not until he was ready.

Next morning the *Slipstream Queen* was already twenty miles south of the Keys when the appointed time for the transmission from Poole arrived. This was deliberate on Marker's part – being out on the ocean, away from prying ears, would make it possible to conduct a normal conversation with the CO.

In fact there was not much to say. Colhoun approved of their plan of action, such as it was. 'The next step will be the tricky one,' he advised, 'depending of course on whether you find out anything. If you do, then one of the most difficult decisions we'll have to take is how much to tell the Americans.'

Cafell raised an eyebrow, but Marker immediately knew what he meant. 'Russell's just a name to them,' he agreed.

'Exactly. Assuming he's alive, I want you to have at least one stab at getting him out of the firing-line before our friends go in with all guns blazing.'

'Agreed, though at the moment I have my doubts as to whether we will find out anything.'

'Take it as it comes,' Colhoun said tritely. 'The "famous frigate", by the way, will be waiting for you tonight, from 19.00 hours, at . . .' He reeled off a series of nautical coordinates, which Cafell took down. 'That's about thirty miles west of our friend's treasure hunt,' he added. 'They have a submersible for you, an electric torpedo, a couple of Kleppers, and the guns you asked for. And they're not going to wander far in the next week or so, just in case . . .'

'Our own frigate on call,' Cafell murmured to himself.

After the connection had been broken, he and Marker studied the relevant chart once more. A cross marked the location of the *Tiburón Blanco*. The question was where they should drop their own anchor.

'If we're pretending to be fishermen then almost anywhere will do,' Cafell said, 'but if we're in the diving business, then we should be somewhere above the edge of this reef.' He ran a finger along the undersea contour line.

'Fishing's a better idea,' Marker said. 'If they see us in diving suits they may start looking for us under their boat.'

'OK, then it's just a matter of how far off we want to be.'

'Far enough not to make them suspicious, close enough to be able to see something. A mile sound too far?'

'Slightly. Those binoculars aren't that good. Make it a thousand yards.'

'We don't need to check their nose-picking style.'

'We don't know what we want to check. If we're as careful as the Yanks must have been we'll end up with what they got – which was nothing.'

Marker grimaced. 'Maybe there's nothing to get. But OK, a thousand yards. Which direction?'

Cafell thought about it. 'South is the obvious bet – between them and the sun. But . . .'

'To anyone with a suspicious mind that'll look a bit too calculated.'

'Yeah. West is the next best bet.'

'Let's go with that.' Marker straightened and yawned.

'I'll get the tub moving again,' said Cafell, moving across to the controls. 'Why don't you make us some more coffee?' he added over his shoulder.

Marker eyed his partner's bare back, bare legs, and the hideous Bermuda shorts which filled the space in between. It was as if some deranged fashion designer had finally found the secret of how to use every clashing fluorescent colour known to man in a few square inches of cloth.

'You do look the part,' Marker admitted.

'The dashing captain or the keen fisherman?'

'The rich prat.'

The sun was almost at its zenith when they had their first sighting of the *Tiburón Blanco*, a dot on the distant horizon, in the gap between the thin lines which marked the two Muertos Cays. The two boats were not alone on the ocean: doing a slow 360-degree turn in the stern, Marker counted twelve others visible to the naked eye. True, most of them were in motion, but at least three seemed to be anchored for one reason or another in the shallow waters of the Cay Sal Bank. Establishing a presence within sight of Arcilla's boat would not seem as automatically suspicious as they had feared it would.

Cafell took the boat slowly towards the position they had decided on, as if he was engaged in looking for the perfect spot. As they approached the more westerly of the two small and barren cays the water grew increasingly clear. Even so, Marker, leaning over the side of the boat as part of the same pantomime, could not make out the bottom. The slope beneath them was steep.

It was, Marker admitted to himself, a good spot for treasure hunting. A wreck that had somehow been snagged near the top of this undersea slope would only recently, with the advances in underwater research technology, have become accessible. Maybe Arcilla really had found a fortune in gold.

As Cafell cut the engines he went forward to lower the anchor, and cast a casual glance over the flat blue sea towards the distant *Tiburón Blanco*. No doubt someone on board Arcilla's boat had been watching them ever since they hove into view. And now it was clear that they were staying for a while the observation would become all the more intense.

'If we're not diving today we can have a beer,' he told Cafell.

His partner obliged, returning from the galley with a couple of bottles. The two men settled into canvas seats in the shade of the awning and appreciatively sipped at the ice-cold beers. Marker had his back to the other boat, Cafell his profile.

'Let's hope they don't have a telescopic microphone,' Marker muttered.

'So what's the next step?' Cafell asked.

'We fish for a while. Then you can head indoors and start taking a closer look at them. After half an hour you can come back out with a couple of microwaved meals, as if you've been cooking.'

'Sounds good to me.'

They finished the beers, collected two more cans, and set themselves up in the stern with the simplest fishing rods they could find among the boat's ample supply. Cafell had not fished for many years, and his enthusiasm for the sport was not much greater than Marker's, who had never held a rod in his life.

The fish didn't seem to realize this, and each man caught a sizeable specimen within the first half hour. They threw them contemptuously back into the sea, had another apparent can of beer – Cafell filled two empties with water – and laughed uproariously at non-existent jokes. A couple of bikini-clad beauties, Marker thought, would have completed the impression they were trying to create.

Cafell got up to go inside, and, with a theatrical

drunken stumble, disappeared from view. He walked through the lounge area and into the galley, where the steam vent had been chosen as the best available observation point. He collected the sheet of gauze veil from the table, and wrapped it around the telescope. This would remove the chances of tell-tale reflective flash with hardly any hindrance to his vision. Kneeling on the counter, he made himself as comfortable as possible and applied the telescope to one of the vent's narrow apertures.

At first he could see only empty sea and sky, but a slight shift to the left brought the *Tiburón Blanco* into view. It more than filled the telescope's field of vision, and Cafell could read the name painted on the bow without difficulty. Behind it, the floating helipad hardly seemed to move in the water.

The boat itself was big, but its lines were graceful enough. Examining it from bow to stern, Cafell counted five men in view, all of whom looked Hispanic. Two of them, one wearing a captain's cap, were talking together in the enclosed bridge; another two, both wearing diving suits but bareheaded, were sitting in the stern taking it easy. Beside them, but not apparently part of their conversation, another man sat with a pair of binoculars around his neck and a shoulder holster draped loosely across one shoulder. As Cafell examined him, the man picked up the binoculars and took a cursory look across the water at the *Slipstream Queen*.

Cafell froze, but if the man had seen anything significant he gave no sign of it. He let the binoculars dangle once more against his matted chest and lit a cigarette.

This scene remained basically unchanged for the

next half hour, and Cafell was about to abandon the observation for lunch when a flurry of movement in the water below the other boat caught his eye. Almost immediately a long, dark shape rose up into view – the submarine.

It was about twenty feet long, and cylindrical. Two bulbous growths had been added: one where the conning-tower on a larger submarine might have been, the other at what was presumably the bow end. This was divided into two large convex windows, which gave the whole craft an insect-like air. There were also large windows in the flanks, through which Cafell could see movement.

Four of the five men on deck were now looking down over the side, while the fifth had resumed scanning the *Slipstream Queen* through his binoculars. A hatch swung open in the top of the bulb on the roof, and a man in a diving suit clambered out through it, swung himself down on to the rungs welded into the side of the boat alongside, and climbed aboard. Another man followed him.

The central bulb had to be a small escape hatch, Cafell figured. Hence the diving suits. It was hard to imagine a craft better suited to treasure hunting.

Its two crewmen had disappeared inside the *Tiburón Blanco*, as had the two who had been relaxing. Even the man with the binoculars had vanished. They were all having lunch, Cafell guessed. He clambered down, found a couple of packets to microwave, and went back to the hatchway leading out to the deck. 'Come and take a look,' he said.

Marker followed him through to the galley, lifted himself up on to the counter and examined boat and submarine through the telescope. He was as impressed by both as Cafell had been. 'I'd like to get a closer look at that submarine,' he said. There were no markings to indicate its Soviet origin – only an outsize number three between the two observation windows on the side.

Nick Russell must have had a much closer view of it in the marina on Provo. But what could he have seen to provoke his own kidnapping?

The microwave pinged to announce lunch. The two men sat either side of the tiny table staring at the little plastic trays containing portions of Chicken Mediterranean on wild rice, carrots and broccoli, and raspberry cobbler. Cafell's cobbler had oozed into the chicken compartment during the cooking process.

It didn't taste bad. It hardly tasted at all.

Marker slid his tray into the rubbish container. 'At least there's no washing up,' he said. 'What do you think about paying them a visit?'

'An announced visit?'

'Yeah.'

'What excuse are we going to use? That we want to borrow some sugar?'

'I've heard worse.'

Cafell switched tack. 'What's the purpose of the exercise? What are you hoping to find out?'

Marker shrugged. 'No idea. Something. Anything.' He leant forward, arms on the table. 'At least we'll get some idea of who we're dealing with. If they really are treasure hunting . . .'

'They'll be paranoid as hell. The guy watching us through the binoculars was carrying a gun . . .'

'Suspicious.'

'Not really. If they think they're sitting on millions in gold bullion, then they would be idiots not to lay on some sort of protection for themselves, wouldn't they?'

'Yeah, OK. You don't like the idea?'

'Not a lot. Whatever excuse we make, it's going to look like we're snooping.'

'If we went and introduced ourselves then at least they would know it wasn't the US Coast Guard watching them.'

'I still don't like it.'

Marker sighed. 'Yeah, you're probably right. I'm just getting itchy.'

'I know what you mean. We'd better get back outside.'

They spent the afternoon alternating fishing with sleeping, keeping both a casual watch and an occasional telescopic eye on the *Tiburón Blanco*. The second crew took the submarine back down soon after two, and reappeared three and a half hours later, by which time the sun was falling rapidly towards the western horizon.

The two SBS men upped anchor and set a course towards it. An hour later, as the last light of the day hung like a luminous curtain across the western horizon, they made first visual contact with Her Majesty's frigate *Argyll*.

Half an hour later Marker was climbing up the rope ladder that had been thrown down to him. The captain greeted him warmly and offered the hospitality of the mess, which Marker declined on grounds of security. The shorter the rendezvous was, the less chance it would be observed.

The Type 23 frigate's winch was already lowering the Vickers Pisces submersible, and in the calm sea it only took a few minutes to attach the tow-line from the *Slipstream Queen*. The electric torpedo and Kleppers followed, straight on to the cabin cruiser's stern deck.

All that remained was the transfer of one large canvas bag, the contents of which Marker checked through in front of the captain. The two MP5s with extra ammo were there, and the two harpoon guns. But no stun grenades.

'We don't have much need of them out here,' the captain told him.

'Let's hope not,' Marker said equably.

The bag was lowered to Cafell in the cabin cruiser below.

'Good hunting,' the captain said, as Marker swung himself back over the side. 'And one day perhaps you can let me know what it was all about.'

Marker grinned and disappeared from sight.

Three hours later they were tying up the *Slipstream Queen* at the Key Vaca dock, having already manoeuvred the Vickers submersible around to the shore side of the jetty arm. Though hardly hidden from prying eyes, it could not be seen from either the open sea or the adjoining properties.

The two men felt both exhausted and vaguely depressed. They might have all the equipment they had asked for, but what were they going to do with it? The day's observation of the Arcilla boat had yielded no new information, and no plan had come to mind which might offer more. If the worst came to the worst they could always invite themselves aboard the *Tiburón Blanco* and see what happened, but such a tactic seemed unlikely to succeed, likely to be dangerous.

'It might look better in the morning,' Cafell said. 'I'm going to bed.'

Marker stayed up another half hour watching a soap on TV, and then reluctantly followed suit. But sleep wouldn't come, and he found himself drifting almost helplessly through angry memories of the last few days of his marriage. How long was this going to go on, he asked himself. Until he found someone else? Certainly after he slept with someone else – Tamara had been proof of that. He had never enjoyed such powerful sex in his life, and yet Penny seemed to loom even larger in his mind. He felt like an animal in a trap, whose struggles to break free only increased the pain.

Two women, he thought sleepily. Two men in a boat. Two submarines. The number three on the side.

Marker jerked himself up on to his elbows. That was it! That was how they did it. He levered himself into a sitting position on the side of the bed and reached for his shorts. He thought about waking Cafell but decided there was no point.

It was about five in the morning in Poole. He collected the keys to the boat, and walked across the sun terrace and up to the path which led to the jetty. The slimmest of crescent moons had risen in the last hour, and was throwing a thin line of yellow-cream light across the rippling water.

He recovered the PRC 319 from the locker in which it had been stowed, and climbed on to the cabin cruiser's roof. After getting an acknowledgement from the duty officer he applied his right index finger to the little keypad for several minutes, watching the letters slip past in the liquid crystal display. He told Colhoun what he had guessed, and suggested one possible source of confirmation. Finally, on the working assumption that he had guessed right, he asked the CO for another PRC 319, and a new, more specialized piece of equipment, to be flown out from England as soon as possible.

He then depressed the key which transmitted the

message in a single burst, carefully refolded the antenna, and packed up the small set.

He didn't go in immediately, preferring to sit awhile on the cabin cruiser's roof, staring out along the narrow swathe of moonlit ocean. For the first time in several days Marker felt a sense of well-being within himself, and he was not about to waste it in sleep.

10

Cafell took one look at his partner and wondered what had happened. Marker had not only made breakfast – fruit juice, pancakes, waffles and coffee – but had also shaved for the first time in four days. Since his last meeting with the Arcilla woman, in fact. He even had a smile on his face.

'What are you looking so cheerful about?' Cafell asked, picking up a glass of orange juice.

'Do you remember that moment on the SC1 course when they remind you that it's an officer's duty to have brilliant inspirations?'

'No. You just made it up.'

Marker grinned at him.

Cafell sighed and reached for the maple syrup. 'You've had one, I take it.'

'Let me ask you a question. Why would someone paint a large number three on something they only have one of?'

Cafell thought about it, his fork poised above the pancake. 'Good question,' he said. His eyes widened momentarily. 'Are you suggesting they have three of them?'

Marker smiled. 'No. You're looking at it the wrong way round.'

Cafell inserted a wodge of pancake between his lips and chewed. 'I don't . . .' he began to say, then his eyes widened again.

'Yeah,' Marker said. 'They have two of them, and they both have the same number. The whole point of the number is to make anyone watching believe that they're seeing the same submarine. As long as no one sees both submarines at once . . .'

'It's a great idea, but what proof do you have?'

'Absolutely none. But it fits, doesn't it. Who would know? There's only the Russian who brought them out here, and he got conveniently blown away . . .'

'And maybe that's what Nick Russell saw, that evening in the marina. Maybe someone overheard him talking about it in the bar. Or maybe someone saw him under the boat – that must be where they keep the second one.'

'Maybe. You remember *Thunderball*?'

'I saw the film.'

'Well, in the book – it must be in the film – the big villain's boat has an underwater hatch. Bond nearly got eaten by a barracuda checking it out.'

'Sounds familiar. But our chum Fidel would need a hell of a big hatch to take that sub of his. And if he has one then what could Russell have seen?'

'Good point. I hope you're right, because according to the master plan we need access to both subs.'

'Ah,' Cafell said, 'the master plan. Are you going to fill me in on the details by any chance?'

Marker looked at his watch. 'In a bit. The boss should be coming through in a few minutes. I called him last night with a couple of requests.'

I see,' Cafell said, following Marker out on to the terrace and watching as he prepared the PRC 319 for reception. 'Did anything else happen while I was asleep?'

'One of those supermodels came round to see you

– I didn't get her name. I told her you couldn't be disturbed.'

Cafell laughed.

Letters started marching across the liquid crystal display.

Marker acknowledged and waited for the Poole operator to send Colhoun's reply.

'Two, repeat two, submarines,' it began, 'missing Murmansk naval research. Fifty per cent reliable technical estimates suggest range 200 miles, subsurface max speed twenty knots. Items requested arrive Miami 18.15 hours. Contact airport FBI office Jim Brandon. Do you require reinforcements?'

Marker gave Cafell a questioning look.

'Not yet,' the younger man decided.

'Agreed,' Marker said, and sent the appropriate reply.

'So you were right,' Cafell said, as he watched him pack up the set.

'You doubted me?'

'The thought did cross my mind that you'd got everything confused with some film you'd seen.'

'Perish the thought.'

'So how about telling me the master plan? I already know what my role will be – I'll be doing the thinking, right?'

'Something like that. I . . .'

'Incidentally,' Cafell went on, 'I find those estimates hard to believe, particularly the speed. Our little beauty can hardly manage half that.'

'Maybe that's why Arcilla went to such trouble to get hold of them.'

'Yeah. And there's not much call for speed in treasure hunting . . .' He stopped suddenly, having just remembered something. 'What items have you requested?' he asked Marker.

'A second one of these,' he said, tapping the radio. 'And a tracking system . . .'

'More James Bond.'

Marker smiled. 'Come and take a look at the map,' he said.

Cafell followed him down the jetty and on to the *Slipstream Queen*.

'The way I work it out,' Marker said, opening up the map, 'the helicopter leaves Provo at around six-thirty in the evening – at least it has on its last two trips – picks up whatever it picks up en route and delivers it to the *Tiburón Blanco* sometime around eleven. The Muertos Cays are about seventy miles from here and another thirty or so from the mainland coast. At twenty knots the sub would have no trouble reaching either long before dawn.' He looked up at Cafell. 'So the radio's for us, because today you're taking the one we have to Frankie. The bugs are for Fidel's two submarines. The idea being that when Frankie sends word that the helicopter has left Provo we take the *Queen* out ten miles or so and wait for a little dot to appear on our screen. And then we follow it to wherever it's going.'

Cafell grinned at him. 'Now that's what I call a master plan.'

It was a hundred and ten miles to Miami, and Marker drove as fast as the traffic allowed, anxious that Cafell should not miss the only plane of the day to Providenciales.

The fifty-mile section between Marathon and Key Largo, which they had only previously traversed by night, was as attractive as the Keys' reputation claimed. Both ocean and bay were studded with pleasure boats, the motels seemed to strike the right balance between seedy nostalgia and soulless modernity, and the bright colours of the foliage blazed in the sunshine. Marker found himself thinking he would like to come back for a real holiday.

Two-thirds of the way down Key Largo the highway took an abrupt turn to the left and headed out along a causeway towards the mainland. As the ocean receded from sight the scenery grew less interesting, with only scrub and telephone poles breaking the flat horizon.

'OK,' Cafell said. 'Some questions. Do you know what the range of the tracking system is?'

'I'm not sure. I seem to remember that it's around thirty miles, but that may be optimistic.'

Cafell drew a rough circle on the map which was balanced on his knees. 'Even if you're right, and assuming the sub will head for the US mainland rather than the Bahamas, we'll have to narrow the angle a lot more than you suggested if we want to be certain of picking up the signal.'

'OK,' Marker said equably.

'Which leads to another question. How are we planning to follow these guys, in the *Queen* or the Vickers?'

'I think we have to play that by ear. If those estimates on the Soviet sub are even half right the Vickers is too slow to keep us in contact for more than an hour or so. And in any case, it only has a range of about seventy miles. We don't want to strand ourselves somewhere with no way of getting back to the boat.'

'Maybe one of us should stay in the boat. One man can handle those subs at a pinch.'

'At a pinch, maybe. I'd rather we were both in the same boat – literally – when we get to wherever it is we're going. It'll give us more flexibility.'

'You mean you want to jump out and have fun while I keep the motor running for you.'

Marker smiled.

'What about our gracious hosts?' Cafell asked. 'Do we tell them anything? They're likely to be pissed off if we don't.'

'Only if they find out. And anyway, as of this moment we still don't *know* that the trail will end on US soil.'

'Right,' Cafell agreed, as Marker sped past a camper in a no-passing section, 'and in the meantime at least you're giving their car a thorough test drive.'

They reached the airport with fifteen minutes to spare, and Cafell went straight through the international departures gate, carrying only the PRC 319 in a plastic bag. Marker checked the time of his partner's return from Provo and visited the British Airways desk for an update on the flight from London. It had taken off on time from Heathrow.

He went back out to the car and sat behind the wheel, wondering how best to spend the next six and a half hours. He would rather have done Cafell's job, but after the staged confrontation at the Ocean View hotel it didn't seem sensible for him to have any more contact with Worrell Franklin than was necessary.

'So go and see Miami,' he murmured to himself. At least he wasn't in a hire car, so the chances of being taken for a tourist and shot had to be better than fifty-fifty.

He followed the signs for Downtown out of the airport and found himself driving down an eight-lane freeway towards the usual clump of high-rise towers. Marker had been to America twice before – for a whole summer as a sixteen-year-old, when his parents were touring with a Shakespearian company, and for a couple of weeks in California with Penny about halfway through their eight-year marriage. There was a lot he had liked, and a lot that he hadn't. Sharing a concrete ribbon with a bunch of people who talked into their car phones as they swapped lanes at high speed came into the latter category. So did the idea of naming the damn thing the Dolphin Expressway. No dolphin of Marker's acquaintance would have been seen dead on it.

The clump of towers was appreciably nearer when an exit sign for Little Havana caught his attention. That was where Arcilla hung out when he was in Miami, which seemed to be most of the time. Marker took the ramp and dipped into his memory for the address which had been mentioned in the American briefing report. Calle Ocho, he remembered. Eighth Street. There hadn't been a number.

The street wasn't hard to find. He drove slowly down it, staring out at the thronging pavements and impressive buildings. Little Havana was an apt enough name – it certainly bore no resemblance to any part of America that Marker had seen before. Several of the buildings clearly dated from the art deco era, but over this Anglo-Saxon skeleton the Cuban exile community had draped their own flesh and blood. The faces were all black or Hispanic, the atmosphere an aggressive blend of Mediterranean and Caribbean. The signs all seemed to be in Spanish. In fact the only English word Marker could see was 'burger'.

A car pulling out into the traffic directly in front of him opened up a parking bay. He pulled over, inserted a couple of quarters in the meter, and walked on in the same direction until he found a coffee bar with tables by the window. He bought a cup of coffee just to get a seat, and found it was the most delicious he had ever tasted. He ordered another, this time with a roast beef sandwich, and sat there watching the Cuban-American world go by.

He was looking at the woman for a couple of seconds before he realized it was her. She had come out of a building on the other side of the street, and had stood outside the glass doors while the man with her finished saying something to someone inside.

She was wearing a short, primrose-coloured dress, a wide-brimmed hat of the same shade, and brown thong sandals. Marker felt an involuntary spasm in his groin as he looked at her.

He concentrated on the man. The photo they had seen at Poole hadn't really done Arcilla justice. Though the face looked much the same he looked taller than Marker had imagined. And there was an air of confidence about the man which no photograph could reproduce. The clothes were both well chosen and beautifully cut. Crockett and Tubbs would have been proud to wear them.

From Castro's version of borstal to this must have been a hell of a long journey, Marker thought. He remembered a history teacher at school arguing that most of humanity's woes could be traced to the widening gap between a caveman's emotions and modern man's ability to transform his environment. Mankind was still swinging a blunt club, only nowadays it was big enough to pulverize an entire rainforest.

And maybe the same principle held true for Arcilla and his sister. Between their Cuban origins and the world they now moved in there was no natural meeting ground. Something somewhere had been bound to get warped.

They were walking away. Marker slid off his stool and

left the café intent on pursuit, but before he had gone ten yards the couple disappeared through the door of a restaurant on the other side of the street. For a moment he felt disappointed, but as he thought about it the full stupidity of trying to follow them became apparent. If she had recognized him there would have been no way he could have explained his presence in Little Havana. At best their whole cover would have been blown; at worst he would have been bundled into a convenient alleyway, killed, and thrown in a skip.

In fact, coming to the area had been a mistake in itself. He was letting his cock do the thinking, rather than his brain. Feeling more than a little disappointed with himself, Marker walked quickly back to his car and took the first road heading east.

He spent the rest of his allotted hours behaving like a conventional tourist, taking a leisurely stroll through the art deco splendours of Miami Beach before taking a siesta on the beach itself. The evening rush hour was worse than he had expected, and the British Airways flight had already arrived when he finally reached the airport. Cafell was waiting for him in the agreed bar, and reported no problems in delivering the radio to Franklin. The ex-SAS man, according to Cafell, had 'looked like Fergie with a new toe to suck'. And he would be watching for helicopter departures from Arcilla's villa each evening until further notice.

The next job was to find the FBI office, which proved surprisingly simple. Agent Brandon, an enormous man dressed in white from head to foot, was expecting them, the bulky package prominent on his desk. Though obviously irritated by the fact that no one had considered it necessary to burden him with knowledge of what it contained, he signed the package over to them with no more than the usual surliness which Marker had come to expect from American law enforcers.

They carried it down to the subterranean parking lot and inspected the contents. The PRC 319 looked identical to the one Cafell had just delivered, the tracking system much as Marker remembered it from the technical aids workshop he had attended a couple of years before. He was relieved to see that Poole had included instructions for its use.

They drove south once more, this time with Cafell at the wheel. 'Are we going out in the *Queen* tonight?' he asked, as they crossed the bridge on to Key Largo.

'I'd say no,' Marker said. 'The first helicopter flight we know about was on a Thursday, and so was the second. It might just be coincidence . . . but if we assume the next one will be this coming Thursday, then tomorrow night seems a better bet for what we have to do. I'd like to be out all day, and give them the chance to get used to us being around. Sneaking up on them in the dark is more likely to make them wonder what the fuck we're doing.'

'I sometimes wonder that myself,' Cafell murmured.

It was just after two in the morning, and the compound on Tortuga seemed fast asleep. Russell was squatting underneath the trees outside his bungalow window, letting his eyes get accustomed to the dark. He could make out the silhouette of a guard standing in the ramshackle tower beside the gates, and there might well be sentries patrolling the outside of the perimeter wall, but within the compound no one seemed to be stirring.

He put his fingers into the dirt and scraped them across his face for camouflage, wishing he had remembered to do this properly before he came out. Well, there was no time now. He started making his way towards the building which housed Joutard's office, not using the path but setting a course which maximized the time spent in the darker shadows cast by the scattered palms.

Outside the barracks which housed the male orphans several were curled up on mattresses. They looked younger in sleep, Russell thought, and told himself to stop being sentimental.

The HQ building was almost directly in front of him now, the bare light-bulb glowing above the doors. Another light was glowing in the outer office where the night guard was stationed. The man was not in sight, but he was probably sitting at his desk, either dozing or reading one of the soft-porn cartoon books which were so popular among his colleagues.

Russell continued on his way, using the barracks on his left to shield him from the guard tower as he circled around to the back of the office. From that position he advanced along its side to the right-front corner and squatted on his haunches in the shadows to wait.

The previous night it had been exactly two-thirty when the guard emerged with the cup of coffee for the man in the watch-tower, but tonight that time went by without his emerging from the office. It was almost three, and Russell was beginning to fear that he had already missed his chance, when the screen door opened and the man emerged, steaming cup in his hand.

Russell watched him cross the parking space and disappear round the corner of the first barracks, waited a long two minutes, and then walked briskly towards the office doors, hoping that the guard's attention was now on his approaching refreshments. He passed inside and stopped, listening for any ominous sounds, either from elsewhere in the building or up on the distant tower.

There were none. He walked behind the desk and started memorizing the map that he had remembered was there from his only previous visit. If that night had been anything to go by he had another two minutes before the guard returned.

Almost thirty seconds were taken up in searching for the compound's location. A combination of logic, luck and the titbits of information which he had garnered from clinic patients finally enabled him to pinpoint it, and he spent the next minute studying the lie of the land between the compound and the island's southern coast. There seemed to be no roads, only paths connecting villages, and none of these crossed the range of hills, some nine hundred feet high, which ran east to west along the narrow island. He would have only five miles or so to travel, but they wouldn't be easy.

His time was up. He turned towards the door, just in time to catch sight of the guard coming back round the corner of the barracks.

He sank to his haunches, cursing under his breath, and then scuttled across the floor towards the passage which led down past Joutard's office. None of the doors was open.

He took a deep breath and opened one, stepped inside, and closed it behind him as quietly as he could. As his eyes adjusted he could see the thin light from the window shining on an iron bedstead and bare mattress. Otherwise the room was empty.

Russell blessed his luck and walked across to the open window. After unclasping the shutters he put a leg across the frame and levered himself out and down, landing in the dirt with what seemed like a deafening thud. He crouched there for a few minutes, decided it was safe to assume that no one had heard him, and made his way carefully back to his bungalow. There he spent the next ten minutes trying to recreate the details of the map he had examined.

It was amazing how much had stuck. SBS training, he told himself, remembering the agony of the film observation test almost fifteen years before. Once he had everything down on paper Russell went back to bed, and fell asleep counting oil drums as they were loaded on to the back of a lorry.

After rising early the following morning, Marker and Cafell were soon on their way. Franklin had made contact shortly after eight the previous evening with the news that the occupants of the Arcilla villa had apparently retired for the night, and that there had been no helicopter departure. If there was one during the coming evening then the SBS men would have to fix the tracking devices before the helicopter's arrival at the treasure boat, and then scurry back to the Keys for their own submarine. Leaving the area in the middle of the night would undoubtedly look suspicious, but a lot less so than towing the Vickers along behind them in full view of the *Tiburón Blanco*.

With any luck, Marker thought as he changed into his wetsuit, the opposition would stick to their Thursday pattern, and they would get another day's grace.

Once they were well beyond the reefs, and before they reached the shipping lane which ran down the centre of the Straits, Cafell cut the engines of the *Slipstream Queen* and let the boat drift. Marker went over the side and Cafell carefully lowered the electric torpedo down to him. Marker practised with the machine for the next fifteen minutes, taking it down around four fathoms and testing its manoeuvrability. He had used them often enough in the past, but not for several years, and in that time a number of modifications had been made.

Nothing basic had been changed though, and the practice session over, they resumed course for the Muertos Cays. This time they had decided on putting at least two miles between the *Slipstream Queen* and the *Tiburón Blanco*, reckoning that what they lost in observational clarity would be more than made up for by the enemy's assumption of their innocence. As luck would have it there were two other leisure fishing boats anchored within a mile and a half of the Arcilla boat, allowing them to set up shop slightly closer than they had expected.

The day proved long and hot. Once again they fished with an enthusiasm that was more apparent than real, and took occasional turns at the telescope. As far as they could tell the men on the *Tiburón Blanco* were following the same routine as before. The only obvious difference was that the man with the binoculars had more boats to keep a check on, and he seemed to be finding the larger of the two other craft by far the most interesting. Marker realized why when one of the two nymphets on board sat herself up, and began replastering her bare breasts with sunblock.

Both the other boats took off in a northerly direction during the hour before sundown, leaving the *Slipstream Queen* and the *Tiburón Blanco* with nothing else to look at but the sea, the sky and each other. The navigation lights grew brighter as darkness fell, and then fainter again as the crescent moon rose in the south-eastern sky, flooding the water with yellow light and turning the distant ship back into a discernible silhouette.

Marker and Cafell ate a light supper, played a few

hands of German whist on the galley table, and listened to a tape of early U2 songs which they had found in the Key Vaca house. They didn't drink any alcohol.

At eight o'clock Marker was ready on the roof for Franklin's incoming message, his body between the small radio and any watcher with a nightscope on the enemy's boat. To his relief the words 'not tonight, Josephine' skipped across the display.

Cafell was already asleep when Marker went back inside – he had always possessed the ability to turn himself off whenever it was convenient. A forte of the truly innocent, the older man thought. Either that or the truly obtuse.

He kept watch until twelve-thirty, then woke the other man so that he could have four hours' sleep himself. At four-thirty he was dreaming his way through playing Stanley Kowalski in *A Streetcar Named Desire* on Brighton Pier when Cafell brought him back to life.

The two men got into their diving suits in the dark, then checked the fastening on each other's breathing apparatus before crawling on their hands and knees out on to the deck. It didn't seem very likely that Arcilla's men would be keeping an all-night watch on the *Slipstream Queen* but Marker wasn't taking any chances. With the bulk of the cabin cruiser shielding them from the enemy the two men fixed goggles and put on their flippers. Cafell slipped over the side and Marker carefully lowered the electric torpedo into the water before joining him. The ocean seemed warmer than it had during the day.

Marker flipped the ignition switch on the electric torpedo, and the motor started up with a satisfyingly low purr. The two men took hold of the grab rail and Marker opened the throttle. They took themselves down about twenty feet and started in the direction of the *Tiburón Blanco*, Cafell doing the steering with the help of the luminous compass strapped to his wrist.

For the moment it was hardly necessary: the sinking moon shone above and behind them like an interrogator's lamp, flooding the water all around them with its ghostly yellow light. On the grey ocean floor plants waved at them eerily as in a nightmare.

But in ten minutes the moon would set, and they would have their window of darkness before the dawn.

Cafell looked as composed as ever, as if he didn't have a care in the world. Marker, on the other hand, could feel anxieties queuing up in his mind. First and foremost was the fear that the *Tiburón Blanco* would prove to have some kind of underwater hatch, and that they would be denied access to the second submarine. Second was the fear that there would be no second submarine, and that the whole business was an expensive waste of time. After all, there might be two subs missing, but they had no proof Arcilla had bought both of them. He might have just needed one for a bona fide treasure hunt; the other one could be anywhere.

But no, Marker told himself. Even if the treasure hunt was kosher it could still serve as a cover. A better cover, in fact.

Cafell tapped him on the hand holding the grab rail, and gestured off to the right where a large fish was watching them. The two similar dorsal fins gave it away as a sand tiger shark, one of the least aggressive members of the shark family. As if it suddenly realized as much, the fish turned lazily away and swam slowly out of their sight.

No other possible threats presented themselves during the remainder of the outward journey. The sea gradually darkened, but the compass was only needed for a few minutes before the navigation lights on the *Tiburón Blanco* were glimmering through the water and providing them with a new beacon. Using all his long experience of underwater operations to judge the distances, Cafell guided the electric torpedo in a long three-quarter circle to bring it around on the far side of their target. He then held the machine in five fathoms of water while Marker swam to the surface with the small hand periscope which had been devised at Poole for such situations.

Some hundred yards to the west Arcilla's boat sat on the near-motionless sea. Save for its navigation lights, the boat was still in darkness. There was no sentry visible on this, the starboard side, but Marker kept an eye glued to the periscope for several more minutes, searching for any tell-tale movement in the shadows. There was none.

He swam back down to where Cafell was treading water, and gave him the good news by means of the prearranged signal. A thumbs down would have meant the younger man returning straight to the *Slipstream Queen*, while Marker went in alone, and then swam the two miles back to their boat. The thumbs up meant they could both get closer without an appreciable risk of being observed.

Cafell put the electric torpedo back into gear and they headed towards the target, gaining depth as they did so. The navigation lights on the *Tiburón Blanco* dimmed and swung upwards until they seemed almost overhead, and at that moment the dark shape of the boat's keel loomed into sight slightly ahead and far above them. A thinner shape hung alongside it – the submarine that was stabled on the surface. If another one was attached to the keel they could not see it from where they were.

Cafell manoeuvred the torpedo until he was directly

underneath the boat, which would then assist in diffusing their oxygen bubbles.

Marker gave him a grin through the mask, waved a farewell, and swam slowly upwards.

It was there, as his instinct had told him it had to be. The submarine was held between two fin-like shields and attached to the keel by a customized system of clamps. There was an underwater hatch, but it was only big enough for divers. Even so, it clearly enabled them to exit the boat above and enter the submarine without any need for movement on the surface. An umbilical air-line was hooked up between the two craft, recycling the air while the sub was attached to the mother craft.

Marker swam from one end of the sub to the other, conscious that every moment increased the danger of discovery, but keen to find as inconspicuous a location as possible for the tracking bug. He settled on a niche inside the propeller casing, removed the two magnetic devices from his belt pocket and dropped one of them into place. Then he swam carefully around to where the other sub was gently tapping against the boat's port side, and fixed the other bug in the identical spot.

Swimming back down he found Cafell without difficulty, and gave him an even wider grin. They headed east once more before turning back in a long arc around the anchored *Tiburón Blanco*.

An hour later they were eating breakfast on the *Slipstream Queen*, watching the sun climb into the sky. By seven o'clock they had upped anchor and sailed off in a northerly direction, with Cafell at the wheel and Marker watching the signal from the tracking devices slowly fade as they slipped across the tiny screen.

They reached the villa on Key Vaca soon after eleven, reported the latest developments to Poole, and took to their beds for the rest of the daylight hours. Cafell was up around seven, and spent the best part of an hour checking and double-checking that anything and everything they might conceivably need was already on board the cabin cruiser. The only obvious omission, he thought, remembering what he had read in the guide book, was the set of beads they would need if they decided to buy the Everglades from the Seminoles.

Marker meanwhile had woken from a broken sleep, and lay on his bed feeling angry with himself. He knew the whole business with Tamara Arcilla was over – it even *felt* over – but it had been like an emotional tidal wave, and it seemed to have swept away almost everything in its path. Including his past with Penny.

He clenched his fist, unclenched it, and walked angrily into the adjoining bathroom. Standing under a cold shower took the edge off his rage, or at least gave it a new focus.

'Time to take control,' he murmured to himself. So far at least, Marker was pretty sure that the emotional turmoil he seemed unable to shake off during his unemployed hours was not affecting his active performance. But sooner or later, unless he found some way to snap out of it, it would. Already he was conscious of the occasional questioning look from Cafell.

He found his partner putting the microwave through its paces. They ate, copiously but less healthily than they would have wished, and then sat watching two dreadful TV sitcoms while they waited for Franklin's transmission. It came at eight, right on time. 'Chopper depart 18.35 hours, heading south.'

The two men looked at each other, eyes shining in the darkness.

'Bingo,' Cafell said.

On this Thursday evening the atmosphere in the Tortuga operating room seemed considerably more sober – and not merely in the alcoholic sense – than it had the week before. The loss of the girl the previous week had apparently disturbed Calderón, at least enough for him to tear a strip off Bodin. Or that was what Russell guessed: he couldn't think of any other reason why Bodin's breath should be so sweet or his temper so foul.

The four surgeons worked in virtual silence, each removing a pink kidney from the unconscious youth in their care. Bodin was the last to fill a plastic box, and Emelisse was almost finished sewing her patient back together before he reached the point of closure. She delegated the rest of the work to her nurse and bent over to examine Bodin's patient, provoking a vitriolic outburst in French. She ignored it, and came across to look at Russell's. 'Good,' she said, and went back to her own.

Russell finished closing his patient, stretched, and palmed the needle he had been using. In the washroom she waited for him, as if having a post-operative drink together was now part of the routine. He told her he was tired and felt like an early night.

'OK,' she said, in a tone which suggested it made no difference to her one way or the other.

He watched her go, feeling sorry that these days he felt awkward in her company.

Back at the bungalow he poured himself a modest shot of whisky, sat down at the table and removed one of the batteries from Dr Barlow's cassette recorder. Then he took the length of insulated wire he had acquired by shortening a light flex and coiled it carefully around the needle. This done, he held the two bare ends of the wire to the battery terminals for five minutes.

The bedsheet supplied him with a piece of thread, and he created a small loop in one end for the magnetized needle. Then he took the improvised compass out to the bungalow's veranda and put it to the test. At this latitude Polaris was too close to the horizon, and hidden by the intervening buildings and foliage, but Russell hadn't forgotten his celestial navigation. From the position of Cassiopeia and the other constellations which circled the North Star he was able to infer its position. The needle knew too.

'I thought you were going to bed,' she said, making him start.

'Changed my mind,' he said, more gruffly than he intended.

'I felt like some company,' she said simply.

He smiled. 'Come in,' he said, opening the door for her. 'Would you like a drink?' he asked, putting the compass down on the table beside the battery.

'Sure,' she said, examining the needle and thread. 'You're going, aren't you?'

He put a glass of whisky in her hand. 'Yes. I was going to tell you,' he added, 'and ask if you wanted to come.'

She shook her head. 'Thank you, no,' she said.

There was something in the way she said it which made him feel defensive. 'You don't have to pay such a price to help people,' he said.

She turned her lovely eyes on him. 'I don't know about other places,' she said, 'only here.'

He sighed and sat down. 'I don't know what's right,' he replied. 'Only . . . I don't know.'

She smiled. 'There's no right or wrong in this place. Except for what you feel here.' She tapped her breast above her heart.

'My heart tells me this is wrong.'

'Then follow it,' she said, almost coldly.

'I intend to.'

She put the glass down. 'When are you going?' she asked.

'I don't know yet. In a few days.'

She nodded. 'I shall miss you,' she said, the words sounding strangely out of sympathy with the coldness in her voice.

He didn't know what to say.

'Don't try the ocean,' she said from the doorway. 'The mainland is your best chance.'

And then she drained her glass and was gone.

11

The night was not as clear as its immediate predecessors, but the army of clouds that scudded across the star-laden sky, concealing and revealing the moon like the folds of a magician's cloak, more than made up in beauty for what had been lost to clarity. The breeze was stiffer too, ruffling the waters of the Florida Straits, and brushing Marker's hair across his eyes.

The *Slipstream Queen* was holding a position about forty miles south-east of Vaca Key, close to the centre of the Straits' shipping lane. It wasn't the most comfortable place to be – they had already twice been obliged to make way for passing oil tankers – but it marked the optimum position for picking up the signal from the tracking device.

On the map Cafell had drawn two lines connecting the position of the *Tiburón Blanco* with the two ends of the Florida keys archipelago. Assuming the submarine was headed straight for US territory its course had to lie inside the relevant segment. Cafell had then drawn a third line dissecting the segment, and found the point on that line which was thirty miles distant – the range of the tracking signal – from its outer edges. And just to be on the safe side he had moved the point forward a couple of miles.

And here they were, with at least another half an hour to wait, staring out across the shining sea.

'It doesn't get any better,' Marker murmured. The emotional knots of earlier that evening had untied themselves, or perhaps been untied by his guardian angel the sea. He felt the tingling sense of anticipation which had always accompanied action, be it a training exercise in Poole harbour, an anti-smuggling operation in the Hsi Chiang estuary or a terrorist alert on a North Sea oil rig.

The minutes ticked slowly by. All thirty of them, and then another ten, and another ten.

'Fuck,' Marker growled, turning away from the screen to stare at the ocean, as if willing the waters to yield up the missing submarine.

'Yes,' Cafell hissed happily beside him.

A faint signal was palpitating on the edge of the circular screen. Both men watched as it slowly took on substance, and worked its way millimetre by millimetre towards them.

'It's coming straight at us,' Marker said.

'Not quite,' Cafell cautioned.

Another ten minutes and it became apparent that if the submarine held to its present course – and there seemed no earthly reason why it should have plotted itself anything other than a straight line – it would pass about a mile or so to their west. 'If it's headed for the mainland I'd put my money on Channel Five,' Cafell said. 'It's between Fiesta and Craig Keys,' he added, pointing them out on the map. 'The water's just about deep enough for them.'

'How about getting there first?' Marker suggested. 'The longer we can keep ahead of them, the less distance we'll fall behind when we have to transfer to the Vickers.'

'OK, but what if they're heading for one of the Keys . . .'

'They aren't. There's too many people around, too many potential witnesses. They're heading for the Everglades. You could lose an army in there.'

'You're probably right,' Cafell agreed.

'We can always turn back,' Marker added.

'Sold.' Cafell engaged the cabin cruiser's engine and turned towards the north, matching its pace to the signal on the screen from the submarine behind them. 'It's doing nearly twenty knots,' he said, shaking his head.

'That's what the sneaky beaky said,' Marker muttered, using the Marine slang for Intelligence.

'Some boat,' Cafell said admiringly. 'It would make a lovely Christmas present for the boss.'

An hour passed by, the dark line of the Keys slowly emerging on the north-western horizon. They were back inside American territorial waters now, and someone was obviously watching, because a call came through on the emergency radio band demanding that they identify themselves and their destination. The former was easy enough, but they didn't know the latter, and given their current course they could hardly claim to be heading home to Key Vaca. After a quick glance at the map Cafell plumped for Naples on Florida's Gulf coast as the destination likely to cover the most eventualities.

'We could have asked them to talk to our friends in Key West,' Marker said, after they had been given a clean bill of health, 'but I didn't fancy having to spend most of the night explaining ourselves in triplicate.'

'Dead right,' said Cafell.

The bridge across Channel Five was now visible through the nightscope, but to the naked eye it was still buried in the dark background. Occasionally a vehicle's headlights would swoop up the long arc of the invisible causeway and down again, like twin planets in flight across the sky.

Another boat was passing under the bridge in their direction, and ten minutes later, as it passed fifty yards or so off their starboard bow, the voice of a silhouetted female could be heard shouting, 'We need another man.' Whether this was because they were numerically one short, or because they were not happy with the one they had, was not explained.

Cafell slowed the *Slipstream Queen* and concentrated on keeping to the deep-water channel under the bridge. Once they were through into the deeper waters of the bay he idled the engines and brought the boat to a drifting halt.

'She's still coming,' Marker said, his eyes on the screen. He looked at his watch. 'About forty-five minutes behind us.'

They settled down to wait, hoping that the Coast Guard was not observing the interruption with a suspicious mind. The palpitating dot on the screen inched slowly across the circular screen as the time passed.

'They're close to the bridge,' Cafell calculated. 'Now we'll see which way they're headed. My guess is that they'll hardly change course at all.'

As the next fifteen minutes went by it became apparent that he was right. They got the boat underway again and set off in pursuit, only slowing to match the submarine's pace when Cafell reckoned they were five minutes behind her. Traversing the bay took about an hour, and it was almost four o'clock when the leading boat approached the twelve-mile territorial limit off Cape Sable. Not much more than ninety minutes of darkness remained.

The submarine changed course slightly, moving in on a diagonal heading towards the coast.

Cafell studied the map. 'It has to be here,' he said, holding it in front of Marker and jabbing it with his finger. 'Lostman's River. It's the only channel into the Everglades which is deep enough.'

'Let's close the gap,' Marker suggested. Staring straight ahead at the dark line of the distant coast, he caught sight of something moving out of the corner of his eye. It didn't take more than a few seconds to make out what it was. 'Oh shit,' he muttered.

The Coast Guard cutter was on an interception course, and at maximum speed if the noise of the 210-foot vessel's engines was any guide. Its powerful searchlight was already on, waiting to bathe them in its glare.

The thought of attempting to outrun the pursuit flashed through Marker's mind, but was swiftly dismissed. For one thing he wasn't sure they could, and for another he knew the cutter carried both a radar-guided three-inch cannon on its foredeck and a fast helicopter on the helipad amidships.

'Heave to,' he told Cafell.

The cutter drew up alongside them, some twenty yards away, and the searchlight was turned full on the two SBS men. Another light picked out the submersible in the water behind them. A megaphone-amplified voice asked them to state their business in United States territorial waters. Shadows dancing on the cutter's deck looked suspiciously like a boarding party preparing itself.

'If they come across turn off the tracker,' Marker told Cafell quietly. Then he cupped his hand and shouted across the gap: 'We are British naval officers engaged in a police action against British citizens. We have clearance from the US Navy and US Coast Guard to operate in your waters. You should have the name of this boat on file. Our password is Key Limey.'

There was a pause, presumably for the Coast Guard officer to swallow his disbelief. 'Please stay in view,' he ordered them, with a hint of courtesy in his tone. 'We'll run a check.'

The two men waited in the searchlight's glare, conscious of the eyes watching them from the cutter's deck, not to mention the fingers that would be sweating on triggers. Five minutes passed, and then ten, without the officer reappearing.

'What the fuck's going on?' Cafell asked. 'We're going to lose the signal.'

'Someone in Key West can't believe their ears,' Marker guessed. 'They've probably decided to wake up Baskin or Jiménez for confirmation. Either that or they're wondering why we haven't shared any new discoveries with them.'

Another five minutes passed, and Marker was wondering whether throwing a tantrum would be counterproductive, when the searchlight abruptly went out. 'You're free to go,' the voice boomed through the megaphone. 'Sorry for the hold-up.'

Marker acknowledged the message with a wave, and tried to rub the light out of his eyes. 'Go,' he told Cafell.

The *Slipstream Queen* surged forward. Looking back, Marker watched the cutter beginning a long turn towards the south. At least it hadn't been given orders to follow them.

'We've lost the fucking signal,' Cafell said.

'Not for long. You said there was only one channel, right? Get in there.'

'And what if I'm wrong?'

'Then we'll have to turn the whole fucking Everglades upside down until we find them.'

The cabin cruiser headed north as fast as its engines and the towed submarine would allow. They were still about twenty-five miles from the mouth of Lostman's River when the signal reappeared, faintly at first but more strongly all the time. Marker took the wheel as Cafell transposed the dot's position from the screen to the map. 'They're about five miles up the river,' he said eventually. 'And they seem to have speeded up,' he added. 'The deep-water channel looks a bastard to navigate. I reckon they're running on the surface.'

'Why not?' Marker asked. 'It's still dark and there's no one in there to see them.'

'It won't be dark for long,' Cafell said, looking first at his watch and then at the eastern sky. Was that the first hint of light above the dark coastline or was he just imagining it?

He turned back to the tracking screen, and for the next half hour the dot's position hardly moved, reflecting the fact that they were travelling in roughly the same direction at roughly the same speed. When it did eventually move, it was to perform a slow U-turn. The distance between the two craft was shrinking. 'They've stopped,' said Cafell.

'Where?' Marker asked from the wheel.

Cafell took the map across. 'Somewhere on the northern shore of this lake,' he said, pointing it out. 'The closer we get, the better the fix we'll get. It's called Hell's Lake, by the way.'

'That figures,' Marker murmured. They were now approaching the mouth of the river, and the sky above the mangrove-covered banks was definitely lightening. As the land grew closer they could hear the swelling racket of the dawn chorus.

'How far up-river can we get?' Marker asked.

Cafell studied the charts again, and then the mangroves off the starboard bow. 'The water doesn't look low,' he said. 'So all the way, if we're careful.'

'I wouldn't like to sink our benefactor's boat,' Marker said.

'I wouldn't like to be in it when you do,' Cafell said, pointing a finger towards the nearer of the two banks. In the dawn twilight a long, dark shape was moving slowly across a flat stretch of grey mud beneath the overhanging trees. 'Are they crocodiles or alligators around here?' he asked.

'Both,' Marker replied, slapping at a mosquito on his neck.

They headed up the river, keeping to the deep-water channel, which mostly followed a line slightly closer to the southern bank than the northern. The river itself rapidly narrowed over the first couple of miles, and then its width stabilized at around a quarter of a mile. On both banks the mangroves looked and felt like walls: dense, impenetrable, almost uniform in height. And nothing rose up behind these walls, no taller trees, no hills, no signs of human occupancy. There was only one escape from this river, and that was the river itself.

There was no longer anything to be gained by speed – the submarine had reached its destination, the darkness was almost gone – but there was a lot that could be lost in waters as treacherous as these. Marker took it slowly according to the chart, with Cafell lending the use of his eyes from the bow in difficult-looking stretches.

Several miles went by, and the mosquitoes grew ever more annoying, but then the river began to widen once more, and the attacks abated. 'We're about two miles from Hell's Lake,' Cafell announced. 'And about half a mile short of what looks like a decent anchorage.'

'How far from there to the sub?'

'About four miles.'

'Sounds good.'

The sun had cleared the wall of mangrove now, and the river had widened to the extent of constituting a small lake. In the lee of a headland on the northern shore they found both Cafell's suggested anchorage and their second crocodile. The reptile ignored them at first, lying resolutely still on its patch of mud, but then it slowly started raising its upper jaw, as if it was miming Tower Bridge.

'They have no strength when it comes to opening their jaws,' Marker said conversationally, as they manoeuvred the submarine around to the side of the cabin cruiser. 'All the power is in the slamming shut.'

'So this one's just getting prepared.'

'I think it's ready,' Marker said. The crocodile's jaws were now at right angles to each other.

The two men concentrated on loading what was needed into the battery-operated Vickers, and then clambered one by one down through the hatch and on to the wooden floor of the submarine's belly. Despite the wide windows the interior felt decidedly cramped. As Marker checked the dials and gauges on the pilot's console Cafell clanged shut the hatch and screwed the locking wheel tight. 'Ready to go,' he said.

Marker switched on the engines, which began to vibrate with an almost melodious hum. He then started the two propellers turning, the starboard slightly slower than the port, as he wanted to move off in a slight turn to starboard. The Vickers edged its way out towards deeper water.

The two men had decided that, for the first half of this short voyage, the risks involved in pranging some uncharted underwater obstruction greatly outweighed the risk that they might be spotted on the surface by unfriendly eyes.

The gamble paid off – only the eyes of several great white herons followed their progress eastward. A hundred yards short of Hell's Lake Marker brought the craft to a stop, and Cafell took a final reading on the exact location of Arcilla's submarine. 'There,' he said, pointing out the spot on the map. 'And here,' he added, pointing out another not too far away, 'looks like a good place to resurface.'

Marker nodded, and reached forward to open the vents. As the water swished into the tanks the submarine sank into the river, three feet, six feet . . . Marker closed the vents and turned on the outside lights. The craft was suspended between the river's bed and surface, with only a few feet to spare in either direction. He started the propellers again, and the Vickers moved forward into the slightly deeper waters of the lake.

The water was not particularly clear, but there was little doubt they would be visible from the air. The thought suddenly struck Marker that a helicopter might have been waiting for the sub, might even now be taking off and wheeling out across the lake . . .

No, he told himself. It would be heading east towards Miami or north towards Tampa.

'How are . . . ?' he started to say, when a dark shape exploded into view through the submarine's front windows, and just as quickly disappeared from view. The second approach, though, was slower. It was a dolphin, no, two dolphins, and they seemed to want to play.

For the next fifteen minutes, as Marker steered the Vickers across the wide lake, the two creatures kept them company, entertaining each other and the SBS men with an underwater display which included everything from looping the loop around their craft to close-up smiles in the observation windows. It was distracting, potentially dangerous, and downright wonderful. When the dolphins, apparently bored by their new friend's rigidity, finally took off for pastures new, the two men felt a rare sense of loss. Both knew that they had seen something few other humans would ever see: one intelligent species trying to play with another.

Cafell, meanwhile, was responsible for navigating them safely to their destination, and at times his powers of concentration were severely tested. But he stuck with it, not least because he knew that their surfacing in the wrong place might well prove fatal. There was no knowing what weaponry the enemy might have on hand, and there wouldn't be much chance of escaping in the submarine once their presence was discovered. Not in water this shallow, anyway.

Finally they neared the appointed spot. The bottom of the lake had been slowly rising for some time, which fitted in with Cafell's calculations. 'Another fifty yards,' he told Marker. 'But slow.'

They had moved forward around twenty yards when the slope of the lake bottom suddenly steepened. 'Here,' Cafell said.

Marker switched off the propellers, turned off the lights and stopped the engine. 'Here's hoping,' he said, and started emptying the tanks. The Vickers rose in the water, rocking gently from side to side. A dark and ragged line of vegetation swam into focus through the ruffled water, and then they were on the surface, and looking quickly round to see where they were.

Cafell's navigation had been spot on. The submarine was sitting in a small cove, surrounded on three sides by a wall of mangroves. Only the open lake was visible through the entrance to the cove. 'They're around that headland,' said Cafell. 'Probably only about three hundred yards as the crow flies.'

Marker did a quick calculation in his head. 'I shouldn't be more than an hour,' he told Cafell.

'Should I wait here or take her back down? If I take her down the noise of the engine might carry,' Cafell said.

'I guess you'd better just keep her where she is,' Marker replied. Having pulled the hood of the black wetsuit over his head he was now applying camouflage cream to his face. Next he double-checked that the camera was in the waterproof pouch at his belt, the silenced Browning High Power in the waterproof holster. He took one look at the Heckler & Koch MP5SD, which was still wrapped in its reinforced cling film, and decided that in this instance mobility was more important than fire-power.

'Ready,' he said.

Cafell was already unscrewing the hatch. 'Watch out for crocodiles,' he said seriously, as Marker clambered up and out on to the top of the submarine.

'Thanks for reminding me,' Marker said sarcastically. The only wildlife in sight was a black cormorant perched on a mangrove root some twenty yards away. 'Won't be long,' he said, and slid down into the water.

He only had to swim a few yards before the bottom came to meet him. He waded ashore, and found his path obstructed by the dense mangroves. 'Should have brought a fucking machete,' he muttered to himself.

He squeezed through a narrow gap, and then another, and another. It was like being trapped inside an enormous hedge, with the added complication that he was standing in three feet of water. Already the hour he had set himself was beginning to look optimistic.

A sudden movement in the water ahead stopped him in his tracks. The snake, striped like a tiger, only in dark brown and beige, swam away into a tangle of roots.

Marker breathed out heavily. Maybe this wasn't such a good idea, he thought. Maybe they should just tell the Yanks the whole story and head on home.

But first he had to find out whether Russell was here. With more than a little reluctance he started forward again.

His luck changed. The swamp and its wilderness of roots gave way to more solid ground and slightly sparser vegetation. Marker rechecked the compass on his wrist and walked on, his boots sinking into the moist soil, his eyes constantly sweeping both ground and foliage for snakes. According to the map it was only a hundred yards or so across this headland to the shores of a narrow creek.

It took almost fifteen minutes, and Marker's relief on catching his first sight of the creek was almost his undoing. He was just about to slide back into the water among the tangled roots when a strangely familiar sound halted him in his tracks.

He crouched down behind a gnarled trunk and found a small window on to the river in the wall of vegetation. He could hear the faint swish of a paddle being deftly wielded by an expert, and the canoe suddenly came into view. In the stern sat a man in jeans, T-shirt and felt hat. The feather in the latter went with the stereotypical Native American face, but the Walkman didn't. The leakage of noise from its earphones was providing the strangely familiar sound, one that Marker had last heard on a bus coming back from Bournemouth not ten days before. At this sort of volume, he reckoned, personal stereos would prove as dangerous to the Indians as white men or alcohol.

The sound faded into nothing, and Marker started making his way forward through the roots. He was within a couple of yards of open water when the view in front of him dramatically expanded. Across the thirty-yard width of the creek another wall of mangroves rose up, but a little way to his left the creek opened into Hell's Lake, and around the far headland, some two hundred yards in the distance, he could see the corner of a wooden jetty. As yet he could see no buildings, but logic put them close to the shore behind that jetty. His spirits, somewhat depressed by the struggle through the undergrowth, began to lift once more.

With only his head above the surface of the green-brown water he moved slowly out from behind the mangrove curtain. The musical canoeist had vanished from sight round the next bend in the creek, and there was no sign of his having a colleague. Marker pushed off through the torpid water towards the far bank.

Getting himself ashore proved as difficult as before. As he fought his way through the interwoven roots Marker promised himself that on his return the SBS would launch a multimillion-pound research programme into the problem of movement through mangroves. There had to be an easier way.

Fifteen minutes and fifteen yards later he was back on relatively dry ground. The trees here were taller and more varied – he was on a hummock, one of those slight humps in a flat land which acted as a magnet to wildlife. There certainly seemed to be more birds in the foliage, and there were flowering plants growing out of tree trunks and branches. Some of these were orchids, he realized. The place smelled like a perfumed Turkish bath-house.

He removed the Browning from its sealed holster, checked that the compass on his wrist tallied with his inbuilt sense of direction, and resumed his progress. He had not gone much further when the vegetation ahead of him began thinning out. Soon he could make out the straight lines of something man-made through the foliage.

It proved to be the roof of a large one-storey wooden building. Marker crawled forward until he could see the end which was facing him. It was about thirty-five feet wide, and boasted two big windows, both of which appeared screened and shuttered.

To his right, behind the building, an area the size of a tennis court had been painstakingly cleared and covered in tarmac, but there was no helicopter sitting on the pad. One had probably departed as soon as the contraband had been transferred from the sub.

To his left, through a gap between the corner of the lodge and the forest, he could see more of the jetty and the lake beyond. There was no cover in that direction. He removed the camera from its waterproof pouch and took several photographs, before moving further back into the trees and starting on a course that would take him around behind the helipad to the far side of the lodge-like building.

The going seemed easy after the mangroves, and it took only a few minutes to reach a spot from which he could study the back of the building. This was about sixty feet long, and contained eight shuttered windows and one door. It had been constructed as a wilderness lodge, Marker guessed, a place to bring boy scouts of all ages for canoeing, bird-watching, orchid picking, whatever.

There had to be at least a dozen rooms inside, and most of them were probably lined with bunk beds.

There was one separate outhouse to its right, and what looked like another closer to the lake shore. Maybe Russell was being held in one of them, Marker thought, though he couldn't think of a single reason why he should be.

He took more photographs, then resumed his march round the perimeter, making sure to keep out of sight inside the trees.

The second outhouse turned out to be a boat-house, built mostly of corrugated plastic sheets, with one side wall resting on dry land, another two on pilings in the lake. The fourth side looked open to the water from where Marker was standing.

He sat on his haunches among the trees, wondering what to do next. So far he hadn't seen a single occupant, but he had to reckon on there being at least two people inside the lodge – the submarine's crew. After a seven-hour voyage underwater it seemed likely that they would take a good long rest before heading back to the *Tiburón Blanco*. And in any case they would need darkness for the return passage through the shallow waters of the bay and the Keys.

They might be alone, though, and quite possibly sleeping.

At the very least, he had to check the outhouse, Marker decided. He carried on round the perimeter until he found the point of approach which offered the most cover, and began crawling out across the ten yards of open ground. There were no cries of discovery from the lodge.

The blind end of the outhouse lacked a window, so he was forced to risk the side facing the lake, which rendered him visible from the jetty and the front veranda of the lodge. One look in the window showed him the building was virtually empty, and certainly not a prison for Nick Russell. Marker turned away, and noticed with a leap of his heart what had previously been hidden from sight by the boat-house – there were two men on the jetty, both sitting in cheap plastic chairs.

Marker sank to the ground, thanking his lucky stars that the men had their backs to the shore. It made sense, since their task was presumably to frighten off unwelcome callers, and here in the western Everglades such visitors could only arrive by boat.

He studied the two men. One was Hispanic-looking and wore jeans, T-shirt and baseball cap. He was smoking a cigarette, and cradling what looked suspiciously like an Uzi sub-machine-gun in his lap. The other one, blond, was wearing a uniform which Marker didn't recognize but which he guessed was that of a Park Ranger. Both men were wearing wraparound sunglasses.

He took out his camera, and was about to take a picture of their backs when the uniformed man got to his feet. He stretched, turned, and said something which made the other guard laugh. Marker depressed the shutter release, and then watched the man walk back up the jetty and disappear behind the boat-house. About half a minute later the sound of a screen door slamming came from the direction of the lodge.

Marker crawled back into the safety of the trees and considered what to do next. He had already exceeded his stipulated hour, but Cafell would give him at least as much time again before he started to worry in earnest. Just the boat-house, Marker told himself, and then he would head home to the sub. The prospect of fighting his way back through the mangroves was not an enticing one.

It took him only a few minutes to come within spitting distance of the lake, but the configuration of the shoreline made it impossible for him to see what was inside the boat-house without leaving the shelter of the trees. Fortunately this didn't seem a risky proposition. There was only a short stretch of open ground between where Marker now stood and the top of the wooden steps which led down to the front of the boat-house. The view from the side windows of the lodge was obscured by the outhouse, and the line of sight of the guard on the jetty was blocked by the boat-house itself. Unless someone emerged from the front of the lodge at the exact moment Marker stepped out into the open there seemed little danger of his being seen.

He walked briskly across the space and on to the steps. The top one creaked slightly, and he took care to lighten his step as he descended the others. From the bottom a wooden walkway led in along the land wall of the boat-house. The Russian submarine and two canoes were tied up against it.

Marker had seen all that he needed to, but for a moment curiosity triumphed over caution, drawing him into the shadowed building for a better look at the submarine.

There was nothing much to see, of course. He would have to climb inside, study the controls, take the craft apart and put it back together again. One day, perhaps.

He crept back down the walkway, turned to ascend the steps, and heard a soft scraping sound from the path above. In the split second which passed before the man came into view Marker had braced his legs and brought the Browning into the classic two-handed firing position.

The Uzi was only halfway towards its target when Marker fired, pumping two bullets into the man's torso and a third through his brain, cancelling the message en route to the finger on the trigger.

The sub-machine-gun clattered noisily down the steps, while the guard sank slowly backwards on to the path.

Marker caught the Uzi on its third bounce, with the unconscious air of a conjuror making a difficult trick look easy. His ears were straining for evidence that someone had seen or heard what had just happened.

All he could hear was the singing of birds, the faint breeze in the trees, the slurping of water against the boat-house pilings. He climbed the steps, grabbed the dead man's feet, and half pulled, half slid him off the path and on to the top steps, where at least he was out of sight from the lodge veranda.

What to do? Marker stood there, his thoughts racing through the possibilities, and lingering for a moment over the memory of the only other man he had ever killed, a Chinese drug smuggler.

He shook his head angrily. There would be plenty of time to worry about his soul – first he had to get his body home.

There was still no sign of an alarm. It didn't look as if he would have any problem leaving by the same route he had used on his way in. Except, of course, that he couldn't take the dead man with him, and the discovery of his body would scupper any chances they had of finding Nick Russell and nailing Fidel Arcilla. The Cuban would put his operation on ice, close the pipeline down, hide away one of his submarines. As of now, they hadn't a shred of proof against any of his men, let alone Arcilla himself.

So how could he get rid of the dead man, and make

it look like an accident? With three bullet holes in him, there was no way they could afford an examination of the body. It had to disappear, either in the forest or the lake.

The canoes riding in the water beneath the jetty caught Marker's eye, and he tried to imagine he was looking down from above at the layout of lodge, boat-house and jetty. He decided that with any luck he could get to one of the canoes without ever putting himself in view from the lodge. It was risky, but no riskier than any alternative he could think of. And he wouldn't have to deal with the fucking mangroves.

He lowered the dead man down the steps and on to the walkway. There he removed the blood stained blue T-shirt and baseball cap, knotting the former around one thigh and stuffing the latter into his utility belt along with the dark glasses. He tangled the Uzi round the guard's wrist, lowered the body slowly into the water, and slid in beside it. Then be began swimming slowly towards the jetty some thirty yards distant, with one hand firmly grasping the dead man's wrist.

The canoe tethered at the near end was not visible from the lodge. With some difficulty Marker bundled the corpse over its side, and then clambered in himself. He took off his wetsuit hood and put on the blue T-shirt, the baseball cap and the sunglasses. The dead man was not that much smaller than he was, and sitting down in a canoe . . .

Marker decided that climbing up on to the jetty to untie the canoe would be riskier than leaving behind a rope that had clearly been cut. They would have no idea why the guard had gone out in the canoe, so how could they expect to understand how much of a hurry he had been in? He reached for his knife, sliced through the mooring rope, and used a hand to push himself off from the jetty.

With the skill acquired by long practice he manoeuvred the canoe around the end of the T-shaped jetty, and then moved it along the other side, with the wooden pilings effectively masking him from anyone watching on land. From the end of the jetty he would have to cross about a hundred and fifty yards in clear view, before the trees on the first headland screened him once more.

He paddled fast, as if he was in pursuit of someone, taking care to keep his face turned away from the lodge. If anyone shouted after him, he would just wave his arms excitedly and point in the direction of the hidden cove, where Cafell was hopefully waiting with the Vickers.

But no one shouted, and when he finally risked a look back all but the empty jetty was hidden from view. He took off the baseball cap and dark glasses, and let the boat drift while he pulled the sodden T-shirt over his head. Marker had no desire to test Cafell's reflexes by confronting him with what looked like a stranger in a canoe.

He rounded the headland beyond the creek, saw the Vickers in the distance and raised an arm in greeting. After what seemed like a long hesitation Cafell waved back.

The sardonic grin on the younger's man's face disappeared when he saw the corpse in the canoe. 'No time to explain,' Marker said. 'Find something to weigh him down with. And hurry.'

Cafell disappeared into the body of the submarine, and re-emerged less than a minute later. 'There's nothing,' he said.

'Shit. We'll have to take him with us,' Marker decided. He hauled the dead man up, and the two of them somehow contrived to lift him on to the roof of the vessel, before bundling him in through the hatchway.

After collecting the sunglasses, Uzi and clothes and passing them to Cafell, Marker leant down, overturned the canoe, and shoved it away from the submarine. There was still no sign of the enemy. 'Let's go,' he said.

Two minutes later they were submerged once more, and heading out across Hell's Lake towards the head of Lostman's River. As before, Marker took the controls and Cafell navigated. Neither man looked back at the body wedged behind them.

There was no sign of the dolphins on the return trip – perhaps they could sense the dead man on board, Marker thought – and the open-jawed crocodile had left his spot on the mudbank by the *Slipstream Queen*. There was no sign of it in the water either, but Cafell wasted no time as he waded the thirty feet which separated the boat from the nearby headland. There he found a heavy enough rock for their purposes.

It was too smooth for a rope attachment, so they wrapped the body in a blanket with the rock inside, and then secured both ends with rope, creating what looked like a human Christmas cracker.

Out in midstream once more, they dropped it into the deep-water channel and watched it sink.

Cafell caught the grim look on Marker's face. 'You had no choice,' he said firmly.

'I know. Let's get out of here.'

'OK.'

Marker went inside to find some fresh clothes, and emerged ten minutes later with a couple of cans. Cafell had one eye on the river, another on the chart, and one hand on the wheel. He reached out the other for the beer. 'So where do we go from here?' he asked.

'Home, I guess.'

'Not England?'

'No. Our villa in the Keys home.'

'And then what? After twenty-four hours' sleep, I mean.'

'Good question,' Marker said. 'Any answers?'

Cafell shrugged. 'I did have a few thoughts on the subject while you were out for your walk. And most of them were pretty depressing.'

'Like what?'

'Well, we may know how most of it works now, but we don't have a fucking thing that could be used in a court of law against Arcilla. We haven't any evidence that any crime has been committed at all. And worse, I haven't managed to think of any way we could get hold of any.' He put down his beer and ran a hand through his hair.

Marker waited for him to continue.

'There are two things we don't know. No, three. One is what they're smuggling, two is where they pick it up in the chopper, three is where it goes from the lodge back there. The obvious way to crack one is to follow the chopper when it leaves Provo, right? And the obvious way is to ask our friendly frigate to track it. But when we find out where it's going we're not really any further ahead. Say it's Haiti – well, the government's hardly going to sanction using the Royal Navy in Haitian waters, is it?'

'No, but . . .'

'Then there's the *Tiburón Blanco*,' Cafell went on. 'That at least is in international waters. We could try and board them during the transfer from chopper to sub, but what's to stop them throwing the drugs into the sea. And there goes our proof. There's no law against having two subs with the same number. The only other option is to intercept the sub with the stuff on board. Trouble is, the bloody thing's faster than we are. We'd have to catch it in a fucking great net or something. And that does sound more like James Bond than reality.'

'OK . . .'

'And one last thing,' Cafell insisted. 'Even if we do catch them with the goods, we still haven't implicated Arcilla. As it is he'll just say that his underlings were acting on their own, and using his treasure hunt as cover. He'll probably be indignant as hell.'

'Probably.' Marker gazed at the wall of mangroves sliding by, an idea beginning to form in his mind. He let his unconscious take over the task of bringing it to fruition. 'We have a more immediate problem,' he said.

'Which is?'

'Our hosts. They may have given us the green light last night, but I have the feeling that this morning they'll be expecting the explanation.'

Cafell laughed. 'Which is?'

'Fuck knows. If we tell them we were chasing a submarine they'll want to know where it went. If we say we lost it they'll think we're incompetent. Either way they'll want to take over.'

'These are their waters.'

'Yeah, but this is our op. They wanted us to nail Arcilla, and that's what we're trying to do. And I'm not sharing anything with the Yanks before I know for certain whose uniform that guy at the lodge was wearing.'

'OK,' Cafell said equably.

'And anyway,' Marker added, 'I always thought the idea of the sea belonging to anyone was a load of bollocks.'

'The Native Americans thought the same about the land,' Cafell volunteered. 'Are you sure the man you saw in the canoe was an Indian?'

'Nope, but he looked like Hollywood's idea of one.'

'Maybe he was just passing through.'

'Maybe.'

They stood in silence for a minute and more, watching the river widen to meet the open sea.

'How about – we were on our way to RV with a possible informant,' Cafell suggested. 'But he didn't show.'

'He was scared off by the Coast Guard cutter,' Marker added. 'I like it. It's thin, but so what – they aren't going to call us liars. Not to our faces anyway.'

'As long as they don't take the *Queen* back,' Cafell murmured.

'Right. We're going to need her for at least another week.' Marker lobbed his empty can into the bin that had thoughtfully been provided. 'And much as it pains me to say it, I think we're going to need reinforcements from Blighty. Two should do for what I have in mind.'

'And that is?'

Marker told him.

12

Neil Colhoun shut the door of his office behind him, propped the umbrella up against a wall, and dropped himself in the tattered chair. The only sound he could hear was the rain beating a tattoo on his windows. It was something of a change from home, where the members of his family were indulging their belief that God provided rainy Sunday afternoons for testing the volume controls on the house's three sound systems. Caught in the crossfire between his wife's country music, his younger daughter's new Björk single and his son's current favourites – the Crash Test Dummies – Colhoun had decided the office was the best place to consider an SBS invasion of the United States.

He picked up the transcription of the lengthy report Marker had sent by burst transmission on Friday afternoon, shortly after his and Cafell's return from their jaunt in the Everglades. And put it down again. By this time he could probably have recited the damn thing word for word.

He reached for the Admiralty and FO memos, which were almost as familiar. The Americans were not altogether happy with their British allies. In fact, they seemed to be a trifle hurt. In future it was hoped that cooperation in this particular endeavour could be more of a two-way street.

Fuck 'em, Colhoun thought sourly, and knew he was

being unfair. If SEALs were conducting themselves on British soil the way Marker and Cafell were behaving in Florida he would be outraged, and he knew it. But . . .

He started leafing through the computer-enhanced blow-ups which the Illustrators' Branch had generated from the pictures Marker had faxed. The quality wasn't that great, but the negatives would be arriving by express post on the following morning and better reproductions would then be possible. There was one picture in particular which Colhoun wanted to examine more closely. It showed the back of the lodge, and in the blown-up version some unusual-looking machines could be made out through the windows of the door. They seemed to be partly made of clear plastic, and their shape had touched a chord in Colhoun's memory. An unresponsive one, unfortunately.

He went on to the next picture, which showed the two men sitting on the wooden dock. The uniform, as Marker had suspected, was that of an Everglades National Park Ranger.

When it came down to it, Colhoun thought, he simply didn't trust the American authorities. He didn't trust their Special Forces to be efficient, and he had no faith in their security. If the man in the picture had been wearing a Coast Guard's uniform he wouldn't have been surprised.

Americans might be no more prone to corruption than Brits, but those working in Florida law enforcement certainly had more than their fair share of temptation to overcome. With so much drug money swilling around in the state the real surprise lay in the continued existence of honest and dedicated officials. The problem was in knowing who they were. Without such knowledge, enlisting American help was like entering a lottery. One in which the losers were apt to die.

It would be safer for all concerned to let Marker proceed with his plan. After all, Colhoun thought cynically, the four SBS men would simply constitute one more armed gang on American soil, and as far as the SBS CO knew, there was nothing against either carrying arms or gang membership in the US Constitution.

He tried to imagine selling this argument to the Foreign Office and failed. But then there was no reason why the FO should be told anything. As far as Colhoun was concerned he had been given carte blanche to sort this business out, and until such time as someone revoked his authority he intended to make the most of it.

Outside, the rain was still falling. He picked up the internal phone and called the duty office to tell them that he was on the premises. 'If anything comes in from London or the States, I want to see it right away,' he added.

'There's a fax here already,' the corporal replied.

Colhoun rolled his eyeballs at the ceiling. 'Send it over,' he said, and hung up.

It turned out to be the intelligence report he had been waiting for. One of the Washington MI6 contingent had done some local research in Florida, and come up with the name and owners of the property on Hell's Lake. Anhinga Lodge belonged to the Friends of Zion Health Care Trust, which ran hospitals in Miami, Fort Lauderdale, Fort Pierce and St Petersburg. It functioned as a weekend wilderness resort for the Trust's two thousand employees. There was a staff of ten on duty from noon on Friday to noon on Monday throughout the winter high season, and sporadically during the summer low season. There were two live-in caretakers. Staff, visitors and supplies were all flown in by one of the Trust's four helicopters.

Colhoun leant back in his chair, hands behind his head. There was something . . .

He had it!

He skimmed through the pages of his address book, found the number he was looking for, and reached for the phone.

'Can I speak to your dad?' he said when the child answered.

'You may,' the girl said primly, before apparently dropping the phone. A few moments later Dick Ferguson came on the line.

'Dick, it's Neil. I need to see you. Now, if possible.'

'We're just about to eat.'

'At four o'clock?'

'We eat late on Sunday, not that . . .'

'It'll only take a minute. I just need you to look at a photograph.'

'Come on over.'

Colhoun hung up, told the duty office he was leaving, and drove into Bournemouth. He had known Ferguson for five years now, since the doctor had performed the operation on his father-in-law. An initial prejudice against money-grabbing consultants had been eroded, if not completely removed, by a common Scots heritage, a mutual taste for malt whisky, and a love of rugby.

Ferguson opened the door himself, napkin still tucked inside his collar, and led Colhoun into the empty living room.

Colhoun handed him the blow-up. 'Those,' he said, pointing out the machines.

Ferguson stared at them. 'They look like Belzer-Kountz machines,' he said at last. 'I wouldn't want to stake my life on it, but that's what they look like.'

'And what are Belzer-Kountz machines?'

'They're for preserving human organs between removal and transplantation.'

Colhoun took back the photograph. 'Thanks,' he said.

'Is that it?'

'Aye, you can get back to your supper.'

'Lunch.'

Colhoun walked back to his car and sat behind the wheel, letting the pieces of the puzzle slip into place. The fact that a health trust owned the lodge, the fact that Russell, a paramedic, had been kidnapped rather than killed.

And Cafell had been right, he thought. It had to be Haiti – there was no way the necessary facilities could be hidden on one of the empty Bahamian keys.

Arcilla was smuggling human organs out of Haiti and into Florida, where desperate people were no doubt paying a fortune for something to which they had no earthly moral right. The more Colhoun thought about it, the angrier he felt.

He gunned the car's engine, and headed for home. He had already decided who Marker's reinforcements were going to be.

Fifteen miles away, Ian and Helen Dubery were parked in a New Forest lay-by, watching gusts of rain sweeping across the road. At least the weather was familiar, he thought unhappily. If this much wind and rain didn't make his wife feel more at home, then nothing would.

'I'm looking forward to seeing Mum,' she said,

confirming his suspicions. She always looked forward to her trips back home. He wondered if she ever told her family on Benbecula that she was looking forward to returning south. Some hope.

But why should she? Her friends were there, as well as her family. In Poole she had only him and a job she hated.

He had no doubt she loved him. After all, they had loved each other since they were about twelve. And he knew that loving him was enough to keep her here. But it wasn't enough to make her happy.

What could he do? He loved his work. Getting into the SBS had been like having every dream he had ever had come true, the realization of aspirations which had begun on the day his father first took him boating in the Sound of Monach. He was only four then, but the green sea and blue sky were still vivid in his memory.

What was he supposed to do – give it all up? For what? There was no work in the outer islands. The fishing fleets were a shadow of what they once had been. All the young people left, just like he and Helen had done.

For a moment he felt angry with her, but what was the point?

The shower was ending as abruptly as it had begun, the sun breaking through the overhanging trees. She turned towards him, a smile on her face. As always, he felt his anger melt away.

'Where now?' he asked.

'Home,' she said.

'Question twenty-nine,' the Scouse voice boomed through the amplifier. Silence settled on the Hardy

Arms. 'What is the average lifespan of an ostrich? That's an ostrich,' the Liverpudlian repeated. 'I'll give you five years either way.'

Three tables away, Stuart Finn leant forward and whispered 'fifty' to the team member who was writing in the answers.

'You sure?' one of his team-mates asked doubtfully. 'My budgie only lasted about six months.'

'That was because you breathed on it,' Finn retorted.

'Fifty does seem kind of old,' Dave muttered.

'How about forty,' his girlfriend Jean suggested.

'Jesus!' Finn said. 'Fifty's the right answer, leave it alone.'

'How come you're so sure of a thing like that?' Jean asked.

Finn smiled at the woman. 'I just am,' he said, placing a beer mat on the edge of the table. He flicked it up and caught it deftly with the same hand.

'The last question,' the quizmaster bellowed. 'That's number thirty to youse who can count. What was the name of the *Titanic*'s captain?'

Finn and the other six members of the Hounds of Heaven quiz team stared blankly at each other. 'What a fucking question,' Dave moaned. 'Finn, you're in the fucking navy,' someone else said.

'The *Titanic* wasn't a warship.'

'They're all boats, aren't they?'

Finn ignored him. The girl on the next table was staring at him again, and this time he just smiled at her. She smiled brazenly back at him for several seconds before turning away. Maybe, Finn thought, the man next to her was her brother or something.

She was going to the bar now, and Finn could see her legs for the first time. They were nice. Shame about the blouse, he thought, but then not everyone could have taste as good as his.

'I'm still not sure about the ostrich,' one of his team-mates lamented.

'I am,' Finn said, getting up, 'and if you change that answer I will go out and find a dead ostrich and stuff it up your arse.'

'He's always right about those things,' Jean said. 'It's depressing.'

'He certainly has a way with threats,' Dave said.

Finn grinned and went to the bar, squeezing in beside the woman. 'Can I buy you a drink?' he asked.

'No thanks,' she said, 'I'm buying one for my boyfriend.'

'Lucky man,' Finn said. 'So why were you staring at me?'

She handed a fiver to the barman. 'I work at the Institute for the Deaf in Bournemouth,' she said with a smile. 'As a lip-reading instructor. No one on our team knew what the average lifespan of an ostrich was.'

Finn was still smiling to himself the following morning, when he and Ian Dubery found themselves waiting for an audience with the CO. At first the summons had given Finn some cause for alarm – not that he could remember actually doing anything worthy of a reprimand – but his fellow-corporal's presence had reassured him. Ian Dubery was not the type to get keelhauled across the CO's carpet.

Colhoun lost no time in telling them what they were there for, and was pleased, if not surprised, by the eagerness on each man's face as he recounted the genesis of the operation and the developments to date. 'You'll be flying out from Heathrow this afternoon,' he said. 'One or both of the others will meet you at Miami Airport.'

'Uniform, boss?' Finn asked.

'No. And as far as US Immigration is concerned, you're just a couple of tourists come to do some diving on the reefs off the Florida Keys. So when they hand round the form on the plane, and you get to the question about purpose of visit, just tick "pleasure", don't write in "illicit military operations on US territory".'

The two men dutifully laughed.

'Captain Marker will brief you on what you'll actually be doing,' Colhoun continued. 'Any questions?'

'Aye,' Dubery said, almost apologetically. 'Do we know exactly what it is these people are smuggling into Florida?'

'Not for certain,' Colhoun admitted. 'But the door-to-door trip takes longer than ten hours, which apparently rules out hearts and livers. According to an expert I talked to last night the best bets are kidneys and corneas, and maybe bone tissue.'

'It must be a pretty expensive business,' said Finn, 'running two helicopters, two submarines, a treasure hunt and a wilderness lodge. They must be either getting an astronomic price or shifting a hell of a lot of kidneys.'

Colhoun checked the notes he had made while talking to Ferguson's friend at the School of Tropical Medicine in London. 'A kidney will fetch $20,000, a cornea about $7000,' he told them. 'A knee joint goes for about $2500. Three small ear bones – $750. You may find this hard to believe, but if you could extract an entire skeleton from a fresh corpse, and powder the bones, you would be talking nearly a quarter of a million.'

'Christ,' Dubery said

'Looks like my Dad is going to leave me something after all,' Finn murmured.

Colhoun smiled despite himself. 'The reason's simple,' he said. 'Supply and demand. The queues keep getting longer, and for the best reasons. Since seat belts were introduced here and in America road deaths – and particularly brain deaths, which allow the organs to be removed from a technically living body – have declined dramatically. So there are less organs for transplant. When they raised the speed limit in some US states from fifty-five to sixty-five the death rate increased again, and the transplant surgeons thought it was Christmas. And then some states started imposing handgun controls, which tightened the supply again.'

'Sick,' Finn commented.

'Aye,' Dubery agreed. 'But if someone you loved was desperate for a new kidney . . .' He shrugged. 'It's a hard call.'

'This smuggling is illegal in America, right?' Finn asked.

'Oh aye,' Colhoun said, checking his notes again. 'The National Organ Transplant Act of 1984 made it a criminal offence to buy or sell a human organ. But it's not illegal in a lot of Third World countries. In India it's quite common for families to sell a daughter's kidney. And even in places where it is technically illegal there seems to be a lot of it going on. In Russia loads of families can't afford to bury their dead unless they agree to sell off the profitable bits. And there was a case in London the other day of a Turkish immigrant caught selling his kidney to some man from Birmingham. In some places in Central America gangs just round up children and help themselves. Even at its nicest this is a very nasty business. And we have no way of knowing if the organs being smuggled into Florida have been donated voluntarily or not. For all we know some bastard warlord in Haiti could just be slaughtering people and cutting them up. Carefully.'

'I think we get the picture, boss,' Finn said soberly.

'Good. I don't want to find out that pieces of you two are on sale in half a dozen Florida hospitals.'

While waiting for the word from Poole on their request for reinforcements, Marker and Cafell found themselves with plenty of spare time on their hands.

This proved a mixed blessing as far as Marker was concerned. Usually there were few things he enjoyed more than simply messing around on or beside the sea, but on this occasion he found that the lack of a controlling purpose left his mind open for the demons to roam. He had hardly thought about Penny over the past couple of days, but now he seemed trapped once more by memories of his life with her.

One part of him wished he had left the Marine Corps, as she had wanted. They would probably have had a child by now, maybe even two. He would have been helping to bring new life into the world, rather than taking life away. He had no name for the man he had killed, and the only face he had seen had already been half obliterated by the bullet from the Browning.

Penny's face also seemed harder to visualize with each passing day, and once, when he tried to conjure it up, he found himself staring into the dead eyes of Tamara Arcilla. Maybe time would untangle these knots of grief, but Marker was no longer so sure. One thing he did know was that any future relationship would have to live and breathe in the shadow of both these women. The past, which had always seemed like a springboard to the future, now felt more like a set of emotional chains.

Rob Cafell had never killed anybody, but he too found himself dwelling on the man whose corpse was now rotting on the bed of Lostman's River. The trip back across Hell's Lake in the submarine had been like one of those black farces on TV, where a body keeps turning up despite the best efforts of all involved. Cafell had laughed at such programmes in the past, but he doubted if he would laugh at one again. And he wondered whether the authors of such pieces had ever seen death up close. For the first time he began to understand his father's lifelong reluctance to talk in any detail about his experiences in the war.

Russell was just finishing putting all the medicines back on the pharmacy shelves when Emelisse came into the room. 'I've got something to show you,' she said.

It was a copy of the *New York Times*.

'Where did that come from?' he asked.

'Oh, Calderón has the Tuesday edition sent up from Port au Prince every week. He likes to read the "Science Times" section. Keep up with developments.'

'I expect Dr Frankenstein was a regular subscriber,' said Russell.

She sighed and tapped the front page. 'Haitian Junta Faces Ultimatum' the headline read.

Russell skimmed through the report, which suggested, without offering any evidence in support, that American military intervention in Haiti was a couple of weeks away at most, and perhaps only a matter of days.

'Maybe it is not worth trying to escape,' she said softly.

'If the Americans bring back Aristide then Joutard's days are numbered.'

He put a hand on each of her shoulders. 'Emelisse,' he said, 'if law and order comes to Haiti it will come first to Port au Prince. And what do you think people like Joutard will do – wait for it to reach out for them?' He answered his own question. 'Of course not. They will cover their tracks, bury the evidence. And we are part of that evidence. All those young men and women with scars on their bodies are part of it.'

She took it in, and her eyes closed as in pain.

'Come with me,' he urged her.

She opened her eyes and looked at him. 'It frightens me,' she said, though as far as he could tell there was not a trace of fear in her eyes. 'But you are probably right.'

'You'll come?'

'Oh no, you don't understand. If you are right, then this is one more reason why I must stay.'

The burst transmission from Poole announcing the dispatch of reinforcements arrived at 09.00 hours on Monday morning. Both the decision and the selection were welcomed by the two recipients. Ian Dubery was as good a boat handler as anyone in the SBS, and Stuart Finn was known to be as effective in a crunch as he was insubordinate.

Marker had 'talked' to Franklin via the PRC 319 on their return from Hell's Lake, and now he composed another message, typed it out on the keypad, and sent it. In a way he felt sorry he couldn't offer the ex-SAS man a more active role, for Franklin had felt like an integral part of the team ever since their arrival in the Turks and Caicos.

Marker and Cafell decided that only one of them was needed to collect the incoming tourists that afternoon, and the younger man drew the short straw. Marker was left to go over the tactical plan once more, take a swim, and watch cartoons on TV. He felt in control again, and told himself that there would be time enough to sort out the meaning of sex, the universe and everything when they had Arcilla behind bars.

Cafell, meanwhile, arrived at Miami International with plenty of time to spare, parked the car, and started circumnavigating the now familiar sights. He bought and started reading a new paperback account of the Battle of Midway, and missed the on-screen announcement of the plane's arrival.

Hurrying down to the relevant gate, he caught sight of them through an open door, as they waited to be processed through Immigration. Dubery was the taller one, with dark, boyish good looks which reminded Cafell of the *Match of the Day* pundit who once played for Liverpool. Finn had lighter hair, swept back and heavily dosed with gel. He looked like one of the lads – Cafell's father would have called him a 'wide boy'. Standing in the Immigration queue, Finn seemed faintly amused by the whole business. Dubery, by contrast, looked slightly worried, as if conscious of how far he was from the presumed simplicities of life in the Outer Hebrides.

The two of them got through Immigration and Customs without any trouble, and Cafell hurried them down to the basement car park.

'Nice motor,' Finn commented.

'Wait till you see the boat,' Cafell told him.

They drove south out of Miami, setting sun to their right, rush-hour traffic all around them. Dubery gazed out of the window with interest, but Finn, happily spread across the two back seats, had apparently seen it all before.

'How many square feet of skin do you reckon you have, boss?'

'What?' Cafell exclaimed.

Finn repeated the question.

'He's been driving me mad all day,' Dubery lamented. 'He bought one of those mini-encyclopaedias at Heathrow, and he's been showing off ever since. When the hostess brought the meal on the plane he asked her when the microwave was invented.'

'And when was it?'

'Nineteen forty-seven,' Finn said from the back. 'And the average human has twenty square feet of skin.'

'I'll be able to sleep at night now,' Cafell said. The light was rapidly fading now, the lights of the oncoming cars like a river stretching into the distance.

'So what's the score, boss?' Dubery asked.

'Marker will tell you the plan. You've got the camcorder?'

'State of the art, according to the Illustrators,' Finn said from the back. 'The man said it would shoot in just about any light short of pitch-darkness. He said the Yanks use something like it for filming their drug busts.'

'Sounds ideal.'

'What are we going to be filming,' Finn asked, 'porno flicks with the boss and this Cuban guy's sister?'

Cafell suppressed a smiled. 'I wouldn't suggest that to Captain Marker if I were you,' he said. 'In fact I wouldn't mention the woman at all.'

'Left a nasty taste in the mouth, did she?' Finn asked mischievously.

'Something like that.'

'Why, was she really ugly or something?'

Cafell grunted. 'She was a stunner.'

'Then . . .'

'Don't ask me. And don't ask him either if you don't want your head bitten off.'

'OK, I get the message.'

They drove on, through Homestead and then on to the two-lane Keys section of Highway 1. As they went past Key Largo's Holiday Inn Cafell asked the other two if they had heard of *The African Queen*. Finn had, Dubery hadn't. Finn expressed his doubts as to whether they had flush toilets yet in the Outer Hebrides. These had been invented, he added gratuitously, in 1589, the year after the Spanish Armada.

For the next half hour Cafell treated the two corporals to a lecture on the defeat of the Armada, something he had studied and modelled in some depth.

'And you thought I was a know-all,' Finn said to Dubery as they arrived at Buena Vista.

Marker was waiting at the door to shake their hands. Supper was already heating in the microwave.

'Invented in 1947,' Cafell said, nodding at it.

'When else?' Marker agreed.

After eating, Finn and Dubery were shown over the *Slipstream Queen*, beers were retrieved from the fridge, and the four men sat in the boat's lounge as Marker went over his intended plan of action.

'My first idea was simply to take over the lodge and round up everyone as they arrived – the sub, the chopper, even the Indian in his canoe if he's part of the set-up. But there's one big problem with that. Either of you two see what it is?' he asked the newcomers.

They both thought for a moment. 'A lapful of kidneys,' Finn said eventually.

'Right. We can hardly expect the bad guys to go ahead and deliver them for us – they'd just make a run for it. And there's no way we could deliver them ourselves. We could just ignore the damn things, but after people have donated them – whether by choice or not – it seems like a terrible fucking waste not to let them go where they're needed.'

Marker looked from face to face. 'So this is what we're going to do instead . . .'

Russell strung the water bottle across his back and checked that he had everything else he needed. The food had been shared out between his pockets, the scalpel he had lifted from the surgery was stuffed in his right boot, inside a sheath made from paperback covers. The length of rope was wrapped around his neck.

It was one o'clock, the time he had decided offered an optimum balance of risks. Later would have been safer as regards escaping the compound, and earlier would have given him more time to get across the island.

Let's go, he told himself, and picked up the grappling-hook he had fashioned from bedsprings. After opening the front door he waited half a minute, watching the compound for any sign of movement, and then walked briskly through the trees and darkened bungalows to the southern perimeter wall.

The grappling-hook caught on the strands of barbed wire at the first attempt, and he quickly pulled himself up the face with the help of the twisted sheet rope. Once at the top he gathered together the sheet to make a cushion, and used it to roll across the barbs. He landed as well as he could have hoped in the bare dirt on the other side.

It had been too easy, he thought. If getting out of the compound was that easy, then getting off the island was likely to be a real bugger.

He stood up gingerly and took his first look at the outside world. It was not the way he had imagined it.

Away to his right a few tumbledown homes were gathered around the gate, and beyond them a line of tall palms followed what was probably a stream bed around the far side of the compound. But that was the extent of the cover. The forested hills he had expected were covered with low scrub up to about five hundred feet, and bare above that. It looked more like Provo than the Haiti he had imagined.

And the gibbous moon riding in the eastern sky was bathing the slopes in pale grey light.

Reckoning that the stream bed probably offered the easiest and most inconspicuous route up into the hills, Russell carefully threaded his way through the shacks beneath the watch-tower, keeping one eye on the guard above. Fortunately the man only seemed interested in what was going on inside the walls of the compound.

The stream bed was full of dry pebbles. Russell followed it uphill, slowly until he was sure he was out of earshot, then as fast as the terrain would allow. The moonlight ensured that he had no trouble finding his way, and until the stream bed petered out in an ocean of scrub he made good progress.

The last uphill stretch was a different matter, and it was almost four o'clock when he reached the ridge top, and found himself looking out across several miles of ocean channel at the distant Haitian mainland. Away to the west, he thought he could make out a few pinpricks of light where the town of Port de Paix was supposed to be.

Below and to his left, some two miles distant, a village was stretched along the sides of a small bay.

The downhill leg proved no easier. The southern slopes of the range were not so bare, and this time he had no stream bed to follow through the scrub. More than an hour had passed when he finally emerged into the cultivated fields above the village, and crawled to the crest of the last small rise overlooking the bay.

There were several small boats moored at a ramshackle dock, and one large enough to serve as a public ferry. Russell was strongly tempted to walk straight down, steal a boat, and take his chances out on the water.

But it was gone five o'clock, and the chances of his reaching the far side of the strait before dawn were non-existent. He would have no time to pick and choose which boat to steal. And he would be a sitting duck if they caught him on the water.

On the other hand, he told himself, if he waited until the following night he could be sure of arriving on the mainland during the hours of darkness, and that would vastly increase his chances of finding some sort of sanctuary in Port de Paix before the local thugs found him.

He didn't much like it, but the smart money was on digging in for the day. He walked back through the cultivated fields, and into the scrub, where he dug out his first hide since the one above Port Stanley twelve years before. This one was blessed with natural cover, and didn't need to be constructed so professionally, but he was pleased with his work just the same.

Which was all to the good. Only a few minutes after incarcerating himself Russell heard the swelling drone of a helicopter. The search was underway.

13

On Russell's watch the second hand momentarily merged with the hour and minute hands. With butterflies dancing in his stomach and adrenalin coursing through his veins he started down the slope to the shoreline.

He had left the safety of the hide soon after dark, and surreptitiously worked his way down through the fields to the hilltop observation point he had reached the previous night. From there he had watched the last ferry arrive, the children dragged home to bed, the cooking fires doused, the kerosene glows dimmed one by one. Now only the two armed thugs were left, sitting on the beach end of the dock, their feet hanging just above the sand.

The four-hour wait had given Russell ample opportunity to both study their habits and work out the safest line of approach. The two men were each on their fourth beer, and though neither was showing any obvious signs of drunkenness – Haitian beer, as Russell knew from experience, was not the most potent in the world – the gaps between their visits to the end of the dock were growing noticeably shorter.

Why they should choose to walk all of fifty feet to piss in the sea when there was a perfectly good beach right next to them, only they could know. In Russell's experience such self-consciousness was refreshingly absent from most 'undeveloped' cultures. But maybe an inability to piss with someone watching was as crucial an indicator of development as cellular phones, microwaves and MTV. Not to mention transplant surgery.

Whatever the reason, he was grateful. It put a distance between the two men, and that would give him a chance.

He reached the shoreline about a hundred yards to the west of where they were sitting. They were talking with their backs to him, but every now and then one would turn his head, and Russell had no desire to play Creeping up on Grandma with two men toting Uzis. Instead he inched his way into the water, wishing the slope of the beach was steeper, but grateful for the noisy swish of the waves. Once the water was deep enough he began to swim, heading in a wide circle for the end of the dock.

The water was warmer than he'd expected, and dirtier too. Reaching his destination, he hauled himself in between the line of pilings and started pulling himself hand over hand towards the land end, where the four dangling feet were silhouetted against the sand. On his way he examined the boats which were tied up on either side, and realized with dismay that the outboard motors had been removed from those boats that normally carried them. He was going to have to row across the strait.

He provisionally picked out a red boat with the name Dolores, and moved on, reaching the point where the waves clawed at the sand about five yards from the four hanging legs. He could hear the two men talking quite clearly now – in Creole, he thought.

Russell lowered himself slowly on to his stomach in the gently breaking waves and began dragging himself slowly up the beach. When he was level with the waving feet he pulled himself up into a crouching position and waited. His breathing sounded far too loud, his heart was hammering like a road drill, and at any moment he expected one of the men to jump down on to the sand and smile at him over the barrel of his Uzi. Or simply blow him away.

But the minutes went by, the men kept talking, and occasionally flexing their feet. Every minute or so Russell would hear the sound of beer glugging out of a bottle and down a throat.

And then two legs suddenly disappeared, and the planks above his head shook with the feet walking away down the dock. Ten seconds, he thought, inching forward towards the still-hanging feet. Another two to get the dick out. And three more to reach mid-piss.

With both hands he grasped one of the offered ankles and pulled with all his might. A shriek split the night, and the man came crashing down on to the beach in front of him, landing head first in the sand. As Russell dived for the fallen gun another shout came from the far end of the dock, swiftly followed by the sound of running feet.

Russell's finger found the trigger and he turned, still on one knee, as the running man's silhouette loomed into view on the dock above. Both guns seemed to open fire at the same moment, but only Russell had a clear view of what he was aiming at. The Haitian was lifted into the air, and seemed to hang there for a moment, like a man bungling a backward somersault, before he crashed down with a sound of splintering wood into one of the small boats parked on the far side of the dock.

The other man, Russell discovered, had been knocked unconscious by the fall.

In the village a couple of lights had appeared, but no one ventured out to investigate, and within a few minutes the lights had been extinguished. Russell used his length of rope to tie up the unconscious man, and gagged him with one of his own socks. Then he walked quickly down the dock to the boat he had chosen, slipped its mooring, jumped aboard, and picked up the oars.

He had more than five hours of darkness left, which should give him all the time he needed. Soon the dock was disappearing from view, swallowed up in the larger silhouette of the hills behind the village.

Half an hour went by, and though the mainland hardly seemed to grow any nearer, Russell felt happy with his progress. With the moon shining down on the sea, the heavens filled with stars, it was possible to forget for a moment what might be waiting on the farther shore, and what he had left behind in the compound on Tortuga.

It was through this precarious sense of well-being that the first shouts of distress reached his ears, and for a moment he thought it was his conscience playing tricks with him.

But it was a boat, a small boat drifting towards him, sitting unusually low in the water. At least two of its occupants seemed to be shouting at him.

He rowed towards the other boat, and soon came alongside. It wasn't much bigger than the *Dolores*, but it was carrying a load more suited to a boat three times the size. A huge mound of belongings filled its centre, and seven people were wedged around its edges. One, a middle-aged woman, was holding a baby in her lap. The other five – two adults and three children all under twelve – were baling for all they were worth.

In vain. The boat was already knee deep in water, the tops of its sides only a few inches above the level of the sea. It was sinking.

'America!' the woman with the baby shouted at him, as if she thought he was waiting for a password.

Other eyes looked imploringly in his direction.

This was what they called instant karma, Russell thought. Someone up there was trying to tell him something.

He manoeuvred his boat alongside and gestured for the Haitian family to come aboard. The woman came first, and the baby was passed over to her. The children were next, and then the mother. With each new arrival Russell's boat let out a creak of alarm and sank lower into the sea.

The father was now beginning to transfer the pile of belongings from the sinking boat.

'No,' Russell told him, shaking his head for emphasis. The man gave him a look which seemed to say: Don't you understand, these things are our life?

Russell shook his head again. Already it was obvious that they wouldn't make it across the strait. He mimed to the Haitian that he could try towing the belongings, and at this the man's eyes lit up. He stepped nimbly into the stern of Russell's boat and reached out an arm for the bow of his own.

Russell turned the *Dolores* back towards Tortuga and begun rowing, conscious of the children's eyes staring up at him. The baby began to cry, and the mother started singing a soft Creole lullaby. Halfway to the shore he heard a despairing sigh behind him and knew that the other boat had taken the family's belongings to the bottom.

The child's wail seemed to grow stronger as they neared the beach, but it didn't matter. Russell's eyes had already picked out the men waiting on the dock.

The dark mangroves slid slowly by on either side, as the *Slipstream Queen* made its unhurried way up Lostman's River. The moon had risen an hour before, and was playing hide-and-seek with the fleet of clouds that were moving across the star-laden sky.. One moment the waters of the river would offer a shimmering carpet, the next a black mirror.

Dubery was at the wheel, Cafell reading the chart. Finn was sitting on the bow with the nightscope, looking out for any uncharted obstructions. Marker was in the lounge, checking through their equipment one last time.

They had been on the move for three hours now, since receiving Franklin's confirmatory message. This time they had secured advanced clearance for their passage through US territorial waters from the authorities in Key West, and had rashly promised a return on their American hosts' hospitality before the night was out. The US Customs Service Air Division at Homestead had been alerted to expect an incoming call sometime around dawn.

It was almost two o'clock now, and they were nearing the spot where they had anchored the cabin cruiser the previous week. As they passed it Cafell showed Dubery where the crocodile had lain, jaws at the ready. He didn't mention that they were passing over the spot where they had sunk the dead gunman.

In the lounge Marker heard both comment and omission, and decided that this team of four had gelled as smoothly as he could have hoped. He wasn't sure he had much in common with either of the two newcomers – Dubery was a bit on the earnest side, Finn still young enough to think the world revolved around him – but then Cafell wasn't exactly his idea of a soul mate either. The important thing was that they all felt confident enough in each other's abilities to make full use of their own, and after three days together Marker was pretty sure they did.

Any lingering doubts about team chemistry had been removed the previous evening. Emerging from his sleep shift Marker had come upon the other three practising cabrioles on the stern deck. Not that he knew them by that name. Finn's pocket encyclopaedia, it turned out, contained diagrams of the eight basic ballet steps, and his SBS comrades were practising number eight, leaping into the air with one arm outstretched, and two legs fluttering against the other. And laughing fit to burst.

Marker smiled at the memory and went forward to join the other two on the bridge. Hell's Lake was not much more than a mile ahead, and it was time to decide whether or not to douse the boat's lights. They were not intending to bring the vessel within three miles of the Anhinga Lodge, but it was always difficult to judge how far sound travelled across water. If the bad guys heard the boat, then it would be better if they could see it too.

'If we leave the lights on,' he suggested to Cafell and Dubery, 'then as far as they're concerned we'll just be one more boat cutting across the southern end of the lake on our way to the Everglades Waterway. There must be several boats a day doing just that.'

'In the daytime, yes,' Cafell said, 'but not in the middle of the night.'

'I don't think the noise will carry,' Dubery said quietly.

'Actually neither do I,' Cafell said.

Marker sighed. The engines seemed awfully loud to him, but maybe that was because he was listening to them. And it would be better not to raise any questions at all in the minds of the enemy. 'OK,' he said eventually, 'let's go for broke. But do your best to keep the engine noise down.'

'You got it,' Cafell said in a mock-American accent.

The entrance to the lake came into view, and a few minutes later the *Slipstream Queen* was venturing out on to the wide waters. Cafell kept them close to the southern shore, where, unless the enemy had acquired state-of-the-art thermal imaging since Marker's previous visit, they would be hidden in the dark line of mangroves.

Lights were already visible across the lake. With the aid of the nightscope Marker could make out two illuminated windows in the lodge, and what was probably a kerosene lamp burning on the end of the jetty.

The *Slipstream Queen* was now far enough away from the course the submarine would take. Marker gave Dubery the cutthroat gesture, and the Scot turned off the engines. In the bow Finn gently lowered the anchor into the lake.

The four men gathered in the lounge, and all but Dubery pulled on their wetsuit hoods. Using the pools of moonlight offered by the windows they applied the dark camouflage cream to the exposed parts of their faces and checked their equipment.

Satisfied, they went out on deck. Once the Kleppers had been quietly let down into the water, Finn and Cafell slid down the rungs and clambered aboard. Marker lowered the waterproof bag containing the camcorder and PRC 319 into the empty seat beside Cafell, and then climbed down to join Finn in the other canoe. Both crews pulled the spray-deck sheet over their heads, clamped it in place, and pulled the paddles from their pockets in the outer skin. Then with a wave of the hand from Marker they turned silently out towards the centre of the lake.

Standing on the deck, Dubery watched them go, frustrated at not being with them, but also remembering the day of his departure from Poole, and Helen telling him on the phone that she had no desire to be a widow at twenty-four.

Some six hundred miles to the south-east, Russell was wondering why he was still alive. When he had been returned to the camp that morning Joutard had made it clear that he would have one more chance to use his surgical skills, and that then he would be given the opportunity to experience the process from the patient's point of view.

But the operations were over, the helicopter long since gone, and he was still in the land of the living. Maybe there had not been enough time for Calderón to harvest both him and the man he had killed on the dock the previous night, several of whose bones, and both of whose corneas, had gone with the helicopter.

Maybe he had another week in hell, Russell thought. But at least he had saved that Haitian family, and he would be going out with a better opinion of himself than the one he had lately become used to. He had tried.

The quality of Joutard's hospitality had naturally dropped. Russell was back in the room where he had first seen Emelisse leaning over his face like an angel. And this time they had thought to board up the window from the outside, as well as lock the door.

He had been given one chance and blown it. And he had the distinct feeling that one was all he was going to get.

As the wilderness lodge grew nearer Marker left the paddling to Finn and devoted all his concentration to the nightscope. Before the angle became too obtuse he was able to pick out an occasional movement through one of the lighted windows, as if someone was walking across the room behind them. But there was no sign of enemy activity outside the lodge or on the jetty.

The mysterious disappearance of a colleague the week before had obviously been attributed to accident. They had found the upturned canoe and made the logical deduction as to the whereabouts of its former occupant.

In the lead Klepper Cafell veered away from the shoreline to pass an unusually ambitious root, and raised an arm to give the following canoe advanced warning. They had paddled about three miles now, on a course that hugged the lake's western shore, and were now not much more than half a mile from their destination. They had gambled on finding a suitable landing spot on this side of the lodge – Marker knew from experience that there were none on the other.

About a hundred yards from the boat-house they were forced to concede that there was none on this side either. At least they had no problem finding somewhere to tie up the canoes – there were about a thousand roots per square yard to choose from. The three men slipped quietly out into the waist-deep water and started wriggling and twisting their way towards dry land, passing the bag with the camcorder and satellite radio forward hand by hand in a leapfrogging sequence. All three men had experience of waterproof containers proving themselves otherwise.

They reached dry ground later than Cafell and Finn hoped but sooner than Marker expected. He unzipped the bag and gave the radio to Cafell, the camcorder to Finn, and kept the bag for himself. Then in single file they started slowly forward in the direction of the lodge. Soon they had their first glimpse of the light on the end of the jetty, and another few minutes brought them to a position just inside the trees which ringed the helipad behind the lodge. The helicopter – an Enstrom 280 FXA Shark – had already arrived.

Marker brought finger and thumb together in the prearranged signal for Finn to use the camcorder, and the corporal squirmed a couple of yards further forward to get a clear shot. Just in case, Marker also spent a few seconds memorizing the helicopter's number.

A raised voice suddenly disturbed the calm, causing all three men to freeze. The silence that followed lasted only a second, before a wail of laughter filled the air. It was only the men inside the lodge, having what sounded like a good time.

'Party animals,' Marker murmured to himself. And their party was about to get crashed.

It was about seventy-five yards from where they crouched to the front of the lodge, and most of it was in shadow. It was worth the chance, Marker decided, if only to check on the strength of the opposition. 'I'm going for a closer look,' he whispered to Cafell and Finn, and before the former could start an argument he was gone, darting over the open ground, along the side of the outhouse, and across the gap which separated it from the lodge.

An oblique look through the nearest window showed there were no curtains, only a mosquito screen. Marker moved away from the lodge, heading for a position in the shadows from which he could get a better look inside the room. Having found one, he took a single quick glance inside and sank to his haunches, letting his mind retrieve the image.

There were four men sitting around a table at one end of what looked like a games room. There was a table-tennis table behind them, and a pool table beyond that. Three of the men looked Hispanic, and none of them was older than thirty. The fourth man was sitting with his back to the window, but the hat and long hair looked more than familiar. It was the Indian he had seen on the creek.

One more look, Marker decided. Like many men with Special Forces experience he was a firm believer in the sixth sense – if you stared at anyone for long enough they became aware that they were being observed. The trick was to keep the vision peripheral, and just take it all in like a camera.

He rose slowly to his feet, took a second look, and sank back down. One of the Hispanics was wearing a shoulder holster, but there were no other weapons on display. If they had SMGs – and there was every reason to think they did – then they were probably leaning against the men's chairs, or maybe out near the main door. There was no way of knowing.

Satisfied he had seen all there was to safely see, Marker took the same route back to Cafell and Finn, and recounted in whispers what he had discovered.

'Can I go and take their pictures now?' Finn asked.

Marker grinned at him and looked at his watch. 'Time we were in position for phase two,' he said.

He collected the three MP5s, wrapped them in the bag which had carried the camcorder and radio, and rammed them into a convenient growth of ferns. Meanwhile, Cafell and Finn had both taken a ball of dark twine from their belts and tied one end around the trunk of the nearest tree. Marker and Finn then moved further back into the undergrowth and turned towards the lake, unrolling Finn's ball behind them. A few minutes later they reached the shoreline close to the spot from which Marker had first seen inside the boat-house, and started looking for the best camera angle.

Cafell had headed off in the opposite direction. According to the largest-scale map they had managed to find, the thick vegetation surrounding the lake rarely extended more than a hundred yards inland, and he was hoping to find a suitably open space in which to use the radio. His hundred yards of twine was nearly exhausted when the light began to brighten, almost imperceptibly at first, but then with increasing speed, as if a bright grey sun was rising. Cafell found himself standing on the edge of a sea of grass which stretched away under the stars as far as the eye could see. He stepped forward on to this strange plain, and found himself up to his knees in water.

He snorted at his own stupidity, and retreated to the dry ground of the hummock. After tying the end of the twine to a convenient tree he wedged the satellite set into a cleft between branches, and set off back through the trees, using the twine as a guide. At its end he transferred to Finn's line, and followed that down to where the other two had set themselves up behind a particularly tangled web of roots, with the camcorder's lens peeking out in the direction of the boat-house and jetty.

It was just after four o'clock, and they probably had the better part of two hours to wait. They did so mostly in silence, occasionally stretching cramped limbs, and intermittently scanning the dark lake for a sight of the submarine. Finn found himself thinking about the boating club on the River Lea where he had first discovered that escape was possible from the oppressive world of Hackney's high-rises. Crouching in a foot of water wondering where the water moccasins were wasn't exactly what he'd had in mind for a career, but he had no regrets. He might be halfway between the frying pan and the fire, but at least that meant he was out of the fucking frying pan. And who knew – he might land in a beautiful woman's lap. Eventually.

Cafell was thinking about his father, and what the old man would think to see him here. It wasn't the sort of war he had fought in, that was certain. But the days of the big boats were over, whether on the surface or beneath it. His dad thought that was sad, but Cafell, for all his love of naval history, didn't agree. In this sort of war, where canoes replaced battleships, the individual counted for more. Every man on this mission had real responsibility, whereas three-quarters of the men on his dad's nuclear sub were just there to keep the damn thing running.

Beside him, Marker was remembering a summer with his parents in one of the south coast resorts. Hastings, he thought it was. They had been playing in some murder mystery on the pier, and he had been given a small part himself, comprising a grand total of three lines. The third of these had been the last of the play: 'Mummy, where are they taking Daddy?'

He smiled to himself and wondered what they were doing now. Probably sitting at home in Highgate, watching themselves on TV, glasses of wine in hand, puffing away at their cigarettes. And here he was five thousand miles away, loitering among the mangrove roots. The whole family was half insane.

The minutes dragged by, and the setting of the moon deprived the lake of its silver sheen. Every now and then they heard laughter or good-natured shouting coming from the lodge. A single bird began to sing, and then another, and almost at once, or so it seemed, the rest of bird-kind was joining in. The sky above the lake's eastern shore began to lighten, bringing the small, dark shape of the submarine gradually into focus.

The men in the house had seen it too. There was the sound of a door slamming, the clump of feet on wood, and then three of them came into view around the wall of the boat-house. The two Hispanics clambered down the steps where Marker had shot their late comrade, one of them carrying the kerosene lamp, the other some sort of customized cradle. The Indian sat down on the top step and lit a cigarette.

Where's the fourth man? Marker wondered. The distant sound of rotor blades turning supplied the answer. He turned and gave the thumbs up to Cafell, who immediately melted away into the vegetation.

Finn looked enquiringly up at Marker, who shook his head. He wanted to be sure that the sound of the submarine's passage would drown out the whirr of the camcorder, and it was still a hundred yards away.

The two men on the walkway were talking to each other in Spanish, a language neither Marker nor Finn understood. Both were wearing open-necked shirts and slacks, and both were carrying handguns, one in a shoulder holster, the other in his belt. The Indian seemed unarmed.

The noise of the submarine was now loud enough, and Marker gave Finn the signal. The phrase 'you're on candid camera' floated out of some deep recess in his mind.

By this time Cafell had retrieved the PRC 319 and was wading out into the sawgrass swamp. The message, giving the helicopter's identification number, had already been keyed in. He sent it in a single burst. In the Poole operations room someone would be noting down the precise time the message was received, and using it as an approximate guide to the helicopter's time of departure. This, along with the location of the lodge and the helicopter's number, would then be phoned through to the waiting US Customs Service.

Back at the lake shore the submarine was being guided into the boat-house. Once it was secure, one of the crewmen clambered out into the yellow glow of the kerosene lamp, and stood there straddling walkway and submarine. His partner began passing out the Belzer-Kountz machines, and he handed them across to the men on the walkway, who placed them side by side in the carrying cradle. There were four of them, and two other containers of a different kind. Once they were all loaded in, the two Hispanics took hold of the rope handles at either end of the cradle and carried it off in the direction of the helicopter. The second crewmen followed the first on to the walkway, and handed a small package across to the now hovering Indian, who stuffed it inside the top of his trousers.

All three men headed up the steps, the Indian carrying the lamp. As they disappeared from view the distant whine of the rotor blades accelerated, and Marker thought he glimpsed a dark shape climbing up into the rapidly lightening sky. The plastic boxes would be delivered all right, and the waiting patients would get what they had paid for, but if the US Customs people were on the ball then there would be no escape for the people who had banked the cheques.

'Time to go,' Marker whispered.

He and Finn extricated themselves from the roots and followed the twine back to its source, where Cafell was already waiting for them. They removed the MP5s from the bag, and replaced them with the radio and camcorder.

Marker led the way to the edge of the trees, and stopped there for a full minute, watching for movement in the dawn twilight. Then all three men moved off at a loping run, Marker and Finn towards the back of the lodge, Cafell towards the front.

Marker had assumed that the door at the back would be in use whenever the helipad was, and therefore unlikely to be locked. In fact it was wide open.

He found himself in a narrow lobby, looking at the spare machines which Colhoun had picked out on the photographic blow-ups. Ahead of him a passageway extended for some ten yards before opening into the wide entrance lobby. In the distance he could see the front door, wide open.

He could hear voices ahead, and decided they were probably coming from the room in which he had witnessed the card game, and which he presumed must open on to the entrance lobby from the right. With any luck all five men would be in the same room.

He remembered his conversation with the captain of the *Argyll* about stun grenades, and allowed himself a bitter smile before advancing stealthily down the passageway to the threshold of the entrance lobby.

The Indian walked into view, his face turned back towards the room he had just left, as if he was listening to a parting comment.

At the same moment one of the two Hispanics walked out past him, took one stride across the lobby in ignorance, and then caught sight of the two SBS men. His eyes almost jumped out of their sockets, and his right hand flashed halfway towards his shoulder holster.

'Freeze!' Marker whispered fiercely, and the man's hand seemed to shift into slow motion as his brain registered the twin barrels of the two MP5s.

The Indian's head had spun around at the sound of Marker's voice, but either his brain was half asleep or he had somehow acquired – five hundred years of American history notwithstanding – a touching faith in the white man's reluctance to shoot unarmed red men in cold blood. Either way he made a break for the door, arriving at it just in time to impale his stomach on Cafell's MP5.

'*Qué pasa*?' the other Hispanic asked as he stepped out into the lobby like one more duck in a shooting gallery. He sounded more irritated than anxious.

By this time Marker had taken several quick steps forward, and there was no chance for the man to miss the menace of the MP5. He raised his hands in the air, and spat a torrent of Spanish in the direction of his fellow-caretaker. Marker yanked the automatic from the man's belt, and took a cautionary look around the corner of the door to the communal room. As he had hoped, the two submarine crewmen were simply standing there looking lost. This wasn't an eventuality they had prepared for.

The SBS men herded the Indian and the two caretakers back into the room to join them.

'OK, boss?' Cafell asked.

Marker nodded. 'And find some rope to tie this lot up with,' he shouted after his second in command.

Cafell disappeared through the front door. A few seconds later they heard the rushing sound of the flare being fired, and through the window Marker caught sight of the bright-green flash in the still lightening sky.

'We are taking you with us,' he told the five men. 'Because we have questions to ask you. Refuse to answer them or make any kind of trouble and you will end up where your friend did, at the bottom of the lake. That's right,' he added, noticing the look of comprehension on a couple of the faces, 'it wasn't an accident. This is not our first visit.'

They looked at each other, and then at the SBS men. The crewmen looked disgusted, the caretakers looked confused, the Indian looked depressed. No one said anything.

After a few minutes Cafell returned, carrying a coil of rope and the package which had dropped out of the Indian's belt. 'Presents,' he told Marker. 'Our stuff's on the jetty. Ian's on the way. I'll take one of the canoes and fetch the Kleppers.'

He disappeared again, and Marker kept the MP5 pointing steadily in the prisoners' direction as Finn went to work tying their wrists together behind their backs. Once all five were securely trussed, he left Finn keeping watch, took out his knife, and sliced open the end of the package. There were three small plastic bags inside, each containing white powder. He cut a slit in one of them, inserted a wet finger, and tasted the powder, just to be sure.

'Icing sugar, boss?' Finn asked.

'The very best,' Marker agreed. 'And just when we thought Comrade Arcilla had abandoned drug running in favour of spare parts.'

'Seems a bit weird,' Finn said. 'They could have brought in a hundred times as much.'

'True,' Marker agreed.

'And why give it to Sitting Bull here? Why not the helicopter?'

Marker looked at the Seminole. 'Maybe in payment,' he said, and a flicker in the man's eyes told him he had probably hit the mark.

It was almost full light outside now, and through the

window the *Slipstream Queen* could be seen approaching the jetty. He looked at his watch. Less than half an hour had passed since Cafell's transmission – they probably had as much time again before the American authorities could put in an appearance. They would probably be too busy tracking the helicopter's deliveries, but Marker was keen to avoid a potentially embarrassing argument over whose prisoners these were.

'Time to go, lads,' he told the five men, and led the way out of the lodge and down to the jetty, with Finn bringing up the rear. Dubery was easing the *Slipstream Queen* alongside, and Cafell was waiting to lift aboard the two Kleppers. Once this had been done the two men hurried round to the boat-house, where they loosed the submarine from its moorings and eased it carefully out on to the lake, before taking to the water themselves, and manoeuvring it across to the waiting tow-rope.

'All aboard,' Marker told the captives.

They filed on to the boat. One crewman and one caretaker were put in one of the two sleeping cabins beneath the stern deck, the remaining three men in the other. There were no locks on the doors, but there was only one narrow exit to the rest of the boat, and Finn was left to cover this with his MP5, just in case anyone had a brainstorm. So far Arcilla's men had seemed too stunned to offer resistance or attempt an escape, and Marker wasn't expecting any trouble in the near future. When the shock wore off they would still have nowhere to run.

As Dubery eased the *Slipstream Queen* away from the dock and took her back across the lake towards the Lostman's River egress, Marker and Cafell went through the questions they wanted answered. Once they had the list, one of the two crewman was brought forward to the lounge area. He was a dark-skinned Hispanic, probably in his late twenties. At first he refused to say anything, other than that he didn't speak English – '*No hablo inglés*,' he repeated sullenly.

'OK then,' Marker told Cafell in a resigned voice, 'we'll have to do it the hard way. Go and get his partner up here, and then we'll throw this guy overboard. His partner will talk.'

Cafell had taken two steps towards the stern when the man rediscovered his flair for languages.

'My name is Miguel,' he said. 'What do you want to know?'

'What time are you expected back at the *Tiburón Blanco*?' Marker asked. 'We shall be asking your partner the same question,' he added as an incentive to truth.

'About four o'clock in the morning,' the man said. 'We leave from the lodge at nine.'

'Tonight?'

'*Sí*.'

Marker went on to extract a detailed breakdown of the *Tiburón Blanco*'s crew, and a sketch map of the boat itself. According to Miguel the two submarine crews greatly enjoyed the treasure-hunting side of their job and hated the long underwater voyages to and from Hell's Lake. Angel Socarras, the captain and head of the operation, was a complete bastard. Miguel had never heard of anyone called Fidel Arcilla.

Nor had his partner, another Cuban-American, whose name turned out to be Jorge. He too thought Socarras was the man in charge.

The two 'caretakers' had never heard of Arcilla either, but they took their orders from a man named Hector Chavez, who ran Anhinga Lodge for 'some corporation in Miami'. Their only job was to look after the place and scare off unwelcome visitors, particularly between

Thursday afternoon and Friday evening. They assumed the contraband organs were going to a hospital, but didn't know which or where. Once they had asked the helicopter pilot, merely out of curiosity, and been told in no uncertain terms to mind their own business.

The Seminole, who told them his name was Ricky Bowlegs, knew nothing of the wider picture. As Marker had suspected, the small shipment of cocaine was payment for services rendered – he and a few friends formed Anhinga Lodge's outer defences, watching and listening out for any hint of danger, either from the law, the Everglades Park authorities or their own people. One Seminole man had needed a strong warning, their captive said phlegmatically. And one Park Ranger had seen more than he should, but he had proved more than willing to jump on the bandwagon.

Marker showed him the photograph he had taken the week before.

The Seminole sighed. 'You boys are good,' he said.

'It's a gift,' Marker told him.

14

The joint operations undertaken by the US Customs Service and the Florida State Police on that summer Friday did not reach the ears or eyes of the press for several days. The hospital staff concerned were bound by confidentiality, the authorities by the hope that bigger fish would still fall into their net, and the donor recipients by sheer ignorance.

But there was no way of keeping the whole business under wraps indefinitely, and soon after four o'clock that afternoon Hector Chavez, the Cuban-American lawyer who had been acting as coordinator between the Health Trust and Arcilla's organization, received a phone call from a worried hospital executive. That afternoon the executive had arrived back from lunch to find the parking lot full of police cars. He had driven away again, and eventually gone home, only to find that there was a police car sitting outside his house. A phone call to a friend at the hospital had confirmed his fears that it all had something to do with the transplants, but he had been unable to get hold of any more specific information. What, he asked Chavez, should he do?

'Pray,' the lawyer told him, and hung up. Chavez then tried to reach his contacts at the other three hospitals in the Trust, but only one proved available, the consultant in St Petersburg, who denied that anything unusual had happened that day.

'Did you have a delivery today?' Chavez asked.

'No, it was . . .'

Chavez hung up on him too, and sat in his Miami office wondering whether he should call Arcilla.

Not yet, he decided. First he needed details. Half an hour and a dozen phone calls later he had set enough investigatory wheels in motion to satisfy a Congressional Committee. Before another hour had passed a picture had begun to emerge, one that was far from comforting. It was possible that the police had been tipped off by someone in the know at the first delivery point, and then followed the delivery boy to the other two hospitals. Possible, but a little too fortuitous, Chavez thought. More likely, and much more seriously, the delivery had been followed all the way from Anhinga Lodge.

He sat at his desk for a few minutes, building up the nerve to tell Arcilla, and finally picked up the phone. At almost the same moment a police detective pushed past his secretary, prised the receiver none too gently from his hand, and started to recite him his rights.

Marker was woken by the hand shaking his shoulder. 'Ten minutes, boss,' Finn told him.

'OK.'

He sighed, shifted his legs off the bunk, and sat on the edge rubbing his eyes and yawning. His watch said it was two-twenty in the morning. Mind and body were telling him that four hours' sleep in twenty-four hours was not enough.

The eighteen or so hours which had passed since the SBS team's hurried departure from Anhinga Lodge had been busy. They had conducted five interrogations, taken lessons in handling the Russian submarine and been through several conversations with Poole. They had sailed the *Slipstream Queen* through the Keys and out across the Straits to its current position some twenty miles south-west of the Muertos Cays. They had rendezvoused with the *Argyll*, and persuaded her captain to offer their prisoners the hospitality of the frigate's brig. He in turn had passed on some up-to-the-minute intelligence – American troops would be moving into Haiti within the next few days. Tuesday at dawn was the current best guess.

Which didn't bode well for Russell, Marker decided. Arcilla's man in Haiti would presumably be shutting up shop.

In fact the whole business was becoming a race against the clock. For all they knew the *Tiburón Blanco* had already received word that the operation was unravelling, and headed out into the wide blue yonder. Or was waiting, guns at the ready, for a visit from the SBS.

There was no way of knowing. The US authorities had promised Colhoun they would do their best to keep the lid on for twenty-four hours, but Marker didn't have the highest opinion of American security. It had also occurred to him, and perhaps the Americans too, that any communication between Arcilla and his captain at this juncture would make it harder for the former to claim ignorance of the *Tiburón Blanco*'s illicit activities. An American might reckon that was worth a couple of British casualties.

They would soon know. Marker got to his feet and walked forward to the lounge area, where Finn was sitting in his wetsuit, encyclopaedia in hand.

'Don't ask,' Marker told him. 'I can't cope with any more interesting facts.'

Finn grinned. 'Time to go?' he asked.

The two of them helped each other on with their

diving equipment, double-checked that everything was working, and went out on deck, where Cafell and Dubery were manoeuvring the Russian submarine alongside. They were dressed in the original crew's clothes, which fitted pretty well.

Marker walked forward into the bow and stood there for a few moments staring out into space. The sea stretched away, empty of other shipping, with only a few small and scattered cays to break the flat line of the horizon. The nearly full moon was almost overhead, and the Milky Way seemed to stream from its sides, north-west towards Florida, south-east towards Cuba. On nights like this Marker knew why men created gods.

It was time to go.

The four men synchronized their watches, and Cafell and Dubery clambered down through the hatch and into the submarine. Marker and Finn slung the cling-film-wrapped MP5s across their chests and lowered themselves on to the submarine's curving back, where they sat splay-legged and facing each other on either side of the protruding hatch, their hands grasping the loop of rope which had been thrown around it.

Inside the sub, Dubery started up the engine. The Russian craft was more uncomfortable than their own, and defiantly devoid of any cosmetic trimmings. But the controls were simple, it was wonderfully responsive, and its capacity for speed was almost unbelievable. Cafell thought he knew a bit about engineering, but he had no idea how the Russians had done it. If the sub survived this particular night the research lads back at Poole would be thinking Christmas was early this year.

Dubery steered them towards the north-east, aiming the submarine towards the easternmost of the three flat humps which made up the Muertos Cays. Assuming that the *Tiburón Blanco* had not shifted position during the last week, such a course should keep the cay between them and the enemy, blinding the latter's radar.

Perched on the submarine's back Marker was remembering the giant worm riders from *Dune*, one of his favourite books as a teenager. Dubery was keeping the sub to about fifteen knots, but the surface was calm, and they weren't in any danger of being thrown off. It was exhilarating, like one of those rides at seaside amusement parks. Whatever his childhood might have lacked, Marker thought, it hadn't been excitement.

The cay grew steadily nearer, the moonlit ocean floor visible beneath them. Dubery brought the submarine to a halt, and the two men on its back slid down into the water. While Finn untied the electric torpedo Marker and Cafell checked their watches again through the window.

They were now only a mile or so away from the *Tiburón Blanco*. Since their means of locomotion was considerably slower, Marker and Finn left earlier. The former steered them in an easterly direction for a couple of hundred yards, and then left Finn with the electric torpedo while he went up to the surface for a look through the small hand periscope. And there the boat was, exactly where they had left it ten days before.

He went back down, gave Finn a thumbs up, and they resumed their journey. The water was clear, and very shallow until they had left the cay far behind them. There seemed to be few fish, and Marker wondered whether the long presence of the *Tiburón Blanco* nearby had scared them away. If so, he was not sorry. The last thing they needed now was a run-in with an irritable barracuda.

None appeared, tetchy or otherwise. About fifteen minutes after leaving the sub they found themselves under the thick black square of the floating helipad, and Marker cut the electric torpedo's motor. After they had tethered the machine to one of the helipad's anchor lines the two men swam deeper before coming back up directly underneath the hull of the enemy's boat. Marker checked his watch. They had two minutes to spare before the sub arrived.

They hung there in the water, watching the bubbles bounce off the hull, Marker cursing the fact that he hadn't thought to wait under the helipad.

The seconds dragged by, but no divers came plunging through the surface. The submarine finally swam into view, and Marker could see the concentration on Dubery's face as the young Scot guided the craft into position just off the cabin cruiser's starboard side. He caught a glimpse of a thumbs up from Cafell as the submarine started rising towards the surface.

He and Finn moved to the other side, waited until the sub was no longer visible beyond the keel, and brought their heads up into the night air.

On the boat above them people were talking excitedly in Spanish. Cafell was presumably following the script and pretending to have trouble with the hatch.

Marker used the rungs on the boat's side to lift himself out of the water, and laboriously removed the cling film from the MP5 with his other hand. Then he advanced another two rungs and hung there while Finn followed the same procedure beneath him.

A tap on his foot told Marker the younger man was ready. He pushed his head up over the side of the boat, saw no one, and climbed over the rail and on to the deck. The voices on the other side of the boat was louder now, and more threatening. There seemed to be no one on the bridge.

Finn joined him, and the two men moved off at a brisk walk in the direction of the stern deck. They were only a few steps away when a cavalcade of noises – the clang of a hatch, the ping of bullet on metal, the reverberation of the shot – erupted from the other side of the boat.

Marker rounded the corner just as the man with the gun turned away from the rail in disgust. His brain registered the gun pointing loosely down, the empty hands of the other two men. 'Freeze,' he heard himself say, his finger poised to squeeze the trigger and send all three men backwards over the rail.

The gunman's hand twitched involuntarily, and then suddenly went limp by his side. The automatic hit the deck with a thud. Finn went forward, picked it up, and tossed it overboard.

Marker was wondering where the other submarine crew was. If they were on board the shot should have brought them out on deck. 'Look after this lot,' he told Finn, and made his way back along the deck to the lounge door. He slipped inside and held still for several seconds, listening for any sounds.

Then it suddenly occurred to him – there had been no submarine tethered beneath the boat. He went swiftly through the rest of the cabins, and came up as empty as he had expected. Back on deck he found Cafell and Dubery trussing up the new prisoners while Finn kept them covered. At this rate, Marker thought, they should go into business as bounty-hunters.

'Take them inside,' he told Finn, and then waited until they were out of earshot before whispering new instructions to Cafell and Dubery. Both men smiled.

While Cafell disappeared down the deck, Marker and

Dubery followed the others inside. 'Where is the second submarine?' he asked the man in the captain's cap.

The man said nothing.

'Your name is Angel Socarras,' Marker told him. 'You work for Fidel Arcilla as a treasure hunter and a smuggler of human spare parts. I will happily feed you to the sharks.'

Socarras shrugged. 'Do what you wish,' he said.

Marker looked at him, sighed, and nodded to Dubery and Finn. The latter looked surprised, but joined Dubery in taking hold of one of the captain's arms. 'Off the stern,' Marker added, and the two SBS men bundled the man out into the night. A few seconds later the men in the cabin heard the beginnings of a struggle, as it belatedly dawned on Socarras that Marker wasn't bluffing. A few more seconds, and there was a loud splash.

'Where is the other submarine?' Marker asked the man who had held the gun.

The man's mouth was gaping open. 'It is gone to Florida,' he said quickly.

'With another shipment?'

'Yes, they go every night now. Because the Americans invade Haiti,' he added unnecessarily.

It was even worse than Marker had feared – Arcilla's man in Haiti was upping production to make the most of the little time he had left. He thought about the cargo that was now heading towards Anhinga Lodge – kidneys probably. They had been taken from someone, but the chances of their finding a new home were distinctly remote. And when the submarine arrived at the lodge the shit would hit the fan . . .

The crew would have to be intercepted. He would have to radio the American authorities.

Every night now, the man had said. 'The helicopter, what time does it arrive?' Marker asked.

The man shrugged. 'Around eleven.'

'See what you can make of their radio,' Marker told Cafell. 'We need to call the Yanks and the *Argyll*.'

Dubery arrived back in the doorway.

'How's the captain?' Marker asked.

'Still out old.'

'What did you throw overboard?'

'A chest full of fishing tackle.'

The gunman's mouth was gaping again.

'The oldest tricks are always the best,' Marker told him.

The following twenty hours were much like the previous twenty. The four men slept in shifts, and devoted their waking hours to the jobs that needed doing. Dubery and Finn went off in the Russian submarine to collect the *Slipstream Queen*, which they then used for transferring the new prisoners to the *Argyll*. The frigate, on station some fifty miles to the east, came to meet them, but the captain failed to show his face.

'Fucking brass,' Finn said. 'They spend weeks sailing their little ships round in circles, and when someone asks them to do something useful they get pissed off.'

'Maybe he didn't join the navy to be a prison governor,' Dubery observed.

Back on the *Tiburón Blanco*, and now relieved of the need to guard their captives, Marker and Cafell contacted Poole via the satellite radio. According to Colhoun the American authorities had so far been successful in keeping the lid on their end of the operation. And Arcilla, who was being watched from a discreet distance, had displayed no awareness of anything being amiss. As far as the Turks and Caicos were concerned, two men from the Attorney-General's office were en route from London with all the necessary powers. They would be there that evening.

The sun went down, and Dubery was entrusted with the task of moving the *Slipstream Queen* a reasonable distance away from the *Tiburón Blanco*. The hours dragged by. At ten-thirty Cafell switched on the helipad's perimeter lighting, and the three men sat out on the bow deck, ears cocked for the sound of an approaching helicopter.

At one minute past eleven they heard it, and soon the dark shape was growing in the south-eastern sky. The pilot landed without difficulty on the barely moving helipad, cut the engine, and jumped down from the cockpit, shouting something in Spanish at the waiting SBS men. Marker advanced towards him in the captain's hat, but the pilot was not so easily fooled. He stared for several seconds, then shouted out a question in Spanish, and finally lunged for the safety of his cockpit. Marker caught him by the legs, pulled him back out again, and showed him his Browning High Power.

'Shit,' the man said, but he seemed more surprised than upset.

Behind him Cafell was examining the plastic boxes, and the organs suspended within them. 'What are we going to do with these?' he asked.

'Feed them to the fish,' Marker said.

There was something in his voice which made Cafell reluctant to argue.

They took the pilot aboard the *Tiburón Blanco*, and sat him down in the saloon cabin. He was not much older than twenty-five, good-looking, and with at least an air of intelligence. And he was certainly pleased with himself – even in these circumstances he had a hard job to keep from smiling.

'Right,' Marker said. 'You understand English?'

'Of course,' the man replied indignantly.

'Good. Your name?'

'Felix Córdoba.'

'OK, Felix. You have two choices. Cooperate with us for twenty-four hours and we'll let you go. Refuse to cooperate, and we'll hand you over to the authorities on Provo, and make damn sure you serve at least ten years in prison. So choose now.'

The man looked at Marker, disbelief on his face. 'Ten years? And you will really let me go?'

'Yes,' Marker said. 'If you help us.'

There was another long pause.

'Felix . . .'

'OK, OK, I cooperate. What do I lose?'

'Not a lot.'

Felix laughed, as if the misfortune belonged to someone else. 'So what you want to know?'

'First off, where do you fly from here?'

'Back to Provo.'

'OK, then that's where we're going.'

'First we must refuel.'

Marker turned to Cafell. 'Tell Colhoun what's happening, and ask him to contact the people Whitehall has sent out to Provo. We need to make sure the people at Arcilla's villa are in custody before we get back.'

'OK, boss.'

'Let's fill up the chopper,' Marker told Finn and Felix.

The helicopter came to rest on the tarmac at Provo's tiny airport soon after four in the morning. To Marker's relief the men from London were not there to meet them. Jet lag had presumably taken its toll, and the hapless Sergeant Oswald had been obliged to form the entire welcoming committee.

There were rooms waiting for the SBS quartet at the Club Med-Turkoise, he said. Marker told him they needed the use of a room here in the airport building for the interrogation of their captive.

Oswald found them one in the west wing, which was not used during the tourist low season. A windowless storeroom next door could be used as a detention room for their captive. Marker thanked the sergeant and gently shut the door on him.

Felix asked if he could have a few hours' sleep.

'Not yet,' Marker told him. 'Questions first, and then you can have some sleep.'

'OK,' Felix agreed good-naturedly.

'Where do you make the pick-up?'

The pilot looked surprised that they didn't know. 'Tortuga,' he said.

'Where on Tortuga?' Cafell asked, pushing a map in front of him.

'Here,' Felix said, pointing with his finger.

'And what is it?' Marker asked.

'What do you mean?'

'Is it a house like the one here on Provo?'

'No, no. It is a camp, a soldiers' camp, but with many civilians. It is Colonel Joutard's camp.'

'How many soldiers?' Marker asked.

'Hard to say. Ten, fifteen, maybe twenty even. They are not army, you understand. More like Ton-Ton. Private soldiers.'

'Armed thugs,' Cafell suggested.

'*Sí.*'

Marker stretched his back in the chair. 'OK, Felix, now we want to know every single thing you can remember about this place – where everything is, where the soldiers are and the civilians are, where this Joutard will be.' Marker grinned at him. 'And the better your memory, the more future you'll probably have, because this evening you'll be taking us in there, and your chances of getting out again are probably going to depend on how well we do once we're on the ground.'

Felix murmured something unhappy in Spanish, but he didn't bother to argue, and for the best part of an hour he answered the questions Marker and Cafell put to him. He knew there were doctors in the camp, but he had not seen them himself, and couldn't confirm that one of them was English. He hadn't been around the camp either, but he had seen it from the air, albeit always in darkness, each time he made a pick-up. And as Marker jogged the pilot's memory with questions, Cafell's diagram of the camp acquired more and more useful detail.

Eventually the well of information ran dry.

'Round up some cushions for our friend here,' Marker told Dubery. 'And you and Finn should get some sleep as well.'

Once the pilot had been locked in the storeroom, Finn said he had a question.

Marker gave him an enquiring look.

'Are we going to get away with this? I mean, isn't HMG going to jump on us from a great height when they find out we've been invading a foreign country?'

'We're going in after one of our own,' Cafell retorted. 'The CO will back us up. He . . .'

'He will,' Marker agreed, 'but it's still a good question.' He ran a hand through his hair. 'And I guess the only answer is – what choice do we have? The good news is that if we fuck up then we probably won't be around to care, and if we don't the most we can expect is a rap on the wrist.' He looked at Finn. 'But if you feel you don't want . . .'

'Fuck, no,' Finn said, looking offended. 'I'm coming. I just like knowing exactly where, if you see what I mean.'

'Up shit creek,' Cafell told him cheerily.

'But with a paddle,' Marker said. He got to his feet. 'Thing that worries me is someone trying to stop us. Like these guys from the Attorney-General's office or wherever it is they really come from. So before they come looking for our guide I think I'll go looking for them. Take them our video, tell them about the prisoners on the *Argyll*. That should keep them happy for a couple of hours.'

'You can tell them to go collect the Americans' boat,' Cafell suggested.

Marker grinned. 'You know, I'd completely forgotten about that.'

'I expect the *Argyll* wants her submarine and Kleppers back too,' Finn suggested.

'You never saw James Bond going round collecting all the equipment he'd abandoned,' Cafell said. 'No wonder Q always looked pissed off.'

Marker's fears of interference from the new arrivals were soon laid to rest. Taking morning coffee with them on the terrace of their luxury hotel, he formed the strong impression that the less the two men from London had to do with him and his men the better they would like it.

They would look at the video in due time, and planned to interview the prisoners on the *Argyll*, probably on the following day. In the meantime, they were waiting for a plenipotentiary from Miami. Nothing could be done, as one of them explained, until they had discussed the ramifications of the whole business with the Americans, and settled any 'potential disputes over jurisdiction'. The man looked across at Marker as if wondering whether he needed to use words with fewer syllables.

Marker left them drinking their coffee, gazing out across the turquoise sea, and probably discussing a convivial round of golf. Back at the airport he woke Dubery, and fell almost instantly asleep on the line of sequestered cushions.

Soon after he and Tamara returned from church, at around ten on that Sunday morning, Fidel Arcilla received a call from a well-wisher in the Dade County Police Department. Two hours, and several phone calls later, he was able to gauge the full extent of the disaster which had befallen his operation.

He lit a rare cigar, and sat back in his orthopaedic office chair.

If the Florida and Provo ends were both blown, he realized, then there was no chance that the *Tiburón Blanco* had escaped. Joutard on Haiti was probably immune, at least until such time as US forces went ashore.

Arcilla picked up the phone to summon his radio operator, then put it down again. Making contact with Joutard in these circumstances might not be the wisest of moves.

He walked out on to the roof garden and leaned over the parapet, looking down at the Sunday promenaders on Calle Ocho. To his right the towers of Downtown split the blue sky, and between them he could see Miami Beach and the distant sparkle of the sun on the sea.

He was not used to set-backs, not any more. He would have to think this through with care, and not let anger get the better of him.

The operation had not been important, or at least not in the financial sense. He could do without such profits fifty times over. The problems were merely legal, and as far as he could tell not particularly acute. He had been careful to interpose numerous cut-outs between himself and the operation, and those who had actually worked in the business would happily go to prison for him, secure in the knowledge that they and their families would all be well rewarded.

The British might try and extradite him, but in a case like this, where the law could be endlessly muddled with moral issues, the process could be delayed for years. US laws had been broken too, but his friends in the CIA would ensure that any legal action against him here would be deferred indefinitely. With Castro's regime crumbling at home they knew they might be needing him at a moment's notice.

No, there was nothing much to worry about. The only obvious crimes had been committed in Haiti, and there was no way he could be held accountable for them.

Still, he thought, turning away from the Miami skyline and grinding the cigar beneath his foot, he would have no more contact with Haiti. There was no point in taking unnecessary risks for a psycho like Toussaint Joutard.

Worrell Franklin arrived at the airport around five o'clock, and made no bones about what his priorities were. 'I'm coming,' he told Marker belligerently.

The SBS man sighed, 'How the hell did you know we were here? And going somewhere?'

'I gave him a call,' Cafell said apologetically.

Marker opened his mouth to say something, closed it again, and eyed his partner with a tolerance born of affection.

'I want to come,' Franklin said.

'Who's stopping you?' Marker said. The ex-SAS man had been in on this business from the beginning, and Marker had no fears he would let the side down. In fact, if Joutard had twenty men, he would narrow the odds from 5–1 to 4–1.

Franklin, who had been expecting more of an argument, looked at Marker, surprise written all over his face. 'My wife would like to,' he said, and then smiled ruefully. 'No, that's not really true. She wants to help Nick. She's just scared I won't come back.'

'I can't guarantee it,' Marker said quietly.

'I can't guarantee surviving my next fucking drive on the Leeward Highway,' Franklin said.

In the Tortuga camp office Joutard handed Calderón a small glass of rum. The doctor raised an eyebrow.

'This is the last night,' Joutard explained. 'I want you to start half an hour earlier. When you've finished the usual, the Englishman will be killed. And the woman too.'

'The woman,' Calderón echoed, but he didn't object.

'She will talk,' Joutard said, as if the doctor had. And because she once spat in my face, he added to himself. It had only been her indispensability that had kept her alive that day. The thought of taking her that evening crossed his mind, but he let the idea go. There would be no pleasure in it. Certainly nothing to compare with the profit her body would bring him on the operating table.

'How will they be killed?' Calderón was asking.

'Head shots?'

Calderón nodded. 'That is best . . .'

'And after you've taken what you can from them, I want you and Bodin to take out the other kidneys,' Joutard decided. There were already two many people in camp bearing the tell-tale scar.

Calderón finished his rum and left. Joutard called in his number two. 'Once they've started with the operations I want you to bring me a girl,' he told the man. 'The one with the perfect body – her name is Françoise, I think. You know the one I mean?'

'The orphan Françoise?' the man said doubtfully.

'Of course the orphan,' Joutard said. Emelisse Alabri's hold over him was a thing of the past, and he could now take whom and whatever he wanted.

Forty minutes after leaving Provo the Haitian coast hove into view. 'Remember, anyone carrying a gun is to be taken out,' Marker shouted over the noise of the rotors. 'And don't wait for them to pull the trigger first. This isn't Tombstone.'

The other four men nodded their agreement.

Marker could now see the cliffs rising from the sandy beach, and the walled compound above them. Beside him Cafell was waiting to check his diagram against the reality.

Felix lifted the chopper a little higher, and they could see the mosaic of buildings, trees and open spaces which lay inside the walls. It was not well lit, Marker noticed with relief. There was electric lighting in some of the buildings, and a few fires outside them, but darkness was the rule. If the watch-tower on the landward side was equipped with a searchlight it hadn't yet been turned on.

The helicopter was coming down now, aimed at a stretch of open ground surrounded by several small fires. At first Marker thought a square had been marked out as a landing sight, but then realized he was looking at a baseball diamond. As the helicopter sank towards the hard dirt surface Cafell made frantic alterations to the diagram.

Two men stood waiting close to one of the fires, both armed with sub-machine-guns. The chopper was still a foot from the ground as Marker stepped off, rather in the manner of a man leaving a moving London bus, and fired a concentrated burst from his silenced MP5. Both men collapsed, sending little clouds of firelit dust into the night air.

The other five men piled out, Felix with rather less enthusiasm than the others. 'This way,' Cafell said, and they were all off at a run, heading for a gap between a long, low building and a stand of royal palms. So far no one else seemed aware of their presence.

Reaching a path Cafell stopped for a moment. 'Is that Joutard's office?' he asked Felix, pointing at a one-storey building a hundred yards or so to their right.

'Yes.'

'The gate's this way,' Cafell told Marker.

'Good luck,' Marker told him, and the group split up, with Finn following Cafell at a run, the others the team leader.

Marker's group sped along the tree-lined path, conscious of the darkened windows in the buildings to either side, and came to the edge of an open space. On the far side was a line of three identical buildings, which would have looked like barracks but for the full-length verandas. According to Felix, the middle one of these contained Joutard's office and living quarters.

Marker paused in the shadows before gesturing the others to follow, and they were only about ten yards short of the veranda when a shout came out of the dark to their right. The SBS men sank instantly to the ground, and their eyes were still seeking out the shout's source when a short burst from an SMG exploded in their ears, and knocked down the still-standing Felix.

Suddenly two men were running towards them like idiots, only to be hurled backwards by the silent power of the MP5s.

The new silence seemed less natural than the old. For a few seconds the birds and the cicadas seemed to hold their breath, and during that time the SBS team could hear music coming from inside the building. To Marker's astonishment it sounded like Elvis Presley.

He managed a quick look at Felix, and realized his wounds were not life-threatening. 'I'm going in. You two get him under the steps,' he whispered, just before another burst of fire erupted out of the night, longer this time, but also wilder.

Dubery and Franklin scrambled for the ground beneath the raised veranda, as Marker leapt up the three steps and hurled himself bodily at the office door. Crashing through, he found himself flying across the room inside, and landing almost at the feet of a running man.

The man's surprise was greater than Marker's, and the SBS man managed to grab an ankle and flip his opponent towards the duty desk, which he hit head first.

As the man slid motionless to the floor the first door in the passage swung open, and Marker had a momentary picture of a naked man looking out, and a naked girl sitting up somewhere behind him, before the door was slammed back shut. He strode swiftly across the intervening yards, raised his right foot, and rammed its sole against the door, sinking down on to his left knee almost in the same motion. The naked man was waiting with pistol raised, but the only shot he had time for went over Marker's head, and the burst from the MP5 stitched a line of momentary agony across his chest. He sank back on to the girl behind him, who lay there whimpering in terror. 'Is your heart filled with pain?' Elvis was asking. 'Shall I come back again, tell me, dear, are you lonesome tonight?'

In the operating room everyone had heard the gunshots, but had done nothing beyond share questioning glances. The Americans couldn't be here already, Russell thought, as he snipped carefully through one of the minor arterial links. It was probably just Joutard's goons entertaining each other. Still . . .

He looked across at Emelisse, whose skin seemed stretched even tighter across her lovely cheek-bones than usual. 'Just keep on going,' she murmured, so softly that he couldn't be sure whether she was talking to him or herself.

Marker put an eye round the corner of the office door, just as another burst of automatic fire ripped across the front of the building. A splinter caught in his cheek, drawing blood. He waited a few seconds and then swung himself through the rail and down to the ground, before rolling instantly back into the shelter of the veranda.

'Hi,' Cafell said casually.

'How's the gate?' Marker asked him.

'It's ours. One man climbed over it and disappeared,

but we had to take out the guy in the tower. Finn's in occupation now. No one'll get past him without learning an interesting fact.'

Marker grinned. 'Good,' he said. 'And Joutard's dead,' he added. 'At least, I think it must have been him. That makes about eight of them accounted for – still a few to go. I think we'd better get to the hospital before anyone gets the idea of taking hostages. Then we can clear up. Frankie, you and Ian keep the bastards busy.'

'OK, boss.'

Marker and Cafell crawled along the front of the veranda to its end, turned the corner and scrambled to their feet. To their right they could see several curtained windows, each with lines of brilliant light seeping through. 'Let's go,' Marker murmured.

They were halfway down the side of the building when someone came running round the far corner. Seeing the two SBS men he had the presence of mind to throw himself on the ground and cover his head with his hands. Marker left him for Cafell, and headed straight for what seemed the only entrance to the hospital building. He was only a few feet from the door when a bullet whizzed past his head and zipped into the vegetation beyond.

He ran even faster, hurling himself through the door as another shot echoed in his ears, and a cry of pain came out of the room ahead.

Russell's head spun round just in time to see Calderón's dead body hit the ground. The kidney he had been holding slithered bloodily across the white floor, and Marker came tumbling in through the open doorway.

For a second no one moved.

'Dr Russell, I presume,' Marker said.

An hour later the compound was secure. Joutard and six of his men had been killed, another ten had wounds of varying severity. The remaining few had escaped across the walls.

Emelisse had spoken to the orphans, many of whom were now wandering around the compound as if they finally owned it. The doctor herself, as Russell told Marker, was back in the operating theatre, sewing the surviving three kidneys back into their donors. 'The tissue match couldn't be better,' he added wryly.

'Some woman,' Marker murmured.

'Yeah,' Russell agreed. 'And I'd better go and see if she needs any help.'

Marker walked slowly down to where Cafell, Dubery, Franklin and Finn were sitting with a bottle of Joutard's rum. But despite the drink, despite the fact that they all had survived, the mood was far from cheerful. The enormity of what had happened in this place was still sinking in.

Marker accepted a glass, but after a while he got up again and walked on alone to where a gap in the cliff-top wall allowed a view out across the shining water. He sat there, remembering the look of terror on the girl's face, and Elvis asking if her heart was filled with pain.

He thought about the other orphans, who had paid with their own flesh for the things which he had always taken for granted, and about the Americans who were no longer slaves to dialysis because of this devil's bargain.

He remembered the haunted loneliness in Tamara Arcilla's eyes, and the hunger in himself which he hadn't even known was there.

He thought about Penny, and knew she was finally gone.

And he stared out across the moonlit sea, drawing on its strength and beauty, so that the healing might begin.